# CONTEMPORARY WESTERN EUROPEAN FEMINISM

# CONTEMPORARY WESTERN EUROPEAN FEMINISM

Gisela Kaplan

NEW YORK UNIVERSITY PRESS
Washington Square, New York

First published in 1992
Allen & Unwin Pty Ltd

First published in the USA in 1992 by
NEW YORK UNIVERSITY PRESS
Washington Square
New York, N.Y. 10003

Library of Congress Cataloging-in-Publication Data

Kaplan, Gisela.
  Contemporary Western European feminism/Gisela Kaplan.
    p.    cm.
  Includes bibliographical references and index.
  ISBN 0-8147-4622-5 – ISBN 0-8147-4623-3 (pbk.)
  1. Feminism – Europe – History – 20th century.  2. Women – Europe –
– History – 20th century.  I. Title.
HQ1587.K37   1992
305.42′094 – dc20                                    91-31639
                                                       CIP

Manufactured in Singapore

*To Lesley J. Rogers*

# Contents

# Figures, tables and maps

# Abbreviations

| | |
|---|---|
| ADM | Associación Democratica de Mujeres (Organisation for the Liberation of Women), Spain |
| APO | Außerparlamentarische Opposition (extra-parliamentary opposition), West Germany |
| BOM | Bewust Ongehowde Moeder (Purposely Unmarried Mothers) |
| CDU | Christlich Demokratische Union (Christian Democratic Union), West Germany |
| CIA | Central Intelligence Agency (USA) |
| CSU | Christlich Soziale Union (Christian Social Union) |
| CVP | Christdemokratische Partei Schweiz (Christian Democratic Party), Switzerland |
| DRP | Deutsche Reichspartei (German Empire Party) |
| EAM | Greek National Liberation Movement |
| ECSSID | European Cooperation in Social Science Information Documentation Programme |
| EEC | European Economic Community (now called EC = European Communities) |
| EGE | Union of Greek Women |
| ELAS | Greek National Popular Liberation Army |
| EPON | Greek Youth Resistance Movement |
| EXON | Christian Social Youth Organisation, Greece |
| FBB | Frauenbefreiungsbewegung (Women's Liberation Movement), Switzerland |
| FDP | Freisinnige Demokratische Parte (Freethinking Democratic Party) |
| FHAR | Front Homosexual and Action Révolutionnaire, France |
| FLG | Gay Liberation Front, Spain |
| FLM | Frente de liberacion de la Mujer (Women's Liberation Front), Spain |
| FPÖ | Freiheitliche Partei Österreichs (Liberal Party of Austria) |
| FRG | Federal Republic of Germany |
| GDP | Gross Domestic Product |
| GDR | German Democratic Republic |
| GNP | Gross National Product |
| ILO | International Labour Organisation |
| JONS | Juntas de Ofensiva Nacional–Sindicalista, Spain (part of the Falange Party) |
| JVP | Young People's Party |
| KDG | Democratic Women's Movement, Greece |
| KEGME | Mediterranean Women's Studies Institute |
| KF | Kvenna Frambothid (Women's Alliance), Iceland |
| KKE | The Greek Communist Party |

| | |
|---|---|
| KDP | Kommunistische Partei Deutschlands (Communist Party of Germany) |
| MDM | Movimento Democratico de Mujeres (Women's Democratic Movement), Spain |
| MLAC | Freedom of Abortion and Contraception Group, France |
| Mld | Movimento di liberazione della donna (Women's Liberation Movement), Italy |
| Mlda | Movimento di liberazione della donna autonomo (Women's autonomous liberation movement), Italy |
| MLF | Mouvement de Libération des Femmes (Women's Liberation Movement), France |
| MFPF | Mouvement Français pour le Planning Familial (French Movement for Family Planning) |
| MOVE | Men Overcoming Violence, USA |
| MVM | Man–Vrouw–Maaatschappij (Man–Woman–Society), Netherlands |
| NATO | North Atlantic Treaty Organisation |
| ND | New Democracy Party, Greece |
| NDP | National Democratic Party, Germany |
| ÖAAB | Austrian Workers' and Employees' Union |
| ÖFB | Austrian Farmers' Association |
| OECD | Organisation for Economic Cooperation and Development |
| ÖFB | Austrian Womens' Union |
| OFRA | Organisation für die Sache der Frauen (Organisation for Concerns of Women), Switzerland |
| ÖSB | Austrian Senior Citizens' Association |
| ÖWB | Austrian Economic Union |
| PASOK | Panhellenic Socialist Party of Greece |
| Pci | Italian Communist Party |
| Psi | Italian Socialist Party |
| RAF | Rote Armee Fraktion (Red Army Faction) |
| SED | Sozialistische Einheitspartei Deutschlands (Socialist Party of Germany), GDR |
| SDS | Sozialistischer Deutscher Studentenbund (Socialist German Student Union) |
| SIA | Solidaridad Internacional Antifascista (International Antifascist Solidarity), Spain |
| SPD | Sozialdemokratische Partei Deutschlands (Social Democratic Party of Germany) |
| SPÖ | Sozialistische Partei Österreichs (Socialist Party of Austria) |
| SPS | Sozialdemokratische Partei der Schweiz (Social Democratic Party) |
| SRP | Soziale Reichspartei |
| SUP | Schweizerische Volkspartei (Swiss People's Party) |
| ÖVP | Österreichische Volkspartei (Austrian People's Party) |
| Udi | Unione Donne Italiane (Italian Women's Union) |
| UN | United Nations |
| UPM | Union Popular de Mujeres (Popular Union of Women), Spain |
| WIN | Women's International Network News |

# Preface

This book was written to give English-speaking readers the opportunity to find out at a glance what has happened in feminism and in the women's movements of post-World War II in western Europe, and to set a record of women's very own history as part of mainstream political, social and economic events. As an overview it has the distinct advantage of being able to show the entire kaleidoscope of European women's movements in its historical and political context, and it can attempt to make some sense of the events of the second-wave movements throughout western Europe as a whole.

The emphasis of the book is thus on breadth and general trends rather than on in-depth analyses, indeed, it is an overview in the true sense. It gives specialists of one country or of one area of study the opportunity to supplement their expertise by new information on neighbouring countries; the theorist may find it useful to consider the context of the ideas of western European feminism; the person interested in social movements may find in it a discussion of paradigms of action; and the student of women's studies will find in it not just an introduction to the movements of the various individual countries but a wealth of proposals and materials.

I have grown up and lived in (mainland) Europe for 24 years and, apart from Iceland, Norway and Portugal, have visited every country dealt with in this book, often not just once but on several occasions and for extended periods. The material for the book took well over four years to compile. It required several research visits to various European centres and an extensive correspondence with European archives, bookshops and feminists. Essentially, however, the strength and the weaknesses of the book are a result of just that experience: of having come into a country and gone out, remaining a visitor and an observer, falling victim to the accidents of encounters and the discoveries of sources as well as enjoying a certain degree of freedom in judgement, unperturbed by local idiosyncrasies.

The bibliography is an attempt to achieve representativeness, if not comprehensiveness, at least as far as English language publications are concerned. There are limits within a book on how far one can take 'comprehensiveness' of course. The choice was made to include only titles cited in the text and such publications as would enable a reader, who is interested in one or another specific problem, to pursue the issue further and in great depth by consulting specialist bibliographies of the titles of texts listed in this bibliography. It will allow readers interested in pursuing topics of special interest in one country to use the bibliography as a starting point. At least one of the selected titles in it will have an extensive and recent bibliography of materials in the original language. In one sense the bibliography is built on idiosyncrasies of the author. The European material is not just difficult to access but, of course, it exists in many different languages. No author should have to apologise for not being able to read all thirteen western European languages fluently. It has helped that I have a reading knowledge of seven of them, with different rates of proficiency. The proficiency determined the ranking order of reading material used for this book: English first, German second, French third, then Italian and, with difficulty, Dutch, Swedish and Spanish. Thus it has happened that Finnish material might have been cited in an English-language edition, a Norwegian author in German, a Portuguese source that happened to be available in Dutch was cited in Dutch and so forth. The main emphasis, however, was on English-language materials, to enable readers to pursue their topic of interest without getting discouraged by the inevitable and, at times, formidable, language barriers and to ensure that further reading may fall into the precincts of reading materials available in English-speaking countries.

G. Kaplan
June 1991

# Acknowledgements

This project could not have been carried out without active, enthusiastic and often unsolicited support from scholars, feminist activists, librarians, institutes and even bookshops. I will not be able to name every person who, along the path of the research for this book, has in some way helped its progress. There are a number of archives and libraries that I am especially indebted to, such as the Feministisches Archiv- und Dokumentationszentrum, Arndtstr.18, 6000 Frankfurt/M-1, and the internationaal archief voor de vrouwenbeweging, Keizergracht 10, 1015 CN Amsterdam. My sincere thanks go to the FFBIZ Frauenforschungs-,-bildungs-und informationszentrum e.V., in Berlin 19, to Wolgang Benz, Institut für Zeitgeschichte, Munich. I thank the British Library, Humanities and Social Sciences, London, the Fawcett Library, City of London Polytechnic and the Feminist Library and Information Centre Hungerford House, London, for their superb and reliable services, locally and in my overseas dealings with them. I would like to acknowledge the particular contribution and fast service of several bookshops, in particular the Silver Moon in Charing Cross, London, the Lillemor's Frauenbuchladen in Munich 40, and the Small World Bookshop in Venice, California, USA. My work on Scandinavian countries was made extremely enjoyable and considerably easier by the open welcome I was given by the Council for Equality between Men and Women, Ministry of Social Affairs and Health, Tasa-Arvovaltuutetun Toimisto, PL Box 267, 00171 Helsinki, Finland. My special thanks go to the Coordinator of Women's Issues Liisa Husu and the research coordinator Merja Hurri, Helsinki, and to Olli Stalstrom, Helsinki. I would also like to thank Kornelia Hauser and Barbara Ketelhut from 'Argument' in West Germany, and extend a warm thank you to my parents for their assistance in Europe when I was in Australia. I am grateful to Allen & Unwin for the rewarding collaboration. My greatest debts, however, are to Maria Markus, University of New South Wales, Sydney, and Lesley Rogers, University of New England, Armidale, who have taken it upon themselves to read the manuscript in full. I am deeply grateful for their advice and suggestions and for providing valuable feedback when it was needed most.

*Suffit-il de changer les lois,*
*les institutions et les coutumes,*
*l'opinion publique et*
*tout le contexte sociale*
*pour que les hommes et les femmes*
*deviennent réellement des égaux?*

Simone de Beauvoir

*Will it suffice to change the laws,*
*the institutions and the customs,*
*public opinion and*
*the entire social context*
*before men and women*
*will become truly equal?*

# Introduction

No one can deny that the phenomenon of 'social movements' of the post–World War II era created a unique constellation in human history. The movements of the 1950s and 1960s, which we now consider 'classical' movements, were followed at once by yet another set of movements of the 1970s and 1980s, of which the women's movements are a part. Not only were these 'new' movements numerous but they often were of a similar kind. This raises questions about the political culture, the social, economic and moral norms of the societies in which they occurred. Some writers of the 1970s and 1980s have begun to consider the implications of these but much remains to be done and written on the subject.

This book deals extensively and exclusively with the women's movements of western Europe. It probes their history and context, their strategies, structures and their culture. The questions that were of particular interest to me were concerned with the possibilities and limits of protest. What were the claims women made? How did they go about getting heard? Did governments take note of their stated aims and needs? What was the role of governments? Did they initiate reform, or did they do so only as a result of the mobilisation of dissent? And if governments undertook reforms, have they made a difference in everyday life for women? Is the very notion of formal equality being translated into practice? What do the statistics describing the social status of women tell us? How do these observations connect with the more elusive issues of a new consciousness and perhaps a new identity for women?

With the hindsight of approximately twenty years since the onset of the new-wave feminist movements, it is time to take stock of what women in Europe have achieved and might or will achieve in the future. We need to gauge, if only tentatively, the degree of change that has been fashioned by the movements themselves and to ask what other forces may have helped the implementation of that change. Not one of the national women's movements would claim that its activity, thought, and protest have been staged without distinct aims in mind. To be sure, sometimes these aims were short term, pragmatic and utilitarian, but, as women took to the streets to fight for the legalisation of abortion or for more kindergartens, other women formulated theories of action, of culture (including the political culture), while yet others produced cultural products such as novels, films, poetry, and the like, presumably also in order to show something about present-day life and its contradictions and problems for women.

The change in social, cultural and even political ways that has been wrought in these two decades is indeed remarkable and to use the word transformation to describe it is not out of order. So vast is the change that young women of today, born in the late 1960s and early 1970s, often need to be reminded that many of their freedoms of everyday life were non-existent and often not even thought about at the time when their mothers, typically the generation of the second-wave movements, were their age. A woman's control of her bank account, even just the right to open one, the possibilities of credit and managing and owning one's own property, the right to equal education opportunities and careers, the mere inclusion into the thinking and planning of present-day western industrialised societies, are altogether changes of vast implication and importance. Moreover, the 1970s and 1980s saw the efflorescence of women's self-discovery, at a time when new identities and a new consciousness were developed amongst women. Much of that thinking filtered through to the general population, even to the most reluctant, and it was hard to dismiss the idea that something in the perception of the (western) world had changed rather dramatically.

We are now witness to a new scenario and a new set of tremendously important changes within Europe. When research on this book began, no one would have guessed and could have predicted that the Europe of the 1990s would be a very different Europe to the one it had been over the post-World War II years. The revolutions in countries behind the iron curtain and the changes in Germany might have been predicted by the most astute political observers amongst us. But it is perhaps true to say that no one would have *dared* to believe these would ever become reality so abruptly, seemingly so naturally, and even without bloodshed in most cases. Romania, Czechoslovakia and East Germany have overturned their governments. The iron curtain is breaking down rapidly and the newly elected governments and the people have entered on the mammoth task of restructuring their societies. The scrambling for US dollars and German marks has started everywhere, the promise of development and of financial aid has given every single event a new dimension of urgency. Enormous problems lie ahead for these countries and any tasks undertaken for Europe will require painstaking discussions over the next few years. One thing is eminently clear. In future, there will be one Germany, which will sit within a new Europe that is on its way towards reaching its own postwar objective: the unification of Europe, targeted economically for 1992.

These new hallmarks in European history in themselves make this book more timely than could have been foreseen, and they make it historically and factually sound to have conceived of the period as ending in the year 1988. For in the latter part of 1989 a qualitatively new set of events had begun to take shape. While the last chapters of this book were being written, news of the Romanian Revolution reached our ears, the Hungarian negotiations with US President Bush took place, the Berlin Wall crumbled, and Czechoslovakia won a freely elected government. These recent events in Europe are like a major dam break, and the flooding of the areas which these barriers had fortified will not stop for a good while. The new political reality in former iron curtain countries has a vitality and a momentum all its own to which western Europe of 1990 has neither been immune nor hostile. Meanwhile, events like the menacing unrest in the USSR and the Gulf crisis and war have created anxiety and economic turmoil.

There is absolutely no doubt that the new developments will have extremely far-reaching implications for the future and might eventually even change the face of Europe, probably beyond recognition. It will be far harder to trace the motives and forces that originally propelled the western European movements once they have been overlaid by these new events, new understandings, new channels of communication, by new problems and constellations.

Thus, ironically, it is because of an innocence unfettered by the knowledge of coming events that this book is more truly a record and reflection of western Europe and of its women's movements than had it been written with hindsight.

For the new women's movements are firmly placed within an understanding of the Europe that was; a pivot undeniably for the whole emancipatory process, be this manifested in the Treaty of Rome, the growing Common Market (of western Europe) or the inter-European women's organisations. The Austrian crest of the eagle looking westwards and eastwards might now not only be a symbol for Austria but possibly for all Europe. It would certainly not have been a fitting one for the pre-1989 era.

This book is thus about western Europe, a large part of a whole continent which up to this day has been classed as 'western industrialised', sharing commonalities of structure, concern and experience with English-language countries. It is seen as a starting point in providing a broad socio-historical introduction to women's status as well as to feminist activities and ideas on mainland Europe. It cannot be more than an introduction but as such it hopes to provide an accessible guide to the most recent developments in western European feminism and give some idea of texts and contexts. Western Europe is defined here as any country outside the iron curtain. This still leaves twenty countries, spanning from Finland to Portugal, Iceland to Greece and Norway to Italy. All of these have been (bravely) designated as western Europe.

The narrative on individual countries in this book has been subdivided into four main groups, falling roughly within four distinct geopolitical areas: the Scandinavian progressive north; the conservative centre; the creative traditionalism of western Europe (France and the Netherlands); and radical southern Europe. It is inevitable that with such sweeping generalisations one risks rebuke for simplification and reductionism. Over twenty national boundaries and thirteen very different languages separate the western European communities from each other. Even the supposed homogeneity within nations is in many cases a myth. 'The Swiss' or 'the Italians' do not really exist. Anxiously guarded vested interests and well-entrenched animosities to other regions make it possible that values and practices in everyday life may not apply beyond one valley, one mountain range, one district or dialect group. North and south may be important differentiators; for instance, Portugal distinguishes between the 'heathen' north and the religious south. In West Germany, catholics dominate the south and protestants the north, while in Italy the north is supposed to signal sophistication of an urban, industrialised kind in contrast to a more conservative rural south. Still other countries are divided linguistically, as are tiny Switzerland and Belgium. There is no denying that European diversity has also meant segregation. Segregation, including cultural and economic delineation, was part of each nation's programme for self-assertion as well as for political and economic independence. All this is commonplace and well known. Nevertheless, simplification has merits when it exposes certain trends and correlations.

In my view, the subdivision into four sectors of western mainland Europe is not particularly arbitrary and rests on a rather long and respectable line of historical scholarship. Ferdinand Braudel, the distinguished scholar of the Mediterranean, was convinced that geographic area and historical development were intertwined in more than banal ways. In 1972, he wrote in his book *The Mediterranean and the Mediterranean World in the Age of Philip II* : 'At bottom, a civilization is attached to a distinct geographical area, and this is itself one of the indispensable elements of its composition. That is why there are cultural frontiers and cultural zones of amazing permanence: all the cross-fertilization in the world will not alter them.'

One of the obvious reasons why, within the four broad groups, countries are then discussed individually is that the western European second-wave women's movements of the 1970s and 1980s manifested themselves also as distinct national events. They were mostly initiated and concentrated in large urban centres (see chapter 1). The publication explosion that accompanied or facilitated the women's movements occurred locally. They were confined and circumscribed by language, culture and, initially, by sheer proximity. Women within Europe needed to expend special energy to break through national barriers and to create their own intra-European discourse. All other issues of history and politics aside, the language barrier alone was and is an obstacle to communication within Europe, even though for intra-European meetings the English language has become the lingua franca. Whatever the intentions of feminists were in the early days of the post-World War II movement, there were practical and linguistic limits that defined the situation. Many Dutch people, for instance, speak several languages but who, outside the Netherlands, can read and understand Dutch (De Vries, 1981: 389)? And how many languages would one need to be able to speak in order to follow trends and ideas adequately? In the European context the answer is: one never speaks enough languages, and even if one did, how would one gain access to publications and know which would be the most important texts to read?

I wanted to write this book also in order to redress, at least a little, the balance in the international feminist debate by introducing the events and debates of western European countries in a comprehensive narrative. Of course, international feminism has long since recognised the communication gaps and inequities and has sporadically solicited papers about 'the women's movements' of countries with a low international profile. But such attempts, by their nature, have remained eclectic and certainly have not been able to result in a sharing of ideas. There have been some specific and some noteworthy studies, many small descriptive articles on the various movements hidden in and dispersed over a wide variety of specialist journals, and a few books of readings. But to date there has been no easily accessible publication that describes, analyses and assesses the phenomenon of the western European women's movements in toto. It is hoped that this book will fill the gap. True to this purpose, the English-speaking countries of Europe (Great Britain and Ireland) receive only marginal attention.

To redress the balance a little in international feminist debate, even in the late 1980s, is an urgent undertaking. That debate, up to the 1980s, has been dominated by English-speaking countries and by the English language as the international lingua franca. Not surprisingly, an English-language feminism has evolved which, over more than two decades, has become highly sophisticated. It is international in the sense that it comes from different countries and supranational in the sense that the discourse no longer requires national identification. Judging by the great familiarity feminist writers of Canada, Australia, England and the USA have with each other, names that appear side by side in bookshops of any of these countries, it has become almost irrelevant from where the texts originated.

There is another side to this, however. English-speaking international feminism, by its own accepted standards of communication, has felt too secure in the belief that it is international when it is so only in the narrowest sense. Spivak noted in the late 1970s that 'International Feminism' in US universities spasmodically included a little French, Italian, German and Latin American feminist information (Spivak, 1981: 155), but most of it was confined to the English-language circuit. Undoubtedly though, there has been a growing interest in feminism in other parts of the world, including western Europe, and there is a growing number of people quite rightly lamenting the fact that so few publications on Europe are available in English. Indeed, few publications on European feminism pre-date 1985. Amongst them are those of French writers, and a few titles by German and Italian writers which have recently been translated into English.

There may be well over 300 million native speakers of English in the world, but just in western Europe alone there are almost as many who do not count English as their native language. Non-English-language countries have partaken in the feminist discourse largely as listeners and as recipients. This challenges the notion that all European feminism has been 'imperial' as Amos and Parmar have suggested. Mainstream feminism is undoubtedly 'white' feminism but, despite their justifiable criticism of international feminism, it has definitely never been Eurocentric (Amos & Parmar, 1984). What these writers demonstrate is that they too have allowed themselves to believe that the English-language voices from Europe, which are almost exclusively British, somehow represent and make up Europe. The Dutch, Greek, Finnish, Portuguese, Swiss or Icelandic woman is usually not found in the English-language discourse.

The channels of written communication have been, and still are, limited by these linguistic barriers[1] and they are not always vastly improved by the possibility of translation. First, it would be ludicrous to imagine that every text in every European language should or could be translated into every other. Second, there are delays in publications of texts that mark important stages in the women's movement of the respective country. Foreign language material must prove its worth before being taken over by a local publisher, and that may take years. Some feminist books are now beginning to cross national boundaries, but often it is five or even ten years after they have first appeared in their original language. Third, there are accidental criteria for a publication of a text, governed by such factors as whether someone happens to have seen and read a title in another language and is willing to promote it and find a suitable publisher. Although these conditions apply to any non-feminist text as well, it must be remembered that the publishing houses which are heavily involved in the publication of feminist texts are usually feminist publishing ventures operating on shoestring budgets and are therefore not in a position to take risks.

How unpredictable and haphazard the communication of feminist ideas via the written text is across western European countries can be gauged by an examination of book titles and authors in different countries. My own visits to bookshops in London, Paris and Berlin revealed that there was rarely an overlap of titles among the bookshops in these cities, apart from those stemming from English-speaking countries. A Norwegian author appeared in one, a Danish author in another, a few Italian authors in this but not that country, a Dutch author (Anja Meulenbelt) had one publication in French, another in English and yet another in German, but her complete works were not found together in one language and one place outside the Netherlands. The flow of feminist books across national borders has not been studied systematically to date but there is a good deal of evidence for the impression that this flow is rarely fast, systematic or based on reciprocity. In 1989, one was still more likely to find American and English texts (in the original or in translation) in feminist bookshops than books and journals from neighbouring countries.

The problem of dissemination of information via the written text has hardly been helped by official national attitudes, which at times almost seemed intent on suppressing feminist material. This is generally not true of English-language countries and there are other exceptions, but I have found, more often than not, that general bookshops rarely carry feminist titles. Some national and state libraries had no stock of the most representative titles; for instance, one of the large German state libraries that I visited only held a handful of feminist texts and most of these were in languages other than German, so that even these few were inaccessible to a wide circle of readers. In response to such an untenable situation, feminists have taken the matter into their own hands and have created special feminist archives: a very diffuse and almost clandestine network throughout western Europe that greets the visitor with the kind of fast, efficient, relaxed and friendly service typical of underground conspiratorial groups.

The funding of these ventures differs vastly between countries and regions but overall, with some laudable exceptions, they are noticeably skewed at the bottom end of funding and subsidy schemes for libraries and archives (Gassen, 1981: 28). Most of the archives that I visited in West Germany were maintained on very small allowances or on no state budgets at all. The excellent archive in Berlin, for instance, at the time of my visit was run entirely without funding and built on strong will, long hours and idealism alone. Such archives cannot hope to build up comprehensive stocks of knowledge in one specialised area, let alone branch out and provide representative material of other countries. It has occurred to more than one devoted volunteer (feminist) archivist that the preservation of records of feminist activism, culture and thought for the future is disconcertingly insecure. In this respect, mainland European countries are at a distinct disadvantage in comparison with English-speaking, including new world, countries like the USA and Australia. In most of western Europe, the seeming resistance of some national and university libraries, and ultimately of governments, to preserve feminist knowledge can actively undermine the formulation and dissemination of western European feminist thought.

Fortunately, ideas do not only travel via the route of libraries and bookshops. European women have taken charge of their own intra-national communication via journals, conferences, meetings and intensive networking. The impetus for doing so came from the self-understanding of the movements as being intrinsically *international,* notwithstanding the fact that they were indigenous and nationally definable. In almost all movements, whether they started in the late 1960s or as recently as the 1980s, a strong sense of solidarity and sisterhood across national and European borders developed almost at once. It was partly built on the small stock of shared knowledge that almost all movements had in common. Apart from the French contribution by Simone de Beauvoir, *The Second Sex,* which preceded any other feminist book of the postwar era by over a decade, there were titles from English-speaking countries, mainly the USA, which found their way into most European countries: Betty Friedan's book *The Feminine Mystique* (1963), Germaine Greer's work *The Female Eunuch* (1970), Shulamith Firestone's *The Dialectics of Sex* (1971) and *Sexual Politics* (1972) by Kate Millet (Lovenduski, 1986: 67; Schenk, 1980: 89; De Vries, 1981: 395).

That these books became so very influential had a good deal to do with the similarity of women's experiences worldwide. Simone de Beauvoir was once asked towards the end of her life (she died in April 1986) what she had learned over the years for and about women and why she was a feminist. Her reply was: 'I have understood the unfathomable depth of women's oppression' (Schwarzer, 1983: 73). Every woman in the movement, even if she was not capable of formulating the agonising truth of women's oppression as Simone de Beauvoir had done, understood that there was oppression and that the experience of the 'second sex' was not confined geographically but was universal. The titles which did much to launch the second-wave women's movements succeeded in doing so because they reassured women that their gnawing (but often suppressed) feelings of injustice were indeed warranted, that they were not alone in thinking about their disadvantage and they were not unique in their predicament. 'Women of the world unite' was not just an empty catch-cry but arose from the firm belief that there was such a thing as a gender-based discrimination that concerned women everywhere.

Within its own national boundaries, each western European country has produced feminists right across the ideological spectrum. Each country has its share of liberal, socialist or radical feminists and a share in public protest actions on such issues as rape, abortion or employment. The price for diversity is often fragmentation, which indeed some second-wave movements in western Europe have experienced. The disadvantages of local fragmentation have often been blurred, however, by participation in intra-national and international forums. If the forum was capable of remaining international, it did so by entering already existing communication channels and networks of English-speaking overseas countries, by supplying arguments, news and general information to international feminist journals, news networks and organisations.[2] A second venue of internationalism was assured for those feminists who joined forces with other international movements of the postwar era, such as international socialism, the peace movement and the gay liberation movement. The feminist and gay movements, as well as the peace movement and international socialism, have a well-established international forum for generalist and scholarly conferences with extraordinarily high participation rates of delegates from all over the world.[3] All these activities ensure a level of continuity of thought and provide a basis for shared knowledge and spontaneous communication, superseding even the efforts of women in the 1920s.

Western European feminists of the second wave have developed unusual strengths all their own. Although each country has produced proponents of every political shade and for any issue dubbed 'women's issue', the European strength lies in what appears to be national specialisations and emphases. As if a division of labour had been planned, western European countries complement each other by difference. French feminism, while it can boast many very important groups, has made its best known contributions in highly abstract philosophical debates. Italian feminism is much more readily identifiable with political activism and political theory of the left than it is with other areas. German feminism is chiefly pragmatic or historical in orientation but has excelled also in film-making. Dutch feminism relies heavily on consciousness raising. Greek feminism, however embryonic, is revolutionary in fervour. Swedish and Finnish feminism is much more a mainstream political reformism than elsewhere, while Norway, Denmark and Portugal have made outstanding contributions to literary feminism. Most countries have produced a wealth of new literature of astounding variety and excellence. Whatever the predominant paradigm of a country may be, together, western European countries offer a very original tapestry, rich in colour and surprising in design and texture, which has helped shape the face of culture, of political debate, of literature and of everyday life.

NOTES

1  Some countries, well aware of their linguistic disadvantage (i.e. speaking a less well-known language), have resorted to producing some of their own journals in English to ensure transnational distribution. The Swedish–English Literary Translators Association, for instance, regularly translates Swedish texts. In addition, they issue a series called *Swedish Book Review*, which at times provides systematic bibliographical information on English translations of Swedish texts or on subjects dealing with Sweden in English. It usually features information on women in Sweden. Finland publishes a journal called *Books from Finland* in which one may find translated short stories, poems and also excerpts from novels, including many written by women. The excellent Dutch feminist archive publishes quarterly bibliographical information, interspersed with titles of other languages.

2  The number of intra-European feminist journals are too numerous to mention. Throughout the 1970s their number grew substantially and most of them are now well established. News-sheets, such as *Women's International Network News* (*WIN*), includes reports on all five continents. One important generalist publication, called *Women of Europe*, provides constant up-to-date information on all relevant aspects of women's lives from all member states, including Europe-wide statistical information on women. It appears in several languages and is issued by the Information Office for Women's Organisations and Press of the Commission of European Communities in Brussels. Apart from the commission's work, there is the European Coordination Centre for Research and Documentation in Social Sciences, which conducts on a regular basis the European Cooperation in Social Science Information and Documentation Programme (ECSSID). The third volume in the Vienna Centre's Series of 'Inventories of Social Science Research in Europe' is called *The Changing Role of Women in Society. A Documentation of Current Research and Research Projects in Progress 1981–1983* (Richter et al., 1985) and is a compilation of women's research in twenty European countries with in-depth accounts on thirteen of these. Such reports are being updated periodically, thus providing useful information on current activities.

3  International feminist conferences, now a regular global feature, have frequently taken place in Europe. One held in Dublin in 1987 was followed in Amsterdam in 1988, by the International Conference on Women's History. In the same year, the eighth ILIS conference (International Lesbian Information Service), congregated in Vienna and brought together the largest gathering of European lesbians ever. Amsterdam holds conferences on gay liberation and gay research. In Los Angeles, a first international Eco-feminist conference was held, attracting a large contingent of European feminists, partly in response to the Chernobyl disaster. Since 1986, socialist feminists meet regularly each year in a different host city (Copenhagen, Hamburg, Madrid etc.).

# PART I

## Western European women: an overview

# 1     The postwar movements

The meaning of the term 'movement' is not at all unequivocal or unambiguous. Broadly speaking, 'movements' are visible collective actions. But such a definition is patently insufficient because there have always been 'collective actions' throughout history: the peasant uprisings of earlier centuries or the collective workers' actions of 19th century Europe were movements of a particular structure, held together by class solidarity and class-specific experiences. What we need, then, is a characterisation of a specific cluster of movements in the post-World War II era in the western industrialised world to which the feminist movements belong. Melucci rightly argued that the classical model of collective action 'has been exhausted under industrial capitalism' and the 'social and political dimensions of collective conflict have diverged', being markedly slanted now in favour of distinct social conflicts (Melucci, 1988: 246).

At the very heart of feminist theory is a challenge to the dichotomous use of terms such as 'public' and 'private', 'personal' and 'political'. Until the postwar movements, 'social' had generally been seen as being inferior to 'political'. Thus it has been said of the French Revolution that its proponents forfeited important political opportunities and rights by emphasising social problems. By having concentrated on the issue of poverty, for instance, the chance of universal suffrage was lost (Arendt, 1973: 60–1). Indeed, it was one of the first tasks of the new movements to challenge the terms 'political' and 'social' and, to a lesser extent, 'cultural'. In 1968 Kate Millet stated in her book *Sexual Politics* that the relationship of one group to another group, or of one individual to another individual, is political when one dominates or rules the other. In 1971 US feminists founded a *political* journal in Cambridge, Massachusetts, called *The Second Wave*, which the editors defined 'as a tool with which we hammer at existing social and economic structures to open up new directions for a women's revolution' (Tuttle, 1987: 288). Whether or not the term 'revolution' is justified in this context is not at issue, but the intention of attacking *social* structures in order to effect *political* change is telling. By contrast, critical observers of women's movements, such as Hannah Arendt, have lamented that those movements have in fact made a fatal mistake by largely remaining social and by not having become political enough (Young-Bruehl, 1982: 76–7; Markus, 1989). It has remained a hallmark of both western European and English-speaking women's movements to question, broaden, change and redefine the use of all of the three terms.

## THEIR CHARACTER

The postwar movements are not class bound, at least not theoretically and by definition, and they are not necessarily definable in terms of the classical political ideological division of 'left' and 'right', although most movements come from specific political traditions. The ecological movement, for instance, has very little to do with traditional political alliances, although it has more often than not flirted with the left. The new movements have generally not arisen (and it is mostly not their stated aim) to take over the power of the state. Most arose to challenge the way in which that power is *exercised*. Yet many new movements of western Europe, such as the women's movements, the ecological and the peace movements, have in fact formed their own parties. The Greens and the 'Women's lists', in countries such as Norway, West Germany, Denmark and Iceland, were created with the intention of being voted into government or becoming the government. The demarcation lines between 'social' and 'political' are indeed blurred and the feminist viewpoint that the 'social is political' is an important conceptual amendment.

One of the salient features of the new movements, according to Touraine, is their link to biological status in post-industrial or rather 'programmed society' (see also Badham, 1984, on post-industrial and programmed society). Touraine argues:

> The specificity of social conflict in a programmed society resides in the fact that the ruling class appears to hold sway over all of social life, a state of affairs that prevents the dominated from speaking and acting from the stronghold of a social and cultural autonomy. They are forced, then, to oppose social domination in the name of the only thing that may yet escape it, namely nature. This is what is important about the ecological movement, which appeals to life against a production ethic, pollution, and the dangers of nuclear contamination. It explains as well the importance of protest movements that rely upon a biological and not a social status: gender, youth, but also old age, membership in an ethnic group. (Touraine, 1988: 111)

The argument is persuasive indeed but raises a problem of a reductionist, socio-biological kind. It has been part of many of the new protest movements to challenge the view that biological status should assign social status, or, more radically, that social status is explained by biology. Simone de Beauvoir said over 40 years ago in her work *The Second Sex*: 'One is not born, but becomes a woman. No biological, psychological, or economic fate determines the figure that the human female presents in society: it is civilization as a whole that produces this creature, intermediate between male and eunuch, which is described as feminine' (Beauvoir, 1952: 249). Monique Wittig, one of the prolific French writers of the new wave, expressed the same sentiment that a substantial number of feminists of the new movement would have underwritten:

> A materialist feminist approach to women's oppression destroys the idea that women are a 'natural group' ... the division from men of which women have been the object is a political one and shows how we have been ideologically rebuilt into a 'natural group'. In the case of women, ideology goes far since our bodies as well as our minds are the product of this manipulation. We have been compelled in our bodies and in our minds to correspond, feature by feature, with the *idea* of nature that has been established for us. Distorted to such an extent that our deformed body is what they call 'natural', what is supposed to exist as such before oppression. Distorted to such an extent that in the end oppression seems to be a consequence of this 'nature' within ourselves (a nature which is only an *idea*). (Wittig, 1981: 47)

The issue of biological and social status becomes even more ambivalent with respect to the gay liberation movement. Some would have said that their movement did not 'rely on' biological status, as Touraine suggests, but that the very premise on which such a biological assignment rested needed to be called into question.

One of the outstanding features of the postwar movements lies in their self-definition. By this I mean the new positive group identity. Leaders of today's movements, unlike movement leaders in the 19th century or earlier, are not just representatives but are an integral part of them. With rare exception, today's movements speak on behalf of themselves. There are no white leaders for black movements, no men speaking on behalf of women's movements. By their own definition, movements based on gender, ethnicity and sexuality tend to view with suspicion any attempts by outsiders to take an active role in their affairs, let alone have control as spokespeople. At best, the role of the outsider can be that of a sympathiser on the fringe of the movement.

There are at least two ways of assessing this phenomenon. One is to argue that a movement will be more effective politically if it musters support from disinterested parties (Arendt, 1973: 167). Such disinterestedness signals to the world that the actor has nothing to gain personally by speaking on behalf of others. There is no 'selfish' motive and no fear that the present (democratic) equilibrium, with its diffusion of power, is in any way usurped by the represented group (Lucas, 1976; Maddox, 1986: 2).

Disinterestedness in a more concrete sense also signals an objectivity of argument which is usefully applied in bureaucratic structures. Bureaucracies, the administrative backbone of democracies, are meant to be value-free and objective. By contrast, the subjective leaders and spokespersons of movements today act as their own advocates and fight their own case for themselves and the group. Anne Summers, an Australian feminist, has rightly pointed out that feminists who have gone into bureaucracies with the aim of effecting change from within 'the system' on behalf of and for women, have played very ambivalent roles. Their position unavoidably defined them as 'missionaries' or as 'mandarins': on the one hand arguing ideologically and, on the other, having special-interest claims in an environment which is not designed to foster expression of self-interest (Summers, 1986; see also Lynch, 1984).

Self-advocacy undoubtedly has very positive features. It is a healthy sign of modern democracies to allow dissent without the intervention of a disinterested (and possibly regarded as more respectable?) spokesperson. Yet some movements have ultimately failed to stake a claim in the world at large because they have not continued to argue their case with reference to that world, but turned inwards, thereby forfeiting the very public space that they had just claimed. Black liberationists have been read by blacks, feminists by women. One oppressed group may have read the literature of another; only rarely has the oppressing majority culture read the literatures of oppression. The exceptions are all the more noteworthy and conspicuous.

Ironically, oppression never means marginality. On the contrary, oppression indicates a firm place within the social construct. Whether as a slave or as a housewife, there is a niche assigned, and society relies on this niche being filled so that it can function in its own preset ways. Only the oppressed actor's *recognition* of oppression actually creates marginality in so far as the actor decides to *leave* the previously assigned role. Then, only then, is the actor without a firm place. Creating a new niche somewhere in that structure is either the aim or the cause for the resistance; creating merely another niche may be possible but it may also mean little if any change within the social structure as a whole. Asking for a thorough revision of that structure and its assumptions, before finding a niche, may be and has been the revolutionary content of many factions of the new women's movements.

By their very nature, movements are circumscribed: they have a beginning and an end; that is, are cyclical. It is rather easy to assume that their disappearance also implies a disappearance of the very force that consolidated them from the outset. This view fails to account for the forces that made the movement a visible collective activity in the first place. Melucci argues that movements would not be possible if it were not for another complementary face of movements, that of *submerged networks*. He writes that it would be hard, for instance, to 'understand the massive peace mobilization if one does not take into account the vitality of the submerged networks'. 'Mobilization', he continues, is only possible by the daily production of 'alternative frameworks which nourish mobilization potential' (1988: 248). In the case of women's movements in western Europe, those submerged networks have existed for most of the 19th and 20th centuries. And even if they change their action potential in empirically measurable terms in the near future, they are likely to persist, probably long after the more dramatic outward signs of protest have disappeared.

Furthermore, women's movements are indebted to industrialisation and parliamentary democracies. Indeed, women's movements are part and parcel and a *symptom* of modern industrialised society. They have more in common with these economic developments than even with the ideals of the French Revolution. The system that has created the impetus for their very existence is also the soil for dissent; it has created the space and environment for its own discrediting. Wittingly or unwittingly, women have become a true embodiment of the spirit of the modern phase of technocracy and are often agents in maintaining and developing the very system that has helped create oppression against which women needed to rally. Likewise, modern women's movements are dependent on the political system of parliamentary democracy. Not one 20th century European movement has survived and run its natural course in a system other than a parliamentary democracy. The Polish Solidarity Movement is perhaps the only example of a fully fledged new social movement outside the precincts of a democratic framework. But it must be noted here too that up to 1981 its activities were legal and this initially allowed for some manœuvrability (Markus, 1985: 17).

Democracy and capitalism, if it must be said, are two systems which do not complement each other but, in their fundamental assumptions, contradict each other. The modern new-wave movements, I would suggest, are a kind of deus ex machina in that their role has been to expose the contradictions of the two systems' coexistence. However, because the social movements are as much a product as they are opponents of these contradictions, they harbour these contradictions themselves and circumscribe their own limits. Chapters 3 to 6 of this book will develop these arguments in detail, in reference to actual situations. Suffice it to say here that the modern ideal of democracy as egalitarian stands in stark contrast to the strictly hierarchical, competitive and discriminatory nature of capitalism. Yet in all nations surveyed in this book, capitalism and democracy seem to coexist in a natural, even supposedly harmonious way. Heller recently explained why this is possible. She contends that one of the paradoxes of formal democracy is that it does not reveal anything of the economic structure of society, its relations of contract, and its power relations. This is 'why formal democracy can coexist with capitalist society' (Heller, 1988: 138).

Our understanding of democracy, however, has altered substantially over this century. Today, we do not understand democracy merely in formal, political terms but also in social terms, taking much more seriously the notion of egalitarianism, of equality of opportunity and so forth. In other words, we have moved to interpretations of democracy that are explicit about its potential social dimensions. Modern political theorists, particularly of the left, tend to welcome this process as one of increasing democratisation (Bobbio, 1987: 32). Such interpretations of the social principles of democracy, however, are then made in *defiance* of the ideological principles of capitalism, and in the case of the women's movements, in *defiance* of patriarchy (Pateman, 1988).

Many political theorists, most notably theorists of the stature of Bobbio and Sartori, have pointed out that 20th century democracies have promoted the growth of bureaucracies. Within bureaucracies, the power apparatus is strictly hierarchical and thus the very nature of bureaucracies in their application of the tasks of democratic government is diametrically opposed to the ideal of democratic power. The dynamics of change work very differently in either model, as Bobbio has recently argued (1987: 38): in democratic societies, power is transmitted from the base upwards, while in bureaucratic societies power descends from the top. Political significance can only be attributed to movements if present democracies can successfully incorporate a concept of grassroots activity into the actual working of the system. Bureaucracies cannot do that because power in them does not rest with the people in the broadest or in the narrowest sense.

Deutsch's cascade model, developed several decades earlier and admittedly concerned with international relations rather than national ones, is still a useful and interesting model. In his view, demands arise among the elites, and cascade downward, until they finally receive support at the mass level (Deutsch, 1968). His views fit well with the analysis of the functioning of modern bureaucracies and they have had support among disillusioned feminists, such as Ingunn Norderval who wrote: 'The popular notion of democracy as the creator of equality receives no more than qualified support. Extension of equal rights to women has not been the result of a "bubbling up" of grassroots demands that are finally placed on the government agenda. Rather, we see an instance of Karl W. Deutsch's cascade model' (Norderval, 1986: 78). Deutsch's model, however, cannot quite account for new 'massive tides of opinion', as Sartori put it (1987: 94), and for new massive counter cultures.

Democracy, in its broadest definition, is rule by majority consent. Having said this, Bobbio points out that minority *dissent* is therefore implicitly an integral part of democracy (1987: 61). Only in the latter model can any movement, including the women's movement, become really 'transformational'. The question is whether social collective action is ultimately futile because it is powerless or whether it is a political force precisely because its political system *invites* grassroots activity as the very essence of its continued existence. In other words, those who argue for the strength and immediate socio-political relevance of a social movement must first believe in a concept of the present politico-economic system that allows grassroots activity to have that relevance. They must also believe that this framework is capable of overriding (or undermining?) the structured, hierarchical nature of bureaucracies, indeed of capitalism and patriarchy.

## THEIR SIGNIFICANCE

Having characterised some of the features of the postwar movements, what can we say of their significance? Alain Touraine argues that it is not that modern societies can explain the movements but that the movements may shed light on the dynamics, structure and essence of modern society. Touraine would have it this way. He detects no 'marginality' in the present-day movements but sees them as holding the *key* to understanding our modern world (Touraine, 1988).

Touraine is not alone in recognising the importance of the movements of the postwar era. The interest in them is informed by a specific set of questions for the future; stated sociologically: the idea of the *social actor,* actively working towards personal liberation; stated politically: the idea of civic society and the rights and responsibilities of the citizen within democracies. The new critical theories of democracy, the revival of the idea of the republic and a new formulation of the 'communal good' by the so-called communitarians for instance, all bespeak the importance of considering movements. In doing so we raise questions of citizenship, of rights and obligations and the possible trajectory of personal freedom and the communal good in the future (Mouffe, 1988; Cohen, 1981, 1985; Arato & Cohen, 1984, 1988).

Most feminist writers will claim that these social movements, despite their departure from the classical political model, are socially *and* politically significant. Katzenstein, for instance, regards the women's movements as transformational in character (Katzenstein, 1987: 5). This is to say that by virtue of their capacity to expose irrationalities and injustices in the political functioning of the dominant modus operandi they can radically redefine politics and challenge dominant values and norms of our everyday life, eventually transforming institutions, elites, laws and even the nature of social relationships. Yet this interpretation of the significance of the women's movements may be too idealistic and endow it with salient features it cannot possess and will not acquire. In later chapters we will see that the impact of women's movements has not and cannot be as unlimited or as 'transformational' as has been assumed or hoped. This is not to be pessimistic, by any means, but merely to suggest that there are real and ideological constraints.

The new women's movements, as other recent movements of the postwar era, were staking very high claims indeed and were part of a postwar upsurge against certain values and against the structured inequality of western capitalist societies. All of them were about renegotiations of value hierarchies and power hierarchies, to some extent demanding a fairer share in the supposed democracies in which they lived, or experimenting with alternative lifestyles and assumptions. The concepts of civil rights and civil disobedience gained great popularity in the postwar years and were embodied so splendidly by extraordinary men such as Mahatma Gandhi and Martin Luther King. Both had shown the world that it was possible to effect political change by peaceful protest, without the use of violence or the threat of weapons. Both had demonstrated that the strategies they used were capable of successful intervention in power politics. And it is this success which gave hope to other movements, especially the women's movements. They too hoped that their social actions would result in change and effectively intervene in power politics.

## WHY CALL IT THE SECOND-WAVE?

What, in historical terms, could be meant by second-wave movements? Our discussion here confines itself to the last twenty years, years of great diversity, activity and innovation, starting in the late 1960s and extending to the present day. The dates were not chosen arbitrarily, but rather were defined by historical context, that is, by the women's movements themselves. It is generally agreed that the so-called 'second-wave' movements in western Europe began in France and West Germany around 1968. In the two decades following 1968, most other western European countries either 'took off' to a full movement or had episodes of publicly proclaimed solidarity amongst women on certain issues. By the end of the International Decade of Women (1985), every western European country had had some experience with women's publicly enunciated demands and ideas and had been forced to reconsider and to amend its legislature and social practices, sometimes drastically revising its thinking about discrimination against women. Most feminists of the late 1980s would agree that the heyday of the second-wave movement is over (Friedan, 1985; D'Souza, 1986). These years are certainly worth exploring in their own right but, of course, there are risks in doing so. Presenting any period in history as if it were self-contained and independent of preceding ideas and events would seemingly deny the dynamics of history and of the importance of specific responses to traditions, ideas and concrete circumstances.

On first exposure to the term 'second wave', a reader may well decide that, logically, this should mean that there must have been a first wave which had forged the way. But this is misleading and applies only to a certain degree, in essence as well as in name. The fact that male historiography has failed to take note of women's activities in earlier ages and has had little interest in recording them for posterity has nothing to do with the fact that there have been many activities by women throughout history which we would now term 'feminist'.

It is one of the very important achievements of present-day feminist historians to have begun uncovering feminist activities and thoughts of previous centuries and continuities of thought and actions from one generation to the next (see, for instance, Mitchell & Oakley, 1976; Bridenthal & Koonz, 1977; Riemer & Fout, 1983). Expressed differently, by terming the movements of this century the 'first', 'second', or 'third', one might imply that there was nothing preceding them. As we now know, this is simply not true. The summary terms of 'first' and 'second' wave can only be used as convenient terms for identifying certain recent clusters in women's activities on a global scale.

In a sense, even these terminological precautions do not save one from causing confusion and from remaining somewhat controversial because, generally, these global statements do not hold when each country is considered individually. The first wave, waning around the 1920s, was certainly the first *international* women's movement. But after it subsided each country followed again its own course of events and local movements began to diverge markedly one from another. The Scandinavian countries, for instance, never really experienced a second wave in terms of their own parameters but continued from the achievements of the 1920s with slow but fairly steady reforms made by left-wing or socialist governments. Italy usually distinguishes three or even four, rather than two, waves of women's movements. In countries like Portugal and Greece, which have emerged from military dictatorships only in the last fifteen years, the women's movements of the 1970s and 1980s are more or less first-wave movements, although even here more and more remarkable predecessors have been rediscovered.

Even in countries where there had been mass movements in the late 19th or early 20th centuries, it is not always historically correct to say that they laid the foundations for second-wave movements. In fact, in some countries the two waves have been completely distinct from one another, the second one rising almost without any foundation on or knowledge of the first. Such discontinuities in social knowledge are undoubtedly related to the two world wars and to the ideologies governing the time: any radical or reformist movement in the western world was swiftly suspended in World War I; and in the years preceding World War II the rising right-wing and fascist ideologies thwarted any progress women might have made to that point. Fascism was an extreme form of misogyny, a political and world view for, by and about men (Theweleit, 1987). In the fascist world that men wished to occupy and rule, concrete measures of policy and moral coercion tactics were devised to convince women that they were highly regarded only when they fulfilled their allegedly innate biological functions of mothering and child rearing in the marital home (Kaplan & Adams, 1990). Under the military dictatorships of Portugal, Spain, Greece and the fascist to-talitarian governments in Italy and Germany of the 1930s, European women were forced back into the narrowest role, that of procreation (Bridenthal et al., 1984). The only women who felt none of these constraints were those who were happy to contribute large numbers of children to their 'fatherland' (and to the armies), or girls and young women who were beguiled by the supposed freedom they enjoyed in girls' and women's organisations.

In the years of fascist terror, a terror which centred most strongly in Germany and Italy but was felt in concentric circles throughout Europe, the progress women had made was not just undermined but actually often reversed, with newly gained liberties being taken away. Worse still, the years of fascist rule often succeeded in eradicating the knowledge of there ever having been a women's movement. But while women were often not in touch with their own history—what feminists came to call, unetymologically but pertinently, 'herstory'—they were keenly aware of the immediate, oppressive past. Hence, the second-wave movements in countries in which there was a strong fascist past were in many ways not so much a resumption of the issues and concerns of the first movement, not a re-claiming of the arguments and beliefs of the 1920s, as a violent rejection of anything vaguely resembling fascist ideology and what it had asked of and done to women. Many Italian feminists today, for instance, are still adamantly against the idea of women's separatism because, under fascism, women had been allowed to occupy a separate space in public life (in organisations and functions) without ever being allowed to expand their economic role, or ever gaining the least amount of political influence (Glaab, 1980: 38). In West Germany, and also in Italy, the legacy of fascism certainly produced demonstrable tensions in many areas where the social values were dramatically at odds with the political systems of democracy and equal rights policies, but first and foremost it did so primarily in those areas concerned with women. In comparison, those countries that had escaped the retrogressive measures of fascism did not lose all the ground that earlier feminist efforts had claimed. In the 1960s countries like Sweden, Finland and even France were able to show female enrolments of over 40 percent of their respective student body at universities (Juillard, 1976: 117–18).

## WHY THE NEW WAVE MOVEMENTS DEVELOPED

It seems to be fashionable to say that the new movements 'grew out of' the student movement of the late 1960s (Vedder-Schults, 1978: 59) or some other phenomenon such as the educational reform movements (Peterson, 1985: 631). This view can be substantiated only partially. It is true that the women's move-

ments of the late 1960s to 1980s have usually been coeval with other movements but it is disputable whether they have been either offshoots of them or
dependent on them. Many women belonged to several movements and participated in demonstrations well before they branched off to form their own organisations. Women learned from such political activism. If they did not know
before, women learned how to organise and voice dissent, but the *content* of
their protest was often substantially different from that of other, previous,
movements. There were instances where women marched and fought with socialists, students, unionists, anti-war demonstrators and other (male) political
activists and these women saw their aims and interests postponed in the name
of 'more important' issues. Although women like Carla Ravaioli saw that alliances in the fight for women's liberation 'could only be with the political organisations of the left' (Ravaioli, 1977: 13; Doormann, 1979: 47), the strength of
the association depended on at what cost to themselves and to the movement
in question women were willing to push that alliance. Years later, many women
regretted having wasted so much time and energy in proffering support for
causes that were not their own (Hellmann, 1987: 120).

If one argues that the women's movements had their own impetus and arose
of their own accord and for their own reasons, it is impossible simply to relegate
the cause and growth of women's movements to other movements of the time.
Although the new movements in western Europe tended to become visible only
in the late 1960s, it would be difficult to exaggerate the importance of World
War II as one of the factors contributing to the ideology of these movements.
When Germany finally capitulated in 1945, Europe rose from the ashes with at
least one immediate idealistic goal: the unification of Europe. This dream was
not a new one by any means but in 1946, at the time when Churchill gave
expression to this view in Zurich (Benz & Graml, 1983: 13), it made very
concrete sense in terms of *realpolitik*. In the eyes of many it was the only future
road for the survival of Europe. Most believed that strong bonds had to be
formed if European countries were in any way to maintain their own political
and economic strength, sandwiched as they were between the two new super-
powers, the USA and the USSR. The period of the Cold War notwithstanding,
the entire postwar period is marked by attempts to translate this aim of unification into reality. In practice, such aims required discussion on standardisation
of economic, political and social matters across European borders. Some of
these identifiably benefited women because they accelerated the implementation
of policies like equality of opportunity at the workplace.

The processes involved in the pursuit of European unification have been slow,
complicated and arduous. Beginnings towards unification were made in two
different directions, one via political and another via economic channels. The
years to come were to show that there was no more than lukewarm support for
any political unification, but the idea of economic collaboration was to take hold
and give postwar Europe a special place in the economic world. In 1948, ten
western European signatories formed the European Council. Although its
membership continued to increase over the years, this body never gained the
political importance which had been hoped for it, just as the European Parliament so far has not acquired any far-reaching powers. One of the first contributors
to a freer inter-European money management and flow of funds was achieved
as a result of the European Payments Union of 1950, followed in 1958 by the
European Monetary Agreement. These agreements, writes Postan (1967: 105),
freed trade 'from the worst of the formalities, restrictions, and shortages which

**Member states of the European Communities and other European organisations**

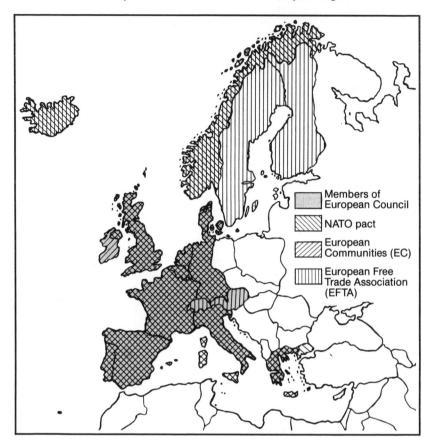

had impeded the settlements of commercial claims before the war'. The Montan Union, formed in 1951, proved to be of more consequence. It was a solid mainland union which at once combined economic, political and defence goals independent of the NATO Pact. In 1957 these and other pacts culminated in the signing of the Treaty of Rome, creating two new bodies, Euratom and the European Economic Community (EEC). The latter has proved particularly successful, or obnoxious, depending on a country's position within the world economy, and has expanded over the years. Belgium, Netherlands, Luxembourg, West Germany, Italy and France have been part of one of the alliances since 1951. Denmark, Ireland, England and Northern Ireland joined the EEC in 1973, Greece in 1981 and Spain and Portugal in 1986. The face of the organisation has also changed over the years. In 1967, the EEC, Euratom and the Montan Union merged into the umbrella organisation of the European Communities, which in 1986 adopted the old European Council flag, representing the twelve member states. Other western European countries which are not members are either neutral in status, as are Switzerland, Austria and Sweden, or have special associative arrangements with the European Communities or other European organisations, such as Finland and Norway.

Table 1.1   Annual average compound growth rate of real output per capita, Europe
1913–1976

| Country | 1913–1950 | 1950–1970 | 1970–1973 | 1974–1976 |
|---|---|---|---|---|
| | % | % | % | % |
| Austria | 0.2 | 4.9 | 4.90 | 3.8 |
| Belgium | 0.7 | 3.3 | 3.64 | 3.3 |
| Denmark | 1.1 | 3.3 | 3.34 | 1.5 |
| Finland | 1.3 | 4.3 | 4.45 | 3.4 |
| France | 1.0 | 4.2 | 4.35 | 3.2 |
| Germany (W.) | 0.8 | 5.3 | 5.02 | 2.0 |
| Greece | 0.2 | 5.9 | 6.18 | 4.1 |
| Ireland | 0.7 | 2.8 | 3.02 | 1.8 |
| Italy | 0.8 | 5.0 | 4.69 | 2.2 |
| Netherlands | 0.9 | 3.6 | 3.67 | 2.7 |
| Norway | 1.8 | 3.2 | 3.31 | 4.0 |
| Portugal | 0.9 | 4.8 | 5.27 | 3.5 |
| Spain | −0.3 | 5.4 | 5.21 | 4.2 |
| Sweden | 2.5 | 3.3 | 3.04 | 2.1 |
| Switzerland | 1.6 | 3.0 | 2.94 | −0.2 |
| UK | 0.8 | 2.2 | 2.31 | 1.8 |

Source: Pollard,1981: 315

Materially and spiritually there was an upsurge of confidence in the 1950s and 1960s. This confidence was partly an offshoot as well as a consequence of technological innovation and advance, particularly in the aircraft industry, in plastics, electronics, artificial fibres, antibiotics and antihistamines. Advances were 'more widespread and rapid than at any time in the past' (Postan, 1967: 143). Contributory factors were labour attitudes and the quality of educational systems, providing university-trained technicians who were the 'sine qua non of technological progress and of economic growth' (Postan, 1967: 156).

Most countries of the EEC, especially West Germany, experienced an economic boom. Pollard noted that Europe climbed out of its economic setback 'with astonishing ease' and exceeded prewar output as early as 1949, showing signs of unprecedented growth by 1951. But, as he also said, the Marshall Plan, passed in 1948, injected US$13 billion-worth of American goods and services and a further US$10.5 billion in counterpart funds into the European economy, giving it 'a shot in the arm at a critical time [which had a] far greater effect than can be measured in dollars' (Pollard, 1981: 13–14). In those two decades daily life improved almost visibly from year to year. Material wealth increased and industries and trade expanded their activities.

The idea of a unified Europe has had some bearing on women and on women's treatment in individual countries, if only as a gentle supranational commitment and as a politics of persuasion. As one of its important packages of collaboration, the Treaty of Rome espoused the principle of economic parity and fair competition which included the rights and costs of female employment. Even though the treaty restricted its interest in women to employment, it actually created a starting point for a change in women's status and self-perception well beyond the employment sphere. I will come back to this later.

Shortages of labour, expressed in guest-worker conscription and a rising demand for female labour, created favourable circumstances for discussions on women's equality with men in the workforce. Between 1948 and 1963 unemployment in most European countries averaged around 1.9 percent or rose, at the most, to about 5 percent. In short, this period was one of 'entrepreneurial euphoria', of high employment and demands 'uninterrupted by crises' (Postan, 1967: 62, 89).

And of course women were now welcome to participate in the labour market, an 'invitation' that was qualitatively different from the conscription of women into war work. During World War II every adult citizen was required or forced to support the war effort, but then released from such imposed duty once the war had ended. The postwar economic boom and rapid rise of living standards in some countries gave women's work a different image. Getting 'back to normal' after the first postwar decade was over should presumably have meant a return to traditional roles. Yet those many women who were widowed or without partners had no way of returning to traditional roles. They raised children whose role models were provided by the single-parent households, by women who managed the lives of their children very adequately. Their daughters, who were in their twenties and early thirties in 1968, are today's feminists. The slogan 'What men can do women can do too' (Schwarzer, 1972) was based on observation of women's experiences and daily combat, rather than on theoretical belief.

Eventually, the increasing participation of women in the workforce and the ongoing negotiation about women's conditions at work were not to remain without repercussions in other areas of daily life. The gradual broadening of women's occupational and educational choices in the 1950s and 1960s amidst a host of discriminatory practices may well have contributed to women's growing awareness of and impatience with social injustices, and it may therefore have been instrumental in bringing about the second-wave mass movements.

World War II's unprecedented devastation of human lives, of families, towns and cities transformed European life. Women helped rebuild nations, the economy, the future. They successfully raised children, worked, borrowed money, and lived without men, transcending previous limited roles as home-makers granted to them by fascist governments.

Undoubtedly also very important were the civil rights movements and the subsequent student movements of the late 1960s, which were coeval with the onset of the women's movements. European universities are generally not autonomous bodies but are directly answerable to a ministry of education (i.e. to the state) and their teachers are public servants employed by the state. The student uprisings in France, Italy and West Germany were thus not just campus revolts but uprisings against the state, and they were taken very seriously as such (Touraine, 1971: 83). It goes without saying that the *models* of these revolts were useful for all of those who participated, including the women whose new experiences could be translated into strategies for women's organisations.

In Europe, civil rights movements began to stir exactly at the time most war-torn countries began to breathe a sigh of relief and notice that the worst was over and one could get on with the business of living. In the USA, the civil rights movement resulted in civil rights Acts in the late 1960s, followed by similar Acts in western European countries. In West Germany for instance, 1968 saw the adoption of the law of the right to resistance (article 20, paragraph 4 of the Constitution). While this civil rights law was conceived of in a very narrow framework, it implicitly provided a legitimate basis for protest and for civil disobedience. It seems more than coincidental that the women's movements of the second wave gained momentum after civil rights Acts had been passed (Evans, 1979).

These contributing factors to macro-level changes are of course not in themselves sufficient to explain the onset of the second-wave movements. Apart from decisive macro-changes in the postwar era, there were a number of important changes at the micro-level which subtly altered infrastructures and perceptions and, over time, expanded women's manoeuvrable space. Again, one will find an interlocking of technological and social change. The results of a survey conducted in Belgium in 1987 are relevant here. The women interviewed were asked what they considered to be the three most important positive changes that had occurred in women's lives in this century. Seventy percent agreed that the contraceptive pill was the most decisive one. The agreement about two further changes was not quite unequivocal as the scores show but they are important to note. Twenty-nine percent thought that obtaining the right to vote was the next most important, and 28 percent named the washing machine (*Women of Europe*, no. 50, 1987: 11). These answers are more astute than they might appear at a glance. They reflect the three bio-social spheres: the body, the public domain and the private domain, or, expressed differently, the biological (reproductive), the political (the vote), and the economic (domestic labour).

It should not come as a surprise that the contraceptive pill ranks so highly in the survey results, nor that there is such a high consensus on this matter. Perhaps for the first time in history, women were given a good measure of control over their bodies and their reproductive potential (Walsh, 1980: 182). For the first time they had a tool by which to plan reproduction according to their own wishes, also opening up the possibility of toying with alternative lifestyles. We know that birthrates may vary substantially across time and that a drop in birthrates is not dependent on new technology. When need arose in the past, couples proved to be quite proficient in finding ways of avoiding pregnancies. But the pill certainly introduced a new measure of freedom for those women who could obtain contraceptives. The drop in birthrates to or below zero population levels since the pill's introduction in almost all western European countries, with the exception of Ireland and Spain, might suggest a number of things, including the possibility that *women* prefer to have fewer children (*Women in Statistics*, 1984: 9).

The pill was first introduced in the early 1960s and quickly spread through most of western Europe. At that time abortion was still a crime in almost all western European countries. In catholic countries, the use of contraceptives was prohibited or severely discouraged. Women continued to die in their thousands each year as a consequence of backyard abortions. Over the last two decades, the use of contraceptives, chiefly oral contraceptives or injected hormone contraceptives, has drastically increased even in countries where the catholic church has rallied against it (see table 1.2). The availability of a contraceptive pill must be seen as an important precondition of the women's movement, especially because it was constrained by one important contradiction: on the one hand technology helped women to gain some control over their own fertility and health (Joeken, 1987: 15), on the other entrenched moral values sometimes forbade them to legitimately exercise that control.

Indeed, once the women's movements erupted it was the abortion issue, as one of the single most unifying issues, which brought together literally millions of women, including those who had little inclination to join a local women's movement. Although the abortion issue was hardly new in Europe, having been the subject of controversy in the late 19th century and in the 1920s and 1930s. It was 'novel' again in the 1960s and 1970s because the issue began to acquire

**Table 1.2    Percentage of European women using contraceptives in the 1980s**

| Country | Percentage | Country | Percentage |
|---------|-----------|---------|-----------|
| Austria | > 60 | Luxembourg | > 6 |
| Belgium | 76 | Netherlands | > 60 |
| Denmark | 67 | Norway | 71 |
| Finland | 77 | Portugal | 62 |
| France | 82 | Spain | 47 |
| Germany, West | > 60 | Sweden | 75 |
| Greece | > 60 | Switzerland | > 60 |
| Iceland | > 60 | United Kingdom | 71 |
| Ireland | 60 | | |
| Italy | > 60 | | |

(comp. with other English-speaking countries: USA 79%, Australia 72%, Canada 68%)

*Source*: Seager & Olson, 1986

new meaning through the rise of the women's movements which view 'abortion as a necessary condition for the liberation of women' (Outshoorn, 1986: 204).

Even before the onset of the women's movements, western countries had engaged in debates around fertility control and the population explosion, because it had become patently obvious that the fast technological changes, the rampant use of resources and the much improved health care were going to present entirely new challenges. These debates brought out innovative social engineering ideas which reflected changes in family life and structure. Such changes, which were as much the consequence of the pill as the reason for its invention, generally resulted in a reduction of women's involvement in traditional tasks of domestic labour and child rearing. Recent figures from the Netherlands, still considered a rather traditional society, reveal that families comprising husband, wife and children account for less than half of all households. The number of unmarried people living together has risen while the average number of children per family has dropped. Voluntary childlessness has become more common, as has the incidence of women with children outside marriage, with or without a partner. The time spent in child rearing, moreover, has decreased. Women tend to have fewer children in a shorter span of time and typically have a complete family by the time they are 30 years of age. Added to this is a change in the behaviour of the young, whose average age at leaving home has dropped by about four years over the postwar period, shortening even further the time spent by women in a traditional role. De Vries concluded with respect to the Dutch situation that a woman who had had a family and reared several children now has at least 25 productive years ahead of her (1981: 47–8).

These Dutch trends, including alternative lifestyles, are quite representative of western European countries as a whole. They began to take shape in the 1960s. It is almost superfluous to add that the ideology of the nuclear family, with its moral coercions and belief in a woman's place being in the home, was very much at odds with these new trends. Indeed, among the first observations made by feminists of the second wave were those concerned with the oppressive expectations of women in the nuclear family.

Since the onset of the second-wave movements, the trends away from the nuclear family, as a union sanctioned by law and/or the church, have accelerated very drastically. Present-day Swedish figures indicate that households of less than three persons, without children, now form the dominant familial culture,

Table 1.3    Ratio of European marriages/divorces in 1981

|  | Italy | Belgium | W. Germany | Netherlands | England | Denmark | Greece |
|---|---|---|---|---|---|---|---|
| No. of marriages | 313 726 | 359 658 | 85 374 | 64 264 | 400 000 | 25 411 | 71 178 |
| No. of divorces | 11 109 | 109 520 | 28 509 | 15 704 | 156 800 | 14 425 | 6 349 |
| Ratio (approx.) | 28:1 | 3:1 | 3:1 | 4:1 | 2.5:1 | 1.7:1 | 11:1 |

*Source*: *Women in Statistics*, 1984: 10

while the traditional nuclear family constitutes a mere 29 percent of present-day households. In 1982, West Germany had a comparable percentage of single-person households (31.3 percent), increasing to almost 50 percent in large cities, while in more traditional countries like Switzerland, the single-person household constituted 11.5 percent. Clearly, the attitude to marriage has changed very drastically, reflected in the decline of marriages, the increase of divorces and the number of children born ex-nuptially. In West Germany the number of marriages declined by 45 percent between the 1950s and the 1980s. The proportion of women living with partners but not marrying them, also in the 1980s, was below 7 percent in Switzerland, around 12 percent in Norway and France and up to 30 percent in Sweden and Denmark. The ratio between marriages and divorces has narrowed considerably in countries where divorce proceedings have been simplified (see table 1.3).

In other words, for reasons which have been explored elsewhere (Mitterauer & Sieder, 1983: 136–41), perceptions of the family changed in the postwar period along with changes in the economic base of the family. An increasing number of people questioned the value of marriage as an institution and the formalisation of love and of parental bonds. In most countries, legislation had not kept pace with these changes and thus the scene was set for major conflict, staged by the so-called hippies, by students and chiefly by the second-wave women's movements.

*MASS PROTEST*

Postwar movements have depended on image-making—not as much for the eyes of politicians as for an elusive, diverse, impersonal audience which may or may not have some influence in exerting pressure on governments. As a *strategy* for protest, this route via public opinion seems particularly ineffective and weak (Touraine, 1988: 132). But how could it have been otherwise? More strictly political movements of the past, such as the labour movement, were in the position of directly confronting 'the enemy'. There was a clearly defined opponent. In most cases, the members of present-day movements cannot declare a common enemy who, when singled out, can be treated as such. Who, in these new mass movements, is the clearly defined opponent and how can that opponent be 'tackled'? Women cannot in practice take to the streets and fight patriarchy by confronting every male, that is, half of humanity. Women continue to live with men and continue to love them, as partners or members of their families. Black liberationists often have no alternative but to continue working amongst whites. Gay people remain surrounded by heterosexuals in their closest family. Ecologists

**Table 1.4   Dates of enfranchisement of women in western Europe**

| Country | Year | Country | Year |
| --- | --- | --- | --- |
| Austria | 1919 | Liechtenstein | 1985 |
| Belgium | 1948 | Luxembourg | 1918 |
| Denmark | 1915 | Netherlands | 1919 |
| Finland | 1906 | Norway | 1913 |
| France | 1944 | Portugal | 1975 |
| Germany | 1919 | Spain | 1931 |
| Greece | 1952 | Sweden | 1919 |
| Iceland | 1915 | Switzerland | 1972 |
| Ireland | 1922 | United Kingdom | 1928 |
| Italy | 1945 | | |

*Source*: adapted from Seager & Olson, 1986: 90–8

may have no choice but to be also guilty of contributing to environmental disasters. The issues of difference and discrimination permeate too many levels of society to be fought in direct ways. There is little else to do but address the largest possible audience and to appeal to that elusive body of public opinion.

Uprisings, revolutions, and demonstrations have a momentum all their own, stirring the masses and, for a time, carrying them in spontaneous outbursts of anger, enthusiasm, etc. At the very least, however, its organising members must have believed that the 'cause' was worth fighting for and, more importantly, that such a fight had a chance of *succeeding*. The high degree of optimism and of activity must, partly at least, be dependent on a social framework in which the right to protest is safeguarded and the social actors and/or the movements have a measurable degree of *autonomy*. Furthermore, one would expect that channels of mediation between the public and the state were efficient enough to make governments at least 'semi-permeable' to pressures of social forces. As we have seen, such is the case, within limits, in contemporary western democracies.

The protest by women in western Europe, as elsewhere in the world, was initially against legal, political and socio-economic injustices and inequality. Women fought for and demanded that these injustices be removed. Formally, and in the broadest sense of citizenship, these goals have been achieved. Every adult woman in every European country is now allowed to vote, for instance. All women in western Europe are now also formally equal before the law, a right that in most countries existed before the second-wave movements started (see table 1.4).

The problem was, and partly still is, that the gap between formal legal and political equality and daily practice has not been bridged. Rights and principles have remained theoretical, especially in socio-economic terms and in terms of women's private lives. Such concepts as job androgyny and domestic role-sharing became important catchwords only in the 1980s; they are still very much in a state of infancy. The new women's movements have introduced new standards and demands. Furthermore, women have understood their rights as citizens as more than just this formal equality, as something that encompasses socio-psychological and economic categories. They are trying to transform their status within the general culture, to become an 'oppositional force' against an 'instrumental and productivist' culture (Touraine, 1988: 151).

There are about 100 million adult women living in western Europe today. Although only 1 percent are members of their respective women's movements, beyond any doubt the post-World War II women's movements in western Europe add up to a mass movement: at least one million women were activists and a further twelve million were sympathisers and supporters in 1983 (*Women and Men of Europe,* 1983). The core of women actively engaged in keeping organisations, programmes and political activism alive must have been much smaller than these figures indicate. The broad basis of membership and supporters suggests, however, that it was possible, and might still be possible, to mobilise large numbers of women almost at a moment's call. These may even exceed the number of identified sympathisers on certain issues. On two occasions in Iceland, for example, over 90 percent of all adult women went on strike (including housewives who refused to mind children, cook dinner, etc.). In Italy, certain rape cases, which included murder, so incensed women that well over 30 percent of Italian women participated in some form of protest. In West Germany, France and Italy more than half a million women (in each country) marched in favour of abortion. The sight of tens of thousands of women marching and protesting is a new phenomenon in European history which has been greeted with surprise, anger and disbelief. It has also met with reluctant approval and moderate conciliation attempts.

The ambivalence about the women's movements, women's roles, strategies and aims has never waned. Sadly, more people in the population in general were against them in the 1980s than they were in the previous decade (*Women and Men of Europe,* 1983). This shift in public opinion over the last decade was not necessarily an indication that women had done anything 'wrong' politically or strategically, but may well have been one indication of the shift to the political right, a shift which was demonstrated by a large-scale European Commission survey of 1983. According to this survey there was a high correlation between the attitudes to women and the political ideology of the day: the further a country was on the political right, the more likely it was to be hostile towards women's claims and the more firmly it would relegate matters of women's status to ones of little significance (see table 1.5).

Some writers have commented that there were strong feminist movements in the UK, Italy, Holland, Finland, Denmark and Norway in the early 1970s,

**Table 1.5** 'The question of women's status has feeble significance': percent of agreement with this statement by country and by political ideology in ten European EEC member states (cross tabulation)

| By country | % | By political ideology | % |
|---|---|---|---|
| | agreed | | agreed |
| Ireland | 66 | extreme political right | 66 |
| West Germany | 65 | | |
| United Kingdom | 60 | political right | 62 |
| Belgium | 59 | | |
| Italy | 53 | political centre | 56 |
| Netherlands | 45 | | |
| Luxembourg | 43 | political left | 44 |
| France | 42 | | |
| Denmark | 34 | extreme political left | 33 |
| Greece | 34 | | |

*Source: Women and Men of Europe,* 1983

**Ideological position of European countries to women's issues**

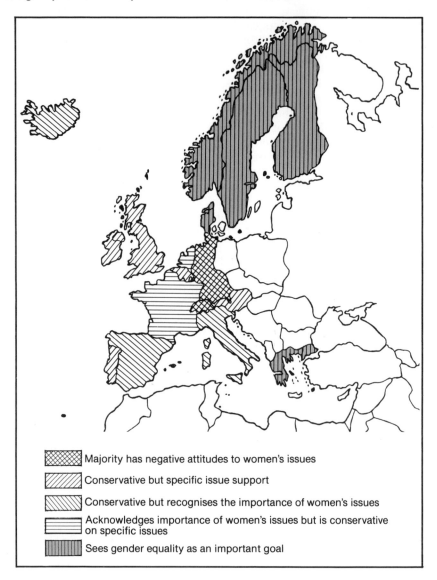

weaker ones in France, Germany, Sweden and Belgium, and weak and belated ones in Spain and Portugal (Lovenduski, 1986: 72). But what does 'strong' and 'weak' mean and by what criteria are these measured? The criteria available for comparison are largely subjective ones. To be sure, it is relatively easy to say that the Portuguese women's movement was intense but short-lived. It was hampered by strong traditional divisions of urban versus rural society, by the split between north and south, emphasised even more strongly by the high illiteracy rate amongst women in semi-rural and rural areas (up to 30 percent) and a multitude of other reasons. Spain's women's movement, according to one highly respected and well-known participant, Lidia Falcón, was 'the most aggressive, explosive, and brilliant feminist movement in all of Europe' (Falcón, 1984: 628). To say that the movement in West Germany was weaker than in the Netherlands is not always particularly useful. Holland is a small country in size and population, West Germany large by comparison. In West Germany, several million women were mobilised into political action and into publications of polemic and scholarly material. In France, West Germany, Italy and Denmark alike, the movements drew public attention. To a feminist in France the local movement was as intense and important as it was to a feminist in Italy. Finally, should one wish to applaud a movement for its strength one has to note that such strength may well be an index of the deplorable status of women in that country, which is hardly worthy of our admiration. In countries which have managed to update their laws and policies to fit contemporary progressive thinking, the 'weakness' of a movement, on the other hand, may well reflect a low level of discrimination.

During the peak of the second-wave movements, a number of protest strategies were employed, all aimed at increasing public awareness of disadvantage. One major form of this political activism, mostly occurring at the very beginning of the second wave, was spontaneous, unplanned action. There were sudden outbreaks of anger, gatherings with singing, dancing through the streets, impromptu speeches and exuberant expressions of solidarity. The second most common form of protest, just as in the civil rights movements in the 1950s and 1960s in the USA, consisted of well-organised campaigns of sit-ins, marches, demonstrations, or court actions. Among the most spectacular campaigns were the 'Reclaim the Night' actions in England and West Germany in 1977, in Italy in 1978 and later in other countries. In addition, women initiated and staged one-off activities which were assured to maximise publicity and even gain national and international attention. One example of this approach was the act of laying a wreath at the monument of the unknown soldier in Paris—a wreath for his unknown wife. Of course, while such actions as this one appeared spontaneous, they were in fact carefully planned, designed to maintain the high pitch of the debate and gain public attention, particularly through the media (Duchen, 1986).

Yet another form of protest was expressed in acts of civil disobedience calculated to reduce the credibility of certain laws and of the state for upholding them. Such acts of civil disobedience centred mostly around the abortion issue. In 1972, 300 French women, among them Simone de Beauvoir, signed an open letter and published it in a daily paper. It was not just about abortion, but it contained the confession 'I have aborted' at a time when such an act was illegal and punishable by law. West Germany followed suit a year later with a very similar action led by the prominent feminist Alice Schwarzer. These acts did not have immediate success but they nevertheless ensured that the issue at hand remained in the public's consciousness and forced politicians to keep it on the political agenda.

The most extreme form of political activism and protest is violence. Most feminists in western Europe shun the idea of violence, not just for reasons of personal inexperience but for reasons of ideological commitment to the goals of the peace movement. There was only a small core of radical feminists who believed that there are instances when violence is the only means of action. Thus the manifesto of the Italian feminist group Rivolta Femminile asks women to think and to act in revolutionary ways stating bluntly that feminism is not pacifism (Chotjewitz-Häfner, 1977).

All of these forms of protest may be called 'movement events'. It is by these events that the broader public assesses, condemns or approves the content and message of a social movement (Dahlerup, 1986: 218). Of all new movements, the western European women's movements were particularly apt at staging such movement events and, probably for the longest period of any postwar movement, they have managed to keep a high public profile over years.

Of all protest actions the written word has been and still is the most sustained form of protest. The prolific number of journals, news-sheets, magazines and books on just about any subject concerning women's lives is one of the most impressive documents of western European feminist activity. This feminist literature—scholarly and literary—has set new standards, new ways of viewing the world, and new demands. It has uncovered a largely untapped creative potential in women and has presented novel world views and analyses. This has been and still is much more than 're-vision', as Adrienne Rich called it, much more than a chapter in cultural history, or an act of survival (Rich, 1979). It is an act of active protest—as suggested within one of her book titles, a protest against 'Lies, Secrets and Silence'. Into this category one might also fit the development of alternative projects of study, looking at topics not just from a different perspective but creating fields of investigation which either had not existed before or were seriously neglected; for instance, Frigga Haug's project on the social constraint/sexualisation of the female body (Haug, 1987). Finally, a woman's refusal to play a role as expected and her insistence on making claims for her own space and rights in the privacy of her home are forms of protest.

It was the achievement of the second-wave movements that these protests did not remain at the defensive level but were translated into concrete and sometimes extremely radical demands.

## THE DIVERSITY OF SECOND-WAVE FEMINISM

Western European feminism of the second wave is not appreciably different in its theoretical diversity and pragmatic goals than is feminism in other western nations. Broadly speaking, feminist writing and activism falls into three large, and sometimes overlapping categories: liberal, socialist and radical feminism. While all advocate change, the extent to which such change should occur, and in which direction, differs significantly in each case. Liberal feminism tends to be organised, hierarchical, negotiative and coalition-building. It seeks to change public opinion by formal networks and via changes in legislature, working in the belief that progressive reforms will lead to the full equality of women. Socialist feminism, while equally well organised nationally and transnationally, avoids hierarchism within its organisations. Socialist feminists also seek to influence public opinion and, when necessary for single issues, fight side by side with women of other persuasions. They do not believe that women's disadvantage is merely a construct of socialisation or a matter of changing legislature. They see that women's inequality is a structural inequality which has its origin in class division and women's exploitation, and the way in which it occurs and is perpetuated is a consequence of the capitalist mode of production. Radical feminists tend to be more separatist than either of the other groups because the primacy of their concern is the concept of patriarchy and with it the problem of sex over class divisions. Sexuality becomes a major focus because it makes men 'intimate enemies' (Lovenduski, 1986: 69), a problem which can be overcome only by understanding and then abolishing patriarchy and/or, at present, by celibacy or lesbianism. The formulation of a lifestyle independent of men, in radical feminist groups, has led to separatist organisations, all-women communes, businesses and book shops, and consciousness-raising discussion and therapy groups. Typically radical feminists tend to express their views, and centre their activities, in small loosely organised groups.

In each western European country the definition of what feminism actually is varies considerably according to differences in the status, role and development of feminism, and it reflects the political and theoretical platform of the authors. One of the most radical definitions appeared in 1977 in *De Bonte Was*, a Dutch feminist journal. As it summarises well one radical perspective, it is worth reprinting here almost in full:

> There is not much time left. The goal of liberating all women and the only way of achieving this, is almost forgotten. And we do want a revolution, so we must finally begin it.
>
> You are not a feminist if you are merely a modern woman: a little more independent, a little more sexual, a little more critical.
>
> You are not a feminist, if you participate in exploiting women sexually, erotically and economically even further.
>
> You are not a feminist, if you only work for the improvement of your own position, if you only meet women of your own profession or class.
>
> You are not a feminist, if you do nothing to improve the status of all women... The personal means nothing without other feminists. It is not enough for you to consider yourself emancipated.
>
> At this stage of feminism nothing is enough. The set goals of feminism are nowhere realised. Oppression cannot be solved personally. Oppression is structurally determined. As long as there are women who are not free, there is no freedom. The oppression of your sister is your own oppression. The only fight is the fight of all of us. All achievements which have not been collectivised by women will be used against us by men. If you can't see that then you are working against us instead of for the women's movement.

At the other end of the spectrum of definitions of feminism one might quote Schenk, who argued that feminism denoted a fight against socially defined roles for women, entailing a psychological liberation process contextualised in a cultural setting (Schenk, 1980: 106). *De Bonte Was* exudes a belligerent enthusiasm for commitment and for political action at grassroots level. Schenk's definition on the other hand is in essence one that betrays the more introspective, considered approach of women in socially privileged positions who need not attempt, in any direct sense, to change the political and economic reality. The political potential of this approach has been translated into psychological categories and is therefore more inclined to relegate the question of consciousness, itself capable of generating considerable political action, into the realm of the private and personal.

If the women's movements in the various countries are seen, as they are here, as protest movements and as blueprints for change, it must also be said that considerable confusion exists generally about the legitimacy of such movements, not in essence but in *name*. Thus, in one western European society it may be regarded as 'wrong' for anyone to be considered a feminist but entirely acceptable to belong to the local/national women's movement. In another it may be approved that women attain equal status but frowned upon if this is meant to be achieved via a women's movement. In Sweden, for instance, a country highly advanced as far as women are concerned, high levels of hostility exist towards feminism, while the idea of women's liberation has very widespread support (Scott, 1982: 158). To say in West Germany 'I am a feminist', so a local German paper reported in 1984, '... is not easy. It is a confronting act which may often lead to a woman gaining a bad reputation' while in Norway, 'it was nothing special and no reason to hide it' (*Weser Kurier,* 1984: 27 February). In West Germany, feminists have been considered to be bra-burning, middle-class, academic and alternative lifestyle people. Doormann points out that the pro-letarian women's movement in Germany was never called feminist and still does not consider itself as such (Doormann, 1979: 37). In the Netherlands, feminism, now even called by that name, has spread all over the country and even the smallest towns have active feminist groups (de Vries, 1981: 389). This new consciousness of a feminist way of viewing the world has apparently permeated several infrastructures of Dutch society. But even here, in the early years of the movement (the 1970s), women did not call themselves feminists because the term reminded them of 'reformist men-hating women' (de Vries, 1981: 392). According to observers of French society, the French women's movement has remained very marginal and is viewed 'as a tiny, left-wing fringe. They are generally considered frustrated women and frustrated intellectuals by both French men and women' (Juillard, 1976: 125; Duchen, 1986).

The confusion over and controversial responses to this ogre called 'feminism' are of course also an indication of the radicalness of women's demands and the threat that these demands might pose to their societies' entrenched values. As did all other new movements, the women's movement learned to accept general resistance and hostility as a sign that their actions were striking at the very foundations of those social infrastructures which were in need of replacement.

# 2   Women's status and employment

The Washington Population Crisis Committee has recently completed a statistical report on women in the world, entitled in part '...Poor, Powerless and Pregnant'. It confirms, after exhaustive studies, that there exists no single place on earth where women enjoy equal status with men or where conditions for women could be classified as excellent. It further stated that 60 percent of people live in poverty or extreme poverty and that this rate is higher for women than for men. These shocking figures rarely concern western Europe. The standards of living vary enormously throughout Europe, and in some countries and many rural areas the lack of facilities, services and modern technology drastically increases women's physical work, the number of childbirths, health risks and the sheer number of working hours in a day. In comparison with the rest of the world, however, especially with developing nations, European women, even in the poorer sections, tend to enjoy reasonable living standards.

In one area the above study does have acute relevance to women all over the world, including western Europe. It confirms a high interrelation of several sectors of status indicators:

> Educational attainment, for example, is related not only to employment but to health, family size and equality in marriage. Patterns of marriage and childbearing have a similarly powerful effect on social and economic conditions for women and are in turn influenced by them. Women with greater educational and economic opportunities marry later and have closer to the number of children they want. (Population Crisis Committee, 1988: 2)

The report also confirmed that it is in education that women universally have made the greatest gains. This gain, they argue, influences a woman's chance in paid employment, her earning power, her age at marriage, her control over child bearing and her exercise of legal and political rights. It seems then that, globally, we should set our hopes for a better future for women on education. There is every reason to support this direction of thinking if control over one's life is improved by education.

The assumption that education is the one and crucial variable to paid employment and economic independence is not, however, always easy to uphold, as this book will show. In western Europe, one may register enormous (but admittedly narrowing) gender discrepancies in incomes and the concentration of women at the lowest levels of payment and in part-time jobs, and then one notes that at the very same time European women have done exceptionally well educationally in the last two decades. Poor job and income performance versus excellent educational performance seems contradictory. Something is definitely mismatched. Put bluntly and simplistically: either the two variables are not as strongly interlinked as proponents for a better education attest or the progress

Table 2.1   **Full-time education ratios by age and sex (in %) in the European Communities
1970–71, 1981–82**

| Age | Year 1970–71 | | Year 1981–82 | | % increase/drop between 1970–82 | | % gain f/m |
|-----|------|------|------|------|------|------|------|
|     | f    | m    | f    | m    | f    | m    |      |
| 15  | 67.1 | 68.7 | 94.1 | 92.6 | +27.0 | +23.9 | = 3.1 |
| 16  | 47.1 | 49.2 | 71.2 | 64.8 | +24.1 | +15.6 | = 8.5 |
| 17  | 33.9 | 36.2 | 55.7 | 48.6 | +21.8 | +12.4 | = 9.4 |
| 18  | 23.4 | 27.8 | 38.0 | 34.7 | +14.6 | + 6.9 | = 7.7 |
| 19  | 16.5 | 22.2 | 25.6 | 25.2 | + 9.1 | + 3.0 | = 6.1 |
| 20  | 12.5 | 18.2 | 19.5 | 19.5 | + 7.0 | + 1.3 | = 5.7 |
| 21  | 9.7  | 15.2 | 13.1 | 14.7 | + 3.4 | − 0.5 | = 3.9 |
| 22  | 7.5  | 12.9 | 11.0 | 12.7 | + 3.3 | − 0.2 | = 3.7 |
| 23  | 5.4  | 10.3 | 8.7  | 12.4 | + 3.3 | + 2.1 | = 1.2 |
| 24  | 3.5  | 7.8  | 7.7  | 11.0 | + 4.2 | + 3.2 | = 1.0 |

*Source*: adapted from *Women in Graphics*; 1989: 98

in women's participation is not as marked as one would wish to believe. There is something to be said in support of the latter.

One error that is generally made with respect to educational statistics is to quote the figures on women's enrolments in toto against the entire population, a method which results in a certain bias. Thus we say that today 40 percent of university students are female, and we can measure that against similar earlier figures to substantiate the argument that over the last decades women have made major gains in educational participation. This is not wrong but, as the figures below show, postwar western European nations *generally* had a need for an increased pool of people with higher educational attainments than before. In every postwar decade, the retention rate at schools, colleges and tertiary institutions has increased. The point is that this is true for *both sexes*. The best that can be said is that women's participation shows an accelerated participation over men's. When taking age groups separately, the most substantial acceleration in EEC countries has in fact occurred at the high-school level and not at the level of tertiary institutions. In Europe the higher school certificate (university entrance certificate) is typically completed at about the age of 19. In most western European countries proper school attendance (post-pre-school enrolment) begins at the age of 6 years, followed by thirteen years of schooling. University degrees, almost never subject to study-time limits, tend to take at least five years.

In toto, the figures reveal that the educational profile of advanced capitalist societies is changing in general and more education is required for the job market than say, in prewar times or even in the early post-World War II decades. Part of that trend, I suspect, is purely inflationary. Compared with twenty years ago, more schooling is required in order to secure the same job as the pool of applicants with higher educational attainment in a given year is increased over and above the demands of the job market; for example, careers in banking, nursing, in secretarial work and even in apprenticeships, over recent years have attracted many more applicants than there are positions available, with the result that employers usually opt for candidates with the highest educational attainment.

Table 2.1 shows that the increase in educational participation of women at tertiary level is not as great compared with men's as might be anticipated. In the age groups in which first degrees and professional qualifications are typically completed in Europe (age 23–24), women's gains over men's are marginal indeed: a mere 1 percent over one decade (see last column, table 2.1: % gain, female over male). In some countries, as for instance in Austria (see chapter 4), women's educational progress shows no acceleration whatsoever over the increased participation of men. Women have indeed made substantial gains in education, but so have men.

This only seemingly conflicts with the other reading that women now make up a larger proportion at universities than twenty years ago. One might assume that the dramatic increase of women at tertiary institutions as a percentage of the *total body* of students (rather than by age) reflects a tendency among mature women to return to study. The return-to-study phenomenon is likely to represent a backlog of needs by those women who, in their days of schooling, either did not think of staying on longer or indeed had no opportunity to do so. The greater encouragement and the more positive attitudes prevailing now with respect to the education of women may result in a continued rise of the female retention rate both at schools and at tertiary institutions. At the moment, however, there is little reason to be overly enthusiastic about women's allegedly enormous strides forward. The new generations of women are only very, very gradually moving towards closing the gender gap.

It is neither assured nor necessarily of intrinsic value to women that this trend will or should continue. This will depend on other intervening variables. In the 1970s and 1980s, women have been able to exploit the general expansionary trend based on the demand for more qualified and highly trained labour. In 1970, only about 5.6 percent of the specific age population (male and female) completed degrees and by 1981–82 it had risen to 9.3 percent. What enticed more young people to stay on for a number of extra years in full-time education was no doubt associated with the rewards they could expect to reap on the job market, such as status and income, as well as the assurance of gaining employment. Cynics may observe that the feminisation of certain professions, such as teaching, has usually gone hand-in-hand with a substantial falling behind of monetary rewards in comparison to other professions or shifted the lucrative income-producing job market to other areas. Alternatively or in addition to comparatively low status and low award structures (in comparison to other professions) women may be clustered at the bottom of the rung of that profession.

Western European feminism has set agendas for non-discriminatory practices in education and employment. It has argued for women's greater access to educational institutions and, at the student level and the lower rungs of academia, women have gradually found entry. Trends for equalisation between sexes in educational institutions have slowly begun to materialise, but the successful translation from educational equality of opportunity into equality in the employment market is yet to be made and its story is one of puzzling complexity.

## WOMEN IN THE LABOUR FORCE

With the economic boom period of several western European countries in the 1950s and 1960s, greater participation by women was welcomed. In the 1970s and 1980s labour market expansion ended and it became apparent that many goals had in fact been set on the assumption of full employment economies. The segregation of the labour market is obviously a related issue. As long as women and men continue to be clustered in certain industries and occupations, the ideal

**Table 2.2   Female percentage of teachers, inspectors and school principals in EEC countries (1981)**

| Country | Teachers | Inspectors | Principals (head-teachers) | | |
| --- | --- | --- | --- | --- | --- |
| | | | pre-primary | primary | secondary |
| Belgium | 57.4 | 19.4 | — | 39.3 (1) | 29.4 |
| Denmark | 41.2 | 4.2 | 97.2 | 1.4 | 6.6 |
| France | 63.1 | 23.2 | 100.0 | 44.4 | 23.4 |
| Greece | 51.2 | 11.4 | — | 40.7 (1) | 43.5 |
| Ireland | 61.6 | 14.4 | — | 47.3 (1) | 35.2 |
| Italy | 72.0 | 15.4 | — | 34.4 (1) | 27.6 |
| Luxembourg | 74.8 | 20.0 | — | — | 8.3 |
| Netherlands | 38.1 | 16.0 | 100.0 | 3.6 | 2.0 |
| Portugal | — | 34.5 | — | 89.7 | 23.5 |
| Spain | 58.5 | 34.7 | — | 46.5 (1) | 19.5 |
| UK | 58.8 | 23.0 | — | 44.4 (1) | 15.3 |

(1) = pre-primary and primary school together

Source: adapted from Women in Graphics, 1989: 102–4

of one job market for all, irrespective of gender, has not become a reality. While we cannot unravel here all of the complexities in the play of women's participation in the labour force, we can at least discuss some of the main contours of the plot as it evolved in the western European theatre: the Treaty of Rome, equality and the full employment ideology.

## The Treaty of Rome and the EEC directives

In the ten member states of the European Communities there are about 35 million women at work today. Their conditions have changed over the years and many of the discriminatory practices, still common in the 1950s, have been outlawed. The reasons for the gradual disappearance of discriminatory practices in most western European countries cannot solely be attributed to the protests by women because the story of women's equity in employment began as a pan-European effort well before the onset of any of the second-wave movements. To reiterate, the chief impetus for change came from the idea of the unification of Europe and the perceived need to gradually implement concrete policies for collaboration and mutual support. The year 1957 was decisive as it sealed the formation of the EEC in the Treaty of Rome. It also marked the beginning of discussions on women's conditions of employment. Although women remained invisible in the many contracts that constituted the Treaty of Rome, there was one clause which contained the single reference to women: 'Each member State shall during the first stage ensure and subsequently maintain the application of the principle that men and women shall receive equal pay for equal work.'

One need not presume that this clause was in any way the product of enlightened men. If it appears progressive now it was only inadvertently so, having been created for reasons of economic expediency rather than social justice. The aim, associated with the creation of the Common Market, was to standardise labour market and employer practices across countries and, as Françoise Remuet-Alexandrou rightly explains: 'to encourage competition between the industries of the Member States by avoiding any distortion of competition stemming from a lower paid female workforce. Its objectives did not result from the general principle of equal treatment of men and women' (Women of Europe, 1986: 2).

Irrespective of the narrow focus and intent that this clause had initially, 'it is in this article that legislation and action in favour of women are based' (*Women of Europe*, 1986). Since 1957, further regulations, decisions and directives have been added to this clause and any country joining, or already a member of the EEC is bound by the community laws and required to ensure their implementation.

The five directives which have appeared between then and 1987 have all further defined and identified areas of discrimination against women and sought ways of eliminating them. Such directives were formulated in a context of policy decisions that aimed at furthering political stability. They came about as a result of a number of test cases which were heard at the European Court of Justice and of investigations of disadvantaged groups within the employment sphere. The most famous of these was the Defrenne case which was heard between 1971 and 1975. It concerned a Belgian airline employee whose retirement provisions (age and pension payment) were disadvantaged compared to her male colleagues. The women in the commission's social affairs directorate seized the opportunity to exert pressure on the social action programme and see that it included special concerns for women (Rights of Women Europe, 1983: 282–3; Hoskyns, 1985, Lovenduski, 1986: 282).

The first directive (1975: 117) argued for the 'elimination of all discrimination on grounds of sex with regard to all aspects and conditions of remuneration'. The second directive (1976: 207), although still expressly referring to the job market, may be regarded as a real breakthrough in principle. It argued for the implementation of the principle of equal treatment for men and women alike. Equal treatment gives a much wider framework than the concept of equal remuneration for equal work because its terms of reference involved discrimination at the workplace on the grounds of marital or family status, access to employment, promotion, vocational training and the right to parental leave of workers of either sex. Later directives covered social security schemes, self-employment and agriculture. Typically, all directives were issued with firm deadlines by which member states were required to make the relevant legal amendments in their national laws where these would have infringed the principles of equal treatment. A publication by the Commission of the European Communities called *Community Law and Women* lists the positive steps taken by individual member states in fulfilment of the directives, and also provides details of judgements and measures against infringements of these laws.

A number of member states may have been none too eager to make any amendments. Yet the pressure applied by the European Commission has achieved a good deal in bringing legislation into line with the principles of equal pay and equal treatment in the widest sense of employment-related activities and social security provisions. One need not deny that, for individual claimants, the complexity of redress to the European Court of Justice is still a deterring obstacle. Likewise, the translation of its directives into national realities and everyday life may, and often does, fall short of the EEC principles. Nevertheless, the commission has moved a good way along the path of creating formal similarities in the social and legal realm of women's status throughout the member states. It has created a yardstick against which all member states and even non-member states are now inevitably measured. This is all the more important since few countries make explicit reference in their constitutions to women's rights and equality in employment, let alone in family law and marriage (see table 2.3).

That the broader European aims, debated at almost exclusively male summit meetings, happen to work in favour of women's interests at least in the one

**Table 2.3  Provisions for equality in European constitutions**

|                | General statement | Employment | Marriage/family |
| -------------- | :---------------: | :--------: | :-------------: |
| Austria        | √                 | —          | —               |
| Belgium        | —                 | —          | —               |
| Finland        | —                 | —          | —               |
| France         | —                 | —          | —               |
| W. Germany     | √                 | —          | —               |
| Greece         | √                 | √          | —               |
| Ireland        | —                 | —          | —               |
| Italy          | √                 | √          | √               |
| Liechtenstein  | —                 | —          | —               |
| Luxembourg     | —                 | —          | —               |
| Malta          | √                 | √          | —               |
| Netherlands    | √                 | —          | —               |
| Portugal       | √                 | √          | √               |
| Spain          | √                 | √          | √               |
| Sweden         | √                 | √          | —               |
| Switzerland    | √                 | √          | —               |
| United Kingdom | √                 | √          | √               |

*Source*: adapted from Seager & Olson, 1986: Section 1

definable area of employment may be seen either as a predictable outcome or as a fortunate accident of history. The timing, however, was useful because the women's movements were able to inject new energy into these programmes and promote from below what most individual countries were not willing to tackle from above at state level. Along with the creation of formal guidelines on employment issues a regular series of publications began (see Introduction), and formal organisations and networks were established aimed at providing a data base and efficient communication channels for women across all member states.

In this spirit Desharmes La Valle, on the publication of the fiftieth issue of *Women of Europe*, was prompted to say: 'over the past ten years, everything has been changing faster than in the previous four decades or so. The European Community has acted as a motive force and a pioneer in legislation on parity, leaving a clear mark on national legislations. The influence of women's associations has been growing. Women have acquired a clearly perceptible awareness, assurance and confidence' (*Women of Europe*, no. 50, 1987: 1). But not all change for European women has come via supra-national or local women's organisations. The Scandinavian countries, with the exception of Denmark, are not member states of the European Communities and are not subject to their directives, although encouraged to comply with UN regulations. Another notable feature of Swedish and Finnish societies is that they have experienced comparatively little feminist socio-political activism. Yet most of the Scandinavian reforms made over most of this century not only occurred well ahead of other European countries but were often achieved without any major debates or opposition by parliaments. Scandinavian countries in general have moved towards the goals of gender egalitarianism in ways, empirically measurable as successes, that still make them the envy of the rest of European women.

The European official networks are important for women by the mere fact that they feature in them. This is a process of formal ratification of women's existence and importance in general European affairs. It is also a process of legitimation of women's issues as issues not just of, by and for women but as *general societal, economic* and *political* questions. This development is unique to Europe and while one should not exaggerate the importance of these networks and their impact on individual practices in different countries they have ensured that certain principles of deep importance to women's lives have remained on the agenda of political and economic summit meetings. Into these transnational networks, women began to inject their own national networks, ideas and energies. The second wave happened well after these networks were in place, and although grassroots movements did not at first take much notice of this European framework (nor did officialdom take note of grassroots movements), both levels of activity moved in the same direction of change.

Whether or not one sees these developments as an example of Deutsch's cascade model is a different matter. Without doubt, there *were* demands that arose from within the political and economic elites of the European Community, among them the idea of parity of the labour force. The standardisation processes, particularly for female labour, however, could not be described as more than a trickle of change, often purposely diffused and rechannelled on the way and therefore hardly capable of 'cascading' down to mass level. This was so partly because the intended changes were not always implemented in the way they might have been but reinterpreted in ways that shifted the problems of gender inequality sideways only; for instance, 'the equal pay for equal work' corollary could only be applied if and when work was seen *as* equal. Instead, particularly in blue-collar work, the *names* of jobs and the value *ascribed* to specific tasks changed on a sex basis. Women's and men's jobs were given different titles and different pay packages, invariably setting those of women's work at the lower end of the scale. Women's job specifications were seen to be of lesser value, certain areas of occupation became feminised and in yet others, subsections developed, in which women formed pockets of cheap labour.

On the other hand, even this evidence does not quite invalidate Deutsch's argument. Once the directives for gender parity of labour were pronounced, the *discrepancies* between policy intention and actual practice became unavoidably visible. At least theoretically, the persistence of such discrepancies could then become an issue and be taken up on the shop floor. Given the enormous time lag between the issuing of the directives and any pronouncements by shop stewards and the (male) union elites that such discrepancies were indeed a fighting issue at all, one might well cynically concur with Deutsch that demands by the elite will only 'eventually' gain mass support.

Indeed, the whole European interest in labour issues—and not only in Europe but in the western world generally (Seager & Olson, 1986: Section 19)—would give plenty of fuel to proponents of the reserve army theory of women's labour. Briefly, this theory argues that women are only called upon to participate in the labour force at times of acute labour shortage and forced out when men can be found to fill their positions. There is ample evidence for this theory and, in the postwar era, more labour was needed to satisfy greater productivity and economic expansiveness in the context of forever present and rising demands. European economic collaboration required standardisation and new competitive guidelines. The demand for more labour had to be qualified too. In line with the fast and reckless economic development, that is, with the intention of raising profits that could be reinvested, what was required was not just more labour but preferably *cheap* labour; cheap labour could help raise profit margins and so assist fast expansion. Its availability was a determining factor for investment (Safa, 1986: 58). The deployment of available labour from all over Europe, such as the controversial if not notorious guest-worker conscriptions, and their employment in the economically fastest growing European countries were part of this development (Castles, 1984). Demand levels after the war were initially extremely high. But by the 1960s further growth did depend on raising household incomes.

## The concept of equality and women's work ethic

One of the fundamental questions that needed to be addressed by feminists in the context of the rising women's movements was why women should work. Linked with this are questions about the meaning of equality and how its interpretation would inform political strategies and social demands. I would like to address the latter first.

Basically, in western European feminist discourse one can distinguish three major perspectives concerning the interpretation of equality. One is called the transformation perspective. The transformation view argues that the status of women is inferior to that of men. Women's status therefore has to be raised to that of men. Implicit in this argument is the view that women need not spend much time in questioning 'the system'. They will enter working life on male terms and will subject themselves to all (male) predefined processes and (male) predefined roles. A second perspective of similar weight and popularity, definable as the justice perspective, argues that women and men have the same innate potential and therefore women have the right to be given the same opportunities as men to express that potential at least in the same way, although this may take different forms.

As to the third perspective, some women argue that there is a special value perspective which, if seriously considered, would lead to true equality. As women have particular experiences and abilities, chiefly in reproduction and mothering, these must be regarded as equivalent in value if not in kind to those of men in terms of their usefulness to society. Therefore women should be given full equality so that in their special way they can reach their full potential (Wistrand, 1981). This view has been called revisionist feminism because it not only threatens the possibility of sexual equality but contains the threat that women's abilities may be best served in the home or in related mothering and nurturing roles to the exclusion of all else. From this perspective it is only a small step to the pre–World War I argument that women would be alienated from their 'true being' if they engaged in roles not suited to their innate abilities. Such roles, for example, would exclude becoming a lawyer, an archaeologist, a motor mechanic or holding similar 'non-nurturing' vocations. Worse still, in its fundamental tenets, the 'special qualities' ideology needs little adjustment in order to become the same as fascist views on women, (see chapter 1). This view seems to surface only in countries which have not experienced fascism first hand as an important or predominant political ideology.

Those who have experienced fascism, as Germany and Italy and, to some extent, their neighbouring countries, usually shun this view precisely because it is too close if not identical to the fascist mode. There is a memory of its implications in practice and most women do not wish this practice to be repeated. The 'celebration' of women's 'special' abilities had once resulted in a systematic removal of women from the workforce, from politics and from any other public social responsibility or role and shunted them back into the home to be condemned to the tasks of child bearing and rearing as the *only* valid and esteemed role. While this view is not very common amongst feminists in western Europe

**Table 2.4    Motivations for female labour in western European countries, 1973, in % of total number of replies**

|                          | France | Italy | Netherlands | W. Germany |
|--------------------------|--------|-------|-------------|------------|
| Necessity                |        |       |             |            |
| (household head)         | 41.2   | 24.5  | 21.9        | 42.1       |
| spouse salary            |        |       |             |            |
| insufficient             | 18.2   | 37.4  | 18.7        | 16.6       |
| other economic reasons   | 6.9    | 3.5   | 2.5         | 22.6       |
| improve standard         |        |       |             |            |
| of living                | 18.4   | 12.1  | 1.8         | 5.6        |
| noneconomic needs        | 4.6    | 8.8   | 25.2        | 11.4       |
| for saving               | 0.6    | 3.5   | 10.4        | 2.2        |
| need for independ.       | 8.1    | 8.4   | 11.9        | 5.6        |
| other                    | 2.0    | 1.1   | 7.6         | 3.1        |

*Source*:  adapted from: *Trente jours d'Europe*, no. 184, November 1973, Information service of the European Communities, Paris; see also Gubbels,1976: 154

(but seemed to have some support in the USA), it had powerful support from a different school of thought in the 1970s and 1980s via the theories of socio-biologists. Sociobiology argues strongly in favour of the innateness of gender-specific traits and characteristics and would therefore support the notion that specific roles, vocations, and behaviour patterns are more suited to one or the other sex (Kaplan & Rogers, 1990). Of course, if we were to discuss issues of a new *identity*, then all these perspectives take on different meaning. In *that* context even the 'special value perspective', if sensibly and sensitively argued around the problematic reductionism, will have a place and possibly quite an important place. But for the purpose of *equality*, the identification of difference is generally not very helpful. (For an interesting and more detailed discussion of women's 'singularity', or 'similarity' perspectives see Liljeström, 1984: 663–66.)

The first two perspectives (the transformational and the justice perspective), while not always explicitly stated, underpin much of feminist literature and they are almost independent of the political persuasion of the writer. They colour the selection of data and determine whether or not a particular development is celebrated as another step in upgrading the status of women. Indeed, the view of equality determines what answer will be given to the question of why women should work. An emancipatory answer argues that women should work in order to have a fair share in the national productivity and an equal share in responsibility. Another view stresses that women should work in order to gain economic independence as a precondition for women's self-determination and autonomy, and yet another points out that work provides an identity and leads to self-actualisation.

Most of these goals sound rather idealistic in view of the employment situation of European women over the last decades. In a survey conducted in 1973 it was found that female labour was largely motivated by economic necessity rather than by the wish for economic independence or for reasons of self-actualisation. In the decade following this survey and in the wake of the second-wave movements one would want to see a rise in the category of women's need for independence. In the early 1970s, however, most women were not in the position to choose and often not in the position to reflect on the issue (see table 2.4 above).

Present economic trends do not support the notion that women in the 1980s have been seeking employment for different reasons than in the early 1970s. The main factor has remained a perceived need to supplement family income. Indeed, there are a host of negative factors embedded, and as yet unresolved, in women's participation in the labour force. Proponents of the dual burden theory have pointed out that as the move of women into the workforce has not been accompanied by a change of attitudes to women's roles within their families, women now face double work loads and are enslaved even further. Then there are problems with the work itself and the value ascribed to it. In many western European countries, women's incomes—despite the directives—are a good deal lower than men's incomes for similar or same job performances. There are obvious and strongly perceived disadvantages for women in the workforce, and the lower awards, indicating 'lesser value', do not provide effective mechanisms for heightening a woman's self-esteem. The EEC survey also claimed that a large percentage of women working in gainful employment perceive their gender as a distinct disadvantage in most job-related criteria (*Women and Men of Europe*, 1983). The problems for women in the labour force, only too familiar to feminists, do suggest that the supposed equality of opportunity in the workplace has not eventuated.

*Full employment ideology and changing labour needs*

It seemed in the early feminist writing, built on the experience of full employment and on the optimism of the early postwar years, that 'progress' (meaning here the technological and economic expansion) was believed to be limitless. Ironically, a 'matching' ideology for this optimism was derived from a very different quarter of the political and socio-historical spectrum, namely from the writings of Engels and Bebel. Both writers saw economic independence as a precondition for human (and women's) liberation. If it was true that women's liberation so much depended on economic independence, it was indeed time to go to work. Paid work supposedly equalled economic independence and economic independence was the identified precondition for true liberation. Inadvertently, these socialist writers of the 19th century thus provided an answer on why women should work at a time when a very different ideology for very different ends was in favour of employing women. We have seen, however, that paid labour for women rarely meant independence. In other words, women of the working class and petty bourgeoisie generally could not 'graduate' to their liberation. In western Europe today, that was and still is the privilege of a well-to-do middle and upper class whose freedom of movement to begin with was less circumscribed than that of their working-class counterparts.

The move from labour-intensive to capital-intensive industries means that more people are becoming redundant and full employment may well be over for good. The labour market has shrunk too, not just for women but for men as well, and many writers question our work ethics and our subdivisions of life into work and non-work in accordance with the gross national product (GNP). Our work ethics may well need to be re-evaluated. In the process of such a rethinking one wonders whether the unreflected and unequivocal support for high participation rates of women in the workforce may not soon become a conservative position. Indeed, it may run counter to a very different set of progressive ideas for the future.

It is conceivable that in future the overall percentage of the economically active (i.e. contributing to the GNP) may decrease. It goes without saying that this does not and should not prevent equality of opportunity and job androgyny. An uncritical view of women's employment as a measure of independence and liberation appears unwarranted. Nevertheless there are feminists in Europe and elsewhere in the western world (including Australia) who watch women's participation rates in the workforce with a certain eagerness and expectation, implying that any overall increase in women's participation in the labour force is a sign of progress. Some European newsletters publish data on the increase of women's percentage in the total workforce as if it indicated some victory.

Women's participation in the labour force in the last decade or so has not in fact increased as much in western Europe as is often thought. In the ten EEC member countries the increase in workforce participation of women between 1970 and 1983 was only 5 percent (from 27 to 32 percent). These increases are hardly cause for fanfares of victory. Equally noteworthy is the fact that most of the increases in the labour force were increases in part-time work, keeping well within the principle of keeping women's labour costs low and maximising returns.

In the EEC countries three-quarters of all part-time jobs, on average, are carried out by women. It is obviously not easy to generalise about these findings. Should one assume that women prefer not to work if the economic conditions of the family permit them not to do so? In some well-to-do countries like the Netherlands, there seems to be some basis for this argument. This is not, however, borne out by the Scandinavian labour force figures. Part-time work is typically badly paid and is characterised by low job security, the absence of fringe benefits and the unlikelihood of promotion opportunities. Clearly, part-time work is no way to economic independence or out of traditional female caring roles. It is designed to supplement income as a measure of necessity or to provide additional family income. For the employer it guarantees a cheap labour force, fine-tuned to immediate production and labour needs.

Worse still was the rising problem of unemployment for women in the 1970s. From 1976 to 1983 unemployment for women in European member states of the EEC rose by 15 percent as compared to a rise in unemployment for men of only 0.6 percent (IMSF, 1978: 36–7). Over two million women in EEC countries and a total of seven million women in eighteen western European countries lost their jobs in less than a decade. One in three women of the member states has experienced unemployment. Women made up half or more than half of the unemployed throughout the late 1970s and 1980s, while they constituted just over a third of the workforce. It would depend on the country's method of data gathering, but in many cases these figures would be understated and the unemployment figures much higher if one included hidden unemployment as well. There are of course substantial variations between countries, but overall the picture for women at work in western Europe looked relatively bleak in the 1980s.

These developments were associated with several interrelated factors. Most western European economies underwent a drastic restructuring process after World War II, of which an expansion of the labour market was a part. European governments generally set themselves four economic goals. Apart from economic growth, a balance or surplus on foreign-trade payments and price stability, most governments saw full employment as a desirable and achievable economic aim. But economic growth slowed remarkably after 1968 and price stability increasingly became a problem. By the early 1970s, inflation was the chief concern, having jumped from 2–3 percent in the immediate postwar decades to over 10 percent in most and over 20 percent in some European countries. These increasing signs of an imminent crisis were coupled with fiscal disasters in 1973 and 1974. The capitalist economy 'suffered a remarkable *volte-face* in its fortunes and prospects' (Gamble and Walton, 1976: 4–5), when the stock exchange collapsed and falls greater than those in the Wall Street crash of 1929–1932 were recorded. Unemployment jumped drastically, reaching four million unemployed in EEC countries in 1975, and even affecting well-to-do countries like Denmark (with an unemployment rate of 14 percent).

Democratic governments of the 20th century have taken on three major functions which firmly placed those governments into the mainstream of economics. Apart from seeking to maintain social peace and political stability, modern democratic governments are committed to managing demands, formulating general economic goals, and also to socialising costs such as public-sector expenditure, employment and so on (Gamble & Walton, 1976: 163). While in the postwar years most governments of capitalist countries expanded public spending on a massive scale, their economic fortunes changed and the commitment to a full employment policy was the first to go in a form of monetary control. Governments no longer upheld their commitment to full employment as either a reachable or desirable goal. Although there has since been recovery in all areas, the commitment to full employment was never again taken up by governments. They ultimately broke this commitment 'not because full employment is impossible, but because it is not profitable' (Gamble & Walton, 1976: 11).

Nevertheless, women were, but are not always as the reserve army theory suggests, the casualties of labour market contractions. The theory overlooks the fact that since the onset of industrialisation, labour-intensive industries have always used female labour, even at times when male unemployment was high. The *choice* of employing women was not necessarily determined by the availability of labour overall but by the cost attached to employing such labour (Tilly & Scott, 1978). Interestingly, women's workforce participation is rising despite a slowing of demand for labour. With the much improved ratios of female students at universities one would expect the number of professional women to eventually rise above present levels. It is noteworthy that the increases in women's labour force participation over the last decades have largely been due to the expansion of bureaucracies and of teaching institutions. The Eurostat Labour Force Survey of 1986 shows that of all women employed in EEC countries, 72 percent fell under the category of services as against 49.6 percent of men (*Women in Graphics*, 1989: 49).

Should one have hoped that women would have done better in the labour force, given the many labour law amendments, the increasingly better education, and the many demonstrations? Should one allow hard-nosed economists to argue that the increased educational opportunities for women have been wasted (in monetary terms) because too few women then take up careers in which their training comes into full effect? Should one argue that women make subject and career choices inappropriately, that is, without consideration of the demand in the market place? Or should one say that discriminatory practices have been curbed most successfully only in environments in which social engineering and control were possible from a central administration? It would seem that the latter has some merit, because there is a stark discrepancy between women's advances in educational achievements and women's success in the labour force. If one thinks, as most feminists do, that labour force participation is an important step towards the liberation of women, then these data and trends matter a great deal.

The quest for equality has so far concentrated on equality of opportunity but, at least in the Scandinavian countries, there is evidence of political and research interest in concentrating on the notion of equality of *outcome*: if two people of different gender are educated in the same way and in the same subjects, will they succeed in their careers equally well? Recent Finnish research on the subject has shown that they will not (cf. chapter 3): so far, even in progressive countries like Sweden or Finland, women need longer to reach career goals and they earn less than their male counterparts (*Naisten asema*, 1984: 134).

## WOMEN AND TECHNOLOGY

Gender-segregated work has hardly diminished, and twenty years of planning, writing, scheming, fighting and arguing have not achieved job androgyny in any western European country. In some areas, such as engineering and purely technological positions, women in western Europe have scarcely made an impact. The reasons for such 'failure' by women—or the 'system', male employers or whoever or whatever might be seen as the 'cause' for the absence of women in these jobs—are likely to be complex. One needs to ask whether women's absence indicates any failure in the first place, and only if this question is answered in the affirmative should one attempt to identify the reasons.

Recently, English feminist Cynthia Cockburn presented a very spirited reply aimed at anyone bemoaning the fact that experimental projects had so far failed to produce the new breed of women technologists and engineers. She rightly says that most of these projects were based on a wrong premise. Encouraging girls into technology was done on the assumption that girls had to be 'given more confidence'. The idea that girls might not have wanted to enter these jobs and could not give a farthing whether or not their decision satisfied egalitarian zealots was obviously never considered as a possibility. She argues that women have not 'failed' but that they have gone on strike (Cockburn, 1985: 56). Might one concur with this? Did those young women go 'on strike'? If so, one reason may be related to the patronising way in which women's entry into non-traditional jobs has been handled. Presumably, in the above example, the underlying assumption was a deficiency model: if only we can get girls to be as confident as boys they might do as well as boys. One experimental work programme in West Germany advertised its 'radical' programme as 'Girls in Men's Jobs', stressing not only the unusual nature of the programme but inferring differences in maturity and thus work status between the sexes.

Second, the list of predictably undesirable and outright unpleasant factors which continue to militate against women entering technological careers is indeed long and impressive. Cockburn feels that women would become 'a kind of de-sexed satellite of a male world' (1985: 58). With the invention of machinery designed to replace human physical strength, women could presumably take up any jobs in technology. That they do not, she suggests, has to do with the extraordinarily male-oriented cultural construction of the work environment. One comparatively small problem concerns the informal set-up at the workplace, ranging from pin-up girl posters on lockers and 'dirty' jokes to a combative style of interaction. More importantly, many jobs require physical postures which are taboo for women. Can a woman be comfortable lying on her back and spreading her legs to repair or maintain a machine? Problems of expectations of female appearance also play a role. Could she use muscle, get dirty and sweaty and still be regarded as a woman, and as a desirable one? These taboos, I like to add as an aside, might be more engrained in western Europe than in other industrialised nations, such as in eastern bloc countries, allowing one to claim that these problems are indeed nothing but constructs that can and should disappear.

Another noteworthy difference between women's and men's work, most conspicuously displayed in technological jobs, is the socialised gender difference in handling space and objects. Cockburn claims that men prefer to move around objects, handle them, do something to them, apply tools and energy (1985: 58). Whether or not women are socialised into a different handling of objects and are meant to prefer less movement and space around the object and area of their work is almost immaterial. What is important is that when women do get jobs in blue-collar work or technology, more often than not they are *assigned* positions of physical confinement. Everyone knows that a classroom full of children is more easily managed when every child is required to sit still and quietly in allocated positions and more difficult to control when every child is allowed to walk around. Perhaps there are similar mechanisms operating between the sexes. The only problem is that women no longer wish to be treated like children and to be maintained in postures and positions that afford others easy access and control.

It is clear from the literature available on technology and women that workshops and sites of technology are not gender neutral. Rightly, women have argued for gender neutralisation of the workplace. But such a neutralisation process is an extremely complex one. It requires not only a change in behaviour but, in fact, a fundamental change in attitudes to work, to living—in short it amounts to a total rethinking of cultural values. If women have fought on *that* front, they have hardly been the passive victims whose work participation fits neatly into the larger economic scheme of things, as Touraine suggested. On the contrary, their critique of such work environments speaks of the active social actor who will try to expose the inequities, fight for change and only then attempt to enter the new field; this is not a fight for a niche in the existing structure but a demand for change before entry into that field.

A different way of arguing the problem of women's entry into technological fields is to reiterate the well-known discrepancies between the moral claims of democracy, such as liberty, justice and equality, and the moral claims of technology as claims of mere practical necessity. Deeply entrenched in our thinking is the idea that technology is autonomous and 'outside society', and, in a one-way motion, has predictable and unpredictable 'effects' upon society with which we have somehow to live. The countless numbers of impact studies of technology on society (see Forester, 1980; Green et al., 1982) are telling verifications of this technological determinism (MacKenzie & Wajcman, 1985). Science is supposed to shape technology and science is value-free. Therefore, technological change can be discussed as if it were an entirely independent variable which creates its own dictates and needs. Many writers have pointed out that science is indeed not value-free (Shapin, 1982), and that the relationship between science and technology is neither a one-way track nor all that easily summarised (Barnes & Edge, 1982). I do not want to enter into this argument here other than to suggest that this technological determinism has a great deal to do with women's absence in technological fields.

Technology, as some spirited writers have spelled out again recently, is *inherently* political. First, it is not 'outside' society in any sense of the word, for the makers of technology are human beings, living and thinking within a given historical and social context. Their innovation potential is shaped by the situation in which they find themselves. Second, as Winner has argued, adoption of a given technical system actually requires the creation and maintenance of a particular set of social conditions as the operating environment. He quotes the example of a nuclear power plant. To accept a nuclear power plant is also to accept a techno-scientific-industrial-military elite in charge of its operations (Winner, 1985: 31). In many technological decisions and anticipated future projects the 'practical necessity' of the project itself seems to diffuse or even cancel any of the moral claims that democracy makes. Ayres gave the extreme example of the intended production of plutonium. He argued that since plutonium was so dangerous, its very manufacture could involve substantial sacrifices of individual liberty. Demands of security checks or covert surveillance mechanisms against individual employees, emergency measures under martial law, etc. would all be part of accepting the manufacture of plutonium. In the process, however, some basic democratic liberties would be forfeited—and forfeited without the slightest protest. Practical necessity overrides moral claims of democracy (Ayres, 1975: 374, 413–14, 443). A less dramatic example of the political nature of technology is its compatibility (in most cases) with highly structured and centralised management, which fosters or even requires social and political relationships of a particular kind. The rational management of large technological organisations such as railways, airlines, communication systems, etc. is again in stark contrast to the philosophy of democracy as an egalitarian system (Winner, 1985: 34).

Women's understanding of entry into the labour force, however, is built not on the 'practical necessity' claims of technology but on the moral claims of democracy. It should not come as a surprise that the formation of the morality (if it is that at all) of practical necessity was shaped by men and for men in a distinctly authoritarian and hierarchical way. Some decades ago Mumford showed that technology need not be 'authoritarian' but could indeed be 'democratic'. He cites the energy industry as his example. Coal, oil, and nuclear power are compatible with large centralised management elites. Solar power is more compatible with an egalitarian and democratic society because solar energy is not centrally controlled, is renewable and thus decentralised in a political and technological sense (see also Argue et al., 1978: 16). If women base their claims on participating in the labour force on the perceived *democratic* right, they become embodiments of one system of thought, of a political–moral paradigm which they inevitably carry with them. The way human beings have shaped technology, however, in its practical everyday application and maintenance is distinctly incompatible with these notions.

The fast, innovative train of technological development boarded after World War II has gone unchecked and unmolested in one direction. Women's entry into the labour force, coupled with the women's movements and their own paradigms of critique, have shown, perhaps for the first time very clearly, that the trains have only gone one way and that other directions, if indeed one wants to remain on that train at all, are in urgent need of exploration. Cockburn has calculated that, if women were to take up their half in technology now, there would have to be 33 000 women scientists and technologists, 106 000 women technicians, and a staggering 250 000 craftswomen in England alone. Obviously, this is not going to happen immediately and perhaps will never happen unless the shaping, use and structure of technology itself is examined and changed.

## WOMEN AND DOMESTIC WORK

Interlinked with the issue of women's work is, of course, the question of women's domestic work and of the status of women in their own home. The subject has been debated at great length in feminist literature but very little has happened in practice. Work in the domestic field has generally remained women's work, even in the ever rising category of women employed outside the home.

The most notable and measurable change in housework has occurred as a result of technological innovation, bestowing upon the modern household such items as the refrigerator, freezer, washing machine, and homogeniser. In chapter 1 ('The diversity of second-wave feminism') we saw that Belgian women mentioned the washing machine as one of the three most important changes for women this century. I doubt whether women anywhere would argue that the washing machine was not an important innovation. But its importance varies somewhat from one social class to another. Middle- and upper-class women presumably had enough money at their disposal to ensure that the washing was done by someone else, such as a laundry service or, in the prewar era, by household staff. Working-class women, on the other hand, and women of the petty bourgeoisie, generally had no choice but to do the washing themselves, devoting more often than not an entire day to the hard physical chore of scrubbing clothes by hand. To those women in particular, the washing machine was indeed a blessing and relieved them of some of the most difficult household work. For middle- and upper-class women, the historical benefits are not as easily identifiable, because now they may be asked to provide services themselves which in the past may have been performed by other (paid) people or services. Someone has to put the washing into the machine, hang it on the line, take it off, iron and fold it and put it back into the cupboard. A laundry service would have carried out most of those chores.

It is ultimately true of any household that technology has greatly assisted in making housework cheaper to complete and, presumably also faster to accomplish. But here we are no longer on firm ground because countless studies suggest that the burden of domestic chores has not been eased overall. Globally one may query this. Some feminists have argued that the innovative technology was never designed to relieve women of work. What household technology, although advertised as promising greater freedom to its users, was meant to do and has succeeded in doing is broaden demand and change the private household into a consumer entity. It has done something for women in so far as they are now supposedly 'free' to seek employment outside the home and to supplement family income.

What it has done for men is enable them to ask their wives to help raise their standard of living by making a financial contribution. Further, it has warded off any suggestions that men should also help in domestic work. If everything was done to make easier the lives of housewives and wives working in gainful employment, it was not always to their advantage; husbands and male partners were encouraged to buy themselves out of any obligation to assist in the running of the household. This message is hammered home in European advertising (and not only there) around Mother's Day. The good husband is not the one who helps with the washing-up, the cooking, the shopping, but the one who buys his wife a washing machine, a dishwasher or a microwave oven. Ownership of any of these items in itself does not shift the responsibility for the work onto someone else or suggest a sharing of that responsibility. On the contrary: as the

**Table 2.5 Percentage of men refusing to help in household chores (1973)**

| Country | Refusing to help | Wife can get help from relatives in more than 30% of cases |
|---|---|---|
| Italy | 49 | √ |
| Luxembourg | 39 | √ |
| Germany/West | 32 | — |
| France | 31 | — |
| Belgium | 26 | — |
| Netherlands | 24 | — |

*Source*: Pross,1973: 93 ff

recipient of a gift, the receiver has to be grateful and is therefore not expected to make demands at the same time as receiving the gift. In a Russian discussion of household chores, as early as 1967, it was publicly stated and admitted that mechanisation of daily life 'paradoxically served as an advantage for men more than for women' (*Komsomolskaje Prawda*: 27 May 1967).

In a comparative study of 1973, the German feminist Helge Pross found that in most western European countries a large percentage of husbands of wives in full-time employment refused outright to have anything to do with housework, while a similar percentage tried to prevent being involved when and wherever they could (see table 2.5). The figures, referring only to men of working wives, would be significantly higher for households in which the wife did not have paid outside employment.

French studies conducted at around the same time (1971) concurred with many of Pross's findings but differentiated domestic role-sharing according to class. Andrée Michel's data indicated that the greatest percentage of husbands refusing to help their working wives in household chores were found amongst blue-collar workers and/or in households where the wife worked in blue-collar work. There was a correlation between the woman's pay packet, her occupational prestige and her position at home. The higher the qualifications and the salary of the wife, the greater the changes, with concomitant decline in the husband's 'authority' and his greater willingness to help in performing daily housework and occasional household tasks (Michel, 1971: 63). In other words, only a very small percentage of households, namely those of two-career couples, had acquired some degree of role-sharing in domestic chores.

Fortunately, there are some really hopeful signs of measurable attitudinal changes that have occurred in the last two generations over all classes and occupational groups. In an attitudinal study across EEC countries of the views of women and men on domestic role-sharing, women and men of different age groups were asked what they perceived to be the best distribution of domestic chores amongst the sexes (see table 2.6). There is clear evidence then that the younger age groups, female and male alike, have far more inclination towards domestic role-sharing than do the older age groups. Some changes are obviously taking place but one must guard against premature assumptions about the reality of domestic role distributions because none of these visibly new *attitudes* needs find reflection in daily *practice*. Indeed, they often do not; for instance, on attitudinal scores, the Swedes and Finns in particular rank highly in favour of domestic role-sharing but, in reality, as Swedish and Finnish women have complained, the overwhelming chores of housework are still theirs. Only in the sharing of child rearing has noticeable change occurred.

**Table 2.6    1983 survey of perceptions of best division of domestic chores (in %)
by country, age and sex**

| By age and sex | Equal | Wife alone (purely housewife) | Wife more | None of these | No reply |
|---|---|---|---|---|---|
| Women | | | | | |
| 15–24 years | 56 | 24 | 14 | 3 | 3 |
| 25–39 | 43 | 31 | 22 | 2 | 2 |
| 40–54 | 34 | 32 | 28 | 3 | 3 |
| 55+ | 24 | 27 | 57 | 3 | 4 |
| Men | | | | | |
| 15–24 years | 47 | 31 | 17 | 2 | 3 |
| 25–39 | 38 | 36 | 21 | 3 | 2 |
| 40–54 | 26 | 34 | 34 | 4 | 2 |
| 55+ | 25 | 26 | 43 | 3 | 3 |
| By country | | | | | |
| Greece | 51 | 22 | 24 | | |
| Denmark | 46 | 30 | 16 | | |
| Italy | 41 | 28 | 29 | | |
| France | 40 | 26 | 29 | | |
| Netherlands | 38 | 25 | 29 | | |
| United Kingdom | 37 | 36 | 23 | | |
| Belgium | 31 | 22 | 35 | | |
| Ireland | 30 | 24 | 39 | | |
| Germany (FRG) | 26 | 34 | 30 | | |
| Luxembourg | 25 | 21 | 47 | | |

*Source: Women and Men of Europe,*1983: 30

Cowan has argued recently (1985: 197) that industrialisation has fostered greater specialisation in its workforce but that, in the domestic sphere, developments have gone in the reverse order: from greater specialisation to less and less differentiation with respect to those responsible for the work. The argument, sweeping enough and meant to entail changes from the 19th to the 20th centuries, cannot be accepted without some careful qualifications. I could find some merit in this if it were confined to middle- and upper-class women. Indeed, the domestic servants left the average well-to-do European households at around the first quarter of this century and later also the upper-class households, although much of the traditional household structure with domestic employees in the monetary and old class elites of western Europe may well still be intact today. Further down the class structure, it may also be true to say that maiden aunts, grandparents and other relatives left the nuclear family units, although their departure would also have saved some work, and their presence may not have been an indication of division of labour. But for the well-to-do woman, the change from the 19th century to the 20th, and even more markedly from the first quarter to the middle of the 20th century, was a loss in delegated housework overall.

Women's role in the home (this should read upper- and middle-class women's role), Cowan argues, became less specialised and eventually relegated women from managerial positions to full-time houseworkers. As the jack-of-all-trades began to disappear in industry, the jane-of-all-trades began to appear in domestic work. Moreover, the savings of work in one area were accompanied by expectations or wishes for activities in another. To come back to the washing machine: it indeed saved time, but to middle-class women that time was apparently lost again in the fulfilment of other chores and tasks related to the raising of the children and the household in general. A modern middle-class (time-consuming) chore, for instance, is to chauffeur children around, to get them to places for extra-curricular activities, to take an active part in school affairs, etc. Cowan argues that time spent in household chores has overall not decreased but in fact increased. Be this as it may, she has proposed a good reason why the second-wave women's movements saw a particularly high presence of middle-class women, suggesting that it was related to the changed requirements of their domestic role (1985: 191).

## WOMEN IN POLITICS

The existence of *rights* need not depend on the existence of movements. Nor is state control a guarantee for social justice. This is obvious. We know that in many eastern bloc countries the socio-political status of women was reviewed and amended by the state without being preceded by movements, albeit in a way that women who had not been consulted often regarded as paternalistic. We also know that in countries like Greece, Spain and Portugal, before their liberation from military dictatorships, there were no women's movements at all and very few rights granted to women. The little that might have been conceded in legislation, as in Spain, was usually not applied in practice.

Expressed differently, in western second-wave feminists movements the existence of parliamentary democracies preceded the movements or began with them. It seems reasonable, therefore, to ponder briefly about democracy per se as the political context of the new movements and on its methods and implied theories concerning pressure groups. Strangely enough, many of the movements wasted no time on such thoughts, even though, as said earlier, participants must have believed that their protest had some hope of success. Democracy is a theory of government, reflected in a government's constitution. As a *method* of government it has no 'end' in view, exists for no ethical purpose and positively excludes the majority from any political activity other than voting (Maddox, 1986: 1). Any other method, such as representative government, Rousseau argued two centuries ago, is a 'sham' and direct democracy is 'possible only in small states' (cit. in Plamenatz, 1958: 2).

One school of thought argues that the political participation of individual citizens in large pluralistic societies is not just unrealistic but in many ways undesirable. For democratic governments to function democratically, however, a larger 'base' is needed. This base is provided by a multitude of organisations and 'bodies' which are not directly linked to state institutions and which, in fact, need to be independent of government and autonomous in their decision making. These have been called 'sub-state' associations which relate only by way of analogy to political democracy (Maddox, 1986: 2) and relegate any influence and power of sub-state associations to a very indirect one, which cannot be guaranteed.

In this paradigm of democracy the process of mediation between the state and the citizens is minimal and their influence on political decisions marginal or non-existent. Extra-parliamentary pressure groups would find it difficult if not impossible to be heard or have any effect at all. The government's refusal to be influenced by such groups would be on the grounds of a mandate given by the people which cannot be jeopardised for the sake of the specific interests of one pressure group. Thus, despite the revolutionary origin of modern democracies, the political participation of individuals is said to be limited or impossible unless that individual is amongst the few elected into government. In return for this exclusion of the individual from any decision making the government implicitly promises to espouse democratic values, and to uphold and foster such values as freedom, equality, humanity, toleration and justice. But the citizen's right to voice political views puts the government under no obligation that these will be considered or applied. If someone, or a group, seeks political influence and seeks to effect change in policies or laws, the logical conclusion, and the only channel open to that person or group, is then to enter formal politics and become part of the government.

In another school of thought, the very method of how governmental power is derived, speaks for minority dissent as a legitimate form of the process of democracy. In the Italian constitution, there is provision for such a minority dissent because it allows for new bills being submitted if they have sufficient popular support. If the submission satisfies the rules concerning the number of signatories (500 000) and has been collected within the specified period of three months, both houses of parliament are obliged to discuss the bill.

Overall, western European feminists have usually adopted one of two strategies. In some cases, these strategies were related to the assumptions of the specific model of democracy at work in their country, but often they were expressions against them. One strategy is oppositional and not collaborative, and characterises large parts of the European second-wave liberation movements. The ultra-radical factions of extra-parliamentary feminist groups have rejected formal government outright and have sought no negotiation or collaboration with it. Those feminists have generally repudiated the idea that change can be orchestrated from *within* formal government. And most have rejected outright the idea that any of the more fundamental issues (i.e. the renegotiation of value and power hierarchies) can be tackled and changed in an unchallenged capitalist economy. They thus purposely stay away from the arena of formal power politics for fear of corruption by 'the system' and for the belief that true change can only come by directing the protest *against* the present democratic framework. Democratic citizenship, so radical feminist groups advocate, is based on a number of moral claims, such as shared rights, social responsibility and solidarity. As movements outside the parliamentary system they say it is the duty of democratic politics to make room for particularity and difference and acknowledge the right of those movements to be heard and dealt with within the political community as a whole. This 'political community' is a much wider concept than the narrow liberal view of government and includes action groups not as *sub*groups but as an integral part of the political community. They inadvertently argue against the liberal, individualistic view that democratic institutions are incompatible with the idea of a common purpose for society as a whole. But they are not alone. The new communitarian thinkers, such as M. Sandel or A. Macintyre, and writers like Walzer or Quentin Skinner have recently endorsed the view that individual liberty and political participation can be reconciled or, more, that individual liberty and social responsibility need to be reconciled (cf. Mouffe, 1988: 28–31).

Another model is based on the idea of collaboration that characterises women's rights movements within the second wave. Such collaboration can take two basically different forms or strategies. In one, feminists enter governments as outsiders or as part of its administrative machinery, by serving either on advisory committees or within bureaucracies. The second model of collaboration is to join forces and to enter the political power structure as one contender. Drude Dahlerup has summarised these trends in a useful schematic outline. Although

Table 2.7  Feminist attitudes to collaboration with the state

|  | Women's rights movement | Women's liberation movement |
|---|---|---|
| State as enemy | no | partly |
| Feminism as non-partisan | yes | no |
| Political reforms the main strategy | yes | no |
| Seeking integration | yes | no |
| Actual integration | marginal | n/a |
| Following the rules of the game | yes | no |
| Using direct action | no | yes |
| Ideology | equality | liberation |

Source: Dahlerup, 1986: 225

this presentation is confined to the Danish situation, it sums up quite adequately the two major directions of approach of feminists vis-à-vis the state in western Europe as a whole (see table 2.7).

There is some, if fairly limited, support amongst feminists for the view that pressure groups should have no influence on elected governments; for instance, Giovanna Zincone, an Italian feminist, has recently redrawn a sharp distinction between social and political groups. In her definition social groups are groups with shared characteristics and markers of discrimination, and political groups are exclusively party groups concerned with decision-making processes. She argues that there is no direct link between the two forms and if there were it would not be desirable. Nor does she support the view that women should have the right to 51 percent of posts in decision-making arenas 'simply because they make up 51 percent of the population'. She does admit that today's democracies represent interests and are therefore partial rather than impartial governments (1988: 160). According to proponents of the views such as expressed by Zincone, the only way for women to gain any influence is to enter the field of formal politics themselves. It is interesting that feminists in Scandinavian countries have reached the same conclusion as Zincone, but for different reasons. Scandinavian feminists have achieved the implementation of a quota system of the number of female candidates a party has to present. In Norway, it is now as high as 40 percent.

Of those who favour the idea of participation in formal politics, this preference is usually couched in terms of one of three predominant views. One belief implies that numerically equal representation of women and men at government level alone is a sign of parity and of democracy at work. Therefore an increase from low representation to high representation is seen as a clear indication of progress, irrespective of the political view and value system of the women in question and irrespective of the backwardness of the party any of them may represent. The mere evidence that the number of women holding parliamentary positions has increased over time is read as a sign of waning discrimination and becomes in itself a symbol of progress.

A second view, contrary to the first, holds that women need to go into politics so that they may be able to do something for women whilst in power. In this case of ideological representation, the political convictions and the level of commitment of the candidate to women's issues is of the utmost importance. This second perspective is probably dominant amongst feminists. Not all women, however, can or want to serve women specifically, but wish rather to serve their party, in which women's issues may or may not feature. Unfortunately, the expectation by women voters may then lead to these female politicians being dubbed 'honorary males' for their failure to act on gender-specific issues. The women currently in power in Europe are neither male nor honorarily so, and they are no less 'real' as women because one may dislike their politics. One may rightly attack them, as any other politician, for their political deeds and omissions, but to engage in these teleological somersaults is, in my view, just foolish.

A third position, mostly expressed in radical feminism, is that women need to get into positions of power because they can do a better job than men. In this meritocratic perspective, the sense of discrimination is probably most acute: if women have no opportunity of proving their aptitude in this field then ways and means will have to be found for them to show it!

One would think that the question of women's participation in politics should also incorporate an appreciation of women's own motivation and reasons for entering into or staying away from politics. Very few studies have actually addressed these issues and asked whether women's low participation rate in formal politics is the result of women being barred from the institutions or not *wanting* to join them. Is it an improvement in the lives of these politically active women to ascend power structures that were created by men or is it hindering them in the expression of their political temperament? Any formal statistics show us that women in Europe, as in other continents and countries, are not chiefly found in formal politics but are noticeably clustered in unstructured direct political action groups, based on the belief that non-hierarchical, direct participatory democratic channels of actions are possible and preferable to existing political channels. As Lovenduski rightly argues in response to studies by Barnes and Kaase, (1979) and by Randall (1982): 'The evidence, although far from conclusive, alerts us to the possibility that women may be less reluctant to engage in the more informal political world of movements, campaigns and direct action of various kinds than in the formal political arenas of parties, elections and legislature' (Lovenduski, 1986: 127).

The absence of or low participation rates of women in politics has generated a number of proposals as to why this is so. A seven-nation comparative study by Verba, Nie and Jae-on made the observation that interest in politics and personal involvement were about the same for men and women when women were educated and employed in the workforce. Even when there was no difference at this psychological and/or intellectual level, women rarely turned that interest into political activity. High levels of interest produced low levels of activity, while for men high interest also resulted in high levels of activity. The process of conversion from one level to another was gender specific, and at that point the gap between men's political behaviour and women's once again widened. The gap then also existed 'even when men in general were compared to the special group of women who are both educated and working' (Verba et al., 1976: 265). They realised that such a male/female difference could only be accounted for in a framework of an inhibition hypothesis, and therefore concluded that very powerful barriers must prevent the conversion of energy and interest into political activism. One needs little imagination to link the inhibition hypothesis to socialisation patterns: women are generally socialised into being nice, submissive, orderly and disciplined. Conceivably, women who turn overtly political will, first of all, have to break out of that paradigm—as a political act of defiance against submissiveness and silence. I am convinced, partly from my own experience, that it is not at all easy to be assertive and vocal in an environment (of politics) that tightly encapsulates expectations of traditional norms of

Table 2.8 Percentage of European women believing 'politics is men's business' (1983)

| | % | | % |
|---|---|---|---|
| Netherlands | 19 | France | 25 |
| UK | 19 | Ireland | 29 |
| Denmark | 20 | Luxembourg | 38 |
| Greece | 24 | Belgium | 40 |
| Italy | 25 | W. Germany | 42 |

Source: Women and Men of Europe, 1983

female conduct, of submissiveness and 'niceness'. Indeed, a recent Finnish study has shown that assertive and vocal women are more likely to be harassed and are more open to attack than their assertive and vocal male colleagues and much more so than submissive women (Högbacka et al., 1987).

Pippa Norris has advanced the thesis that women are relatively numerous in national office where they are also well represented in local government (1985: 90). Although this may be true overall, such a correlation cannot tell us very much. It seems more important to establish a correlation between attitudes of the general population and women's success as office bearers. A different formulation of the thesis might propose that in those countries where the majority of the general population believes that women can do any job as well as men, the representation of women at national and local level increases. Scandinavian countries have a consistently high representation of women at local and at national level, while England, France and Italy are consistently and substantially below European averages. France had 5.7 percent of women in the lower house in 1987 (as compared to 11.2 percent average in European Community countries), and a mere 2.5 percent in the upper house, the Sénat.

But even such correlations between general attitudes and women's participation rates are ultimately tenuous. There is, for instance, an interesting discrepancy between the *actual* presence of women in politics in the UK and the *attitudes* held by English women (and men) to women's presence in politics. In the European Commission's survey, one statement said: 'Politics is men's business' and women were asked to agree or disagree. The breakdown of this 1983 survey in percentage of *agreement* with the statement by women is shown in table 2.8. As this table indicates, only 19 percent of English women (but about the same percentage of men) agreed with the statement. The vast majority of English people readily concedes politics to be men's *and* women's business. But having established this, where *are* the women in politics in England?

Inglehart's investigation of several western European countries led to the claim that in countries which are predominantly protestant—and she includes England in this—political interest is much higher than in catholic countries. The interest may well be higher but, as the figures in table 2.9 below show, such an interest is not reflected in actual *presence* in political power positions (Inglehart, 1981).

The discrepancies do not end here. Swedish women have amongst the highest public profile, with 28 percent representation in government in 1984. Sweden can also boast one of the highest female labour forces in Europe and the highest unionisation of women. But, surprisingly, women are particularly underrepresented in top management union positions (6.7 percent in management while half of all members are women). Italy, by contrast, has 16.7 percent in top management positions of the leading union, with the total membership of women

**Table 2.9 Women in European public office 1979–1984 (%)**

| Country | Date | Lower House | Upper House | Cabinet | Regional | City |
|---|---|---|---|---|---|---|
| Finland | 1983 | 31 | n.r. | 18 | — | 22 |
| Sweden | 1983 | 28 | n.r. | 6 | 31 | 29 |
| Norway | 1983 | 26 | n.r. | 22 | 29 | 23 |
| Denmark | 1983 | 24 | n.r. | 15 | 20 | 21 |
| Netherlands | 1984 | 19 | 19 | 12 | 16.5 | 13 |
| Iceland | 1983 | 5 | n.r. | 10 | — | 12 |
| Switzerland | 1979 | 11 | 7 | — | 10 | 14 |
| Luxembourg | 1982 | 10 | — | 8 | — | — |
| Austria | 1981 | 10 | 21 | 26 | 21 | — |
| West Germany | 1983 | 10 | 5 | 6 | 8 | 11 |
| Portugal | 1982 | 10 | — | 8 | — | 2 |
| Ireland | 1983 | 9 | 10 | 8 | 5 | — |
| Italy | 1983 | 8 | 4 | — | 4 | 3 |
| Belgium | 1983 | 6 | 12 | 16 | 8 | — |
| France | 1982 | 6 | 3 | 11 | 14 | 3 |
| Spain | 1982 | 6 | 4 | 5 | 6 | 8 |
| Greece | 1983 | 4 | — | 7 | — | — |
| UK | 1983 | 4 | 7 | 9 | 16 | — |

*Source*: Norris,1985: 92

at only 33 percent. Sweden had a continuous socialist government for 44 years. Much of postwar Italy was under more conservative governments, although often under pressure from left-wing parties. Both countries developed strong and well-organised union systems. While Sweden forged ahead with policies of egalitarianism, Italian women were still protesting against very basic gender inequalities. Yet it is in Italy where the representation of women in unions is greater and more vibrant. There are complex historical reasons for this, of course. The point here is simply to suggest that the proposal of a dichotomy between protestant and catholic does not explain the low participation rate of women in politics.

Finally, to illustrate further the contradictions that surround us: when the figures on women in politics and women in employment are compared, a very peculiar imbalance emerges: in England, where attitudes to women in non-traditional jobs are actually amongst the most favourable, women's participation in politics is the lowest in western Europe, and women there express the least sense of disadvantage in the workplace. By contrast, in Denmark, with the highest participation rate of women in politics among European Community member states, women are particularly disgruntled about gender disadvantage in most job-related criteria. If making the simple equation that women should be in government so that they may do something for women, should one then not expect a correlation between parity at the workplace and women's presence in politics? Vice versa, if the proponents for higher representation of women in politics are right, should not an absence of women in government also mean that the greatest disadvantages for women are reflected in the treatment of women at work? We will not solve these issues here. They are far more complex than advocates for or against gendered representation argue them. Lovenduski's careful study provides useful points of analysis for these questions.

At least this much is clear: in the area of politics, research and experiences have shown that women are not less likely to enter politics than men, provided the political environment explicitly welcomes women into its ranks. The research

Table 2.10   Women in parliament in EEC countries in the late 1980s (in %)

| Member state | Parliament | Women rep. | Election date |
|---|---|---|---|
| Denmark | Folketing | 30.7 | 1988 |
| Netherlands | Tweede Kamer | 21.3 | 1986 |
| Netherlands | Eerste Kamer | 21.3 | 1987 |
| West Germany | Bundestag (federal) | 16.0 | 1987 |
| West Germany | state governments | 13.4 | 1988 |
| Italy | Camera dei Deputati | 12.9 | 1987 |
| Luxembourg | Chambre des Députés | 10.9 | 1984 |
| Portugal | Assembleia da República | 10.0 | 1987 |
| Belgium | Ch.des Représentants | 8.5 | 1987 |
| Ireland | Dáil Éireann | 8.4 | 1987 |
| Ireland | Seanad Éireann | 8.3 | 1987 |
| Belgium | Sénat | 8.2 | 1987 |
| Spain | Congreso/Diputados | 7.8 | 1986 |
| United Kingdom | House of Commons | 6.5 | 1987 |
| Italy | Senato della Republica | 6.3 | 1987 |
| Spain | Senado | 5.9 | 1986 |
| France | Assemblée Nationale | 5.7 | 1988 |
| United Kingdom | House of Lords | 5.6 | — |
| Greece | Vouli ton Ellinon | 4.3 | 1985 |
| France | Sénat | 2.5 | 1986 |

*Source*: European Parliament document PE 128, 465, 7 Feb. 1989 (cit. in *Women in Graphics*; 1989: 14)

by Verba et al. confirmed that all matters of education and social position being equal, men and women had no different degrees of psychological involvement or commitment to politics. The difference occurred in the application or use of that commitment through a variety of strong inhibitors and social sanctions (Verba et al., 1977: 265). Inglehart found, not surprisingly, that in countries where authoritarian attitudes had prevailed the longest there existed two different gender effects of politicisation: women either had a noticeably low rate of political commitment, or large sex differences in political interest between men and women existed (Inglehart, 1981: 313). The barriers and inhibitors that have prevented women from seeking public office twenty years ago are slowly being removed either by women insisting on a minimum percentage of representation (as in Norway), as a result of new party formations, such as the Greens in West Germany, or by public pressure from the electorate to have more women stand as candidates. To varying degrees of success, the number of women in formal politics has steadily increased over the 1980s (see table 2.10). None of these figures stands up to a comparison with gender profiles in Scandinavian countries and, for all their rhetoric, some countries, like Italy and France, still have abysmally low participation rates of women in formal politics (as do the USA and Australia). Nevertheless, over the last decade the rates for western Europe have improved overall. It remains to be seen whether this is indicative of a trend or merely one of the final consequences of the feminist movements, destined to peter out.

## WOMEN AND CIVIL LIBERTY

The distinction between and the dichotomy of the 'public' and 'private' has occupied feminists since the beginning of the second-wave movements. By arguing that the personal was political, feminists were found guilty of transgressing well-entrenched philosophical traditions and well-established political ideas. Hundreds of years of European jurisprudence (see also chapter 7) had defined the boundaries of the private realm as the area of 'desire, affectivity and the body' (love, sex and woman) and the political realm as public and rational, ruled by impartiality (men). The separation of the two spheres was anything but arbitrary (Young, 1986: 382, 387–9; Pateman, 1988: 115; see also Elshtain, 1981). Laws penetrated deeply into the private sphere and they decreed in surprising detail how women were to behave within the marital home. Feminists discovered that the issue of child bearing was just one of the many aspects of the private life of a woman that had fallen under state control, presumably in an effort to control women's behaviour and men's desire. At the same time, laws had little to say about protecting women from male violence, as long as it happened in the home.

## Abortion

We will see in later chapters that on the issue of abortion a vast proportion of European women was mobilised. Once women decided to speak up, they also realised that a woman's body was her own. If feminists of the second wave brought the issue of abortion into the public arena for debate, amendment or abolition, it was, ironically, not because the personal wasn't private but because the public had intruded into the private realm of individuals. The chief aim was then to make laws pertaining to pregnancy and abortion disappear from the public statute books. The difference here is that 'private' in the feminist sense means the *right* to retreat into the private sphere on matters concerning the individual and not the *inability* of something considered private to become political and public. Feminists showed that private concerns were indeed capable of becoming political issues but they also showed that in civil society the right to private and personal decisions was inalienable and not a matter for state intervention. Here women wanted to wrest the issue *away* from public control and put it in the lap of the individual. The argument across western Europe was, if one may put it this way, for the 'privatisation' of the body away from state control and nationalisation.

Abortion, widely practised although always officially prohibited by the church, had been a relatively obscure issue until the 19th century. Present-day feminists often do not know that laws prohibiting abortion are a modern phenomenon in Europe no older than the Industrial Revolution. Abortion was not always a crime written up in legal codes. In the Netherlands, for example, the first law to be explicit about abortion was passed in 1836. Under this law, abortion practices were hardly affected; for a woman to be charged with unlawfully aborting a foetus, the prosecution had to prove that the foetus was alive at the time of the abortion. If abortion were not available the child would not then necessarily stay in the household but, as is still happening in some poorer sections of Europe, would be sent out as a foundling. Infanticide of the newly born was also quite common.

Some writers have argued that, during the latter part of the 19th century, abortion was one issue around which the medical profession began to fight for its monopoly over the female body. There is evidence for this in the USA (Gordon, 1977; Mohr, 1978) and also in Europe (Outshoorn, 1986: 16). Yet this explanation is not sufficient. New anti-abortion and anti-contraception regulations came in either towards the end of or at the beginning of the 20th century, and were perceived as necessary to boost populations. Most western European countries, in fact, introduced anti-abortion laws for the first time in the 20th century. In the Netherlands, the law was tightened in 1911, making abortion a crime in all cases except for severe medical reasons (Francome, 1984: 135). Anti-abortion laws occurred at a time of nationalism and racism, fascism and the preparation for war. Many countries had criminalised abortion by the time World War I broke out in 1914, and several others (e.g. Germany and Italy) had tightened the laws by the 1920s or 1930s, introducing strict penalties and long prison sentences for offenders and for those who volunteered to become accessories. In most cases the new regulations on childbirth, coinciding with the maturing of modern nation-states, must be regarded as one of the aberrations of the perceived new role of national governments.

The criminalisation of abortion and contraception in Europe at that time served several purposes, and law-makers were in league with a variety of interest groups at the top of the power elites. The force of nationalism, then often couched in racist terms, the readiness for war and, in the 1920s, the much publicised 'discovery' of an alleged international Bolshevik (and Jewish) conspiracy all combined in a confused but extremely volatile scenario. It helped to create an atmosphere of hysteria about the fact that local birthrates were falling. It fuelled fear that their 'race' (i.e. their nation) was going to die out unless something drastic was done at once. It was alleged in newspaper propaganda that their nation could be swamped and superseded by other 'races' of 'lesser value' unless women produced more children than before. Even academics of some standing debated earnestly the need for a strengthening and invigoration of the 'race'.

These fears were underpinned by a profound class bias, for it became apparent that the birthrate was falling not indiscriminately but mainly amongst the working classes. European feminism of the 1910s and 1920s certainly went about educating working-class women in the art of contraception, and they were obviously successful (Bridenthal et al., 1984; Kaplan & Adams, 1990). The new radical movements had taken it upon themselves to argue that much of the abject poverty of the working class could be stemmed if it were taught how to prevent large numbers of offspring. The political echelon, be this the aristocracy or the upper bourgeoisie, was alarmed that a drop in birthrate amongst the working classes would deprive them of cheap labour in peacetime and the rank and file in wartime. Indeed, Mussolini and Hitler made it quite clear that their desire to increase the population was bound up with military plans.

In other words, the question of abortion and contraception, or rather of childbirth, was no longer considered a private matter at all but perceived as a matter of national concern, with all its unsavoury racist, classist, and nationalistic overtones. Indeed, power elites raised the dictum 'populate or perish' to a national issue seemingly of the utmost importance and urgency. The church, from its point of view, found little to object to because the family policies of the right and of fascism did not represent a rival set of ethics, which was the case with the radical movements. Making abortion illegal and the advertising of contraceptives punishable was something that the church could support wholeheartedly. What had been purely part of church doctrine before was now underwritten by the state. Inadvertently, the authority of the church and its dogma was thereby increased in the social domain, at a time when its political power was generally being diminished by growing secular state control.

In fascist countries (Italy and Germany) or in those with strong dictatorships

(Greece, Portugal and Spain), state intervention in personal and intimate matters reached a new pitch. Women not only suffered during fascist dictatorships but also in the aftermath because many of the fascist laws were not rescinded once the dictators had gone. The state continued to exercise the right to intervention and to punishment in areas of the most intimate kind, such as pregnancy and childbirth, and it was up to the second wave to question that right of intervention. It had to take on powerful interest groups that had defined abortion as either a medical or a national issue. It had to grapple with the church. It had to make giant leaps over additional hurdles erected by other powerful lobbyists on the question of morality. Morality was an effective shield against abortion law reform, for one could not reason with it. It is remarkable that the greatest doubts and the most deeply felt personal qualms were expressed by the very people who were in power. An additional problem was that the political machinery was not really equipped to deal with an issue that had assumed a popular position with everyone voicing an opinion. Because it took on these characteristics, as did the issue of capital punishment in England and Australia, it was bound for high-profile conflict. Feminists had to muster the full force of public opinion in order to keep their view of the issue on the forefront of the political agenda. The morality aspect, cleverly pushed as the only reference point, clouded the issue successfully for a good many years, even after the movements had fully mobilised against the abortion laws. It managed to supersede and to overlay arguments of civil liberty and personal responsibility, but these were precisely the issues that women wanted to raise. This happened in just about every western European country with the exception of Sweden, and in eastern European countries.

Of course, there are valid arguments against abortion, but these lie in a different direction altogether. Monique Pelletier, when she was Minister for Women in France, argued strongly against the symbolic value that abortion law reform/liberation had acquired. She said then:

> Abortion must remain a last resort and it must be granted under strictly observed conditions. We must refuse to encourage the practice or to make it commonplace. I repeat, it is neither a right nor does it represent progress, and although I do not talk of blame or guilt, I again say loudly and clearly abortion is not a symbol of freedom. (cit. in Mossuz-Lavau, 1986: 103)

Pelletier is not entirely wrong. The fact that we can perform abortions more safely and quickly and less painfully is progress only in the limited sense of better technology and better medical methods. To subject oneself to the ordeal of an abortion is not a symbol of freedom. Medically speaking, abortion is a violent interference with a woman's body, and it would be far preferable not to have to undergo it. At this point, however, the arguments always get confused, for it *is* a new freedom for a woman to be able to determine the number of offspring she is to produce. This freedom is bestowed partly by modern medical technology but also by a public recognition of a woman's right to choose what will happen in and to her own body.

The counterargument by anti-abortion groups, most fiercely promoted in Italy, is that a woman may make a choice about her own life but, since her body carries another life, she has no right to prevent that 'child' from living. The problem is that the foetus is not yet a 'child' but an organism with a potential to become one. Medically, ethically, philosophically, and legally no clear definition of 'life', or more aptly of *independent* life, has so far emerged. There has never been apparently a philosophy of birth (Pateman, 1988: 114). There are grey areas surrounding birth and death that may never be resolved. Ironically, the more sophisticated our medical methods for intervention become, the less likely it seems they will be resolved.

Meanwhile, a new population ethic has developed worldwide which considers it immoral, undisciplined and rapacious of the human race to continue multiplying in numbers which are so destructive to the environment. These too are life and death questions that should no longer be ignored. At no time, however, has any of the many western European pro-abortion lobbies ever argued that women *must* have abortions, but instead they have merely advocated freedom of *choice* for women, something that the anti-abortionists have never considered as a principled option. Clearly, the emphasis should be on better contraceptive methods (without side-effects) than on promoting abortion as the chief form of birth control. No woman would argue for abortion in *preference* to preventative methods. Indeed, in eastern bloc countries, where abortion has been practised as the main form of contraception, many women now regard this method of birth control as a sign of 'the brutality of the communist system' (Rosen, 1990).

The chief task of the feminists then was to get the state to agree that neither it, the church or the medical profession was to pass judgement on the number of pregnancies a woman had to undergo. Tatalovich and Daynes (1981) have probably best analysed the new feminist demands as a 'deregulation' claim, an insistence on the privacy of a matter in which the state should have no business at all. To varying degrees, feminists in many western European countries have succeeded although, in most, the shadow of medical control, as distinct from purely medical supervision of a health issue, has not vanished (see table 2.11). Historically, a public profile on abortion as a matter of state control is a very recent phenomenon which the feminist lobby has now almost returned to the private domain.

The issue, however, has settled uneasily. It keeps flaring up and the new ground gained causes subcutaneous discontent. This is also true for the rest of the western world. In Louisiana, USA, for instance, new abortion legislation was debated in 1990, and some bills have so far been proposed which, if any of them was passed, would make Louisiana perhaps the most anti-abortionist state in any western country, and possibly in the world. The issue of abortion is certainly not dead, and any pro-abortion changes in the last decades will have to be carefully guarded against landsliding into dictatorial rules and curtailment of civil liberties.

*Domestic violence*

The debate on the distinction between public and private, and with it the political actions feminist movements took to ensure that the personal *became* political, have led to a number of interesting contradictions. The drift towards the exclusion of the state in affairs, now more adamantly than ever defined as private and personal, has not been universally supported by feminist thinking. One of the most noted exceptions has been the issue of domestic violence. While feminists have vigorously argued for the law to stop intervening in personal and private matters, their stand on domestic violence was diametrically opposite. Domestic violence included not just physical violence but psychological cruelty and, perhaps the most controversial of all, rape in marriage.

Until the second-wave movements erupted throughout western Europe, the

**Table 2.11  Abortion legislation in nine western European countries**

| | Austria | Denmark | France | Germany | Italy | Netherlands | Switzerland | Sweden | UK |
|---|---|---|---|---|---|---|---|---|---|
| Women's request | √ | √ | √ | × | √ | √ | × | √ | × |
| Social grounds | √ | √ | √ | √ | √ | √ | √ (?) | √ | √ |
| Medical grounds | √ | √ | √ | √ | √ | √ | √ | √ | √ |
| Notification | × | | √ | √ | √ | √ | × | √ | √ |
| Second doctor's opinion required | × | × | √ | √ | √ | × | √ | × | √ |
| Compulsory waiting | × | × | √ | √ | √ | √ | × | × | × |
| Parental consent for minors | √ | √ | √ | √ | √ | √ | √ | √ | √ |
| Obligatory advice re alternatives | × | × | √ | √ | √ | √ | × | × | × |
| Non-residentials | √ | × | × | × | √ | √ | √ | × | √ |
| Part of health insurance | × | √ | √ | × | √ | √ | √ | √ | √ |

(legend: √ means 'yes', × means 'no')

Source:  adapted from Ketting & Van Praag, 1986: 160–1

law rarely, if at all, interfered in matters which it had itself defined as private—these included fights and problems within a marital and domestic setting and, in view of the sanctity of the family, nothing was considered more private by law than the sexual relationship between married partners. To restate this here, a man's marriage was seen as a private matter while a woman's body was not. We know that the laws of many countries permitted violence against women in wedlock and some laws actually encouraged it. It was never called violence but 'chastisement' and was seen as acceptable in cases when the wife's behaviour displeased the husband. Such displeasure presumably meant that the husband knew best and acted in the best interest of his wife and family as the state's appointed head of the household. In some countries, such as Germany, the law encouraging physical violence against women disappeared around the turn of the century (in 1900), while in others they were only rescinded in the 1970s (as in Portugal). The position that feminists generally took on this issue was to invite the state to intervene with a heavy hand, to punish the perpetrator and to protect the women and children at state cost. The 'conspiracy of silence' which often surrounds victims and their families and friends suggests, however, that a residue of opinion remains which condones violence against wives for specific reasons. Attitudes die hard.

More importantly, the concept of 'privacy', in the tradition of mainland European law, is one of those sacrosanct concepts inherited from Roman law, reinforced over and over again through the centuries, especially from the 17th century onwards. It was, and to an extent still is, one of those laws that has become the chief guardian of civil liberty, the very thing for which women have been fighting. In Montesquieu's interpretation of the Roman concepts of *libertas* and *civitas* in his famous book *De l'Esprit des Lois* (1748), he espoused the idea that personal liberty meant not only freedom of religion and conscience, and opinion and word but, most significantly, it meant *freedom of domicile*: the house as a refuge, an asylum, a place in which one was protected and secure from state intervention. This interpretation of Roman law by the French philosopher played a significant role in the French Revolution and it became enshrined in the new code of citizenship that Europeans and the western world have generally followed: no emissary of the state, be this a policeman or any other official, is permitted to enter one's domicile without a warrant; no one can make an arrest in a person's own home unless a warrant is presented. Indeed, in most countries of the western world, it is permissible and legal to order police off the premises. This code has such importance as a guardian of privacy and personal liberty that fascists, and other dictators did nothing faster than to violate it, a sure sign that the state would arbitrate wherever it pleased. It was one of the first rules that democratic governments resurrected, realising it laid indeed one of the most important ground rules of any form of democracy.

After parliamentary democracies were in place and vows for a commitment to democratic principles had been made, feminists argued that the state *should* intervene in what the law had considered a private domain. Conceptually, this was a very difficult step to take. That it was possible to take that step at all is related to the interpretation of violence. Feminists argued that violence against a person must be considered in terms of the statute books *wherever* it occurred. Their case rested entirely on the legal practice of charging offenders with murder, wherever it occurred. Any assault, therefore, should also be regarded as criminal irrespective of the place of the event. Law agencies falsely assumed that domestic violence was the result of a fight within the marital relationship and was therefore a private matter. Only research and documentation has clearly substantiated the feminist argument that domestic violence has nothing whatever to do with a 'family squabble' but is, in fact, a power game. It needs no provocation and is not an isolated incidence, not a 'squabble'. Within the debate on the 'private' and the 'public', however, the whole issue of domestic violence appeared a contradiction in terms and contravened not just misogynist laws but some of the most progressive ideas of the French *philosophes*.

Feminists themselves helped to solve the deadlock in some ways by opening refuges for women—places to go to if the domicile is no longer safe. Refuges reflect a sad truth: the violence has occurred more than once and has become so unbearable for the victim that she has to run away. Feminists have used their own initiative here in providing this service for women, but it took years before governments, hesitantly, stepped in and provided assured financial support for such refuges. Consistent with women's abhorrence of it, feminists have condemned violence not only as a means of controlling women but also violence in general (Hanmer, 1981).

## SOME HYPOTHESES

The accumulation of concrete empirical data on women's status in western Europe will increasingly invite scholars to make comparative studies and to analyse why women in one country have fared better than those in another. Publications attempting macro-level analyses of European women have begun to appear and include Lovenduski's excellent book *Women and European Politics* (1986). Although it is probably too early for general theory constructions, it is more than tempting to hypothesise about differences of achievements in various European countries precisely because the differences in political systems, religious beliefs and economic status and national wealth are often very marked (see table 2.12).

Given the history of Europe, a history of competition and constant warfare amongst its nations, one needs to guard against judgemental comparisons and single-variable statements. These have occurred from time to time. I will name only a few of the most common ones I detected, and I do so in order to eliminate them from further discussion rather than to build on them.

### General hypotheses

One hypothesis is that a country may be less likely to adopt progressive ideas when it is predominantly catholic. As table 2.12 shows, well over half of western Europe is catholic and only four countries are predominantly protestant. It would be foolhardy to suggest that only these four countries have developed progressive ideas while catholic ones have stayed behind or, vice versa, that catholic countries are more discriminatory against women than protestant ones. Portugal and Spain, two predominantly catholic countries, now have perhaps the most advanced constitutions in western Europe, incorporating rights for women not just in the public but in the private sphere as well (see table 2.3). Denmark and France, also predominantly catholic countries, have a record of achievement comparable to or exceeding those of other countries. The attitudes of the Danish people to women in professions and employment are particularly enlightened (see table 2.13). The list could be extended. Surely, it is not a question of which religion predominates in a country but the *role* religion plays

**Table 2.12  Structural data for European countries, 1989**

| Country | Area (per 1000 km²) | Population ( millions) | Religion | Political format | GNP (per capita income in US$) | Affiliation |
|---|---|---|---|---|---|---|
| Austria | 84 | 7.57 | cathol. | republic | 9.150 | neutral, EFTA |
| Belgium | 31 | 9.86 | cathol. | monarchy | 8.450 | EEC |
| Denmark | 43 | 5.12 | cathol. | monarchy | 11.240 | EEC |
| England | 244 | 56.62 | mixed | monarchy | 8.390 | EEC |
| Finland | 338 | 4.89 | protest. | republic | 10.870 | |
| France | 547 | 55.17 | cathol. | republic | 9.550 | EEC |
| Germany (West) | 249 | 61.12 | mixed | republic | 10.940 | EEC |
| Greece | 132 | 9.93 | orthod. | republic | 3.350 | EEC |
| Iceland | 102.3 | 0.24 | protest. | republic | 10.720 | |
| Ireland | 70 | 3.55 | cathol. | republic | 4.840 | EEC |
| Italy | 301 | 57.13 | cathol. | republic | 6.520 | EEC |
| Liechtenstein | 0.16 | 0.027 | cathol. | dukedom | 17.625 | |
| Luxembourg | 2.5 | 0.367 | cathol | monarchy | 13.380 | EEC |
| Malta | 0.315 | 0.380 | cathol. | republic | 3.300 | EEC |
| Netherlands | 42 | 14.56 | mixed | monarchy | 9.180 | EEC |
| Norway | 324 | 4.17 | protest. | monarchy | 13.890 | neutral, EFTA |
| Portugal | 92 | 10.29 | cathol. | republic | 1.970 | EEC |
| Spain | 505 | 38.82 | cathol. | monarchy | 4.360 | EEC |
| Sweden | 450 | 8.36 | protest. | monarchy | 11.890 | neutral, EFTA |
| Switzerland | 41 | 6.46 | mixed | republic | 16.360 | neutral, EFTA |

*Source*: *Fischer Weltalmanach*, 1989

in the political running of a state and whether or not its inherent rigidity and mythology make it unwilling to accept any change running counter to its dogma. Perhaps it should be said that *any* religion, as long as it has a stronghold on the state and can wield real power, will be a great stumbling block for substantial change in secular matters. In the areas concerning the family and reproduction, which the new women's movements have raised, the church has done and will do its utmost to prevent the very changes that, in the eyes of feminists, would best benefit women. Most, but not all, European states have partially or fully succeeded in relegating church power outside political precincts. The mechanisms involved in this often slow, historical process are extremely complex as is an assessment of any power of the church today, be this legitimate, condoned, tolerated or invisible; it is a question of the degree of influence the church might have on public opinion or on party politics. Indeed, these issues might be fruitful starting points for analysis.

Another hypothesis relates to the relative wealth of a country. The economically poorer Mediterranean countries of western Europe are supposed to be slower or 'behind' other countries in relation to women's issues. There are several things wrong with this view. First, countries like Greece, Portugal and Spain, the poorest western European countries, have all had just over a decade to recover from long dictatorship or fascist rule. It is in these countries, and in Italy, that Eurocommunism flourished in the 1970s and firm commitments were made for restructuring and reorganising their societies, cleansing them of fascist and military

**Table 2.13    Degree of confidence expressed by women for women in non-traditional jobs**

| Driver | | Surgeon | | Doctor | |
|---|---|---|---|---|---|
| % | | % | | % | |
| Denmark | 86 | Netherlands | 81 | Denmark | 78 |
| France | 75 | Denmark | 79 | Netherlands | 68 |
| Netherlands | 71 | France | 67 | France | 63 |
| UK | 58 | UK | 63 | UK | 62 |
| Belgium | 58 | Belgium | 61 | Belgium | 62 |
| Luxembourg | 54 | Luxembourg | 58 | Luxembourg | 59 |
| Italy | 45 | Ireland | 51 | Ireland | 50 |
| W. Germany | 44 | Italy | 49 | Italy | 44 |
| Ireland | 43 | W. Germany | 46 | Greece | 43 |
| Greece | 33 | Greece | 41 | W. Germany | 34 |

Percentage figures refer to 'yes' answers to the statement:
'Women are as good in these jobs as men'

Source: Women and Men of Europe, 1983

right-wing values. All of them have in fact made vast strides forward, not without great political unrest, and have included women's activism as part of a new democratic process. Moreover, Italy, still regarded as a poor country although its annual GNP figures now show its to be leaving that category, can claim perhaps the most impressive feminist activism in western Europe. To be sure, this activism has typically originated in the more sophisticated urban environment of the north rather than in the depressed rural south.

Conversely, the notion that technological progress and a generally high standard of living, by way of 'trickle down effect', gives an assurance of women's greater parity in public and private life, is also a myth. West German society, for all its economic achievements and political success in building the first stable German democracy, is also one of the most conservative countries in western Europe. Denmark, Norway, Sweden, and the Netherlands compare well in living standards with West German society, but attitudes of Scandinavian men and women to women in all aspects of equality are far more liberal than German ones. As shown in table 2.8, almost half of the population interviewed in West Germany believed that politics was indeed only men's business, while in the Netherlands less than 20 percent adhered to such prejudice.

The responses to a question measuring tolerance to women in skilled but non-traditional female jobs were equally disconcerting. Women were asked whether they had equal confidence in the job performance of a female bus driver, a surgeon and a doctor (delivering babies). Table 2.13 gives the percentage of women who have equal confidence in women performing these jobs as well as men. On this measure West Germany appears as one of the least egalitarian, scoring consistently lower than other, poorer countries. One can of course query the sample size, the method of data collection and argue for or against the representativeness of the findings. Unfortunately, several details, such as the method of collecting the sample, were not stated in the commission's findings. The instrument used for gaining the data was a closed and structured questionnaire. (To my knowledge, the European Commission takes these findings from statistical surveys commissioned by it from established survey groups/institutions in the country of origin of the data.) Some feminists inside and outside West Germany have dismissed these figures as nonsense because the findings did not correspond to their own personal experiences. To make this quite plain here: the sample concerned the *general* population, and not a small group of progressive feminists. But even if one deals with these figures with caution and a sense of reservation, they should at least lead one to accept the general point that a correlation between wealth, high technology and social progressiveness is not all that easily made.

Citing the case of Switzerland well demonstrates that wealth is not an index of progressiveness. Switzerland, the hub of wealth in Europe, postponed signing the Declaration of Human Rights in the Charter of the United Nations of 1948 because it contained the clause which allowed basic freedom irrespective of race, sex, language or religion. As late as 1968 Switzerland, in all seriousness, suggested signing 'with reservations' and with certain amendments in order to exclude sex from the agreement (Woodtli, 1975: 209). Most Swiss women gained the vote only between 1971 and 1975 (in stages through the various *Kantons*, in a few small regions even later). In Liechtenstein, the tiny but extremely wealthy dukedom, male voters decided in 1971 to turn down women's suffrage. Despite scathing international criticism in the press, such as the *Time* article 'Keeping up with Kuwait' (*Time*, vol. 97, 15 March 1971: 39), accusing Liechtenstein of practices akin to certain feudal middle-east countries, women's suffrage was effectively postponed for another fourteen years. Liechtenstein's women were allowed to go to the polls for the first time in 1985.

Another hypothesis, at times implied in feminist writing, is that backwardness and progressiveness correlate with the size of a country or, rather, its population; for instance, an Austrian feminist recently claimed that her own country, together with Switzerland and Iceland (all countries with very small populations) make a 'strange trio' amongst the industrialised European countries as they are the most backward (Pauli, 1986: 7). As we saw, however, Norway, Luxembourg and Finland, countries to which the label backward cannot be applied on any measure, have very small populations (under five million people) while the populations of Denmark, Sweden and the Netherlands are under ten million. By European standards, all of these countries are small *and* progressive, if to varying degrees.

Finally, there is a tacit assumption that new countries like the USA, Canada and Australia, supposedly unfettered as they are by the weight of tradition, would have made democracies work in much more progressive ways than the old countries or those less experienced in democracy. This is a prejudice that relates back to the English-speaking world, but it is not true. The English-speaking countries, headed by England, have the dubious distinction of having the poorest record of women participating in political decision-making processes anywhere in the western industrialised world. Figure 2.1, a comparison of women's legislative participation in English and non-English-speaking European countries, may suffice to illustrate the point.

*The seesaw effect*

We tend to think that if one area of women's advancement into equality lags behind other spheres (private, political, economic), it is only a matter of time before changes occur to bring the three areas on a par with each other. The figures for the status of western European women do not support this optimism. On the contrary, it appears that when women succeed in one or two spheres there are certain backlashes in the other one or two; for instance, when women

**Figure 2.1    Percentage of women in national legislatures in European and English-speaking countries**

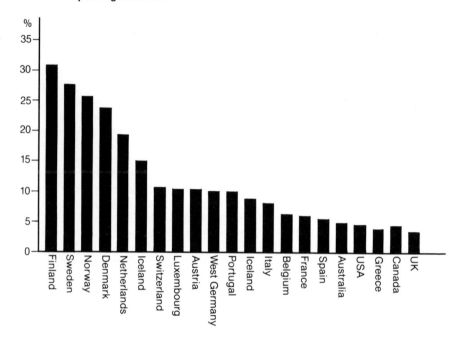

*Source*: adapted from Pippa Noris, 1985: 90

have achieved fairly high representation in politics, it is highly unlikely that they will have any equality either in economic terms or in their private lives. Or, when women have made large strides in their personal relationships, conducting these in egalitarian ways, it is highly likely that their presence in politics will be very weak and/or their economic status far lower than that of men. This observation is best demonstrated in countries or regions where *most* effort has been expended in the eradication of disadvantage. In countries, where changes have been sporadic and basic formal changes only introduced recently, we may not easily detect the differences from one area to the next. Disadvantage may simply be present more or less equally in all areas of women's lives. Uneven development only begins at a certain level of 'progress'.

I have called this hypothesis the seesaw effect. If one brings down a seesaw on one side it will go up on the other. Expressed more seriously: when and where women have achieved visible success in one or two of the three areas (political, economic or personal) one or two areas will show marked signs of regression or maintenance of traditional gender divisions.

To the philosopher of history the idea that gains will be accompanied by losses is far from new (Heller, 1980). The distribution of gains and losses, at least initially, is understood by feminists to mean that men will have to accept some losses while the gains are reaped by women. When all discrimination is removed, then men and women alike will reap the benefits and there will be no losses at all. In the reality of present-day industrialising or industrialised western societies, the predominant economic paradigm with its inbuilt system of inequalities cannot tolerate the counteractive forces of equalities beyond a certain limit, or it will be transformed altogether. Thus, despite the revolutionary potential of the women's movements in western Europe, the supple system of capitalism harnessed it so that it was whittled away to small step reformism, accommodating women's demands by degrees within the given framework.

The hypothesis proposed here may appear contradictory. It supports the radical position that without *fundamental* changes the dominant socio-economic paradigm will continue to exert itself and retain structured inequality. On the other hand, the hypothesis refutes the notion that women's integration into the workforce, that is, women gaining economic independence, will take away all the inequalities. August Bebel's proposal, radical enough in the 19th century, has been proven insufficient. Capitalism, not as he saw it then but as we now know it from empirical evidence, is resilient enough to integrate women without altering core value hierarchies in the slightest. In order to renegotiate all value hierarchies it is obviously not enough to propose a change of one, two or even three variables. At the moment, the seesaw effect appears to be rather prominent, especially in the most progressive countries, and unless further changes of a more substantial kind occur it may well remain so. Stated less pessimistically, the contradictions and irrationalities associated with women's status will continue to be absorbed and, in a number of cases, even be accepted. Although human beings are often quite comfortable in living with irrational spaces, as Karl Mannheim argued (1969), these need to be exposed and analysed in order to replace a shallow victorious mood with a more considered understanding of the limits of women's liberation.

The differences in women's status in different countries and the manner in which changes have been effected raise important issues for women, issues which will be tackled in more detail in the chapters to come. In Part II of this book, I have identified the theoretical paradigms of individual countries as falling into progressive, conservative, marginal and revolutionary clusters which shed light on the complex issue of the freedom and limits of action in a given context. More importantly, by examining the various action paradigms separately and in some depth, the known and practised alternatives reveal their relative successes and weaknesses and may give us some idea of likely future achievements.

# PART II

# Characteristics of individual countries

# 3  Progressiveness in Scandinavia

This chapter will deal with some of the salient features of Scandinavian social management that are generally regarded as progressive. It may as well be said from the outset that this progressiveness is inherently linked to the broader social aims of Nordic societies and to the way these social democracies have understood their commitment to social justice issues, resulting in the formation of fully fledged welfare states. In Scandinavia, the foundations of the so-called modern welfare state were generally laid in the 1930s or even earlier. The plan then was to ensure that no citizen would fall below subsistence level and, indeed, that there would not be a single occasion in an individual's life when income would fall as low as subsistence. From the 1970s on, the problems of the welfare state have been to keep pace with a constant rise in the inequalities generated by the market economy. Nevertheless, as recently as the 1980s, writers on the subject concluded that the high standards of benefits and the breadth of coverage make the Scandinavian countries exceptional worldwide:

> It has raised the standard of living of the worst off markedly above the subsistence level, abolishing the material deprivation and obvious penury that continues to characterize life for substantial numbers in other industrial societies, such as France, West Germany, and the United States. The mesh of the welfare net is very fine indeed; to fall through virtually requires that you cut a hole first. Moreover, the net is cast widely, encompassing those who in other societies, like the American, would enjoy no benefits during their economically active years. Perhaps this is the reason for the breadth of political support that the Scandinavian welfare states have enjoyed; if you do not benefit today, you are likely to tomorrow. (Logue, 1983: 244)

Logue explains that one of the crucial ingredients for the success of this welfare state was not the intention of creating welfare but *equality*. Thus, even though social welfare was a goal it was 'secondary to a more fundamental egalitarianism ... that extended beyond equality of opportunity to economic equality and to equality in control of one's own destiny' (Logue, 1983: 245).

Women, in general it seems, are better off in Scandinavian countries than women in other western European nations and the western world. A great historical advantage, in comparison to other western European nations, lay in the mere continuity of reform over a long period of time. Changes in the status of women not only occurred earlier than in other countries but, crucially, were then not forfeited through war, dictatorships or fascism. Women's right to vote and be voted into government was generally established in Scandinavia earlier than elsewhere. Throughout the 1980s each Scandinavian country has had a considerably higher representation of women in politics than any other western nation. Indeed, except for Iceland which was a latecomer, women have had, for many decades, considerably higher representations in parliament and government than other European countries.

**Table 3.1 Percentage of women in Scandinavian parliament, 1929–1984**

|          | 1929 | 1949 | 1966 | 1977 | 1984 |
|----------|------|------|------|------|------|
| Finland  | 3    | 12   | 17   | 23   | 31   |
| Sweden   | 1    | 10   | 13   | 21   | 28   |
| Denmark  | 3    | 9    | 11   | 17   | 26   |
| Norway   | 1    | 5    | 8    | 24   | 26   |
| Iceland  | 3    | 4    | 2    | 5    | 15   |

*Source*: adapted from E. Haavio-Mannila et al., 1983: 91

One factor contributing to women's significant participation in politics was Scandinavia's economic development in the 19th century, based as it was on a free peasant economy rather than on large landed estates. Pollard writes that the success of the northern countries 'must be sought in such factors as favourable location in terms of sea transport, early commercial and banking development, and human capital in the form of an active, healthy, law-abiding and enterprising population enjoying the advantages of a relatively good education and early emancipation from serfdom' (Pollard, 1981: 234). Perhaps, given the advanced and emancipated nature of these societies even in the last century, it is not surprising that for most of this century the issue of women's equality has been on the agenda of political parties and that it has been fought for in small steps throughout this time. In the 1960s, when the USA, England, Australia, or any other western European nation had barely any women in politics, be that in parliament, in the legislature or any other decision-making bodies, women in Scandinavia already played an important role in politics.

Equally, in such areas as sexuality, contraceptives and family counselling, the Nordic countries, except for Norway, were in general far ahead of other western nations, both in legislation and policy initiatives. The issue of abortion was decided earlier and usually with far less public uproar than in other countries. The change occurred almost quietly and, in Sweden, even without much debate (Wistrand, 1981: 5). Thus abortion never became the catalyst for women's movements, as has been the case in other western European nations (Bergman & Vehkakoski, 1988: 86). Iceland, Sweden and Denmark liberalised their abortion laws in the interwar period (1918–1939), Finland in 1951 and Norway in 1965. Abortion on demand was introduced in Denmark in 1973 and in Sweden in 1975 (Francome, 1984: 132).

Space will not permit me to dwell on the highly complex separate issue of the Scandinavian developments in belief systems and the role of the church in the state. The evolution of present-day church–state relations and the processes of secularisation, whatever secularisation means, have been thoroughly investigated elsewhere (Gustafsson, 1987). It appears from these accounts that church–state relations have stabilised. In some instances it is not the church assembly but parliament which has the final say in some church matters. This is only relevant to us here in so far as the ordination of women is concerned. Like abortion and changes in family law, the issue of ordaining women as priests has usually been considered a good deal more controversial and emotive than mere issues of equality, and change in this area has been hardest to achieve. In Denmark and Iceland there was least resistance to the idea of ordaining women and this happened relatively early, in 1948 in the former and in 1974 in the latter case. In Norway, women were granted the right to become priests in 1938 but resistance from within the church was so profound that the first woman was ordained only in 1961 and the number has remained small to this day. In Sweden, that right was granted in 1958, but in Finland, surprisingly, it had to wait until 1986.

The formation of the Scandinavian states as we know them today occurred rather recently. Sweden, still a monarchy today, in 1848 called its first liberal government under King Oscar I (1844–1859), a member of the Bernadotte dynasty. Under his son, Karl XV the old estate system was replaced by a parliamentary system of upper and lower house (1865–66). In 1905 it ended its union with Norway and up to 1921 it instigated a series of election reforms. The Socialist Party (social democrats) grew into the strongest party and was in power continuously for 44 years (1932–1976), regaining power in 1985. Sweden was neutral in both world wars. Norway, which had been under Swedish or Danish rule for centuries, became a sovereign state in 1814. It abolished its aristocracy in 1821 and finally seceded from the union with Sweden in 1905. In 1907 Norway elected its own king and since then it has remained a monarchy with a system of parliamentary democracy.

Norway was formally neutral in both world wars. In World War I, however, Norway sympathised with England and in World War II lent half of its navy to England. In 1940 the king and government were forced to flee the country, returning from London in 1945. Norway is one of the founding members of the UN. Like Sweden, Finland and Iceland, Norway is predominantly protestant, but while the political power of the church was broken long ago in these other countries, the Norwegian church has remained influential, as the relative importance of the Nowegian Christian People's Party attests.

Denmark is a monarchy like Norway and Sweden but unlike other Scandinavian countries it is predominantly catholic, a fact that should caution one against the temptation of drawing hasty conclusions about the adverse or positive relationship between religion and the progressiveness of a society (Lovenduski, 1986: 48, 53; Evans, 1979: 70). For a long time Denmark was led by socialist and radical-left governments. The radical left under Zahle (1913–1920) created the democratic constitution of 1915, the year in which women were enfranchised. The social democrats, although not as radical today as they used to be, were reelected in 1984. Like other Scandinavian countries, Denmark was neutral throughout both world wars, true to the principles espoused in 1864, but it was occupied by Germany from 1940 to 1945.

Finland was part of the Kingdom of Sweden from 1154 to 1805, when it became an autonomous grand duchy subordinate to Russia. Independence from Russia was declared in 1917 and the Finnish republican constitution drafted two years later. Although Russia and Finland had signed a peace treaty in 1920, in 1939 the USSR attacked Finland in retaliation for strong fascist activities clearly designed as a bulwark against Russian power. Despite strong Finnish resistance in the so-called Winter War, Finland lost important territory, regaining some of it later as leases from the USSR. Nevertheless, in the entire postwar period the tensions between Finland and the USSR have never quite ceased. From its beginning, Finland was a parliamentary democracy, dominated alternately by communists or social democrats, and often coalition governments were formed. For a period of almost three decades, Finland was ruled by Prime Minister Kekkonen (Jutikkala & Pirinen, 1984: 262). The 1987 elections saw the first conservative president (Harri Holkeri) in Finland since 1946. Iceland became an independent monarchy only in 1918, after the final breakaway from Denmark, and was proclaimed a republic as recently as 1944.

In other words, Iceland, Norway and Finland fully asserted national independence only in the 20th century, and Denmark and Sweden saw their political power, terrain and economic gains substantially reduced as a result of the secessions in the 19th and 20th centuries.

Scandinavian history has largely evolved independently from mainland Europe. Enmeshed as the Nordic countries are with each other, they share a number of structural, demographic and ideological features which may have some socio-cultural relevance (except Iceland, which because of its extreme isolation has developed rather differently). All Scandinavian countries have in common small populations and, with the exception of Denmark, extremely low population densities. In all of them, population growth is below zero and life expectancy at least 70 years for men and 78 years for women. Scandinavian countries are noteworthy for their homogeneity. Ethnic and religious differences are rare and confessional warfare or disputes have been alien to them throughout this century (Meissner, 1980: 149). Equally noteworthy are their wealth and the general high standard of living. Of all Scandinavian countries Sweden has the highest standard of living and, after Switzerland, the highest in western Europe. Finland has the lowest in Scandinavia. Nordic countries have followed the system of proportional representation and consequently there are numerous parties in parliament; for instance, Denmark has thirteen major parties and most of them are represented in parliament. In Finland, the 1987 elections voted representatives of nine parties (out of ten) into parliament, resulting in a coalition between the left, centre and right-wing parties, as had been the case for two decades before. Contrary to the expectations of some critics who see numerous parties as a sign of political weakness and instability, the political multiparty system of parliamentary democracy, with some isolated exceptions, has bestowed decades of stable government. Most Scandinavian countries have experienced periods of militant nationalism, but not one of them has undergone a revolution.

The Scandinavian economies emerged more or less intact after World War II, but most of them suffered severe shortages or were forced into new directions. In several countries, capital stock had not been renewed and rationing was often necessary up to 1950, by which time full employment was realised. This was generally followed by about two decades of fast growth (Fitzmaurice, 1981: 29) and a sudden downturn into economic crisis in the early 1970s. The oil crisis of 1973, the increasing problem of inflation, and the balance of trade deficits all led to a sudden rise in unemployment, to drastic cuts in public expenditure in some cases, and to a general rethinking of social and economic paradigms. The women's movements were coeval with these events and often formed part, and a novel part at that, of the rethinking process.

With the exception of Iceland, which is still largely a fishing nation, every other country subsequently experienced very substantial shifts in its respective economy. Denmark and Finland, for instance, although there had been a long span of industrial development reaching back into the 19th century, began to industrialise in earnest only after 1950, although Denmark in particular had already rationalised its agricultural activities in the 19th century and had moved to high technology agriculture in the 20th century (Pollard, 1981: 235). As much as 50 percent of the labour force in Finland was employed in agriculture and forestry in 1950, but 30 years later the figure had dropped to 9 percent (Ministry, 1987: 5). Denmark, as Fitzmaurice observed, 'drifted from agriculture to industry [because of a] widening difference in earnings' (1981: 33), and agriculture soon started sliding into crisis (Christensen, 1983: 183). Norway remained a fishing and agricultural country well into the 1970s. Just after the dramatic rise in oil prices in 1973, however, Norway discovered its own oil and gas supplies (1974), became independent in the energy sector and shortly thereafter began to export. Yet, as Benz has argued, the discovery and exploitation of these new resources also brought immediate economic problems, such as sudden increases in inflation and large-scale mining disasters like the oil spill in 1977 (Benz, 1983: 150). In the early 1970s, pragmatic welfarism—including deficit financed public works and subsidies—came under attack because it was based on the assumption of continued economic growth (Fitzmaurice, 1983: 36), and those expectations of growth could not be upheld. The women's movements in part also fell prey to that thinking, and this had important ramifications for their strategies, as was mentioned before in chapter 2, 'Women and technology'.

In other words, postwar Scandinavian societies were socio-economically in flux: the changes in material wealth, the possibility of upward mobility and of social justice—often seen by right-wing parties as unaffordable luxury items— were all indicators of new social, political and economic spaces being created in the wake of abandoned traditions. One may surmise that groups of minority status, such as women, would have gained from this fluidity and to an extent they did, but with certain qualifications, as we shall explore later. At the same time, the belief in social justice for all as a yardstick for democracy at work was adamantly upheld. Ways and means were sought of translating these beliefs into practice, whether in the expansion of welfare measures, the number of provisions for children, or other expenditure in the public sector.

*SWEDEN*

The Swedes are noted for their stand on a number of important contemporary concerns including women's issues and environmental questions. Sweden was the first country to make legal provisions for environmental protection, women's issues and nuclear power. As early as the 1960s, Alva Myrdal, then Minister of Disarmament, sharply objected to the use of nuclear, chemical and biological weapons, and in 1982 she was awarded the Nobel Peace Prize for her work. Except for Austria, Sweden is the only European country so far to have taken active steps against the use of nuclear power, but the ultimate goal, the abolition of the nuclear power plants, might have to wait a little longer. The social democratic government had resolved in March 1987 that nuclear power plants would cease operations as of 1993, but it then lost the election.

Women's issues have been on the political agenda in Sweden for a considerable time, in fact since the 19th century. Well before any other country (in 1810) women in Sweden gained permission for entry into trade and sales occupations. In 1845 they obtained the right to inherit property. From 1859 onwards they were able to become primary schoolteachers, and by 1870 they were allowed to matriculate. Three years later their right to go to university as fully enrolled students (not as guest listeners as in some other countries) was granted. In 1876, all schools became coeducational. In 1883, the first doctorate was awarded to a woman and in 1914, Selma Lagerlöff became the first woman to be appointed to the Swedish Academy (Anthony, 1915: 30–39). The first large-scale women's movement originated in the 19th century. Before it died down in the 1920s, divorce by mutual consent was made possible (1915), women gained the vote (1919), were declared of legal age at 21, and a new family law of 1920 abolished the husband's guardianship of wife and children. The

**Table 3.2   Household size and composition in Sweden, 1983**

| Households | Without children % | With children % |
|---|---|---|
| 1 person | 30 | 5 |
| 2 persons | 28 | 25 |
| 3 persons or more | 8 | 4 |
| | 66 | 34 |

*Source*: Wistrand, 1981: 17

reform efforts slowed down after that time but there were amendments and changes throughout the coming decades. The year 1938, for instance, saw the introduction of maternity benefits, and the abolition of the rule that barred married women from paid employment (1939). In 1944, homosexuality was decriminalised and about ten years later the high court ruled that sexual preference was an irrelevant criterion for parental fitness. The Swedish Riksdag actually decreed in 1977 that two people of the same sex living together 'shall be fully accepted by Swedish society' (Morgan, 1984: 658), a decision un-paralleled nearly anywhere else.

For all concerns of the body and reproduction, I believe, Sweden has devised excellent laws and facilities. Sex education, first pioneered by Elise Ottesen-Jensen, has been part of the school curriculum since 1956 and counselling in sexual matters is free of charge (Adams & Winston, 1980: 37–8). Schoolgirls of 15 years and over can ask for contraceptives from the school nurse without parental consent, and abortion is available on demand. Laws concerning reproduction are, of course, interlinked with the entire complex of family law and the protection of the child. In Sweden, up to 30 percent of adults (highest in urban and lowest in rural areas) between the ages of 20 and 30 years have partners but are not married and the nuclear family has lost its predominant position (see table 3.2). These changes are partly the consequence of legislative changes in Swedish family law introduced in the 1960s. The new and repeatedly amended legislation is based on several fundamental principles:

1   that every adult ought to be responsible for his/her own support independent of marital status;
2   that marriage is a voluntary form of cohabitation;
3   that no form of cohabitation is superior to another; and
4   that the child's needs ought to be fulfilled irrespective of circumstances and social (family) constructs into which the child is born (Wistrand, 1981: 18).

In other words, the Swedish government has purposely moved away from legally safeguarding marriage as the only legitimate form of cohabitation. Interestingly, the Committee Concerning the Situation of Homosexuals, a government committee formed in 1977, has moved rather the opposite way and in 1984 recommended that same-sex couples be permitted to marry and to adopt children. But this was as much a decision to foster inclusion of sexual preference rights into the non-discrimination clause of the constitution as it was a genuine attempt to create the same options for any couple. The legal changes concerning the family have removed the moralism inherent in the notion of the 'sanctity' of the (nuclear) family along with the abolition of disadvantage for children born outside marriage. Women's perception of themselves has altered accordingly

Table 3.3 Marriage/divorce ratios and ex-nuptial births in Sweden, 1950–1979

| Year | Marriages | Divorces | Ratio | Ex-nuptial births % |
|------|-----------|----------|-------|---------------------|
| 1950 | 54 222 | 8 008 | 7:1 | 9.8 |
| 1955 | 52 250 | 8 785 | 8:1 | 9.8 |
| 1960 | 50 149 | 8 958 | 5.5:1 | 9.9 |
| 1965 | 59 963 | 6 563 | 6:1 | 13.8 |
| 1970 | 43 278 | 12 943 | 3.5:1 | 18.4 |
| 1975 | 44 103 | 25 383 | 1.7:1 | 32.4 |
| 1979 | 37 300 | 20 322 | 1.8:1 | 37.6 |

Source: Wistrand, 1981: 18

and a growing number of women have elected to sever marriage ties and to bear children ex-nuptially (see table 3.3).

In my opinion, none of these changes is a sign of a deplorable loss of morality or a lamentable breakdown of 'the family' but a sign of a growing maturity of a people who have learned to take responsibility for their own actions, who can act responsibly without need of coercion by law. Clearly, Swedish society has chosen to make no moral decisions on forms of cohabitation and to withdraw from legal punitive measures should any less common option of cohabitation be chosen by individuals. It may be interesting to note here that the birthrate in Sweden is no lower than in other European countries, despite its liberal approach to contraceptives and abortion. It is perhaps *because* of its mature approach to matters of reproduction that Swedish families may be planned more responsibly. As early as 1974, 92 percent of Swedish women planned the size of their families and almost all Swedish women over the age of 16 years used contraceptives. This means that most children both in and out of wedlock are wanted children, which is indeed a worthwhile outcome, though still so much opposed in some other countries.

It will not come as a surprise that the chief beneficiaries of such conscious family planning are indeed the children themselves, whose welfare and care are very high on the Swedish national agenda. In child care provisions, a German paper admits, Sweden is exemplary, granting parental leave of eighteen months to either parent (or taken in turns) after the birth of a child. In the first year, 90 percent of the person's income will be paid by the state. Upon return to work, either partner may work a six-hour day, although on reduced income, until the child reaches school age. When a child is ill and requires home care, there are sick leave provisions, applicable to mothers and fathers (Wistrand, 1981: 33). It is recognised, however, that these provisions for the home care of children are not sufficient and others are needed to enable parents to seek work. Adams and Winston speak about an 'impressive array of social services for children' (1980: 20). Between 1965 and 1974, the number of child day-care places for preschool children alone increased by more than 500 percent. The costs are borne to 15 percent by parent fees, 50 percent by local government and to 35 percent by the national government (Adams & Winston, 1980: 50–3). Interestingly, the focus on outside activities of preschool children has somehow deflected attention away from the home; for instance, Adams and Winston found that the Swedish family, in general, was far less child-centred than the family in the USA. A possible explanation might be that an interesting and stimulating life for the child outside the home eliminates the necessity for the overbearing attention by one adult at home who somehow has to signify and stand in place of the entire socio-cultural context and content of the child's society.

We said before that the idea of progress and change was anchored to the term 'equality' for all. The Swedes call their society '*samhälle*' which, translated, means 'community' or 'the home which has been built by all and for all'. Petersen argues, perhaps a little optimistically, that the Swedes have an untroubled relationship to their state: 'the state is us' is the basis for individual collaboration (Petersen, 1981: 8). But whether it is untroubled or not is not as important as the perception of issues vis-à-vis the state. The issue of equal pay was raised in parliament as early as 1944. In 1960, Sweden was one of the first countries to sign the UN convention on equal pay, which was followed by equal pay policies and the Equality Programme of 1968 within the governing Socialist Party. In 1980, Sweden framed a new policy for equal pay and equal opportunity. Women's hourly incomes relative to those of men rose from 68 percent in 1960 to 98 percent in 1985. Women's participation in the workforce steadily increased between 1974 and 1986, from 60 to 80 percent, a fact that was registered throughout Europe (*Tagesanzeiger*, Zurich: 18 March, 1982). In 1986, the Ministry of Labour foreshadowed that 'if the present trend continues, women and men will have roughly equal employment participation rates—between 85 and 90 percent—in five or ten years' time' (Preface, *The Swedish Act on Equality between Women and Men at Work* 1986). It is doubtful, however, whether one can call participation rates equal, even if they are the same for men and women because of the part-time factor. The rate of full-time employment for women has barely changed over the last decades. Almost all increases were

**Figure 3.1    Gender distribution of part-time and full-time work in Sweden, 1970–1980**

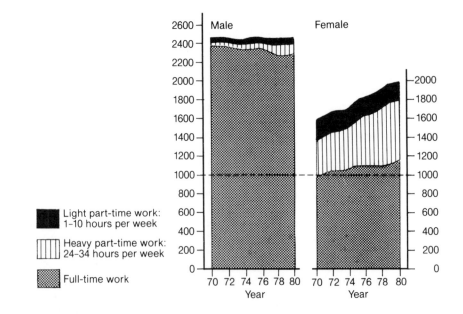

*Source*: The Central Bureau of Statistics; figure from Wistrand, 1981: 61

in so-called 'long' or 'heavy' part-time positions and some in 'short' part-time work (see fig. 3.1).

It is clear that in Swedish policy the aim of employment androgyny is taken seriously. Sweden is one of the very first western European countries to have recognised that such an aim needs to be accompanied by reforms and publicity efforts which encourage domestic role-sharing and some re-education of both sexes. It has also recognised that in order to reach this goal it is necessary to address the question of male roles and values. Anita Gradin, the Minister for Equal Opportunity in the early 1980s, set up a working party for the role of the male in 1983. She did so on the basis of a survey conducted earlier that year which showed that men of the younger generations were willing to take the idea of equality seriously in the home, but not at work and amongst male friends. In the report by that working party, the (male) writer stated that, 'We men are the prisoners of a system for which we ourselves are primarily responsible. A system that is not only detrimental to us as men but also postulates a role for women that renders any equality between the sexes impossible' (WIN, vol. 12, no. 3, 1986). The experimentation with new concepts of males roles had just begun in earnest and the report found that 'many men attach considerable importance to a change in the role of the male'. One suspects that this broad framework has only been possible because of a long-standing commitment to equality by governments, unions and the population alike. Interestingly, the term 'equality' (*jämlikhet*) seemed outmoded once the women's question again came to the fore in the early 1970s. Instead, a new term, *jämställdhet,* came to be used widely. Inherent in this was a shift to new considerations of what equality might mean in gender terms. Wistrand explains that it refers to *equivalent* conditions, opportunities and responsibilities between the sexes but not on the grounds that men and women are presumed to be the *same*, as the term equality might imply, but that they are *different* (1981: 7). The entitlement to the same opportunities arises from the rights of citizenship and not from an assumption of social or biological sameness.

Given the magnitude and structure of change in Sweden throughout this century, it may appear peculiar that until 1977 Sweden actually had no national laws against sex discrimination in employment and no equal-pay provisions. This stems partly from the government's reticence against interfering in private business and in employer affairs, but also from union attitudes. Many Swedish unions have argued that women ought to receive *unequal* treatment, that is, have the right to be overcompensated in order to counteract the effects of discrimination (Adams & Winston, 1980: 117). The Swedish argument alerts one to the complexity of the concept of equality and is a reminder that centuries of deeply ingrained practices of discrimination cannot be wiped out with simplistic models of egalitarianism.

Sweden has not really had a second-wave women's movement. One of the main reasons Sweden never developed a strong new feminist movement was probably because most demands that brought women together in other countries had actually been met (Adams & Winston, 1980: 138–40). There are two major women's organisations in Sweden today. One of them, the Frederika Bremer Association, dates back to 1894, while the other one, called Group 8, was formed in the 1970s. The latter has only a small membership of around a thousand women living in and around Stockholm (Lovenduski, 1986: 98). Since 1982, there has been a women's university in Umeå, the most northern part of Sweden, based on a lively feminist research that has a long tradition (Liljeström,

1984: 661). A number of small feminist organisations stem from the early 1970s, usually established around specific issues, but in only a few of them were women's issues the sole concern. Peterson has analysed these organisations and found that 45 out of the 58 were concerned with violence against women either within the context of anti-violence/peace debates or in addition to these broader peace issues (Peterson, 1985: 633). Today, all major cities in Sweden have refuges and rape crisis centres. Nevertheless, it is surprising that the first rape crisis centre was opened relatively late, in 1978, well after many other countries had established this kind of service and support for women. This happened, one suspects, on one level because the overt assumption about Swedish society, held by Swedes, is that of a consensual peaceful democracy (Elder et al., 1982), and violence simply did not fit into that model.

More importantly, Swedish women themselves believe that self-help groups are counterproductive because they take away from the mainstream political focus by relieving pressure on the government (Lovenduski, 1986: 99). By and large, although this attitude might have delayed the establishment of crisis centres, it has continually ensured that women's issues are not a matter of marginalised self-help groups of women. As part of a major *political* platform, their concerns are not merely social questions but questions of state, of government, of the country. The notion of an integrative approach to all individuals within Swedish society is also apparent in the treatment of groups which, for personal or physical reasons, have special needs. There are strong and well-developed networks for disabled and mentally retarded people and for alcoholics and many other special-interest groups. These networks are not simply social support groups but formal channels of representation and consultation for government bodies. They cannot be sidestepped in cases of political decision making (Petersen, 1981: 24).

Furthermore, this insistence on the participation of women in political life, the insistence that women's issues are an integral part of the mainstream life of the nation, sets Sweden apart from most other European states. This thinking also removes the barrier between the public and the private. If the individual is convinced of her/his rights to be safeguarded by the state, the individual exists as a politically accountable member of that state and is free to move between the spheres of informal and formal, public and private, intimate and open, without change of status. Consequently, no distinction can be made legally or morally between the public and the private spheres of an individual's life. Employment androgyny and domestic role-sharing, for instance, must therefore be regarded as part of the same issue. Violence in private or public is an intolerable infringement of human rights and individual freedom. Conversely, the right to decide about pregnancy, marriage or cohabitation are then touchstones for the individual's autonomy as an intrinsic part of a socio-moral platform of an elected government within a fully fledged and functioning democracy.

Swedish society, to the onlooker, appears genuine in its wish to combat discrimination in gender-specific cases as well as generally at all levels of society and to change welfare thinking into a consideration of political, democratic rights. To achieve this end, Swedes are willing to regard infringements on human rights in their society as infringements against themselves. In that sense, the questions that Swedish society raises are less specifically women's or welfare issues but rather society's issues. For these reasons, consciousness-raising for women has never become popular in Sweden. As Adams and Winston so aptly put it: 'In Sweden's collectivist culture, an effort to solve the women's problems at the individual level is seen as merely disguising the need for structural solutions.

What good does it do an individual to "raise" her consciousness if she then cannot find a job because of the structure of opportunities in the labour market or the lack of adequate support services?' (1980: 137).

## NORWAY

Norway was the first sovereign state in Europe to give full citizenship rights to women, a process that began in 1901 and ended with full suffrage for all women in 1913 (Anthony, 1915: 225). As early as 1908 the country passed a law granting women equal pay for equal work (Anthony, 1915: 227). Many of these improvements, including amendments to family law granting women rights to control and inherit property, were the result of a widespread suffrage movement which had been active since the mid-1880s. Despite these early demonstrative changes, the formal statistics would seem to indicate that Norway is one of the conservative countries of Scandinavia: its divorce rate is lower than in other Scandinavian countries, and so is the rate of singles living together, but the number of marriages is higher. Global interpretations, however, can be misleading. Until recently, the church had a relatively strong influence which was felt particularly on the issue of abortion. The possibility of an abortion law reform was discussed at length in the 1920s and again in the 1940s, but the first definitive bill was not proposed until twenty years later. Finally, the abortion law was liberalised in 1978 and only a year later amended to abortion on demand as a free health service. Interestingly, since the law permitting abortions, the number of abortions has stabilised and even declined as it has in most Scandinavian countries (see fig. 3.2). This demonstrates that the right to abortion on demand does not necessarily affect birthrates, as some politicians in various European countries have feared. Typically, only in countries in which contraceptives are not easily available or their correct use not well understood, would one expect a high rate of abortion. In Norway, as in other Scandinavian countries, abortion on demand was granted at a time when the knowledge and availability of contraceptives were already so widespread as to prevent most unwanted pregnancies. One hastens to add that politicians' (irrational and indefensible) fears of a drop in the birthrate should never enter into the debate on the individual's freedom of choice over reproduction.

Norway is in some ways not as lavishly endowed with social service provisions as Sweden, although it is better equipped than most western European countries. It has as many progressive ideas as other Scandinavian countries and these are reflected in the kind of service Norwegian society provides. Also, in matters that are usually regarded as highly controversial elsewhere in the world, the Norwegian people occasionally show a spirit not easily found in other countries; for example, the 'conservative' parliamentarian Wencke Lossow declared during a national conference on homosexuality that she was a lesbian, a confession that was widely publicised in the daily press. Contrary to expectations one might have, her political career did not end at that point. She was neither asked nor forced to resign but was reelected at the next elections with more votes than she had attracted before (*Weser Kurier*, 1984).

The women's movement in Norway, although fairly contained in comparison to central European events at the same time, was a good deal more angry and confrontational than in Sweden. In Norway, the student movement and the women's movement coincided in the late 1960s and early 1970s (*Working Paper,*

**Figure 3.2  Scandinavian abortion statistics, 1970–1985**

Legal abortions per 1000 women during their reproductive period

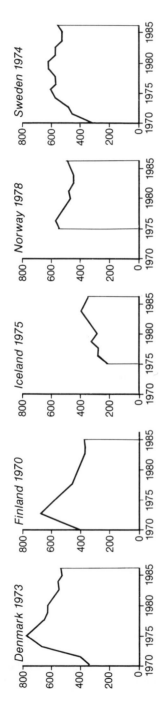

Legal abortions per 1000 live births

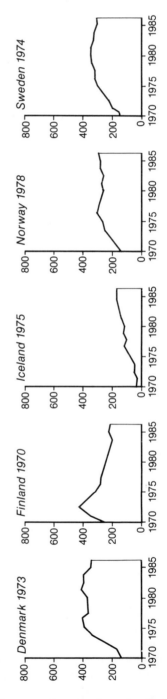

Oslo, 1987: 5). These movements had been foreshadowed in the postwar era by a revival of resistance movements one of which was the renewed struggle of the Lapps, who form an ethnic minority not just in Norway but also in Sweden and Finland. The Lapps are still seeking recognition and a fair share in the life of the societies to which they now belong. The onset of anti-nuclear and anti-Vietnam demonstrations also preceded the women's and students' movements (Ambjørnsen & Hæfs, 1988: 157).

One of the first feminist campaigns concerned female representation in parliament and in municipal councils. The campaign began in 1967 when a special investigative action committee was set up. By the time of the 1971 elections, the strategies and action plans for enhancing female participation in politics were firmly in place. Altogether Norway has 450 municipalities, of which 78 at that time had no female representatives at all. Using loopholes in the election system, the lobby group succeeded, in one coup, in restructuring the gender composition of politics. After the election, the number of municipalities without women had dropped to 22, and nine of the largest municipalities (including Asher, Trondheim and Oslo) were able to boast that 40 to 50 percent of their governing bodies now consisted of women (Haukaa, 1988: 171). The ensuing uproar by male politicians against this victory for women actually altered electoral law and diminished the influence of voters on the choice of candidates representing the party. This amendment also instantly reduced the number of women eligible to stand for office.

The point had been made, however. Under public pressure the parties themselves had to amend their ways in the 1975 and 1979 elections and now had to be seen to allow women into the ranks of membership and party leadership (Skard, 1981: 79–80). Indeed, both the Liberal Party and the socialist left introduced a quota system between 1973 and 1974. The Labor Party managed to resist this change for another decade but finally yielded to the quota system in 1984 (Benn, 1987: 89). In Norway, these changes have resulted in what some might call a 'feminisation' of politics by at once raising women's presence in parliament, local councils and political parties to almost half of the governing body in some cases. This shows that concerted political action outside the mainstream political system can be a very effective tool for manipulating and changing public opinion.

In 1970, there were many spontaneous gatherings and marches, punctuated by outbursts of anger and calls for revolution, and new women's groups and organisations sprang up everywhere. Amongst the most important ones to appear that year was a radical, but not socialist, group called Nyfeministine (New Feminists). Two years later, a socialist and Marxist–Leninist group was formed, called Kvinnefronten (Women's Front), which today is still the strongest and most influential group. By 1974, the lesbian movement had been organised (Lesbisk Bevegelse), followed by the foundation of yet another group which called itself Brod og Roser—Bread and Roses (Haukaa, 1988: 172–73).

The years between 1972 and 1977 are generally regarded as the most active period of the second wave, but marked as they were by internal strife within the movement itself (in which the media chose to take great interest) this periodisation is disputable. Such media interest, designed no doubt to discredit the movement, cannot be taken as an historical measure of the level of the movement's activities. Indeed, the Kvinnefronten has remained very active throughout the 1980s. One of its main aims in recent years has been a persistent lobbying for a six-hour working day. Kvinnefronten women hope that by changing working conditions in this way, more women will have the opportunity of engaging in full-time work, of seeking out career-oriented work in which they can remain throughout their lives, while fewer women will be forced into part-time work with its many disadvantages. Another issue which in the 1980s gained wider support than the six-hour work day was the fight against the pornographic industry, seen as 'a struggle for women's worth as human beings against the business interests of the pornographic industry [and as] a rebellion against the role of victim' (WIN, vol. 12, no. 4, 1986: 59). This campaign has been successful in so far as the Norwegian government passed a law in 1986 prohibiting in all media and movies sexual descriptions which are humanly degrading. The campaigns against prostitution have, so far, not succeeded.

Apart from changes in legislation, the women's movement has also brought about a number of useful and practical changes. For instance, in 1974, the University of Oslo opened a free legal advice centre for women and in 1975 began teaching women's law (*Working Paper*, Oslo, 1983: 6 and 11). In 1978, the first women's refuge was opened and a further 36 refuges opened their doors to women within the following ten years (Ambjørnsen & Hæfs, 1988: 136). In 1982 a foundation meeting of the Nordic forum for women's research on women took place in Oslo. The Centre for Research on Women started in 1977 and was then expanded and given more funding for interdisciplinary research in 1982. Norway has a long record of so-called 'social justice research'. The new feminist research of the 1970s and 1980s draws on that history. It is socially committed and action-orientated research (Hernes, 1985: 773–7).

Strangely enough, Norwegian feminism has never developed the kind of every-day subculture that we have come to associate with many post-1960s women's movements in the western world. In the mid-1980s there were no specialised women's bookshops, cafés or health centres.

Literature is another thing. As in other western European countries, Norway has produced its own feminist writers. Indeed, Norway has a long-standing tradition of feminist literature, starting with *Amtmandens Dottre* (The Bailiff's Daughter) of 1854, written by Camilla Collett, who is credited with having written the first feminist novel in Norwegian literature (Hanson, 1984: 9). The work of Cora Sandel (1880–1974) has been translated into English and many other languages. Her novel *Krane's Café* (1946) particularly bears the stamp of feminist analysis. It is regrettable that little of this literature trickled into other European countries at the time. By contrast, *The Doll's House* from the pen of Ibsen won critical acclaim and ironically became, internationally, one of the most noted early 'feminist' literary pieces. Since the 1970s, Norway has produced a wealth of feminist literature, both light-hearted and serious, examining women's position in everyday life. Margaret Johansen (born 1923), for instance, became one of Norway's very successful satirists in the 1970s. Also in a light-hearted vein, but a work that wants to be taken much more seriously, is the parody on the entire sex-role socialisation process by the Norwegian writer Gerd Branten-berg, entitled *The Daughters of Egalia*, originally published in 1977. The recipe for her book is quite simple: save for the actual biological difference of giving birth, the social roles in this book are reversed. In a different class of novels is the beautiful narrative by Herbjørg Wassmo, entitled *The House with the Blind Glass Window* (1981), a sensitive sparingly written novel dealing with the childhood and teenage experiences of a girl who grows up in northern Norway. Herbjørg Wassmo won the Nordic Prize in 1986 and her international reputa-tion has grown ever since. Lesbian literature in Norway had few forerunners, but notable amongst them were Borghild Krane's book *Følelsers forvirring* (A Confusion of Feelings) of 1937, and Ebba Haslund's *Det hendte ingenting* of 1948, translated into English for the first time in 1987 as *Nothing Ever Happened*. These books have been made to disappear from the bookshelves very quickly. But in the 1970s, the story was different. Gerd Brantenberg's book *Opp Alle Jordens Homofile* (1973), translated as *What Comes Naturally* (1986), has become a cult book in Scandinavia.

The status of women in Norway, in practice, is not very different from other western European countries, despite its better welfare net. Norwegian women claim that the egalitarianism has not reached gender, and discrimination is experienced in all areas of everyday life. Thus, Berit Ås wrote in 1984:

> In Norway *the conditions of men have improved more than those of women*. Women are victims of institutional rules of discrimination which affect them economically and politically. For example, husbands do not participate more in household and child care activities when an increasing number of women enter the paid labor force. It is much more difficult for women to obtain paid work than for men, and, when hired, women get lower salaries. Women with education equal to that of men are promoted less often and fired at an earlier stage when crises occur. Quota systems, demanded as affirmative action to improve women's positions in the educational system, have been used to a greater extent to guarantee less-qualified *men* educational opportunities within traditionally *women's* areas. And women have understood that mere 'equal opportunity' rights are unjust—because they favour those groups which already have the greatest resources, and increase the gaps between weak and strong, poor and rich—in plain text, between women and men. (Ås, 1984: 510)

It is of course not a new discovery that policies of equal opportunity do not lead to equality when implemented within the context of structured inequality. In many western industrialised countries, however, politicians and large numbers of women alike had hopes that non-discriminatory policies and explicit equal opportunity measures would eventually lead to equality. Even if this approach was a failed attempt of social engineering, it was probably a necessary social experimentation.

In politics, however, Norway is unique in the world today. It not only has had a woman as a prime minister for some years now, but in her government of eighteen ministers, eight are women. The near equal representation of women in government is of particular interest since all of the women's organisations in Norway fought their battles not from within political parties, but from the outside as autonomous groups. By the standard of other western industrialised countries, the changes made within the political parties are profound. Even the reluctant Labor Party, when it introduced the quota system, did so by agreeing that 40 percent of its parliamentary candidates be women. Also noteworthy in this context is Ingunn Mean's article of 1972 in which she lamented not only that so few women were active in Norwegian politics but that so few women were attracted by politics (Means, 1972: 492 ff).

Irrespective of a host of reasons that might keep women away from formal politics, surely the degree of access to a career in politics for women is a determinant of attraction or repulsion. Norway's political composition of 1988 has proved Means wrong. The changes that have occurred in less than two decades also empirically show women's capability and readiness to join the ranks of politicians when and where *women perceive it as legitimate* to do so. It is a measure of the degree and intensity of social barriers that, in order for women's active participation in politics to be perceived as a right, that is, as legitimate, it had to literally allocate 'reserved seats' for women. But these seats have not remained empty. Such evidence would also modify speculations about women's nature and temperament, as was alluded to in chapter 2, 'Women and the labour force'.

Denmark's feminism goes back a long way, with its roots in the 1850s and 1860s (Welsch, 1974), and a strong unionised working-class women's movement from the 1880s onwards (Morgan, 1984: 180). The first bourgeois women's movement began in 1871 with the foundation of Dansk Kvindesamfund (Danish Women's Union), an organisation which fought for the equality of women and for women's suffrage, granted, however, only in 1915, 46 years after the beginning of the movement.

Denmark's second-wave women's movement fell into approximately three stages. The first, an active and direct protest stage, lasted for about four years (1970–1974), the second stage represented the period of strongest proliferation of groups and of formation of counter-cultural activities (1975–1980). The third stage, as a stage of 'professionalisation' of feminism and concretely working on legislature and specific projects, has continued up till now (Dahlerup, 1986: 230–3). The movement began with the public demonstrations of the so-called Redstocking group, first in April 1970 in a 'Keep Denmark Clean' action against fashion and authoritarianism, followed, one month later, by a demonstration against gender differences in pay. A year later, a permanent women's camp was established at Femø Island and the first Redstocking publication appeared, called *med søsterlig hilsen* (with sisterly love). Most of the Redstocking members were middle-class women with socialist leanings. The initial number of demonstrators had been small but, as in Norway, membership numbers grew very quickly and a host of other groups sprang up, such as the socialist women's group in Tåstrop (1972), the Alexandra Group (1974–1976), Group 27 (1976) and organisations which promoted the position of lesbians (1974). In 1979, the first flats for abused women and children were occupied and in 1980 the Danner refuge was opened as a response to the perceived violence and oppression of women in Danish society (Gerlach-Nielsen, 1980: 5–10; Søndergaard, 1988: 54–60).

Women's organisations are particularly strong in Denmark. The largest of them is an umbrella organisation called Danske Kvinders Nationalråd (National Council of Women in Denmark) to which about 40 organisations belong, and whose total membership of one million women accounts for almost a fifth of the entire population of Denmark (*Women in Europe,* 1988). Denmark is the only Nordic country with a separate union for women workers (Kvindeligt Arbejderforbund) and, up to 1970, almost all political parties had very active women cells. Denmark, therefore, has strong socio-political organisations which act as watchdogs for women's interests and can be mobilised very quickly. Many of these existed before the onset of the movement in 1970.

One wonders why the Danish movement started when it did. There must have been important and politically alert submerged networks for a large-scale and vibrant movement to evolve out of the small group of twelve women protesting in the streets against makeup and fashion in 1970. In the absence of student or Vietnam demonstrations of any size as in other countries, the catalysts for the second wave are more obscure. To be sure, Danish women were influenced by other women's movements already under way in the USA, in Britain, and the Netherlands. Dahlerup writes that the women's cells within political parties were suddenly dissolved in 1970, supposedly as a step towards egalitarianism (Dahlerup, 1986: 222). No doubt, there is a connection between their dissolution and the onset of the new women's movement in Denmark, even though the first Redstockings were members of the Department of Literature at the University of Copenhagen and not directly from the pool of active party politicians. Fitzmaurice has argued that other socio-economic upheavals benefited the women's movement (1981: 38) but this is simply incorrect in the chronology of events. The women's movement arose in 1970. The upheavals Fitzmaurice cites as catalysts for the women's movement began two or even three years after its onset. In 1972, Denmark's position in the EEC gave rise to the so-called 'people's movement' against the EEC and brought together people of very different political persuasions. In 1973, the oil crisis sparked off the environmental movement. The main point of these movements was a critique against western capitalist materialism and against political establishments. Feminists of the Danish women's movement were certainly to be found in these demonstrations and might have belonged to several movements at once, but the women's movement certainly preceded rather than succeeded either of the socio-economic ones.

Søndergaard points out that the Danish women's movement had a strength all its own and possessed an unusual degree of cohesion compared to other western European countries. She attributes this to Denmark's long tradition particularly of the union movement. It was also rather exceptional in that most of the women in the movement had children and lived in family settings (Søndergaard, 1988: 63). More importantly, this history of union movements has been shaped by a strong commitment to women's solidarity, irrespective of class, which has been maintained to some extent in the new feminist movement of the 1970s. Some writers claim that workers and feminists often work together on women's questions (Doormann, 1979: 19). This is certainly true in those cases where feminists supported equal pay and strike activities in factories. But some Redstockings were critical of their own limited effort to mobilise working-class women (Vammen, 1984: 183).

Interestingly, over recent years the women's movement has continued to lose ground in Denmark. Popular support for it waned between 1975 and 1983. Although no anti-feminist movements developed in Denmark as they did in the USA, the criticisms of the women's movement were substantial. In the survey of the European Commission in 1983, as many as 83 percent of Danish women were adamantly against the women's movement. One needs to qualify this. According to Dahlerup, and as mentioned before, there were two strands of the new movement, one concerned with women's rights and one with women's liberation. The former, an 'old-style' feminism, survived in the old and strong organisations like the Dansk Kvindesamfund or the Nationalraad, and also characterises the membership in the Equal Status Council (Ligestillingsraadet) that the government set up in 1975 (Vammen, 1984: 184). The latter, the women's liberation strand, evolved as an ultra-radical group that was explicitly anti-capitalist, like the environmentalists and factions of the anti-EEC groups later, and saw little value in mere numerical equality because such 'equality' for women would mean participation in an exploitative system (Dahlerup, 1986: 222). Yet the two strands together made up the new wave. I have not seen any explanations as to why Danish women outside the movement have drawn such a sharp distinction between the women's movement on the one hand and women's issues on the other. It may be that the methods of their protest, particularly of the liberationists, were considered objectionable, because much of the *content* of the protests had in fact already been accepted by the Danish population, men and women alike. The idea of women's right to equal opportunity, for instance, had general support.

The 1983 survey results tallied with observations by Redstocking feminists in Denmark that the new feminism had more widespread ideological influence than political clout. General attitudes of the population showed a high acceptance of some of the most important feminist ideas. Thus, in the same survey, Denmark emerged as one of the EEC countries with the most positive attitudes to women and the most egalitarian ideas. Almost 90 percent of both women and men had equal confidence in women's ability to carry out jobs which were once considered to fall into the male domain: professions such as parliamentarian, doctor, lawyer and other non-traditional jobs such as bus driver. The idea that women may be less competent than men had almost entirely disappeared from Danish thinking and the percentage still believing in women's lower competence was the lowest in all EEC countries (*Women and Men of Europe*, 1983: 102). Most importantly, both men and women believed that women's issues were of great social and political importance and needed to be dealt with as a matter of urgency. These views were not confined to the public sector but included the private sector as well. The majority of Danish men and women, for example, believed that household chores and child care should be shared equally between marital/cohabiting partners (*Women and Men of Europe*, 1983). It may be noted here that Denmark's immediate neighbour, West Germany, scored almost consistently at the other end of the scale on all of these attitudinal surveys. This should dispel any myth that geographic proximity or similarities in culture by themselves imply similar cultural habits, value systems and norms.

Denmark may not have the same maternity leave provisions as other Nordic countries and may lag a little behind Finland and Sweden in parental leave provisions (*Kvinnor och Män*, 1988: 101), but it is far better equipped to deal with child care up to 10 years of age than any other Scandinavian country (see fig. 3.3).

It has generally been argued that family life patterns (marriages, divorces, number of children, etc.) have changed gradually over the postwar period. The Danish figures indicate that the changes there were anything but gradual, being compressed into a mere span of five years in the latter part of the 1970s. When Andersen compared some of the structural and demographic data of the early 1970s with those of the beginning of the 20th century he found that the percentage of marriages in the period 1901 to 1974 had actually increased and that first marriages were contracted earlier in 1974 than in 1920. In the 1920s women married on average at the age of 25.9 and men at 27.8, but in 1974 the average marriage age was 23.5 for women and 26.6 for men, while the divorce rate remained low and rather stable (Andersen, 1977: 62–7). Statistics for the decade 1970 to 1980, by contrast, show that within this period, the number of divorces jumped by 40 percent and the number of marriages dropped by 30 percent. In 1973, the first stage of the new Danish movement, free abortion became a reality and the few attempts to create anti-abortion movements failed completely (Dahlerup, 1986: 239). Bearing in mind that Denmark is a predominantly catholic country and that church opinion emanating from Rome was explicitly against abortion and even against contraceptives, the secularisation of morality in Denmark is particularly remarkable. As predicted, the birthrate

**Figure 3.3    Municipal child care for ages 3–10 years, Denmark**

Municipal child care for children 3– 6 years

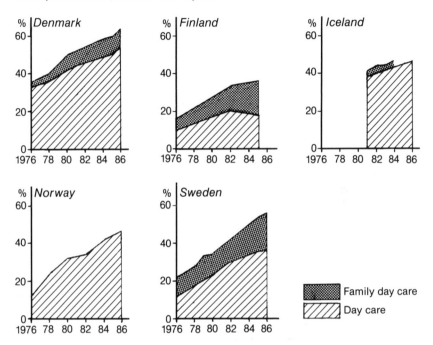

Municipal child care for children 7 – 10 years

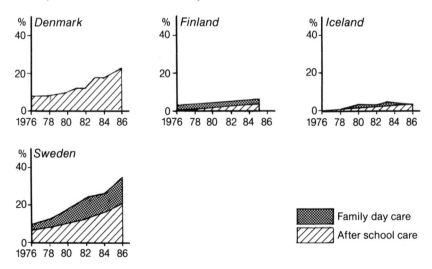

*Source*: adapted from *Kvinnor och Män*, 1988: 103, 105– 6

declined, showing a birth deficit for the first time in 1981. In 1983, the divorce to marriages ratio was 1:1.7 (25 000 marriages as against 15 000 divorces) while the number of unmarried adults about equalled the number of married adults (Hansen et al., 1985: 3).

A recent publication called *Women in Denmark in the 1980s* (1985), has seen a link between these dramatic changes, women's large-scale entry into the labour force from the 1960s onwards, and the onset of the women's movement in the late 1960s. These may well have been contributing factors. More importantly, Denmark underwent drastic changes in its economy in the postwar years through the sudden and growing importance of industry at the expense of the rural sector (Christensen, 1983: 180). At the same time, Denmark committed itself to a policy of pragmatic welfarism within its mixed economy and did so at a time of full employment and growth. The decisive challenge to Denmark's economic and welfare policies came in 1973: the oil crisis, with its ensuing recession, brought new economic pressures which came to a head in 1976 when balance of payment deficits suddenly reached crisis proportions, jumping from 3 billion to 11 billion kroner in one year (Fitzmaurice, 1981: 34). The cost in the public sector by then had increased to 49 percent of GNP. Given the fiscal problems, there were many Danes who felt that welfarism was draining the economy. As Fitzmaurice points out, this economic crisis resulted in a critique of the welfare state from every political quarter. The political right argued that the spiralling costs could no longer be ignored and that the country could no longer support welfarism at the then current rate. The centre parties saw welfarism as a way of undermining the morality of society by allowing the transfer of family re- sponsibilities to the state and by encouraging a purely materialistic outlook on life. The critique by the left, including new-left splinter parties which had formed in the mid-1970s, was perhaps the most substantial and disconcerting. They also agreed with other parties about the prohibitive cost of the system, but their attack focused on the system that administered public welfare and questioned the outcome of its services. First they called the system ineffective, expensive and wasteful. Moreover, it had not lived up to its own pronounced goals because poverty continued to exist in Denmark. As the system had failed to redistribute incomes towards the lower-income groups the claim that Denmark was a welfare state was an empty phrase (Fitzmaurice, 1981: 131).

Women were affected by these changes in several ways. Their role in agriculture, sometimes a rather independent position, diminished and all but disappeared. In the period of postwar economic boom women began to enter the labour market in large numbers, but this economic honeymoon soon passed when changes in industry, the effects of the 1973 oil crisis and its ensuing recession, and fiscal crises increased unemployment and general redundancies. Women had benefited from the expansion of the bureaucratic apparatus by filling the positions that arose with the need for additional staff, but they were at risk of losing these positions again once demands for cuts in public expenditure were voiced from the entire political spectrum. Women had taken the plunge of seeking divorce or of not marrying at all, but then became the chief victims of the recession and were forced into the position of welfare recipients. In 1983, a total of 20 percent of all families with children were single-head families, of which most (as many as 85 percent) were women. Most of these women (three quarters) belonged to low-income groups, or no-income groups, and were in need of assistance (Hansen et al., 1985: 4). Economically and ideologically, women found themselves in a very vulnerable position.

Despite these crises in the Danish economy, Danish expenditure priorities have not appreciably altered after the 1970s. In Danish government expenditure, health ranks in second and education in third position. Noticeably, in all Scandinavian countries health and education are given high priority, ranking in first to fifth position of overall spending. Military expenses rank between tenth and nineteenth position. In most other western European countries the trend is reversed and education and health have a much lower budgeting profile. In West Germany, France, Belgium and England, military expenditure is higher than that for education. In England, Ireland, Italy and Spain, educational and health concerns rank even lower than twentieth position (Heidenheimer et al., 1983: 19).

Denmark has also responded to its various crises in the housing sector developing innovative ideas from socially undesirable situations, particularly those affecting women. In Danish society, the majority of the population (over two-thirds) live in owner-occupation situations, but single-head families are usually excluded and have to resort to rented accommodation. Eighty percent of all rented accommodation is occupied by single-head households. Typically, these flats are rented in large housing complexes which are not conducive to the formation of friendships or of a larger community, or to communication generally. A sense of isolation, coupled with financial problems largely caused by high rental costs, was found to be too high a price to pay for the wish for independence. The social and psychological problems were not only recognised quickly but the inadequacies of such housing complexes led to a large and widespread movement of residential collectives. These are new architectural designs meant not only to put a roof over people's head but also to fulfil the occupants' social and personal needs. They are designed like villages in whose centre there is a community house, usable by all occupants as the focal point for gatherings (Hansen et al., 1985: 9). Innovative ideas, such as this response to a housing crisis, were often the result of women's efforts and directly or indirectly of the women's movement.

Feminist research in Denmark is remarkably active, given the size of its population. For 1979 alone, a research register for Denmark included 941 specifically feminist research projects. Directories of feminist researchers were first published in 1980. The research has concentrated on labour market research, women's daily lives and Marxist theoretical work. In more recent years, however, research has investigated various approaches to structural oppression (Richter et al., 1985: 747 ff). In 1982, a women's studies centre was set up in Copenhagen and women's studies courses have grown ever since to become an integral part of tertiary education.

*FINLAND*

Finland's national history, like that of Iceland and Norway, began only this century, but unlike the other Scandinavian countries, its domination by a foreign power in the 19th century led to a nationalist movement which indirectly benefited Finnish women in gaining entry to public life. Finnish nationalism was largely a middle-class affair concerning a very small group of people and as such it could not afford divisiveness within its own ranks. How deeply entrenched these divisions were, however, became clear because, once the Republic was proclaimed, civil war broke out almost at once, splitting the country ideologically into 'white' and 'red' factions. But before Finnish independence, overriding nationalist interests swept aside other divisions and vested interests for a while and women entered politics as soon as the Finnish Republic was proclaimed. Haavio-Mannila suggested that women's entry into politics was possible so early because it happened at a time when Finnish male politicians had not yet become entrenched in the political system (Haavio-Mannila, 1979; see also Lovenduski, 1986: 153). Perhaps this view somewhat devalues the efforts of the women in the first Finnish women's movement, which peaked at various times: in 1884, 1892 and again in 1907. In 1884, the first Finnish Women's Association was formed (Suomen Naisyhdistys), followed by two others in 1892 and 1907 (Jallinoja, 1986: 160). Juusola-Halonen has argued that 'the Young Women's Union struggled hard to gain the vote, equal salaries for women and men and the prohibition of prostitution, etc. and sent many of its members to the first Finnish parliament' (1981: 454). Thus, even before Finland seceded from Russia, a number of important reforms had taken place. Women were allowed to be educated (1886), and they were allowed to vote (1906). The constitution of 1919 only confirmed women's equal status with men (Anthony, 1915: 39, 223). Women were economically active outside agriculture and participated in the workforce in higher percentages than elsewhere in the western world. In 1910, 39 percent of the labour force was made up of women, steadily rising to 47 percent by 1980 (*Finnish Statistical Yearbooks*). In Finland, women's roles and women's experiences were shaped by this history and determined the way in which women responded at the time of Finland's 'radical movement'.

In education and equal opportunity policies as well, Finland was far ahead of the rest of Europe. As early as the 1940s, marginally more women than men sat for the matriculation examination, and throughout the postwar period women have had higher participation rates in adult education than men (*Naisten asema*, 1988: 43). If anything, in Finland the pendulum has swung the other way as, overall, most university places now go to women. In 1977, the ratio was 5:3 in favour of women (Kandolin & Uusitalo, 1980: 17), and the trend has increased since then. These figures are, however, global, with substantial variations across faculties, and they hold true only for undergraduate levels. At postgraduate level, in research, and university positions the participation rates of women drop considerably. In 1985, 39 percent of all postgraduates and less than 10 percent of academic university staff were women. By 1988, in research, women represented roughly 20 percent, but most of them worked at the level of research assistants (Ministry of Social Affairs, 1988: 16). Despite this minority status of women in the higher echelons of education, the Finnish figures compare very favourably with other western European nations, as will be shown later. Irrespective of such comparative allowances, one cannot help noticing that for such a very large pool of female undergraduates the number of university teachers seems particularly low.

On the other hand, Finland prides itself on having more women in the various professions than anywhere else in the western world. Almost half of Finnish architects are women as is a little over half of all medical practitioners. Some areas (in addition to teaching) are now dominated by women, such as pharmacy (83 percent), veterinary science (76 percent), psychology (72 percent) and dentistry (70 percent) (Ministry of Social Affairs, 1988: 15). In Scandinavian countries, unemployment rates generally compare very favourably with the rest of Europe, but Finland is also the only Nordic country in which unemployment of women is lower than the unemployment of men (see figure 3.4). One suspects that the

**Figure 3.4   Unemployment of women and men in Finland (by age)**

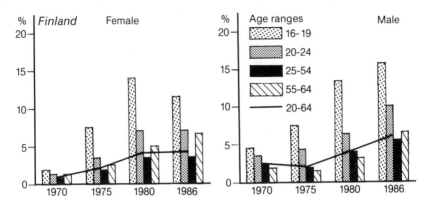

*Source:* *Kvinnor och Män,* 1988: 77

reason for such a difference lies in the greater diffusion of women in the Finnish job market and the high percentage of fully qualified and trained women.

Finland's greatest advertisement for its high standard in health care is the present infant mortality rate, which is one of the lowest in the world. But Finland has responded differently to the need for the care of infants when both parents work. It has been slow in creating adequate child-care centres but instead has created excellent paternity leave provisions, encouraging parents (without loss of position or career) to care for their newborn and infants at home. In all, parents can claim about eight months of paid leave (158 working days), of which up to five months may be granted to the father. For this entire period of absence, the leave-taking parent is awarded 80 percent of the last wage or, if that parent had not been in gainful employment, is paid a basic rate by the government. After the expiry of the eight months, a parent may request one to three years of leave without pay (Törnudd, 1986: 114).

Apart from a basic law providing for maternity leave granted in 1963, most of the progressive regulations pertaining to work and child care were adopted between the late 1970s and in the 1980s, and not without concerted action by women. In Finland 75 percent of women with children are in full-time employment and it has been in their interest to make work more profitable by removing the double taxation of family units earning double income, as this often substantially affected the take-home pay of women: women and men are now taxed individually (Törnudd, 1986: 257); to find ways and means, other than public care, of parents looking after their children themselves: at present, less than half of Finnish preschool children can be accommodated in day-care centres; and to remove the punitive effects of having to pay for expensive alternative child care: since 1988, child-care expenses have become tax-deductible items (Bergman & Vehkakoski, 1988: 79; Räsänen, 1984: 147 ff).

Finnish life changed pace noticeably after 1945 due to the sudden and intense processes of industrialisation and urbanisation, changes that were especially visible in the 1960s and early 1970s. Literature gained a new lease of life by describing 'the great move' of people from rural areas into urban environments (Mäkelä, 1987: 36). In the Finnish tradition of critical realism writers seized upon the opportunity to highlight social changes and their social cost in great detail. Thus, almost at once (around 1965), a strong new-left counter culture formed.

Women played a leading role in this new counter culture, generally referred to as 'the radical movement', and were highly visible as early as 1965 when dissenters in most other western European countries had not yet begun to mobilise. It was marked by and enmeshed in the transformation of the evolving society, despite its critique of the latter (Jutikkala & Pirinen, 1984: 265). Bergmann and Vehkakoshi noted that the tenor of this new culture was coloured by the economic boom of the early 1970s and was very optimistic in outlook (1988: 83). Many women of the new women's movement in Finland believed, however, that socialism was a necessary condition for the liberation of women, a view that often made collaboration with other existing women's groups difficult (Jallinoja, 1986: 159). Most Finnish feminists were part of an organisation called Group 9 (Yhdistys 9), formed in 1966. Theoretical and practical discussions focussed chiefly on sex roles in the home and at work and this was part of general sex-role discussions in the Nordic countries. A pioneer in the new research on women was Anna-Liisa Sysiharju with her doctoral thesis 'Home, Equality and Work' of 1960 (Haavio-Mannila & Husu, 1985: 755). At the same time, one of the main spokespersons for this new feminist wave, Elina Haavio-Mannila, criticised women's low income, their double workload, the long hours of work and women's lack of political resources, and so helped publicise women's grievances.

This episode of the second wave was short-lived as far as widespread public debate was concerned. A Finnish survey conducted a year later (in 1966) showed, however, that the public relations exercise of the previous year had reached its target groups since as many as 80 percent of the urban and 60 percent of the rural adult population had followed the gender debate (Haavio-Mannila, 1968: 196–7). Neither the student movement nor the women's movement produced an independent political culture, but rather they expanded the range of interests and influence of political parties. Bergmann and Vehkakoski suggest that this development was an undesirable outcome of the protests (1988: 86), but it may well be that the absorption of grievances into mainstream politics was a very healthy one.

The legislative changes in favour of women, first made after women's public appearances in 1965, have continued to be made to the present day. The movement itself was revived again in 1977 with Riita Auvinen's PhD thesis entitled 'Women in a Man's World', which sparked off renewed interest in women's affairs and created a strong demand for knowledge about women's lives and problems (Richter et al., 1985: 755–8). Within political parties, women have formed their own cells; for instance, in 1982 an autonomous women's movement spontaneously formed within the Communist Party, even though (or because) the party itself had become deeply split into pro-Russian and pro-Eurocommunism camps. This autonomous group survived into the late 1980s because women from the various factions found that there were far too many gender-related issues that the party itself did not adequately tackle (Benn, 1987: 88).

Just as in Sweden, the debates on women's status and on the subject of equality have led Finnish writers and policy makers to conclude that any changes in sex-role behaviour, expectations and norms must involve men as well as women. Thus Törnudd, in a discussion on Finnish laws and the international norms of human rights, argues, 'much too often international instruments, also those adopted by the ILO [International Labour Organization], take as the target when speaking about women's opportunities, the levels and choices open to men. But one has not taken into consideration that the traditional role of men might need change too' (1986: 256).

## ICELAND

The information on Iceland in both English-speaking and western European countries is scanty at best, and details on specific topics are in many cases non-existent. From the information available it appears that Icelandic society has developed differently from other Scandinavian countries but, in its very recent history, it has also undergone some decisive transformations as a result of the local and overseas women's movements of the 1960s and 1970s.

Iceland's rather small population of 240 000 people, scattered over a sparse island, can look back on an ancient and highly developed culture. Tomasson points out that the ancient Icelandic laws were particularly liberal and accorded women a higher status and a greater measure of independence than any other culture in Europe. In the 10th century they had the right to own property, were allowed to divorce and to remarry, to vote and to take an active role in the political and social events of the time. With the onset of christianity, these rights disappeared and with them women disappeared from history and recorded culture altogether (Tomasson, 1980: 106-10).

Iceland still claims to be a very egalitarian society with a low degree of class consciousness, but women are certainly no better off in Iceland than elsewhere in Europe. Up to the beginning of the 1980s, formal statistics tell us that women were underrepresented in the labour force generally and they were rarely found in the professions. In the 1970s, women constituted 29 percent of the workforce; 34 percent of students were women, but this translated into only 22 percent of teachers both in primary and high schools and, in other professions, women's presence averaged around 2 percent. At the same time, women earned 30 to 40 percent less than their male colleagues (Tomasson, 1980: 110). Changes then occurred rather suddenly and drastically. In 1964 only 28 percent of women worked but by 1980 the percentage had risen to 65. In university studies, only 15.3 percent of graduates were women in 1970 but in 1980 women formed 40.9 percent of graduates (Styrkársdóttir, 1986: 142).

Iceland's women's movement began in 1968, with the formation of a new women's group of schoolteachers, within a women's rights organisation called 'Raudsokkahreyfingin' (Redstocking Movement). They were concerned especially with the low status of women and they planned to change this by focusing, as in other Scandinavian countries, on political institutions (parliament, administration and unions). They were helped to some extent by the fact that the coalition party in government in the 1971 to 1974 period was leftist in character and somewhat sympathetic to women's demands. These demands were largely couched in leftist language and had leftist aims. The Redstocking Movement had as its slogan: 'No women's struggle without class struggle, no class struggle without women's struggle' (Styrkársdóttir, 1986: 142-5). Both slogan and name were later taken over by the Danish movement. In 1980, Vigdis Finnbogadóttir, who had been the director of the Reykjavik Theatre, became the first woman in the world elected to the position of president. It is noteworthy that Mrs Finnbogadóttir is a single parent, a fact that, unjustly, would have made an election victory rather unlikely elsewhere in the world. In 1981, Kwenna Frambothid (KF), the Women's Alliance, was founded. It issued its own feminist newspaper, called *Vera*. This important new organisation formed the basis of a new 'women's list' which could be launched as a feminist political party. As a result, the Icelandic Redstocking Movement was formally abolished a year later and its active members joined the Women's List (Kwenna Listin). This fast transition from social movement to political-interest group, and its seemingly total absorption into the political arena, is unique to Iceland.

Icelandic feminists noted that the situation for women had not improved since the Redstockings had begun and pointed out the disadvantages for and discriminatory practices against women. In 1982, only 5 percent of parliamentarians and less than 7 percent of all councillors were women and there were only two women on the Icelandic trade union central committee. A mere 5 percent of women earned the equivalent of or above the average male wage and the total earning capacity of women was a mere 66 percent of male wages. They argued that if they earned just 66 percent of the wages they should be asked to pay only 66 percent of the cost of consumer items. The supermarket demonstration of 1984 was certainly an original movement event. At the time, Iceland suffered from a severe economic crisis and the inflation rate had reached 50 percent. Feminists decided to make their point in a colourful, non-violent confrontational manner. They went to supermarkets, taking a good many items from the shelves and then offered to pay 66 percent of the total cost. Supermarket managers and police were called in but they stood by helplessly as women filled the supermarkets singing and dancing. As in other countries, feminists also objected to the sexism in the media and in the public sphere generally. It was unfortunate for the mayor of Reykjavik that he had made sexist comments in public, an act which immediately sparked off another demonstration, now known as the Beauty Queen Action of 1985 when women, dressed in nothing more than bikinis and wearing heavy makeup, entered the council chambers during a session and paraded noisily in front of the consternated male councillors (Dominelli & Jonsdottir, 1988: 36–53).

There may not have been as many movement events in Iceland as, for instance, in France or West Germany, but the ones that were chosen were certainly extremely effective in terms of gaining media attention and alerting the wider public to the problems that feminists wanted amended or eradicated. In one respect, the Icelandic movement was unique in the history of new European women's movements, at least as far as the degree of solidarity among women in general was concerned. On 25 October 1975, in support of the International Women's Year, feminists called for a general strike and a most unusual thing happened: almost 90 percent of *all* adult Icelandic women literally went 'on strike'. Housewives went out for the day leaving small children and household chores to their husbands, working women stayed away from their jobs and almost the entire island came to a standstill. Women wanted to show that their society would stop functioning without them and that the injustices and discriminatory practices at the workplace were neither morally nor practically defensible (Einarsdóttir, 1976: 18). The speaker for the Icelandic women's movement, Gerdur Steinthorsdóttir, said at the time, 'We are not demanding any specific pay rises here. We only want to show that it is a great injustice that women receive less pay' (*Frankfurter Rundschau*, 25 Oct. 1975).

In 1985, exactly ten years later, women again called a stoppage in order to remind their male compatriots that a whole decade had gone by, and the UN

Decade for Women had ended but the injustices had not disappeared. The *Boston Globe* reported that the mood of the women at this mass rally was angry and disillusioned. It claimed that the law of equal pay, which had meanwhile been introduced, 'was being flouted by firms making secret payments to men'. Women numbering a quarter of the capital's population (25 000) gathered in Reykjavik, making public their view that in the previous ten years things had become worse for women rather than better. The mass protest was supported by the Republic's President Vigdís Finnbogadóttir. Even though parliament had voted for a ban on the strike, its nine women legislators staged a walk out in sympathy for the stoppage. The newspaper claimed that, in 1985, 80 percent of women worked outside the home but earned up to 40 percent less than men, owned only 10 percent of the country's property and were 'virtually excluded from top jobs' (WIN, 1986, vol. 12, no. 1: 72). Apparently the resistance to women's claims for justice and for participation in both the economy and politics was very pronounced, more so than in other Scandinavian countries. Under pressure, political parties only then began to nominate women candidates (Lovenduski, 1986: 154).

In 1983, the Women's Alliance made its first parliamentary breakthrough. In the next election of 1987, it very nearly doubled its vote and won six seats in its own right in the country's 63-member Althing (parliament). Nevertheless, Iceland's women MPs have retained a cautious and suspicious distance from the institution in which they now work. Gudrun Agnarsdóttir, one of the Women's Alliance's representatives in parliament pointed out in an interview that her party was neither left or right and that it 'refuses to allow itself to be pigeon-holed within the traditional political spectrum'. She said that the party is prepared to participate in government but that it 'will make very firm conditions, especially on improving the status of women and children'. One of the leaders of the Feminist Party, Siguridur Kristmundsdóttir, however, sounded more determined to effect change when she stated in the same interview, 'Promises are no longer enough. Now we want real influence in the running of the country along with the men' (*Financial Times*, UK, 6 May, 1987, repr. WIN, 1987: 59).

There is no doubt that the women's movement in Iceland, however brief or sporadic it might have been as a movement, has had a profound impact on Icelandic society. Women themselves have instigated a women's refuge and a women's centre and have created a network for legal aid and advice. More importantly, the swift success of Icelandic women in changing the participation rate of women in education and work, their concerted efforts in creating and maintaining a women's party as a pressure group within the political system, their achievement in lobbying successfully for a woman candidate for presidency and their unique national strike actions make the Icelandic women's movement remarkable by any standard.

*THE MODEL EXAMINED*

By comparison with formal statistics for other nations Scandinavia has achieved a greater measure of social equality for women than anywhere else in western Europe. Indeed, by any measure of international standards of human rights, the Nordic countries are exemplary, and often considerably ahead of other western European countries. Being 'ahead' here means that goals for the implementation of human rights have been interpreted in innovative and often radical ways, and that these new regulations have partly or fully achieved the elimination of injust traditional moral codes; Sweden's radical statement that no form of cohabitation is superior to another has removed the moral, economic and legal advantages of marriage and the nuclear family from the statute books and has therefore largely eradicated the inequalities and injustices forced on women, and also on children born ex-nuptially.

Progressiveness here denotes change in the desired direction of equality of human rights and awards, irrespective of sex. It also connotes a conception of justice which embraces equality as well as equity. Ginsberg summarised the meaning of progress by saying, 'I believe that the eighteenth century thinkers were right in regarding progress as a movement towards "reason and justice" and in laying stress on equality as the core of justice' (1953: 68). I think that it is still appropriate today to use the term in the sense in which Ginsberg and the 18th century *philosophes* understood it. Progressiveness is then defined as a cluster of actions and purposeful changes in attitude that will allow progress to be made in the direction of or even beyond a standard of values as laid down by international commissions (e.g. the Human Rights Commission) and other international bodies (e.g. the UN).

No doubt women's options have expanded greatly in this century, if mainly for women of middle-class background and for those women living in the wealthier countries. Still, there is a risk of overestimating and misinterpreting the changes that have occurred in women's daily lives. One does not deny that some progress has been made, but there are substantial formal statistics available which show clearly that by any measure of equality (equal representation, equal pay, equal awards) societies and governments have so far failed to uphold the promise of equality and make true the demands of the moderate factions of the women's movements.

Indeed, amongst Scandinavian scholars, politicians and feminists there appears to be widespread agreement about the inadequacies of the present position of women. The authoritative Scandinavian statistical handbook of 1988, called *Kvinnor och Män i Norden* (Women and Men in the North), states categorically: '*There is not yet any area in which women and men are equal*' (p. 136). Politically, women have no equal representation anywhere in the Scandinavian countries, incomes are lower for women than for men, women's employment is more vulnerable to market forces, with often much higher unemployment rates, and women are much more often employed part time than are men. Men have more leisure hours, more money, more power and far less involvement and participation in domestic duties than women (*Kvinnor*, 1988: 136–7). Some publications in recent years have adopted a despondent tone. After all, the Scandinavian struggle for women's equality is now over a century old (Herman, 1972: 45 ff). Even if writers have conceded that socio-economic and political developments were intercepted by two world wars and by industrialisation, many women feel that progress has been too slow and that changes in the position of women relative to men have been far too small to warrant enthusiasm or undue optimism.

In education, socialisation and the actual pay packet many sharp inequalities have remained, and some of the incipient practices of discrimination have largely been left untouched. Or perhaps one should say, in the light of our discussion on market forces, that there are many events, processes, and circumstances which reinforce traditional gender segregation and gender inequalities. To the surprise of Swedish social planners and educationists, decades of non-sexist

**Figure 3.5 Proportion of all gainfully employed persons in Scandinavia who work within totally segregated, heavily segregated, and non-segregated occupations**

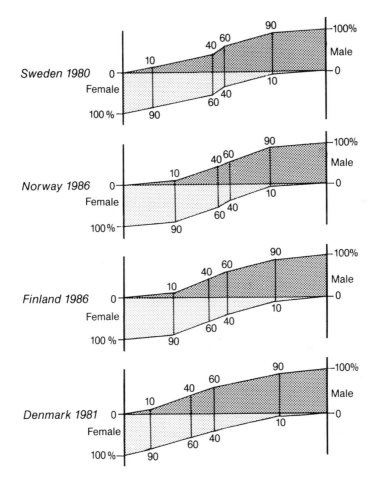

Source: Kvinnor och Män, 1988: 83

educational curricula have barely made an impact on subject choices at school and on occupational structures. Both have remained gender based and sex segregated. The large increase of women in the labour force between 1960 and 1970 did not lead to 'any considerable decreases in occupational segregation between men and women' (Kandolin & Uusitalo, 1980: 33). Despite rigorous reform programmes, surveys of 1975 and 1977 (Wistrand, 1981: 54–5), and again in 1988 (*Naisten asema*) found that Sweden has one of the most segregated labour markets in western Europe. Women cluster mainly in about 30 occupations, with a further 70 dominated by them as against 200 which are dominated by men. The most common study areas for women and men, even at school level, show this segregation. In Finland today, only 6 percent of employees work in gender-mixed work places. The remainder is subdivided into segregated areas: over 60 percent of women work in caring professions and in the service industry, while men are found almost exclusively in positions of power and decision making (Bergmann & Vehkakoski, 1988: 80). An overview of recent facts about fields of study and occupational distribution has been provided by *Kvinnor och Män i Norden* (1988), and is shown in figure 3.5.

In Finland, the seesaw effect is very striking. On average, women earn 40 percent less than men and 63 percent of all women in the labour force are low-income earners. Simultaneously, however, women are very well represented in politics and have a much greater presence in the professions than women in other Scandinavian countries. As said earlier, however, the numbers game in politics (i.e. the sheer numerical presence of women in politics) is not in itself a sign of women having a voice in gender-specific issues. Thus, Juusola-Halonen found in 1981 that it was difficult for feminists to get their point of view accepted or supported in parliament. She writes: 'One of the main problems is that although there are women in positions of power in Finland, this does not necessarily mean that these women work for feminist interests' (1981: 459).

The Central Statistical Office of Finland admitted in 1984 that, irrespective of educational attainment, *men earn more than women* (*Naisten asema*, 1984: 129). It calculated income levels in relation to educational attainment, an important exercise that should be done in other countries as well, particularly by those which claim to follow equal opportunity and equal treatment policies. The statistical inquiry established a number of noteworthy facts. When men and women have the same educational attainment, men will achieve certain income levels in a few years while women will achieve the same only towards or at the end of their working lives. In medium educational groups, women's incomes increase at only half the speed of men's. When women are much better qualified than men, the income inequality is exposed even more dramatically: in the public sector men with primary school education, earn, on average, only 5 percent less than women with completed university degrees. In private industry, the failure of making true the promise of equality is still more pronounced. In a 1979 survey women with degrees and fields of high specialisation, on average, earned less than primary school-trained men, while men with similar high degrees of specialisation earned much more (see table 3.4). These findings, while seemingly outdated, well reflect typical western European trends indicating that equality of opportunity is not translated readily into equality of outcome.

In a 1981 study by Haavio-Mannila and Eskola, educational background and likely career patterns for women were correlated. It was found that educational success was an important predictor of later career advancement among women while this was not an important criterion for men (Haavio-Mannila & Eskola, in Epstein & Coser, 1981: 69; see also Eskola & Haavio-Mannila, 1975). These findings suggest that career prospects for women exist only when women are

Table 3.4   **Average earnings (in Finnish mark) by sex and levels of education in Finland in 1979**

| Education | Female | Male |
|---|---|---|
| Basic schooling to leaving certificate | 25 000–30 000 | 38 000– 52 000 |
| Matriculation and further study | 41 000–45 000 | 65 000– 70 000 |
| Completed degree and/or postgraduate | 58 000 | 90 000–100 000 |

*Source*: adapted from *Naisten asema*, 1984: 134

willing to subject themselves to long vocational and tertiary training courses. Career women generally spend much longer than men in preparing for careers but, even so, the latter still have greater success in terms of income. Ironically, a completed university degree has at least some unexpected side benefits as a protection against sexual harassment at the workplace. Finnish studies showed that women in token positions were more often harassed than other women and this occurred particularly in medium-level occupations. University-trained women, on the other hand, reported the lowest incidents of sexual harassment—a small consolation for the gap in monetary awards, one would imagine (Högbacka et al., 1987: 38).

Taking the example of Scandinavian countries, I would like to come back to the issue of women's role and place in the labour force. In the last decades, the number of women at work has risen substantially in most western countries. What does this information tell us? By itself, very little, and we must be careful of not exaggerating its significance.

First of all, many of the supposed changes are not as marked if measured over a longer period than some publications on the status of women have presented. Figures read over the whole of the 20th century show that the participation of women in the labour force often emerges as fluctuation, depending on labour power needs at a given time, rather than as a gradual increase. As argued before (see chapter 2, 'Women in the labour force') these global figures gave rise to the theory that women function as a reserve army for the capitalist economy. We might debate its validity, as Baldock and others have done (Baldock & Cass, 1983: 22 ff), but the picture is not unequivocal. Even during the postwar years (after 1945), the changes are sometimes not as marked as one might want to believe. Between 1963 and 1979 in Sweden, for example, the total number of women in employment and study together rose only by 4 percent for the 16- to 19-year-old group, and when compared to changes in men's participation of employment and study for the same period and the same age group, only very marginal gender differences emerge. In the 20- to 24-year-old age bracket, the percentage of women engaged in full-time study rose only by 2 percent. However, in the same age group the participation of women in the labour force jumped by 15 percent (Rehn & Petersen, 1980: 65–6), as shown in table 3.5.

These figures may look promising here and there but they have to be viewed with reservation, because they do not distinguish between part-time and full-time work. Apart from Finland, most increases in women's labour force participation have occurred in part-time work. Overall, almost 50 percent of women in Norway, Sweden and Denmark are in regular and short-hour part-time work with all the disadvantages and job insecurities usually intact. Part-time work, 80 or 90 percent of which is exclusively carried out by women in Scandinavian countries, must now be classified as a specifically female job market which has nothing other to offer than short hours. In exchange for this 'privilege' employers are allowed to give less job security, fewer if any of the benefits, and no promise for career prospects. The trend of the 1960s and 1970s towards part-time work has generally continued in the 1980s, as figure 3.6 shows.

The fact that so many women work in part-time positions also betrays the belief that the role of women as chief home-makers and child carers has not appreciably changed but has contributed to the new discrepancies and problems for women at work. In the 1980s, Denmark had the highest proportion of

**Table 3.5  Women and men in full-time study or in the labour force in Sweden, 1963–1979**

|  | Aged 16–19 | | | | | |
|---|---|---|---|---|---|---|
| Year | In labour force | | F/t students | | Unemployed | |
|  | M(%) | F(%) | M(%) | F(%) | M(%) | F(%) |
| 1963 | 62.5 | 59.6 | 27.0 | 26.8 | 2.9 | 4.7 |
| 1965 | 62.2 | 50.7 | 27.5 | 29.0 | 1.9 | 5.1 |
| 1970 | 52.8 | 50.9 | 37.2 | 35.1 | 3.4 | 4.8 |
| 1973 | 53.7 | 49.8 | 36.1 | 38.4 | 5.8 | 8.0 |
| 1975 | 59.0 | 56.2 | 32.1 | 33.4 | 4.2 | 7.1 |
| 1977 | 56.7 | 56.1 | 33.8 | 34.1 | 5.4 | 7.9 |
|  | Aged 20–24 | | | | | |
| 1963 | 81.2 | 64.9 | 9.6 | 7.0 | 2.1 | 2.3 |
| 1965 | 79.7 | 63.6 | 10.3 | 7.4 | 1.2 | 2.9 |
| 1970 | 77.1 | 64.3 | 12.2 | 12.1 | 2.5 | 2.4 |
| 1973 | 78.4 | 67.6 | 11.8 | 12.2 | 4.2 | 4.7 |
| 1975 | 82.7 | 73.7 | 9.3 | 10.4 | 2.1 | 3.5 |
| 1977 | 83.4 | 77.1 | 9.0 | 9.7 | 2.9 | 3.5 |
| 1979 | 83.7 | 79.9 | 8.4 | 9.4 | 3.6 | 3.8 |

Source: Rehn & Petersen, 1980: 65–66

women at work (49 percent) out of all the EEC countries (*Women and Men of Europe*, 1983: 17) and even more women wanted to work in 1983 than in 1975 (*Women and Men of Europe*, 1983: 81). Since most women are in part-time positions, however, they do not perceive themselves as equals of their male colleagues. The 1983 survey mentioned before found that in job-related criteria, such as salary or job security, promotion potential, etc., Danish women see themselves at a distinct disadvantage vis-à-vis men (*Women and Men of Europe*, 1983: 107).

Women have a high profile at work and in politics. Ideologically, government bodies, policy makers and educational institutions are on the side of women; so is the general population whose attitudes reflect egalitarian norms and standards. It is an astounding fact that in Denmark women and men *think* positively and progressively and yet women's lives have not improved appreciably (relative to men's). The laws, policies and public attitudes are enlightened, as occurs only in a few other places, yet women earn less than men (proportionately), are in lower-status positions at the lower-income end of the scale, and suffer from the double burden of paid and unpaid work. In Denmark, as in Sweden and Finland, this seesaw effect is particularly striking.

It is also worth noting here that the persistence of discrepancies between formal equalities and reality has a rather long history in Denmark and Norway, which demonstrates the ineffectiveness of progressive laws if the social actors are not willing or ready to implement these. In Denmark, women have had the right to be voted into parliament since 1915, but after the appointment of one female minister in 1924, there was no other such appointment for 50 years (Hansen et al., 1985: 35). In addition, the equal pay law, awarded to women in Norway in 1908, is not yet a reality. In 1986, Norwegian women earned 84 percent of male wages, did almost all the part-time work that the labour market had to offer, were clustered in about 30 occupations as against about 300 for men, and had

Figure 3.6    Proportion of all employed persons who work full time, 'long' part time, and
'short' part time, 1975–1985

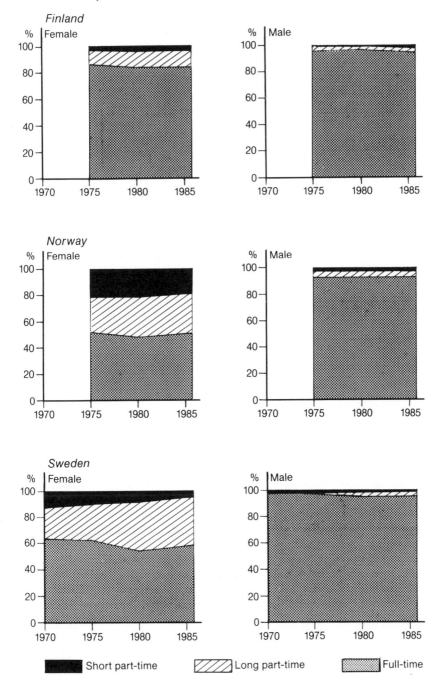

Source: Kvinnor och Män, 1988:79

Figure 3.7    Proportion of all employed persons working within the public sector

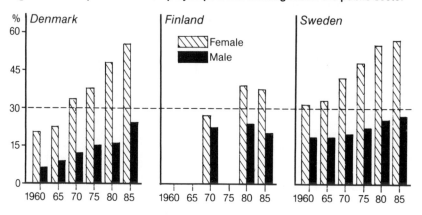

Source: Kvinnor och Män, 1988: 86

far less economic independence and less job security than men. In other words, the global figures showing the steep increases of women in the workforce are hardly impressive once the distinction between full-time and part-time work is made.

One also needs to consider the quality, content and concomitant disadvantages of the work situation for women. Finland, for instance, has the longest working hours of any Scandinavian country. It is moreover the only western European country that has such a high proportion of women, 88 percent, in full-time employment (*Naisten asema*, 1988: 72). Of course, as long as women suffer from the dual burden of paid and unpaid work, they cannot win either way: in part-time work they do not gain high income or prestige and in full-time work, especially if this entails very long hours, they do not get a moment's reprieve, let alone leisure time, and are thus severely overburdened. This is hardly a commendable state of affairs.

Finally, before drawing hasty conclusions on the meaning of women's rising participation in the workforce, one also needs to consider into which employment sector women have gone. For Sweden, Denmark, Norway, and Finland there is evidence that the greatest increase in women's employment has occurred in the public rather than in the private sector. Thus, many women, if they have not gone into part-time positions, have actually been absorbed by bureaucracies (see fig. 3.7). Governments may be congratulated for having provided employment for women and for doing what they preach. Conversely, it may be argued that government initiatives have failed to make an impact on the private sector of the labour market: there has been very little 'trickle down' effect from government policy and legislature to the private sector, that is, to the broader economic infrastructure of society. Instead, the issue of women's status has led governments into becoming the caretakers of women.

Women, whether as welfare recipients, welfare providers or general workers in government bureaucracies have become wardens of the state and are exposed to its whims and dictates. Women are allowed to live under its protection, a protection that is much more fickle than is generally admitted. The example of Finland has already shown that the 'big brother' protection is flawed and rather impermanent: of all long-term unemployed women, a total of 33 percent comes from the social service sector alone (*Naisten asema*, 1988: 72).

Governments, as we saw in chapter 2, are chiefly caretakers of broad economic goals and economic management and therefore have a considerable influence on the economic direction and development of their nations. It is not just that governments have failed to make an impact on the private sector, but the problem of inflation which besieged almost all western European nations, including the Scandinavian countries, from the early 1970s on, has shown clearly where their hearts and their ideology lay. Inflation can be vastly reduced by forcing private companies not to increase prices. But western industrialised countries in general regarded such price control as an unacceptable extension of 'state interference'. What they did pursue instead was a course of action called 'monetary correction' which results in nothing other than unemployment (Gamble & Walton, 1976: 24). Yet causing high rates of unemployment and severely affecting the livelihood of masses of people has never gone by the name of 'state interference'. Hence it would be incorrect to say that governments fought for social policies *against* the private economic sector but rather more correct to assume that their role has been ambivalent. Their simultaneous policies on the economic and social front have often been contradictory. Scandinavian governments have guarded against the detrimental effects of their economic policies a little better than other nations but, by the very nature of the late capitalist mixed-market economy, the fundamental contradictions remain an integral part of their management, though to differing degrees depending on the political ideology of the party or government in power.

We need not herald large bureaucratic apparatuses as a singular blessing nor rate them as a sign of progress but, for better or for worse, this is the environment into which women have been accepted most readily. This is the labour sector in which women have forged careers and come to maintain livelihoods. We all know that governments change and with them their ideologies. The arguments for or against small or big government styles and expenditures have been argued ad infinitum in the postwar years. Of late, however, with the shift to the right of the political spectrum, voices in favour of small governments (including privatisation of government-run and owned industries and organisations) have become noticeably louder and sharper. The move towards privatisation has already been made in England and in Denmark and is likely to be made by other western European countries very soon. In most cases, privatisation, as a way of reducing government liabilities and administration, has led to redundancies with, inadvertently, the large pool of female public servants as the first target (Coyle, 1985). Women's jobs are again in jeopardy, and the process of privatisation in western Europe has deprived women of incomes and careers. Indeed it will deprive many more in the years to come (Søndergaard, 1988: 65; Bergman & Vehkakoski, 1988: 80). These developments in Scandinavian countries should indicate to us that neither part-time work nor work in the public sector alone will suffice to give women the same job security and chance of economic independence as men. As long as women have not infiltrated all levels of the labour market and have not obtained firm job security they can be made to vanish from the labour market at a moment's notice.

Moreover, it was argued in chapter 2, 'Women in the labour force', that before one regards increases of women in the labour force as a sign of progress, one must also consider for what reasons women choose, or are forced, to work. Only a small proportion of women work because they want careers or self-determination and autonomy. Most women see their entry into the workforce as an unavoidable consequence of economic pressures. 'Economic pressure' is of course a malleable term. It does not bring tears to our eyes when we hear of someone who claims that she 'had to' work for a second car or a trip to the Bahamas. But such excesses should not entice us into feelings of cynicism. No matter how broadly based the well-to-do middle class and the extremely prosperous upper class may have become in the rich western European countries—although in the last two decades, market forces have begun to undermine the comfortable position of the middle classes—most people have only a limited share in the nation's wealth. Even in the wealthiest European nations there are substantial numbers of people, chiefly women, who live in extreme poverty or very circumscribed conditions, a fact that tends to be forgotten or not believed. Increases of GNP have generally not signalled a redistribution of wealth either through economic infrastructures or through welfare measures. One of the problems of being poor in a country classified as having a high standard of living is that its price structure, including that for the most basic items like food and shelter, is adapted to the purse of the highest bidders. It is obvious that the highest bidders are not from the bulk of the population, not the working class, the lower middle class or in some cases even the middle class.

Norwegian industrialisation, albeit late and timid, and the exploitation of Norway's own natural energy resources have brought in their wake a loss of the importance of agriculture and fishing and an ever growing prominence of the city. As elsewhere in the western world, urban space itself has become a commodity that is flaunted, horded, collected or displayed as if it were some luxury item for investors only. If anything, the trend has intensified in the 1970s and 1980s and is particularly obnoxious in cities which have established themselves as money or tourist centres of their respective nations. In Norway, perhaps more so than in other countries, the consequences of this free-market exercise have been disastrous in several ways.

I would like to digress for a moment, however, into giving a specific Norwegian example of a type of poverty in a wealthy nation that is also found elsewhere in Europe and demonstrates well a particular conflict between social policy and financial management.

Norway's housing market provides a good case of how pernicious the economic pressures that impinge on women's lives can be. The high cost of living in Norwegian cities favours two-income partnerships and appears to work as a force to maintain the incidence of marriage. In Oslo the housing shortage has for years been maintained artificially, keeping up demand and raising prices to such levels that most people cannot afford even the most modest accommodation. Yet, in the absence of alternative rental accommodation people will continue to buy apartments even when this cost far exceeds their means. Ambjørnsen and Hæfs argue that people's need for shelter irrefutably enslaves them for the rest of their lives, lives dominated by repayments for housing. Mortgage repayments for a small two-room flat for *two* people in Oslo, for example, would now require an income equivalent to *three* adult wages in order to be within reason. Every additional room adds to the cost, disproportionate to the income (Ambjørnsen & Hæfs, 1988: 122).

Other large centres have similar housing problems. The situation is not unique to Norway. Lisbon and Sydney come to mind at once as two other cities where the cost of accommodation in the 1980s has sharply risen well beyond anything compatible with average middle-class or even upper middle-class incomes. The point here is not that housing has simply become expensive but that it is entirely mismatched with income. The cost of accommodation in Norway also affects social and family relationship patterns and determines lifestyle choices. On the basis of formal statistics I previously described Norway as one of the most traditional of the Scandinavian countries, its having, for example, a considerably higher marriage rate than Finland, Sweden Denmark or Iceland. One tends to deduce conservatism from such information. But this claim has to be modified now by interposing evidence of a different kind that might well account for the high marriage rate. Communal living and de facto relationships, for example, are hampered by the housing costs because banks are extremely reluctant to lend money to couples or to groups of people amongst whom no legal bonds or obligations exist. In other words, the high marriage rates at early ages and the low divorce rate may well not be an indication of Norway's conservatism but a reflection of economic dictates which have simply priced other lifestyles out of the market. Moreover, 'singles living' is a viable lifestyle option only in the rarest situations because one income is generally not sufficient to cover housing repayment or rental costs. There is a similar demise in having a large family or in looking after aging parents. In each case, the addition of family members needs to be translated into added rooms and greatly magnified costs in an unchanged or barely changed income structure. This economic situation in housing, by itself, has created a blueprint for living and for social relations against which social policy directives have been powerless. One cannot stress enough that free-market exercises such as these work against women in particular as women only very rarely attract the kind of incomes capable of sustaining independent living.

The housing market in Norway has been so grossly out of step with people's social needs and material capabilities that it does not just undermine but completely destroys any chance for implementing the feminist notion of woman's self-determination and autonomy. It is a silly argument to say that Norwegian men are in the same position and that they too have few options. Traditionally, men have reaped the benefits from marriage in social, psychological and economic ways. The present constraints imposed by the housing market have not greatly altered men's traditional privileges, if any of them have been affected at all. There is a good deal of evidence to suggest that women's lifestyle choices differ from men's. The majority of divorces today are filed by women. Women usually elect to have fewer children and, if given a choice, now tend to marry later or not at all. The percentage of 'never married' women in their thirties and forties has increased sharply over the postwar period in many western European countries, when and where women have had options for independent living.

The specific issue of Norway's housing situation was meant to demonstrate an important principle of market forces versus social policy. Yet the important question remains. Why have the patterns of inequality altered so little considering the magnitude of reforms and the changes in lifestyles, education and general opportunities which have occurred in the 20th century? Our western thinking is explicitly goal-directed and oriented towards change. The arguments about progress and the status of women usually imply a linear relationship between the aim and final goal, from a particular standpoint at a given time. Thus, in much of feminist writing the words 'already' or 'not yet' appear frequently, presumably meaning that something that has not as yet been achieved will be achieved in the near or distant future, as if these programmes were a step-by-step construction of a new edifice. We are used to hearing about new policy directives and new laws and expect that these will be implemented. The problem with this approach, which governs all our western democracies, is that the 'edifice' is society as a whole, while the construction process for women's equality occurs almost entirely in only one corner of the society.

Most reform movements, by implication, are firmly embedded in the social rather than the political realm, and they are even less likely to be at home in the world of economics. In the 20th century we have invested a good deal of energy in the belief that social justice for women can be obtained via *social* and *legal* means. We have talked at length, in all western countries, about needs and wider human rights. We have sought to translate our understanding of social justice into everyday life. Yet while we may have talked about the economic structure and its relation to individual needs, we have never seriously tried to alter the economic structure and its rationale—despite the fact that much of our social existence is inextricably enmeshed with the productive forces. We have lived and continue to live with one of the major ideological contradictions of this century: we seek fulfilment of daily human needs but organise production around profit motives and economic demands (Heidenheimer et al., 1983: 330). The contradiction, all too familiar, commonly surfaces as public expenditure *versus* economic dictates. If fiscal problems arise, measures are taken rather swiftly to cut public expenditure, but little if anything is done to change the economic dictates. Much has been written about this contradiction and there is no need here to expound the entire debate yet again. It has to be borne in mind, however, that with the idea of progress towards social justice for women and, ultimately, for all, we often presuppose that the social realm can exist by itself and find expression of itself independently of other forces. It seems unlikely that anyone would see matters quite as crudely and naively as this, but part of our wishful thinking possibly lies somewhere near such a construct. Thus we participate in a mystification of the real relations of production and of power relations.

We have seen in the Norwegian case that there are rather obvious problems between the free-market economy and the implementation of social justice. The latter, referring here to social justice for women, requires social engineering and planning, especially so since the systems which have created the injustices are well entrenched and need to be broken down. In the Nordic countries, partly because reform programmes are so much further advanced than in most other western nations, the discrepancies and problems emerge with much greater clarity than elsewhere. Here, more than anywhere else, the *absolute* incompatibility between social engineering and the free market economy is dramatically and demonstrably evident, irrespective of the seemingly necessary function of governments to socialise costs in order to manage demand and accumulation effectively (Gamble & Walton, 1976: 163). While public policy in Scandinavia supports the notion of women's equality and strives to make this belief a livable reality, the free-market economy may pull in the other direction, according to the whims of amoral market forces. Ultimately, the role of even the most progressive social democratic governments 'has lent itself better to repairing the ravages of capitalist production than to preventing them' (Logue, 1983: 253).

For the Scandinavian feminist engineers of change, such a stocktaking exercise for the last decade or so creates headaches and uncertainty. The surprise generated by such data should not result from so little changing over such a long time, but rather from hardly anything changing despite very concerted efforts by policy makers, feminist groups and the population in general. Sociobiologists and similarly hardened deterministic, reductionist thinkers might now exclaim how these obviously failed social experiments demonstrate most convincingly that, after all, men and women are not equal, and that women are possibly inferior and will behave according to some innate biological mechanism. I do not think that these figures show anything of the sort (Kaplan & Rogers, 1990a). What they do show is that there are limits to change if the most fundamental variable, the economic system, with its inbuilt system of structured inequality, has remained unchanged within that same period. This is why the Danish faction of the liberation movement expressed anti-capitalist sentiments and why it insisted on claims of *liberation* rather than mere equality. But even those moderate Scandinavian feminists who espoused a belief in women's rights as a legitimate moral claim to lay before democratic governments have been less than happy with the progress. Haavio-Mannila, aware of the discrepancies between promises and reality, has aptly called her last book *Unfinished Democracy,* in itself a powerful reprimand to those who believe that democracy is already a fully fledged system rather than an evolving one.

There are recently more feminists who support the idea of a politics of difference, implicitly succumbing to the view that there may be innate differences in talents and intelligence between males and females. There are others whose belief in the continued existence of surreptitious discrimination has led them to search for answers in micro-psycho-social research. Hence, some studies have found now that teachers in Sweden devote twice as much of their time to boys as to girls (Wistrand, 1981: 39) despite the social progress of Sweden towards equality between the sexes. Whatever conclusion has been drawn from such experiences over time, all writers agree that inequality has persisted often in such crass and obvious ways that these are discouraging even the most rugged feminist optimists. Other sources have suggested that the reason for the limited success of resocialisation programmes has been the exclusion of the male in the whole process. In a 1985 publication entitled *A Report on Equality Between Women and Men in Sweden,* one chapter, called 'The new man', pointed out that men had largely been omitted from the debate on equality and needed to be included:

> Women are still the prime movers in the debate on sexual equality. *In order for any further progress to be made*, men will have to approach women in debate and reality. The sex role of women has been greatly transformed; they have assumed economic responsibility but also look after homes and children. Although nearly all women nowadays are gainfully employed, many men still behave as though they were married to full-time housewives. Through this division of labour, men are able to preserve a dominant superior position. Men still occupy practically all positions conferring power and influence in society, although it is also true that not all men have power. This has not changed by women also being gainfully employed, because for the most part they are employed in low-paid service and caring occupations. To achieve equality between women and men, the man must also strike the same balance between paid and unpaid work, i.e. gainful employment and care of the home and children, as women have done already ... [emphasis added] (cit. in WIN News, vol. 12, no. 1, 86: 69)

Whether these lines contain the essence of a new resocialisation 'package' for boys and men or whether this is a rather limp appeal for reasonableness to those in power is not entirely clear, nor for that matter important. It is significant that the writers base much of their hope for *any* further progress on psychosocial categories. The argument on the economic structure and its inherent ideological ramifications, which I would regard as the most perspicacious one for any fundamental change, only surfaces in relation to the domestic sphere. The economic and power hierarchy remains untouched. To my mind, this demonstrates an inexplicable confidence (or naivety?) in the suppleness of the present economic structure in being able to accommodate any changes, even those that must of necessity run counter to the very essence of this structure, and an unlimited confidence in the political system of social democracy.

Notably, in all Scandinavian countries, the effect of the social movements has been a swift transition from remaining outside government and outside the political sphere (in the most limited sense) to an integration into politics. The crassest example is Iceland, where the entire movement was officially abandoned once a separate women's party (the Women's List) was formed. In Norway, the present governing elite consists of many women, while the movement has almost waned. Also in Finland and even in Denmark where factions of the movement resisted integration into the existing political paradigm, the change from social movement to political interest group (Costain, 1982) is rather dramatic. If this is the best way to go, that is, if the change from a supposedly politically mute (social movement) to a politically participatory role (member of political party and of government) is the one democratically viable, correct and presumably most *effective* way to ensure change, then why are the changes in infrastructure not as dramatic as changes in women's participation rates in politics? Is it really a matter of time before change will trickle down, if not 'cascade down', to mass level, or is the assumption that all the desired transformation of society must come from formal political activity wrong from the outset? Are the sceptics and the disillusioned feminists right in regarding political parties as marginal to social and economic reality?

# 4   Conservatism in the Germanic countries

In chapter 2 we saw that in the postwar period West Germany, Switzerland, Austria, and Liechtenstein had at times shown extraordinary reticence to reforms. In particular, Switzerland and Liechtenstein surprised the western world by their long-standing and remarkable hostility to enfranchising women. This issue occupied Switzerland throughout the first half of the 1970s and Liechtenstein until 1985. Austria and especially West Germany had very different histories in their reform and welfare programmes but, in terms of the second-wave feminist movements, the governments of both countries were at times opposed to pressure groups and non-responsive to women's demands. Today in these countries there may be few if any major differences in women's status in comparison with most other western European countries, but throughout the entire 1970s and even 1980s the behaviour of all governments, often with substantial support by the general population, was markedly skewed towards conservatism.

Both Austria and West Germany developed a commitment to welfare programmes, but it cannot be said that any of the Germanic countries actively pursued goals of egalitarianism, as in Scandinavia. Rather, the chief interest of these countries lay in the relentless development of a strong economy, and in creating social, economic and political stability that would permit unimpeded growth. Social justice issues were ultimately of secondary interest. West Germany has certainly achieved its goal as one of the most economically powerful countries in the European Community and one of the leading economies in the world. Austria is on a similar path, and Switzerland and Liechtenstein have maintained per capita national incomes that are almost legendary, these being amongst the highest in the world. Of course, such aims do not only put social justice issues into a low-priority category but, in many instances, they are entirely incompatible with free market forces.

## WEST GERMANY

It is difficult to try and sketch even some of the elements of a German past which are relevant to postwar feminism without falling at once victim to the peculiarities of Germany history. Since unification in 1871, Germany has undergone many dramatic changes in political structure and has again experienced sharp caesuras and fragmentation in the 20th century: the collapse of the monarchy in 1918; the collapse of the Weimar Republic in 1933 when Hitler seized power; and in 1949 when Germany was split into two parts, the FRG and the GDR, before being reunited 40 years later. The problem with German history is that it needs to be reinvented anew in almost every generation. Thus

Hagen Schulze, when he published the first of six volumes on German history in 1982, lamented:

> When the French nation recognizes herself in her history, it is always the same nation and the same history, the same dates and figures, the same myths. The thread of identity spans from the Merowingian Empire to the present. The picture that the French have of their history does not change: the key words, the names, the epochs, the judgements remain immovable, sedimental stone in the collective national consciousness, in which unity and identity are rooted. Mutatis mutandis, this is the common relationship that the European peoples entertain to their respective histories. What is different about the Germans? Their incapacity to find a picture of their history which, in the long run, will guarantee identity and self-confidence of the nation, has a host of reasons ... Germany ... throughout centuries, is a European 'no-man's land', a host of 'German lands'—les Allemagnes, as the French say. (H. Schulze 'Die Deutschen und ihre Nation' Report in *Die Zeit*, 24.9.1982, Feuilleton: 8)

Equally, there are several layers and strands of German tradition, such as socialist, catholic, and reactionary ones (Pinson, 1966: 173, 194 ff), each of which has dominated at one time and then been submerged again, adding to the sense of discontinuity and fragmentation of German history.

*From the 'first wave' to dictatorship (1871–1933)*

When German principalities achieved unification in 1871, they did so at a high price and in an extremely contradictory manner in the sense that the effects of sudden industrialisation in the 1880s were felt under Prussia's leadership. It foisted an agrarian, land-owning aristocratic ruling élite (the Junkers) onto this new state, which was pre-industrial in outlook and the least likely group to lead the new empire into the industrial age (Evans, 1976). The strictest anti-socialist laws introduced by Bismarck forced socialist thinkers into exile or prison: Karl Marx, who had been forced to leave German territory twice in his life, died in London in 1883, August Bebel was imprisoned, and Clara Zetkin moved to Paris. The socialist tradition in German territories which had gained considerably in strength throughout the second half of the 19th century, now found itself brutally suppressed by Bismarck.

Under the constitution of the German Empire, women lacked the most basic and fundamental civil liberties. The 1851 Prussian prohibition of women's right to assemble for political purposes was never repealed. Police had the right to disperse gatherings of women if they considered these to be subversive and/or political. The husband had the right to chastise his wife, keep her property and income and control all her affairs. The Civil Code of 1900, although it barely changed the position of women at all (Evans, 1976: 13), gave women the right to keep money they had earned in gainful employment. Nevertheless, this freedom over finances did not extend to assets or other property, all of which remained with husbands.

Also from the time of Bismarck's rule stems the notorious paragraph 218 (actually paragraphs 218–220) of the Penal Code, which was introduced in 1871 and occupied feminists of the second wave throughout the 1970s. It made abortion punishable by up to five years' imprisonment, and for anyone assisting in the abortion a prison term of up to ten years was decreed. The sale and use but not the production of contraceptives were strictly prohibited. At the same time, the effects of industrialisation made themselves felt in rapid urban growth, overcrowding and a hopeless impoverishment of the new and growing working class which was now condemned to bear children it could not feed.

Yet no matter how stifling this atmosphere was, both politically and socially, it failed to prevent the spreading of socialist ideas and party politics. During the very years of Bismarck's repressive laws, the socialist party grew from half a million members in 1877 to one and a half million by 1890 (Hunt, 1964: 9). Socialist debate also broached the subject of women. August Bebel, for instance, the co-founder of the Socialist Democratic Workers Party (Sozialdemokratische Arbeiterpartei) in 1869, was one of the first men to devote considerable time to the subject. Whilst in prison, he wrote his later famous book *Women and Socialism* (*Die Frau und der Sozialismus*). Due to strict censorship it was first published in Switzerland in 1879 but via the 'red postal service', the underground socialist publication distribution network, knowledge of the book spread quickly. It was soon translated into fifteen languages and became one of the most widely read works of socialist literature. The later, revised version of this book incorporated ideas expressed by Engels in *The Origin of the Family, Private Property and the State.*

Two other formidable figures who helped promote the development of socialist feminism need to be mentioned here. One is Clara Zetkin and the other Rosa Luxemburg. Clara Zetkin (1857–1933) was particularly relevant to many of the World War I and postwar currents of the 1920s because she became the instigator of, and one of the most important theoreticians in Europe on, the proletarian women's movement. As early as 1889, during the Paris meeting of the Second International, she was successful in getting the socialist movement to accept issues pertaining to girls and women as part of its overall programme. The socialist emancipation theory which she espoused in her book *The Women Workers and Women's Question* (1889) became the ideological blueprint for leftist parties in western Europe. One of her chief arguments, all too often forgotten in the contemporary feminist movements of the western world, was that every class has its own women's question. Her devotion to proletarian women's issues carried a great deal of weight. She remained one of the heroines of women workers and, at least in Italy, she was rediscovered by the new postwar feminist wave of the 1970s.

Rosa Luxemburg was born in Poland, and later studied in Zurich. She then did all her political work in Germany where she was imprisoned and ultimately murdered. She was a co-founder of the Communist Party in Germany. Her famous thesis: 'Freedom is always the freedom of the dissenter', classified her as the founder of democratic communism. Some of her best-known works were the popular *Reform or Revolution* (1899), *Mass strike, Party and Union* (1906), *The Accumulation of Capital* (1913), and *What is Economics?* (1925).

In the late 19th century, countless women's groups and women's associations sprung to life. Of these, the most important were the General German Women's Association (Allgemeiner Deutscher Frauenverein), formed in 1865, and the powerful Federation of German Women's Associations (Verband Deutscher Frauenvereine), formed in 1894. Women began to fight for their right to be educated and partially succeeded in this endeavour, but petitions for equal status of women, made shortly before the codification of the new Civil Code, were unsuccessful. The suffragette movements, particularly the English movement, became an inspiration to German women. Membership of the federation had grown substantially by the turn of the century and in 1902 a separate German Union for Women's Suffrage was created. The number of associations and their publications are too numerous to mention here. (For a listing of the most important feminist journals of the 19th and early 20th centuries see Weiland, 1983: 100–1). By the time World War I ended, there were at least sixteen different feminists journals, and a large number of organisations which were explicitly devoted to feminist issues. Every branch of the movement, be it proletarian or bourgeois, had its own political subdivisions and clubs in radical and moderate wings. There was a women's suffragette movement under the leadership of Anita Augspurg, and finally, after the war, also a peace movement headed by feminists. Internationally, German feminism, particularly socialist feminism, had assumed a leading role. In the women's conference of Stuttgart in 1907, preceding the international socialist conference, Clara Zetkin was elected secretary of the international women's movement and her journal *Gleichheit* (Equality) was chosen as the organisation's international voice.

In 1918, on the collapse of the monarchy after Germany's defeat in World War I, the Weimar Republic was proclaimed and this constituted the Germans' first genuine, but rather uncertain, attempt at democracy. A wave of strikes engulfed Germany, and also Austria, and led to the spontaneous formation of revolutionary workers' councils and soldiers' councils in 1918. Major uprisings followed, including the so-called November Revolution of 1918 and the Spartacist Uprising of early 1919 (Waldman, 1958). Tragically, the moment for establishing a different order passed, and at great cost to those who had attempted to turn Germany into a democracy. The Spartacists, among them Rosa Luxemburg and Karl Liebknecht, were murdered. The revolution was defeated, the revolutionary councils disappeared and the democratisation process was only partially achieved, weakening the new republic from the outset: 'The old social ruling groups retained their positions; the bureaucracy continued to rule rather than parliament. The Kaiser went, the generals remained' (Carsten, 1972: 335).

Despite the precariousness of the democratic framework, the Weimar Republic (1918–1933) was politically, economically, culturally and socially a very significant period and nonetheless so for women, who began to organise and lobby vocally in well-organised and numerically strong groups. It was a period in which several feminist movements arose and a number of substantial claims for women were granted. Indeed, the first large-scale international women's movement was dominated by German women, particularly in the socialist camp. We need not dwell here on the German feminist movements of the 1920s as there are already several publications available covering this period (Bridenthal et al., 1984; Grossmann, 1983; Koonz, 1986, 1987; Stephenson, 1983). Suffice it to say that women gained the vote in 1918 and were allowed to attend schools and universities. While the period saw a resurgence of anti-feminist movements (Jeffries, 1983) and religious groups, the rise of fascism and Nazi propaganda, and a new virulent anti-semitism fuelled by fears of an international 'Bolshevik conspiracy', it also spawned artistic creativity and socially critical art (Käthe Kollwitz, George Grosz, the Bauhaus), and saw the development of highly progressive feminist activity and views. In particular, traditional views concerning work, love and sex and the use of contraceptives among working-class women (Grossmann, 1983a) were to some extent successfully challenged during the few years of the Weimar Republic. In 1926, the penalty for abortion was changed from imprisonment in high-security prisons to imprisonment in low-security prisons. By 1927 abortion was decriminalised for cases in which the woman's life would have been seriously endangered if she carried the child to its full term. The post-World War II dramatic anti-abortion law demonstrations in France and West Germany were not all that new. In 1931, a spectacular 'I have aborted' campaign against the abortion law was publicly staged, and there was every indication that the law might have been modified or repealed had the Nazis not won the election.

The Weimar Republic folded within the span of a mere fifteen years, leading in 1933 to Hitler's election to power, and thus directly into dictatorship and ruthless totalitarianism. These events came in the wake of the world depression of the late 1920s and early 1930s, of extremely high unemployment rates and a general plummeting of living standards. The victory of the National Socialist (Nazi) Party went hand-in-hand with a reassertion of the 'Kinder, Küche, Kirche' (children, kitchen, church) mentality, in which womanhood was once again defined in the narrowest role of motherhood and housewife. Worse, such views were now firmly anchored to the pathos of a fateful German nationalism and whipped up as a new 'pride', a pride Germany had lost with its defeat in World War I. Germany's fall into the darkness of national socialism (1933–1945) was punctuated by the Holocaust, by World War II, the brutal elimination of opponents and by the eradication of any progress feminists had wrought in the first quarter of the century. The Nazi period was to become a time when biology indeed became 'destiny' (Bridenthal et al., 1984). The majority of German women followed Hitler despite the misogynist laws (Kaplan & Adams, 1990), the horrific excesses practised on women, such as rape, forced breeding, forced sterilisations, etc. (Bock, 1984a, 1986), and the role Hitler had decreed for women (Stephenson, 1983; Koonz, 1987). Hitler did not just unleash total war and cause the death of tens of millions of men. Millions of women also perished as a consequence of National Socialist orders—if they were Jewish, Gypsies, mentally retarded or physically deformed, and if they had been political activists on the left, or dissenters for humanitarian or other reasons.

*The FRG and the 'economic miracle'*

We will not attempt here to deal with the twelve years of the Nazi regime and the destruction of Germany. Suffice to say that the damage done by the Nazis to humanity was so great that 1945 has often been regarded as a 'zero hour', a moment in history when the past is wiped out and human life begins anew as if after a great natural disaster. This issue has been debated at length in German historical scholarship but rarely with reference to the perception and traditions of women. Those who scrambled back to their feet after World War II may have been victims, supporters or opponents of the Nazi regime but, irrespective of their role during the Nazi period, all who lived through the experience of the war were deeply affected by it and, in more than a superficial way had, wittingly or unwittingly, absorbed much of the Nazi propaganda.

In some respects, zero hour never happened for women. One of the legacies of the Nazi period was its misogynist views of women, and these died only slowly. Many of the Nazi laws were not revised until the 1960s or 1970s, and the failure to revise them was more often than not a reflection of the views held by the newly appointed (male) policy makers. For a good while after the inception of the West German democratic state, attitudes to women remained extremely unfavourable and in line with Nazi attitudes. In 1960, for instance, fifteen years after the end of the war, a survey was conducted throughout West German universities which, at that time, had a female student contingent of about 20 percent. Male teaching staff were asked whether they minded female students or female colleagues. Sixty-four percent of male respondents were against the acceptance of female students at university and a staggering 79 percent entirely rejected the idea of employing women at lecturer level or above (Menschik, 1977: 120). Such high levels of contempt for women in career positions or higher education sit well with pre-industrial (Evans, 1976) and fascist ideology, but they were less fashionable in the 1920s, if only for reasons of upper- and middle-class solidarity. In the highly class-structured Weimar society, men were more likely than now to support the demands of middle- and upper-class women as long as the newly accrued benefits did not flow onto the working class. Some of the Nazi views obviously persisted in the population at large despite the fact that even the Nazis, after 1939, had not in practice been able to eradicate women from the professions (Schenk, 1980: 74), and despite the efforts of feminism in the postwar years.

In some instances, however, a general amnesia about Germany's prewar history had overtaken the population. Records were destroyed, and people exiled. The Bauhaus, which was closed and exiled, has retained a low profile in the Germany of today, while in the USA there is no dearth of information on this significant art movement (Whitford, 1984). Feminism also suffered: women's history, the knowledge of the existence and achievements of the German women's movements of the early 20th century and of the period of the Weimar Republic, was wiped out. Unbelievably, in the 1960s, young West German feminists confessed that they knew absolutely nothing about the women who had fought for women's rights before the war. Thus, in many ways, women of the 1960s and later were not the beneficiaries of the work of the earlier generations of feminists (except for the right to vote). They started afresh, reinventing feminist arguments rather than beginning where their predecessors had left off (Schenk, 1980: 7).

This total break with the past, which was brought to light in the 1970s, made the second-wave movement in West Germany something qualitatively very different to movements in countries where feminist ideas had managed to survive or develop unimpeded. Moreover, Germany's radical and socialist tradition had equally fallen victim to Nazi extermination programmes, at least in West Germany. The story of Marx and Engels, of Rosa Luxemburg and her party colleague and friend Karl Liebknecht, of August Bebel and Clara Zetkin and many more on the socialist left, was appropriated by East Germany, by the new socialist German Democratic Republic (GDR) which was created in the Soviet occupation zone. In April 1946, a historic congress united the two anti-fascist worker's parties, the Socialist Democratic Workers Party and the Communist Party, to form the new Socialist Unity Party of Germany (Sozialistische Einheitspartei Deutschlands—SED). Its aims were to strive 'for the complete eradication of fascism, for the construction of the country on an anti-fascist democratic foundation, as well as for peace and friendship with all nations.' (Zeit im Bild, 1978: 59). The publication is in English and gives a good overview of the legal amendments and policy changes to assure women's access and equity concerning work and life. (For a very brief introductory note on women and the GDR see Morgan, 1984: 241.)

Here, this particular German tradition not only survived but was seen as the true German history from which a new Germany could rise from the ashes. East Germany entirely rejected the responsibility for the atrocities under Hitler, pointing out that there had been another radical Germany that fought as hard against Hitler as possible. On the basis of Engel's, Bebel's and Clara Zetkin's work, the

SED immediately outlined a programme for women's equality: 'The struggle to implement equality for women, which is one of the unalienable demands in the programme of the revolutionary working-class movement, had now become an integral part of our anti-fascist democratic transformation' (SED history, cit. in Zeit im Bild, 1978: 59). We know in the light of recent events, such as the fall of the Berlin Wall in 1989 and the resounding defeat of the SED 40 years after its foundation, that the party, and with it the country, had failed to turn this new German republic into an economically and politically viable state. It remains to be seen how the traditions of East and West Germany will affect each other in future.

Our discussion here concerns only West Germany which, at least from 1949 to 1989, had its own and more or less entirely independent history. In 1949 West Germany was established as a parliamentary democracy (the Federal Republic of Germany—FRG) under the auspices of the Allied Forces (British, US and French). There can be no doubt that the West German exercise in democracy has been successful in the sense of being stable and functional. The political history of West Germany, Roth argued, cannot be understood, however, without taking into account the failure of its first democracy and the experience of nazism (Roth, 1985: 26, 28). West Germany's model of democracy arose not as a result of a bourgeois revolution nor from a grassroots level, but on the Allies' insistence and in response to national socialism, Stalinism and generally the fear of communism. Thus, it was defined almost more as an anti-totalitarian weapon than as a political system in itself. Its guiding principle was the politics of integration into the western bloc, truncating possible political innovation and restructuring from the start. The new regulations were marked by an extreme rigidity and by an attempt to safeguard 'the system' against too much power of the people; such as maintaining the principle of representative elections throughout its new constitution and thereby eliminating direct elections of the president. Notions of and the hopes for a democratic renewal of life, a new humanitarianism and ideas of a reorganisation of property and social innovation were largely thwarted (Brand et al., 1986: 40). The new Christian Democratic Union (CDU)–Adenauer government (1949–1969) was anxious and intent on succeeding economically. Adenauer's foremost goal was to create an unimpeded environment for business. Political openness certainly was not part of the government's political agenda.

The beginning of the Adenauer rule ushered in an unprecedented economic boom. West Germany experienced the longest period of prosperity ever known in a capitalist economy (Fetscher, 1978: 11). This so-called 'economic miracle' of the postwar years, while it baffled economists, was helped by several factors. The Marshall Plan injected substantial funds. Ironically, the total destruction of German industry during the war now helped speed up its modernisation. The Korean War and a belated rearmament also benefited productivity. In addition, West Germany received literally millions of people, either as guest workers or as refugees, who poured into the country, swelling the population from around 46 million at the end of the war to 60 million by the late 1960s. Amongst them were highly qualified people from eastern bloc countries and from East Germany once the GDR was proclaimed. Abelshauser considers this transfer of human capital as one of the chief ingredients of the West German postwar economic success. Between 1952 and 1963, counting only moderately qualified labour, West Germany gained human capital estimated at around 30 billion DM. In addition, around 20 000 engineers and technicians, 4500 medical practitioners and 1000 university teachers were granted the status of political asylum and residency. While this injected the much needed know-how at the right time, the FRG was able to keep its overall training and education budgets at a low level (Abelshauser, 1983: 96).

From the start, West German industry was able to employ the latest technology and build up its potential almost entirely unimpeded by competing international interests or by union claims. Its economic principles of a 'social mixed market economy' (*soziale Marktwirtschaft*) prevented monopolies and price-fixing and gave great weight to entrepreneurs. The postwar years saw the formation of very strong employer associations which began to wield considerable political influence. Union activities, by contrast, remained relatively tame. There were some strike actions in the early postwar years, muted to an extent by the scarcity of commodities and basic food items, but also swept aside by dramatic politic events such as the Blockade of 1948. After the subsiding of a large-scale union strike in 1948, the unions appeared cooperative. This was so for several reasons. National socialism had destroyed the organisations of a class-based workers' movement and, due to a variety of factors such as demographic ones, the former (pre-1933) strength of the labour movement could never be recouped. Furthermore, after 1949 the labour shortage persisted for more than a decade so that employers themselves had to think of ways of attracting labour. Special packages were devised for much sought after labour, such as the thirteenth monthly income per year and a special Christmas bonus. Wages, to a point, were negotiable, at least much more so than in most other EEC countries (Childs & Johnson, 1981: 71). Union and worker representation on committees and boards of directors were introduced, although in a much more limited sense than had been hoped for by the union. It was also in this period, in the late 1950s and throughout the first part of the 1960s, that foreign guest labour and women were enticed into seeking employment.

In the 1950s West German life revolved around the notion of economic progress and fast growth. Indeed, its productivity outstripped prewar output as early as 1949, and growth was maintained throughout the 1950s at the rate of 8 percent per annum. In the 1960s growth slowed to a still-high rate of 4.9 percent per annum. These developments were obviously highly approved of by the majority of the population. In 1957, the Christian Democratic Union (CDU) again won the election and did so with an absolute majority of 52 percent, a rare event in democratic elections. The *political* climate that Adenauer (i.e. the conservative CDU) created in its twenty years of rule was hardly free and cooperative. It was a period of political repression. Any opposition party in which movements and protests of the 1950s were involved, for example, the anti-rearmament movement and the census movement, were destined to be short-lived (Roth, 1985: 32).

In the immediate postwar years, the general wish (and need) for rebuilding the devastated nation lent itself to discipline, order and hard work, which resulted in a stern conformism that continued well after the dictates of survival had been removed. Most West Germans of the 1950s and 1960s, as countless studies have shown, suffered from political apathy and ignorance. Publications by writers such as Horkheimer or Habermas in the early 1960s, for instance, commented that right across the educational and class spectrum people were ignorant of the most basic political structures of both local and international political events, too ignorant in fact to make any political decisions themselves. Pross laments that in such a climate of political apathy democracy itself is at risk because it requires political judgements and a certain degree of identification with the processes of decision making in order to maintain a stable democracy. Society as a whole can become susceptible to and even support authoritarian and anti-democratic solutions to problems (Pross, 1972: 23–26) if it is unaware of when and how the limits of democratic power can be exceeded.

The degree of the postwar boom led initially to a sense of euphoria, so well portrayed in the film *The Marriage of Maria Braun*, and allowed the substantial social costs and political sacrifices to remain largely hidden by-products of a reckless 'bigger and better' philosophy. After all, West Germans had just emerged from a totalitarian system in which everything had been political and politicised. As Fetscher argues, the newly gained individual liberty and the new depoliticised space in which people could just get on with their own business of living was a relief for many (1978: 21). There was a price to be paid but the bills only started arriving from 1967 onwards. Indeed, the CDU was able to extend its powers, in part because the principles and functions of political parties in West Germany are also governed by the constitution, which is rare amongst democratic nations (Childs & Johnson, 1981: 27). Under the guise of protecting liberty and democracy, the government firmly denounced and smothered whatever political debate might have taken place. In 1957 the 5 percent clause was introduced, preventing the entry of smaller parties into government and effectively curtailing the possibility of a multiparty system. Parties which were deemed to be a risk to democracy or to be destructive of the FRG could be declared unconstitutional and therefore vanquished. Thus the Communist Party of Germany (KPD) was banned, following considerable clashes with police. Interestingly, the Soziale Reichspartei, (SRP) a neo-Nazi party, was not initially considered to be a constitutional risk. It was only declared so after Britain insisted on its eradication and it was finally banned in 1952. Later on, other radically right-wing parties such as the German Reichspartei (DRP) or the National Democratic Party (NDP) did not suffer the fate of the SRP (Nagle, 1970). This political climate persisted well into the 1970s despite a gradual shift to the political left.

A change of fortune for the CDU arrived with the first German economic crisis of the postwar years in 1966. Suddenly demand faltered or drastically diminished; the car industry, for instance, suffered a 21 percent downturn of sales that year. Overall, production capacity began to exceed demand over a broad range of consumer items and this had an immediate effect on the labour market. West German economy had more or less operated on full employment throughout the postwar years.

This fact determined the consciousness of the social movements as they erupted in the late 1960s, including the women's movement, even though for the first time the West German economy now experienced a shortage of available work. Unemployment figures, however, did not rise steeply at first, but this was so because guest workers on short contracts from other countries had filled much of the gap in the demand for labour and, where possible, contracts were simply not renewed. In 1967, although 300 000 guest workers lost their jobs, this did not appear in the unemployment statistics. Between 1961 and 1967 the figures of those seeking work and those indicating available work reversed (see table 4.1).

This first crisis heralded what was to become and remain a feature of postwar (late capitalist) economies: periodic unemployment, structural crises in industries and a growing threat of unemployment through automation. These mounting

**Table 4.1   The West German job market in 1961 and 1967**

| Jobs advertised | | No. of unemployed |
| --- | --- | --- |
| 1961 | 536 000 | 161 000 |
| 1967 | 220 000 | 636 000 (+ 300 000 guest workers) |

Source: Mandel, 1969: 22

problems also signalled to some a growing concentration of economic power in a few hands, that is, in 1954 the largest concerns possessed 25.4 percent of total wealth, increasing to 44.5 percent in 1969 (Brand et al., 1985: 43). They also indicated a trend towards the authoritarian state with a reduction of democratic freedoms (Mandel, 1969: 53). Yet the overall stability of German society belied the ever increasing political pressure building up and hiding a profound unease inside its construct of a concensus democracy. This was due, in part at least, to its sudden wealth. To an important degree it also had to do with a political style known for its contempt for and swift measures against dissent. A low trickle of dissent that might have been dissipated by appropriate negotiation was instead harnassed and held back; when the pool of grievances was filled to capacity it broke through the barriers with enormous force.

Thus 1966 saw the formation of a radical oppositional group, called Außerparlamentarische Opposition (APO—extra-parliamentary opposition), which evolved because social critique and political debate were apparently all but dead. The calm that had prevailed for a time, as it turned out, was just the calm before the storm. The Vietnam War, while never highly publicised in the media—and partly ignored for reasons of expediency as the government's interests were directed towards protecting West German export markets to the USA—did attract the attention of a number of left-wing groups and students. The official attitude to the Vietnam War roused anger and criticism in vocal subsections of the community.

Another rather more mundane event a year later set the scene for countless clashes and conflicts to come. It created an atmosphere in which radical groups and substantial numbers of left-wing participants and sympathisers began to see the state as a hostile, alien and punitive power structure that needed to be smashed. The 'we' and 'them' confrontational politics was at first merely an undercurrent but later it almost reached the proportions of a civil war. One of the first occasions was the visit of the Shah of Iran to West Germany in 1967. The Shah's visit had been preceded by bad press denouncing him as a dictator whose army elite and court lived in splendor while his people were poor and starving. Many Iranian dissenters were students in Berlin at that time. A series of mass demonstrations turned at once into violent clashes with police and the Shah's Iranian troops: his personal bodyguards who were not shy of using force in German crowds. Most tragically, an unarmed student (Benno Ohnesorg) was shot dead by a police officer. He was accorded the status of a political martyr, a victim of an oppressive political system. The image of the state and of the police was not helped by the fact that no criminal charges were laid against the police officer who killed the student.

International events at the time also influenced the local mood. There was the Chinese Cultural Revolution, the ghetto and student uprisings in the USA and, closer to home, the 'Spring of Prague', the May Movement revolt in France and similar student uprisings in Italy. It was in this politically explosive climate of 1968 that the German student uprising began. In West Germany, student demonstrations were chiefly under the leadership of the SDS (Socialist German Student Union) and violent clashes with police were recorded on most large city campuses. One of the outstanding public figures in the West German student uprising, Rudi Dutschke, almost suffered the same fate as Benno Ohnesorg. He received bullet wounds to the head, from shots fired not by police but by a right-wing extremist, and barely escaped death. Bloody encounters became the order of the day. Explicit tactics of violence became part of the SDS repertoire. This violence was directed against objects such as cars, buildings, equipment, etc. but not against people. Yet, in one sense, the *risk* of violence against people (i.e. against participants in protests) was almost welcomed as a way of temporarily creating publicity, and as a device for creating antagonism towards the state to foster internal solidarity (i.e. against 'them'). Of course, this is just one view. From another perspective it could be argued that bloody encounters might also have been welcomed by the police as a (common) tactic to help isolate a group, leading to its being crushed.

Clearly, a leftist counter culture was growing in strength and awareness, encouraged by the events internationally and at home. The student uprising of 1968 addressed a number of issues vital to the new postwar generation. Fetscher perhaps goes a little far in psychologising the causes for the uprisings. After the collectivism of Nazi rule, he writes, loneliness and freedom were gladly accepted by the generation that had lived through the Nazi period. To the new generation, however, both were alienating and meaningless, expressing themselves as 'spiritual dissatisfaction' and 'spiritual unrest' (Fetscher, 1978: 21). This assessment is, I think, rather esoteric and it diverts the focus from the real issues at hand at that time. The university system was indeed in urgent need of reform, the authoritarianism of the *entire* educational system, to many, was unbearably inappropriate for the *democratic* model the postwar political system had formally proposed. The hopelessly pre-modern orientation of universities that had restored an academic cast with all professional privileges intact (Roth, 1985: 35), was indeed inappropriate for modern educational and social needs. Ironically, the student uprising of 1968 originated from the Free University of Berlin, the one West German university which had been founded after the war as an explicitly democratic institution. Its constitution 'included equal rights, open and non-discriminatory education'. But it was here that foreign students, largely Arabs and Algerians who sought asylum, were treated with contempt by officialdom (Cohen, 1983: 303–4). The students understood that the ideals were not translated into practice and that they did not seem to apply in West German society in general.

There was also the problem of Germany's '*unbewältigte Vergangenheit*' (unresolved past). Students felt that there was far too little, if any, critical debate apart from literary works such as Wolfgang Borchert's *Draußen von der Tür*, Günter Grass' *The Tin Drum*, some works by Heinrich Böll (e.g. *Das Brot der frühen Jahre*) and Siegfried Lenz (*Die Deutschstunde*), the intellectual presence of the Frankfurt School of Sociology and the critical theory of such men as Adorno, Horkheimer and the early Habermas. The fascist past was treated as a 'closed book'. Such omissions were not without repercussions for the younger generation. As this new generation well understood, West Germany had an historical heritage that was, internationally at least, scandalously irreputable. The challenge to the authority of the state was a challenge to the parents who had obviously been part of a system of terror. These past, unatoned deeds and the silence surrounding them had left the new generation in a void. Partly because it was almost impossible to escape the unmentionable past, it was difficult for the new generation to build a positive national identity, free from the guilt (assumed or real) of parents or the parents' generation. The student protests in the late 1960s were born out of frustration and were a belated sign that the new generation no longer wished to be weighed down by parental history.

The direction of the leftist counter culture was inspired by enlightenment ideas and the SDS projected itself as an emancipatory and egalitarian movement. The idea of emancipatory educational concepts, for instance, took hold very quickly and resulted in the very rapid formation of so-called *Kinderläden* (children shops), child-minding centres to which children could come freely (Doormann, 1983: 239). Within the SDS women began to form their own women's councils with the explicit aim of fostering the liberation of women (1969). The reason for the creation of such councils, which were abolished once the new women's movement was under way, lay in the perception of their role within the SDS. They noticed quite rightly that there was a substantial difference between the emancipatory, egalitarian speeches of their male 'comrades' and their actual behaviour towards their female 'comrades' (Schenk, 1980: 84). Women continued to type the speeches and make coffee while their male colleagues discussed politics (Schmidt-Harzbach, 1981: 227).

## The new women's movement

The beginning of the new women's movement in West Germany dates from around 1971. In 1971 the single most outstanding 'movement event' was the publication of a letter in the magazine *Der Stern*, in which 374 women, among them well-known figures, all publicly announced 'I have aborted', at a time when abortion was a punishable crime. In another magazine, *Der Spiegel*, 329 doctors signed that they had performed abortions (illegally). Clearly, abortion was perceived as an issue of great importance. In 1969 alone, the number of illegal abortions was estimated to have been between 350 000 and 1 million (Beyer et al., 1983: 9). These 'confessions' created a furore in the media and amongst the general public, sparking off demonstrations against paragraph 218 of the Penal Code (*Strafgesetzbuch*), against which feminists in the Weimar Republic had already rallied. Throughout West Germany, it brought tens of thousands of women into the streets (Doormann, 1983: 241). In March 1972 a women's congress was organised which had an unexpected attendance of about 400 women. The congress turned into a tumultuous affair in which pent-up emotions and enormous energy reserves were unleashed (Schenk, 1980: 84).

The first phase of the movement (1972–1975) was dominated by the issue of abortion, or rather, solidarity of women was created around paragraph 218. In 1972, the first handbook on abortion and contraception was published by the women's organisation which, like its Norwegian sister, was called Brot und Rosen (Bread and Roses). Mass demonstrations recurred throughout that year, climaxing in 1973 in the march on Bonn, the political capital of West Germany, where over 5000 women gathered to demand abortion law reforms. Surveys taken at the time showed that more than 60 percent of West German women were against paragraph 218.

Of course, West German women also had other immediate concerns, such as the oppressive nature of the church and its influence on the reactionary politics of West Germany at the time. These fostered the sudden formation and growth of a multitude of women's groups and women's organisations. A mass exodus from the church made women's position quite clear. This act of leaving the church was regarded as a very radical move indeed. Yet the unifying spirit of the movement at first rested on the abortion paragraph. Despite the strength of this issue, however, signs of polarisation in the movement became visible almost from the start. On the one hand, there were socialist women who relied on the Marxist classical authors and sought links with working-class women, on the other were groups which relied more on the feminist literature from the USA, delving into theoretical issues of patriarchy and forming consciousness-raising groups.

The second phase of the new women's movement (1975–1979) was defined by a number of caesuras, one of which affected West German life in general. In 1974/5 an economic crisis worse than that experienced in 1966 hit the country. The first crisis had ultimately ousted the CDU from government and had brought about the election of the moderately left-wing Social Democratic Party of Germany (SDP) in 1969. Although the new crisis did not bring down the SPD government, it changed its position and, along with other important political events in the early 1970s (discussed later), helped to change the political climate. As briefly alluded to in chapter 3, the economic crisis was not confined to West Germany but gripped most of western Europe and capitalist markets elsewhere, partly as a consequence of the oil crisis in 1973. In April 1975 in EEC countries alone there were 4 million people unemployed, of which over 1 million were in West Germany and Italy (Gamble and Walton, 1976: 415).

The other important caesura which occurred within the movement itself was brought about by the fate of the abortion issue. Abortion as an issue had finally been taken up by the political parties and drafts were prepared for an amendment of paragraph 218, and put to the test in federal court. It was there that the unbelievable happened: in 1975 the application for amendment was defeated. The years of lobbying it seemed, had been in vain. After this defeat the movement, although it did not disperse, lost direction and in fact never regained its former strength (Doormann, 1983: 243).

The government made a clear statement that it was not going to be coerced into political action by a social movement in favour of just one interest group. Expressed differently, the thread of authoritarianism in German politics, never too far below the surface, showed again with an insistence on law and order well supported by a pre-modern, pre-democratic professional public service apparatus and a conservative legal body.

One of the main features of this second phase was the movement's political retreat. Some critical commentators noted that feminists were not just behaving appallingly apolitically but that they were also doing nothing to help the women who most needed help during the economic crisis (Doormann, 1979: 60). Instead of taking up these causes, women of the movement spent time in highly psychologised consciousness-raising groups which were influenced by US feminism. Political activity diminished in favour of cultural feminism. Feminist literary and scholarly publications became prolific. This second phase also saw a concentration on women's projects. This project movement, if nothing else, was a variant of the alternative lifestyle movement at the time. Its importance lay in the creation of a large network of women's services and the outward manifestation of a strong, separate women's culture. Separate bookshops, journals, magazines, calendars, publishing houses, and cabaret, film and music groups were formed. Journals like *Courage*, now defunct, had a circulation of 70 000. A magazine for women and about women's issues, called *Emma*, started in 1977 by Alice

Schwarzer, almost immediately had a circulation of 120 000 and is still going strongly today. Women's refuges became another project. The first one went into operation in Berlin in 1976. By 1979, fourteen such projects existed and by 1982 there were 99 refuges throughout West Germany (with a population of 61 million people). Feminist therapy and health centres came into existence and in 1976 the first women's summer university programmes were offered in Berlin, which attracted and still attract large numbers of women. In this period, a new democratic women's organisation was formed and grew quickly, but it was at odds with other feminist groups.

It was a specific characteristic of the West German women's movement that its leading feminist activities emanated from networks which called themselves 'autonomous'. There was no centre, no central organisation and no official spokespersons for the movement. While this had been a conscious decision, based on a deep mistrust of hierarchy and hierarchically run institutions and organisations, the absence of a centre made it also more difficult for the movement to gain political clout. Contact between groups from one town, city or state and the next were incidental (Schenk, 1980: 113). The movement as a whole fared rather badly in those years, both within its own factions as well as with the media. According to Tröger, the mass media presented a distorted, myopic and often downright hostile image of the women's movement (1978: 178) and there was no one in particular who could act as a spokesperson for the movement in order to eradicate the misconceptions, distortions and outright untruths. Furthermore, the liberal women's movement and the autonomous socialist movement never saw eye-to-eye. The liberal faction regarded the socialist position with 'mistrust and even enmity' and every leftist woman was suspected of 'harbouring a male comrade' (Schlaeger, 1978: 63).

Hilke Schlaeger sees in those years a 'deplorable de-politicising of the movement', partly demonstrated in its inability and unwillingness to overcome internal rifts and struggle together for goals common to women throughout West German society, and partly in its inability to tackle the class bias. In her view, the movement was only for privileged and well-to-do women who had little interest in the affairs of the socially disadvantaged (1978: 63–4, 66). Indeed, neither faction of the women's movement in West Germany, unlike the women's movement in the USA, took the most downtrodden of all women into its fold or fought in any specific way on their behalf. The large number of foreign guest-worker women was never made part of the movement. This, Feree suggested recently, was largely the result of a fundamental prejudice against other cultures (such as the Turkish culture): the belief that women from those backgrounds were backward and helpless within their own cultures and thus presumably not capable of useful collaboration within the movement (1987: 178). There were feminists who participated in giving guest-worker women and their children German-language classes, and helped and supported these de-culturalised children (no longer part of their own culture and rejected by their new culture) in kindergartens and creches. Apparently, some shelters for migrant women were set up but, in general, there was little integration into the movement. By the late 1980s there were hopeful signs of changes in attitude, accompanied by a new steady flow of immigrants and refugees. The German Women's Council (Deutscher Frauenrat) in a meeting in November 1988 adopted an agenda endorsing the view that the situation of migrant women had to be improved (*Women of Europe*, no. 47, Nov.–Dec. 1988: 15).

The third phase of the movement (1979–1982) saw a revitalisation in political terms and a dissemination of political alternative movements in which women played a crucial role. Gassen said somewhat apologetically that the politicisation of West German women was a slow process partly because it seemed generally frowned upon for women to become political (Doering, 1981: 46; Gassen, 1981: 219). There were two immediate concerns in 1979. One was once again the abortion paragraph. Although the amendment had been defeated in 1975, it was finally accepted in 1977. Instead of the simple time-clause solution (*Fristenlösung*), however, the amendment restricted legal abortion to specific categories and conditions (*Indikationslösung*). This regulation allowed women to have an abortion in specific situations—for grave health reasons, eugenic and/or circumstantial problems, as for instance, pregnancy resulting from rape, or for severe social or psychological reasons. Politically and legally, this amendment was much more vulnerable to further (reactionary) amendments than any law which had put the right of control and responsibility into women's hands. Women were well aware of this when, in 1979, the paragraph once again came under attack by the conservative CDU. The second concern arose when Joseph Strauß, an extremely right-wing mysogynist member of the Bavarian Christian Social Union (CSU) in 1979 was put up as a candidate for the position of federal chancellor. This stirred women from the various factions of the movement into action because it was clear that the abortion law reform and any other positive change that might have occurred for women would come under threat and could be lost entirely.

Interrelated with the Strauß threat, which was averted when the SPD won the elections again, came another issued by the army (*die Bundeswehr*). It ushered in a new, strong political movement. The army announced in 1978 that it took women's emancipation seriously and intended to see women conscripted to the army in the same way as men, that is, for a compulsory military service of eighteen months. The answer to this idea, considered preposterous by most West German women, was very prompt and in May 1979 resulted in a series of demonstrations which did more than just register a protest. It signalled, in fact, the beginning of a new movement and in a way 'saved' the flagging women's movement from petering out. The army's proposal was unmasked as yet another ploy for armament and militarisation of West German society and as a purposeful misconstruction of women's fight for equality.

In Hamburg and Cologne large anti-military and anti-nuclear congresses of the women's movement were held and thousands of women pledged their solidarity. By 1980, the West German contribution to the international women's peace movement was substantial. During the UN world women's conference in 1980, 'women for peace' organisations presented General Secretary Waldheim with 500 000 signatures of European women against nuclear weapons and militarism. Women argued that the money being squandered on militaristic expenditures should be used to give women the much needed chance for equality (Doormann, 1983: 265 ff). This opposition, particularly against nuclear power stations and nuclear weaponry, steadily drew wider circles and began to spread across West Germany, involving men and women alike. One of the many widely publicised actions took place in Brokdorf in February 1981. The action, taken in reprisal for the intention to build a nuclear power station, was based on the principles of the US civil rights movement of non-violent resistance (Kleinert, 1981); and there were other such demonstrations, such as in Grohnde, Kalkar and Gorleben.

The fourth phase of the women's movement (1982–present) in a sense is one that is least identifiable as a movement. It has few if any individual 'movement events'. The trend towards right-wing values, resulting partly from repeated economic problems and crises of overproduction, saw the reelection of the CDU in 1982 after thirteen years in opposition. The very things women had feared in 1979 when Strauß was a candidate for the position of chancellor now happened anyway. The Kohl governments were not noted for emancipatory policies. At the same time there were also voices amongst feminists who played directly into the hands of the conservatives. The CDU resolved to minimise the unemployment problem chiefly by a concerted but oblique policy to coax women out of the workforce and back into the home. Unfortunately, since the late 1970s, a new motherhood ideology had also developed within feminist ranks which could now be very easily incorporated into reactionary politics. Women themselves created the new motherhood mythology, by demanding a fair recognition of 'special qualities' (Beck-Gernsheim, 1984).

Even if in some ways the conservative parties and the opinions of some feminists coincided, the overall CDU women's policy package was not in the interest of women. Some of the similarities between the party and the ideas of feminists were too great to be accidental: the CDU advocated child allowance and some feminists lobbied for wages for housework; the CDU lamented the drop in birthrate and feminist factions began to glorify motherhood. Schlaeger rightly recognised in 1978 that the movement itself had developed traits that were reactionary (1978: 64). One might add that the 'special qualities' perspective had been adopted by the Nazis and on it their politics for women had rested entirely. Again, the issue is tricky and to date unresolved, for on one hand, the assignment of specific roles could logically lead to exclusion of other roles, as it did under fascism generally; on the other hand, the formation of a new identity was not and should not be tied to specific role concepts. Judging by the sudden jump in the sale of books on mothering, breastfeeding and the like, one wonders how far the distinction is made.

If this new feminist 'special value' perspective failed to acquire a prominent status, this probably had to do with the increasing politicisation of yet another movement. Apart from the peace movement, but to some extent interrelated with it, there was the ecological movement which had also gained credence, if rather belatedly in comparison to other countries. West German women saw that there was a connection between their claims for emancipation, the environment, peace and the programmes of destruction both in the military and economic camps. And here, for the first time in the history of the FRG, the protest of a movement achieved a measure of success in entering politics. In the formation phase of the Green Party, with such people as Rudolf Bahro, Rudi Dutschke and Herbert Gruhl, ecological and feminist considerations became explicit concerns. In 1983, the Greens were not just the first new party to enter the parliament (*Bundestag*) in 30 years of West German history but women, usually feminists, were part of this new political structure. In 1984 and 1985 all of the Green Party's leadership consisted of women.

*Terrorism and its effect on the women's movement*

The West German women's movement and its limitations cannot be understood without some reference to the political extremism and to terrorist activities from the late 1960s through to the first half of the 1980s. One suspects that these activities, which ran parallel to and sometimes overlapped with the women's protests, did the movement a great deal of harm and sapped some of its energies. The phenomenon of terrorism, claimed one writer, was used 'to cast aspersions on and actively suppress criticism of the government from liberals, leftists and feminists' (Jacobs, 1978: 165). Extremist activities at times stole the limelight from feminist action. On other occasions, the public confused the origins of these public acts and wrongly attributed violent actions to feminists, so that politically less astute observers ultimately blamed any dissent on the one conglomerous group of 'radicals' against whom the government should act.

Right and left extremist groups in West Germany had several elements in common, one of which was the youthful average age of their members. Of those who were tried before the courts, 72 percent of extreme-right terrorist groups were under the age of 30, with as many as 40 percent under the age of 20. The remaining 28 percent were usually well over 40 years old and had been active supporters of the Nazis. In extreme left-wing organisations, the age profile was consistently young (86 percent under the age of 30) with few, if any, over the age of 40. Very few were under 20 years old (9 percent). Thus, the overwhelming majority of terrorists in either camp belonged to the generations which were born after World War II, mostly at a time when the rebuilding of cities and towns and the worst postwar hardships were over. These were the children of the 'economic miracle' (*Wirtschaftswunderkinder*).

Both groups concentrated their efforts on a fundamental but rather abstract attack against the capitalist state and specifically against democracy, albeit for very different reasons. Right extremist groups regarded democracy (and socialism) as decadent and, for Germans, as *alien* forms of rule which ought to be smashed and rebuilt to accommodate a strong *Führer*. Extremist groups were not alone in that opinion. In 1981, a representative large-scale survey found that 20 percent of all those interviewed agreed with the statement 'We should have a *Führer* again' (Sinus, 1981: 215). They generally extolled the Nazi regime and revelled in racism, but this time, in the absence of Jews (Kaplan, 1989: 72–3), it was expressed as a hatred of foreigners and guest workers and a fear of racial mixing with Turks, Yugoslavs or other 'foreign races'. Left-wing terrorist groups by contrast had concrete political grievances, often shared by feminists and other left-wing groups. They accused the government of not being democratic enough, and regarded the parliamentary system as corrupt and its politics in domestic and foreign affairs as warped by authoritarian, imperialist and capitalist self-interests. Many of the methods for maintaining the sanctified 'law and order', they argued, were illegal within the terms of the democratic constitution, such as the police raids and handing over defenders for trial. West Germany's membership in NATO, and the government's kowtowing to it, were seen as a symbol of US imperialism. Left-wing extremists particularly objected to the US nuclear weaponry that was to be installed on West German soil. In its social and economic policies at home, the government was accused of acting more or less exclusively on behalf of employer interests rather than on behalf of the population as a whole. A broad spectrum of those on the political left, including feminists, found it easy to sympathise with these objections, and indeed often shared them, if at a more sophisticated level. Yet most shunned the violent methods as too extreme. Furthermore, these acts of violence, especially against people, often had the opposite effect of making the extremists and their cause odious to the wider public.

In the late 1960s the left-wing Red Army Faction (RAF), was formed with Andreas Baader and Ulrike Meinhof, and almost immediately assumed political terrorist action (Baumann, 1977). In 1967 a bomb was found in America House in Berlin, a message of disapproval against US imperialism. A year later two large shopping complexes in Frankfurt were set aflame as a protest against the 'consumer terror'. In another set of mass demonstrations, bombs, stones and abuse were hurled against the Alex Springer publishing house in Berlin because it had sharply condemned the demonstrations and the violence used in them. This act was largely attributed to socialist students (SDS), but apparently had also involved the Baader–Meinhof Gang, as it came to be called. These activities marked the beginning of a long drawn-out battle lasting into the 1980s between the RAF, other terrorist groups and the authorities, expressed in guerilla tactics, extensive property damage, highjackings, murders and extortions. The 1970s were dominated by left-wing extremists while the 1980s saw more right-wing terrorism. 1977 is generally regarded as the peak year of the confrontations with left-wing extremism (Mayer, 1978). Apart from 1973, every year of the decade saw victims of terrorist acts (a total death toll of 23). In the same period, thirteen young people, students, terrorists and demonstrators were killed or found dead. Most of the terrorists died in prison, all allegedly having committed suicide, a few of whom, it was known, starved to death as a consequence of hunger strikes. Amongst these was Holgar Meins, one of the RAF members, who died in prison in 1974. Like Benno Ohnesorg, Meins was widely mourned as a martyr and seen as a symbol of a system whose injustice and inhumanity, according to the sympathisers, were rightly 'under fire'. Right-wing terrorist acts were particularly prevalent in the early 1980s. In 1980 and 1982 there were cases of arson and bombings of guest-worker homes, murders of foreigners, the murder of a Jewish publisher and the bombing of the Munich *Oktoberfest*.

Unfortunately, the government's response to all these activities was similarly aggressive and ushered in a counter-terror which was widely felt throughout West German society. For a period of at least five years (1972–1977), at the height of the women's movement, those events led to judiciary and other changes which can only be described as anti-democratic. There were also violent reprisals, such as the so-called Radical's Decree (*Radikalenerlaß*) of 1972 which gave the state significant legal powers. Issued under the social democrats, it set into motion a horrible Salem-like witch hunt, repeating with at least as much venom as the McCarthy era in the USA the horrors of a 'suspicion hysteria'. In 1976, Peter Weiss, one of the foremost German-language playwrights, published an article in a New York journal called: 'Joe McCarthy is alive and well in West Germany. Terror and counter-terror in the Federal Republic'. Indeed, the Radicals' Decree opened the door to a misuse of power. While it was meant to eradicate anti-democratic forces, it became itself an anti-democratic instrument, expressed chiefly through the activities of secret police and the Office for the Protection of the Constitution (*Bundesverfassungsschutz*), which was empowered to search and investigate people on the faintest suspicion of left-wing sympathies and anti-constitutional activities.

The Radicals' Decree was no doubt an overreaction and entirely unnecessary as a measure of fighting terrorist acts. The criminal code covered well all the offences committed by terrorist groups and these crimes could have been dealt with in the same manner as any other criminal offence. The Radicals' Decree was obviously more than merely a measure to capture the offenders but a reprisal against radicalism of all sorts. Radicals were declared enemies of the constitution and fought as enemies of the FRG, a move which only too clearly showed that the government wanted to get at the submerged networks of the radical movements and to eradicate even the vaguest sympathetic leanings. Ultimately, it demonstrated that this new German democratic state was not yet ready to behave democratically when put to the test. It could not take any criticism, or as a book title of 1978 aptly suggested, these crises constituted *The Puberty of the Republic* (Jungwirth & Kromschröder, 1978).

Mayer thought that the government suffered from a paranoid need for allegiance (1978: 163). Such demand for allegiance to the state was seen in totally black-and-white terms. Either one was for or against this state and, in the case of the latter, one had to be officially branded an enemy against whom the state could rally seemingly at will. That indeed is the behaviour of a totalitarian rather than of a democratic state. The terrorists had overstepped their rights and no democratic government need tolerate such grave infringements. The Radicals' Decree, however, left the door wide open for the judiciary, the police and the secret police to define an 'enemy of the state' in the widest possible terms. Margret Mitscherlich wrote in those years: 'Whoever dares to express criticism of circumstances and laws in the Federal Republic ... is in danger of being categorised as a so-called "sympathiser"' (see Jacobs, 1978: 165). At the height of the hysteria, the status of sympathiser and enemy of the state could be acquired by being a member of or fraternising with legal left-wing parties, by signing petitions and attending demonstrations.

The mobility of the women's movement was of course more than just hampered by the new law. It put members of the movement at risk both in their jobs and even in their private lives. Women's centres which were involved in organising abortion trips to the Netherlands were regularly raided by police for 'supporting criminal organisations'. Teachers, of whom half were women, who had ex-pressed or shown any left-wing sympathies were dismissed or were not employed. The Office for the Protection of the Constitution screened well over one million people throughout West Germany. It had permission to declare a black ban on public employees, such as teachers, who were denied the right to practise their vocation if they were found to have any radical tendencies (*Berufsverbot*). In all, it initiated and succeeded in obtaining the dismissal of around 4000 people (Jacobs, 1978: 165–67). In 1978, a women's congress was called in Frankfurt with the telling title 'The Women's Movement and Political Oppression in the Federal Republic of Germany'.

There were a whole host of judiciary changes and prohibitions which, in essence, constituted infringements to democratic, civil rights and were open to abuse by the judiciary, by secret police and the courts. It was a kind of 'martial law' declaration that curtailed freedom of speech and, without any doubt, severely interfered with people's freedom of alliance and freedom of thought. It was a time when students, with plans of becoming teachers, were usually too afraid to enrol in courses identified as left wing or Marxist, which were all but wiped off the curriculum. Books were confiscated, such as *Wie es Begann* (How it all began) written in 1977 by Bommi Baumann, an early member of the RAF. The secret police conducted countless raids and house searches, sometimes with the flimsiest of excuses; for instance, the house of Heinrich Böll's son was searched simply because he was the son of one of West Germany's most famous, prolific and critical writers. Another writer, Luise Rinser, had her house searched because ten years prior to the terrorist trials she had once been interviewed by the selfsame Ulrike Meinhof who later became a terrorist (Fetscher, 1978: 84–101). The police training for street combat was stepped up and more equipment and weaponry for the dispersal of demonstrations was acquired. At court, confiscated material, up to then only available to the judge, was handed over to the prosecution. Defending lawyers could be excluded from a trial and dismissed from a case if doubt arose about their allegiance to the state. The mere suspicion of being a 'sympathiser' was enough. A trial could be commenced without the presence of the defendant (a measure against the terrorist hunger strikers in prison) and unlike the court rules in other countries such as the USA, could not be reopened once the defendant had recovered from his/her indisposition. The idea of a trial in absentia of a defendant has very wide implications indeed. Crown witnesses against terrorists generally obtained amnesty, and for self-confessed murderers a maximum of three years jail was offered in exchange for information on other terrorists. State (*Land*) governments now declared political organisations as unconstitutional when they had no power to do so (it had been reserved for the federal courts to deal with matters of the FRG constitution).

The power of the RAF and other extremist organisations was declared broken by about 1984. Most of the leftist terrorist leaders were dead (none of the right-wing extremists was, however). The job practice prohibition (*Berufsver*bot) was withdrawn, and once the frenzy was over the West German state seemed to return to normal. None of the legal changes was rescinded, however, and count-less writers have since suggested that the terrorist activities were merely used so that the state could acquire powers that it should not possess in a democracy. After all, the extremist groups were numerically very small. The number of deaths they brought about over a fifteen-year period was much smaller than the number of fatal car accidents each year. The importance of the RAF and later of the 2nd June Movement (Bewegung 2. Juni) was totally overrated and as groups they had little significance other than that given to them by the govern-ment. (Since the reunification of Germany in 1990, the RAF has made a 'come back' and claimed responsibility for at least one murder.) It is important to note how the state reacted and failed vis-à-vis a series of crises that in themselves were no real threat to democracy, as the federal Ministry for Domestic Affairs seemed to suggest (*Bundesministerium*, 1982).

It is noteworthy that in very few other western European countries has there been such persistent protest actions by young people over such a long span of time, almost uninterrupted for two entire decades and running parallel with the women's movement. In the third phase of the women's movement (1979–1982) for instance, there was yet another movement apart from the peace and the ecological movements, namely that of the 'house occupiers'. The protesters here were not just students but apprentices and young unemployed. At the peak of this movement in 1981, about 500 privately owned houses were taken over by these 'squatters'. The protest concerned the unchecked and officially condoned speculative exploitation of real estate. Through special taxation rebates it was actually encouraged. At a time of an acute housing shortage and high rental costs, there were houses left empty or, in a state of delapidation, rented out to foreigners at exorbitant prices. Those practices the protesters considered ex-ploitative and as exacerbating the difficult housing situation.

The women's movement had its own new and specific grievances which were based on a new consciousness and on a recognition of the failings of democracy, as it pertained to women. Our consideration of events in other political quarters has merely highlighted the fact that women had to conduct their protests under what, at times, were extraordinarily difficult circumstances. The women's move-ment has never used violence, although for a brief period the frustration levels and the anger reached such levels that some began to toy with the idea (Plogstedt,

1984: 336). The small Red Zora splinter group (women who practised armed resistance) never became influential. The new women's peace movement and the ecological movement have not just carefully avoided violent conflict; in the tradition of the civil rights protests they have made non-violence part of their strategy and platform.

## The status of women in West Germany today

By the late 1980s the nation had made some crucial amendments to its laws and attitudes, if only falteringly or belatedly. Corporal punishment in schools was abolished in 1971. Divorce law and general family law reforms in 1976 eradicated the notion that women had the right to seek gainful employment only if this did not conflict with the interests of their families. To all intents and purposes women are equal within the family, and within society at large, but the translation into practice is certainly less evident here than in the Scandinavian countries. West German women are less likely to seek employment outside the home and part-time jobs are not easy to find. They are less likely to be actively involved in politics than their Scandinavian neighbours and less likely to be seen in leading positions and in the professions.

More importantly, the West German commitment to social welfare has remained largely reactive and geared towards repairing the worst ravages of the free-market economy rather than towards providing a net of services as a right for all. The West German welfare net, while in some ways excellent by international standards, is certainly not knit as tightly as in Scandinavian countries, and it is far easier to fall through that net and suffer the miseries of poverty and deprivation than in the north of Europe. Thus, the structured inequalities tend not to be minimised as in Scandinavian countries and this has a number of immediate consequences for women.

In social services that benefit women and families it becomes apparent how vulnerable and how dependent on government philosophy they are. In West Germany, services in general fall under federal government funding and therefore have been at risk since public spending cuts were deemed a necessary measure in the economic crises that have beset the West German economy at a rather regular rate. The SPD under Helmut Schmidt began a process which was continued in a more concerted fashion by the Kohl government after 1982. Rationalisation of the bureaucracy, continuous cuts in the service sector, even though pertaining to all social groups, have hit women hardest and have partly obliterated the gains that had been made in the 1970s. There have been cuts in special apprenticeship, work and retraining education programmes for women, unemployment benefit, child endowment and rental rebates. Creches and kindergartens, while expanding in Scandinavian countries, are being shut down again in West Germany. The so-called nought-tariff for low income-earning parents of preschool and kindergarten children was abolished again. Fees for such childminding and pre-education services have drastically increased while such services as women's health centres, refuges, family advisory programmes, even education and youth centres have all experienced some, often severe, pruning to their budgets in the 1980s. Women's archives are barely funded, if at all (Nienhaus, 1981: 28). In all these cases, financial stringency has been given as the reason for the cuts.

In some cases it is not even clear whether West German governments regard some service features, for which feminists had asked, as *legitimate*. The women's refuge movement is a case in point and the fight here is certainly not over. When the first refuges opened, the initiators had to 'prove' that violence against women existed, that such violence was neither welcomed or condoned by women and was not a woman's fault or the result of her 'masochism' and/or an element in her sexual pleasure. Moreover, federal social security law does not know such values as autonomy and equality. According to the pertinent law of the Penal Code (paragraph 72), women who have escaped from domestic violence are legally regarded as being in the same category as those who have just been released from prison. They are classed as being incapable of handling their own affairs, and are therefore in need of close state supervision and scrutiny (Beyer et al., 1983: 93).

A lack of commitment to the ideal of equality is reflected clearly in the way women's position at work has been handled in the postwar period. Changes towards greater gender equity were half-hearted and slow. The West German Basic Law of 1949 made equal rights provisions for women but in reality these were never taken seriously (Schuster, 1982, Ferree, 1987: 177). In 1973, a 'women and society' commission was formed to enquire into the status of West German women. This body lingered on despite the EEC equal-pay and equal-treatment directives of 1975–76. As late as 1980, a law on equality for women in the labour market was introduced, but apparently only under duress by the EEC directives (Lovenduski, 1986: 273). Objections to women's treatment in industry were in fact not articulated very strongly by women themselves, partly because a 'separate but equal' tradition had existed for a long time. It had supposedly been introduced to 'protect' women. Thus, in order to safeguard their health, women were excluded from certain heavy work and even from entire industries, such as mining and construction. Criticism against the protection view, as a means of keeping women in low-paid jobs (*Leichtlohngruppen*) has only been raised more frequently in recent years (Lappe, 1981; Slupik, 1982; Demmer et al., 1983).

After the initial influx in the 1950s and 1960s, women's participation in the workforce has not appreciably altered (an increase overall of 1 percent) throughout the 1980s (*Fischer Weltalmanach* 1982; 1987: 538; 1989: 191). If there was any increase in women's participation, it was in the part-time sector, gradually rising from 3.9 percent in 1960 to 24 percent in 1983. In the last five years, however, available part-time work has been on the decline again and this will have an effect particularly on women with small and school-aged children.

In the late 1970s a new concept of part-time work, 'the capacity-oriented variable work time' (*kapazitätsorientierte variable Arbeitszeit*, abbreviated to *Kapovaz*), was introduced with the idea of creating and maintaining an on-call reserve army of labour which could be mobilised at differing rates of capacity so that labour needs would be 'fine-tuned' in accordance with productivity requirements at any given time. For obvious reasons, the scheme was greeted with great enthusiasm by employers. The pool of workers/employees/special-skill personnel was conceived of as a roster system which required the potential casual employee to remain at home near a telephone for the time allotted on the roster, irrespective of whether he or she would be called in to work. There were no provisions for reimbursement for the waiting time. Most of these rostered casual employees were women and, perhaps not surprisingly, it took the unions the better part of six years before they openly rejected the scheme as one being solely in favour of employers and heavily slanted against the interests of employees. The system was still in operation in the late 1980s and, although some

Table 4.2   **Percentage of women and men in part-time work in 1983 in select western European countries**

| Country | Women | Men |
|---|---|---|
| Sweden | 46 | 7 |
| Denmark | 43 | 2 |
| England | 38 | 1 |
| West Germany | 24 | 1 |
| France | 15 | 2 |
| Italy | 6 | 1 |

*Source*: *Aktuell*, 1984: 659

legislation has prevented the worst abuses of this situation for employees, it remains an ethically dubious practice.

Women's strongest presence in the self-employed groups, altogether accounting for over half of all those earning an income in this category, suggests that the private sector, that is employers in secondary and tertiary industries, have not been very keen on employing women. A women's congress on economic power and women, which was held in November 1988 in Berlin, ascertained that less than 1 percent of women employees in West Germany hold key positions in private companies, that is, less than 2000 of a total of 52 000 key positions censused (*Women of Europe*, 57, Nov/Dec. 1988: 16). Instead of seeking admission to employment from the state, however, they have opted for taking the initiative themselves with other family members. An area in which women now have a very high profile is the hospitality business. Roughly 50 percent of restaurant management permits were granted to women in the late 1980s, two-thirds of restaurant employees and almost half of all chefs in German restaurants are now women (*Women of Europe*, 47, 1988: 16). One might suspect that the impetus came partly from the strongly perceived disadvantages and discrimination practised at workplaces in general, a problem that could only be avoided if the woman became her own boss. The *courage* to undertake such business ventures, as well as a profound distaste for any form of discrimination, may well have come from the activities of the women's movement. The number of women who registered their own businesses in the 1970s and 1980s could attest to this.

Women's participation in union elites and representation from industries in which women constitute the majority of workers is low, although some small signs of change have become noticeable at the level of membership recruitment. Generally, women's presence in union elites is as low as parliamentary membership of women in the most conservative parties. It is questionable, however, whether membership in West German union elites is an effective political channel for the pursuit of change in women's affairs. Unions are considerably weaker organisations in West Germany than, for instance, in Italy or Denmark. Women's voices in union matters are in themselves rather weak because most West German women work in self-employed categories, either in independently run businesses or helping in family ventures, and therefore they are numerically strongest in groups that would seek affiliation in employer organisations rather than in employee groups (see table 4.3).

In matters of reproduction, the German catholic tradition is still more than faintly noticeable. It is true that abortion has been decriminalised. As in England and Switzerland, however, the law attempts to limit the use of the service by

**Table 4.3　Labour status of women in the West German economy, 1969 and 1977**

|  | 1969 | 1977 |
|---|---|---|
| Category | % | % |
| Self employed | 20.5 | 20.6 |
| Helping in family business | 83.9 | 86.3 |
| Tenured public servants (incl. teachers) | 15.1 | 16.3 |
| White-collar workers | 48.9 | 51.3 |
| Blue-collar workers | 27.6 | 28.4 |

*Source*: Childs and Johnson,1981: 182

**Table 4.4　Abortion incidence and rate in selected countries (1980)**

| Country | Abortion incidence | Abortion rate in % (women aged 15–44 ) |
|---|---|---|
| West Germany | +– 300 000 | 2.28 |
| France | +– 250 000 | 2.21 |
| Denmark | 23 300 | 2.13 |
| Sweden | 34 800 | 2.05 |
| Italy | 222 400 | 1.88 |
| England and Wales | 128 900 | 1.13 |
| Switzerland | 14 900 | 1.07 |
| Netherlands | 19 700 | 0.62 |

*Source*: adapt. from Ketting & van Praag,1986:163. Most of these figures are estimates.

declaring that it is up to the law and the medical profession to decide whether a woman has sufficient reason for a termination of pregnancy. Ketting and van Praag have recently shown, however, that restrictions in the abortion law do not achieve the purpose of the law-makers and do not necessarily correlate with social custom. In the Netherlands, where abortion on request is accepted practice, the rate of abortion is the lowest in Europe. West Germany, on the other hand, despite its restrictions, has almost the same rate of abortions as Sweden with its extremely liberal laws (1986: 163) (see table 4.4).

The law is thus not entirely workable in practice and the many forms of by-passing authorities indicate that laws, if they are not in line with social practice, have severe limitations. In most countries, including West Germany, abortions need to be reported to the health authorities, but such attempts of controlling behaviour have generally resulted in substantial under-notification. Moreover, the decision of 'sufficient grounds' in England is best achieved by a claim for medical reasons, in Switzerland for psychiatric reasons and in West Germany for social reasons. Thus, the *naming* of the problem varies according to the way the law is framed. West German women accommodated themselves, if reluctantly, to the new law. Abortion was no longer a burning issue but only, one suspects, because the social practice has been able to avert legal strictures. It became a frontpage issue again when the advanced legislation of the former GDR clashed with FRG legislation on abortion.

By contrast, maternity leave provisions are excellent for both working and non-working mothers. In West Germany, maternity leave provisions come under the auspices of a women's labour protection legislation package, particularly in secondary and tertiary industries. Thus the package allows for transfer from

Table 4.5   **Percentage of women in West German parliament in 1983, by political party**

| Party | Political position | Women representatives in parliament (in %) |
|---|---|---|
| CDU/CSU | right to extreme right | 7.1 |
| FDP | centre to right | 9.4 |
| SPD | centre and left of centre | 11.6 |
| Greens | left | 55.6 |

Source: Aktuell, 1984: 271

strenuous to light work and from late shift to day shift without loss of pay during pregnancy. It grants six weeks maternity leave and a further leave of half a year on part pay. Recently, maternity leave payments have been increased in amount and in length (from six months to one year). In 1984, the conservative government initiated the special Mother and Child Foundation to support pregnant women in difficult socio-economic situations and to persuade these women not to abort but to carry their child to full term. Yet women's groups have rightly been suspicious about the motives and they also fear that this new support scheme serves to erode, in an oblique way, the freedom given by the abortion reform and may lead to new attacks on the amendments of paragraph 218 (*Aktuell*, 1984: 440). It is therefore doubtful whether women want to regard these motherhood support structures, under the circumstances in which they were implemented, as an achievement of the movement.

Women's active participation in politics throughout the 1970s and most of the 1980s had been low and consistently below European average. In the latter part of the 1980s, however, there have been substantial increases in women's membership in government. According to the 1987 and 1988 election results, West German gender inequalities in government have diminished to an extent that West Germany is now above the EEC average, with 16 percent of women in federal and over 13 percent in state governments. The real breakthrough for West German women has occurred via new parties and movements. In 1979, the Women's Party was formed (Frauenpartei) which, up until now, however, has not broken through the '5 percent of the vote clause' to get into parliament. The other, at the moment more important, political change has been achieved via the Green Party, which is the only one of the newly formed parties which managed to secure seats in parliament. The platform of the Greens was not specifically intended for women, but in its rhetoric it generally fostered women's presence although, in practice, women had to fight for their place in that party too (Brox-Brochot, 1984: 315 ff.) and eventually had to create their own women's lists. The Green Party in West Germany, unlike the Green Party in Austria, has mustered more and more support for women over time and has continued to grow since its inception. The gender profile of the Greens suggests a very new era for women in West German politics (see table 4.5).

One is reminded here of Ingunn Means' description of the Norwegian situation (see chapter 3, 'Norway'). Just as she believed (wrongly) in 1972 that Norwegian women were not interested in politics, so women and men in West Germany told me in 1988 that there was no interest in entering politics among West German women. Attempts to attract more women into politics had apparently constantly failed. Not one of the traditional four parties, however, the CDU, CSU, the Free Democratic Party (FDP) or SPD, can claim to have been particularly progressive on issues concerning women, the environment and nuclear disarmament. The present situation in Norway and these Green Party figures suggest a very different prognosis. Here we can extend the conclusion reached earlier: it is not just a matter of access to politics, not even just a matter of understanding whether male colleagues will be overtly hostile to women's presence, as is apparently the case in West German, Austrian and Swiss politics, but surely also a matter of the ideology on which the party rides (see Gassen, 1981: 245).

In education, there have been some promising changes towards greater equity between the sexes. Student enrolments of women at tertiary institutions have slowly climbed since the 1960s, from 23 to 38 percent in 1987 (Childs & Johnson, 1981: 182; *Fischer Weltalmanach '79: 293; Fischer Weltalmanach '87*: 204). In university positions, however, women rank very low in comparison to Scandinavian and some other western European countries. In the mid-1980s only 5 percent of all tenured positions (including professors) and only 11 percent of untenured (research and assistant staff), were occupied by women.

Feminists are keenly aware that the general tenor of conservatism that pervades West German society has made their work arduous, the recognition of women's abilities slow and their active participation in the public sphere tenuous. In 1980, Habermas, once considered a supporter of student protests, edited a prestigious two-volume *Suhrkamp* edition, entitled *Stichworte zur Geistigen Situation der Zeit* (Key Words on the Spiritual Situation of our Times). It was on a topic that was meant to represent West German thinking and the new 'spirit' of West Germany. In this *œvre* of over 840 pages, written by 34 authors, only two contributors were women. Their contributions, moreover, filled only a total of 28 pages or 3 percent of the material; one of the articles is about childhood, the other about jeans and fashion consumerism. Comments on the state, the nation, authority, politics or culture were obviously not entrusted to any of the available outstanding female minds. This book is perhaps a true reflection of the level of consciousness and the gender division of West German culture and politics of the 1980s. The two-volume work ends with a quote from Samuel Beckett's play *Waiting for Godot* which, on behalf of women in West Germany, I think might well be quoted back to the publishers themselves:

Estragon:  ... It can't be helped.
Wladimir:  ... Soon I will believe it too ... I have long fought against this idea. I said to myself: Wladimir, be reasonable, you haven't tried everything. And I took up the fight again.

In 1978, an autobiographical story written by a young German waitress, entitled 'Waiting for a miracle', contained these lines: 'I still ... still believe—well, in truth, in something that has to come ... And still, I'm still waiting for a miracle ... ' (Ruth, 1984: 175).

## AUSTRIA

Austria, first came into existence as a separate entity at the end of World War I (1918) when the Habsburg Empire, to which modern Austria belonged, collapsed and Czechoslovakia and Yugoslavia became new nations. Hungary and Austria were left to form their own republic. This development was greeted with enthusiasm by the strong Austrian socialist force, almost entirely working class in character. It prided itself as having overthrown the monarchy and having won a bloodless revolution (Carsten, 1972: 78 ff). But even though the Habsburg monarchy had been corrupt, decadent and crumbling from within, as Szabo's film of 1984, *Colonel Redl*, admirably showed, there were some who found it difficult to live without the former 'glory' of the Habsburg Empire. The disappearance of the Habsburg dynasty proved anything but a solution to the problem of central Europe. The dynastic empire, said Taylor, had 'sustained central Europe, as a plaster cast sustains a broken limb' (1970: 272). The new nations were now faced with two significant problems: the internal problem of authority and the external problem of security. In addition, there were complicated issues of historical identities vis-à-vis the political realities at hand; the Austria to which its former state elite was loyal was now a historical memory rather than a territorial state. Even for the left-wing forces, the new Republic of Austria presented a conceptual problem of considerable dimensions. Under the dual monarchy of Austria–Hungary, Austro-Marxists had pledged their support to proletarian internationalism and to a multinational state, and had, more than implicitly, condemned the divisiveness of nationalism (Lindemann, 1983: 247).

The political success of the young republic was rather short lived in that the debates about democracy led to ever increasing internal rifts. By 1934 civil war broke out. The Social Democratic Party was dissolved and replaced by an authoritarian government under Dollfuß, who, however, was murdered the same year by the Nazis. The next four years were governed by attempts to safeguard democracy and Austria's independence, ironically by Austria putting itself under Italian protection. But Chancellor Schuschnigg's talks with Hitler in February 1938 failed. Hitler marched into Austria a month later, annexing it to Germany and declaring that, historically, Austria had always been German. This was doubly ironic, for Hitler himself was Austrian. From Georg Ritter von Schönerer (1842–1921), an aristocrat and prominent anti-semite, he had learned about nationalism and from Karl Lueger (1842–1921), a former mayor of Vienna and the founder of the Christian Social Party of Austria, he had learned to develop his anti-semitism and the appeal to the 'little man' (Taylor, 1970: 272). Hitler's view had a good many supporters in Germany and in Austria itself, for the debates about the possible borders of Germany, in view of the size and complexity of the former Holy Roman Empire of German Nations, had always been contentious. Some Germans still perceive Austria as something of an appendage to Germany. While Austrians, now more than ever, would generally strongly disagree with this presumption, matters were not quite as clear cut in the 1930s. Austria had created its own strong fascist movement and many were vulnerable to nationalistic sentiments after shedding their former identity as members of the Habsburg Empire. Others, like the Austrian Social Democrats, had been strong proponents of German nationalism and had actively supported Hitler's annexation policy. After World War II Austria was neither unscathed nor without blame, but in view of its size vis-à-vis the powerful Nazi state, the Allies allowed Austria to hold its first elections without foreign interference as early as the 27 April 1945 (a few weeks before the official end of the war).

Austria's second republic was proclaimed in 1945. In 1955, when it signed the final round of peace treaty documents (*Staatsvertrag*), which assured full sovereignty, Austria was on its own and determined not to repeat the mistakes of the 1920s. One of its first acts was to pledge neutrality forever, following the example of Switzerland and the Scandinavian countries. Built on the basis of parliamentary democracy, Austria's political parties reconstituted themselves or were newly founded. The Austrian Socialist Party (Sozialistische Partei Österreichs—SPÖ), for instance, had been prohibited in 1934 and was only able to resurface in 1945. Today, it has about 700 000 members, an enormously large number considering the size of the population (almost the same number as the CDU has been able to attract in all of West Germany, a country with almost ten times the population). Indeed, Austrian Socialist Party membership is one of the strongest in the socialist international movement of any country. Another party, a christian democratic party, called the Austrian People's Party (Österreichische Volkspartei—ÖVP), was founded in 1945. Although one would hesitate to call this party even moderately progressive, it has nevertheless an interesting structure, signalling its willingness to be a representative democratic organisation. It consisted of members of six associations: the Austrian Workers' and Employees' Union (ÖAAB), the Austrian Farmers' Association (ÖBB), the Austrian Economic Union (ÖWB), the Young People's Party (JVP), the Austrian Senior Citizens' Association (ÖSB) and, interestingly, the Austrian Women's Union (ÖFB). Of all the other splinter parties which either formed immediately after the war or, like the Green alternatives just recently, only the Libertarian Party of Austria (Freiheitliche Partei Österreichs—FPÖ) and the Greens are represented in parliament. In the 1980s, the major parties (SPÖ and ÖVP) have lost seats in parliament to the smaller and newer parties. Just as in West Germany, the Greens in Austria have been able to record almost instant victory, and unlike other smaller and recently formed parties, have been able to secure a role in parliament.

In 1945, Austria's currency and financial situation was chaotic and, despite reforms, the monetary situation of Austria only began to stabilise by the early 1950s. Its economic development is also attributable to the Marshall Plan which, between 1945 and 1955, injected over US$1.6 billion into the economy and lifted Austria into a period of fast economic growth developing its secondary and, especially, its tertiary industries. The shift from primary and secondary to tertiary industries has been particularly obvious throughout the 1970s. While the economically active population generally drifted away from agriculture, Austria, however, produced 102 percent of its own national needs in the same period (1983). The secondary industry is particularly active in steel and iron ore production, in energy resource processing, and otherwise in electro-industry, textile, glass and porcelain production. Heavy industry in Austria was nationalised in 1946.

Austria has bilateral agreements with the EEC at present, which has freed it from the burden of tariffs. In view of the European market goals of 1992, it has already considered closer ties with the EEC and even membership. In the tertiary sector, one of the most successful industries has been the tourist industry, with rises in income over the years. In 1960, Austria derived just over US$6 million from tourism, US$25 969 million in 1970, and by 1983 the total annual income had increased to a staggering US$83 242 million. Austria in the 1990s is the strongest tourist country in western Europe.

In some ways, the Austrian model of economics and government can be compared with the Swedish model, and for that matter also with other smaller countries such as Belgium and the Netherlands. Van der Wee saw the model of the mixed-market economy of these countries as neither neo-collectivist nor neo-free-market, but as a model of central consultation between representatives of various social partners in the context of bipartite and tripartite structures. In Sweden and Austria, government controls social planning centrally but has allowed employers and unions to decide with them on issues such as the share of prosperity growth (Van der Wee, 1987: 310, 313). Austria, like Sweden, has declared in its neutrality that it will not make use of nuclear power. In both countries, socialists and social democrats form the majority political culture. Internationally, Austria has made a name for itself as a neutral and peacekeeping body that has supplied expertise and leadership to such institutions as the UN and the European Council. The country has grown in confidence, both economically and politically and has gradually developed a positive concept of its own separate identity.

## The position of Austrian women

In women's issues the new Austrian Republic had little to offer on which it could build, although there had been some promising moves throughout the 19th and early 20th centuries, worth reiterating here. In the German principalities and in Austrian territories, the women's movement started most conspicuously in 1848. On German soil, it was the result of the March Revolution which many women had supported. The revolutionary fever of 1848 had its special variant in the Habsburg capital of Vienna. At the height of the unrest the then labour minister announced that wages for women would be drastically cut and the measures would be imposed from the following day onwards. Eight thousand women workers were affected by those cuts and these prompted them into a large-scale public demonstration which, however, was dispersed by the National Guard. A few days later, a much larger and more determined crowd demonstrated against the low wages and this time the uprising ended in a bloodbath (the so-called *Praterschlacht*). Out of sheer outrage against the deaths and injuries of the protestors, a new women's organisation was formed. This Democratic Women's Association under Karoline von Perin, a member of the aristocracy, was the first political women's association which advocated democratic ideals. In its ideals, it was far ahead of the political reality surrounding it. It existed only for two months, after which Vienna then was firmly back in the hands of counter-revolutionary forces. Perin, despite her privileged position and her advanced age, was taken into custody, apparently beaten but later released. The same year (1848), a women's rights commission was formed across the Atlantic Ocean in New York which published the well-known *Declaration of Sentiments*, signalling the start of the American women's suffragette movement. These developments were not as ill-fated as similarly spirited attempts by European women at the same time. Austrian and German women were forced back into their traditional roles (Weiland, 1983: 188).

Such efforts, however, were not entirely in vain. The spirit was rekindled by Iduna Laube in 1866 and many ideas incorporated when she formed the Wiener Frauen Erwerbsverein (The Viennese Women's Employment Union). There were other abortive changes, such as the Austrian Code of Law of 1812, which made provision for a separation of property, irrespective of sex. In 1861, women obtained the active voting right in the principalities of Austria, Bohemia and the Steiermark, but this right was abolished in 1888. Nevertheless, there were signs of a radicalisation of women towards the end of the 19th century, fostered and supported by the international socialist movement, to which women like Louise Kautsky, Amalie Seidl and Anna Boschek belonged. In 1893, Amalie Seidl had been instrumental in the organisation of a major strike action of 600 women workers in several factories. Adelheid Popp was a member of the workers' movement and generated a working women's lobby in speeches and through her newspaper *Working Women*. Bertha von Suttner made her name as a leading pacifist for which she was awarded the Nobel Peace Prize in 1905.

Women's rights to education and to enfranchisement generally came to be recognised at about the same time as in Germany. In the Habsburg Empire, women were allowed to complete high school. In 1892 they were permitted to enrol in philosophy, in 1987 in all liberal arts and in 1900 also in medicine. As in the Weimar Republic, the new (first) Austrian Republic granted women the vote in 1918 and a year later opened all universities to women, but further ideas for change were smothered in the political struggle for survival of independence and of democracy. The first republic, however, saw the beginnings of an effective social service legislation (Zöllner, 1974: 566).

The creation of modern Austria, the second Austrian Republic (1945– ), has been shaped by its special dual heritage, a mix of 'authoritarianism, repression, and rigidity on the one hand, and progressive liberalism, socialism and innovation on the other' (Benard and Schlaffer, 1984: 72); its fascist past and the contradictions of these strands of tradition are all still evident today. The layers of tradition, inherited from the Habsburg Empire, underpin Austrian life but they are set in a context of socialist ideals, entrepreneurial economics and progressive environmental and peace strategies. In other words, the country is riddled with contradictions. The socialist leader, Bruno Kreisky, was able to go on the election trail with photos of himself sitting in front of a painting of the last Habsburg emperor! These traditions have influenced women's position and the women's movement in curious ways.

Benard and Schlaffer have made the important point that Austria's monarchic past implies not just the negative tradition of authoritarianism and repression but that it was precisely only through enlightened rulers that reforms were possible, more often than not inflicted on recalcitrant and backward provinces (1984: 72). Reforms from above have happened not just under the Empress Maria Theresa or her son Joseph II, but again in the 1970s. Apart from the efforts that had gone into shaping its modern constitution, Austria's main bout of social reform, as this pertained to women, occurred in the mid-to-late 1970s and, at a much slower pace, in the 1980s. When these occurred, under the socialist Chancellor Bruno Kreisky, they caused a stir throughout Austria, particularly the statement that reform was needed whether the public wanted it or not. When he proposed the introduction of a Secretary of State for Women's Affairs he had to threaten to resign as leader should this not be accepted by his party.

Throughout the 1970s and early 1980s, women in Austria still laboured under very basic forms of discrimination, and the changes, partly as a result of new legislation, have begun to be felt only in the last few years. The chief emphasis of these reforms concerned the family and reproduction. The legal changes that were effected show how backward and antiquated Austrian laws had been. The changes that have occurred within *that* context must then be described as radical and fundamental, hauling Austria into the 20th century within a few decades. In 1974, Austria repealed its abortion law and instead granted the right of abortion for the first twelve weeks of pregnancy, a move that put catholic Austria ahead of West Germany, where the fight for abortion law reform continued unabated for several more years. This reform was indeed a reform 'from above', initiated by the government against staunch catholic opposition voiced not only by the church but also by the population. The Austrian abortion law is one of the most progressive in Europe today, allowing women full self-determination, requiring no notification, no special doctor's expert opinion, and not even parental consent for any woman over the age of

14 years. It can be performed anywhere and needs no special licensing of health care institutions. Of course, even such a generous ruling is modified by social custom and, given the resistance of catholic doctors and nurses to involvement, has severely restricted access in reality.

In 1975, the first family law reform bill was passed, formally decreeing equality between spouses. Up to 1976, for instance, husbands had the right to prohibit their wives from seeking work outside the home. Until 1978 men had absolute power over their children. A woman could not make as much as a passport application for her child, even if she had been divorced for years. A father had to sign that application and also had the right to refuse if he saw fit to do so. The new custody and family laws of 1978 removed these relics, as the divorce and property law reforms removed the worst injustices from the legal statute books. Up to 1978, all property and assets were assumed to belong to the husband. If the couple had bought property during their marriage, it was usually in the husband's name because the mutual signature attracted a gift tax against the wife and acted as a very persuasive deterrent against joint signatures. The gift tax was removed along with the change in property settlement reforms in cases of divorce. The same set of laws also made possible divorce by mutual consent or after separation of six years, prescribing maintenance payments to be made by the husband if his former wife was still caring for a minor at home or if she was over the age of 40 years and the marriage had been of at least fifteen years duration. In 1983 the discriminatory marriage prohibition for a woman was abolished. Up until then she had not been allowed to remarry within a ten-month period and/or had to prove that she was not pregnant. Tax exemptions, hitherto only claimable by the husband, were made to apply to the sole, rather than just the male, breadwinner, allowing women who were either unmarried or divorced to claim these exemptions as their right. By the same token, the accountability for the partner's debts after divorce was waived. The same year also saw changes in citizenship requirements that had affected any Austrian woman and her children married to a person of another nationality. As from 1983 onwards an Austrian woman could pass on her Austrian nationality to her children regardless of the father's nationality.

Maternity leave (*Karenzurlaub*) was made available for one year. For a woman who had her first child and had worked continuously for an entire year before pregnancy a set daily allowance was payable, giving the mother an opportunity to stay at home on a minimum monthly equivalent of a wage. A higher rate was set for single mothers. In 1985, 95 percent of eligible women used the scheme, 90 percent of them to the full extent. In addition, it was made possible for women to claim an allowance (*Sondernotstandshilfe*) up until the third birthday of the child. This allowance, however, was made dependent on the last income of the woman. Despite these restrictions, the scheme has been very popular. In it first three years of operation, the number of claimants almost doubled (4700 in 1980, 8500 in 1983). The law has also permitted parental sick leave for up to one week per year to be taken by either working partner for the care of a sick child and a family allowance to be paid tax-free per month according to the age of the child (Feigl, 1985: 22–5).

There have been visible demographic changes in recent years: more women than ever choose to live alone (20 percent of the 19-plus age groups) and in two-person households (25 percent); women with higher educational attainments (matriculation and/or university training) tend to remain single longer or never marry (see table 4.6). Divorces have doubled between the 1960s and

**Table 4.6    Percentage of Austrian women as singles (by educational attainment)**

|                         | Age | | | |
| Highest education level | 25–30 | 30–35 | 40–45 | 45–50 |
| --- | --- | --- | --- | --- |
| University | 40 | 22 | 19 | 21 |
| Matriculation | 42 | 16 | 13 | 14 |
| Vocational certificates | 27 | 14 | 11 | 13 |
| Basic schooling | 19 | 10.5 | 7 | 7 |
| Apprenticeship | 20 | 8 | 6 | 5.5 |

*Source*: adapted from Feigl, 1985: 12

**Table 4.7    Percentage of Austrian husbands helping in housework and child rearing, 1977 and 1983**

|                      | 1977 | 1983 |
| --- | --- | --- |
| Help in household |  |  |
| Daily | 20 | 29 |
| Never | 62 | 58 |
| Sometimes | 18 | 14 |
| Help in child care |  |  |
| Daily | 30 | 54 |
| Never | 52 | 32 |
| Sometimes | 18 | 14 |

*Source*: adapted from Feigl, 1985: 17

1980s (in 1985: 29.5 percent) and the trend in Austria, as elsewhere in western Europe, is clearly towards the three-to-four person household, excluding grandparents and large families. As the figures on domestic chores suggest, most of the double burden of work—housework and raising children—falls to the woman. The amendments in family and divorce laws have not led to a questioning of the family and of marriage as an institution on any broad scale. They also have not led towards the concept of domestic role-sharing, although there are small signs of some attitudinal and practical changes. A longitudinal survey of 1977 and 1983 established that the proportion of men who never helped with housework had decreased slightly while the proportion of husbands/partners helping in child care and child rearing had gone up rather dramatically (see table 4.7).

In 1979, one of the milestones in Austrian social reform was the industrial decision to grant equal pay for men and women in work of equal value. A commission was set up to supervise the implementation of these new directives but it was 1983 before Austria ratified the UN directives on social and economic gender equality.

In education, especially at upper high school and at university level, there are clear signs of change in the postwar years. In 1988, 48.8 percent of university students were women. These increasing enrolment figures might augur well for the future. In moderate ways, they have already resulted in higher levels of professionalisation amongst women than in previous years. In medicine, for instance, women's enrolments in 1970–71 stood at 26.4 percent and at 46 percent in 1983–84. Those women who completed their medical degrees in the winter semester of 1979–80 constituted 30.1 percent of all successful graduands while, in 1982–83, these had risen to 37.1 percent. There are still noticeable gender differences in the areas of medical practice and these might not disappear all that quickly. As a rule of thumb, the least promising careers with the lowest monetary awards are generally filled by women such as, for example, rural or governmental general medical practitioner positions. Amongst specialists, 37.5 percent of paediatricians are women, but only 10 percent of radiologists and 2 percent of surgeons (Pauli, 1986: 101). Some of the gender segregation in study areas has been minimised, or has even disappeared. The humanities have remained dominated by women, and in a range of science areas women have entered in larger numbers than in the 1970s.

Feminists in academia pointed out in 1989 that the situation for academic women was, however, far from promising. Only 19.1 percent of assistant academic staff and 2.9 percent of professorial staff (equivalent to all tenured staff from lecturer to chair included) were women. In as many as two-thirds of all faculties there were no women professors at all. In 1988, at the University of Vienna, for example, the law faculty had one woman who occupied a full chair/professorship (out of a total of 23), so did the faculty of medicine (out of a total of 70). Catholic theology, economics and architecture had no women and only the 'intergrative faculty', one of the few new inventions of the old Viennese university, could claim three out of a total of 27 full professorial positions (ÖH Frauenreferat, 1989). The few appointments of women that have been made in recent years, as the Union of Socialist Students has estimated, represent a rate of 'progress' that would ensure equity of women's representation in academia, not in the near future, not in this century or the next, but probably by about the year 3429 (VSSTÖ, 1988: 5). It has been established that women with qualifications equal to men's (and all other things being equal) need about ten years longer than men to tread the same steps upwards on a career ladder. Moreover, academic qualifications obtained by men have so far been fully absorbed, or rather their skills and knowledge have been translated into leading positions or upper-middle levels of responsibility. For women, however, even doctorates have been no guarantee of employment in career positions. Of university-trained women below age 40, the percentage of underemployed in 1983 was 12 percent; between 40 and 50 it was 18 percent, and between 50 and 60, 29 percent (Pauli, 1986: 99). While these statistics suggest that the position of women with doctorates has slightly improved over time, they also suggest that educational qualifications are not the only way out of discriminatory situations: in Austria in the 1980s every fifth woman with a doctorate worked in a position in which the doctorate was superfluous.

Austrian students have furthermore highlighted the fact that study completion rates of women are lower than those of men. In the 1980s, the drop-out rate of women was at least twice as high as men's. Indeed, it is very useful to compare the enrolment figures of men and women for the same period, an exercise that is all too often omitted in statistical accounts, especially when the intention is to show women's emancipation and increasing integration into the economy and into society in general. Therefore, it often escapes detection that universities, and tertiary institutions in general, have undergone significant growth periods somewhere between the 1960s and late 1970s, along with increases in the population and changed needs for the economy. The growth in female clientele at tertiary institutions is thus not necessarily a sign of their greater

**Table 4.8    Changes in Austrian women's educational attainment compared to men's**

| Highest educational standard | Women | | | Men | | |
|---|---|---|---|---|---|---|
| | % | | (% gain/loss) | % | | (% gain/loss) |
| | 1971 | 1981 | | 1971 | 1981 | |
| Basic school (*Pflichtschule*) | 73 | 62 | (−11) | 48 | 40 | (−8) |
| Apprenticeship | 13 | 17 | (+ 4) | 6 | 39 | (+3) |
| Technical schools | 9 | 13 | (+ 4) | 5 | 7 | (+2) |
| High schools (upper levels) | 4 | 6 | (+ 2) | 7 | 9 | (+2) |
| University | 1 | 2 | (+ 1) | 4 | 5 | (+1) |

*Source*: Feigl, 1985: 29

participation, as the comparisons in table 4.8 effectively show. Clearly, according to these figures, women's participation in higher education relative to men's has not increased in the last ten years because the growth rate for men is the same. The distribution of women across faculties has changed but not the most essential variable, that is, the completion of higher education that will lead to different vocational roles within Austrian society.

Women have also made little progress in occupying leading roles in politics. As voters, they form the absolute majority (52.7 percent) in Austria today but as active participants are barely visible or appreciated. In 1983, three ministerial positions were occupied by women. In 1986, two of the fourteen ministerial posts were held by women: one was the portfolio for education, art and sport (SPÖ), and the other for environment, youth and family (ÖVP). Altogether in the 1980s, women have accounted for 12 to 19 percent in parliament, a percentage not significantly different to that of 1919. The social democrats can boast about the same percentage amongst their representatives while the Austrian Green alternative, surprisingly, is described by critical commentators as being decidedly anti-women since it has reluctantly allowed only one token woman into its (parliamentary) ranks. Indeed, women's right to participate actively in politics has been questioned informally by male colleagues in less than charming or civilised ways. Pauli renders a long list of public statements by politicians which can only surprise us for their low level of wit and their clumsy and parochial sexism and general prejudice. One example here may suffice to illustrate the point: a male minister, newly appointed to the portfolio of building and construction, was asked how he felt about being given a female assistant minister and how they would work together. He allegedly suggested: 'Well, she can always paint the planks on the freeway' (Pauli, 1986: 10–11).

Women's position at work began to change marginally in the 1980s. In 1978, women constituted 39 percent of the total workforce as compared with 38 percent in 1934. In the 1970s there was a brief rapid growth period for women's entry into the labour force but this slowed again in the 1980s and left no clear mark, particularly since women's unemployment in the 1980s remained constantly above that of men's. Unemployment in Austria has always been extremely low. Yet even at this level of unemployment for women (at 3.9 percent as compared to 2.9 percent for men in 1985) there is a constant erosion of women's participation in the labour force. Nevertheless, the areas and composition of the workforce have changed over time. In Austria, as elsewhere, there has been an increase in part-time work. Increasingly, women with small children take paid employment outside the home. Thus, in 1985, almost half of all married women with small children and 80 percent of unmarried mothers worked (Feigl, 1985: 40); 41.6 percent of all employees were women, dominating the areas of service (67 percent), office work (66 percent) and trade (56 percent) and, as in other countries, showing very clear traits of gender segregation. In technical, semi-professional and vocational jobs, women formed less than half of employees (41 percent), while in such areas as building and construction, women's participation decreased to around 3 percent.

In distribution of prestige and income structures, the gender inequalities in Austria emerge very clearly. In an official report on the social situation (*Bericht zur sozialen Lage*) of 1984, it was admitted that women overall earned only 67 percent of the average male wage. Expressed differently, the Austrian average income was not reached by two-thirds of white-collar women workers (as against a fifth of men) and by 85 percent of blue-collar workers (as against 40 percent of men in this category). Only 4 percent of women ranked amongst the top incomes, as against 30 percent of men. In the 1982–1985 period, the number of women in this category increased by 0.2 percent (as against 0.6 percent for men), while, overall, women's presence in four-digit incomes decreased by 12 percent in the same period. In the public sector, women constituted by far the majority of employees but only 26 percent of the upper income brackets were women. In private industry, the most noticeable change has occurred in the category of self-employed. Here the proportion of women has increased over time. Of all self-employed in the mid-1980s, 33 percent were women and the number is slowly rising. Of those, almost half of the women founded the companies themselves, while the other half have either inherited a business or taken it over from a spouse. The greatest presence of women in the self-employed category was in travel (47.7 percent of the total) and in the insurance and credit money market (42 percent). As already mentioned, one of Austria's chief industries is the tourist industry so that women's participation in this sector of the economy is anything but marginal.

Writers on women's issues in contemporary Austria seem agreed that women have not made much progress, either in the more limited framework of 'emancipation' or in the wider sense of 'liberation'. There was a women's movement in Austria. It rarely agitated. Either it negotiated or its leaders were co-opted into government committees. It had some links with the workers' movement of the past and the leftist parties but relatively little impetus of its own. Indeed, some writers called it 'derivative' because it borrowed and copied from French, Italian or German movements, whatever seemed a good idea at the time, being a little slapdash about reforms initiating anything that seemed to be the latest flavour (Benard and Schlaffer, 1984: 73, 74). The women's movement, starting in about 1972, was barely conspicuous at any time, and is said to have disappeared completely, notwithstanding the network of feminist groups and feminist activities. Austria has procured no feminist mass movement; this could not happen, so one feminist writes, for the family structures are 'too catholic, too authoritarian, too traditional patriarchal' (Fischer, 1988: 185).

The refuge movement and 'women help women' projects have thrown a net of activities and strongholds over the country. University students today are active in polemic as well as concretely aimed activities. But I have not seen a single comment that would indicate a positive prognosis for feminists or for significant social change in the near future. One of the Austrian feminist publications of the 1980s was aptly subtitled 'The long march into the dead-end road'. Indeed, at best, Austrian development in women's policies has been uneven, hampered not just by unwilling politicians but by a trenchant traditionalism that is fairly secure and difficult to shake off, particularly in rural areas. A recent governmental survey asked for views on its proposed introduction to pay women a basic income/allowance for three years after childbirth. Sixty-four percent of peasant women and 56 percent of female pensioners were against this idea, and among the younger and partly urban generations 40 percent of women shared these views (Pauli, 1986: 91), although not always for the same reasons.

It used to be said that the German and Austrian mentalities could be summarised by one small alteration in a single sentence: a German (Prussian) might say 'The situation is serious but not hopeless', while an Austrian would say 'The situation is hopeless but not serious'. I doubt whether this description continues to have jocular or even anecdotal relevance. Feminists in Austria do not take matters lightly. To them, the situation is hopeless *and* serious, a perception that is aided by the observation of women's improved status elsewhere in Europe, including West Germany.

## SWITZERLAND

To the economist, Switzerland is a highly successful country. Over the entire postwar period, it has had unemployment figures around 1 percent, inflation rates of under 4 percent, a level of taxation not exceeding 10 percent, no value-added tax on consumer goods, and it can boast GNP figures which are the highest in western Europe (Liechtenstein excepted) and amongst the highest in the world. By law it is required, and able, to balance the budget annually. Internationally and within Europe, tiny Switzerland has played a prominent role in innovation in chemicals and machine industry (Van der Wee, 1987: 232). Even politically, Switzerland is in some ways exemplary. Since 1959, it has been governed jointly by four parties which provide a fixed number of places in government: two seats to the FDP (Freethinking Democratic Party—Freisinnige Demokratische Partei), two seats to the CVP (Christian Democratic Party—Christdemokratische Partei), two to the Social Democratic Party (SPS) and one seat to the Swiss People's Party (SVP—Schweizerische Volkspartei). The Swiss do not rely solely on representative government, however, but engage in exercises of direct democracy, probably more often than anywhere else in the world. As many as 50 percent of important political and economic decisions may be made via referenda. Examples of such referenda are the decisions not to increase taxes above 10 percent and not to introduce value-added tax.

From the point of view of social justice there may be few hymns that could be sung in praise of Switzerland. Switzerland has far fewer services and a far smaller and less well established net of service provisions than West Germany and even Austria. When Switzerland faced inflationary tendencies, the Swiss government responded by reducing, among other things, government expenditure and government subsidies. Of all western European nations, Switzerland now has the lowest budget allocation for social services, although minor increases from the 1970s to the 1980s have been noted (from 17 to 21 percent of total budget costs). The assumption is that all adult inhabitants of Switzerland must look after their own affairs. Indeed, Switzerland has been able to maintain the highest proportion of an active labour force (earning coefficient) of anywhere in Europe and its citizens enjoy high incomes as a result of the very low taxation rate. There are of course connections between levels of taxation and social services. Sweden has possibly the best network of social services and also has the highest taxation rates in Europe. Switzerland instead has opted for minimal taxation rates and few if any services. There are for instance no maternity leave provisions. In cases of special need, money for maternity leave is paid out of unemployment funds.

There are indices that commonly disadvantaged sectors of society may not suffer as much as in other nations in which the contrasts between rich and poor may be more pronounced. In 1981 for example, pensioners' incomes fell proportionately into the same categories as the economically active population. Two-thirds of pensioners lived at or below the average Swiss income while just over half of the economically active were in the same categories.

Social welfare, it seems, is not necessarily perceived as a concomitant of responsible government, and services in this area may well be expected to, and often do, come from private sources. Guest workers cannot expect, and will not easily find, any social infrastructure that will support them, nor, unlike West Germany, will Switzerland promise them anything that falls outside the immediate contract provisions. The roughly 200 000 female guest workers are usually married, earn least within Swiss society and have no or few rights. They and their husbands are the Swiss labour reserve army which can be called upon and dispensed with at short notice. At one point, immigrant labour in Switzerland reached a total of 30 percent of the labour force. The tough, but often less than commendable, foreign-worker policy has of course contributed to a low unemployment rate of Swiss citizens and in a small way also to a maintenance of the Swiss high standard of living (Kindleberger, 1967: 201, 209, 211). As late as 1987, Switzerland decided not to ratify the Social Charter of 1965 of the European Council, which has so far been ratified by most other western European countries. The charter spells out the basic rights for work, for equal pay for equal work, for health protection at work and for the right to form unions. In a sense, this is similar to Switzerland's decision of 1968 not to sign the UN Charter without amendment because it demanded a promise of non-discriminatory policy on the grounds of sex, religion, race, etc. (see chapter 2).

But there are signs that social tensions have grown below the shiny and well-polished surface of Swiss economic common sense. The economic recession, which hit other western European countries in the first part of the 1970s, slowly descended on Switzerland in the early 1980s, albeit in a less dramatic form than elsewhere in Europe. In addition, family structures have begun to change, if ever so slightly, affecting particularly women who, as Hinn writes, experience in full the contradictions of Swiss society in law, social security, housing and working conditions, and in the lack of social services and backward public education (Hinn, 1988: 208). At least 1 percent of women are single parents (around 35 000 women), a further 65 000 are sole breadwinners for a family, women who are made to feel the full weight of gender discrimination in their pay packet. Women have little say and they play a marginal role in the economy. They have little or no opportunity to add to Swiss technological and professional know-how, to cultural and intellectual life. Only 20 percent of working women are in jobs requiring any training and/or certificates. In the late 1980s, only 13.9 percent of students at universities were women, and throughout the entire country there were only 66 women in tenured lectureships and none above, constituting a total of 3.9 percent of Swiss academic staff (Hinn, 1988: 209).

Swiss women never had a movement comparable to that of West Germany or even Austria. Yet the voices of protest by individuals and/or by small groups have been strong throughout the entire postwar period. The publication of a book by Iris von Roten, a Swiss lawyer and feminist, is a case in point. Called *Women in Play-Pens*, it was published in 1958 and is said to have had more influence on Swiss women than Simone de Beauvoir's books and possibly even the feminist publications from the USA a decade later. Indeed, less than a year after its publication women's campaigns against the status quo began on a relatively large scale (for Swiss conditions). Women were then not enfranchised at all. It was chiefly a fight for gaining the vote, although many other feminist ideas were part of their agenda. Unhappily for women in Switzerland, the decision of 1 February 1959 brought defeat for their demand for the right to vote. Only three small estates (*Stände*) of the Swiss Romande (French West Switzerland) and one state (*Kanton*) had adopted the principle. Such can be the price of direct democracy that each, even the smallest, community in Swiss society, has a right to adopt or reject a legal proposal as it sees fit. Thus, women in Switzerland had to fight the battle for implementation of women's enfranchisement separately in towns, cities, and country alike. They were at the mercy of referenda and a general (male) population that had to be won over separately in each state and community, and there are still, apparently, some small pockets where women have no voting rights.

Women in Switzerland had to fight long and hard over a decade before they finally gained the right to participate in their own democracy. In 1960, the German-speaking Basel women organised a day of mourning and demonstrations to commemorate the first anniversary of the day when their wish for enfranchisement had been defeated. But six years later, Basel rather suddenly accepted women's right to vote, a decision which in turn sparked off virulent anti-enfranchisement campaigns in Zurich. These campaigns for and against women's right to vote continued throughout the 1960s and led to the formation of an organisation calling itself the Women's Liberation Movement (Frauenbefreiungsbewegung—FBB). In June 1968, it published the so-called Zurich Manifesto, decrying Swiss institutions as outdated, immovable and inflexible and ultimately against the interest of the Swiss people. On the tenth anniversary of the defeated women's vote in Basel, the movement once again organised a march of mourning (1969) and this time was able to count among its supporters men of letters and well-known public figures. The movement also formed close ties with the Swiss new left and on certain occasions undertook combined actions, as on Labour Day in May 1971 when they demanded the vote, equality and, notably, equal pay.

The student movement, appearing belatedly in Swiss society in comparison to other western European countries, founded an autonomous Progressive Organisation of Switzerland. This was important for women in so far as another separate organisation for women grew out of it in 1977, one which at times has been very influential. This Organisation for Concerns of Women (Organisation für die Sache der Frauen—OFRA) has functioned as a voice for women and as an identifiable body which was willing and able to defend claims, and announce aims and policies. In the late 1980s, the importance of OFRA has waned again despite the fact that the number of reform attempts were few, lukewarm and barely capable of redressing the balance of social, economic and political injustices against women. Since the early 1970s, to be sure, almost all adult women in Switzerland have had the right to vote, even though in one *Kanton* as late as 1982 male citizens voted against allowing women to participate in local elections (Flanz, 1983). The mid-1970s also saw an abortion law reform. In 1978, a new child law equalised the rights of nuptial and ex-nuptial children and brought about new regulations for maintenance and custody rights and duties for the father of a child. In 1988, the amended marriage law conceded women and men equal status in marriage, without going as 'far' as allowing the couple to choose between spouses' names. Hinn's exasperated comment on these reforms was that it was incomprehensible that women would waste their energy on reforming the family law when the very concept of it, not the details, should have been challenged (1988: 208).

It was well within the tenets of Swiss democracy that women should initiate their own projects. Of course, to find the private financial sources for these projects has been another matter. One of the most adamantly pursued tasks for feminists was the campaign against domestic violence. In 1977, women in Zurich founded an Association for the Protection of Mistreated Women. In order to persuade the Swiss public that domestic violence existed 'even in Switzerland', they conducted large-scale surveys amongst Swiss doctors, marriage counsellors, family advisory centres and other relevant organisations. Seventy-one percent of doctors and 88 percent of various services answered that they had been confronted with domestic violence in dealing with their clientele, on at least a weekly basis. Over two-thirds of interviewees also confirmed that violence against children was a concomitant factor in spouse abuse (Pletscher, 1977: 85). It was after the publication of these findings that a women's refuge was opened. The enormous energies women have invested in getting programmes off the ground can only be gleaned from the fact that the government is not readily approachable with respect to providing money for social causes. The Swiss population would have to agree in a referendum that it was willing to pay more than 10 percent in taxes. Such voluntary action seems unlikely in the near future, and may well prevent Switzerland from signing the Social Charter of the European Council for some time (unless certain amendments are made possible).

The reforms that have occurred in Switzerland tend to be the ones that cost little or no money to implement. Services, however, do cost money. Social provisions for the disadvantaged cost money and for these to be regarded as a government responsibility one would expect that a substantial rise in taxes was unavoidable. The oldest democracy in modern times in Europe has chosen to be democratic in ways long considered a luxury in other western European countries, namely in participatory decisions concerning the treasury. But this right, it seems, may now also prevent other and often more important democratic principles from becoming a reality.

*THE MODEL EXAMINED*

Germanic countries appear to be a good deal more conservative and change resistent in their thinking than the Scandinavian countries. Women's movements and their claims are a very good measure of the level of modernity of a society. In Switzerland, the fight for such a basic right as the vote in a country regarded as having high democratic principles and a respectable tradition in democracy must strike one as odd. But of course, although the contradictions here may be more pronounced than in other democracies, they signal the same problem as elsewhere. In each case the protests of women make a statement that the country in question should live up to its own assumed principles of democracy. Austria is a curious case amongst western European democracies because of its exceptionally uneven development. Irrespective of its traditions and contradictions, the Austrian variant of democracy on one level is arguably the same as the West German model, as it is basically autocratic, if not 'absolutist', as Nagle would have it (Nagle, 1970). But at the same time it has a firmer grip on economic control (via nationalisation of economic enterprises) than has West Germany. Switzerland, by contrast, is a free-market economy and its system of power, despite or because of its rigidity, is also relatively incapable of social change.

In all three countries women have found it particularly difficult to get their governments to respond to demands made by them from outside the parliamentary (i.e. the immediately political) environment. We have seen in chapter 1 that concepts of democracy (in terms of function *and* structure) vary widely both in theory and practice. Ideologies on the political left and right usually differ markedly one from another in the way they perceive the role of government. But even within political ideologies there have been pronounced differences. It might seem remarkable now, although historically it is not surprising, that governments as unlike one another as the right-wing German and the socialist Austrian ones have responded with similar disdain to women's attempts to win public debate and to bring about change in gender inequities. Both governments have said that they will not be told what to do by pressure groups. Both have made amendments in the legislature, with the important difference that, in Austria, some of these amendments were against the will of a conservative public. The Kreisky government was obviously strong enough to risk a number of unpopular reforms, such as the abortion law, the setting up of a women's secretariat within government and the like. Nevertheless, in all three countries governments ensured that the impetus for political decisions was seen as coming from them. Initially in Switzerland and West Germany, these political decisions were clearly in opposition to feminists and were expressed as resistance and hostility. Generally, it seems, there is little acknowledgement, let alone respect, for extra-parliamentary opposition and the governments of Austria and West Germany have ignored protest groups as far as possible. They were able to do so, however, by rightly judging that the voting behaviour of the public at large would generally not be affected by gender issues. This may be less true of Austria than of West Germany and Switzerland.

The concept of democracy has also varied over time and has undergone some profound changes within the short span of the post-World War II period. In the 1960s, the *Dictionary of the Social Sciences* listed as the basic tenets of western democracy such things as equality before the law, and freedom of speech, of the press, and of religious as well as other civil liberties. It also included government responsibility to majority vote and the obligation to obey laws which express the will of the majority, provided that they are based on 'universal' suffrage by free secret ballot and regular elections with more than one political party (Gould & Kolb, 1964: 187). Over the last two or three decades, however, our expectations of democracy at work have changed or, rather, expanded to include a variety of other rights and obligations. First and foremost, such rights are now considered not only within the sphere of the politico-legal arena but also within the economic and socio-economic spheres: economic freedom and equality of economic opportunity have become inherent in our contemporary notion of democracy. Of a yet more recent date is the claim that social equality of opportunity, including formal education and personal realisation of abilities are also part of democracy at work.

Not all governments of western European countries would readily embrace this new self-understanding of democracy which, for want of a better word, has been classified as social democracy. In most of western Europe of the post-World War II period, however, the trend was towards social democracy and West Germany has not escaped that trend. We are told that this trend, for some time, has resulted in a 'profound unease' about present conditions and future prospects of social democracy, expressing itself as a constant tension between the parties' commitment to social change and their commitment to democratic values. The various countries have tried to solve these tensions in different ways. In West Germany for instance, the commitment to a range of democratic values was taken more seriously than was the commitment to social change (Kolinsky & Paterson, 1976: 209). The argument contrasts social change with democracy as if democracy, per se, epitomised a static situation to which social change was an alien and possibly deterring element. Indeed, the West German emphasis on law and order, no doubt fostered by fears of slipping into the morally lawless society of its immediate past experience, in more than one respect hampers the very idea of social change. But in West Germany, the uncertainty goes deeper than just the question of how much social change a society should and can bear, and for whose benefit it is. The issue is with democracy itself. In this regard a critical observer of West German society, Theodor W. Adorno, queried the West German attitude to democracy. With the hindsight of the turmoils of the 1970s, his remarks of 1963 have not lost but gained in poignancy. He wrote then:

> This much we will be able to say, that the system of political democracy has been accepted in Germany as something that in the US is called a working proposition, as a functioning entity which up to now allowed for, or even fostered, prosperity. But democracy has not settled in well enough for people to experience it as their own and for them to know themselves to be subjects in a political process. It is regarded as a system amongst others, just as if one had a sample chart from which one could choose between communism, democracy, fascism and monarchy, but not as a system which is identical with the people itself as an expression of its maturity (Mündigkeit). Democracy is assessed according to its success and failure in which one's own interests play a part but it is not assessed as a unity of one's own interests within the totality of interests of society ... (Adorno, 1963: 130, trans. GK)

West German governments during the years of the most active feminist movement have demonstrated that they followed a method of democratic rule which clearly stated that special-interest groups have no right to interfere with the programmes of a democratically elected government. Feminists in turn have stayed outside the political party machinery and their position has been weakened politically by a refusal to mirror party politics in terms of structures and hierarchies. They have formed no representative bodies and they have resisted hierarchisation, but at a cost. For the West German autonomous movement had no spokespersons for the movement, and no way to respond, in representative ways, to media and political criticism. Autonomy was certainly achieved within the movement but, as a consequence, it remained an extra-parliamentary opposition with very little political clout. In West Germany, the jealously guarded autonomy of the women's movement has now broken down a little and, in recent years, members of the movement have sometimes been willing to work with and through government institutions (Ferree, 1987: 184). Whether this is a blessing or whether it signals the final collapse of the movement and the spirit behind it remains to be seen. In Austria, negotiation with and co-option into the government had been a feature from the very beginnings of the weak Austrian

**Table 4.9    Drop of population from economically active age groups to 0–14 age groups**

| Country | % | Country | % |
|---|---|---|---|
| West Germany | 53.6 | Italy | 44.2 |
| Switzerland | 50.4 | Greece | 43.7 |
| Austria | 48.5 | Norway | 43.1 |
| Denmark | 47.8 | Spain | 41.2 |
| Netherlands | 47.3 | Portugal | 39.7 |
| Sweden | 46.5 | Belgium | 35.6 |
| UK | 45.5 | Ireland | 30.0 |
| France | 44.6 | | |

*Source*: calculated from Höhn,1985

movement in the early 1970s. Indeed, the method of co-option may have partly contributed to the weakness, since strong and vocal feminists were removed from the movement and brought into the fold of the government (Benard & Schlaffer, 1984).

Since the crises of the 1970s, West Germany has once again decided, where possible, to stay away from anything that might be perceived as social experimentation or change. Environmental and gender issues belong in the uncomfortable category of events and demands that will cost money and some social engineering. Change has occurred, falteringly, but in many cases it has been reversed in recent years. The issue of motherhood and reproduction, however, has remained to the forefront of government activity, less so as a consequence of a feminist lobby than as a result of changing demographic factors. Here, governments often provided unsolicited comments. Statistics have revealed that, proportionally, the central European Germanic countries have the smallest contingent of young generations (see table 4.9).

This narrowing population base has led to policies for women which, on the surface, look promising but barely hide a pro-motherhood ideology. Especially in West Germany, these birthrates below zero-population growth have raised concerns for planning (e.g. education) as well as for fiscal management (e.g. pension payments). The 65-plus age group is one that continues to increase in number as death rates fall. The left- and right-wing parties alike have questioned how pension provisions for the elderly can be upheld at the present level if the ratio between the economically active and the economically passive is changing in the direction of having fewer to pay for more.

More than indirectly, West German governments have expressed distress with women for their refusal to produce sufficient numbers of the next generation, which is supposed to pay for the economically inactive (Radusch, 1981: 21). They have sought ways of 'encouraging' women into marriage and motherhood. I would like to raise two points in connection with this concern: one is that headaches about 'underproduction' of children in an overcrowded world seem ludicrously out of place; the other acknowledges that most people in West Germany make substantial contributions towards their own old-age pensions, and thus it is irrational, or dishonest, to argue that there is no one to pay for the aging population when that same aging population in fact will have paid for itself. Governments may well choose to spend the money held in trust for pensions on other budgetary items, but they cannot then make the perverse claim that their budget deficits or mismanagement of fiscal matters should be alleviated by a higher birthrate! Since the CDU returned to power in 1982, the trend towards an outspoken reproduction policy has become more obvious. In Austria, as in West Germany, the net of maternity provisions and safeguards for women who become mothers is excellent. Earlier than West Germany, Austrian governments decided to improve this area of service for women. By the late 1970s, Austria had one of the highest maternity leave payment structures in Europe and even the world (Oakley, 1983: 119).

There are some substantial changes in other areas as well. Post-1945, many democratic rights were granted automatically, and freedoms were bestowed on German women which had either previously been theirs for a short period during the Weimar Republic or had never been granted before. Throughout the 1970s, West Germany and Austria decreed new laws for the elimination of gender discrimination in education and work. Switzerland has slowly followed suit with reforms that have at least eradicated the most archaic and discriminatory practices against women. Conceptually, however, very little has happened in Germanic countries (in comparison to the Scandinavian countries) that would really threaten traditional beliefs. On any scale of attitudinal values, statistical analysis of macro-data identifying gender distributions, power, income, and even visibility structures, shows that women are at a substantial disadvantage in all three countries, even though the belief that a woman has complete freedom of movement is widely shared by those women. In many ways, the Swiss and Austrian reforms have not yet grown beyond the 19th century British practice of democracy, understood then in purely political and legal terms (Pickles, 1971: 60). 'Time-honoured' traditions in both countries have a recalcitrance all of their own and make it fiendishly difficult for progressive feminists to even dent prevalent societal, and basically unthreatened, value hierarchies. Such concessions as have been made do not require a thorough revision of value hierarchies. On the contrary, the idea of giving concessions is often a way of preventing an examination of prevalent values. In all three countries, marriage and the family, for instance, are regarded as sanctified institutions and protected by laws. This is far removed from the Swedish model of cohabitation which places no particular value on any specific form of human adult bonds, and is explicit in not ascribing superior value to one form of cohabitation over another.

Abortion law reforms have usually not broken with the nexus of control over the female body. In Austria, despite the very liberal reform of 1974, the law has not led to a changed and freer practice. Abortion has largely remained a taboo subject and 'it is only by word of mouth that women can find their way to the scarce facility' (Outshoorn, 1988: 212).

In all three Germanic countries, equal pay provisions have at times not broken through the most fundamental barrier of a basically discriminatory perception that women may not be *capable* of performing work of equal value as men. In addition, in all three countries there are more than just remnants of the belief that men should be the breadwinners and women stay at home. Indeed, a worldwide opinion poll of the late 1970s found that Switzerland had the highest percentage of respondents of any industrialised country agreeing with this view (Hastings, 1980). The poor participation rates of women in politics, in positions of power and leadership, whether in the private or the public sectors, do not so much reflect a lack of opportunity as an at times negative attitude and a poor self-image on the part of women. Curiously, Switzerland is an exception here, with increasing numbers of women in politics in the late 1980s. Work-related organisations and union politics in all three countries have noticeably fewer women in them than in most other western European countries (see table 4.10).

**Table 4.10   Percentage of women in union elites in 1981 in selected western European countries**

| | | | |
|---|---|---|---|
| France | 25.5 | Austria | 8.1 |
| Italy | 15.9 | West Germany | 7.8 |
| Iceland | 15.5 | UK | 6.9 |
| Denmark | 12.9 | Switzerland | 3.0 |
| Sweden | 9.4 | Belgium | 2.8 |

Source: *Information 6. Women's Representation in Trade Unions*, European Trade Union Institute, 1983

We have seen in our description of attitudes and distribution of leading positions that attitudes of the general population (women included) reflect considerable doubts about the merits of a basic integrative egalitarianism. The idea of liberation, as need not be stressed, fades from view altogether. One ought to remain aware that equal rights policies in themselves need not be progressive at all and it depends on where they start and what they amend. Reforms of relatively small scale may have vast implications while a whole host of reforms in another area may not even scratch the surface of the problem.

The feminist counter culture certainly looks as if it is going to remain a permanent feature of West German (and Austrian) society. Feminist bookshops, publishing houses, and various other cultural activities have become businesses like any other and serve a well-established network of women. Thus, a substantial change has occurred in this cultural domain: a women's culture has been created that goes well beyond the club culture of earlier days, which was defined in terms of women's roles as wives, mothers and housewives. This new feminist counter culture is strongly separatist. Some of the bleak prognoses made in the 1970s about the possible disappearance of feminist debates and viewpoints have thus turned out to be incorrect. Nevertheless, the implementation of the ideal of women's equality, let alone of women's 'liberation' is a long way off.

Some writers have blamed the 'mentality' and the 'soul' of Germanic countries for the apparent reluctance to adopt change. I cannot underwrite such spirituality, as I do not believe in such notions as the 'soul' of a people. Switzerland, Austria and West Germany, despite some similarities, have undergone very different historical and political experiences. That they have ended up as being the conservative core of Europe, at least where women are concerned, is not explained by such nebulousness.

What then of the seesaw effect? How can the hypothesis be tested here? I believe that the hypothesis is not rendered invalid, but that in environments of conservative reformism the seesaw has nevertheless begun to swing. Common to all three countries is the conservative position on gender issues which, superficially, might even appear, in certain instances, as a curious contradiction of the economic goals of 'progress', advancement, and innovativeness. An earlier point needs to be reiterated here, and it confirms the hypothesis of the seesaw effect. All three countries, whether in relation to their size, their destruction in World War II or their ensuing problems, have achieved astounding economic feats in the postwar years. The wealth of Switzerland and of West Germany is almost legendary. Even Austria, given its size, limited resources and small population, has survived and grown economically far beyond the most daring predictions. In all three countries, the chief energies have gone into economic endeavour, with more than average success. The principle of inequality, as was said in chapter 1, however, is not just a concomitant but an inherent part of capitalist economies, and this in itself is a powerful deterrent against any attempt to deal with, let alone eradicate, socio-economic inequalities, of which women are a glaring manifestation.

At the same time, values have begun to change and certain allowances for new egalitarian views have had to be made. It seems to me that the perception of equality, particularly in West Germany, stems from two factors. In personal freedom, women in all three countries are free; they can go anywhere and indeed choose to do what they like; and in personal relationships, women have considerably more freedom than ever before. Added to this is the general wealth of these countries which is shared, to a great extent, by a very broadly based middle class. The women's movement and the increasing emancipation of women is firmly based in that middle class. As far as this class-based structure is concerned, it has helped to propagate the myth of women's achieved status of emancipation. But not all are middle class and not all can take up the advantages of middle-class living, and not even all middle-class women could claim to live well or without discrimination. Feminists have done little practical work to help their blue-collar working sisters. Schlaeger laments that the ideology of an affluent society 'only allows misery to be viewed as an individual problem' (1978: 65). We have seen that this is not the case in Scandinavian countries and the claim that affluence prevents alliances across classes is simply not true. Rather, they are prevented as long as class hierarchies are firmly in place. Despite Schelsky's remarkable attempt in 1965 to persuade readers that West Germany was a 'classless society'—in the sense that its affluence had made it a unitary middle class (1965: 332–40)—West Germany has remained a class-structured society (Dahrendorf, 1972: 86 ff, ch. 6). This is not to say that many of the demands of feminists are not, in essence, directed towards undermining or eradicating inequalities. In the most radical groups, such as socialist feminist and communist feminist groups, the recognition for the need to break down gender inequalities *together* with class inequalities is more than apparent. But to those proposals the *resistance* by German society seems to have been profound.

In West Germany, influenced by the US models, consciousness-raising groups and other spiritual feminist endeavours have had a firm place in the movement's agenda. Many women may have a new consciousness now, but this consciousness may have become an end in itself. Moreover, consciousness-raising groups belong in the broadest sense to a western individualism. That individualism implicitly argues that one can get anywhere as long as one makes the right moves oneself. But will it change anything of the structured inequalities that the particular society has set up? For the seesaw to stop swinging, conceptual changes need to be made first. In not one of the three countries has this occurred so far.

Argued on concrete examples, the seesaw effect can become very pronounced. In personal expressions of freedom, Austrian and West German women have achieved a great deal but in political participation and economic independence they are often poor cousins of neighbouring countries. In Switzerland, personal attitudes and economic management have remained very traditional while women have gained substantial access to politics. Ironically, while women were and still are not permitted to vote at every level and in every part of Switzerland, participation of women in politics has increased sharply throughout the 1970s and 1980s. In 1971, it stood at 5 percent and by 1979 at 10.5 percent. By the mid-1980s the figure had risen to 15 percent, leaving West German and Austrian women behind (Norris, 1987: 131).

As early as 1931 Leonard Woolf, in his book *After the Deluge*, made the important distinction that civil liberties aim at the protection of the individual *against* authority, while political democracy aims at the just and rational organisation *of* authority in human society. Clearly, the women's movement in western Europe, not just in the Germanic countries, was and still is a civil rights movement, but more than that—it is also a civil liberation movement. All western European democracies have organised their societies in 'rational organisations of authority'. Whether they are always 'just' is one of the debatable issues of the movements of the postwar era. However, the civil liberties aspects of democracies were, and still are, promises to be fulfilled. There can be no liberty where there is inequality. This French Revolutionary insight has either not been fully grasped by those in power, or it has been purposely ignored. I think that the latter is generally true of all three Germanic countries and moves towards equal rights policies have not been volunteered. If pressure is brought to bear on these countries it may have to be continued internationally, and first and foremost come from the EEC. Deutsch's cascade model might possibly fit this supranational frame of the EEC, which is to become the European single market in 1992.

# 5 Fringe upheavals and creative traditionalism in France and the Netherlands

At the risk of overstating the case, the Netherlands and France have been categorised under one specific paradigm despite the fact that they are in many ways so obviously different. Our interest here, however, lies in the discovery of patterns of interaction between protest movements, society at large and the government of the day. Indeed, in this respect, there do appear to be important similarities which must rouse our interest. In both countries, the degree and intensity of the movements stood in no relationship to the outcomes that were achieved. Relative to the efforts made by the grassroots movements, women seemed to have received more in return than one would have expected. Before the second wave began, the status of women and the attitudes towards family, reproduction and gender roles were not appreciably different in the Netherlands and in France from those in the Germanic countries. After the Dutch and French movements had subsided, however, everything had altered so substantially that some writers even doubted whether the name 'reform' adequately described the turn-about of laws, rules and social practices which occurred within a few decades (Stetson, 1987: 101).

One is tempted to ask why change in France and in the Netherlands was so rapid and so thoroughgoing when the manner of protest was generally no different to that employed by German-speaking women? I am afraid that one will need to resist this temptation to avoid simplistic and reductionist arguments. But it is useful to remember that the traditions of both France and the Netherlands include a conservative *and* an equally strong radical strand. Both countries have strong traditions of dissent, have repeatedly insisted on the freedom of expression and, concomittently, have condoned or *counted on* critical and speculative thought. I have called this 'creative traditionalism', indicating that historical experience has turned protest and change themselves into a tradition.

In the Netherlands that tradition began in the 16th century with the 'golden age' of its provinces both as a leading European power and as a model of freedom of expression. The Dutch (Northern) Provinces, as they were called then, had fought for and won their freedom from Spanish oppression in 1579 and later even aided in defeating the Spanish Armada. This was a feat widely admired in Europe and also greeted with disbelief. The Dutch Provinces were but a tiny conglomerate of provinces, while Spain, apart from the Ottoman, was the most powerful and largest empire in the world. David had won against Goliath. By the middle of the 17th century, the Dutch were arguably the most powerful nation in Europe. They had created a large colonial empire, they commanded the only standing army that came close in size to that of the Spanish Empire, and their merchant ships dominated all major sea routes. More than 70 percent of the Baltic trade was controlled by Dutch ships. Dutch was the diplomatic language throughout the Baltic region (Huizinga, 1968: 150) and contemporaries valued the provinces as the high school of every tradesman.

Much more impelling than their economic leadership, however, was their spiritual leadership. They were a 'working model of free institutions' (Sombart, 1967: 144) and the 'centre of light for the rest of Europe' (Figgis, 1956: 168). Their freedom of press and their willingness to publish foreign language material gave the Dutch Provinces a unique role in European life as mediators and as a forum of opinion. They provided the venue for otherwise unpublishable material and were the one and only sounding board for controversial European ideas in toto. From the provinces emanated the richness and diversity of foreign heterodoxy. Faster than the Vatican was able to put works onto the Index of banned books, the provinces printed new 'heresies' and uncovered old ones. Dutch publishing houses like Elsevier diffused books more widely, more efficiently and promptly than anywhere else at the time. For the history of ideas, the Dutch book trade had enormous implications. The freedom of the press also created within the provinces themselves a climate that was most conducive to speculative thought. Bertrand Russell points out that, with respect to philosophy, it was this 'Dutch freedom of speculation which made possible the most notable advances since Greek times', and he rightly concludes that it was therefore 'impossible to exaggerate the importance of Holland in the seventeenth century' (Russell, 1945: 525).

Of course under Louis XIV the hegemony of Europe quickly switched to France. It was Versailles which eventually provided a refined European audience with a new focal point and a new cultural leadership. France was important to 17th and 18th century Europe not just because of Versailles and its military might. There was another French tradition which was to prove of lasting importance for France and for the rest of the western world. This 'other' tradition, the radicalism and enlightenment that had its roots in the writings of the *philosophes*, culminated in 1789 in the French Revolution. The principles of *égalité, fraternité, liberté,* its declaration of human rights, set new agendas for Europe and the world. It taught the French the lesson that there were ways of forcing rapid and fundamental change, even against powerful vested interests.

While these histories may seem far removed from present-day France and Holland, they have been kept alive and have been passed on from generation to generation, intertwined, as they are, with each countries' sense of national identity and heritage. In recent history there has been ample opportunity in both countries to practise resistance and rebellion. The last occasion in the Netherlands was furnished by the Nazi occupation, which united the Dutch people in their will to survive and to oust the oppressor. To an extent that was also true in France, but French history of the postwar era was stormy enough in itself to ensure that political skills needed for effective dissent were never lost. French and Dutch societies have developed and nurtured a high degree of political consciousness that not only readily *responds* to political and social actions but *initiates* action. The issue is not always whether others agree with the content of dissension, and indeed Dutch and French public opinion on the new feminism has often been less than supportive, but whether the public is willing to consider grievances in the first place, and perceive their utterance as a legitimate or illegitimate exercise. Once dissension as a political act is regarded as legitimate, the ground rules of protest and response are fundamentally different from those contexts in which there is no legitimate space for dissent. In France and the Netherlands, the fights for change were no easier just because of this sense of legitimacy. But while the battles were hard and long, they carried the reforms a good deal further than did like battles across their eastern borders.

The Netherlands and France also remind one of another important historical phenomenon. It is rarely made clear in current feminist debate that, in earlier centuries, women at certain times and in certain places had significant rights or at least pockets of individual freedoms which had then been lost. The Netherlands, like Italy, could boast famous Renaissance women (Morgan, 1984: 468) who excelled in the fine arts, and even in universalist scholars such as Anna Maria van Schuurmann (1607–1678), who was at once a musician, a painter, a poet, an engraver, sculptor and linguist. Possibly the most pronounced loss of freedom for women occurred in the 19th century with the subjugation of the family and a pro-motherhood philosophy that was pursued especially vigorously in the second half of the 19th century by competing catholics and calvinists. The potential for equality between the sexes had existed well before that, partly because of the Dutch free-thinking tradition and also as a consequence of the French Revolution (Hogeweg-de Haart, 1978: 20). As said earlier on, in many cases, restrictive legislation, which was directly or indirectly against the interests of women, was in fact usually not introduced before the 20th century. In the Netherlands, the first law to be explicit about abortion was passed in 1836. As late as 1911, the law was tightened, making abortion a crime in all cases except for severe medical reasons (Francome, 1984: 135). Likewise, in most western European countries up to the 17th century, women were also able to run businesses and farms independently. Increasingly, women of the bourgeoisie (of the merchant middle classes) were shut in at home as a sign of the prestige and income status of the male, while women of lower status tended to be co-opted into the processes of the Industrial Revolution. Thus, it was not just a matter of liberation for women as a whole. Rather, the marked differences that urbanisation and industrialisation had created made working-class women hope for an end to their involuntary ordeal in factories and allow them to stay at home, while middle-class women, over most of western Europe, felt so stifled in the home that they wanted to break out of their gilded cages.

The Netherlands adopted their first constitution in 1815, after the fall of Napoleon. It was then the Netherlands ceased to be a French possession, which had been the case for a few decades. The monarchy was made constitutional and hereditary in the house of Oranje-Nassau by primogeniture of males, with the possibility of rule by a female. The crown bearer was automatically the executive. Interestingly, for the past 100 years the Netherlands have had female monarchs: first Wilhelmina (1890–1948); then Juliana (1948–1980); and, since 1980, Beatrix. All of them have been very capable political leaders, irrespective of whether one agrees with their politics or not. The examples they set, as is the case with female monarchs in several other countries, should have refuted long ago the notion of women's inferior ability in politics.

The fight for equal rights gained ground from the 1860s onwards. In 1867, the town of Haarlem pioneered a new type of school that was exclusively for girls. Girls were beginning to be educated and the trend towards liberation had begun, leading in 1884 to the formation of De Vereniging voor Vrouwenkiesrecht (Association for Women's Suffrage). So disconcerting were these developments to male politicans that in 1887, during a revision of the constitution, a special clause was inserted explicitly stating that women were not to vote. This prohibition not only increased the vigour of the resistance, but also the zest for more liberty, for the vote, and for better conditions for women. Under such able women as Wilhelmina Drucker (later called *Dolle Mina*—Mad Mina), and Aletta Jacobs, the Dutch suffrage movement soon gained momentum. In 1889, Mina Drucker founded an Association of Free Women (De Vrije Frouwenbeweging) and later edited its magazine *Evolution*. She embraced the new socialist ideals and spent her life fighting for women's rights; she was, for instance, instrumental in safeguarding women's right to go to work. The suffrage movement commenced mainly due to the initiative of Aletta H. Jacobs, the first woman medical doctor in the Netherlands. Aletta Jacobs (1854–1929) was a woman of exceptional perseverance. In 1870, she was the first girl ever to be admitted to the Higher Burgher School, only, however, as a 'listener'. Until 1906, no girls had been admitted to these high schools without specific approval of the inspector of schools. She became the first female student at the University of Groningen and later devoted her life to women's issues. She established a free clinic for poor women of Amsterdam and also pioneered the introduction of birth control methods, where this appeared to be medically or socially advisable. Her work pioneered contraceptive methods all over Europe (Brugmans, 1961: 287). She is a much revered personality of Dutch history now, as her statue in Amsterdam testifies.

The enfranchisement of women was granted in 1919 and the Internationaal Vrouwen Archief[1] was founded in 1935. In general, though, the post-World War I years, with the setting in of the recession, saw the women's question recede into the background and the few rights threatened that had been obtained (Hogeweg-de Haart, 1978). Holland was neutral in World War I and intended to remain so in World War II, but it was occupied by the Nazis in 1940, forcing the royal household and cabinet into exile in London. From here the ousted government ran a strong and well-organised resistance movement in which women played an important part. The German occupation had two immediate consequences. It almost entirely destroyed the Dutch economy, and it made Holland give up its traditional neutrality.

After the war, the monarchy was reinstated and the Netherlands began to embark on a course of heavy industrialisation. As with other European powers, its colonial empire crumbled, first with the loss of Indonesia (in 1949), then of Dutch New Guinea (in 1963) and finally of Dutch India and Surinam (in 1975). The loss of Indonesia was economically not as catastrophic as had initially been predicted. This was helped by internal political collaboration on economic matters and a concerted programme for industrialisation. Between 1950 and 1960, the Netherlands doubled productivity and raised it to three times the prewar level (Woller, 1983: 162). Petrochemical industrial centres sprung up west of Amsterdam, notably in Rotterdam, now one of the largest such centres in the world. Interestingly, industrialisation in the Netherlands did not result in a sharp rise of female labour, a fact that is noteworthy in the context of the reserve army labour theory of women. At least up until the 1970s, participation rates of women in the labour force had not appreciably altered since the turn of the century. In 1909, 23.9 percent of the labour force were women and in 1979 the percentage had just crept up to 27.4 percent (*Emancipation*, 1980: 66). It has increased since but only to 34.3 percent, and is still amongst the lowest in western Europe.

Dutch society is largely a homogeneous country, 95 percent Dutch, with a sprinkling of ethnically different groups from Surinam, the Mediterranean and other places. If one can speak of pluralism at all, it is of a pluralism mostly created by differences of opinion, as in religious and political ideologies (Meissner,

1980: 16), vertically cutting across all sections of society (*vertikale pluriformisme*). This vertical ideological separation split Dutch society in the 19th century and still needed to be overcome in the 1970s. Dutch sociologists call this phenomenon *verzuiling* (pillarisation) but argue that it has gradually eased in virulence in the postwar years, partly due to the waning importance of religion in people's lives. One would assume that this pillarisation had to become more transparent before a national women's movement could effectively take off. The coincidence between these elusive processes and the onset of the women's movement in the Netherlands would generally support this view.

It may be argued, however, that the political and institutional life of the Netherlands was anything but geared for social and political change, leaving dissenters to face a myriad of brick walls and institutional tangles. Unlike West Germany, the Dutch political party system does not have a 5 percent clause and is therefore multiparty (i.e. including even very small parties), as are all Scandinavian countries. On average, there are thirteen to fifteen parties in the Dutch lower house (*Tweede Kamer*) but there are instances in recent history, as in 1977, when as many as 27 parties have been part of the coalition government. Admittedly, 1977 marked the longest government crisis in Dutch postwar history and it was eventually resolved by an uneasy coalition between the Labour Party and the Christian Democrats. Yet this system has obvious advantages in the Dutch case, such as creating a buffer against the pillarisation of Dutch society. It is clear that such a diversity of parties governing together makes it difficult for one world view or one political ideology to dominate.

Unlike other multiparty systems in western Europe, the Dutch system, in fact, proved a particular stumbling block for feminist activists. Its complexity has shown time and again to be supple enough to resist change partly because of certain tactical disadvantages when and where change is desired. One of its effects is that parties invariably vote en bloc. Dutch feminists learned that there was little value in lobbying individual members for a certain course of action. In all instances the whole party needed to be influenced (Briët et al., 1987: 47). This, coupled with the general conservatism in the Netherlands, has made it more difficult for the second feminist movement to affect change. Yet another set of circumstances militated against political change. In the early 1970s the Dutch welfare system was decentralised so that many battles had to be carried on at local rather than national level. Moreover, Dutch unions were allegedly the most bureaucratic within the labour movement of western Europe. In other words, Dutch feminists were faced with a bewildering complexity of bureaucratic and political structures, and their position did not appear an easy one from the outset.

The Dutch women's movement began as early as the Finnish movement (in 1967). Unlike the Finnish movement, however, which was at first barely noticed elsewhere, the Dutch movement in some ways set a model for the rest of western Europe. Unique in western Europe was the Dutch movement being preceded by public discussions of sexuality, homosexuality, and love and marriage. These public discussions throughout the 1960s created an atmosphere of openness on such issues (De Vries, 1981: 391) so that the gay groups and lesbian associations which developed during the years of the women's movement were far less marked by the 'coming out' trauma experienced in other countries.

In 1967, the social democrat and now well known feminist Jok Kool-Smit wrote an article entitled 'Het onbehagen bij de vrouw' (The discontent amongst women) which has been regarded as the starting point for the new feminist wave

(Rang, 1988: 165). At that time, there existed a number of well-run traditional women's organisations, such as the Dutch Federation of Country Women and the Dutch Federation of Housewives. These were largely sworn to remain non-political. Hence Dutch feminists, as feminists elsewhere, had to create new structures and organisations (Outshoorn, 1986a: 64). The members of the various organisations had usually been politically active before the onset of the women's movement, for instance as students or in the anti-Vietnam movement. As were other movements in western Europe, the Dutch new wave was also influenced by publications from the USA, and it counted amongst the seminal US literature *Notes From the Second Year* (1970) and *Voices from Women's Liberation* (1971).

One of the first groups was called Work Group 2000. A year later, in 1968, the MVM was formed (Man–Vrouw–Maatschappij—Man–Woman–Society), followed in 1970 by Dolle Mina, named after Wilhelmina Drucker. Thereafter a multitude of other organisations sprung up such as the Purperen Mien, Paarse September, married women's groups such as '7152', and *praat groepen* (consciousness-raising groups). The MVM largely consisted of well-educated members of the middle class. It was not just a well-organised, well-informed lobby group, but as such it was probably unique in the western European new-wave movements because, as the name suggests, it consisted of women and men. Unlike other organisations with male and female membership, the Dutch MVM never deteriorated into generalist political issues. Yet its energies more or less dissipated within seven years. It is debatable whether its disappearance was indirectly a result of its strength or an inherent weakness of its approach or possibly both. The organisation had played such an important role in the public debate of women's issues that members of the group were approached as 'experts' on women's questions and its leadership was increasingly co-opted onto special advisory and government committees. Unavoidably, the government's appreciation of its skills and knowledge drained the movement of its leadership and best talent. The MVM eventually dissolved, not least as a consequence of co-option. No doubt, co-option can function as a powerful political weapon to eliminate political pressure groups in the community.

The strongest energies of the women's movement emanated and still emanate from the socialist feminist camp, largely outside the political system, while the Communist Party tended to remain strongly anti-feminist. Socialist feminism has been the driving force in Dutch feminism and has become best known outside the Netherlands, with such outstanding literary figures and prolific writers as Anja Meulenbelt, Joyce Outshoorn and Petra de Vries. Dolle Mina, operating within a socialist framework, was a much more radical organisation than MVM and apparently became generic for 'liberated women' (Outshoorn, 1986a: 65). Its members published and engaged in a series of protest actions in order to attract public attention and gain public support for their claims. One of its early brochures bore the telling title *Een rebelse meid is een parel in de klassestrijd* (A rebellious woman is a pearl in the class struggle). Dolle Mina remained in public view throughout the 1970s, partly for its strong pro-abortion stand and its methods of conveying women's views on the subject. Campaigns like '*Blijf van mijn Lijf*' (keep away from my body) and the women's refuge movement followed similar patterns as in West Germany. In 1980, the government supported financially at least 30 rape crisis centres. Feminist therapy groups and women's health centres were opened, first in Amsterdam but eventually throughout the country. At the same time, a profusion of publications and new journals began to dot the literary landscape of the Netherlands, as *Dolle Mina, Vrouwen, Opzij, Serpentine, Vrouwenkrant* and *Lover* appeared. Feminist publishing houses such as De Bonte Was (1972) and Sara (1976) started operating in Amsterdam (Dittrich, 1980).

Amongst its spectacular actions was the gate crashing of a gynaecologist congress in 1970. Women disrupted the congress and paraded in front of the gates and the gynaecologists with slogans written across their bellies. The action *'Baas in eigen Buik'* (boss of one's own belly) was able to win widespread public support at a time when the estimated annual figure of illegal abortions was 10 000 to 15 000. Ironically, most abortions performed within the Netherlands were serving women from other countries (such as West Germany) while Dutch women usually had to travel to England if they wanted an abortion. It is probable that the risk of being tried for illegal abortion was generally perceived as being greater in one's own country of citizenship than in a foreign country. The travel industry benefited greatly from these 'abortion travellers', but this alone made a farce of the illegality of abortions everywhere. The social practice had long been otherwise and gynaecologists reaped substantial additional incomes, literally at women's expense. In addition, only the well-to-do were able to undertake the journey, leaving the poor to bear the unwanted pregnancies. But unlike other countries, abortion was also practised widely within the Netherlands and the government rarely interfered or laid charges.

By 1967, abortions were available legally on some social grounds but the method was cumbersome and obviously did not apply to every woman who sought a termination of her pregnancy. In 1971, the first outpatient abortion clinic opened its doors in Holland, and by 1980 there were already fifteen such clinics. Between 1970 and 1981, there had been eight abortion bills before parliament, and each step of reform or amendment was juxtaposed by demonstrations and actions. In 1974, for example, the then Minister for Justice determined that the abortion clinic Bloemenhove would be closed down, but women, mostly Dolle Mina women, effectively prevented police from entry and held out a siege for two weeks, during which time the action received widespread support from the public. The clinic remained open (Outshoorn, 1986: 78). Indeed, for a short period of time in 1974, the abortion issue was the only one that brought all women's groups together in a coalition named Wij Vrouwen Eisen (We Women Demand). Their demands have been published in various publications, see for instance the ones put out by the Emancipatieraad and by the Breed Platform. Later attempts to achieve similar coalitions of women's groups, such as the Breed Platform (Broad Platform), were not nearly as successful as the action *'Wij Vrouwen Eisen'* had been eight years earlier.

The coming years were again dotted with demonstrations and strike action. One of the largest of these occurred in 1981, in response to an abortion bill unacceptable to Dutch feminists. On 31 March, over 20 000 women went on strike, either at home or at work. Eventually, the abortion law reform lobbies had more or less achieved their aim and this ended a long-standing political battle which had begun even before the second wave had started. In specially licensed clinics abortion was made available on demand for women up to their twentieth week of pregnancy and, as part of the national health insurance, it was delivered free of charge (Francome, 1984: 137).

About the same time, in the mid-1970s, the media began to lose interest in the women's movement, but the snowball effect of the first years of the new wave was clearly evident. The women's liberation movement, says Oudijk, 'has created a change in Dutch society so fundamental that it's impossible to turn it back' (1984: 474). By the mid-1970s women's cells within political parties had become radicalised. In the political parties of the left *rooie vrouwen* (red women) organised themselves as pressure groups. Feminism had penetrated deeply into Dutch culture and even small towns had women's groups, cafes, bookshops or some educational activity specific to women. In 1977 the movement had groups in about 37 towns. Five years later, the number of towns with feminist groups had grown to nearly 160. Effectively this meant that in every fourth town in the Netherlands the women's movement was represented and active in one way or another (Briët et al., 1987: 46). De Vries suggests, however, that in those years feminism was better described in terms of consciousness rather than in terms of actions and activities (1981: 391). But it should also be described in terms of increased educational opportunities. Women chose to enter access education, continuing education and night school programmes, which mush-roomed throughout the country as a consequence of the feminist endeavour to educate women and to reach specifically working-class women. The feminist adult education groups and the high school for adults, called Mothers Mavos, have many feminist teachers (Lovenduski, 1986: 84). Curiously, while generalist educational courses have received such a boost, the spin-off effect of turning education into careers has been small and slow.

In the Netherlands, the years 1974 to 1975 saw an important turning point for the women's movement, and not just because of the economic crisis that had beset western Europe. From the mid-1970s onwards, the Dutch government finally began to respond to EEC directives and to feminist lobbies, to set in place a number of new structures and programmes, and to embark on a series of far-reaching reforms. One needs to bear in mind here that the Dutch social security system is considered to be one of the best in the western world. Enshrined within it is a guarantee of each citizen's right to social assistance. It has wage-related and means-tested schemes and, like Australia, functions on the notion of a minimum income below which no individual should fall. In other words, a good many things had already happened in the social security area in support of greater equity between the sexes even before the women's movement began. The divorce law liberalisation occurred rather early, in 1971, and allowed for divorce after one year between mutually consenting partners and after three years of separation if one party was unwilling. Only civil marriage was regarded as legal and all property was considered jointly. In the same year, contraceptive services were made available free of charge and two years later sterilisation was also covered as a free service under the National Health Insurance Plan. These laws and amendments followed the debates of the 1960s and preceded the women's movement.

In 1974, however, the government signalled its willingness to do something very specific for women, at first by establishing a Committee on the Status of Women (an emancipation commission) in order to construct a comprehensive and consistent policy on the emancipation of women. In 1975, the Nederlandse Vrouwen Raad (Netherlands' Council of Women), which today has over one million members, began to be funded by the government. The same year, an equal pay for equal work act was released, following the directives of the EEC. In 1977, the Dutch government appointed a state secretary for emancipatory politics. In 1980, the Equal Treatment of Men and Women Act was introduced, specifically aiming at any discriminatory practices against women at work. The 1982 Civil Code reform introduced other sweeping changes, amongst them those concerned with inheritance of children born out of wedlock, and discrimination. The new draft bill included in its identifiers of discrimination, marital status and sexual preference. Sometimes the *absence* of laws is also emancipatory. Thus, in the Netherlands, there are no laws specifically dealing with homosexuality. It may indeed indicate truly progressive thinking that a government feels that there are areas in which it has no business at all to make rules, and others, like discrimination, in which it feels obliged to protect the individual citizen.

Presumably on the same assumption of needing to protect individual citizens against discrimination and any form of abuse, the government has also stepped into controversial areas such as prostitution. The law forbids pimping and brothels (i.e. any profit making on behalf and by the use of prostitutes), and new policies established government aid services for prostitutes. A 1989 inquiry into physical violence against prostitutes by the Ministry for Social Affairs and Employment Opportunities has revealed that they do not make too much use of that service despite an alarmingly high incidence of rape and other mistreatment experienced by them. Ter Veld, a female junior minister and Secretary of State, filed a report in response to this and asked parliament for major changes in the area of assistance for prostitutes (*Women of Europe*, no. 63, 1990: 26).

In the 1980s, governments sank considerable funds into universities, supported women's research at universities and made concerted efforts to ensure that women's studies could be undertaken and followed up by employment. For the years 1978 to 1981, the Dutch government set aside 46 million Gulden in order to foster the process of emancipation, not just in large cities but in any town. It advertised and offered money to any community with convincing ideas and plans that would work towards enhancing the status of women (Dittrich, 1980: 656). In later years, the government established a prize for the best such efforts, the *Joke Smit* award. Local administrations also have funds available (emancipation prizes) which are awarded to individuals, groups or government bodies that have contributed most 'to improving conditions for women in the Netherlands' (*Women of Europe*, no. 63, 1990: 28). The issue of prize giving, of course, can be a double-edged sword. It may help the government gain political kudos while diverting attention from areas of real urgency. I have found little evidence of this in the Dutch case. In the best sense, prizes can work as ongoing publicity, and they function well as a clandestine method of monitoring legislative change.

Nevertheless, the Dutch government itself is not all that exhuberant about its own achievements in the UN Decade for Women (1975–1985). Between 1985 and 1986, the Dutch Ministry of Social Affairs and Employment published a series of booklets on women's rights. In one entitled *A Decade of Equal Rights Policy in the Netherlands 1975–1985* it named the areas in which the government had been active, such as anti-discrimination legislation, subsidies to support equal rights and opportunities in society and the women's movement, measures to combat sexual violence against women and girls, experimental projects and help for women from minorities and women and employment, but it repeatedly allowed the reader to see the government's own level of frustration with the slow progress. In the introduction to another booklet, called *Design of an equal rights policy plan for women in the Netherlands*, the government apologetically states that it can act only 'within the limits of governmental responsibility and within the margins that are determined by the efforts to reduce the burden of social security charges and to conduct a socio-economic policy designed to bring about structural recovery in the Dutch economy'. Another booklet of the same period, called *Equal Rights and Opportunities for Women in the Netherlands* states laconically that 'the average workload for women, including paid and unpaid work, has risen while for men it has diminished'.

This self-critical attitude of the Dutch government is not without foundation, both in terms of the actual status of Dutch women in the 1980s, as well as in terms of its own legislative efforts. Not all reforms have worked well for women, as one of them, the revision of the taxation system, which came into force in January 1987, exemplifies. It highlights the difficulties of implementing social justice (i.e. equality) within the context of deep structural inequality. One of the complaints was that the taxation system indirectly discriminated against families with one breadwinner, seemingly arguing that married women who stayed at home to raise their children were not worthy of some taxation relief. So the balance was redressed, decreasing the tax burden on single breadwinner families and raising it for double income earners. The inevitable happened: the system now inadvertently discriminates against working women. The sudden rise in taxation on women as spouses or wives was such that the many women in part-time jobs suddenly saw their meagre incomes dwindle. Over 10 000 women left their part-time positions once the new system came into force. Likewise, a woman's income is now taken into account when her disabled or unemployed spouse receives security benefits. If *she* stays at home, *his* benefits increase. Again, it will mean that women may be discouraged to seek work or even just part-time work if there is so little financial benefit to be derived from it. Other changes, clearly aimed at lowering public expenditure, have removed discrimination but increased the contributing costs for individual women who have chosen forms of cohabitation other than marriage. As from 1986, unmarried partners, homosexual as well as heterosexual, have been treated as married couples for old-age pension benefits. Each person now receives 50 percent of the total pension benefit instead of the previous 70 percent for singles. Unmarried women in de facto relationships will have to make higher contributions to the scheme throughout their working lives but, in the end, will derive fewer benefits from this (Sjerps, 1988: 101–2).

In the work situation, Dutch women have found themselves generally in an unhappy transitional state. A longitudinal study, for instance, found that in 1967 by far the majority of married women stayed at home and described their position then as 'highly satisfied'. In the intervening decade of the women's movement, perhaps due to its influence or to other factors, attitudes of housewives changed substantially. The 1978 figures show that the level of high satisfaction for housewives had dropped to 37 percent (*Emancipation*, 1980: 71).

Indeed, women's direct participation in the country's GNP is among the lowest in western Europe, be this in the category of the gainfully employed generally, in decision-making positions or, as a future indicator, in education and preparation for a career. There are usually two reasons given for this low participation rate. One concerns the traditional bourgeois attitude, often expressed as 'my wife does not have to work'. As in France, where the *femme de la maison* has also not quite lost the nymbus of status, the Dutch division of labour and roles has persisted precisely because of the general affluence. Another not entirely unrelated cause is the excellent social welfare system, which permits single women, whether unmarried, divorced or widowed, to bring up their children on pension payments.

These views are too narrow, however, and there is a multitude of complicating factors. As we have seen, some of the recent changes in social security laws and the taxation system implicitly discourage women from seeking work. Furthermore, as a consequence of the economic crisis, workplaces were *not* readily available. Between the 1960s and 1970s the number of married women joining the workforce had risen from 7 to 31 percent and surveys showed that more would have joined had more jobs been available. Women who entered the labour force usually went into part-time positions. In the mid-1980s, over 50 percent of all working women were in part-time positions, as against 5 percent of men (Sjerps, 1988: 100). Women's unemployment rate was consistently higher than men's. Working women with children also found few, if any, support structures outside the home. In 1980 only 120 creches were available to cover childminding for a working day for children between the ages of 0–10 years of age, but by then 85 000 married women with children under 4 years of age were part of the working population and more than 20 000 children were on waiting lists (*Emancipation*, 1980: 75).

Moreover, women's participation rate in the labour force is inflated by a strong age bias. In fact, the majority of women in the Netherlands work, but usually do so only in preparation for marriage and a family. Women's participation rate drops off very sharply from the age of 25 years of age, comparable only to trends in Ireland and Luxembourg. In other western European and western industrialised nations women's employment figures by age suggest a much longer involvement across time. In addition, the Dutch labour market does not show the signs of a retrieval of women's labour after child bearing is over, as do other countries (Norris, 1987: 57–8).

These figures are further complicated but not entirely inconsistent with another finding that from the turn of the century to the 1970s, marriage rates for men and women alike have actually increased. In 1899 as few as 33.3 percent of women and 32.5 percent of men were married by the age of 40. By 1976, nearly 50 percent of men and women were married by this age (Gadourek, 1982: 225). The 1970s, however, also saw alternative lifestyle organisations, such as the BOM group, Bewust Ongehuwde Moeder (Purposely Unmarried Mothers). The trend in the 1980s has been towards postponement of marriage, higher divorce rate—it has tripled since the 1960s—and increased single living. Child bearing has dropped off from 2.6 to 1.6 children for each woman since the availability of contraceptives. But such changes in marital status have not been as apparent in workforce participation as one might think. Recent studies have shown that 60 percent of divorced women with children became recipients of government payments rather than participators in the workforce.

Women's participation in higher education has risen gradually, although the mid-1980s figures for women in professional occupations hovered around 18–22 percent. In 1980, only 25.4 percent of all graduands were women. Women in professions and in public offices were rare: only eleven of the 533 members of the diplomatic service (2.3 percent), 22 of a total of 902 lawyers (2.4 percent) and eleven of 759 mayors (0.9 percent) were women (Dittrich, 1980), but all these figures have risen since then. The overall percentage of female university students has just increased to over a third of all students and represents the lowest in western Europe. One may expect that the percentage of women in professional training and university courses generally will approach western European averages much more closely in the early 1990s. Eventually, this will mean that the professions will have to accept a larger share of women into their ranks.

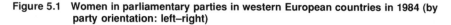

**Figure 5.1   Women in parliamentary parties in western European countries in 1984 (by party orientation: left–right)**

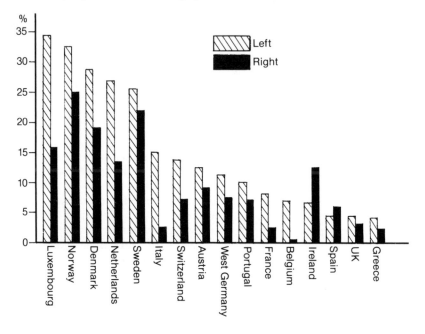

*Source* : adapted from Mossuz-Laveau et al.,1984, in Norris, 1987: 127)

All in all it appears to the onlooker that the changes towards a more egalitarian society have happened very swiftly and suddenly in the Netherlands and that the government pays more than lip service to the new social and political demands made by women. Government policy and public debate have gone far beyond simplistic issues of discrimination at work. It has dramatically cut discrimination at all levels. Equal pay has been achieved in most areas and women now earn, on average, just 2 percent less than their male counterparts. Women's participation in politics is especially noteworthy, having drastically increased within the last ten years, now ranking amongst the highest participation rates in western Europe, comparable only to Scandinavian countries, and, interestingly, Luxembourg (see fig. 5.1).

This fact is clearly attributable to the activities of the second-wave movement, or rather to the feminists working actively towards change, particularly in the four left-wing parties and in some of the unions, such as the teachers' union and the civil service union (Meulenbelt et al., 1984: 6). Contrary to predictions, feminists in unions succeeded in forming their own caucuses and organisations which effectively work together with other branches of the unions (De Vries, 1981: 396–7).

Irrespective of the limits of many of the changes, Dutch society has made substantial adjustments to a new way of thinking. Dutch attitudes to women and gender issues are now amongst the most egalitarian in western Europe (together with France and Denmark). In the Netherlands, the emancipatory policies for women worked hand-in-hand with the emancipation of homosexuals, a move that was not only supported by government and legislators but by the general population at large. Arguably, the Netherlands are to Europe what San Francisco is to the USA: a haven for people with same-sex preference who can go about their lives more freely (although even there not too freely) than probably anywhere else in Europe. There are lesbian archives and radical lesbian women's groups. There are national gay/lesbian radio programmes. The various unions and political parties have special gay/lesbian cells within them. While in most other European but also western industrialised countries in general, teachers usually choose or are forced to hide their sexual orientation for fear of dismissal, the Dutch Teachers Union officially has a lesbian and gay teachers' section. There have been parliamentarians who wear a pink triangle to indicate that they identify with lesbian/gay rights. There are countless homosexual political groups, and politically active umbrella organisations such as the COC, which brings together about 70 groups, twenty or so of them lesbian (Morgan, 1984: 467). The new taxation law and the social security system now treat gay and lesbian partners as couples. Financially, for the couples, this move was of course to their detriment, but imbedded in these rules is the core of a new way of thinking that is not unlike the Swedish model. Cohabitation is the determining factor, and not marital status, a change of view that no longer draws clear divisions in favour of the nuclear family. One is tempted to think that public opinion changed before the government moved to ratify it and that the government took very few risks. Yet the changes that it did bring about also show a commitment to making the new policies work.

## FRANCE

The French are a nation unusually experienced in political upheaval and in overthrowing monarchies and governments. French history is also about the only national history that has a fairly unbroken record of exceptional women scholars, scientists and revolutionaries, too numerous to mention here (Morgan, 1984: 227–8). The French Revolution of 1789 which ended the *ancien régime* and declared France a republic, was echoed in 1830 by the July Revolution which again overthrew a monarch and reclaimed the republic for a brief spell. The February Revolution of 1848 toppled Louis Philippe and for four years France was a republic again only to be lost to Napoleon III, crowned emperor. It was not until 1870 that the republic finally won within a context of war (the Franco–Prussian War) and uprisings. In Paris, which instituted the Paris Commune in 1871, the socialist lobby contained many women. Nearly 20 000 people lost their lives when government forces brutally put down the rebellion. France had to number its various stages of republicanism. It is now in the fifth republic. The third republic ended when the government was forced into exile due to Nazi occupation in World War II. The problematic fourth republic which, in twelve years had no less than 25 cabinets, ended in martial law as a result of the crisis surrounding Algiers (the military putsch of 1958). Charles De Gaulle, who formed the fifth republic, had to resign nine years later as a result of socialist and other left-wing pressure during the turmoil of the May Movement student uprising of 1968.

In France, protesters and governments take each other very seriously. In 1986 for instance, students protested again, supported by a general strike of the unions. The 'reform' programmes proposed by Education Minister Alain Devaquet (higher fees and stricter quotas) were swiftly dropped by the Chirac government.

Everyone knew that the alliance of students and unions was powerful enough to topple yet another government. Demonstrations are a part of French tradition. The previously mentioned EEC survey of 1983 established that every third French person interviewed had participated in a demonstration at least once and every second person interviewed said that they were willing to demonstrate should the need arise (*Women and Men of Europe 1983*). France, which is still predominantly catholic, fought its battles with the church during the last century. By 1909 the separation between church and the state was achieved and the secularisation of state power became a reality. Thus, despite strong traditional forces and vested interests, France has had a strong extra-parliamentary culture of protest and a strong intellectual network outside universities. In the last 200 years of French history these counterforces have always been able to be mobilised very quickly.

The rise of dissent in the postwar years was promoted by a number of very substantial changes. France, as other western European countries, had suffered major defeat and losses in World War II and needed to rebuild its economy. One of the most important plans was the *Plan Monet* which set out to modernise France, restructure its economy and change it from an extensive to an intensive regime of capitalist accumulation with intensified patterns of individual consumption. Batiot points out that by the late 1960s social relations, 'deeply altered by state-encouraged new relations of consumption, home-ownership, management, family and education' (1986: 91), had not adapted to the economic transformation and its demands, causing alienation and tensions. It is rarely mentioned that between 1950 and 1970, despite a sharp increase of full-time employment of women after 1962, the socio-economic status of women in France, as in Switzerland and Ireland and new-world countries like Canada and the USA, actually declined (Brooks, 1983), probably adding to the general level of discontent.

In addition, France was troubled by the growing local resistance in French possessions outside Europe, a battle for which France paid the high price of war. Although France is one of the few western European countries still with a substantial number of overseas holdings, it has lost political clout in many of these. In 1954, the Battle of Dien-Bien-Phu signalled the end of French control over Indochina. The same year saw the beginning of the Algerian War which became a protracted and costly affair for France, ending six years later in the declaration of independence for Algeria. By 1959 it was clear that Algeria, conquered in 1847, would not remain French.

Moreover, the status of French democracy over the postwar years was not altogether clear and it suffered a number of severe setbacks. Recent typographies of western democracies have classified France as one of the interrupted or limited democracies of western Europe. Indeed, the fourth republic had ended in martial law and, in order to coax De Gaulle back into politics in 1958, he was granted concessions regarding his personal powers as president of the fifth republic (Lijphart, 1984; Norris, 1987: 41–2). Rather than a fully fledged democracy, De Gaulle's republic had elements of a 'benign' dictatorship with very little consideration for the 'common people'. As Françoise Giroud said of De Gaulle: 'Seated there on his pile of gold, De Gaulle could see a long way, all the way to the United States, but he couldn't see directly beneath him. And his Prime Minister, in dealing with the miners' strike in 1963, had shown that he too had no feeling for labor [*sic*]' (Giroud, 1974: 269).

Despite the lessons of Algeria and Dien-Bien-Phu, De Gaulle continued to pursue militaristic goals for France. He supported and encouraged French nuclear armament and his government held the first nuclear tests far away from French home territory in 1960. In 1966 France left NATO and three years later refused to sign the nuclear disarmament contract. By the 1980s military expenditure was swallowing up as much as a third of the entire French budget (Raulff, 1983: 315). This pro-nuclear policy has never been seriously contested, either by later right-wing French governments under Georges Pompidou (1969–1974), and Valéry Giscard d'Estaing (1974–1981) or by the left-wing government of François Mitterand (1981–). In 1982 Mitterand stated, like his predecessor, that the government intended to increase French nuclear power and that it was not interested in participating in disarmament talks in Geneva. Despite some isolated criticism, the issue of nuclear power has not been a focal point of attention or protest by the public. The catastrophe of Chernobyl had none of the strong repercussions in France that it had in other western European countries; nothing was recorded for and open to public debate, as in West Germany for instance. Tests of the degree of contamination by the Chernobyl cloud were either not made or not publicised. The environmental issues, so closely tied with the peace movement internationally, never took off in France to the same extent as in other countries. An ecological party was founded but up until and including the 1988 elections it had never risen above the crucial 5 percent necessary for parliamentary representation (the same 5 percent clause as in West Germany). There have been a few ecological feminist groups, such as Écologie Féminisme (1972) under the prolific writer Françoise d'Eaubonne, but ecological issues have generally not achieved political agenda status.

At the time, De Gaulle's politics inadvertently strengthened the new left in France, saw the rise of a vibrant, critical intellectualism and fuelled anti-imperialism, spawned by the Algerian but encouraged by the Vietnam and Cambodian wars. In this general climate of dissent, the position of women also began to occupy an ever growing terrain. The gradual increase of publications about women and the slow but steady reformism concerned with women's status over the postwar period prepared the ground for an independent women's movement after 1968. In 1944, women were enfranchised and in most instances the constitution of 1946 recognised the equality of women before the law. Simone de Beauvoir's seminal work, _The Second Sex,_ was published in 1949. It was then well ahead of its time and the inflammatory quality of this work only came to the fore once the new women's movement got underway. In 1956 M. A. Weill-Hallé founded the French Movement for Family Planning, (the Mouvement Français pour le Planning Familial—MFPF) chiefly to seek the repeal of a 1920 law that prohibited the sale of contraceptives. The Neuwirth law of 1967 actually rescinded this law and authorised the sale of contraceptives. Anachronistic elements of the Napoleonic Code, many of them related to women, were finally removed by 1965 (including one that had denied women the right to open their own bank accounts). Throughout the 1960s there were seminars and publications on the situation of women in modern French society, such as the work by Geneviève Aimée Texier and Andrée Michel, entitled _Condition de la Française Aujourd'hui_ (1958) (sometimes also entitled _La Situation des Femmes Françaises Aujourd'hui,_ but both mean the same thing: The Situation of Frenchwomen Today). Some feminist groups bore movement character (Sauter-Bailliet, 1981: 410), such as Petites Marguerites, Polymorphes, Pervers, Les Oreilles Vertes, and a group named Féminin–Masculin–Avenir, which initially had started out as a mixed-gender group in 1967, as in the Netherlands, but within months had lost all male participants and was renamed Féminist–Marxist Action.

These reforms and the occasional debates on women may not have done much in preparation for events, but often they and the women's own educational backgrounds provided ready-made tools with which to take up the fight. For instance, women at tertiary institutions generally had a much higher profile than elsewhere in western Europe and, except for some Scandinavian countries, their numbers were greater than anywhere else at the time. In 1963, for instance, 43 percent of all university students were women, as compared to 32 percent in England and 24 percent in West Germany (Juillard, 1976: 117–18). Thus, at the beginning of the second wave there was a large pool of well-educated women whose intellectual abilities had been sharpened and who had been well prepared in expressing ideas in writing. One peculiarity of the French tertiary system is that those enrolled in literature, of whom the majority were women, had to also take a major sequence in philosophy. It is perhaps not surprising then that of all western European second-wave women's movements it was the French that provided the greatest and most novel input into feminist theory.

The uprising of 1968 has at times been dubbed as the most important French event, sociologically speaking, since the Paris Commune in 1871, partly because it erupted as a combined effort of unions and students and led to general strikes. Indeed, in present-day western industrialised societies, the nexus between workers' unions and university students is unique, and has proved to be a powerful weapon against the government. Moreover, it showed that unions and workers still played a considerable role in power politics, unlike so many other western European nations. The women's movement of the second wave quickly made its own name a year later and burst into activity with an unprecedented number of public demonstrations and publications. It even had its own hymn: 'Reconnaissons-nous, parlons, regardons-nous, ensemble nous sommes opprimées, faisons ensemble la révolution. Levons-nous, femmes esclaves, dressons-nous pour rompre nos chaînes.'[2]

In English-speaking countries, especially outside Europe, the French women's liberation movement is probably the best documented and best known of all western European second-wave movements.[3] The writings of the main proponents of a group called Politique et Psychanalyse, women like Hélène Cixous, Luce Irigaray and Julia Kristeva, have had their works translated into English and have won international, that is, English cultural circuit, acclaim for their theoretical contributions to the contemporary feminist debate.

Yet often the impression created abroad is that this handful of writers is synonymous with 'the movement' and that therefore the French movement was perhaps one of the most important European events. It is true that the movement as a whole, dubbed by the French press the 'Mouvement de Libération des Femmes' (MLF) in 1970, at first attracted considerable public attention. This was partly because there were some rather flamboyant and effective publicity stunts, and partly because the French press responds very quickly to any protests, however small. But overall, most writers agree, the French women's movement was weak and rather short-lived (Juillard, 1976; Chafetz et al., 1986: 182; de Beauvoir, 1984; Duchen, 1986). Less than 1 percent of adult women belonged to it and they formed a tiny fringe of French society. According to Sauter-Bailliet, the entire MLF at best consisted of around 4000 women. Most of the activities of the MLF were based in Paris, with some spin-off in Toulouse, Lyon (1981: 412) and later also in Marseilles. 'Popularity' would hardly be the term to describe the MLF in

France; Choisir, which had been a highly successful and vocal group in the abortion law reform with a great deal of public support for the *issue* and for the sober methods of its impressive leader, the lawyer Gisèle Halimi, failed once it turned to political activism. Its candidates for the 1978 election of representatives for the European Parliament scored a mere 1.5 percent. Moreover, of all EEC countries, women in France expressed the greatest degree of hostility towards their own 'second wave'. Only 7 percent said that they could conceivably join the movement (as against a European average of 18 percent), whilst 85 percent of all women interviewed (against a European average of 65 percent) were totally against the movement (*Women and Men of Europe*, 1983: 41–3).

If the MLF has enjoyed a high profile—and undoubtedly also a degree of notoriety—it is partly because it was quickly usurped and turned into an enterpreneurial enterprise by the small group Politique et Psychanalyse, or Psych et Po for short, that had formed around Antoinette Fouque, a wealthy psycho-analyst. Under her leadership, the MLF was turned into a very profitable business. In 1979, she registered the name MLF, given to the whole movement, as her trade name, ran three bookshops (called 'des femmes'), her own publishing company (Éditions des Femmes) and a series of magazines, such as *Le quotidien des femmes* (1974) and the *Magazine des femmes en mouvements*, a weekly publication with a circulation of 150 000. The objections to these practices were widespread, not so much for the entrepreneurial format of the companies but for the fact that a small and indeed the most elitist group of the French second wave had the audacity to claim that *it* was the movement. The Féministes Révolutionnaires, to whom women like Simone de Beauvoir and Monique Wittig belonged, the socialist Cercle Dimitriev, the communist Les Petroleuses and even abortion reform groups like Choisir or the Parti Féministe Unifée Français were hardly pleased by this coup.

Duchen felt that one of the most objectionable features of Psych et Po, and hardly conducive to further political action, was the self-congratulatory tone of the *Magazine des femmes,* which claimed that the oppression was already over-come and all was well now because women of today were in charge of their lives (Duchen, 1986: 37). To my knowledge, such development in a woman's move-ment is unprecedented. Ironically, it is this part of the movement which has become perhaps the most influential of all. Psych et Po was accused of having utilised to the full the class structure and the economic system—both of which most of the other feminist groups in France see as a major source of women's oppression. The group has also used, borrowed and absorbed most of the mainstream (male) intellectual tradition and has placed their debates firmly within that tradition. They were heavily criticised in France for doing so but that was in the best French intellectual tradition. They were attacked inter-nationally at the women's congress in Copenhagen in 1980 for these practices (Lovenduski, 1986: 96) and accused of 'intellectual terrorism' (Marks et al., 1981: 31). Nevertheless, in 1981, the unperturbed group added 'international' to its MLF trade name and logo. Apparently, none of the criticisms levied against Psych et Po by other feminists was ever answered. Antoinette Fouque eventually left France for the USA. Initially at least, the writers associated with Psych et Po had more impact abroad and became French export articles, mostly to the USA and Australia, a fact that Simone de Beauvoir particularly regretted:

The French women's movement thus is alive and well. But it is in constant danger, because of the existence of such groups as Psych. et Po. which pass themselves off as *the* women's movement and exert considerable influence, thanks to the unfortunate all—too warm reception the general public has given their ideology—a convenient neo-femininity developed by such women writers as Hélène Cixous, Annie Leclerc, and Lucy Irigaray, most of whom are not feminists, and some of whom are blatantly *anti-*feminist. Unfortunately this is also the aspect of the French women's movement best known in the United States. Such books as Elaine Marks's *New French Feminisms* give a totally distorted image of French feminism by presenting it, on the one hand, as if it existed only in theory and not in action and, on the other, as if the sum of that theory emanated from the school of neo-femininity. (1984: 234–5)

A less hostile reception of Psych et Po in France had to wait till the 1980s, when more conservative and even anti-feminist women's writings on 'femininity' came back in vogue.

The new French women's liberation movement is perhaps best subdivided into three phases, although all of them were overlapping to a certain extent and were never as clearly marked as in some other countries. The first phase lasted until about 1975. The movement undoubtedly started in 1968, signalled by the founding of Politique et Psychanalyse, by Françoise Parturier's published 'Lettre Ouverte aux Hommes' (An Open Letter to Men) and by Monique Wittig's book *Les Guérillères* (1969). The radical feminist journal *Le torchon brûle* (1970–1972) only published seven issues in those years but it was important in the early stages of the new French feminism. A piece published in 1970, called 'Combat pour la libération de la femme' (Fight for the liberation of women, Wittig et al., 1970) is generally regarded as the first manifesto of the new women's movement in France (Moreau-Bisseret, 1986: 76).

The formation of most of the feminist organisations, the *groupes femmes de quartiers* (local women's groups) and most of the protest actions fell into the years 1970 to 1974. Amongst the most important groups was the Féministes Révolutionnaires (1970), the revolutionary feminists, who declared war on the patriarchal order, and chose flamboyant public protest actions as their main strategy. They were strongly separatist from the beginning, with a weighty contingent of political separatist lesbians, like Monique Wittig, who was one of its chief proponents; the 'lesbian front' was a later development and took form only in 1983. Female homosexuality in France was much more 'closetted' than male homosexuality. When the (male) Front Homosexuel d'Action Révolu-tionnaire (FHAR) formed in Paris in 1971, after the May Movement revolt, it was in the wake of a publicly known tradition of gay male French writers and intellectuals who had had 'little compunction about "coming out"' (Reader, 1987: 71). Jean Cocteau, André Gide, and later Michèl Foucault and Barthes had lived quite openly as homosexuals. Lesbianism, by contrast, had largely remained shrouded in silence, despite such flamboyant figures as Colette and Gertrude Stein. Nevertheless, the revival of this issue by the Féministes Révolutionnaires played a large part in the discussions on male sexual domination and the formation of vocal lesbian groups. In French feminism, the issue of sexuality has probably played a much larger part in the discussions on liberation than elsewhere in western Europe and very original and often very radical notions of sexual liberation were developed.

Consciousness-raising groups in the American style never took off in France, but there were spontaneous groups usually organised by radical feminists, which clustered around interests, life experiences and similar views. Neither the local neighbourhood groups nor these interest groups had any particular structure. As with German autonomous feminism, there was no organisation, methods of communication were often extremely poor, and, most importantly, there were no spokespersons.

In a different vein, but in terms of concrete goals and achievable legal changes, not less important for French society, was the formation of Choisir in 1971. The group was first conceived of at the beginning of the Bobigny trial near Paris, which brought the issue of abortion and the cruelty of the abortion law to public attention. A 17-year-old girl had aborted a foetus which had been the consequence of rape by a schoolboy. The boy, who had not only raped but denounced her for having aborted, never stood trial. Most probably as a result of public pressure the girl was finally acquitted in 1972. The lawyer Gisèle Halimi was the co-founder of Choisir, which devoted its energies to legal battles in abortion and rape cases (such as the highly publicised rape trials of Colmar and Aix-en-Provence defended by Halimi and Choisir) and to the clarifying of women's needs and demands in public areas such as education, politics, law, and medicine. In 1973 Halimi first summarised these in a publication called *La Cause des Femmes*.

In 1972, two other noted groups were constituted. One was Spirale under the leadership of the writer Catherine Valabrègue, which saw as its aim the study and liberation of women's creative ability to help create and foster a 'smothered' women's culture. The other, the Cercle Dimitriev, named after the founder of a women's group during the time of the Paris Commune, was interested in the relationship between class and gender and aimed particularly at the working classes. In 1973, the MLAC (Freedom of Abortion and Contraception Group) and an organisation for feminist film-makers and actresses, Musidora, were founded, followed in 1974 by one of Simone de Beauvoir's initiatives, a league for the rights of women, the Ligue du Droit des Femmes. Some writers have suggested that the movement began to crumble as early as 1972, partly because of an ever increasing number of splinter groups and the total lack of coordination and organisation between them (Léger, 1988: 99). Yet, this same spontaneity and lack of hierarchy and organisation were also amongst the strengths of the new wave of feminism.

The main methods of French feminist protest were demonstrations and publications and these protest actions were well chosen, hitting hard at cherished notions of masculinity and at the core of French nationalism and traditions. French society over the ages has developed inviolable, important symbols of French life and history, intrinsically tied to its own identity. Instead of attacking the state, French feminists were thus able to attack these inviolable symbols. This was a new feature of the May Movement revolt of 1968, with its chief spokesperson Daniel Cohn-Bendit, and it was a firm belief of activists in general that they had no desire to oppose the government using traditional methods of attack, implying that they did not wish to be implicated in a system that they had rejected from the outset (Duchen, 1986: 5). By choosing to stage events which had long since acquired symbolic significance in French history, they were able to arouse public feelings at once. The placing of the wreath for the unknown wife on the tomb of the unknown soldier (1970) is one such example, and it created furore in the press:

> ... as if a sacrilege had been committed. And so, in a sense, it had. The tomb of the unknown soldier occupies a sacred place within the French symbolic order and within Western mythology. Located in the centre of Paris it signifies patriotism, nationalism, and the masculine virtues of heroism and courage. The Arc de Triomphe is one of the most explicit signs of a French, and, by extension, of a victorious, universal, male

order. It is the shrine of shrines that glorifies war and the cult of the dead. (Marks et al., 1981: 31)

Another example concerned the right to abortion and contraception, demonstrated in a march from the Bastille (1971), symbolising clearly enough the beginning of yet another French revolution.

There were many other demonstrations in those years, aimed especially at protecting women's bodies (against such as rape and domestic violence) and at giving women the right to control their own bodies (abortion and contraception). The 'Manifeste des 343 "salopes"', was published in *Le Nouvel Observateur* in 1971. Like its West German counterpart, it was a public confession to having aborted, signed by a number of women of prominence, including de Beauvoir, Halimi and well-known actresses such as Jeanne Moreau, Catherine Deneuve and Delphine Seyrig. The *Manifeste* and the word '*salopes*', meaning slut or bitch, shocked the public and, as many writers have suggested, this action was chiefly responsible for putting the abortion issue on the political agenda. Later demonstrations against the abortion laws involved the gatecrashing of a gynaecological congress, with accusations of hypocrisy in that profession. The most active phase of the movement concluded with the repeal of the abortion law. The majority of the medical profession was in favour of the change, despite staunch opposition from the Association of Doctors Respecting Human Life. All leftist parties were strongly behind the change but the governing parties needed considerable persuasion. They finally settled on allowing the abortion law repeal for a trial period and on the proviso that abortions were not to exceed a quarter of all hospital operations (Francome, 1984: 139).

Noticeably, all of the new feminist organisations were outside the party machinery of French politics, and to date this has remained the case. France of the late 1980s had one of the lowest participation rates of women in power politics (under 8 percent), higher only than Greece, Spain, Belgium and the UK. In France, however, one wonders whether the low participation rate is not the result of a choice that women themselves have made, coinciding with the thrust of the feminist movement of the early 1970s that had branded any political institution as male dominated, patriarchical and therefore not just untrustworthy but something to be avoided at all costs. We have seen earlier in Dahlerup's models of the second-wave movements that those groups adhering to liberationist ideas rather than equal rights ideas consciously chose not to be co-opted by the state. French feminists, it seems, have remained true to their ideals. Alternatively, I think one needs to take note of Lovenduski's analysis of the change of the voting system, first brought into effect with De Gaulle at the beginning of the fifth republic in 1958. She argues that the multiparty system in combination with the first-past-the-post electoral system in two rounds in France led to an under-representation of women, shown by the drop of women in the national assembly (Assemblée Nationale) (Lovenduski, 1986: 148).

The second phase of the movement between 1974 and 1978 was marked by a sudden explosion of feminist publications and the foundation of feminist journals and magazines with enormous variety in content, style and aims. Particularly since 1975, the media has given much space to feminist issues and women have become highly visible (Rogerat, 1988: 108). It is tempting to argue that amongst the features of nationalism there is also a reluctance to import foreign ideas and to perceive of crises in rather strictly national terms, be they social, political or otherwise. This is at least the impression created by the history of the second wave in France. American imports played a much smaller role than elsewhere in western Europe. Instead, French women created, discovered or rediscovered their own heroines in writing and politics. Simone de Beauvoir's *Le Deuxième Sexe* of 1949 had at least the same, if belated, catalyst effect as did the books of Friedan and Millet in the USA in the 1960s. The four-year span is circumscribed by the publication of such hallmarks as Julia Kristeva's *Des Chinoises* (1974), Luce Irigaray's *Speculum de l'autre femme* (1974), Hélène Cixous's 'Le rire de la méduse' in *L'Arc* (1975), Irigaray's *Ce sexe qui n'en est pas un* (1977) and in 1979 *Les écrits féministes de Simone de Beauvoir*. Writings by Annie Leclerc, Christine Delphy, Françoise d'Eaubonne and Gisèle Halimi, Monique Wittig, and other creative writers such as Nathalie Sarraute, Dorothée Letessier, Marguérite Duras, Christiane Rochefort added highly original publications to French culture. Within the same time span the first histories of the French women's movement and French feminism were published (Albistur, 1977; Pisan et al., 1977) and a host of feminist journals and magazines were founded.[4]

The belief that the control of sexuality was the key to the powers men had enjoyed over women was shared by all groups of radical feminists (Stetson, 1987: 161). They fought the all-pervasive patriarchal, phallocratic system and its incipient misogyny, and thereby steered a path of confrontation against all male systems, of which the political system was a part. In other words, as most writers agree, the French new wave was strongly feminist in ideology and created a rich new culture, filling the spaces of silence and omissions of women, but as a socio-political movement it was weak and often, apart from Choisir, it lacked a direction that could be translated into political action or into legal reforms.

One of the interesting features of the French situation is that the influence of the movement on social, legal and policy changes was not altogether clear. To be sure, in the abortion issue and in the laws concerning rape, the movement exerted considerable influence by winning over public opinion. In 1974, under the then Minister for Health, Simone Veil, the law forbidding abortion was repealed, the change being made on a trial basis for four years. It was permanently ratified in 1979 and allowed for abortion in the first ten weeks of pregnancy. In 1980 rape was reclassified as a crime, rather than as a *délict* (misdemeanour). The change in law with respect to rape has worked in the sense that there has been a significant increase in the number of reports on rape. In 1975 there were 1695 cases of rape reported and in 1984 there were 2859 reports (Stetson, 1987: 171). Whether or not the incidence of rape has actually gone down as a result of publicity and legal changes is not ascertainable.

A number of important initiatives by feminists led to better support services for women. In 1974, more or less simultaneously with women's refuge movements elsewhere in the world, the first house for battered wives, the Flora Tristan Centre near Paris, opened its doors. In 1975, GLIFE, an information centre for women was established, as well as the so-called SOS Femmes Alternatives, a 24-hour emergency telephone service for women. Those activities, while initiated by women for women, eventually received funding from the government.

Irrespective of women's activities, so it seems, there were a host of legal and policy reforms trickling down the maze of French bureaucracy through the 1960s and the 1970s. In 1970, family law was changed, stipulating that parental duties and responsibilities were to be equally divided between husband and wife. Shortly thereafter the wording was changed, 'paternal' authority being replaced by 'parental' authority. In 1972, well before the EEC directives were pursued vigorously, France brought in an equal pay law. It also granted women with newly born children permission to take two years leave without pay without affecting retirement benefits. Divorce by mutual consent was granted in 1975.

There were also changes of a structural kind and of new services appearing for the first time in French history throughout the 1970s. In 1971 a committee for working women was established with a brief to make recommendations for proposed legislation. In 1974 the government itself created the new cabinet post of Secretary of State for the Condition of Women. It appointed Françoise Giróud as its first minister to this post. Françoise Giróud's appointment was understandable, and somewhat ironic. She was no doubt not just one of the best known, if not *the* best known, woman journalist in France at the time. She was also considered to be one of the best journalists in Europe, having been the long time editor-in-chief of *L'Express*, the largest French weekly news magazine. In addition, she was a co-founder and editor of the leading woman's magazine *Elle*. Unfortunately, in her association with *Elle* she had made many enemies amongst radical feminists, who found the limp reformist stance of the magazine extremely irksome and had expressed those feelings very noisily in demonstrations, at the meeting of the 'Estate General' of *Elle* in Versailles in 1970. Giroud's rather conservative position and her marginal involvement in the women's movement of course suited the conservative Giscard government well. On the other hand, her international standing was impeccable and elicited praise by such well-known feminists as Betty Friedan. In 1974, when Françoise Giroud's translated version of her book *Si Je Mens ... Conversations avec Claude Glayman* ('Should I lie ...' translated as *I Give You My Word*) appeared in the USA, Betty Friedan said on the jacket of Giroud's book:

> Françoise Giroud gives us a sense of what self-realization for a woman can be all about: her abilities fully and freely used in a life of passionate commitment to society —her voice heard in the largest decisions of her time—her passionate personal involvement in love and motherhood without denying their complement of pain and joy—and her struggle to somehow put it all together in a way that few women have yet been able to do.

In one sense, Giróud's appointment was clearly a public relations exercise for, within half a year, the portfolio was shifted to an office of much lesser importance and it then vanished completely until the 1978 elections, when Monique Pelletier was appointed to a new minister's position for women's issues (*Ministre déléguée à la condition féminine*). Giroud, however, was certainly not idle in the little time she had at her disposal. She compiled a bulky brochure containing policy suggestions, entitled *A Hundred Measures for Women*, which was passed and accepted by cabinet and became a blueprint for governmental action. After the election of the Mitterand government in 1981 the position was given to Yvette Rondy.

The beginning of the third phase of the movement could be placed in 1981, when Mitterand's Socialist Party won the election after 25 years in opposition. François Mitterand had been going to the polls since 1965 and had lost every election against Charles De Gaulle and Valéry Giscard d'Estaing. But he was to become the first president of the fifth republic who was re-elected for a second seven-year term (in 1988). For feminists, Mitterand was 'a breath of fresh air' (Duchen, 1986: 138). Ironically, however, it was chiefly the women's vote which had prevented his election previously (see table 5.1).

Mitterand's election was helped by several factors; the most important one

Table 5.1   Voting pattern according to sex in French presidential elections, 1965–1981

| Year: | 1965 | | 1974 | | 1981 | |
|---|---|---|---|---|---|---|
| Political orientation | left | right | left | right | left | right |
| Candidates | Mitterand | De Gaulle | Mitterand | Giscard | Mitterand | Giscard |
| Women's vote (%) | 38 | 62 | 46 | 54 | 49 | 51 |
| Men's vote (%) | 52 | 48 | 51 | 49 | 56 | 44 |
| Total vote | 45 | 55 | 48.5 | 51.5 | 52.5 | 47.5 |

*Source*: adapted from Stetson,1987: 38

was probably the economic situation of France. Under Giscard, and in the aftermath of the economic crisis in Europe, the annual growth rate plummeted from 5.6 percent to 2.8 percent between 1974 and 1981. The GNP fell to 0.1 percent in 1981. The number of unemployed had risen from 0.4 million to 1.7 million and inflation had gone up to 12 percent within the same period. The election was a landslide victory for the left and it secured almost 60 percent of all seats in the new parliament (as against 23.1 percent in 1978). Curiously, every third person in the new parliament came from a professional background in education and, as expected, employers from the private sector were underrepresented. According to his election promises, Mitterand nationalised banks and large industrial concerns, raised the minimum income, increased annual holidays to five weeks, and lowered the number of weekly working hours to 39 and the pensionable age to 60 years. In new labour laws, workers were given a stronger position on the factory floor.

It is a little arbitrary to define this period post-1981 as a third stage of the *movement*. Within our definition of social movements one might well prefer to call the period after 1981 a new phase in women's rights legislation rather than fit it into the parameters of movements. There were attempts to form new organisations, as for instance the autonomous current within the French Social-ist Party, but this folded in 1984, after only five years in existence. The move-ment had waned; yet at least the structures of many of the organisations, then formed or strengthened, still existed and were ready watchdogs for any change in government policy: the French Family Planning Movement (MFPF—Mouvement Français pour le Planning Familial), for instance, had been around since the 1960s and had grown in strength and feminist content; Maison des Femmes and especially Choisir, which had a strong role to play in the heyday of the movement, had never dissolved but had continued to work for specific feminist goals. Their viability was demonstrated in 1985 when three assaults on women, which occurred in broad daylight (with witnesses who felt that nothing needed be done to prevent a rape because it was 'nothing special'), created headline news. These organisations together with the Collectif d'associations contre le viol (a collective against violence) immediately organised a campaign 'Ne laissons pas le viol se banaliser' (let's not trivialise violence). From a legal and policy perspective, the changes accelerated under the Mitterand presidency, and more: the new government gave political recognition to a new philosophy which was, if not always applauded by feminists, egalitarian in principle.

One of the government's first acts in this regard was the creation of the Ministry of Women's Rights. The new name (including 'rights' instead of just 'issues') clearly enough indicated a change in philosophy. The budget for this ministry was ten times that of the preceding government and with this improved funding and the government's backing a number of measures were swiftly put into action. In 1981, a TV campaign was launched advertising contraception as a woman's right. The ministry had found that abortions had remained high as a result of lack of availability and adequate information services on contraceptives. Only 32 percent of French women used modern contraceptives and only a total of 377 information services existed throughout France in 1977 (Stetson, 1987: 68). The number of family planning centres was raised from 150 to 374 and in 1981 over 1000 specific contraception advice centres were opened. The number of illegal abortions that were still being performed after the repeal of the abortion law also suggested to the ministry that the delivery of the service posed serious problems, partly because of the reluctance of doctors and of hospital staff to perform the operation. In 1981, it was estimated that 250 000 legal and illegal abortions were performed in France. Of those, one-third were on women under the age of 20. Overall, only 32 percent of women of reproductive age used modern contraceptives (the pill, IUD). Older, married women had the highest use of contraceptives or preventative measures while only 15 percent of women under the age of 18 used any precautions at all (*Womenspeak*, 1982: 14). The figures were alarming enough to result in a series of new regulations. Thus, in 1982 the government announced that 70 percent of abortion costs would be reimbursable through the health service. In the same year, a new *décret* (no. 82–826) was announced which obliged all hospitals with surgical or maternity services to perform abortions. This directive at once increased the number of available hospitals by 40 percent and by more than 100 percent within a three-year span (Stetson, 1987: 71).

In the field of employment, a number of changes were effected in the 1980s. In 1982 a new labour law required employers to keep basic statistics on the gender of employees (*Code du Travail*, L432–3–1), and in 1983 a law 'on equality in professional matters', which established the principle of equal pay for equal work, forbade any discrimination against women in hiring, training and promotion. In this area, the nationalisation of banks and large industrial concerns worked well for women in the sense that there was more leverage for ensuring that the new laws would be implemented fairly promptly and according to the letter. Thus, one of the nationalised banks put into action a new management plan and also outlined steps towards achieving a 30 percent presence of women in management by the end of the 1980s. In 1984, a major television campaign was launched by the Ministry for Women's Rights, in conjunction with the Ministry of National Education, entitled 'Jobs do not have gender' (Coquillat, 1988: 178–9). Another more recent change required employers to give full justification for giving lower pay to women (*Code du Travail*, L140–8). These changes were important not just because women, on average, had earned 30 percent less than their male counterparts but also because, throughout the 1960s to the 1980s, participation rates of women in the labour force had crept up at a steady rate. In 1962, they made up 34.3 percent of the workforce, 39.2 percent by 1980 and 42.4 percent by 1984 (Stetson, 1987: 130). This is noteworthy for several reasons. In France, and also in the Netherlands, the position of the housewife as an index of male breadwinning capacity remained an important status symbol. The *femme au foyer* symbolised comfortable middle-class life freed from the hassles and petty realities of 'gainful' employment. Yet unlike several other western European countries, women's employment in France had not shifted into part-time work. In the mid-1980s, EEC countries employed 11 million part-time workers of whom 9 million were married women. As we have seen, in some Nordic countries such as Denmark and Sweden the largest percentage of women workers were found in part-time work. The French ministry explicitly stated that it had learned from the Swedish experience and wanted to avoid the 'ghettoisation' of women in poorly constituted work situations (Coquillat, 1988: 183). France today has one of the lowest EEC percentages of women in part-time work, a total of 17 percent of all working women as compared to 28 percent in West Germany and 46 percent in Denmark (*Women in Statistics*, 1984; Barry et al., 1988: 85–6).

Well before the start of the new wave, French women had a high participation rate in education, including tertiary education, but, as in other countries, women in academia typically occupied the lower ranks. Since 1981, a campaign has been operating under the auspices of the National Centre for Scientific Research, called 'Women and Research', to encourage women to continue into research and higher degrees by providing funding for them to do so. Four university posts for women's studies have been created, as well as prizes for professional women in cultural fields. Annual prizes and awards for women include the George Sand Prize for literature, another the Alice Prize for a (non-sexist) children's book, awards for musical compositions and the Camille Foundation, a purchasing fund for plastic arts by women (Coquillat, 1988: 182). From February 1984 to December 1985, a special commission was employed to eradicate sexist language from official documents and official use.

The prolonged rule of the French left under Mitterand, due to remain in office until 1994, has had certain repercussions on feminist debate about women's role in politics. The journal *Nouvelle Questions Féministes* devoted an issue to this problem. The feminist clubs Flora Tristan and Ruptures have each held seminars on the subject and the former has published an issue (1986: *Cahiers*, no. 16) entitled *État de droit, droits des femmes?* (The lawful state, rights for women?). The old confrontationist stance of feminists vis-à-vis the state has mellowed and today there is a new subsection of feminists that believes in collaboration with the state. French feminists are only too aware that this *féminism d'État* (state feminism) is in stark contrast to the avowed autonomy of the second-wave movement (Rogerat, 1988: 111). At times reluctantly, feminists have deemed it necessary to participate within the confines of French institutional and bureaucratic life, even when this has not fundamentally altered their perception of the state and the government as male institutions.

*THE MODEL EXAMINED*

One of the most notable features of the Dutch and French second waves is the strong cultural revolution each created in its own country. Valabrègue's fears of a 'smothered' women's culture were quickly allayed in both countries. As in several other nations, there were bursts of unprecedented writing and publishing activities by women. In the Netherlands, the *praet groeps* (consciousness-raising groups) and the educational efforts by feminists spread throughout its territories. While the second wave remained more on the fringe in France than in the Netherlands, what the two movements had in common was the feminists' relationship to the power politics of the day defined largely by volunteer 'outsiderism.' Autonomy, as in West Germany, was also important in both these countries. Apart from the abortion issue and the discussions surrounding rape, women's groups in either country could not find much common ground and there was little, if any, centralised activity that could turn the movements as a whole into strong lobby groups.

Both in France and the Netherlands the media gave considerable attention to feminist debates. More importantly, in both countries the governments responded and instigated change from above with surprising speed. The question is: why did the governments give so much when relatively little pressure was exerted on them? Or, expressed differently: even if there were considerable pressures exerted, as was the case in West Germany, why did the governments of France and Netherlands respond when the German and Austrian example had shown that it was possible for governments to resist pressure groups? Neither France nor the Netherlands embraced the concept of participatory democracy in the way the Swedes do (i.e. *sämhalle*—the state is us). Neither country suffered terrorist activities, as did West German (and Italian, and Spanish) society, and in neither, to understate the facts, were women in politics a noteworthy force. Despite or because of the absence of these criteria the French and Dutch governments responded in ways that seemingly went far beyond immediate political expediency.

In both countries, the willingness for change was demonstrated by the funds that were set aside. Social engineering costs money, and it needs to go beyond the publication of a few pamphlets and making more services available. The issue is not just whether a government is willing to provide new services. Services can mushroom and disappear, justified each time by fiscal considerations. They may be a necessary part of a new infrastructure, but by themselves they cannot remove inequalities. On the contrary, many services are merely responses to needs created by persisting inequalities rather than measures of eradicating the sources of those inequalities. In each case, the funds were substantial. One suspects that in both countries the notion of social democracy won the day, each government (in France belatedly under Mitterand) accepting broad definitions of democracy which entailed equality of opportunity irrespective of sex, race, religion, sexual orientation and marital status. Beyond this, the governments accepted that *social change* was a desirable goal, even though social change is often not measurable in monetary terms and awards. Unlike economic policies, which are meant to increase profit and the wealth of a nation, social reform tends to cost money and its benefits are more ephemeral and related to the quality of life. Of course, this is not entirely true as far as work is concerned: standardisation measures in the cost of labour have economic ramifications, but in either country, these considerations were least important. In the Netherlands women's participation in the workforce has remained low, and in France, the position of women in the labour force has only come into focus in the late 1980s.

Perhaps it is more important that in these two countries protest actions formed an intrinsic right of citizenship. But here it also became apparent that the population as a whole seemed ready for change, if not for a transformation of their society. It needed the catalyst of the women's movement and that of several other movements (environmentalist, student, peace movements, etc.) to make outdated values crumble, and with them various social and cultural habits. The course of confrontation and making evident the shortcomings of governments that both protest movements so admirably pursued did not result, as in West Germany, in an inflexible and anxious official response that saw only the power struggle and the maintenance of authority before all else. In the Netherlands and in France, the content of the grievances was quickly seen as legitimate and was adopted, albeit sometimes in watered-down versions.

Of even greater importance is the conceptual change that has occurred in both countries. The reforms in France and in the Netherlands, although not more plentiful than in other countries, have often been more far-reaching than elsewhere. It has been mentioned before that reforms need not be an index of progress or of conceptual change. Reform may not require any change of values and in its name retrogressive ideas can be hidden. Nor is the apparent magnitude of the reform necessarily an index of a substantial political or social change. We can only speak of substantive reforms in cases in which the change involved a transformation or an abandonment of previously held traditions, beliefs and customs. The most radical changes that have occurred in the postwar era typically address questions related to value hierarchies. Moreover, it is not just a negotiation of values but an acknowledgement of the validity of a plurality of views.

The Dutch example demonstrates these issues well. One may well ask what has changed in favour of Dutch women amidst so many blaring cases of apparent disadvantage? These changes to date may not be many, but most of them are substantial in what they *represent*. One change has been implemented in lieu of the equal pay policy. Indeed, the equal pay policy programme must be described as one of the most successful ones in western Europe because by 1980 Dutch women earned just 2 percent less than their male counterparts (Dittrich, 1980), a fact that has only been matched by some Scandinavian programmes. In most other western industrialised countries women, on average, earn about 25 to 30 percent less than men in comparable positions. Although fewer Dutch women are part of the labour force than in other western European countries, the present success indicates that the Netherlands have done away with the concept of cheap labour and second-class citizenship in the production of the country's GNP.

Another example, that of abortion, has already been mentioned. Comparable only with a few countries in the western industrialised world, Dutch society in reality has introduced abortion on demand as a free health service. France has followed suit by further amendments to its original abortion bill. A right is qualitatively very different from a concessional framework, which may not require any change of thinking at all and may only mean granting a benefit for expediency—a benefit that may be quickly curtailed, or even partially withdrawn. Instead, the governments of the day have condoned the simple, but politically and socially highly important, claim that a woman has a right to decide about her body by herself without policing, paternal supervision and state control. It is telling that the liberal approach to abortion in the Netherlands has had one concrete result: by the early 1980s, Outshoorn claimed, the Netherlands had the lowest abortion figures per 1000 inhabitants in the world (1988: 212).

A third area, no less significant for its far reaching implications of freedom of ideas, is that of the role of women's studies in universities. In 1976, the University of Amsterdam resolved to make room for women's research at its university. It launched the 8 million Gulden project (approximately US$4 million) which specified that each year 1 million Gulden were to be spent on women's studies projects. Included in the package was a guarantee of employment for women who completed the course and assured expert supervision for women's higher degree studies. Today, most Dutch universities teach the subject area and have chairs in women's studies. They are well funded, at least as well as any other area of thought and research suitable for higher education studies. Holland is also the only country in western Europe that has created a chair for gay and lesbian studies. Brita Rang, a German feminist now living in the Netherlands, still cannot believe her good fortune in having ended up at a Dutch university. When she undertook to organise an international women's congress in Berlin, she writes, she had no funding or government help and the activity was barely condoned within the university itself. In the Netherlands, by contrast, no fights ensued and no pleas had to be made. Two historians were employed for a year to undertake the organisation of the international women historians' conference. They were given an office and a telephone and additional allowances for stationery and other costs, forwarded by the Emancipation Council (Rang, 1988: 165). I am almost certain that the euphoria in Rang's writing is not shared by all feminists working at Dutch universities. This congress organisation is a small matter, and perhaps even an isolated event. It is, however, a starting point. There is no implicit assumption made about the relative value of an international congress according to subject matter: who can say whether rewriting history, for instance, is ultimately of greater or lesser benefit to human society than neuroethology. In a way one wonders whether the Netherlands want to recapture their position as the 'centre of light in the rest of Europe' by showing a 'working model of free institutions'? (Sombart, 1967: 144). We need not dwell on this, but these conceptual jumps that have been made in the Netherlands in the postwar years are certainly in its own best free-thinking tradition, or a revitalisation of that tradition by new, innovative ideas.

Of no lesser importance are the changes in attitude to gender and marital questions that the Dutch people have demonstrated in the last two decades. In 1965 almost half of all Dutch people were against divorce, a figure that dwindled to 11.5 percent by 1977. Most Dutch people, men and women alike, would prefer to see social differences between the sexes disappear to include domestic role-sharing and equality in parenting (Gadourek, 1982: 54, 222). Even a study of 1973 found that Dutch men, of all western European groups examined, were the least likely to refuse helping in the kitchen (Pross, 1973: 94). The idea that only women are suitable for raising children has lost support in a mere decade (80 percent against) and so has the idea that it is unnatural for women to supervise men (from 30 to 10 percent in a decade) (*Equal Rights and Opportunities, Introd.*). Of all EEC countries Dutch men and women are now least discriminatory about women in politics or in non-traditional jobs and view women and men in those positions with equal confidence (*Women and Men of Europe 1983*). France, like Sweden, has also considered men's responses and roles within the new framework of democracy. A 1978 survey established that men's views on women's roles and status had changed in those cases when women had also changed. The most positive attitudes were recorded from men under 35 who had wives or girlfriends in careers and/or had given up the traditional concept of housewife and mother (Henry, 1978: 118–19). Attitudes need not be accompanied or underpinned by action, as we have seen. The same criticism cannot, however, be made of the Dutch. Twenty years ago, the representation of women in political office was below 3 percent, but it has risen well beyond English or West German percentages in this time and now is just behind Scandinavian countries. The change in such a brief span of time is astounding and, if anything, is evidence of the intention to translate ideas into practice.

Dutch feminists believe that feminism has carried a good deal of political weight in the Netherlands (Meulenbelt et al., 1984: 6). French feminism, de

Beauvoir said, also 'had an impact on French society disproportionate to the number of its active members, its limited means, and above all its limited media access' (1984: 233). They base this view on both governmental and elusive popular support for their campaigns. These campaigns more or less coincided with the EEC directives, enabling government elites and the unions to bring pressure to bear on the legislature for the elimination of legal inequalities pertaining to gender. It is interesting to note that a Dutch survey conducted in the 1970s found that over three-quarters of those women surveyed regarded the women's movement as unnecessary and as something entirely alien to themselves (Briët et al., 1987: 56). Largely, then, support was not given for the movement as such but rather for specific issues of women's rights. This would also suggest that the movement itself remained politically and, in the view of the public, much more marginalised than the presence of a feminist culture would suggest. Nevertheless, the speed with which the government acted and the population responded is surprising, particularly in view of the problem of *verzuiling*, the strongly oppositional camps of catholics and protestants, which is still not entirely a matter of the past. It was as if an old, rotten edifice only needed to be touched in order to collapse. In its stead, within a little over a decade, there emerged a changed society, modern and progressive in its ideas, with changed agendas and new issues announced and debated on television and radio, long after the spectacular activities of the movement were over.

The starting point for the substantial change (not just industrialisation) may have occurred in World War II as a result of the experience of being occupied and economically ruined. These horrors were fresh in the minds of survivors. The Dutch resistance movement created a strong sense of national identity and a counterweight against pillarisation. Within the resistance movement, women played a particularly important, if not predominant, role. Indeed, as in France, the resistance movement relied heavily on women as often the only remaining adult (civilian) population in certain areas. As in France, the courage and skill of women to act on behalf of their country and for the liberation of their country was greatly admired and acknowledged, and it made a mockery of the suggestion that women were the weaker sex in need of support and so held in a state of minority. The French gave women the vote as a gesture of gratitude at a time of a resurgence of nationalism. More broadly speaking, it probably encouraged the view that *any* form of oppression was simply no longer acceptable. It was a matter of uncovering those oppressions in order to eliminate them. The waning importance of religion in people's life may also be a contributing factor. Over 40 percent of the Dutch population now considers itself atheist or humanitarian, openly rejecting religious ideologies. In France, too, rights issues have begun to overtake considerations of conscience bound to religious affiliation. In neither country can one yet speak of a humanitarianism unfettered by the weight of religious doctrines, but clearly choices have been made in favour of secular human rights, reaffirming more strongly than ever before that citizenship is a political right, no longer marred or bound by property ownership (i.e. class), religion and gender, or even by sexual preference.

NOTES

1 The 'Vrouwen Archief' is unique in the world today. Some of its books date as far back as the 16th century. In the 1980s it had over 25 000 volumes, and arguably the largest and best single collection of books solely on women's writing and women's

issues in the world today. Its information and archival service is also superb and readily accessible for researchers and interested parties from outside the Netherlands.

2   'Let's recognise each other, speak, and look at each other. We are oppressed together. Together let's make the revolution. Rise, enslaved women, let us get ready to break our chains.'

3   Our discussion of the French movement confines itself therefore to some essential points, relevant here. Detailed descriptions of the movement and outlines of some of its main ideas can be gleaned from recent and relevant publications such as those by Marks and Courtivron (1981), Duchen (1986), Moi (1987) and Grosz (1989).

4   Amongst the many journals, and special issues of journals devoted to feminist concerns, apart from those already mentioned, are *Les femmes s'entêtent*, as a special issue of *Les Temps Modernes* (1974), *Les Pétroleuses* (1974), and *Nouvelles Féministes* which ran from 1974–1977. *Sorcières* was edited by Xavière Gauthier in 1976, and the *F Magazine* by Claude Servan-Schreiber (1978). The *Questions féministes* (1977–1978), was run jointly by Simone de Beauvoir, Christine Delphy and Monique Wittig.

# 6 Revolutions and radicalism in southern Europe

In many ways the political and economic development of southern European countries in this century bears no resemblance to the rest of western Europe. Only Italy is in some ways an exception. Up to the 1960s at least, all four countries (Portugal, Spain, Italy and Greece) were considered the poor cousins of western European economic life. Living standards were low and poverty widespread. Their GNP was then, and still partly is, substantially below that of all other western European countries. More importantly, the tale of their political fortunes over this century has provided a dismal record of oppression and dictatorships. Portugal under Salazar suffered 42 years of dictatorship, and it took half a century before free elections were again possible. Spain, under Franco, lagged not far behind the Portuguese record with 39 years of dictatorship. Under Mussolini Italy experienced the longest rule of a fascist 'leader' (over twenty years) of any country, and Greece fell back into military dictatorships several times in the post-World War II period. It is only since the 1970s that Portugal, Spain and Greece have been freed of the yoke of dictatorships and one-party rule.

The post-dictatorial phases in these countries set in motion a hasty restructuring of the economy and a transformation of social life, giving politics a new lease of life by introducing and maintaining a parliamentary democracy. All this happened among peoples who had no experience of normal political practice (Duran & Gallego, 1986: 209). Political turmoil was perhaps an inevitable concomitant of such a restructuring process and the price to pay for severance from dictatorial rule. Portugal had no less than nine governments in three post-revolutionary years, Italy had 31 governments in less than 25 postwar years. The Greek form of government vascillated between military junta and parliamentary democracy and Spain has suffered a similar fate to Portugal. All of these upheavals, some of them as recent the mid-1970s, were growing rather than dying pains, and signalled the birth of new and modern nations.

The battles that each of the southern European countries had to fight in the postwar decades had been fought elsewhere as well, though much earlier. They were concerned with the question of who should hold the power in a nation: the armed forces, the church, or a secular body of democratically elected people. In the 1970s and 1980s Portugal, Greece and Spain had to sort out the military pre-eminence in politics. In Italy, the power of the church had to be confronted in new and challenging ways, a process that has barely begun in the other southern European countries. And finally, the influence of the old established ruling classes had to be broken.

In all these countries political parties had been prohibited or made mute during their respective dictatorship periods, but underground resistance movements had existed, led by socialist and communist forces. These re-emerged in Portugal and

Italy with great vigour, whereas in Greece they had been almost completely wiped out. But in each case, it was this clandestine resistance, or the existence of an identifiable resistance movement, from which a new positive identity for a new nation could be forged. Each country eventually established an open economy in which revolutionary change took place at a breathtaking speed.

The role of women during the time of these dictatorships, which were supported by the institution of the church, was of course highly circumscribed. Social norms and laws were not just strongly in favour of men but afforded women a status that was little better than slave, rendering them totally dependent upon the mercy of the male heads of households. Until rather recently, the economies of most southern European countries were predominantly agriculturally based and still steeped in the pre-industrial manufacturing mode of highly exploitative rural home-based labour which typically fell to women and sometimes children. Women thus had few if any rights and rarely if ever any reprieve from total paternal/patriarchal supervision, from child bearing and lowly paid or unpaid work. Topics like sexuality or any form of birth control were entirely taboo and a large number of women, mostly in rural areas, received little or no medical attention. With the exception of Italy, death rates of mothers in childbirth and infant mortality rates were high until the 1970s. The ability of women to organise and to respond to their plight, however, varied markedly, for reasons which shall be explored in this chapter. Italy had a very powerful women's movement, and Greek women's organisations were particularly radical. Spain had a relatively short movement and Portugal stood out as one country in which the obviously oppressed were generally not able to muster wide mass support.

The transformation of these countries into western-style modern societies has not been painless and cannot be regarded as complete. In Portugal, Spain and Greece, governments have taken it upon themselves to drastically revise and change the social, political and economic life and have usually been seen to include women in the programmes of change. Only in Italy was a strong and very impressive grassroots feminist lobby at work in demanding change for women and for their society. The Italian feminist movement, in my view, has perhaps been the most impressive of all feminist movements of the second wave. But even in Portugal, Spain and Greece, women have stirred to form their own networks and organisations and have spoken out openly for their own rights. In all countries the revolutionary fervour and language is unmistakable, as is the readiness for confrontation and radical change within a context of powerful traditions and institutions such as the church.

## PORTUGAL

In our discussion of the Scandinavian and other western European countries there were a number of assumptions made, about things that one tends to take for granted as being part of the infrastructure of a modern European society: compulsory schooling for ten or so years, health care, social security, and an array of services and provisions which form the dynamic context in which women and some men seek to implement equal rights and opportunities in their daily lives. A mere glance at the social life of southern European countries provides ample evidence that these social infrastructures are indeed fragile in their infancy and vulnerable in their novelty. Nowhere could that be more apparent than in Portugal.

Portugal awoke after its bloodless revolution of April 1974, the so-called Carnation Revolution, from semi-feudal slumber, into which it had been cast by its falling from world empire status hundreds of years ago. Portugal had experimented with republicanism in 1910, but as with the Weimar Republic, the dream was short-lived. It lasted for only sixteen years, after which a military coup finished it off in five days. Within those sixteen years the country had had 44 governments and eight presidents. Yet Portuguese women were as much part of European emancipation events either before, and, or during, the republic. Portugal's first woman to graduate in medicine (1891) was Armelia Cardia, the first woman to graduate in law (1913) was Regina Quintanilha. In 1911 the first woman university professor was appointed. The National Council of Portuguese Women, with distinctly emancipatory goals, formed in 1914 and two large-scale feminist congresses were held in Lisbon, one in 1924 and the other in 1928, two years after Salazar assumed power. It was to be the last one for 47 years. When the republic disappeared so did women's right to equality in marriage, the divorce law and many other freedoms. What followed were 42 years of iron rule by Antonio de Oliveira Salazar, a former professor of economics at Coimbra. In 1924, his book *Bolshevism and Society* (*O Bolchevismo e a Sociedade*) was published, and with it Salazar became the undisputed spiritual leader of the Portuguese political right.

Gradually, Salazar created his own brand of dictatorship, though it had some of the usual characteristics: extensive use of secret police, prohibition of all political parties, outlawing of strikes and dissidents and imposition of strictest censorship. In 1933 he presented a new constitution—(his) *Estado Novo* (New State). It legitimised what Harsgor called 'a subdued Lusitanian, catholic version of a fascist regime' (1976: 4) which, although it refrained from the scale of brutality perpetrated by Mussolini and Hitler, was nevertheless an extremely rigid and uncompromising dictatorship. The new constitution established the equality of citizens before the law, except for women, 'in view of their differences deriving from her nature and interests of her family' (Stocker de Sousa et al., n.d.: 5). He abolished what few social services had been available and took little interest in the people, their needs or education. But he amassed a fortune in gold reserves for Portugal and keenly watched the maintenance of the remainder of the Portuguese world empire. He left untouched the old economic monopolies but renewed ties with the Vatican, signing the Concordat under which Portuguese couples marrying in the catholic faith were not permitted to divorce.

It was as if Portugal had become frozen in time and space—a cynical interpretation of the idea of 'stability'. Salazar was clever enough not to involve Portugal in World War II and to stay away from the Axis Pact between Hitler and Mussolini. After the Allies' victory, attempts were made to force him to liberalise his *Estado Novo*, but it was soon recognised that 'Salazarism was incapable of democratising itself. It stood out in its grim and eerie immobility' (Harsgor, 1976: 5).

In 1968, Salazar suffered a stroke and resigned. After his death in 1970, the *Estado Novo* he had created survived him for another four years, under Caeto's rule with the army's backing. It finally collapsed when the Armed Forces Movement, led by General de Spinola, dealt it a swift and bloodless death knell in the successful revolution of April 1974. There was a chance that the new military leadership might have led Portugal into a new dictatorship. Due to some extent to the power struggles amongst the military itself and largely due to the efforts of António Ramalho Eanes, the way was opened for the first parliamentary elections in 1976.

In 1974, the country saw itself faced with massive tasks. Social immobility was extreme. The upper class, a semi-feudal oligarchy, was a small, rich and separate entity that controlled most of the country's economic fortunes. Eighty percent of the national economy was in the hands of eight families. The middle classes were weak and had been rendered ineffectual. Universities had been cleansed of any liberal tendencies. The bulk of the population was proletarian— chiefly agricultural (over 80 percent of the population lived in rural communities). Every third woman and every fifth man were illiterate. In rural and semi-rural communities the figure might have been as high as 80 percent for women (Lovenduski, 1986: 105). General ignorance was aided by the unavailability of newspapers, of books, and often of radio and television. Social security provisions hardly existed. Schools and hospitals were run down and medical services only functioned in some of the largest cities. Basic services such as transport, electricity and water were often absent from rural and semi-rural areas. Beggars were a regular feature of Portuguese life. In and around Lisbon, the beautiful capital of Portugal, over half a million people languished in slums, often lacking even basic sanitary facilities. The rural sector was depressed and hardly any changes, technologically or socially, had occurred here over centuries (Schümann & Müller, 1986: 24–32). It had been in the interest of the ruling class to freeze the social structure to maintain control over the latifundia in the south and the fragmented small holdings in the north, as well as over the few large business corporations and the banking activities. In other words, as Lomax writes:

> ... it was an archaic social system that provided considerable economic benefits for a few at the cost of low overall productivity, and that resulted in the lowest per capita income in Western Europe, together with the highest rates of illiteracy, infant mortality, and infectious diseases. (1983: 110)

Women were, if not in name but in reality, the property of their husbands, who could determine every detail of family life or veto any decision their wives had made. By law, domestic work was compulsory for women after marriage. The Penal Code went so far as to implicitly permit a husband to kill his unfaithful wife because the crime had no prison sentence attached, merely stipulating that a husband leave his province for three months (Barbosa, 1981: 477). The limp attempts under Salazar to introduce an equality law for men and women were dismissed as an absurdity, given the alleged innate differences and inequalities of the sexes (Schümann & Müller,1986: 73). In 1970, infant and maternal mortality matched the worst in the world: fifty infant and seven maternal deaths per 1000 live births were the stated figures, though the real figures were probably higher than the official records revealed. Contraceptives were not available and not known. Abortion was a serious crime, punishable by at least eight years' imprisonment. Under Salazar, no women's organisations were permitted other than associations run by the catholic church, such as the Obra das Maes (Mothers' Circles).

In its foreign policy Portugal had been particularly resistant to giving up any of its vast colonial empire, which had been amassed at the time of Portugal's golden age in the 15th and 16th centuries. Portuguese East India had been discovered and conquered by Vasco da Gama, and was later ruled by Alfonso d'Albuquerque who had also taken Goa, Ceylon and Malacca. Pedro Alvares Cabral conquered Brazil in 1500 and further possessions were claimed on African soil. Brazil declared its independence as early as 1822, but up to that time, especially since the discovery of diamond and gold fields, it had substantially enriched the Portuguese economy. Indeed, Portugal had failed to develop its home markets and industries because for centuries local production was less important than the imported goods from its colonies. It had ultimately failed to restructure and modernise its economy because it had been able to rely on external sources of income.

Moreover, the Portuguese colonies (called *ultramar*) provided Portugal with a source for an image of its own greatness, which became deeply embedded in Portuguese thinking and in turn fostered a yearning (*saudade*) for a resurrection of that former 'greatness'. *Ultramar* was not merely a term for overseas possessions but a concept which formed part of a Portuguese national identity. Salazar knew how to exploit this Portuguese mentality well and held onto *ultramar* in a way no other European nation had managed or had dared to do. Thus, in the 1960s, Portugal still reigned over the biggest colonial empire of any western European country. Half of Timor Island, Portuguese India and Sao Joao Batista da Ajuda went first, but there was still Angola, Mozambique, Guinea Bissau, the Cato Verde islands and the provinces (islands) of Sào Tomé, Príncipe and Macao. In the 1960s Angola and Mozambique became 'Portugal's own Vietnam' as the liberation movements in both countries gained momentum. Up to 50 percent of the Portuguese budgets went towards financing the costs of the wars and one in four Portuguese men served in the military deployed to these colonies (Morrison, 1981: 12).

Indeed, every single element in Portuguese society and political life seemed to pose insurmountable obstacles for a new Portugal, especially since not one of the Salazar opponents had any practical experience in governing a country. Old vested interests of the military and the upper-class elites quickly surfaced. The old mistrust between north and south and its fundamental differences re-emerged—the 'heathen', communist, that is, anti-clerical population (especially the Alentejanos) in the south, and the devout catholic north. Sectarianism, a burning suspicion of everyone (fuelled by over 40 years of secret police activity), and a fear of the outside world were characteristics of the possible political elites (Harsgor, 1976: 13).

The creation and/or resurfacing of political parties occurred, however, with surprising speed in 1974. Two major right-wing parties, the Popular Democratic Party with its offshoot the Social Democratic Party and the Social Democratic Centre, were more easily constituted than any of the left-wing parties, whose leaders had been imprisoned or exiled. The Portuguese Communist Party was the oldest of the parties on the left. It had been founded during the years of the first republic, in 1921, but had quickly become illegal and had remained so until 1974. Within five months of the revolution, 136 local headquarters were established throughout Portugal. Membership in the party grew tenfold between 1974 and 1976 (to 115 000 members). The 30 communists who emerged as leaders in the re-established party had astonishing and tragic life records. On average, each had been a member of the Communist Party for 30 years and had had 23 years of full-time political activity. On average, each had served about ten years of imprisonment. Jose Magro and Francisco Miguel had the longest prison terms with 21 years each, and a further fourteen members, including three women (Georgette and Sofia Ferreira and Alda Nogeira), had each spent well over ten years in prison and had suffered severe deprivations and torture.

The Portuguese Socialist Party, which is apparently comparable to the right wing of the British Labour Party, evolved from the Socialist Portuguese Action Group (Acção Socialista Portuguesa) which was formed in Geneva in 1964 and was enrolled in the Socialist International in 1972. This group had developed in exile through the strong support and links with the West German SPD. In 1973, in West Germany, it formed the Portuguese Socialist Party under Mário Soares who in 1976 became Portugal's first prime minister under the new constitution. The party was strongly anti-communist and so the stage was set for major confrontations not just between left and right parties but within the left as well (Ferreira & Marshall, 1986: 210–13).

Portugal's leadership changed several times between 1974 and 1976 and since the first free elections in 1976, elections have been held frequently. It was not until the end of the 1980s that the first signs of political stability appeared accompanied by a gradual shift to moderate and centre parties. An ideological explanation for this development was offered by Poulantzas, who argues that the budding domestic bourgeoisie of Portugal needed a different framework in order to express its own self-interest but was too weak to achieve a break with the dictatorship by itself. It therefore aligned itself temporarily with the popular masses. Portugal only apparently had a revolutionary movement with a proletarian base and a socialist ideology, but its real agenda was the attainment of bourgeois democratisation (Poulantzas, 1976: 135–6, 144; Lomax, 1983: 124). Whatever the underlying causes may be, workers and especially feminists would probably concur with the view that a revolutionary transformation of Portuguese society has not yet occurred—although it is never quite clear what a revolutionary transformation *ought* to achieve. To all intents and purposes, I believe, a transformation process has in fact commenced.

In the three years from the beginning of 1974 to the end of 1976, Portuguese governments under leftist military leadership began the arduous process of re-building the country by focusing at first on three major changes, often referred to as the 'three d's': decolonisation, democratic freedom and the dismantling of the old economic monopolies. In the years 1975 and 1976, Portugal recognised the independence of most of its overseas colonies. Angola won its independence in 1976, with Cuban help. This was not against the ideas and wishes of Portuguese industrialists who had forcefully argued against the colonial wars and had expressed a strong wish to see their money used for the development of local industries. The system was cleansed (*saneamentos*) of supporters of the old Salazar regime. In the dismantling of Salazar's economic system, the government first of all destroyed the old economic monopolies. It confiscated the properties of large property owners, and nationalised not just transport and basic services but about one quarter of the GNP (including banks, petrochemical plants and breweries). The communist-led confiscation of property created considerable unrest and strong anti-revolutionary movements in Portugal's so-called 'hot summer' (*o verão quente*) of 1975, and in a way threatened to undermine the gains made by the revolutionary coup of 1974. The Communist Party made similar claims about the workers' movement which gained in strength in the summer months of 1975—the number of strikers has been estimated as high as 200 000—and openly denounced the postal workers' strike in June 'as playing into the hands of the reaction' (Lomax, 1983: 115). But such actions probably revealed more about the conservative and bourgeois nature of the Portuguese Communist Party and about its fear of losing influence than about the nature and source of the strike actions. At the same time a popular movement initiated all sorts of spontaneous actions and formations of workers' organisations.

As far as Portuguese economic fortunes were concerned, Ferreira and Marshall rightly point out that the Portuguese revolution could not have come at a more inopportune moment than in 1974. We recall that 1974 saw the worst economic recession in the western industrialised world and economies suffered everywhere. Moreover, the revolution itself had several immediate negative consequences. The Portuguese economy had come to depend to a significant degree on two foreign sources of incomes. One was derived from Portuguese people as guest workers elsewhere in western Europe and a second was derived from the tertiary industry of tourism. Portuguese guest workers, afraid about the meaning of the revolution, stopped sending money back home, and tourism was drastically curtailed, depriving one of the country's largest tertiary industries of much needed revenue. In addition, foreign investment dropped off sharply by a staggering 80 percent and capital left the country with the employers and property owners who chose to flee. This somewhat negatively counteracted the government moves to allow rural and urban workers a greater share in the GNP. The confiscation of land, particularly in southern Portugal, resulted in some redistribution of wealth, and incomes of workers were generally increased, but eventually higher inflation rates took away some of the benefits (Ferreira & Marshall, 1986: 207–8). Moreover, the Portuguese settlers of Angola and Mozambique returned to Portugal (*retornados*) and, for a time at least, they added further negative weight to the fragile new republic. The *retornados* were usually strong opponents of the decolonisation policy and in addition they began to swell the large numbers of people looking for housing and employment. This development went hand in hand with a drop in annual emigration. In 1975 the net annual emigration was 120 000 but by 1979 it had dropped to 45 000. These basically short-term problems might have been weathered had the oil crisis and general recession not also happened at this moment as well (Morrison, 1981: 61).

In 1976, the new constitution was finally written and proclaimed. A German paper hailed it as 'the most progressive in all of Europe' (Pollman, *Deutsche Volkszeitung*, 1979), and indeed such a claim is not entirely unfounded. It is noteworthy that, apart from the UK, the only western European countries which made *full* constitutional provisions for women's rights and women's equality in all areas of life (employment, and family/marriage) were Portugal, Spain and Italy, all countries in which socialist forces came to dominate at the time when the constitutions were drafted. The Portuguese constitution has been amended several times since 1976. Throughout the 1970s there were political forces that wanted the left political bias removed from the constitution, but they did not succeed until June 1988.[1] The constitution aimed at a mixed market economy with the state as a major partner. The constitutional revision of 1982 was an important one, for it defined fully for the first time the role of the military, and relegated it firmly to the civilian control of parliament. Presidential powers were reduced so as to make it more difficult for a president to dismiss a government, a right that was of tremendous importance immediately after the 1974 coup. The 1982 revision also replaced the Council of Revolution which had served its role, with several other bodies (Ferreira & Marshall, 1986: 226).

At the same time the government began to create the social infrastructure that Portuguese society had almost totally lacked. It set out to improve energy and water distribution, and sanitary conditions. It began to introduce and rationalise a national health care service along British lines and changed medical training requirements to entice young doctors into rural areas, at least for some time in their professional lives. It set up primary health care centres in rural areas and began to dispense contraceptives over the counter, contrary to the dictates of the church. It started making social provisions for old age and unemployment, and in the areas of housing and infant care.

In schooling tremendous changes were forged in a mere decade. The general political unrest of the 1970s had allowed Soares to restructure the entire educational system without much opposition. Basic schooling was for six years and had been compulsory for a mere four years, but even this rule had never been enforced. An examination after four years of schooling, coupled with the award of a certificate, ensured that most of the students usually left at that time. Soares abolished this examination, increased the years of compulsory schooling and introduced a single stream secondary education system. Democratic school governments were created, teachers were allowed to unionise and the whole syllabus was thoroughly revised (Ferreira & Marshall, 1986: 232–4). Formal adult education was introduced and expanded quickly, partly to combat the exceptionally high illiteracy rate. A decade later, in 1986, Portugal joined the EEC as its youngest and poorest member, and pledged to improve the position of women along with a multitude of other obligations and rules.

The new constitution of 1976 was a milestone in Portuguese women's history. Women regained the vote and were declared equal in all aspects of life—in marriage, the family and at work. As time went on, statutes and amendments were added to the constitution. Much of what has happened in Portugal to improve the lot of women occurred because of government initiatives and legislation. In 1979 a separate law decreed equal rights for men and women at paid work (piecework at home) and in employment (outside the home). In 1980 Portugal ratified the UN convention on the elimination of any discrimination against women. Civil divorce was also made available for couples who had been married in church. By the mid-1980s the divorce rate stood at 9.2 percent.

In 1973, Maria de Lurdes Pintasilgo, who later became Portugal's first woman prime minister, was the founder of the first commission for social policy for women. From it, today's Commission for Women's Condition (Comissão da Condição Feminina) emerged. It was set up in 1978 and is attached to the prime minister's office. Like similar offices of government in other western countries, the commission has been active in eradicating anachronistic laws and has initiated programmes and policies for women. It also has its own documentation centre which houses a substantial number of books and regularly publishes statistical information on women (*Folha de Informação Bibliografica*).[2] There is also an Executive Council of the Committee on Women's Status which hears complaints and proposes changes in areas that affect women. One of its recent activities (in 1989) was the organisation of a seminar and information gathering exercise on the topic of sexual harassment in the workplace (*Women of Europe*, no. 60, 1989: 28). As elsewhere in western Europe, women of the urban and rural upper class have always had educational opportunities and venues for self-expression. The shift that has now occurred is the realisation that women, irrespective of their background, should be accorded such rights and opportunities. In order to put such injunctions into practice, large-scale changes in lifestyle and values have been made and are likely to continue to be made.

The centuries of oligarchy and the four decades of right-wing dictatorship, however, have left a deep mark on Portuguese life. Some of the problems inherent in this legacy of oppression will continue into the next century. Inflation rates soared in the 1970s and real wages fell. The foreign debt reached astronomical proportions that austerity measures were unable to curb. Just when the economy appeared to recover, it was dealt a new blow by the worst drought Portugal had experienced since the turn of the century (1981–82). This affected not just agricultural production but also energy production, which had just begun to rely in part on hydro-electric forces. Moreover, because of economic parity adjustments in Europe in 1982, the country effectively had to devalue the escudo by 9.4 percent, which was harmful in terms of its import requirements and its foreign debt. When in 1984 Portugal celebrated the tenth anniversary of the revolution, it was still the poorest country in western Europe and needed to import 50 percent of its food. Foreign debts had reached over US$14 billion, inflation was up to 34 percent and unemployment was over 12 percent. In the late 1980s there have been signs of improvement, but to date Portugal has not fully recovered from its economic problems. Neither rural nor urban poverty has yet been effectively curbed.

It needs to be emphasised that Portugal is still one of the most rural countries in the western economic system. Its urban population accounts for just over 30 percent of the country's total. The supply of modern amenities and networks of communication and transport are usually geared towards urban-dominated environments and can be afforded because they are limited to concentrated clusters of human habitation with a high per capita use. By contrast, in predominantly rural Portugal, the great majority of families lives far apart from each other. Areas which have a low per capita return and use are less likely to be provided with services.

Acquiring standards of education, health and social services to which most other western European countries have been accustomed for some time has necessitated drastic steps. The great need for educating the population, even at the most basic level, is often beyond the scope of available resources. In many areas primary school classes, for instance, now accommodate up to 100 students. Teaching is done in shifts and school buildings are often used until 11:00 p.m. at night for routine instruction of students. There is also a drastic teacher shortage at all levels of schooling, trade and post-secondary education, partly because Portugal suffered a constant brain and skill drain during the Salazar rule. Such skills are not replaced quickly, particularly since demand for skill has drastically increased in line with the reform intentions. Nevertheless, the illiteracy rate is falling steadily, although in 1988 it still stood at about 11 percent for men and 21 percent for women.

In rural areas the acute shortage of doctors and health-care provisions has not been alleviated. Despite such failings in the delivery of health care, improved health standards generally drastically decreased infant and maternal mortality within a decade, halving both by 1980. Despite these improvements infant mortality, now standing at about 26 per 1000, is still four times higher than in Sweden (6.5 per 1000). Medical services relating to childbirth are often entirely insufficient, especially in rural areas. In 1981, the majority of births still took place outside hospitals, many without any medical assistance or even a midwife (Barbosa, 1981: 479). From the very beginning of the new republic, women tried ceaselessly to impress upon governments the need for abortion law reforms. It ran a number of concerted campaigns, especially after 1977. But even with support from feminist parliamentary delegates, the campaigns led nowhere. So it was that Zita Seabra, a woman of extraordinary vitality and intelligence who had spoken strongly in favour of abortion, was dismissed from the Communist Party and the government because she had been allegedly fraternising with the 'enemy', that is, the reform communists (Sá e Melo, 1988: 193). In 1984, after four years of parliamentary indecision, the government finally passed an abortion law which permitted abortion in cases of rape, severe health problems for the mother and in cases of foetal deformity. This legislation was not and is not in line with social practice and with general opinion. The number of illegal abortions in Portugal has been estimated at about 200 000 per year, often carried out under such appalling conditions that many women die (Barbosa, 1981: 479). A Portuguese survey in urban centres found in 1984 that 70 percent of that population was unequivocally for the right to abortion and only 4 percent was strictly against it (Schümann & Müller, 1986: 70). Noisy demonstrations accompanying the 1984 bill proposal had no effect and within parties the debates led to increased hostilities. This abortion law has not changed anything for women in rural areas. Their ability to secure contraceptives has been marred by ignorance, fear of consequences from the church and sheer unavailability. The stories of foundlings remain heart-rending.

It is not surprising that the position of women has changed little in the rural environment. Apart from the health concerns in pregnancy and childbirth, women have remained particularly disadvantaged in many other ways. This is partly to do with the gradual shift to urban life as part of the industrialisation process. When men from rural areas have no choice but to seek work in the city or even abroad, they typically leave their wives behind to deal with children, aging parents and the running of the farms. Those women who are lucky enough to have their entire family around them also find it difficult to make ends meet and are now, more often than not, forced to find paid employment outside the home. The jobs they can get tend to be limited in supply, usually of a menial kind and poorly paid, and often involve extremely long working hours and little or no paid holidays. Rural women in those positions rarely get any relief whatsoever from work, for the time-consuming domestic work still waits for them after a ten-hour working day away from home. They depend on relatives for the supervision of their young children because, still in the late 1980s, there were kindergarten places for only 8 percent of preschool children. Pre-marriage life for young women has its own pitfalls. Throughout the post revolutionary period unemployment has remained unabated and severe. In 1981, for instance, an average of 28 percent of women aged between 15 and 24 were unemployed as against 8 percent of men in the same age category. On a farm, there is never a shortage of unpaid work of course, but this does not help the combined family income nor help prepare the young woman for marriage. In towns and cities, the situation is changing rather drastically. The female employment rate of 1989 stood at 39.5 percent as against 13 percent in the 1960s. This rate is now twice as high as that of men and only 6 percent of women, as against 14 percent of men, are employed in senior and middle-management positions and higher skilled jobs (*Women of Europe*, no. 63, 1990: 29).

There are, however, some positive changes overall for women and work. Women's earning capacity, for instance, has increased markedly. Before the revolution, women earned about 53 percent of male wages but by 1977 it had gone up to 72 percent, a direct result of the 1974 statutory national minimum wage fixation. Such rules tend to be enforcible more readily in towns and cities than in rural areas but at least they have been effective to some extent. In 1971, almost 83 percent of women were in the lowest paid jobs, and by 1978, only two years after the constitution was proclaimed, the figure had dropped to 54 percent.

Portugal has never had a women's movement comparable to any of the countries already discussed. But women have stirred and subsequently did organise. After Salazar's resignation in 1968, women and men who had stood close to the Communist Party secretly formed the Movimiento Democrático das Mulheres (Women's Democratic Movement) which burst into considerable activity after 1974. They later also published a journal, called *Mulheres* (Women), which achieved the relatively large circulation of 25 000 in urban areas (Pollman, 1976).

If anything looked like the beginning of a movement, it was the act of arresting the 'three Marias' (Maria Isabel Barreno, Maria Teresa Horta and Maria Velho da Costa) for the writing and publication of their book *Novas Cartas Portuguesas* (*New Portuguese Letters*) in 1973. In it the authors had been particularly frank about matters of gender and sex, and female sexuality and sensuality, for the book was intended as a revolutionary examination of gender relations. The three Marias argued in it that what men do to women was barbarous: 'bodies torn apart by the member' (*New Portuguese Letters*, 1975: 188). Male lovemaking was termed a 'slithering' over a woman's body (p. 156) which eventually led to pregnancy. 'A woman's only role is to give birth and to remain stillborn herself' (p. 107). Marriage, men and the sexual act were all reviewed in the negative. Men were enemies and there was nothing women could do but stay far away from them. The *New Portuguese Letters* became known worldwide when the trial opened in 1973 in pre-democracy Portugal. Fierce demonstrations accompanied the authors' arrest and trial in Portugal. Thousands of letters poured in from all over the world (chiefly the USA, France, and England) to save the writers from prison. The defence case began in 1974, but the charges were dropped once the Carnation Revolution began.

After the revolution, a Movimento de Libertação das Mulheres (Women's Liberation Movement) sprang up. It was this rather small group which organised demonstrations in 1975 to ensure that women's rights were written into the constitution. These demonstrations, ushering in the International Women's Year, were met with substantial hostilities. Apparently thousands of men turned up at these demonstrations in order to boycott them. 'They attacked and insulted the women ... in every possible way,' wrote Barbosa (1981: 478). A year later an information and documentation centre for women was formed and it was this group that published a charter of women's rights in 1977 along with another journal, *Lua*, which had to cease publication two years later due to lack of funds. Amongst these early women's organisations was also the Union of Antifascist and Revolutionary Women (União das Mulheres Antifascistas e Revolutionárias), an extreme-left Maoist group. It published a small journal, *Mulheres de Abril* (Women of April), referring to the month of April in which the Carnation Revolution occurred. In 1989 this group changed its name to Movimento pela Emancipaçoa Social das Mulheres (Movement for the Social Emancipation of Women).

A landmark in women's affairs was the first national meeting of working women, Encontro Nacional de Mulheres Trabalhadoras, in Lisbon in 1976, organised by Intersindical, the general workers' union. Over 800 delegates attended this meeting. Under Salazar, a women's section of the union had existed but the segregation between male and female workers at the workplace and at the union level had been so complete that workers of either sex never met and women had no idea of their status and pay in relation to that of men. This first national meeting of working women created a new basis for women's rights in the unions and at the workplace (Pollmann, 1976).

Women's activities and organisational formations increased throughout the 1980s. The Women's Democratic Movement has continued to act with and on behalf of women and has given particular support to rural women and to the arts. In 1989, for instance, they honoured Clementina Caneiro De Moura, a well-known feminist, for her work as a painter, teacher and craftswoman. They have supported and commended a women's collective for farm reform in the development of the Alentejo area in the south. The Association of Portuguese Women in Agriculture (Associação de Mulheres Agricultoras Portuguesas) now exists and has created a much needed network amongst rural women. It has addressed, among other things, the problematic legal status of women in family agricultural businesses. Several autonomous groups have sprung up particularly since Portugal's entry into the EEC. In 1986, for instance, a Liga dos Direitos das Mulheres (League of Women's Rights) was formed which, under the leadership of a lawyer, Rose Nery Sttau Monteiro, and a judge, Helena Maria Lopes, has begun to look at areas of legal discrimination against women. Another, called Feminist Intervention (Intervenção Feminina) consists mainly of professional women in freelance or independent positions who have begun to meet feminists from other countries. In 1987 the Socialist Association of Women (Associação de Mulheres Socialistas) was formed in response to the Socialist Party's dissolution of its women's section. In the late 1980s there was discussion about coordinating women's organisations into a national body. One of the chief aims of the women's organisations, no matter how different their views may be otherwise, has been to take on the political parties to ensure that more women can become politically active (Sá e Melo, 1988: 191).

It remains to be seen what industrialisation and Portugal's entry into the EEC will eventually do for the status of women. Social emancipation has not occurred yet (Schümann & Müller, 1986: 24). Many of the changes so far have been formal rather than substantive and have not resulted in a significant improvement of women's status and freedom of movement. It is noteworthy that the Portuguese government has largely circumvented the power and influence of the church by enforcing such rules and regulations as the divorce law, the open sale of contraceptives, and an abortion law. These reforms are extremely limited but they have partly broken the nexus with the church. The government has also relegated the armed forces to civilian control and created a parliamentary democracy and a republic, which appears to be stabilising. Of equal importance is the fact that Portuguese society is a now a learning society. Social democracy, indeed any modern democracy, cannot function without having a population that is able to read and write and participate in the political events of its country. Portugal had developed a tradition of silence. Finding a voice, be it expressed in literature, in politics, in social concerns or in women's issues, is a formative process that cannot be completed overnight. The 1974 revolution was the start to overcoming the *fado* (fatalism), the *saudade* (yearning) and the much cultivated art of *paciencia* (patience).

Immediately after the revolution, in April 1975, a Lisbon lawyer told a foreign correspondent, 'We have made a considerable anatomical discovery this April: the Portuguese have teeth'. The foreign correspondent thought that this remark was a reference to the revolution. 'No,' the lawyer replied. 'What I mean is that you can see us smile.' The correspondent then retorted that it was not only a discovery of teeth but also of the tongue. 'This has been', he wrote, 'the revolution not of the gun, but of the word' (Eder, 1974). Some have doubted whether it was a revolution at all (Riegelhaupt, 1983: 3, 8; Lomax, 1983: 105). I cannot see that the working classes have had a good deal to smile about. Economically at least their situation actually worsened. But in terms of a bourgeois democratisation process, indeed the smiles and the words have not waned. Professional associations, parent groups and women's groups have taken up their roles in a functioning democracy.

All of these things need time. Political participation needs experience and the development of workable structures. No one can learn the rules of democracy under a dictatorship and no democracy can be maintained without the imput of large numbers of people. Oligarchies and small power elites together with low or non-existent levels of education of the general population are perfect recipes for dictatorships. Portuguese women, emerging from this oppression, have the ominous task of helping their sisters to overcome their incredibly high rate of illiteracy in order to communicate effectively in a political arena. Women, I would like to add, do not need literacy to know and understand their social reality, but it is the task of the literate to point out the stark physical misery in which women live. The small but vocal group of educated Portuguese women in the 1920s and 1930s had had the nearly insurmountable task of identifying, without funds or experience and a large pool of women to draw on, what was a feminist issue. The new Portuguese movement is better off: the pool of working women and educated women is larger than it was in the 1920s, and they have been active, critical and vocal elements of Portuguese society, fighting for political representation and for rights. The translation of these rights into practice will take time. In the 1989 municipal elections, only five women out of 305 mayors earned office (1.6 percent), even though 18 percent had presented as candidates. If not in politics, the number of women in the professions, at universities and the vocations is, although still small, steadily increasing. It will take *paciencia* indeed to see changes in daily life, particularly in family life, as a new reality.

## SPAIN

Spain began its history as a series of territories and rival kingdoms, unlike Portugal which has the unique position in European history of having existed as one kingdom and nation since the Middle Ages. The various Spanish kingdoms were not always under christian rule either. For 600 years, up to the late Middle Ages, Spain was ruled by the muslim Morisquoes and was only gradually regained by christian kings. These traits of its history are still apparent today, both in its cultural muslim influences and in the strong particularisms and linguistic differences of the Basque Lands and Catalonia. Like the Portuguese, the Spaniards became maritime voyagers and conquerors of new worlds. In the late 15th and early 16th centuries Spain began exploiting the newly found continents and lands even more thoroughly and brutally than other countries before it. The cultures of the American subcontinent (such as Peruvian and Aztec) were destroyed and the riches brought back to Spain. Spain's 'greatness' partly rested on this unimaginably large bounty of precious metals and partly on the clever dynastic policy of the Spanish House of the Habsburgs. By the 16th century Spain had become unified, held sovereignty in Italy and in much of Northern Africa, and exercised suzerainty over the Dutch Southern Low Countries. With remarkable speed, nearly all of Central America and South America had been brought under Spanish rule. In this semi-universal *monarchía española* the sun never set.

By the 17th century, however, its *siglo d'oro* (golden age), the riches were slipping away and the glory could no longer be paid for in copper. While the conquest and exploitation of the Americas had represented the 'single most spectacular act of primitive accumulation of capital' (Anderson, 1974: 60), the use that was made of it did not fully benefit the Spanish economy: from the Americas the gold and silver were spent on goods from other countries. Thus, the precious currency failed to develop home markets and instead gave rise to economic parasitism. The benefits were reaped by foreign economies, mainly the countries that finally overran Spain—England and the Dutch Low Lands (Vicens-Vives, 1969: 443). This occurred in a very short time span. Literally within 50 years the huge empire went into total decline. It had produced an outstanding literature and culture in this time, among them Cervantes' *Don Quixote* and in the same century the works by Calderon and Lope de Vega. In the 18th and 19th centuries Spain sank into oblivion, into poverty and into political uncertainty. Its American empire crumbled and by the mid-19th century there was nothing left of the Spanish might in South America.

If Spain has shown signs of any recovery from its dramatic fall from 'greatness' in the 17th century, these must be sought in the years after Franco's death in 1975. Before that, its political fortunes were as uncertain as was its economy. Alba took the trouble of counting the number of upheavals in Spain from the time of the death of the last absolute ruler in 1833 and the death of Spain's last dictator in 1975. In those 142 years he counted thirteen changes in political regimes, nine monarchs who were either dethroned (3), exiled (2) or assassinated (4), and a further five heads of state who were assassinated. It had two republics, nine constitutions, four civil wars and a total of 127 governments—109 in 103 years and eighteen in Franco's 39 years (Alba, 1978: vii). Spain was neutral in World War I but it was locked in permanent colonial conflict in Morocco. Foreign trade suffered and the majority of the population became even further impoverished. In 1917, social tensions almost led to a revolution. There were general strikes and unrest was widespread. In 1923, these were suddenly brought to a halt by the military coup orchestrated by General Primo de Rivera with the support of the king. But the restoration of order was not accompanied by economic growth and none of the causes of the unrest was removed.

The fact that Spain was able to survive as one country at all through those many political upheavals may well have had to do with the consciousness of her identity which, not unlike that of Portugal, was strongly tied to the glory of the *siglo d'oro*. In addition the *monarchía española* had laid claim to having 'saved' christendom from the 'barbarian' muslims twice, and that it therefore had a crucial role to play in European history. Spain had not only fought the Morisquoes in the Middle Ages but, in a second *reconquista* of the 16th and 17th centuries, had also fought battles long and hard against the Ottoman Empire. Such a crusader spirit was unlikely to lead to a separation of church and state powers (and it never did) or to allowing a transformation of the social fabric. Indeed, during the Franco regime of the 1960s, 2.9 percent of landowners owned 80 percent of all pasture lands in Spain and the 18 percent of the upper echelon of Spanish society collected well over 50 percent of the nation's total GNP (Alba, 1978: 223). The problem with the 'former glory' consciousness in Portugal and in Spain was that it produced a thinking in which progressive ideas could not thrive, and in which traditions, however outmoded they were, were bitterly fought for and able to hold sway. In Spain, the many attempts at political change and social revolutions were repeatedly thwarted.

The most sustained fight for reform and thorough change was of course fought in this century. It occurred during the second republic, founded in 1931, and became the ill-fated Civil War (1936–1939). The war ended with the victory of the (extreme right) Falange movement and Franco's dictatorship. (The original Falange Party (Falange Española Tradicionalista y de las JONS) had been founded in 1934 and prohibited in 1936 during the republic because of its fascist ideology. Reinstated as early as 1937, it was destined to become the only political party in Spain.) Although the second republic may have been nothing more than one stage in the ruling-class crisis (Fraser, 1981: 196), it was nevertheless a very important stage in the Spanish move towards modernisation and change, not the least so for women. Unlike Portugal which has a fifth of the landmass of Spain and a quarter of its population, Spain did develop a much stronger bourgeoisie and urban culture than Portugal ever had. That bourgeoisie eventually demanded some living (i.e. social, political and economic) space of its own, as it had done in countries like France and England several centuries earlier. In addition, urban culture included an urban proletariat which worked and lived under extremely harsh conditions. The urban proletariat was joined by a rural proletariat, a glut of seasonally unemployed landless labourers who worked for starvation-rate wages. In other words, Spain had developed a strong leftist political culture. These forces came to the fore most strongly in the second republic, but they had begun their work years before the republic was proclaimed.

The role of women was an explicit agenda item within the context of republican and democratic ideas. *La Revista Blanca*, an anarchist paper published between 1923–1936, promoted radical ideas of change, as did another paper, *Estudios* (1923–1939), first called *Generación Consciente*, which had a circulation of approximately 70 000. They led the campaign on sexual matters and on the emancipation of women, arguing strongly for the 'religious detoxification of sexuality' and for a very new appraisal of women's role. In a 1927 edition of *La Revista*, the Spanish feminist Federica Montseny published an article with the telling title 'La mujer, problema del hombre' (The woman, a problem of men) which set the gender debate in motion (Nash, 1979: 14–15). It is noteworthy that the Spanish Second Republic, like the Portuguese Republic earlier, gave women the vote and the status of equality before the law, and permitted divorce. In a whole range of concerns its constitution and legislation attempted to remove the gender bias and the oppression of women.

One of the republic's remarkable offshoots was the foundation, in 1936, of Mujeres Libres (Free—or Freethinking—Women), an explicitly proletarian feminist organisation in Barcelona and the first autonomous feminist organisation in Spain (Ackelsberg, 1985: 63). It was the brainchild of three women, Lucía Sánchez Saormil, who worked at a telephone exchange, Mercedes Comaposada, an academic, and Amparo Poch y Gascón, a medical doctor. They targeted working-class women and within three years their organisation had a membership of around 20 000 and possibly more, mostly in Catalonia. In 1937, Mujeres Libres held its first national congress in Valencia. Its main platform was a fight against the triple enslavement of women workers: through ignorance; as production workers; and as women. They stood firmly against the major leftist parties (socialist and communist) because, as they claimed, their policies were aimed at the middle class and the petty bourgeoisie but not at the working class (Nash, 1979: 21). The only collaboration it sought and the only groups it hoped to influence were the anarchists, such as the Federación Anarquista Ibérica (Iberian Anarchist Federation). Many of them were also members of an inter-

**Table 6.1    Illiteracy rates (in %) in Spain, 1900–1985**

| Year | 1900 | 1910 | 1920 | 1930 | 1940 | 1950 | 1960 | 1970 | 1985 |
|------|------|------|------|------|------|------|------|------|------|
| Women | 54 | 47.5 | 41.2 | 32.0 | 23.2 | 18.3 | 14.8 | 12.3 | 11 |
| Men | 36.8 | 32.1 | 28.1 | 19.5 | 13.8 | 9.9 | 7.3 | 5.1 | 5 |

Sources: González, 1979: 268; Seager & Olson,1986: 'country table'

national anti-fascist organisation, called Solidaridad Internacional Antifascista (SIA), and they contributed to other journals such as the important *Tiempos Nuevos* (1934–1938). In line with the aims of Mujeres Libres, they published a journal by the same name, founded an institute for women and funded a massive literacy drive in order to educate female workers. Their view was not that illiteracy had anything to do with women's ability to judge their social reality correctly but rather that literacy turned working women from passive recipients of their triple oppression into women capable of taking up the political fight for their rights (Ackelsberg, 1985: 70). Indeed, the most pronounced reduction of illiteracy amongst women, and also amongst men, occurred in those twenty years (1920–1939) when radical parties were bringing new demands to the fore (see table 6.1).

When the republic was proclaimed in 1930, the new government inherited a treasury crisis, large debts, and a rapidly falling currency. On the pronouncement of the republic, it had to contend with the flight of capital, with the worldwide depression and with the substantial internal problems of agriculture. It was asked to tackle its inadequate cultivation and irrigation, its unjust tenantry system and the exploitative employment of landless labour. While the republican governments tried to do some things to amend the situation, such as agrarian reform (expropriating land and settling peasants on it), the changes were too slow, the problems too profound and the opposition from the landowners, the industrial and financial bourgeoisie, the clergy and small-holders too formidable to be dealt with peacefully (Fontana & Jordi, 1976: 479–97).

The Spanish Civil War was not just a Spanish tragedy. To all those who feared the advance of fascism through Europe, it was an international one. Rarely has a civil war been able to muster support from so many other countries. Volunteers for the republicans arrived from all over the western world and included well-known writers who left moving and fitting epitaphs for this hopeless war: George Orwell's *Homage to Catalonia* (1938) and Ernest Hemingway's *For Whom The Bell Tolls* (1940) amongst them. The civil war was finally won by the champions of the anti-bourgeois, anti-urban and anti-republican elites and clergy. This was due to the help of the Axis powers and the inhibitions of western democracies. With this the idea of liberty in Spain was buried for another 40 years. At the end of the war, the Spanish economy was seriously run down. Roads and railways were in indescribably bad condition. Industrial equipment was worn out and electrical power was in such short supply that it affected industrial and agricultural productivity. For Spain it was the beginning of a long period of poverty.

Some of the changes set in motion during the time of the republic were never entirely lost, as the continuous drop in the illiteracy rate testifies, but for women in general much was lost. Legislation reverted to 19th century concepts, based on the Commercial Code of 1829 and the Civil Code of 1889, with all the restrictions on women resurrected. The 'ghost of the Inquisition moved through the lives of many unfortunate women', wrote Lidia Falcón (1984: 628), and, indeed, the re-entry of ecclesiastical tribunals, which once again became the sole arbiters on love, marriage, sexuality and child custody, spelled doom for women. Thus, the defeat of the organised working class in 1939 saw a dramatic and devastating reversal of those women's rights which had already been gained. Women's organisations, the Socialist Party, Communist Party, and the unions, such as the Unión General de Trabajadores, a socialist union federation, and the Confederación Nacional de Trabajo, an anarchosyndicalist union federation, were all brutally suppressed (Fishman, 1982: 281) and would not be allowed to surface for another three and a half decades. In 1939, Franco reinstated the old Spanish power elite and returned to it its old authority and 'rightful' place. He reversed all republican decisions and rules, abolished parties, introduced censorship and persecuted anyone who had been active in the opposition. Spain once again became a 'Hobbesian state' of indivisible authority (Carr, 1977: 258), but this time destined to be isolated and forgotten. Although Spain kept out of World War II it was not for reasons of neutrality but because it could not afford to enter it. Nevertheless, after the war the Allies remembered Franco's sympathies with Hitler and Mussolini and punished Spain by not offering any loans or other financial assistance. Spain was starved of foreign exchange and the effects were catastrophic.

Spain calls the decade of the 1940s 'the years of hunger'. It was ushered in by the glibly perverse words of Franco who, in 1940, said: 'We do not want an easy, comfortable life... We want a hard life, the difficult life of a virile people' (Carr, 1982: 740). The decade brought intense suffering to the majority of the Spanish population in towns and countryside alike. Moreover, the general economic demise was exacerbated by a series of severe droughts and the absence of (imported) fertilisers. Bread rationing ended only in 1952. The general experience was that of 'food queues, of patched-up clothes, of fountain pens bought on the instalment system, of reconditioned tooth-brushes' (Carr, 1982: 742). Tuberculosis was widespread, people ate thistles and weeds, the black market thrived and police started fining those who gave alms. The taxation system, described by observers as 'the most socially unjust in Europe' derived 65 percent of its revenue from indirect taxes which 'lay heavily on the poorer classes' (Carr, 1982: 749). Spanish per capita income in 1954 was the same as that for 1936.

Spain never experienced an 'economic miracle' of the same dimensions as West Germany or Italy, but it began to climb out of its recession in the 1960s. Reforestation and irrigation programmes began in the early part of that decade. A number of reforms were aimed at stabilising the economy and especially at reviving its industry. The bad recession of 1959 had forced many Spaniards to seek work abroad[3] and they typically sent back their remittances, which came to exceed income from citrus fruit export and soon accounted for twice the revenue from traditional exports. Private foreign investment began to pick up, at first gradually and then rising dramatically (around US$100 million in 1960 to about US$6000 million by 1973). In the 1960s, the OECD paid aid to European countries which it considered 'underdeveloped', such as Spain, Yugoslavia, Greece and Turkey.

If there was a 'Spanish miracle', it happened in industry. Between 1950 and 1956 industrial production tripled. In the 1960s the industrial growth rate was exceeded only by that of Japan. Industrialisation had taken off particularly in shipbuilding and automobiles (Tipton & Aldrich, 1987: 125). The progress was not only rapid in the production of goods (such as chemicals, energy, machinery), and in the production of steel, aluminium, cement and sulphuric acid, but the transport and communication needs were such that these sectors grew even faster than industry itself (Fontana & Jordi, 1976: 522–24). The growth in industry was entirely at the expense of agriculture. Within two decades, agricultural and industrial production had swapped places: in 1950, 40 percent of the workforce were in agriculture and 25 percent in industry; by 1970, the percentage had reversed completely, with 26 percent in agriculture and 40 percent in industry (Logan, 1977: 389).

Carr called the period between 1951 and 1975 the 'paradoxical' years (Carr, 1977), and indeed they were paradoxical in several respects. Politically, the country remained immobile but economically it was beginning to be transformed, inevitably affecting the social fabric of Spanish society. Coupled with the population explosion—the population of Spain doubled between 1940 and 1980—industrial development fostered the emergence of a new middle class consisting of white-collar workers (sales, service, office workers) and an increasing pool of skilled tradespeople. As Logan has shown, it was the new affluence, that is, this new middle class, which added a new and volatile element to Spanish society (1977: 390). Moreover, Spain needed money from foreign investments and loans and therefore had to pander to western ideologies and wishes to some extent. In 1953 it finally succeeded in obtaining some economic aid from the US in exchange for permitting the US to set up military bases in Spain. In the new economic climate of the post–Treaty of Rome (1957) period, Franco had to write off 'twenty years of aggressive nationalism, acute protectionism and arbitrary interventionism' (Fontana & Jordi, 1976: 517). The Stabilisation Plan of 1959 was one other such attempt that began to encourage foreign investment. One might add that multinational companies found both Spain and Portugal attractive in terms of their cheap labour. The tourist industry was beginning to be a feature in Spain's annual revenue and had reached US$2000 million by 1969 (Carr, 1977: 280–82). In 1970 one million Spanish workers worked outside Spain[3] and the number of tourists per year had increased to 23 million.

Francoism, pushed by a new technocratic elite which sought integration into the European and world markets, made several further concessions to the west, such as in 1962 passing a law abolishing the illegality of strikes. This was a rather two-pronged issue, for the new law allowed only economic strikes and it was never quite clear which was economic or political. Clearly the rule could be used at will. In 1966 press censorship was abolished but severe punishments were established for newspapers publishing material against official ideology or not in the interest of the security of the state. More books were allowed to be published in Catalan, and some intellectuals were even permitted to make public statements without reprisals by the regime. In 1965 a group called the Christian Democrats, which had the semblance of an opposition, was able to publish its views in a magazine called *Cuerdenos para el Diálogo*. All this, so Alba observed, was part of the official and superficial liberalisation of Spain which had been set in train 'to present an image of the regime to European Institutions that would be acceptable for admittance' (Alba, 1978: 224). Franco succeeded in this and in 1970 a trade agreement between Spain and the Common Market was finally approved.

Clearly, politically, Franco tried to make as few concessions as possible while actively seeking Spain's economic improvement. In practice this meant that the two economic and political spheres were mismatched: loosening in one sphere and tightening controls in the other. Nevertheless, the dictatorship had become somewhat 'semi-permeable' and had begun to be open to criticism, propelling its own self-destruction. Trade unionism, which had all but been dead for two decades, began to revive under a new generation of trade unionists, both in Spain and amongst the exiled population of unionists (Paris, 1979: 30). In the 1960s, the Spanish workers' strike rate had begun to be comparable to those in other parts of western Europe. The first large strike wave originated in the mines in Asturia in 1962, where 80 000 miners had gone on strike. Franco's response was to declare martial law, which resulted in a solidarity strike action throughout Spain, involving a quarter of a million workers, but also spokespersons from universities and an ever rising number of dissenting students. Workers were radicalised, ironically because of the consistent repression of unionism, amongst them many women who were part of the new industrial proletariat. In the midst of the rising prosperity of Spain, workers were asked to be content with a lifestyle that had changed little since the austerity measures of the civil war and, clearly, they were no longer willing to accept passively the brunt of social and economic disadvantage. 1974 saw the highest number of recorded strikes in Spanish history about the government's ineptitude in dealing with the new (European-wide) economic crisis and Spain's soaring inflation (Carr, 1982: 737).

A rising discontent due to the fossilisation of social and political structures erupted in student demonstrations in Madrid and Barcelona as early as 1965. Like other countries, Spain had also massively increased its educational institutions. In Britain, a total of 28 universities have been opened since the 1950s; eleven have been opened in Spain and five in Portugal (Tipton & Aldrich, 1987: 186). The number of student enrolments had grown astronomically in only fifteen years: in 1961, there were a total of 65 000 students in Spain. By 1976 over 400 000 were registered. A small group of students were anything but politically illiterate. They formed secret societies, and new members were carefully screened and selected and then trained in a new political discipline of dissent. Later on, numbers were increasing so rapidly that the secretiveness could no longer be maintained. Student organisations eventually became strong enough to appear in public where they were promptly met by Franco's reprisals and an overwhelming police machinery in the service of the state. Over many years of student resistance throughout the 1960s, thousands of students were arrested, questioned, mistreated and condemned to prison sentences. The presence of police and their dilly vans became a 'normal' feature of university campuses. The teaching staff at universities, newly hired to deal with the expansion, tended to be on contract employment, a sure recipe for discontent. Indeed, in view of their precarious position those university teachers became the focus for dissent and revolution (Bernecker, 1984: 149).

The contradictions between the 1940 Falangist proposals of universities serving a Spain of 'centuries of crusades and cathedrals' (Carr, 1977: 288) and the needs for institutions serving as mass education institutions had become all too apparent. University professors who had participated in the uprising were dismissed but by 1967 the demonstrations erupted again, this time closing eight universities. Newspapers began to report strike actions. The Democratic Union of Students, although illegal, was tolerated and in 1968 a series of university 'reforms', described by observers as 'anti-democratic reformism', were initiated, leading in 1970 to an entire reorganisation of the educational system (Alba, 1978: 226). Illegal groups thrived. Student unrest in 1969 actually led to the abolition of basic constitutional rights and martial law was declared again. Before this happened, a wave of mass arrests and decrees of exile swept through the country.

University professors, student leaders, intellectuals, priests and leaders of workers and catholic organisations were captured and tried. But this time the general response of wide sections of the population was not so much fear as anger (Bernecker, 1984: 152).

Regionalism found a new vigour to express its demands for separatism and regional nationalism. Particularly in the Basque Lands, the frustration of not having been heard turned into terrorism among a group that called itself Euskadi Ta Azkatasum—Basque Land and Liberty, modelled on the Bader-Meinhof Gang (Janke, 1980). In 1970, the Burgos trials against terrorists caused a crisis of Francoism. The claim by the Basques, so Carr points out, was not only one of regionalism but really 'also a claim of an underdeveloped region neglected by central government' (1980: 178). The Basque Lands, Andalusia and Catalonia suffered the heaviest unemployment in Spain. In the last year of Francoism, an anti-terrorist law came into effect which made the death sentence mandatory and gave widest powers to the police. When the new law was put into effect several terrorists were immediately court-martialled. It became clear that the accused had been tortured and, from the way the trials were conducted, that their guilt was not manifest, a fact which caused deep shock in all of western Europe and further strengthened the anti-Francoists (Alba, 1978: 244).

Illegal women's organisations, largely linked with equally illegal communist and socialist parties, had also extended into a vast net of clandestine activity. In 1963 the Movimiento Democrático de Mujeres (Women's Democratic Movement) was founded in Madrid and quickly spread to Zaragoza, Valencia, the Basque country and Galicia. It was led by strong feminists such as Merche Comavella, Lidia Falcon and Carmen Alcade. In 1968, the Federation of Housewives was formed which also began to be infiltrated by feminist ideas, but the communist women in it were discovered by police and expelled (Duran & Gallego, 1986: 210). Illegal trade unions harboured groups of feminist sections so that, in all, there existed at least 90 feminist groups and organisations in the last years of Franco's rule (Lovenduski, 1986: 105). Although largely unknown to a wider public, there were already a number of publications on women's issues, chiefly by Lidia Falcón who, in 1962, published *Los derechos laborales de la mujer* (Women's labour rights), followed in 1964 by *Los derechos civiles de la mujer* (Women's civil rights) and in 1969 by *Mujer y sociedad* (Women and society). All of these activities indeed constituted 'a submerged network' of which Melucci had spoken (see chapter 1).

It was perhaps uniquely in Spain that the catholic church began to liberalise its views before the state. Catholic unions harboured illegal workers' organisations and the younger generation of priests in particular refused to form any alliance with Francoism and often actively supported dissenters. More dramatic still was the open declaration by the bishop of Bilbao that he defended Basque national-ism. Franco thought that this crumbling of his alliance with the church was an 'incomprehensible stab in the back' (Carr, 1977: 286). Indeed, it was an unex-pected development, even in the eyes of the remaining republicans who in the 1920s and 1930s, saw only the old ruling classes and the church as their enemy but, quite wrongly, had not recognised the Falange as one (Fraser, 1981: 198).

Franco's death in 1975 created a euphoria in Spain only matched by that of the proclamation of the second republic. The new freedom of the press in particular swamped the country with the publications of dissenters, of long-forbidden papers and of writers who had long since been banned from Spanish life. In 1976, after 37 years of being banned, the Catalan paper *Avui* published

**Table 6.2   Ratio of police to inhabitants in various European countries (1975)**

| | | |
|---|---|---|
| Spain | 1 policeman per | 138 inhabitants |
| Italy | 1 policeman per | 275 inhabitants |
| W. Germany | 1 policeman per | 413 inhabitants |
| France | 1 policeman per | 481 inhabitants |
| UK | 1 policeman per | 500 inhabitants |

*Source*: Alba, 1978: 273

its first post-Franco issue. In the same year, *El Pais*, perhaps today Spain's most important daily paper, first appeared. The paper had asked since 1972 for permission to go to print but had always been denied. That it now was able to start operations signalled to Spaniards the great change that had taken place. The return of Rafael Alberti to Spain, after 40 years of exile, was no less an occasion than the release of Nelson Mandela from his long imprisonment in South Africa. The works of noted Spanish writers, banned for years, suddenly reappeared from oblivion. The theatre experienced a truly remarkable renaissance (among its products were plays by Alberti). Vicente Aleixandre received the Nobel Prize for literature, and Spanish films distinguished themselves by overseas successes. All sorts of minority groups crawled out of their hiding spots. Bohemian culture, nightlife, nudists, homosexuals, transvestites, songwriters and political commentators were part of the new scene, as were new democratic bourgeois initiatives, new liberation movements, such as the women's liberation movement, and an array of new papers and journals. All of these events were part of a 'catching up' syndrome, of a way of demonstrating a reality that had been hidden for too long. The disappearance of taboos overnight produced an onslaught of euphoric self-confessions, debates, discoveries and analyses (Bernecker, 1984: 217).

Franco had left a formidable legacy, and in many ways the post-Franco years were years of trying to come to grips with the immediate past and of somehow living with its trauma. The victims of the Franco regime were also keen to ensure that no one would forget the scars that the regime had inflicted not just on individual lives but on a whole society. Lidia Falcón, a lawyer and journalist who was one of many women who became a political prisoner under the Franco regime, stated in March 1976, during the first International Tribunal on Crimes Against Women:

> In the last 100 years ... no other epoch has been so continuously sinister and ferocious as the one we have lived through in the last 37 years. The suppression and exploitation of women has been intensified on all levels. We have been humiliated as human beings, as sexual persons, and as laborers. We have been used as brood mares and we have been manipulated as economic tools of the family unit, which is the basis of the new state. (Russell & Van de Ven, 1984: 165–6)

What remained after Franco's death was a police state 'intact'. Indeed it had more police per capita than any other western European nation (see table 6.2). Franco's 'liberalisation' in concert with the economic changes and a highly oppressive set of political tactics had created a 'schizophrenic' society (Carr, 1982: 769), an Orwellian 'double-think' in the governing classes and masses alike. There was confusion as to what was permissible or desirable and even as to what it was that needed change most urgently.

Another of Franco's legacies was the appointment of Prince Juan Carlos as his successor well before the end of his own rule. It was his wish that Spain never revert to democracy and republicanism, or pluralisms of any kind. As his support from the church, formerly a pillar to his power, waned, he turned to the military and to the old aristocracy. Juan Carlos had given no indication that he would make any substantial changes after Franco's resignation or death. It was no surprise then that after Juan Carlos had been sworn in as King of Spain in 1975, economic growth slowed to half, monetary reserves fell dramatically and tourism decreased at once. There were also numerous strikes and a feeling of great uncertainty about the political future of Spain.

To the surprise of western European nations, Spain's transition to democracy occurred peacefully and rapidly under the guidance of King Juan Carlos and his prime minister, Suárez. In 1976, the king granted amnesty to political prisoners, except terrorists, and followed this a year later by another amnesty decree which freed a further 170 prisoners, some of whom were serving life sentences. Among them, I believe, were many women who, in 1976, were still condemned to life sentences, such as Maria Jesus Dasca, Concepcion Tristan, Beatriz Rodriquez, Luz Fernandez, Eva Forest and Jone Derrensoro (Russel & Van de Ven, 1984: 205).

In 1976 Juan Carlos recognised Catalan as a co-official language with Spanish in Catalonia. He passed a bill later that year giving universal suffrage, and in 1977 he legalised political parties and the right to strike. In 1977 the various parties signed the important Moncloa Pact addressing some of the most urgent socio-economic problems. Via a referendum the king obtained support for the idea of a constitutional monarchy within a parliamentary system. In 1977, Juan Carlos signed an agreement that would permit the first free elections, which was the death knell to the Francoist power elite. To ensure that this move would not spark off another right-wing revolt, the king had formerly sought alliance with the military (Alba, 1978: 264–71).

Parties emerged from underground and many new ones were founded in a scurry for a place in the new government. Altogether 161 legal parties, 50 illegal organisations, half a dozen terrorist groups, anarchists and other splinter groups vied for the support of the electorate. The political climate showed that no one had any experience in governing a country or in running an effective election campaign. Few had any experience of ever going to the polls: less than 15 percent of the 22 million adult voters. A political culture had existed but only as clandestine secret societies, never as an opposition in the political arena. Party organisation was poor, the speeches were vague and passionate, and the electorate was utterly confused (Alba, 1978: 276–8).

In this free-for-all political euphoria, it was easy to suspect that chaos could ensue and that no one would be able to win sufficient votes to form a government. Nevertheless, this did not happen. In the end there were only two major parties which shared most of the votes and a further two which just made it into parliament. Prime Minister Suárez's own coalition, now a conglomerate of the Social Democrats, Liberals, Christian Democrats and the Union of the Democratic Centre together won 34 percent of the vote, followed by the Socialist Party with 28 percent, the Communist Party with 9 percent, and the Popular Alliance with 8 percent. Suárez emerged as the victor of this election. Not one of the well-known Francoist candidates won a seat.

The first task of the new Cortes (parliament) was the drafting of a new constitution, which was adopted in a national referendum in December 1978. The new constitution in many ways reconfirmed over 40 years later the constitution of the second republic. After the completion of this task, new elections were held in 1979 and the Centre Party succeeded in gaining the majority of the votes. The Socialist Party remodelled itself into a more moderate party, in line with election results. The election results of 1977 and 1979 were seen by many as a victory for democracy and, at the same time, as a victory for moderation (Carr, 1980: 176), promising at once greater stability of government, it was thought, than the more radical governments of Portugal and Italy.

Nevertheless, all was not well in the new *monarchia española*. Many had far too high or inappropriate expectations of what a democracy could do (Carr, 1980: 179), others questioned whether a monarch appointed by a fascist dictator and backed by the army would initiate any qualitative change in Spanish life. Yet others were convinced that the change from Franco to Juan Carlos would mean little in the political and social reality of Spain. During the International Tribunal on Crimes against Women in March 1976, the Popular Union of Spanish Women wanted to have included in the proceedings 'a resolution of censure against the monarchy and fascism of Juan Carlos, condemning him as inheritor and perpetuator of fascism in Spain' (Russell & Van de Ven, 1984: 206).

The economic problems did not disappear; at first they worsened. In 1977, inflation was running at 20 percent and foreign debts had escalated to US$14 billion. As in Portugal, workers were returning from other western European countries and they swelled the number of unemployed at home. Restrictions on credit very nearly paralysed the construction industry, increased rental costs and generally reduced real standards of living. University unrest had not been curbed because the only 'reform' programmes in universities were those instigated under Franco. Funding for and conditions in elementary schools were poor. 'Health care was pure fiction. Social security was a joke. Urban politics were a sham for dirty deals' (Alba, 1978: 275). The nationalist claims, particularly of the Basques (and its terrorist groups) had not gone away, and Guipúzcoa and Vizcaya were in a state of 'permanent agitation', earning with their protests much sympathy from foreign media. By 1979, Basque terrorism had become more aggressive and insistent, with threats to plant bombs in the middle of Spain's Mediterranean tourist resorts (Carr, 1980: 175, 178). This happened despite the fact that the new constitution of 1978 granted statutes of autonomy to the various regions. The political right (members of the military) exerted pressure because they were enraged at the king's total disinclination to support the deposed Francoists. Feminist groups drew up a set of demands with the greatest urgency, to ensure that these demands would be written into the new constitution, including such issues as legal equality; laws prohibiting discrimination at the workplace, in education and leisure; shared rights over children; legalisation of abortion, divorce, contraceptives; amnesty for women; abolition of the Law of Social Danger (*Peligrosidad Social*), which was used against homosexuals; an insistence on equal rights for unmarried mothers and their children, for the foundation of family planning centres and for inclusion of such cost in a national health scheme. As in Portugal, all these problems should have been addressed at once in order to avoid major upheavals and new unrest.

Clearly, there was a good deal that could and needed to be done by the post-Franco governments if the promise of liberalisation and a more equitable society were to be fulfilled, at least in line with UN conventions and the Treaty of Rome. Throughout 1976 and 1977 feminists had been prominent in the media and had contributed their bid for change so that to some extent all parties had to take note of women's issues. In the first elections of 1977, twenty of the newly elected delegates were women, among them the well-known feminists Carlota Bustelo and Maria Dolores Calvet. In 1978 the new Spanish constitution underwrote once again, as in the second republic, that women and men were equal before the law. It is not difficult to assume that the influence of feminists and the public attention they attracted during the period of the drafting of the constitution had some effect on the actual wording and details of that constitution. In the same year the prohibition on the sale of, and information about, contraceptives was removed, not without substantial pressure to do so being exerted by the parliamentarian feminist Carlota Bustelo, and after strong protests and demonstrations. In late 1979, the *Estatuto del Trabajador*, the principal labour legislation of the new regime, was passed. The *Ley de Relaciones Laborales* (Labour Relations Law), which came into effect in 1980, eradicated the archaic rule that husbands had to authorise their wives' work outside the home. In 1978, the government set up a Subdirección General de la Mujer (Women's Sub-directorate) under the auspices of the Directorate General for Youth and Socio-Cultural Advancement. Its budgetary allocation was reasonably good from the beginning. It had the task of campaigning for a 'new image' of women and women's new rights, it encouraged women to take a more active role in Spanish political life, and sought to provide information relevant to women. It has formed a women's information centre, publishes a monthly newsletter and has also published a series of valuable reports on the position of women in Spain. It has a documentation centre and offers financial and technical assistance to women's associations. It supports and sometimes runs seminars and lectures aimed at women who are housebound and unable to participate in regular associations (Ottolenghi, 1981: 80–2).

Some years later, in 1983, this 'sub-department' for women's affairs was transformed into the Women's Institute (Instituto de la Mujer) at a higher administrative level of the bureaucracy and with a substantial budget increase (3.5 million pesetas in 1984). This institute is very active today and represents the chief government body for women's issues. It has formed employment promotion teams (Equipos de Promoción de Empleo) and regularly runs campaigns aimed at improving women's status. In 1989 a campaign called '*Reparto de Responsabilidades*' (sharing of responsibilities) went on national television to drive home the point that sharing of domestic work is just, particularly when the wife works outside the home (*Women of Europe*, no. 63, 1990: 31). By 1984, the institute had supported 204 different projects and its top positions were occupied by leading feminists (Threlfall, 1988: 217).

The legal provisions which affect women in the areas of family and reproduction however, have been of dubious success. The few that have been achieved were accompanied by extensive feminist demonstrations, as was the case with the Bilbao trials, in which nine women were put on trial for having aborted. Two years of demonstrations and sit-ins (1979 to 1981) were punctuated by police brutality towards demonstrators, which sparked off further actions. A total of 25 000 signatures was collected in solidarity for the women on trial and a further 1200 women publicly confessed to having aborted. The charges were dropped (Threlfall, 1988: 216). Lida Falcon estimated in 1976 that 30 percent of female prisoners served sentences purely for having had abortions (Russel & Van de Ven, 1984: 166). Despite these demonstrations, the ensuing legislation was anything but in line with feminists' demands. With the support of the Communist Party, an abortion bill was finally passed three years later. The abortion law of 1984 was, and still is, an extremely limited piece of legislation.

Table 6.3  Number of abortions carried out in Britain on resident and non-resident women,1985–86

| Total number of abortions: | 1985 | 1986 |
| --- | --- | --- |
| Spanish women | 17 688 | 11 935 |
| Total non-resident women | 30 772 | 24 667 |
| Total resident women | 141 101 | 147 619 |

(The overall percentage for late abortions, 18 weeks and over was 1.4 percent for resident women and 8 percent for non-resident women in the two years)

Source: Spanish Women's Abortion Support Group, 1988: 73

Like the Portuguese law, it makes concessions for abortion only in the severest circumstances. Although the law was likely to benefit only 5 percent of women who sought abortions, there were, one should note, massive demonstrations against the bill, chiefly by catholic women from the Confederación Católica de Padres (Catholic Parent Confederation), while demonstrations for a more comprehensive abortion bill were rare (Duran & Gallego, 1986: 203–04). Yet the reality is that in 1983, for example, more than 23 000 Spanish women went to London for abortions (Benn, 1987: 86). In 1985 to 1986, almost half of all the non-resident women on whom abortions were carried out in Britain were from Spain (see table 6.3).

In 1988 the law sought to permit abortions to be carried out only within the first twelve weeks of pregnancy even in cases of foetal deformation (the Alton Bill). The conscientious objection clause for doctors built into the law further complicated matters so that of all women who had actually requested termination under the legal guidelines, only 1.1 percent were able to obtain it from the time the law took effect to the end of 1986, that is, in a period of eighteen months (Spanish Women's Abortion Group, 1988: 72). This medical reluctance to act explains why so many abortions were carried out overseas on women who were well over twelve weeks pregnant (see table 6.3). Even the abortions that have been legalised are not covered by health insurance. One can assume therefore that the present situation strongly favours women from social backgrounds with some money, able to pay for an abortion at home or abroad, usually in the Netherlands or England.

Before the abortion legislation in 1982, the government had approved a limited civil divorce bill. Despite the law's limitations, the divorce rate jumped to 20 percent in the first year and then stabilised at about 5 percent per year. In 1983 the Instituto de la Mujer established that half of the cases for divorce filed by women were on the basis of domestic violence. Indeed the high incidence of violence in Spanish marriages began to surface fully only since the Minister of the Interior had insisted on establishing police records on domestic violence. In the first year of its operation a staggering 1300 cases of domestic violence were recorded, but, of course, not all of these would necessarily lead to divorce. Wife abuse is not illegal and there are no mechanisms in policy and law to help victims. It is noteworthy that in the mid-1980s there was still no law prohibiting incest and the law regarding sexual abuse is rarely enforcible in cases of incest. Rape is severely punished in Spain (twelve to twenty years imprisonment), but it is rare that a sentence can be pronounced on a rapist. The restrictions are twofold. One is the result of one important clause: the victim has the 'power' to pardon the rapist. In a small community especially the mechanisms of 'persuading' the victim to let the rapist go free are extremely powerful and rather unsavoury. A second restriction is the definition given to rape. Legalistically, they are so strict that most rapes do not fall into the legal parameters, but are reclassified as 'dishonest abuse' (Morgan, 1984: 623). There are an estimated 15 000 rapes per year in Spain but less than half of 1 percent are reported. In the 235 cases on record for the entire period of 1977 to 1981, the circumstances were unusual, or especially cruel: 27 died, 111 were gang-raped, fourteen had been raped by their fathers, eight by the police and fourteen by minors (Morgan, 1984: 623). In 1982, the Spanish women's movement managed to open its doors to victims of domestic violence in Barcelona.

It is difficult to generalise the status of women. In Spain, less so than in Portugal, there is still a rural segment of Spanish society that has barely begun to notice the overall rise of living standards and the new official attitude to women; here change has been much slower. The Franco years froze the country-side in time and space, as a participatory study of southern Spanish peasant women of 1978 showed. It was reported that water was in short supply and needing to be carted from wells. This was done only by women, irrespective of whether they were old, pregnant or sick. Electricity was often non-existent. The entire burden of raising children, washing by hand, looking after the men and a rural household not cluttered by a range of appliances, fell exclusively on the women. In addition they very often had to help in the harvest or cook in the family restaurant or sell goods in the family-owned store. Cooking, it was noted, constituted an especially time-consuming task because no set hours for dinner were observed; younger children ate at one time, older children at an-other, the husband was served his tea whenever he got home and only then the woman ate her meal as well. If husbands were employed in other towns and cities or even abroad, the burden on women was even greater.

Young unmarried women often worked in factories and were subject to the most incredible exploitation by employers. Here women worked for well below the national minimum wage, longer hours than elsewhere (twelve-hour days), and were given no holidays to which they were legally entitled, while continuing to be under the strictest parental supervision (Kavemann, 1978: 128–39). An article in the Civil Code, abolished in the 1960s, had stated that a woman had no legal right to leave home without parental consent if she were under the age of 25. In rural areas, the abolition of that rule was little known and rarely followed. In rural areas, piecework done at home, and almost exclusively done by women, has remained quite common in certain regions. In the early 1980s there were still no specific regulations on home workers' legal and social security status (Ottolenghi, 1981: 31).

Conditions for married women remained problematic in many other ways. When, for instance, they were beaten by their husbands there was nowhere for them to turn for support. The researcher said that in the towns under investigation the conditions for childbirth could only be described as 'barbaric' (Kavemann, 1978: 150). Even in cases of difficult births no painkillers and no anaesthetics were given. To prevent some problems at birth, the vaginal opening was cut automatically while the woman was fully conscious. Women were often so traumatised by the experience of giving birth that they never wanted to have another child, but because they were not able or not forthright enough to get contraceptives, and had very little idea of the working of their bodies and the alternative methods of contraception, they continued to bear children (Kavemann, 1978). Although the national figures are high in comparison with the rest of Europe, they indicate, however, that birthrates have been falling steadily in

Table 6.4  **Number of children per woman and maternal mortality in western Europe in the mid-1980s**

| Country | No. of children per woman (average) | Death rate of women per 100 000 live births |
|---|---|---|
| Austria | 2.1 | 10 |
| Belgium | 1.6 | 12 |
| Denmark | 1.5 | 6 |
| Finland | 1.6 | 7 |
| France | 1.8 | 15 |
| Germany, West | 1.4 | 24 |
| Greece | 2.3 | 17 |
| Iceland | 2.3 | 22 |
| Ireland | 3.5 | 15 |
| Italy | 1.9 | 21 |
| Luxembourg | 1.5 | 50 |
| Netherlands | 1.6 | 9 |
| Norway | 1.8 | 8 |
| Portugal | 2.3 | 40 |
| Spain | 2.6 | 16 |
| Sweden | 1.7 | 6 |
| Switzerland | 1.5 | 9 |
| United Kingdom | 1.8 | 10 |
| Average | 1.9 | 16.5 |

*Source*: Seager & Olson,1986: 'country tables'

Spain since the early 1970s. Interestingly, the majority have clung to 'natural' contraceptive methods, such as withdrawal and rhythm. By 1984, only 26 percent of women used the pill, and 10 percent of men, the condom. It remains to be seen whether the AIDS problem will change men's reluctance to use condoms. Within the changed medical environment, maternal mortality has fallen to the European average (see table 6.4).

Despite the new legislation which gives women equal rights in work and in marriage, there are still acute problem areas for women which have not been resolved. One may be tempted to regard the considerable drop in the marriage rate throughout the 1980s as a sign of resistance on the part of women. By the end of the 1980s it stood at 5 percent per year and was lower than in most other western European countries (Threlfall, 1988: 221).

If not in moral legislation, then in education women have made great strides forward. They have increased their numbers in secondary and tertiary education and, since 1979, have also been permitted to enter non-traditional occupations— most notably the navy, as deck officers, ship engineers, and radio operators. The railways now employ women as mechanics and engine drivers and women may join the police force (Ottolenghi, 1981: 32). In the late 1980s, the number of boys and girls attending primary and secondary schools was about evenly matched, and the same was true, overall, for enrolment figures at capital city universities. For Spanish universities in general, the present enrolment of women at universities is just over 40 percent as against 32 percent in the early 1970s (Threlfall, 1988: 222), although the choice of courses has remained very gender bound. The majority of teachers are women, but in technical jobs women's participation rate drops well below 10 percent.

Not much has changed in the last fifteen years since the death of Franco in either work or politics. Women's participation in the workforce stagnated at around 32 percent in the late 1970s. Unemployment has always been a good deal higher for women than for men (often as high as 20 percent for women as against 10–15 percent for men) and especially high for women with university training. Job offers were and often still are strongly biased in favour of men. In the late 1970s and early 1980s it was extremely rare to find a job advertisement that was applicable to both sexes (only 2 percent of all jobs) and only every fifth vacancy was explicitly for women—the other four-fifths being reserved exclusively for men. Labour legislation has at least made some strides in giving some rights to pregnant women. At first the law allowed for twelve weeks maternity leave, but by the mid-1980s that was raised to sixteen weeks, during which the woman could claim 75 percent of her last pay. Women with infants up to the age of nine months were granted one hour off from work per working day for breastfeeding purposes. There were, however, no legal provisions which would prevent an employer from dismissing a pregnant woman. In effect, this means that employers were under no obligation at all and were merely asked to volunteer to comply with the legislation!

In politics, women's participation has actually dropped off since the first election in 1977, and women's presence in political parties has remained low. In 1981 the first woman minister since the second republic was appointed. In the right and centre parties, the presence of women is greater than in leftist parties (around 30 percent as against an average of 12 percent), but this is partly due to the way entry to the parties is controlled. In leftist parties, entrance is selective and based on the individual application while in the centre and right parties men are allowed to automatically enter their wives or daughters as members. The only real exception is the membership in the Basque Nationalist Party, which has a female membership of around 35 percent (Threlfall, 1988: 223–24). One might suspect that nationalism, particularly of an oppressed group, may override sexism, as it did for instance in Finland. Now, however, all parliamentary parties and *comisiones obreras* (union committees) have women's sections dealing specifically with women's issues.

Spain had its own women's movement, which erupted at once after the death of Franco, and it showed considerable strength and staying power despite its initially small nucleus. Apart from the case of Greece, Spain's new-wave women's movement is perhaps unique in western Europe in that it started in fear and secrecy with clandestine meetings. Assemblies were dispersed by police, arrests were made, women stood trial and even had to flee into exile (Threlfall, 1988: 210). The number of organisations grew, however, throughout the 1960s and 1970s and was part of a general upsurge of the Spanish population against Franco's dictatorship and political immobilism. While Franco was still alive, the only members who could attend meetings organised by the United Nations' International Women's Year committee were those who belonged to the Secciòn Femenina de la Falange Española, the official fascist women's organisation and the only 'political' one permitted under Franco. Thus the International Women's Year and Spanish feminists at first had problems coming together. Two weeks after Franco's death in Madrid, in December 1975, the 'Jornades por la Liberación de la Mujer' (Days for the Liberation of Women), were celebrated in secret meetings by about 500 women. These were euphoric occasions (González, 1979: 143–5).

By 1976 Spanish feminism had really begun to take off with a series of large-scale meetings, such as the 'Jornades de la Dona Catalana' (Catalonian women's days) and the formation of a multitude of feminist organisations (Rague-Arias,

1981: 472). As elsewhere in western Europe, the number of organisations and groups grew very quickly, starting in the major cities of Barcelona and Madrid and spreading to other regions and towns. As in other countries, many had developed out of a leftist party culture, such as the relatively short-lived Frente de Liberaciòn de la Mujer (FLM—Women's Liberation Front), which pursued socialist goals and openly promoted women's double militancy for party and feminist ideals. Another was a communist Marxist-Leninist group called the Union Popular de Mujeres (UPM—Popular Union of Women), and yet another, far less radical group associated with the Spanish Labour Party was the Asso-ciación Democratica de Mujeres (ADM—Women's Democratic Association). From this latter group came the Union por la Liberaciòn de la Mujer (Organisation for the Liberation of Women), which had ties with a revolutionary workers' organisation.

In 1977, the anarchist group Mujeres Libres made its reappearance and called their renewed activity 'the second epoch'. In the first issue of their journal, *Mujeres Libres*, the editorial stated:

> A tender and heart-felt homage to Lucía Sánchez Saornil, Amparo Poch y Gascón, Mercedes Comaposada, the founders of the journal *Mujeres Libres*, and all the com-rades who worked on the paper within the context of the great task of the liberation of women.
>
> Suceso Portales

> Forty one years have passed since the *Mujeres Libres* was published for the first time. While I am writing these short lines for the first issue of the second epoch, I want to commemorate with all my heart and deeply felt sympathy two of the unforgotten comrades who first initiated the journal: Lucía Sánchez Saornil and Amparo Poch y Gascón, the first of whom died in Spain and the latter in French exile. I also want to send a sisterly greeting to Mercedes Comaposada ... (Nash, 1979: 127)

These words clearly established that the four decades of Franco's dictatorship had not been able to kill progressive ideas. Somehow the ideas had persisted and had begun to resurface as soon as the stifling censorship was removed. Unlike West German feminism, which had to begin afresh in the postwar era, Spanish women were able to draw on a feminist tradition which was in fact as far removed in time as had been the case in West Germany, but which for some reason had not been stamped out entirely. The Mujeres Libres established them-selves again in Barcelona, Madrid, Andalusia and in several other places. They had few if any links with political parties and espoused an autonomous position, demanding fundamental changes in society. Theirs was clearly a platform of revolutionary fervour. They also rejected the idea of getting women into leading positions, claiming that women's participation in existing structures would change absolutely nothing and systems needed to be restructured first.

There were other radical, often utopian, feminist groups who simply rejected everything patriarchal civilisation had created and in its stead wanted a culture 'created by women in freedom' (Rague-Arias, 1981: 473); such were Las Brujas (the Witches), Las Magas (the Magicians) and Lucha Anti-authoritaria de Mujeres Antipatriarcales y Revolucionarias (Anti-authoritarian Struggle of Revolutionary Antipatriachal Women). Apart from these groups with very spe-cific ideological platforms there were also those with more limited and concrete ideas on self-help, such as the interest of the Movimiento Democrático de Mujeres (MDM—Women's Democratic Movement) in nurseries or the socialist women's interest in family planning centres (the first one appeared in 1977 in Madrid).

There were a host of consciousness-raising groups and neighbourhood collectives, and eventually lesbian groups evolved in some large cities. The Gay Liberation Front (FLG) is now a political party and the Institute Lambda, a homosexual rights organisation, also has a lesbian caucus (Morgan, 1984: 623). It has generally been observed that the Spanish new-wave movement had a fairly high inner consistency on the left for the first four years (1976 to 1980), but then began to fragment in the following years, although the various strands collaborated again on the issue of abortion (Lovenduski, 1986: 105).

Although Spanish feminism is generally regarded as being weak in comparison to other western European countries, this was certainly not true for major cities like Barcelona and Madrid. It is true that many organisations and groups folded after an initial few years burst of feminist activity (Falcón, 1984: 629). Catalonian women in particular, however, have been extremely active in the post-Franco era, both in social and political concerns. Apart from countless autonomous organisations, 1979 saw the formation of a feminist political party, Partido Feminista de España, which was legalised in 1981 and was able to hold its first party congress in 1983. Its magazine *Poder y Libertad* (Power and Liberty) is an important publication. As yet no one from this party has managed to get into parliament but support grew steadily in the 1980s. The political views of feminists and the range of their concerns are in essence no different to those expressed by feminists in other western European countries. This is an interesting phenomenon in regard to Portugal and Spain, since, due to strict censorship controls, neither country had the benefit of immediately obtaining material from the second-wave movements elsewhere in the world.

If there is any difference between Spanish and northern European feminism, it is most apparent in the way the past impinges. In Spain, women are constantly aware of and concerned with their experience of the immediate fascist past. The political ineffectiveness of women under Franco made Spanish feminists wish for coeducation and gender-shared living and working spaces. It made the question of single and double militancy of feminism perhaps more virulent than in other countries. The issue was not just whether one should devote one's energies to party ideology and to specifically feminist issues (double militancy) or whether one had to concentrate purely on women-specific fights (single militancy), but whether or not a political party was at all the kind of organisation that could be trusted to take women's issues seriously. The official fascist 'women's section' of the Falange had only believed in safeguarding women's role and place in the home. For those feminists who argued that even anti-clerical parties were still patriarchal, little could be gained by joining such parties. Yet an autonomous, non-aligned status carried with it a self-imposed segregation that, because of past experience, feminists wanted to avoid. It was and is a difficult situation that has never been entirely resolved. It is true that women (and men) in Spain have a poor record of participation in organisations and in political parties generally. Only 9 percent of the entire adult population is part of any organisation or club, and membership in political parties and unions hovers around the 1 percent mark. It has been suggested that membership of women in feminist organisations is probably fewer than 0.1 percent of the adult female population.[4]

Duran and Gallego have argued that the Spanish feminist movement has been far removed ideologically from the rank and file of Spanish women (1986: 204). This assessment of Spanish feminism and the criticism of its alleged elitism in the past and present does not seem entirely justifiable. It is true that, as in other countries, the leadership was dominated by urban educated middle-class women but, unlike several other movements already discussed, working-class women in fact formed part of the new wave in Spain. The problem was rather that the movement remained largely urban and was initially unable to reach rural women. Yet the number of feminist conferences and meetings held annually in Spain would suggest that feminism and women's issues have acquired a firm place in Spanish social life. In 1979, a meeting in Granada was attended by about 3000 women and the nationally coordinated meetings, which have been held since 1985 in a different area each year, regularly attract 3000 to 5000 delegates. In addition, Spain has developed a unique movement in Europe: a girls' movement which sprung up in Barcelona in 1986. It may not only have the function of spreading feminist ideas to much younger age groups but also to a socially wider net (Threlfall, 1988: 218).

Knowledge about women's status and role in Spain has expanded considerably throughout the 1980s due to research and teaching courses which have become a lively and important feature of Spanish groups and universities. The Instituto de Derechos de la Mujer (Institute for Women's Rights) regularly undertakes applied research in order to provide documentary material for parliamentary debates on the status of women. It is hoped, of course, that the research will act as a guideline for legislative changes in the status of women. Furthermore, since 1979 women's studies courses have sprung up which have coordinated and disseminated knowledge of women and of feminism at tertiary institutions. The first of these courses, the *Seminario de Estudios de la Mujer* (seminar for women's studies), began to run in Madrid at the Universidad Autónoma. It too held annual conferences, the *Jornadas de Investigación Interdisciplinaria sobre la Mujer* (days of interdisciplinary inquiry into women), from which emanated a number of important feminist publications. Trade unions have done important groundwork on unemployment, retraining and the informal economy, and a whole host of feminist centres have devoted time and funds to a wide variety of research topics on women (Folguera, 1983: 780–81). Spanish feminism has created a social network of some magnitude and the many self-help groups have begun to deliver services to women for the first time since Francoism. An important network was established to help women get abortions abroad. Socialist and communist parties financed family planning centres, run by women.

The chief elements of Spanish feminism may be summarised as a search for a non-sexist culture and a building of a feminist culture. As a political force it was and has remained weak (Duran & Gallego, 1986: 206). To build a non-sexist and feminist culture is not such a modest aim as it may appear. It is a pursuit aimed not only at eliminating discrimination and disadvantage but at creating a culture that is both inclusive of women and indicative of new cultural values of citizenship for men and women alike. In a society built on strong honour and shame sanctions associated with rigid sex-stereotyping, the development of a non-sexist culture is a major cultural and social undertaking because it involves not just a change of social role perception and of behaviours but also the abolition of an entire elaborate moral code: it is, for instance, against the honour of a man, and not just a matter of his masculinity, to help with housework; it requires the overcoming of a double barrier to achieve change. When a woman's entry into the workforce is seen as 'ugly', as it was still regarded in many villages in the 1980s (Carr, 1982: 757), the issue is not just of a role perception being defended, but the honour of the family being at stake and a woman shamed by possible contacts with men outside the immediate family circle. Finally, the complex code of honour and shame has to do with a repressed sexuality which, officially, is only allowed to find expression within marriage, possibly between partners whose reason for marriage was not love or who have reason to be afraid of further pregnancies. Many of the barriers have been undermined since the years of Spanish industrialisation and are in conflict with economic opportunities and necessities. Yet the church has remained extremely powerful and the part of its teaching that involves the repression of sexuality and the prohibition of interfering with reproduction has not helped in breaking the vicious circle of the shame and honour system.

Lack of funds was a further problem. Nevertheless, over the years there have been publications of some journals, the most important amongst them being *Vindicación Feminista*, edited by Carmen Alcalde between 1976 and 1979. It then had to cease publication for some years due to shortage of funds. An important journal open to all aspects of feminism, it has recaptured its market since going back into publication. There are also magazines such as *La Mujer Feminista* (Feminist Women), *Tribuna Feminista* (Feminist Tribunal) and *Mujeres* (Women) published by the Women's Institute, and *Donnes en Lluita*. The leftist newspaper *Liberación* and *El Pais* occasionally deal with women's issues. Theatre and cinema rarely deal with women's concerns, although there are now a number of remarkable feminist film-makers; the two most famous are perhaps Pilar Miró and Josefina Molina. The Women's Institute offers prizes and awards for women artists, but women have distinguished themselves in the arts beyond special prizes for women; Soledad Puertolas, for instance, has just won the *Planeta de Novela*, one of the most prestigious literary awards in Spain, making her the sixth woman to win this prize since 1975 (*Women of Europe*, no. 63, 1990: 31). In several universities, courses in women's studies have been established—in Barcelona and Madrid in 1978, and later in Valencia, Granada, Alicante, Navarra and Zaragoza.

One needs to remember that many of these events took place within five years of the end of a protracted and highly misogynist dictatorship and that many of the activities and events staged by Spanish feminists, with or without government help and support, represent a tremendous achievement. Moreover, it was an achievement which often went beyond that of other western European countries. Change in Spain has happened rapidly and resolutely. It bore the marks of a determination rarely displayed in countries like Australia, the USA or Britain, which claim to have all the ingredients of social justice. Women in these parliamentary democracies, without any scars of past dictatorships, without the ingrained state powers of such institutions as the catholic church, without traditions such as the Inquisition, have now no appreciable margin, if any, over the situation of women in Spain.

*GREECE*

Up to the 1970s Spain, Portugal and Greece found themselves in the less than flattering position of being regarded as underdeveloped and as shameful exceptions to the alleged peaceful parliamentary concensus which ruled elsewhere in western Europe (Tipton & Aldrich, 1987: 205). The marginalised position of these three nations, the problem of their regimes aside, was ironical in terms of their historical self-perception. Along with Spain and to some extent Portugal, Greece believed that it had fulfilled a special role in European history. At least up to pre-World War I its nationalism was fuelled by the mythology, spun mainly by the Greek orthodox church, that the Greeks were a selected people because from them stemmed the occidental civilisation and culture which was eventually spread to the rest of Europe. Greek was the language of the New Testament and therefore endowed with divine qualities. The utterances made in that language were consequently complete knowledge systems, whole in themselves and not surpassable (Choisi, 1988: 84). Yet all three nations in the modern era had to fight for 'integration' into Europe.

In Greece it was never quite clear whether such an integration into a *western* Europe was desirable and actually suited the Greek mentality and past. After all, Greece had been part of a Byzantine Empire and its eastern interests were expressed in a value system very different from that espoused by westerners. Today the differences in views of the proponents of a Byzantine easternism and those of a western orientation (called 'hellenisers') are still relevant (Kourvetaris & Dobratz, 1987: 3). Greece had ceased to exist as an independent country after the Ottoman victory at Constantinople in 1453 AD. For nearly 400 years Greek territory was under Turkish dominion and many Greeks lived in areas which are now Bulgaria, Romania, Albania, Turkey or part of the USSR. Indeed, when the Greek War of Independence, fought in the 1820s with the help of the French and the English, turned into victory, there were many more Greeks who lived outside the borders of the new small Kingdom of Greece than inside. The total population of this newly proclaimed Greece (in 1830) was a mere million people, while outside, in the *diaspora*, a further 3 million Greeks lived under Ottoman rule.

Greek society had never been really suited to monarchy. Yet western nations decided that monarchy was to be instated in the new Greece. They had to hawk around for a suitable monarch, suitable only in the sense of his puppet status. The young (17-year-old) and mentally handicapped Otto I (1832–1867), from Bavaria, was a prime example. So too, to some extent, was the Danish contender who later came to the Greek throne as Georg I (assassinated in 1913). This monarchy had nothing to do with an organically grown indigenous class hierarchy of which a monarch could be considered a 'sovereign'. When Greece was founded, it entirely lacked a landed aristocracy, the chief class support for a monarch. There was no middle class to speak of and the Turkish landlords had been driven out. A law of 1920 broke up the large estates (*tsiflikia*) and these vast lands were given to peasants. Greek society was 'like quicksand' for a ruler (more so for a foreign-born ruler) and promised an 'inauspicious start' for any bureaucracy (McNeill, 1978: 58) because it had neither mass support nor specific class support. Instead, a political class of upstarts formed, mostly in the military, which was opportunistic and guided by the motive of gaining whatever measure of power could be taken. This gave rise to the obnoxious clientele system of political favouritism and corruption, not organised around party platforms, programmes and ideas but around individuals who wanted to get into or stay in power. It furthermore gave rise to internal rifts between monarchists and republicans, a battle which raged and tore the nation apart well into the 1970s.

The story of the new Greek nation throughout the 19th century and well into the first quarter of the 20th century was one of active expansionary politics in line with the idea of a 'Greater Greece'. Greece partly succeeded in expanding its territory, for example, in 1864, 1881 and in the Balkan War of 1912–1914. Despite tensions between the *antochthones* (native born) and the *heterochthones* (born abroad) there was some unity of purpose. After World War I and the Asia Minor War in 1922 Greece not only gained more territory, there was also a massive repatriation of Greeks from Asia Minor, an endless stream of refugees and forced repatriations totalling well over 1.2 million people. They brought with them different views, experiences, skills and even languages and almost doubled the indigenous population within a decade. If there was anything that could forge the disparate groups into a nation it was the language, maintained through religion, and of course the orthodox christian faith itself to which the resettlers had clung within the largely muslim environments. Their values, forged by the orthodox religion but also by Ottoman customs, with their emphasis on communal and family life (*koinovion*), on religion and other-worldliness, often stood in strong contrast to the secular humanist and cosmopolitan hellenisers, who accepted western institutions and values.

The story of this period was of course more complex than these few lines may suggest. Suffice it to say that the forging of the modern Greek nation would have been unthinkable without its religion, a fact that has more than marginal importance for Greek women. This inextricable link between nationalism and religion could not possibly augur well for women's emancipation. While the secular nationalism of Finland, for instance, assisted women in gaining entry to politics and public life at the very beginning of its independence, the religious nationalism of Greece actually inhibited or prevented women's social and economic progress. At the same time, the economic situation of many of the refugees who arrived penniless and in rags from Asia Minor and other areas north and east of Greece, added a potentially radical element to Greek society (McNeill, 1978: 63). The road to political certainty and economic survival was perhaps the hardest for Greece of any 'western' European nation and frought with instability, uncertainty, political upheaval, poverty, cruel bloody wars and dictatorships. Its western orientation was cemented by its entry into the European Communities in 1981, but for reasons yet to be examined, that alliance has not been a particularly happy one to date.

Yet throughout its troubled history, progressive ideas, including women's ideas and organisations, nevertheless flourished whenever there was the slightest easing of any of the dictatorships or ruinous wars. As early as 1804, before Greek independence, Greek women founded institutes and schools for the education of girls, such as The Greek School for Young Girls, the Professional School for Greek Women and the Sunday School for Girls. The first secondary school for girls was founded in 1835. In 1855, the first 'feminist' magazine called *Kypseli* (Beehive) was published by the Greek poet E. Samadinou, and the first organisation for women's rights, called Filanthropiki Omada Gynaikon (the Charitable Women's Group), was founded in Athens by Kaliori Parren. The same woman later founded Enosi gia tin cheirofetesi ton gynaikon (the Union for Women's Emancipation) and in 1897[5] this was followed by a Union of Greek Women. In 1872 leading feminists founded the Union for Women's Education and regularly published their views in several magazines, one called *Thalia* and the other *Euridice*. Names like those of Sevasti Kallisperi, the first doctor of letters in Greece, and Alexandra Papadopoulou for their educational contributions, and foremost Kalliopi Papalexopoulou (1809–1898) for her political work as the mother of the revolution of 1862 which toppled King Othon, stand out amongst an ever growing number of Greek feminists and writers (Riot-Sarcey et al., 1986: 449–51, Roïdis, 1896; Xiradaki, 1898).

In the 1890s, influenced by international socialist feminism, Greek feminists were as politically active as were suffragette movements elsewhere in the world. They demanded the vote and fought hard for the abolition of a law that forbade women to become scientists, merchants or civil servants. A conference held in 1898 was the first large-scale gathering devoted to discussing the status of women in Greece (Stamiris, 1988: 114). Ten years later the National Council of Greek Women's Organisations encompassed 50 different women's organisation, and the number of associations was still growing. In 1910 Athine Gaitanou Yannou founded the Socialist Women's Group and from this group the most radical changes were demanded, such as the right to abortion, the abolition of the dowry, the introduction of civil marriage, as well as the legal protection of 'illegitimate' children. Throughout the 1920s further women organisations were founded, such as the League of Women's Rights, which was another important radical feminist group, and a number of feminists gained a national and international reputation for their work on women's rights. Some of these were Rosa Imvrioti, Anna Theodorapolou and M. Svolou (Molvaer et al., 1984: 145–7).

Further movement in the direction of social change was brought about by a set of political events in the 1920s that was to alter the face of Greece yet again. After the Treaty of Lausanne in 1923, which ended a complicated and protracted series of wars, it was clear that the Greek dream of a new Byzantine Empire with its heartlands in Asia Minor had come to an end. Instead the country had to be content with forming a Greek nation on the Greek peninsula and Aegean islands, worsening the internal struggles between monarchists and republicans. In 1924, at the time of massive resettlements and the beginning of the world depression, Greece declared itself a republic. Not unlike Spain and Portugal, the Greek Republic suffered from great instability, the royalists and republicans being unable to reach any sort of modus vivendi. In the twelve years of its existence it had eleven governments, two coups and was forever beleaguered by threats of assassinations and further coups. Greece's major exports were luxury items like wine, olives, tobacco and currants, and in the years of the depression they were increasingly without buyers.

As in other countries, the departure of monarchy was timely, for it left the blame for a socially and economically unmanageable situation to the 'commoners'. Meanwhile the monarch expected to return in due course to 'save' the nation. In Germany, this expectation proved to be a miscalculation on the part of royalty, but not in Greece to which King Georg II returned in 1936. Under Ioannes Metaxas, his prime minister, a dictatorship was forged which led Greece into one of the bloodiest periods of its modern history. As with dictatorships elsewhere, political parties were prohibited and most of the progressive women's organisations were dissolved, their files burned and their leaders sent into exile or prison. Only the most conservative groups, such as the Christian Union of Young Women, the Union of Greek Women Scientists, the Greek Women's Council and the Greek Women's College, were allowed to exist.

Greece was a British Ally in World War II and was thus in formal terms an enemy of Italy and Germany, although Metaxas himself more than toyed with fascist ideas. Mussolini offered Greece an ultimatum because he wished to occupy strategic points on Greek territory. The Greek government, fearing the response of the people, said no (*ochi*). *Ochi* Day is still a national holiday in Greece. In 1940 Greece repelled an Italian invasion only to succumb to a German invasion the following year. Greece became an occupied country, subdivided between Bulgaria, Italy and Germany. Through those war years Greece suffered terribly from the burning, pillage and sheer brutality carried out by the occupying forces. Civilian populations, if they had not been tortured or shot (or raped) were left to die of hunger. In the winter of 1941 to 1942 the whole nation was on the verge of starvation and the high death rate was curbed only to some extent by the intervention of the Swedish Red Cross. In 1943, the 'final solution' of the 'Jewish problem', imported by German occupation, was translated into practice. Ancient flourishing Jewish communities were rapidly destroyed and over 80 percent of Greek Jewry died in German concentration camps.

It was at this time that a resistance movement took shape and quickly spread through the entire country. The brief spell of republicanism now proved to have been of tremendous value in one crucial way, namely in that organised political life of the people which had been strengthened during the 1920s, particularly in the left-wing parties. The resistance sprang from precisely those groups that Metaxas had wished to silence and these now became a major force in Greek society (Kourvetaris & Dobratz, 1987: 48). In fact, in facing a common enemy, ousted leftist parties combined forces under communist leadership, and organised themselves chiefly into two camps: the National Liberation Movement (EAM) and the guerillas known as the National Popular Liberation Army (ELAS). As in other resistance movements against Hitler and fascism in western Europe, women were an integral and important part of the resistance. But women did not just serve the resistance. Within their own ranks they discovered a new solidarity which, within a few months of the budding resistance movement, turned into a growing women's liberation movement. It became 'a mass-movement of impressive dimensions' (Molvaer et al., 1984: 148). In 1944, the resistance established a revolutionary government under the name of the National Council and Provisional Committee for National Liberation, which at once proceeded to elect a provisional government. Here, women were fully enfranchised and four of them were voted into the council as a recognition that women and men together would rebuild Greece after the liberation from fascism. In 1944 German forces withdrew and the period of occupation finally came to an end.

The occupying forces had barely withdrawn when women began to be active with their own concerns, well aware of the need to build political support structures for the time when free elections would be possible and women could hope to be enfranchised. Early in 1945 they founded the Panhellenic Union of Women and participated in the international foundation in Paris called International Democratic Foundation of Women. Women's conferences were held in Thessaloniki and Iraklion in the following year, accompanied by the publication of a journal called Nea Thesi. One of the last organisational feats before the onset of new crises was the formation of a Panhellenic Federation of Women and a conference in May 1946, in which 600 representatives from over 150 women's organisations took part.

By the time the war ended, the National Liberation Movement had over one million members. In addition, a specially organised Youth Resistance Movement (EPON), had at least 350 000 members (Choisi, 1988: 137). Hence a substantial percentage of the Greek population (total under 9 million in 1970) was formally organised into anti-fascist and anti-occupation forces and became active supporters of democracy. These resistance movements consisted largely of shopkeepers, peasants from the hills and from the lowlands, women, students and school leavers. If ever a group of Greeks could claim to represent the interests of their country, the people of the resistance were exactly that: representatives of a nation of small shopkeepers and peasants. The revolutionary government demonstrated that it was ready to lead the people out of war and into a new Greek democracy.

This, however, was not to be. While the rest of Europe was preparing peace treaties, Greece began to slide headlong into civil war. The Greek Civil War (1946–1949) was as tragic as the Spanish Civil War had been, largely as a result of the interference of western 'allies'. If western allies had been the making of the modern Greek nation in the 19th century, they were very nearly the unmaking of the new nation in this civil war and thereafter. The resistance movement was firmly based in the masses, predominantly in the peasant populations and small farmholders who, at the end of the 1940s still constituted over 70 percent of the Greek population. It was a highly anti-authoritarian, staunchly independent stratum that was determined to be liberated from monarchs, right-wing militarists, fascists, foreign intervention and anyone who prevented a democratic form of government based on the will of the Greek people. The energy, even the very heart of Greek thinking, sprang from these resistance groups.

Yet in 1945 Churchill thought it 'wise' to support a Greek return of the monarchy as a 'bulwark against communist takeover in Greece' (McNeill, 1978: 71), and to do everything in his power to support the monarchy and the national army under its command. In addition, the USA intervened and gave the necessary muscle to these plans. Misguided and paranoid as these steps were, Britain and the US supported the right-wing national army and thus contributed not only to the civil war but also to the rifts in Greek politics that would eventually lead into yet another dictatorship. The very countries that defended parliamentary democracies on their own turf, thought it 'unwise' to allow another country to establish a parliamentary democracy. The USA sent soldiers and considerable financial assistance in order to 'crush the rebels' and allow 'order' to be restored to Greece. It is one of the tragedies of modern European history that the USA and its allies, rightly celebrated in 1945 as one of the liberators of Europe from fascism, should so have misjudged the Greek situation. One might venture to speculate that, had the Greeks been left alone, the situation might have been similar to that of Portugal: going from a bloodless revolution to parliamentary democracy. Instead, the British and US intervention actually supported the very forces that had prevented parliamentary democracy, and one suspects that the reasons were no more profound than an irrational fear of communism which might have taken the lead in the restructuring of modern Greece, as it did in Portugal.

The Greeks paid dearly for this international political bungling and ignorance. They fought a desperate fight. By 1948 at least one third of the population was destitute and on relief (Kourvetaris & Dobratz, 1987: 51). A tenth of the population was forced away from its villages into refugee camps around Athens, a move to deprive guerillas of a food base and of their support. The United Nations relief and rehabilitation funds began to run out by 1947 and the new Labour government in England, understandably, stopped supporting the right-wing Greek government (McNeill, 1978: 80, 87). Leftist forces were weakened and communists outlawed (1947). Women's organisations were crushed and prohibited, women again were imprisoned or forced into exile and their publications were burnt. One writer bitterly noted that women at least had equality in suffering, in torture, exile and imprisonment. In Trikeri alone there were 5000 women in the local concentration camp (Stamiris, 1988: 120). Meanwhile the CIA helped the Greek military to build up an extensive net of secret police and information services which ensured that any expressions of democratic leanings were smothered and that only the fanatically anti-communist and those who were totally loyal to NATO would be supported (Choisi, 1988: 69).

In 1952 Greece became a constitutional monarchy and was led by Papandreou's government, which was clearly opposed to communism and any leftism. The political power was vested in the king, the army and the secret service and paramilitary police units, and this allowed nepotism and corruption to continue to thrive (Raulff, 1983: 344). Internal politics, the unavailability of labour and the clear signs that Greek democracy was a long way off caused many Greeks to leave. One of the immediate consequences of these postwar developments was that Greece, with the emigration of 25 percent of its entire workforce (McNeill, 1978: 117), suffered one of its worst brain and skill drains in this century. Some went as guest labourers to other European countries, chiefly to West Germany, but most of the departures were final, as Greek families settled in the USA, in Canada and mainly in Australia. By 1970, Australia alone had received over 130 000 settlers, most of whom had come as unassisted migrants in the 1950s and early 1960s (Dept. of Immigration and Ethnic Affairs, *Australian Immigration*, Consolidated Statistics, no. 13, 1982, Canberra, 1984). Melbourne became the city with the largest population of Greeks outside Athens, perpetuating Greece's reputation as a *diaspora* nation. Today, there is one Greek living elsewhere in the world for every three Greeks in Greece (Kourvetaris & Dobratz, 1987: 18). But, of course, these desperate measures and protest actions unwittingly supported the government of the day by drastically reducing the pool of dissatisfied unemployed and actually creating a labour deficit. In addition, the remittances from guest workers assisted the economy at home.

Under US influence the political right maintained a decisive parliamentary majority in Greece throughout the 1950s and 1960s. This position was certainly helped by a complicated voting system which had elements of majority and proportional voting, and not only disadvantaged smaller parties but 'invited' election manipulation; it was possible, for instance, for a party which had received 10 percent of the primary vote to end up with no seats in parliament (Choisi, 1988: 65). Women had received the right to vote (in 1952) but few of them made use of it. The unions and the army remained under the spell of their former dictatorial management, but the stability and the kind of economic planning and development that the US advisers had hoped for never eventuated. The chief problem was that of revenue for the government. The political clientele system, unrevised as it was since the beginning of the century, was 'entirely incompatible with the wholesale restructuring of public expenditures and taxation that American advisers wanted' (McNeill, 1978: 94). A progressive income tax proved completely unworkable. It seemed as if the Greek people took revenge on a government that in many ways was alien in structure and ideology. From this point of view, ruling Greece indeed resembled walking on quicksand. Personal income tax, as a percentage of gross domestic product (GDP), was less than half of the European average (11.5 percent), and almost 70 percent of central government revenue had to be obtained by indirect taxation. Tax evasion in Greece was probably the highest in Europe and no measure seemed to be able to overcome the problem. As soon as the government initiated one scheme, the Greek population sought ways of circumventing it (Kourvetaris & Dobratz, 1987: 138–9). This was aided in many ways by the fact that, even after the war and with the beginning of industrialisation, still well over half of all Greeks lived and worked on their own farms, and a larger than European average (about half of all people in the labour force) were small shopkeepers, independent in their bookkeeping.

Throughout the 1960s, the Greek mood was despondent and restless. But for some time at least, economic progress was made in secondary and tertiary industry. Threefold increases in industrial output were recorded and a fivefold increase in tourism by 1964. These economic changes, however, were not accompanied by any social adjustments or new policies. The gap between rich and poor widened. No policies over wages and salaries existed, social welfare was not considered on any statement of priorities, and there was little effort made to create a new educational elite that was able to deal with modern economic demands. It had a growing and parasitic tertiary (service) sector, a large but inefficient agricultural sector and a very low labour absorption capacity. In 1960, more than 50 percent of the labour force was still employed in agriculture, only 19 percent were craftspeople, process workers and labourers, and just over 3 percent were in technical and professional fields (Kourvetaris & Dobratz, 1987: 53). One might add that women were among the educational elites of the 1950s but, like the Greek educational elite in general, they were too small in number to have any impact on the prevailing political and economic climate. The political unrest continued, exemplified in 1963 by the murder of Gregorios Lambrakis, a politician with some allegedly leftist leanings, and the resignation and ensuing exile of the prime minister, Konstantin Karamanlis. Any signs of controversial movements were short-lived and the few women's organisations founded at that time, such as the dynamic and militant Panhellenic Union of Women (Stamiris, 1988: 120), had only a brief spell of existence; in the intensification of political struggle, the military coup of 1967 abruptly ended all organised social activity, even the mildest forms of it.

The self-appointed junta of army officers, which ruled between 1967 and 1974 was, many Greeks believe, a direct consequence of dependence on the USA and NATO. The junta's ability to stay in power for seven years was at least partly due to US financial and military aid (Choisi, 1988: 170, 178). Led by G. Papadopoulos, this military dictatorship was thoroughly brutal. It concocted a series of special laws, threw a net of spies over Greece, orchestrated mass imprisonments and deportations, and permitted torture as a routine method of 'investigation'—all manner of cruelty and extortion to combat the constant and passive resistance by the Greek people (Raulff, 1983: 346). The European Council condemned the Greek junta under the Declaration of Human Rights in the Charter of the UN and forced it to leave the council. One of the feminists who suffered under Papadopoulos' regime recounted her experience in the following way:

> My experience, together with that of so many others, began on the first day of the military coup on the 21st of April, 1967, when they knocked on the door of my house for the first time. Fortunately, because a friend had warned me, I had the opportunity to escape. After that I lived underground.
>
> The first month after the coup, we began to form an organisation with the name E.K.D.A. Unfortunately after the first pamphlets were distributed, they arrested us. I was arrested by the police in August 1967. They took my books, personal things and anything else they wanted. For the next one and half months I was in complete isolation from other prisoners. Every day for one month I was interrogated day and night. When they did not interrogate me they would put me in the dirtiest and darkest cell, full of dirty water and mice. I will never forget how I was constantly standing up, being afraid to touch anything because the cell was so full of mice.
>
> ... When I was finally freed I left for Paris. In 1969 I decided to go back to Greece, where I was arrested again and interrogated about the organisations abroad and my participation in them. They let me go, but in August 1971 the military police (E.S.A.) arrested me yet again. I was told that if I would not speak, I would not leave the E.S.A. alive ... They would talk outside my cell, saying that my mother was dead, and they

threatened my mother that if I did not speak, she would find me dead. One month later they let me go. But then I suffered amnesia and my left side was paralysed. (Russel & Van de Ven, 1984: 167–8)

It might appear contradictory that Papadopoulos and his military regime would want to give Greece a constitution, but this was precisely what he did in 1968. It was, however, inoperative until 1973. There are several reasons which could account for the move. Amongst these were western European pressures on the colonels to liberalise their regime, and giving a country a constitution was the kind of international gesture that might have appealed to western allies. It is more sinister to suspect that the charade was staged in preparation for the intended abolition of the monarchy and in order to extend the regime's own power. The colonels had probably learned their lesson from Mussolini's mistake in not abolishing the monarchy while he was in charge. Indeed, the constitution involved guarantees of civil rights *and* included the monarchy's abolition. In the latter, they could actually count on the support of the population which had long since wanted to rid itself of the monarchy. A referendum of 1973 voted in the republic by a resounding majority of 69 percent, and Papadopoulos was sworn in as its new president.

The double game played by American and European countries could not have been more evident than in Spain or Greece. Politically, they supported any party or group that was clearly anti-communist and against leftism of any shade, which resulted in the support of anti-democratic, militaristic and extremely right-wing (even fascist) groups. At the same time they demanded democratic structures in order to justify economic dealings with the nations in question! At least in Greece, the military junta was ultimately caught in its own web. It was supported by the USA but needed to show some liberalisation in order to be eligible for further support and large-scale economic investment. Economic investment, tourism and other forms of foreign exchange gradually increased standards of living and expectations. Thus the rampant urbanisation process that had begun in the late 1950s invited new standards and considerations of urban problems and issues. The acquisition of modern amenities was just one small measure of the substantial change that took place (see table 6.5).

The paradoxical situation began to result in some form of overt resistance by about 1973. The christian social youth organisation EXON published the only christian resistance paper (*Christianiki*) at the time. An anti-dictatorial student union called EFEE had existed since the early 1960s but by the end of 1972 it began to take up the fight more actively. The most notable of its protests was the uprising in the Athenian Polytechnicon in November 1973. It has been said that this event aided the toppling of Papadopoulos and his military regime (McNeill, 1978: 245). Students and other dissenters barricaded themselves in the Polytechnicon; their slogan was 'freedom, bread, education'. Tanks rolled through the iron gate and into the masses of students, killing 34 and wounding many others.

**Table 6.5  Percentage of dwellings with modern amenities in Greek cities in 1961 and 1970**

|  | 1961 | 1970 |
| --- | --- | --- |
| Running water | 39 | 80 |
| Electricity | 50 | 90 |
| Flush toilets | 14 | 46 |
| Baths | 10 | 35 |

*Source*: McNeill, 1978: 219

These student deaths are still commemorated on their anniversary each year as epitomising the struggle for civil liberty (Kourvetaris & Dobratz, 1987: 154).

Further instability was caused by the Cyprus crisis coming to a head in July 1974, when Cyprus was invaded by Turkey. It took just three days and a series of what were believed to be fundamental errors of judgement to bring about the downfall of the colonels. Papadopoulos was put under arrest by Greek army commanders, Karamanlis returned from exile and was widely celebrated as if he were a hero. He was at once installed as the prime minister of a new, interim civilian government. The nightmare of the military junta under the colonels was over. Greece breathed a sigh of relief.

After the junta, political parties immediately reappeared on the scene. The Greek Communist Party (KKE) which had been banned since 1947, reorganised. Most other western European communist parties had long since dissociated themselves from the USSR after either the uprising in Hungary or the invasion of Czechoslovakia, however, the KKE still adhered to a hard pro-Soviet line. Andreas Papandreou founded and became the leader of a new non-communist, left-of-centre socialist party, called the Panhellenic Socialist Movement (PASOK), which managed to bring together old factions of resistance fighters. Its main platform rested on key issues such as national independence (i.e. against US interventionism, NATO and multinational takeovers), power to the people, social emancipation and democratisation (Choisi, 1988: 63). PASOK had a remarkable career as a party for it took only seven years from its foundation to its becoming the government. The 1975 elections, however, favoured the conservatives under the leadership of Karamanlis. On his return from exile he had revamped his conservative party into a new party, the New Democracy (ND), with a platform of parliamentary, pluralistic democracy based on a free-market economy. The KKE paid the price for its unadapted programme and thinking by gaining only 1.8 percent of the vote.

Just as the political parties, the women's movement also became visible in 1975. It was spearheaded by Margaret Papandreou, the wife of the prime minister, together with upper-class women in Athens (Kourvetaris & Dobratz, 1987: 159), who were no longer willing to passively watch government activities. They began to campaign against the pre-modern Byzantine family law. Their slogan 'No women's liberation without social liberation—no social liberation without women's liberation' remained its chief form of self-advertisement. Feminists then established a coordinating committee of women's organisations and began to campaign in earnest. Women's publications, journals such as I *Skouba* (the Broom), and the *Sphinx* began to appear in the late 1970s. Women's organisations also regathered at once, usually in concert with the political parties. Thus the first mass movement of women, the Democratic Women's Movement, (KDG), was founded by women who belonged to the Greek Eurocommunist Party (1974). The Union of Greek Women (EGE), formed in 1976 under Margaret Papandreou, had close ties to PASOK, and in 1976 women of the Communist Party created the Federation of Greek Women.

All three groups were, and still are, fundamentally different in outlook and approach. The KDG, despite its political affiliation, has always aimed for autonomy and it addresses a wide range of radical issues, spelled out in its regular publication *Deltio* (the Bulletin). In these aims it is close to the Movement for the Emancipation of Women which was founded in Athens. The PASOK-influenced EGE, which calls itself a socialist feminist organisation, has become a powerful organisation of over 10 000 members. It had several immediate goals

in response to the inequality of women. It sought to increase women's participation in the workforce and wanted more women in decision-making positions,
together with security provisions for women in the workforce and in home
piecework. It was adamant about the need for mass education on family planning (i.e. sex education, contraceptives, etc.) and demanded legalised abortion.
It saw the need for nurseries and day-care centres throughout the country and
intended to fight against sexism in advertisements. It too has a regular journal,
called *Anoikto Parathyro* (the Open Window). The Federation of Greek Women
on the other hand, which has at least 50 smaller groups as members, has never
believed in autonomy and, as a matter of principle, has argued for the essential
participation of women in the main political struggles. Its bi-monthly periodical,
*Synchroni Gynaika* (the Woman Today), is still being published today (Molvaer,
1984: 150). Other, smaller feminist groups were conceived of as civil rights
groups, such as several founded by lesbian women, and are less interested in
legal reform than in autonomous political activism and public education concerned with sexuality (Morgan, 1984: 271).

The years since the fall of the colonels have been perhaps the most exciting
and stimulating ones for Greece in this century. All the forces that had been
suppressed for so long were eventually coming to the fore. During the junta,
writers had been exiled or imprisoned and much of their writing had been put
on the Index (church list of forbidden books) or had never been seen. Now that
freedom of the press and freedom of expression were again permitted, a flood
of publications, largely dealing with political themes, poured onto the Greek
market and reached an audience thirsty for some politically diverse views and
opinions. Amongst these writers were women of some renown like Mitopulu,
Megah Seferiadi, Papadimitriu and Meleagru (Choisi, 1988: 92). Greece has
experienced a tremendous cultural and artistic renaissance, and this has included
literature on social and women's issues. One might add here that the role of the
Minister for Culture from 1981 onwards had a great deal to do with this
cultural renaissance. After the 1982 elections, the portfolio of the Minister for
Culture was given to an extremely impressive woman, the singer–actor Melina
Mercouri. She instituted a programme of widespread reforms and her reputation
amongst friends and foes alike was that she was the 'best Culture Minister
Greece has ever had' (*Sydney Morning Herald*, Nov. 4, 1989: 22).

Politically, however, the years after the junta under the Karamanlis government
were generally conservative and uninspired by any great wish for sudden change.
The best that can be said for the ND regime, especially in the first few years, is
that for the first time in Greek history it provided a comparatively stable political
life. This stability has been attributed to Karamanlis' extraordinary ability to steer
Greece very gently and very gradually into the new waters of a republican democracy (Diamandouros, 1984). His strategies for the transition from dictatorship to parliamentary democracy were in fact not unlike those of King Juan
Carlos of Spain. Both heads of state made minimal commitments, cautiously
steered a middle road, carefully watched the military over their shoulders, and
hesitantly, if not deliberately, postponed major reform. The only immediate and
clear display of the new powers was as much a symbolic act, a signifier of the new
regime, as it was a matter of national safety. King Juan Carlos of Spain declared
amnesty for political prisoners, as did Karamanlis, who also brought the chieftains
of the military junta to trial but then converted their death sentences to life
imprisonments. Both Don Carlos and Karamanlis immediately legalised all political
parties, a move that would help both to gain mass support. In Spain, as we have

seen, the first free elections completed ousted the Falangists from power. In Greece, the first free elections gave Karamanlis a resounding vote of confidence after the first months of his interim rule. Issues concerned with women's rights, or anybody else's for that matter, were low on the list of priorities.

Karamanlis was rather fortunate in that the European economic crisis of 1974 to 1975 had not nearly the detrimental effect on Greece as it had on Portugal and Spain. This was partly due to Karamanlis' diplomatic and public relations skill in assuring the population and foreign investors of a continuation of peaceful conditions, balanced by rational and cautious government. Indeed, tourists never stopped coming to Greece and guest workers continued to send their remittances. Neither did foreign investment decline. But there were other extraneous circumstances. Greece was able to enter into a new round of negotiations with the EEC and in 1975 it became an associate. Very timely indeed was the discovery in 1975 of oil in the Aegean, which helped Greece with its escalating energy consumption (McNeill, 1978: 135).

On the level of reforms, the Karamanlis government performed poorly. It was not just an up-and-coming lower middle-class stratum which had emerged from the drift towards urban dwelling. Students, peasants, and women all had their own set of grievances. To be sure, according to the constitution women were now formally equal but the translation of these rights into practice left much to be desired. In their campaigns women soon learned that the ND regime under Karamanlis had no intention of changing anything, at least not at once (Stamiris, 1988: 121). A committee was set up to reform the Family Code, with the brief to come up with new reform proposals in seven years' time. In this, as in many other cases, the policy of going slow on changes eventually backfired on the government. Some of the few things it began to tackle were often the least important; for instance, the ND government made a decision on the old issue of language use. It decided in favour of *dimotiki*, which had been the spoken language and the language of literature for a long time, and raised it to the national language. Until 1975, however, the language of government, law, scholarship and education was *katharevousa*, a cleansed and artificial language that was closer to old Greek than to *dimotiki*. While this rationalisation seemed a good idea at the time, it created endless problems in deciphering official and scholarly documents, and finally Old Greek had to be reintroduced in schools to overcome this situation (Choisi, 1988: 85).

Student dissatisfaction did not disappear either and student opinion, it has often been claimed, is a good barometer for the political mood of the Greek public in general. Their criticisms, like that of many European student movements of the 1970s, were directed against the USA, against US bases in Greece, Greek membership of NATO, foreign interference in Cyprus and exploitation by multinational companies. But their grievances were also very specific. The *numerus clausus* (quota) system was extremely harsh. Only 20 percent of those wishing to go to university actually secured a place and many had to go overseas to study. Professors were accused of ruling their departments and students in a despotic manner, dictating what students had to learn and to think, a behaviour hardly in line with the democratisation and social emancipation at which the new Greek state allegedly aimed. Moreover, the issue of conscription also affected a large number of male students in adverse ways. Military service was compulsory for two years and in cases of misdemeanours could be even longer. Pocket money 'earned' during the time of service was not even sufficient for a packet of cigarettes. If a young man had family who in any way depended on him, there was no financial support given to the family. Worst of all, for many, were two other interrelated concerns. The army had not been 'cleansed' of its right-wing proponents and often it was sufficient for a drafted person to be suspected of 'democratic leanings' in order to be singled out for severe and inhumane treatment. Secondly, the long service made reintegration into educational training more difficult. In 1979, students rebelled more forcefully again and considered it a minor victory that the proposed government plans for limits on study time and further limits on academic freedom were thwarted (Choisi, 1988: 33, 83).

In summary, the Karamanlis government created a nagging dissatisfaction in the population about what ought to be done and what was in fact being done. The measures that worked well in the period of immediate transition and highly inflammatory political climate were one thing. But once the transition was over, there were large sections of the Greek population that wanted to see substantial reforms. From 1980 onwards, the political fortunes of the Karamanlis government changed for the worse. In 1981 the government earned the mistrust of the population when it did little to rectify right-wing mob activity and murder. During a peaceful demonstration at the Polytechnich in Athens to commemorate the tragic student deaths of 1973, right-wing terrorists had intervened and caused the death of a student. There was also the government's lack of response to the catastrophic earthquake in 1981. Ten months after the event high school students were still taught in tents because none of the damaged buildings had been made reusable (Choisi, 1988: 162).

Greece's entry into the EEC in 1981 created great concern amongst sections of the population. Steep price rises of up to 20 percent followed almost immediately, and the fears of a possible flood of cheap imports later proved well founded. While Greek manufacture remained weak and its output began to stagnate, there was a growing bias in favour of foreign products. Greece had been given some years of grace before it had to allow cheap imports into the country but that time of grace was over in the mid-1980s, and the worst predictions came true. Even formerly unique Greek foodstuffs such as feta cheese became import items. Initially at least, leaving aside the substantial payments made to Greece in the mid-1980s, Greece's entry into the EEC cost it dearly. By the late 1970s it also became clear that corporate profits were deteriorating while capital flight increased and rises in energy consumption led to a sharp increase of energy imports. The economic management of the government in toto was not considered particularly healthy. Since a large proportion of the economy was under state control, such as transport, communication, energy, banks, education and public utility companies, the blame was laid squarely at Karamanlis' feet. By 1980 public sector spending had increased to 70 percent of total expenditure and its deficit stood at an extremely high 13 percent of GDP, compared to 2.5 percent in France and West Germany (Kourvetaris & Dobratz, 1987: 126–7).

When the time of the elections arrived, the Greek population was ready for a change and impatient for more radical policies. Some were even willing to let a government try measures towards a fundamental transformation of Greek society. Women's organisations had analysed and recorded all the ills that they observed, compiling a formidable list of discriminatory practices, which were delivered when the PASOK government took over in 1981 (Stamiris, 1988: 122). The mood of the Greek public was well captured in the European survey mentioned previously. In this comparison of EEC member countries' views, the

Greek population scored highest in all areas expressing a need for change. To reiterate: when asked what the best division of roles within the family was, over 50 percent of Greek women and men answered that equal-gender sharing was the best.[6] This was by far the highest score in all EEC countries, and a very radical reply indeed. Likewise, when asked whether the situation of women was of any real concern, 37 percent replied that it was of great importance and was one of the priorities to be addressed, and a further 25 percent said that women's right to equality, along with other gender issues, was of great importance. No other EEC member states came anywhere near the Greek results, with an 11 percent European average for the former and 20 percent for the latter question (*Women and Men of Europe in 1983*: 58). In their willingness to demonstrate for rights, Greeks were amongst the EEC member states with the highest score, having either done so in the past or being prepared to do so in future. It is also remarkable that 18 percent of Greek women had participated in demonstrations (only the French and Italian figures are higher). One has to bear in mind that until 1974 one demonstrated only at great risk to life and personal liberty. PASOK, the socialist party which came to power in 1981, combined elements of the old resistance with progressive secular ideas. It had grown substantially in membership (about 150 000) and in support, and under the leadership of Andreas Papandreou it won a clear and overwhelming election victory.

PASOK inherited a stagnant economy with a high balance of payment deficit, high public-sector borrowing, high inflation, low productivity and profitability, and stagnation in investment (Kourvetaris & Dobratz, 1987: 119). Its occupational structure, with a marked lack of technically skilled and trained people, was unhealthy, and high unemployment was recorded overall, with employment and manufacture being over-concentrated in the Athens area. Over one-third of the Greek population lived in rural areas, often with poor access to schools, hospitals or other services. Peculiar to Greece is that only 29 percent of land can be used for agriculture or grazing and the peasant population is therefore concentrated into small farming properties, usually of less than ten hectares (90 percent of all farms are this size or less). These farmers are therefore economically extremely vulnerable.

The educational system, despite some reforms in the 1970s was outmoded and too few partook of it. In 1981 the overall illiteracy rate was 19 percent, but that of women was considerably higher, about 24 percent, and it was higher still in some rural pockets. Altogether four-fifths of all illiterates in Greece are women. Success at high school was commonly very expensive because the demands of examinations, particularly of entrance examinations for university, were such that those who wished to succeed usually had to go to one of the privately owned *Frontistiria*, a special tutorial and remedial school which prepared students for examinations. Such tuition was of course not free. Any school attendance overall had been low and has only risen gradually in the postwar years:

**Table 6.6   Greek school and university attendance according to sex, 1961 and 1981**

| Year | School attendance | | University attendance | |
|------|------|------|------|------|
| | F % | M % | F % | M % |
| 1961 | 36.6 | 50.3 | 0.9 | 2.9 |
| 1981 | 51.6 | 60.9 | 3.5 | 6.8 |

*Source*: Stamiris, 1988: 130

Under the PASOK government one of the entrance examinations for high schools was abolished, so student numbers increased. This was, however, at the cost of severe overcrowding in classrooms. The student quota at universities has only increased from 20 to 30 percent of the high-school leavers, because the competition has continued to involve costs in preparation for university. Evening classes have been created to stamp out the high illiteracy rate, with some success, for in 1988 it had dropped to 11 percent for women and 5 percent for men. Nevertheless, even today as much as 50 percent of women farmers in Greece have completed only the first six years of schooling, and many have less schooling than that (*Women in Agriculture*, 1988: 28).

Prior to PASOK coming to power, the health and social security services were extremely poor. The cost of illness often brought a family to the brink of financial ruin because even the best insurance demanded a 20 percent payment of cost and parts of doctor's and hospital fees were not covered. Peasants had no social security at all and in many cases where young people migrated to the cities and other countries, the old were left to fend for themselves. Of all hospitals about 40 percent were private and expensive. Only a third of all nursing staff was qualified, doctors were often only trained to deal with epidemics rather than with modern illnesses. They were not only in extremely short supply in rural areas, but other supportive health services usually did not exist. Infant mortality was three times higher in rural areas than in towns and cities. Family planning and general health centres were rare, and child care, if it was available, was only for children aged 3 and up (Choisi, 1988: 76–8).

The PASOK government attempted to deal with many of the poor social conditions, but improvement has been slow. Since 1982 peasants have been able to receive some form of social security. Women who were farmers were considered for the first time as having self-employed status and entitled to a pension at the age of 65. While such a recognition was long overdue, the pension was so low that in 1989 a new complementary insurance scheme had to be introduced. The drawback is that farmers have to contribute financially to it throughout their working lives, adding a very real burden for the low-income small farm holders (*Women in Agriculture*, 1988: 27). Education and the health services have generally been stepped up, but they have remained inadequate, especially in rural and semi-rural areas. The problem partly was (and still is) the stagnant economy, which is not a good precondition for stamping out social ills. Social engineering takes money and thus, in general, the changes are neither as drastic nor as thorough as the government or the people would like. Overall, one may therefore register only trends of social reform.

In political matters, since these were less dependent on the public purse, PASOK acted rather swiftly and more successfully; the military, for instance, was brought under firmer control to be relied upon only in foreign affairs, no longer to participate in domestic matters. Greece joined Austria and Sweden in their endeavours to contribute to nuclear-free environments and to support a freeze on nuclear weapons. In this it was supported by other Balkan countries (Kourvetaris & Dobratz, 1987: 113).

Perhaps the most remarkable changes under Andreas Papandreou were those that contradicted church dogma. After PASOK came to power the relationship between the government and the church clearly deteriorated, mainly for two reasons: one concerned a direct intervention against the church and the other concerned a number of sweeping changes and legislative initiatives, especially in the area of family law and women's rights. The tension between the government and the church, smouldering over the women's and family law issues, came to a head in 1987 with the government's decision to nationalise monastic land. The Greek church is extremely wealthy but is violently opposed to the mere suggestion of rendering any services to the community apart from prayers and church services. It runs or funds no hospitals or schools, has no social services and does little with the land in its possession. It still owns 1 percent of all Greek property and this is more or less fallow land, used neither for agriculture nor for anything else (Choisi, 1988: 75, 193).

But this experiment against the church failed, as did others in practice, demonstrating that secular power had not gone far enough and did not always have general support. The government decreed in 1982 that all Greeks had freedom of religion, but this rule has not always been adhered to however, and even the law courts have repeatedly taken the side of the church. Thus, in 1984, three missionaries were condemned to prison sentences of over three years each for giving a 16-year-old school boy a New Testament written in English! In 1987, four protestants were condemned to long prison sentences simply because they made it known that they were protestants. Ninety-eight percent of the Greek population is Greek orthodox. The idea of religious freedom therefore rarely needs to be tested but, where it has been, the law courts have clearly decided in favour of the church and against existing legislation. The church itself has also not looked passively on the reform programmes in schools and universities. In 1985, for example, 5000 priests were seen marching in the streets to protest the introduction of Darwin's evolutionary theories into Greek schoolbooks. On the issue of nationalising church land, the clergy went on strike and refused to deliver church services. Again they took the matter to court and won, the law courts overriding government wishes.

The PASOK government had more success in activities that were related to gender which, at least indirectly, staked a claim for the pre-eminence of secular government and its legislative apparatus over church power. In the political history of Greece, the Papandreou government was the first to identify and deal with particular women's issues. The real hallmark of the new regime, although work on it had begun some time before, was the passing of a new family law in 1983. It took considerable pressure from women's organisations to ensure that it would be passed. It removed all the privileges of the household head, so that women could now open their own businesses and were no longer obliged by law to do domestic work in marriage. Women and men were placed on an equal footing in marriage, be this in terms of property matters or of child rearing. The marriageable age of girls was raised from 14 to 18 years to prevent women from entering into arranged marriages against their will. Civil weddings were recognised as being of equal status to church weddings. Civil divorce was granted after four years of separation with a no-guilt clause attached to the separation, irrespective of whether the wedding was a civil or religious one. Women were given access to health insurance and social services independently of husbands or male guardians. Maternity leave provisions were improved so that women would not lose jobs due to pregnancy.

Still more remarkable were perhaps the sudden and effective legal changes concerning the controversial area of reproduction and sexuality, controversial because the issue of abortion and contraception was clearly raised against church will. Contraceptives were made available cheaply and readily. In June 1986 one of the most advanced abortion laws in Europe was passed in Greece, allowing abortion on demand for the first twelve weeks of pregancy and up to 24 weeks in cases of rape or for medical reasons related to the mother or foetus. In any case, the decision for abortion was the woman's and, even though there was a time limit on the freedom to choose, acceptance of this law was a milestone in Greek social history. Abortion, moreover, was free and covered by health insurance. This measure curbed the number of illegal abortions in Greece, estimated to have been as high as 300 000 annually.

The issue of sexuality also began to be faced in legislation and in law enforcement agencies, if only very falteringly. Incest, rape and sexual harassment are now prohibited by law, but it requires people to lay charges in the first place, and courts that will recognise the guilty party. In 1982, with the help of the national feminist organisation the Movement of Democratic Women, a woman in Northern Greece won a case against a rapist who was then convicted to eight years' imprisonment. Before the PASOK government came to power, courts had tended to put the blame for rape on women. In 1980, a woman who had wounded a man in his attempt to rape her received a three-year goal sentence while the attacker escaped lightly with a five-month sentence! (Morgan, 1984: 268)

In 1982, the government also made a number of structural changes. First, it appointed an adviser to the prime minister on matters related to the equality of the two sexes, followed by the setting up of a Council of Equality, which was upgraded in 1983 into a General Secretariat for Equality of the Ministry to the President. It is an autonomous department with its own independent budget. It does not merely have observatory and advisory capacity but can make policy recommendations and can create mechanisms for implementation of its own policies. It has set up further committees in all prefectures to look at local problems of inequality. Since the rural/urban dichotomy is relatively sharp in Greece, this structural feature is of some importance, particularly to rural and semi-rural areas (Papandreou, 1984). The general secretariat can deal with day-to-day problems of discrimination brought before it and can provide grants for retraining or special training programmes for women, particularly in non-traditional occupations. One such was the recent women's house-painters' co-operative, the first of its kind, which was founded in 1988 in Kalamata on the Peleponnese.

These new committees and political structures for women's issues were accompanied by increased activities within the women's movement itself. One of the important foundations of the early 1980s was the opening of a research and documentation centre by the League for Women's Rights and the foundation of the Mediterranean Women's Studies Institute (KEGME) in Athens which is a non-governmental organisation with consultative status to the United Nations' Economic and Social Council. It conducts feminist and action-oriented research, and has gathered an impressive body of information on women at work (women in cooperatives and women and technology) and 'women of migration' (immigration and repatriation and their specific health, education and employment status). KEGME holds seminars and conferences and actively promotes peace, runs anti-pollution campaigns and supports anti-nuclear initiatives. It has established its own information and documentation centre and regularly runs women's studies programmes. The universities of Athens and of Thessaloniki run regular women's studies series and lectures, usually free of charge and accessible to women outside the university. Almost all women's organisations hold conferences and meetings regularly. Perhaps the most noteworthy are those by the Greek Women's Federation which held its fourth conference in 1988. This was attended by representatives of foreign women's organisations and some 960 delegates from all over Greece and was of special importance as it outlined the priorities that the women's movement should adopt up to the year 2000. Social security and health issues were chief amongst such items as peace and social protection (*Women of Europe*, no. 54, April/May 1988: 17). In 1988, the first centre for battered women was opened in Athens and the Women's Rights League published a wide-ranging inquiry into sexual harassment in the workplace. In the same year, the Greek Feminist Anti-Nuclear Movement of Athens took the international Messenger of Peace Award given by the United Nations Secretary General and, during the Reagan–Gorbachev summit meeting in Moscow, was able to hand over a disarmament appeal to the two superpower leaders (*Women of Europe*, no. 56, 1988: 20).

No doubt, the new legislation moved very much in the same direction as feminists wanted. Thus, in the first years of the PASOK government the women's movement and the government were allies. Women's equal status in Greece was long overdue and PASOK, with its link to the resistance movement of the past, knew this only too well. By the late 1980s, however, the honeymoon phase was over. Equal status was one thing and active participation in politics obviously quite another. For here, not even PASOK showed any interest and feminists felt they were getting nowhere. To let the government and the public know, they staged a mass rally on International Women's Day, 1989, in support of women's greater participation in politics. Feminist organisations were in favour of a quota system forcing parties to have women make up at least 35 percent of their electoral lists. A little later in 1989, in the election for the European parliamentary representatives, PASOK and other parties presented women candidates in the order of a mere 7 percent of all candidates and in addition put them low on the list of their candidates. The conservative Nea Demokratia was the only party which deliberately placed one woman candidate (Giannakou Koutsikou) in second place on the ticket and, as it turned out, she became the sole female Greek representative to the European Parliament (*Women of Europe*, no. 60, 1989: 19).

PASOK enjoyed six years in power but in November 1989 it lost the election and was replaced by an uneasy, three-party coalition, formed after days of negotiation. Once all the portfolios were decided and the government finally in place, politicians presented themselves to the public. A storm broke out when it became clear that this new government contained not a single woman. The protest was by no means just confined to a small feminist lobby but was unleashed in the daily papers, within party rooms, and amongst the general public. As an afterthought Martha Handrinou-Mathiopoulou was appointed General Secretary to the Minister of Justice, but this did little to cool the rancour of women (*Women of Europe*, no. 63, 1990: 19).

Women know that their fight for representation is not just a gender issue but, in Greece, also a fight strongly tied to class and a fight against a specific political culture. Psacharopoulos points out, for instance, that women's representation in top administrative and professional positions has often been higher than that of men in the same stratum: 7 percent as against 5 percent (1983: 353). It has been true in most western European countries throughout most of this century that women from upper-class or well-established wealthy families were likely to be able to receive a good education, and were able to make use of their talents if they so desired. In Greece, the question is not related to aristocracy, as we have said before, but the family name and its accrued prestige. Bottomley makes the point that a study of women parliamentarians in Greece had revealed the importance of family connections, observing that all these women had families of political note with an established 'clientele'. Melina Mercouri, for instance, is the daughter of a former mayor of Athens (1986: 187). Andreas Papandreou is the son of George Papandreou. Andreas Papandreou's wife Margaret played a weighty role in government and in the women's movement. This is not to argue that their appointments are based purely on privilege. Their background secures a basic entrance ticket, but thereafter they are on their own. They have to prove their merit exposed as they are to the full misogyny of male power politics. It is debated in present-day Greece that only competence should decide entry into politics, neither the family connections nor the gender. But this involves more than a strategic change: it requires a radical departure from previous political practice. It would require a move away from the hidden political oligarchies and the clientele system to party platform politics and open recruitment practices. One might add here that the nexus between gender and class, and class and positions of authority is not necessarily broken in other western countries, certainly not when it comes to senior positions and to politics.

It is more than apparent in the Greek case that legislation against discrimination has been an attempt to legislate against social custom. Greece, perhaps more clearly than any other western European nation, lives on at least three levels of tradition and modernity. Large segments of the urban population are western in outlook, progressive and even radical. Another stratum lives in a state of tension between traditional values and some modern 'imports'. In a third group, most readily found in rural areas, there is little evidence of a change of pace, lifestyle, customs or views. One example is that of the *prika* (dowry), which the government abolished along with its family law reforms in 1982. In several parts of Greece the system of the dowry is still maintained. In families that adhere to it, a girl is an expensive item. In exchange for her lifelong obedience and (hard) work, brothers usually cannot afford to marry until the sister is married off, for they, along with the father, have to save for the dowry of the girl. Dowries are substantial contributions to a new household, either as large sums of cash, investment papers, land or an apartment. The mother tends to contribute a wide variety of household items, jewellery and linen. Arranged marriages are still being practised and in many families girls are unable to move about by themselves. They have to be accompanied by a male member of the family, even if this may be a younger brother. This is deemed essential for three reasons. A chaperon, or male guardian, acts as a protector of the family honour and prevents the girl from being talked about or falling into disrepute, even through no fault of her own. It is also supposed to prevent the young woman from falling in love before the dowry is ready. In the case of an arranged marriage it ensures that she will not gain too much exposure to the opposite sex so that she is unable to compare the relative merits of her husband-to-be with other possible contenders. In some families the new bride is still judged by the mother-in-law in terms of whether she is likely to accept the mother's regime. In some mountain regions the chief criterion for approval or disapproval of the new bride is made on a judgement of how much weight she can carry on her back (Choisi, 1988: 17–20). Women in rural areas usually put in working days of fourteen to sixteen hours as unpaid labour in rural family concerns (Stamiris,

1988: 118). In large areas of (male) Greek society the issue of sexuality, especially of female sexuality, is still taboo because its possible existence may well be a threat to the male honour system (Kourvetaris & Dobratz, 1987: 158), an honour system that also forbids men to help women in the household. We can see in the context of these traditions how radical the answers were in the above mentioned European survey. It is likely that the data were gathered in major cities. Nevertheless, they are not invalidated by the existence of social customs contrary to views on domestic role-sharing, gender parity and equality of status before the law. Breaking down such social customs as the ones described is certainly an agenda item for many feminists (Papandreou, 1984). With the crumbling of old beliefs and practices, however, there has also been an increase in loneliness, isolation in old age, and in other miseries associated with modern urban living.

Kourvetaris and Dobratz do not believe that much will change socially or economically in the near future. Major economic changes seem unlikely. The trade union movement and the working classes have remained weak and so, in a fashion, has the middle class (1987: 119). The link between Greek nationalism and its religion weighs in favour of a religious state, even though religion in the cities is beginning to be far less of a factor of daily life than it was. The church continues to stand in the way of breaking down entrenched social practices and adherence to a tradition which helped to forge the Greek nation in the first place. One needs to note that in Greece more women are members of women's liberation organisations and more claim to be feminists than in any other western European country—4 percent overall membership in feminist organisations as against a European average of 1 percent (*Women and Men of Europe in 1983*: 47). This is all the more remarkable as overall Greek affiliation patterns are amongst the lowest in western Europe. Whether Greek feminism will ever become the kind of strong, political mass movement that is capable of taking on the church, which I believe it will have to do, appears doubtful at the moment. It seems more than likely, however, that the army's might has been checked, if not broken. With the disappearing predominance of the army went much of the worst machismo of Greek society. At least of the three traditional enemies of women's emancipation (the government, the military and the church) the Greek government has shown itself to be more of an ally of women than one might have expected, given the continuing pressure exerted by the church.

## ITALY

Compared with any other country in western Europe, Italy probably had the most impressive, politically active and far-reaching women's movement of the 1970s. It was large scale, extremely well organised, and strongly confrontational. The new Italian feminist movement included women from all strata of society. It claimed the strong support of working-class women and it engaged in political theory construction. Italian feminists were and are highly vocal, politically aware and engaged in politics to a degree one rarely finds anywhere else in Europe or, for that matter, in the world. Their movement managed to hold mass rallies simultaneously in various parts of Italy; in no other country were so many feminist slogans, songs and banners created, and so many hundreds of thousands of women mobilised; and perhaps in no other country were so many women injured, imprisoned or killed in their fight for liberation.

Many Italian feminists in the late 1980s believed that their struggle has not led to anywhere near the hoped-for changes (Hellman, 1987: 195). In Italy, however, it is perhaps more evident than elsewhere that the women's movement is largely responsible for many of the changes in the last two decades, be these in the legislature, in social policy, or with respect to political party successes or failures. If one were looking for effective grassroots activity against powerful political elites, one could choose Italy as an example. The modern Italian women's movement has been indeed the 'longest revolution' in postwar Italy. It came in the wake of a fundamental modernisation of Italian society and it has perhaps been the most important catalyst in the long process of transformation of Italian society (Pasquinelli, 1984: 132). The church and the ruling class, the male political elite, the patriarchs in families, the institutions of education and the bureaucracy all came under fire. Italian society needed to be transformed and uprooted from its sinister and misogynist fascist past and the medievalism of the catholic church.

Italy has always claimed at least two traditions, one democratic, emanating from the Renaissance cities of the north, revived by the freedom fighters of the *risorgimento* (national reawakening), and evidenced in the participatory principles of the workers' movements of the late 19th and early 20th centuries. The other, a machismo steeped in violence, spanning the rural Mafias and fascism, surfaced regularly as a reactionary force throughout the postwar period. It was the task of the new wave to confront the latter and to help the former to dominate public debate and political thinking. Women in Italy have done more than their share in the process of democratisation of Italian society.

The period from the 19th to the 20th century saw a continuity of left-based political culture and of women's active participation in it, complemented by women's independent organisations and political activity at grassroots level. This culture became a tradition that has flourished either openly or otherwise throughout the history of modern Italy. It is this tradition in which women were trained and they held onto it even in the worst of times. The strength of the new wave, I believe, was partly a consequence of the political culture in which it was spawned and it was based on a rare display of political literacy.

*From Renaissance to unification*

Italy, like France, can to some extent boast a *visible* women's history well before the onset of industrialisation and, in Italy's case, this was well before unification. Such a visible history, when typically confined to recounting the lives and achievements of exceptional women, is barely capable of teaching the political lessons necessary for political, social and cultural change. Yet at times when women have actively participated in political change and formulated their own platform for change on gender politics, the existence of such forebears can be psychologically strengthening. One of the messages conveyed by their memory is that not all women were victims and not all accepted their 'station' as predefined by an oppressive society.

Italian history, especially of the wealthy merchant centres of the northern principalities and kingdoms, furnishes many examples of successful independent womanhood and female scholarship, as for example during the Renaissance. Whether or not this phenomenon of learned women was simply a transitory mark of a time and its related beliefs, such as Renaissance individualism and 'an egoism of creation' (Heller, 1978: 199), is not the issue. In our context it is merely important that the memory of these women and of their achievements was never entirely erased, as a 19th century publication shows. Stanton wrote of these women in 1884:

> ... during the Renaissance women distinguished themselves not only in prose and poetry, thereby proving their equality and sometimes even their moral superiority to men, but they filled with distinction several of the most important chairs in the universities of Italy ... At the epoch when the famous medical school of Salerno flourished, in the fourteenth century, Abella, a female physician, acquired a great reputation in medicine and wrote books in Latin, and in the follwing centuries women professed the sciences and the classics in the universities of Bologna, Brescia, Padua, and Pavia. It is during this period that we encounter the names of Bettina Gazzadini, of Mazzoloni, whose bust is found among those of the most distinguished savants in the anatomical museum of Bologna; Laura Bassi, who lectured on physics in Latin; Marie delle Donne, Elena Cornaro, Clotilde Tambroni, and the celebrated Gaetana Agnesi whom no women and few men have ever equalled in the extent and profoundness of her learning and in the goodness of her heart. I shall not speak of the beautiful Novella di Andrea, of Laura Cereta-Lerina, at twenty professor of metaphysics and mathematics at the University of Brescia; of the celebrated Neapolitan, Martha Marchina, professor at a German university, an honour enjoyed at that epoch by Italian women alone; of Pellegrina Amoretti, of Isotta da Rimini, and of so many other heroic souls who, toiling in isolation and surmounting unheard-of difficulties, ever protested with word and pen against the inferiority attributed to their sex, and finally won the admiration of men. (Stanton, 1884: 312–13)

Curiously, Stanton omitted some of the most famous intellects of the Renaissance, such as the sisters Beatrice and Isabella d'Este, Vittoria Colonna, a poet and friend of Michelangelo, and the (in)famous Lucrezia Borgia, suspected of being a poisoner, who attracted many thinkers and artists to her court in Ferrara.

In later periods there were fewer women of renown recorded. During the period of *risorgimento* (national reawakening), which occupied the energies and ideas of its most progressive leaders for most of the 19th century (1815–1870), the issue of women and women's rights was almost entirely swamped by the urgent question of unification. There was one notable exception, namely the Casati Law of 1859, which permitted women to become teachers. But even then there were women amongst the dedicated nationalists, such as Sara Nathan and Carlotta Benettini, Garibaldi's wife Anita, and one ardent nationalist, Cristina di Belgiojoso, who combined these nationalistic pursuits with new ideas of feminism. In 1866 she published her *Scritto sulla Condizione della Donne* (Writings on the Condition of Women) (Morgan, 1984: 369).

Unlike Spain or Portugal, Italy had been split for centuries into a multitude of kingdoms and principalities, usually under the sovereignty of foreign rulers. Hundreds of years of history passed as different countries separated the various parts of Italy. Indeed, the north and south of Italy had not been united since the Roman Empire. The Bourbon monarchy had ruled in the south, the papal one in the centre, and Austrian domination had determined the fate of northern parts of Italy. Aristocratic elites in the south kept the peasantry in a state of bondage while in the north industrialisation had already begun to shape a modern industrial urban culture. Only in 1870, largely through the achievements of Garibaldi, Count Benso di Cavour and Mazzini who continuously kindled the movement of *risorgimento*, was Italy unified.

*From unification to Mussolini (1870–1919)*

Usually, three phases of feminism are identified within modern post-unification Italy (Bassnet, 1986: 93). I would like to claim, however, that there were at least four distinct phases, identifiable not just in terms of historico-political circumstances but in terms of their own agenda. The first phase began immediately following the unification of Italy. It was a suffragette and rights movement, spanning the time from the first unification in 1870 to the time of the monarch's consignment of power to Mussolini. During this first phase of Italian feminism (1870–1920) women began to make their mark on the new nation. In the 1870s and 1880s there were such able orators and writers as Anna Maria Mozzoni, Malvina Frank, Emilia Maraini and Gualberta Alaide Beccari. Beccari founded a journal called *La Donna*, published first in Venice just before unification and then in Bologna. It was devoted entirely to immediate social and political concerns for women. Under the patronage of Margherita, the Queen of Italy, another journal, called *La Cornelia*, flourished in Florence and attracted distinguished women jurists like Forlani, Gabba, Macchi and Urtoller who wrote about the women's question from a legal point of view. Everywhere women's organisations (*leghe*) sprung up. In 1878, De Sanctis opened two institutions of higher education for girls for training as primary school teachers.

Female worker organisations were formed and took very active political steps to fight for an improvement in wages and conditions. One such example is the initiatives of the rice pickers of the Emilia who organised themselves in 1883 and carried out a series of rather desperate struggles, confronting police and often losing their lives in the process. In 1889, textile women workers created the Union of Sisters of Work (Società delle Sorelle del Lavoro) to fight for a cut in working hours and an increase in wages. Before the elections of 1897, Anna Kulscioff established her fame by calling for an end to the dehumanising working conditions of one and a half million Italian women. It was her initiative that caused the Socialist Party of Italy to include the legal and political equality of men and women in its political programme, if only as a programme of emancipation (Fiocchetto, 1988: 24). In yet another violent demonstration of 1898 in Milan, this time against the rising cost of bread, Anna Kulscioff was one of many women arrested (Bassnet, 1986: 98–9).

Mozzoni, by contrast, stressed the need for the liberation of women. As early as 1864 she advocated the right to divorce, and in 1881 she founded a league for the promotion of women's interests (Lega promotrice degli interessi femminile) in Milan. This group has been identified as the feminist socialist forerunner of the important Unione Donne Italiane (Udi), founded in 1944, which existed throughout the post–World War II years, and retained an important voice even at the time of the new movement of the 1970s. In 1897 the first National Women's Union was formed in Rome, followed in 1899 by the National Women's Association in Milano, in 1903 by the National Council of Italian Women, and in 1910 by the National Committee for Women's Suffrage. In 1912 in Milan, a newly founded journal entitled *La difesa della lavoratrice* (The Defence of the Working Woman) espoused militant socialist ideas. Women's rights and the right to vote remained issues up to the takeover by the fascists.

It was significant that at least one part of the newly formed Italy had begun to industrialise at about the same time as several other western European nations. The new political ideologies of the left, gaining credence in the second half of 19th century Europe were, after all, based on the existence of an exploited working class whose labour was used in newly created factories for the production of a mass market. These ideologies made little sense in societies in which the new spirit of capitalism and industrialisation was absent. But in Italy, at least in Italy's industrialising north, the ideas had a material basis. When unification came, the disparities between the different parts of Italy showed up all the more clearly. In the light of the fundamental differences between north and south, the high level of illiteracy, the lack of national cohesion of customs and the historical experience and lifestyle, the introduction of a parliamentary democracy in 1870 within the setting of a constitutional monarchy was a mammoth task. There was little that could grow organically in this new nation. Combined with this was the lack of coherence within social interest groups and classes. Indeed, regional jealousies and competitions amongst aristocratic elites of various parts of Italy were the order of the day. As a result, the aristocracy was less effective in exerting its influence on a national scale than it had been on a local scale. Aristocrats tried to maintain power, of course, but as a class they were not as united as aristocratic elites elsewhere. The Vatican held its own sway, often against the interests of the ruling classes as well as the wider population. Indeed, much of the centre of Italy was marked by a strong anti-clericalism. Moreover, in the north and in the centre of Italy, particularly on the Italian shores, a lively merchant tradition (Genoa, Venice, Florence) and a strong renaissance bourgeoisie were still evident, even after the economic decline of these centres.

In the complex constellation of these historical developments, and of class, power, vested and new interests, Italy at once became receptive to the new worker's parties and the whole 'international' labour movement of Europe. Barely twenty years after the establishment of the nation, it was steered on a course of worker radicalism based on the new communist and socialist philosophies and party politics. Syndicalism developed as an attempt to bring industry and governmental power under labour union control by means of strike actions. Radical groups (anarcho-syndicalists) advocated the abolition of the state and its governmental structure and demanded the rule of workers by workers. Unions organised the first general strike throughout Italy in 1904, a good deal earlier than anywhere else in the western world, with the exception of Australia.

Italian unions of the early part of the 20th century were not just seeking monetary gains but political power vis-à-vis a state which had so obviously shown its lack of interest in the new urban and industrial problems of workers. In Turin a workers' militant political tradition began which some writers regard as 'one of the most exciting and inspiring chapters in modern Italian history' (Hellman, 1987: 113). Here, as well as in a few other northern centres, a factory council movement took hold that preached self-management (*autogestione*) and encouraged workers to express their views openly, if need be in strike actions. Under the leadership of Antonio Gramsci, a practically and theoretically well-founded leftist workers' culture emerged. It ushered in the 'red biennium' of labour struggles and became a visible driving force for action in international and local events which included a wave of strike actions involving as many as half a million workers throughout Italy at any one time, and lively anti-war demonstrations between 1911 and 1915. Women formed an active part of this workers' movement. We need not dwell here on the rifts within the political camps of the working class itself, nor on the oppositional stance between the working classes and the liberal bourgeoisie, who would have needed to unify in order to ward off the rise of fascism. Our interest here lies only in this fact: that a very lively political leftist culture had thrived in Italy and influenced power politics for longer than anywhere else in the western world.

## The Mussolini years and World War II

As happened in other countries, such worker influence was eventually doomed. The crisis of the power elites resulted in a regrouping of forces in order to break the grassroots movements, which had been aimed at toppling state power. In Italy, this regrouping took similar form to those in Portugal and Spain, ending in an alliance of sorts between the monarchy, the military, the church and the new fascist ideology. After 1919, with the formation of the fascist party under Benito Mussolini, any strike action and labour violence were brutally suppressed.

The second phase of Italian feminism coincided with these years of fascism. It lasted from 1922 to 1946. For women it was a significant period on two accounts. On the one hand, Mussolini's dictatorship manufactured a series of laws which were particularly directed against women. On the other hand, it created and fanned a resistance amongst women and men which, while largely fought underground, was often very active and typically very radical. If women had not been trained in political skills in the workers' movement, they certainly gained that experience in the resistance movement.

One of Mussolini's decisions, as retrogressive for women as for Italy's future, was to end the long-standing cold war with the Vatican by taking it back into Italy's political fold. The same man who, in his younger years, had rallied against the catholic clergy, saw it expedient in 1929 to sign the Lateran Concordat with the Vatican, reinstating the church into the power structure of the state and re-establishing the importance and pre-eminence of canon law in Italy. For one, the Concordat confirmed the indissolubility of the family and reconfirmed the dictum of Pope Leo XIII of 1880 that 'a man rules a woman as Christ rules his church'. It is not clear whether the church helped the dictator or whether Mussolini helped the church, but clearly on certain issues both benefited from the union.

Vatican views on women and family-related issues are well known and need only a brief mention here. What is important is that against the new secular Marxist thinking the catholic church became all the more reactionary and belligerent in defending church doctrine. In 1909, that doctrine was affirmed anew. Woman's contribution to the world was to be in the preservation of tradition, in her reproductive role as a mother, in her home-making, in her ability to look after others and in her devotion to making the family happy. Gainful employment outside the home was therefore seen as a severe corruption of women's role and, as it could have detrimental effects on the family, was also considered perverse. Embedded in the catholic doctrine was the belief that women had to be kept under firm male authority throughout their lives, by fathers, by brothers and by their husbands. In 1931 the encyclical *Quadragesimo anno* once again confirmed women's place as being in the home and thereby underlined some of Mussolini's decrees of the 1920s. The church regained control over divorce and marriage, a right that had long-ranging consequences for postwar Italian society, and it regained the power to pronounce judgements on abortion and reproduction. In some ways the fatal marriage between the fascist dictatorship and the church proved even more obnoxious than the totalitarian misogyny of the Nazis. Dictators could be deposed, defeated or killed. Neither Mussolini nor Hitler survived the nightmare of World War II, but the church was there to stay, as an institution in the very heart of modern Italy. Its reappearance in the politics of state and secular matters was indeed a severe setback, far more difficult to overcome than fascism itself (Glaab, 1980: 35–9).

Mussolini's consistent policies against women throughout his twenty-year dictatorship were also cheap and politically simple. In their implementation he needed to fear little resistance from the monarch, from the military or the church. Fascist anti-women legislation in fact began with a decree by the monarch, who in 1923 forbade the promotion of women to the position of school principals. Mussolini continued the trend. In 1926 he abolished council elections so that the few women who had gained an administrative vote for their work in World War I were deprived of making use of that right. Gradually, he discouraged women from working altogether and, if they did work their earnings were only half that of men.

Two further factors restricted women in new and threatening ways. One was concerned with population politics. Mussolini wanted to see a rapid population increase 'for the reinvigoration and increase of the race' and advocated that the ideal Italian family consist of parents and twelve children. To promote the process of 'maximum fecundity' he proclaimed in 1924 that any form of contraception and birth control was punishable by law. In 1930 it was declared that abortion carried extremely severe penalties; even those who simply aided abortion faced at least five years in prison. If, however, the husband, or any male relative, insisted on an abortion, even against the woman's will, there was little or no punishment. Mussolini levied taxes against 'unjustified celibacy' and he founded the Opera Nazionale Maternità e Infanzia (National Foundation for Mother and Child). Italian women, unlike German women, effectively resisted this invitation. The statistics reveal that under Mussolini the birthrate actually dropped, and in 1929 the rate of abortions was thought to be as high as 30 percent of all pregnancies (Birnbaum, 1986: 37).

Of immediate consequence were the new laws under the so-called Code Rocco, named after the minister Rocco, which fostered and permitted a degree of women's subordination never known before. They effectively disenfranchised the woman in her own home and made her a powerless sexual object and convenient tool in the hands of men. Adultery was made punishable for women but not for men. Physical chastisement of women and children was explicitly permitted by law and this form of 'control' was even encouraged under the guise of its being the husband's duty to 'correct' his wife's and children's behaviour when seen relevant. In case of death of the wife or children after severe beatings the punishment was extremely mild, if carried out at all. By law, women were not allowed to refuse intercourse with their husbands. They were not allowed to leave or 'stray from' the domicile against the husband's wishes, an act which was punishable by one years' imprisonment. Rape of a female prisoner by an officer was reclassified as misconduct and, if brought as a charge at all, was dealt with as an administrative matter.

As far as the affairs of women were concerned, this agreement between the *Duce* and the Vatican was a double-headed monster. The misogyny of one fed on that of the other. But matters are more complicated than suggested here. There were plenty of women as well as men who willingly followed Mussolini, believing that he was a liberating force for Italy, and they barely, if at all, saw or cared how his policies enslaved women more than ever. This is still a contentious point for feminist historians today and not easily resolved. Macciocchi explains it this way, if not entirely satisfactorily:

In a political regime the question of the influential and active support of women is connected with the superstructure of its most dense form, namely religion. It is at the very moment when religion, the centuries-old scourge of women, is no longer adequate as an ideological shield for the power apparatus of the rising bourgeoisie (the entry of female power as a force in the struggle occurred in the nineteenth and twentieth centuries with the Paris Commune and the October revolution) that fascism comes to the relief of the church guards. It is able to do this because of the submissiveness of women, whose instincts it can channel into a sort of new religious fervour which serves to support mass dictatorships and mass totalitarian regimes. The seizure of power by fascism and nazism uses as levers the martyred, baneful and necrophiliac femininity of Woman as Reproducer of the Species ... (1979: 68)

As a dictator Mussolini was certainly no more benign than Hitler but, leaving aside a number of rather crucial differences and similarities, he was certainly less efficient and less thorough. Mussolini never restructured the administration but allowed the power of local and regional bodies to remain largely intact. The infiltration of the Gestapo (Geheime Staatspolizei) into every corner of every one of the institutions in Germany contrasted with Mussolini's rather limp attempts to keep institutions and powerful subordinates in check. In Italy it was possible for the renowned thinker and activist Gramsci, at least in the early years, to compose much of his original work in a fascist prison. Lindemann maintains that such a feat would have been unthinkable in a Nazi concentration camp (Lindemann, 1983: 294). Nor did Mussolini have the undivided loyalty of his staff that Hitler had of his. For one, there was the Italian King Victor Emanuel who, despite his political insignificance for the twenty years of Mussolini's rule (1922–1943), still had his own loyal circle, and the oath of allegiance was sworn to him and the country rather than to Mussolini. Second, and more important at the time, was the fact that Mussolini never created a militia with either the thoroughgoing devotion to the leader or the unbending organised brutality of Hitler's Waffen SS, which functioned as a highly effective countervailing force against the military establishment. He also had far less control over his generals than Hitler.

Some of these weaknesses had important consequences. But first we need to retrace our steps to the beginnings of the fascist party in 1919 and point to the other, democratic Italian tradition which found its most significant expression in the foundation of the Communist Party in the 1920s. It was of course conceived of as a counterforce to the rise of fascism, and the fact that it survived twenty years of fascism, in a manner of speaking, can only be attributed to the slipshod way in which fascism was practised in Italy. The Communist Party at that time was an extremely progressive force which had attracted highly competent and intellectually brilliant people. The foundation of this party was certainly also one of the hallmarks in the history of women's emancipation and liberation, because under its umbrella the feminist movement stayed alive.

The Italian Socialist and Communist parties were generally no less patriarchal or misogynist than elsewhere in the world, but they were fortunate enough to be led by men or influenced by men and women who were far ahead of their times in promoting views of equality amongst the sexes, and who began to address women's issues as part of a national agenda for change. One of the most important people was without doubt Antonio Gramsci (1891–1937), editor of the communist newspaper, *L'Ordine nuovo*. He lent weight to the launching of another paper devoted entirely to women's issues, called *Tribuna delle donne*, renamed *Compagna* in 1922, which was edited by Camilla Ravera. Both Gramsci and Ravera were amongst the many who paid dearly for their political work. Gramsci was sentenced to twenty years imprisonment, a term which he did not survive, and Ravera was incarcerated for thirteen years before she was released in 1943. Another of the undoubted leaders of the left was Palmiro Togliatti, who served as general secretary of the Italian Communist Party (Pci) from 1926 to 1964. The role of Palmiro Togliatti cannot be exaggerated. His value to the party from prewar to postwar restructuring lay precisely in his long service: it ensured internal cohesion and continuity of party and ideas. He saw an intimate relationship between the women's question and democracy and socialism. In his view, the women's question was neither an issue of one single class nor of one single party but was an essential problem to be tackled if mass democracy, that is, participatory democracy was to become a reality at all.

There were also a number of leading intellectuals abroad who directly influenced Italian political ideals. The most famous and relevant of these leaders of international socialism, the women who had a profound effect on Italian feminist thinking during the 1920s and again during the 1970s (Birnbaum, 1986: 26–7), were Rosa Luxemburg and Clara Zetkin. Another of great renown and importance for socialist women's movements at the time was Aleksandra Kollontaj (1872–1952), a Russian activist who became a socialist after seeing the misery and exploitation of women workers in factories (Mullaney, 1983). She combined socialism and feminism, but insisted that women's rights could not wait until after the socialist revolution. In 1917, she was the only woman in the first Russian Bolshevik government and a year later she organised the first all-Russian Congress of Working and Peasant Women. She was also a prolific writer and amongst her influential works were her books *The Social Basis of the Woman Question* (1908), *Society and Motherhood* (1916) and *The New Morality and the Working Class* (1918). Unlike her contemporaries she also broached highly controversial issues such as sexual love and relationships freed from the bondage of marriage. It is noteworthy that, to my knowledge, the Italian Communist Party was the only party in the world which took up the *questione femminile* (women's question) at that time, not just as one of the urgent *social* problems, but instead as 'one of the great unresolved *national* questions' (emphasis added, Hellman, 1987: 29).

It is true that by the end of the 1920s Mussolini had either exiled, jailed or killed nearly all socialist and communist leaders. Irrespective of this, the strong organised political left of the working class was never so completely thwarted in Italy as in Salazar's Portugal or in Hitler's Germany. Thus, while socialist and communist-led movements were suppressed for almost a generation, there were just enough loopholes in Mussolini's system to permit the survival of ideas and of those people who could give them weight. In a clandestine fashion they lived on, and as the brutality of Mussolini's system became more apparent they gained in strength to become a strong underground resistance movement under the auspices of communists, socialists and christian democrats.

The *partigiani* (partisans), unlike the hired soldiers of Mussolini, were known and respected for their bravery and heroism. Italians called this resistance to fascism their second *risorgimento*. The racial laws, for instance, that Mussolini introduced to Italy in 1938, copying the German example, never became entirely enforcible and certainly never led to the mass extermination of Jews as was happening in other western European countries. In Italy, as in Bulgaria, Luxembourg and France, the majority of Jews survived. Altogether 80 percent of

Italian Jews were saved by Italians in well-organised underground activities (Dawidowicz, 1986: 403; Birnbaum, 1986: 34, 43; Zuccotti, 1987).

Women played an important role. It is estimated that of the 200 000 partisans throughout Italy over 70 000 were women. There is, however, considerable disagreement on the numerical strength of the partisan movement. Some agree that these official figures are far too low and their estimates range from 200 000 to as high as 2 million (Bassnet, 1986: 104). Women were sometimes organised in war groups like the Gruppi femminile di assistence ai combattenti della liberazione (women's groups for aid and resistance fighters) and Gruppi femminili antifascisti (anti-fascist women's groups). By 1943 the protests became visible, especially in centres like Milan and Turin, demanding an end to deportations to Nazi concentration camps and the end of fascist and Nazi massacres. Women's defence groups (Gruppi di difesa della donna) formed in 1943 providing strike support to partisans (Beckwith, 1985: 22). Clearly it was the anti-fascist unity which gave the feminist movement its strength in those last war years. Camilla Ravera, the grand leader of women's resistance against fascism, rejoined the resistance once her prison term was over. She said of that time:

> There were hundreds and hundreds of women who enrolled in the ranks of the partisans as fighters. But there were thousands and thousands of women active in the liberation movement: they stored arms, carried arms, relayed orders, looked after the wounded, kept lines of communication open and so on ...
>
> The participation of women in the movement to liberate Italy from fascism and build a more just society actually signified their place under the new conditions. Not for nothing was one of the first depositions among the laws established after Liberation the granting of the vote to women. And in the first Parliament of the Republic there were more than fifty women representatives. At that point in time women gave such a convincing, clear display of the fact that they did know how to think politically, how to choose, take decisions, get together even in struggle ...
>
> And during the reconstruction, when there was still a sense of anti-fascist unity, women worked miracles. (Scroppo, 1979: 26; translation Bassnet, 1986: 104–5)

In 1944 women openly celebrated International Women's Day in Milan. If anything, the war which Italy entered in 1940 began to act as a cover for clandestine activities at home, the government's attention being firmly focused on international events and on the Italian losses.

One of Mussolini's worst strategic errors, which ultimately led to his downfall, was his inability to judge correctly Italy's capacity for military action. He entered the war when Italy could ill afford it and was not prepared for it. He led Italian troops from one defeat to the next. Indeed, he won no victories at all. Italians failed to occupy Greece, eventually doing so only after the German army had intervened. He lost his Ethiopean war to a handful of British troops, saw the Italian forces annihilated in North Africa, and was unable to ward off the occupation of western Allies only weeks after he had promised publicly that Allies would never set foot on Italian soil. It is not only that his brand of fascism ran out of steam, but that Mussolini himself lost credibility, and this 'bred a profound cynicism' in the Italian people (Latey, 1972: 299–300). The power elites, such as industrialists, chiefs of staff of the army and the king himself began to criticise him openly. Eventually they succeeded in deposing Mussolini by a simple but well-planned coup. In 1943, workers, especially women, in Turin and Milan went on long-lasting strikes. The population was tired of the charades. They, as well as the power elites, wanted separate peace treaties, independent of Hitler's plans. The country felt deeply humiliated by the war and mass desertions became the order of the day.

The importance of the organised resistance lay less in their faint political clout during the war than in the assessment of their role after the war. There was a good deal Italians wanted to forget after 1945, such as the accusations that the Italian soldiers were cowardly, Italy's alliance and collaboration with Hitler, and the excesses of fascism within Italy. The discovery of the courage of the partisans and the existence of a strong resistance movement furnished just the right ingredients to rid many Italians of their feelings of shame. Hellman perhaps goes a little far in suggesting that the sacrifices of the *partigiani* 'cleansed the country' of the 'stain of collaboration with fascism and opposition to the Allies' (Hellman, 1987: 12), but they did contribute to this process. The success of the resistance movement lent a new respectability to those who had been its participants, and this helped to reconstitute communist, socialist and other parties after the war. More than that, irrespective of the ensuing events of the cold war, including the excommunication of communists by the Vatican, the spirit of the *partigiani* resistance movement took the *leadership* in the creation of Italian democracy, and was behind the forging of a new constitution for Italian society, the society that Italy wanted to become.

## The postwar years

The immediate postwar years were a time of considerable rhetoric and idealism and we may well ignore a good deal of its pathos with the hindsight of historical rationalism. But it was an important time, not just in terms of the good intentions of a people who had to rebuild their society but in terms of the immediate actions that were taken. The Italian Communist Party (Pci) and the Italian Socialist Party (Psi) were instrumental in the drafting of a new republican constitution. It gave women the right to vote and it enshrined the concept of equality between men and women. Like the French, the Italians too took these measures in recognition of women's crucial role in the resistance movement. But unlike the French, they were willing to concede that now, in peacetime, women should retain an important political role in order to create and defend democracy. The king's role in the fascist era led to the abolition of monarchy and to the declaration of the republic by public referendum in 1946. And women used the vote at once. In the 1946 communal elections 53 percent of voters were women and as many as 81 percent of all adult women went to the polls (Glaab, 1980: 47). Palmiro Togliatti exerted influence by continuing to support the rights of Italian women and contributing to their involvement in the restructuring of Italy. It was partly his initiative that women's cells were organised within the Pci and that a good number of women, 22 altogether, became delegates of the constituent assembly (Camera dei Deputati). Yet, as far as women were concerned, the role of the Pci must not be romanticised. For women to enter parliament after the first free elections in 1946 required a little more than just party-room discussion. Indeed, women had to gather in mass demonstrations to exert enough pressure for this to happen. We need to note here that women who had for the first time formed a mass movement during the period of resistance were skilled and experienced enough to orchestrate mass rallies. They continued to be a force with which to be reckoned.

Italian leftist politicians were concerned that the new system of free elections in postwar Italy might lead to a resurgence of fascism amongst an uneducated electorate. They therefore created the Italian Women's Union, (Unione donne Italiane—Udi), which initially consisted of women from all political parties, though it was financed and run by the Pci. This women's union developed directly out of several resistance groups, among them the partisan Gruppi di difesa della donna. The latter had published its own newspaper, *Noi Donne*, which had been founded in France in 1936 by exiled Italian women. By the end of 1943 it first appeared underground in Milano, Turin, Florence, Genoa and Reggio Emilia. By 1944 it was officially the new paper of Udi (Fiocchetto, 1988: 26). Initially therefore, the core membership of the Udi largely consisted of women who had been anti-fascist activists experienced enough to take on an important leadership role for the large masses of women who were known to be conservative or ill informed. One such typical example of a resistance veteran in the Udi was Elina Zaghi, a working-class woman from northern Italy who had spent much of her life in the communist resistance movement (Kertzer, 1982).

The Pci and Psi knew that granting women the vote would initially work against their own political interests because women would favour the more conservative and traditional centre beliefs of the christian democrats (Beckwith, 1985: 19–21). Indeed, this is what happened. Moreover, just a year after the foundation of Udi, a conservative catholic women's centre, called *Centro Italiano Femminile*, (CIF), was formed. This attracted a large membership at once and split Italian women into two camps, a division that even in the heyday of the 1970s was barely overcome by the feminist movement. While the CIF stressed family life and women's rightful place in it, the Udi was more concerned with reforms of a broader nature. Yet the Udi's chief role was still to eliminate fascism, and in women's issues it acted under the direction of the Pci rather than of its own accord.

The period after these first postwar struggles, which I have called the third phase of Italian feminism (1946–1968) was a diffuse period. At first, feminist political activities increased. In 1948, for instance, women within the Socialist and Communist parties formed an *alleanza femminile* (women's alliance) and the Udi was initially able to attract more women. By 1949, it had one million members and *Noi Donne* was selling over 200 000 copies weekly throughout Italy (Birnbaum, 1986: 55). The Udi was also the first women's organisation that openly discussed abortion and did so in print (in 1961). Women's membership in the Pci gradually declined, however, and issues pertaining to women were seen less and less on the political agenda. The initiatives of the Udi tended to focus around *assistenziali* (aid and support) for veterans and striking workers, and for services of use to women, such as day-care centres and communal laundries (Hellman, 1987: 115). The political work of the Udi began to falter around 1959 under the onslaught of the new materialist revival of capitalism and the growing recovery and economic expansion of Italy. But this meant that there were just ten years between the waning of feminist activity and the onset of the new movements of the 'hot summer' in 1969.

Thus, despite the momentary flagging of direction and of political programmes of organisations like the Udi, it is clear that their ongoing existence provided a certain ideological continuity from the prewar years onwards. The organisation and the party eventually had to learn that in the postwar years it was no longer enough to be just *against* a political foe, and one that was fading from view, but that concrete plans and programmes for the present and future had to be forged which would be applicable within the altered social, political and economic conditions of Italian society.

In the post–World War II years, Italian society became more clearly split into Marxist and catholic blocs and Italian governments had to accommodate their own short-lived status and extreme instability. Amidst this instability, however, there was an element that has often been referred to as 'immobilism', suggesting that there was very little movement in postwar Italy. I prefer to agree with Tarrow and replace the term 'immobilism' with that of 'political continuity' as an important feature in Italy's postwar political culture. His observations here certainly tally with mine concerning the continuity of political culture, not just in terms of ideas but in terms of individuals who continued to be involved in political activism. He writes:

> What shows through all the existing studies, however, is the tremendous continuity of the political elite, and the origins of even today's leaders in the crisis period of the 1940s. This is frequently taken as evidence of immobilism, and it is certainly true that the experiences of the anti-fascist resistance and the early cold war did little to prepare today's leaders to deal with the problems of an advanced industrial democracy. But our concern is with the maintenance of democracy, and not with its efficiency of operation: where this is in question, the content of the Italian elite's formative ex-periences—anti-fascism, the establishment of democracy, national unity—seems more important than its age or lack of expertise. We may even suppose that a political class forged in crisis would possess more resources to deal with the crises of today than one that grew up amid the routine problems of administering the prosperity of the 1950s or 1960s. (1980: 171)

The high degree of political 'literacy' of women in the new postwar movement of the 1960s and 1970s has thus at least two origins. Clearly, the existence of a long-standing political culture in which women were active was one precon-dition. Another must be sought in the fact that as long as modern Italy has existed, women have never been struck off the agenda of political parties or off the social policy calendar for any length of time.

*New-wave feminism*

The new wave, itself a sign of crisis and upheaval, was preceded by years of substantial unrest and economic growth. Between 1945 and 1983 (i.e. in a mere 38 years) Italy had a total of 44 national governments, mostly, however, under the leadership of the Christian Democrats. This constant change in government has sometimes been attributed to Italy's multiparty system, but this is nonsense. Scandinavian countries have long since had multiparty systems and very stable systems of government. If anything, as Tarrow observed, other western Euro-pean countries have moved towards multiparty systems in recent times and, as he suggests, have become 'italianised'.

The instability of the Italian political system in the first of the postwar years was not so much an indication of shortcomings in the political structure or of the politicians at the helm but rather of the vast and overwhelming changes in Italy's economic structure and international role. Italy's rise in economic for-tunes followed on almost immediately from the signing of the Treaty of Rome in 1957. The growth rate jumped drastically between 1958 and 1962, doubling Italy's GNP in a period of less than ten years in the wake of increasing in-dustrialisation, urbanisation and a rapid secularisation. Italy simultaneously suffered a population explosion, with pressure on available housing and resources, and an increased demand. In 1947, Italy had a population of 47 million; by 1978 it had risen to 57 million.

Italy clearly had its own postwar economic miracle, accompanied by a re-markable rise in living standards, which was aided by a number of factors. One was the temporary emigration of labour to other European countries. Like the Spanish and Portuguese people, Italians signed contracts as guest workers, mainly in West Germany and Switzerland, and returned remittances to their families at home. Money was also imported via the tourist industry. As in Austria and Spain, tourism became a chief source of income. Italy's favourable position with respect to the rest of Europe made the country a much sought after holiday playground for wealthier Europeans. Italy has never lost its position as the European supplier of summer sun, beaches and good food, and its tourist industry has continued to show staggering increases in financial returns. In 1977 Italy made over US$14 million and in 1986 over US$53 million in tourism alone (*Fischer Weltalmanach '90*, 1989: 927; *'81*, 1980: 899). This contributed substantially to Italy's postwar economic development.

Nevertheless, Italy's economic miracle was mainly based on the availability of cheap labour from its south and from the rural areas of the north. This, in turn, had a number of important social and political consequences. In only fifteen years, between 1940 and 1966, the agricultural workforce dropped from 40 percent to 24 percent and by 1977 it had gone down still further, to 13 percent. Expressed differently, in the early 1950s only half of the population was dependent on salaries and wages while in the late 1970s well over three-quarters of the population relied entirely on payments from employers (Barkan, 1984: 9). The steel industry boomed and by 1975 Italy had become the largest supplier of steel in Europe after West Germany and France. Out of this agricultural pool a new working class developed which was not just unaccustomed to city life, but which was unwilling to accept without complaint the poor conditions that their new life offered amidst the rising living standards of Italian society. The combination of this new urban working class with the established, highly sophisticated, disciplined and well-organised working class of the industrial triangle in the north was indeed a volatile combination that promised industrial trouble (Tarrow, 1980: 177). In addition, there emerged yet another new, disenfranchised group, the urban *lumpenbourgeoisie* which had little patience with prevailing conditions.

The first severe test of the Italian economy came between 1963 and 1964 when demand began to falter, resulting in sudden and unexpected massive unemployment. Women were particularly hard hit: a total of 700 000, or 11 percent, lost their jobs within less than a year (Glaab, 1980: 73). By the end of the 1960s, the situation was extremely explosive, particularly in the northern industrial cities like Turin. Here, a variety of movements began to coincide, such as the squatters' occupation of houses, the student movement, workers' actions and a somewhat generic urban movement, concerned with a shortage of housing, services and schools. Young people and students began to protest against US involvement in Vietnam (Hellman, 1987: 22, 137).

1969, the year of the 'hot summer' of mass strikes, marked a turning point in Italian postwar life and the beginning of a social and economic crisis which did not subside until more than a decade later. It saw the extraordinary alliance between the catholic working-class trade unions and the left-wing student groups, an alliance not too dissimilar to that which brought about the May Movement revolt of 1968 in France. It saw the spectacular rise of a militant working class united for the first time in its fight for new qualitative social demands. The spontaneous waves of worker and student uprisings in 1968 and 1969 were an attempt to establish mass participation and rank-and-file democracy (Frogett, 1981; Torchi, 1981). The worker militancy, especially pronounced in the years of 1968 to 1972, eventually altered the nature of organised labour and the balance of power within Italy (Hellman, 1987: 21). In 1970 the council movement of the 1920s finally bore the fruit of official recognition of the *consiglio di fabrica* (factory council) in the Workers' Statute. But such victories were not sufficient to keep the general unrest in abeyance.

The years from 1969 to 1975 were particularly intense. Italy slid into a headlong crisis. Capital flight, high inflation rates, high unemployment (especially in the south) and a high number of strike days became the order of the day. The oil crisis of 1974 hit Italy at a very vulnerable stage and sent the inflation rate soaring to 25 percent. At the same time, Italy continued to expand extremely rapidly both in its industrial operations and in transport and communication. The number of freeways alone almost doubled between 1968 and 1978. Clearly, Italy underwent profound changes and at a rate in which social, geopolitical and political adjustments were severely lagging behind economic developments and general realities of the day. In this process of development, increasing segmentation and fragmentation was unavoidable. An Italian observer very poignantly remarked of the time: 'We Italians are in transit from the past to the future of industrial capitalism without having lived through its present' (cit. in Tarrow, 1980: 176).

During this period Italian women who participated either in student or worker strikes began to learn a lesson that French and German feminists were also learning at about the same time: their participation in a class-based programme of dissent left no room for women to express dissent on a gender basis. In the class war about to be unleashed in Italy, the universalistic appeal, despite some lip-service being paid, was decidedly lacking when it came to women's issues. If women were to voice matters of immediate concern to them, they would have to find that voice outside this political subculture of dissent. Balbo rightly observed that much of the debate on the Italian crisis and its transformation was, and partly still is, gender-blind (Balbo, 1988: 67).

The survival of more than just remnants of the terrible legacies of fascism had not gone unnoticed by women. For women, the fascist era would not be over until the oppressive laws against them had been removed from the Italian law books. In many cases this did not occur before the 1970s, partly because conservative forces, chiefly the church, had more than tacitly supported the fascist family laws and had little or no interest in supporting any law reforms. Well into the 1960s, for instance, fascist employment laws remained intact, barring women from law and diplomatic careers and limiting their numbers to 10 percent of jobs in the public service. The law that allowed employers to dismiss female employees upon their marriage was not repealed until 1963. When the new wave began in 1970, there were substantial salary differences for work by men and women, and women occupied the lowest rungs of the educational ladder (Merkl, 1976: 134). Indeed, fascist laws had effectively eliminated women from the workforce, except for young girls working towards marriage. In 1871, 48 percent of the total workforce had been women. Exactly one hundred years later, the participation rate of women in the workforce had declined to 17 percent (Glaab, 1980: 74). In 1971, 5 percent of Italian women were illiterate, 27 percent had not completed primary school and a further 44 percent had no education beyond elementary level, that is, seven in ten Italian women had had just the minimum exposure to formal education (Glaab, 1980: 52). In areas of family law the influence of church and fascism remained equally strong for at least two decades after the new Italian Republic was founded. Up to 1967 adultery was punishable only for women, and up to the change in family law in 1976 girls could be married off at the age of 12. Abortions were of course strictly prohibited and it was not before 1971 that the fascist law forbidding the advertisement or sale of contraceptives was rescinded (Barkan, 1984: 133). Most intended law reforms in the areas of family law, reproduction, and women and work were bound to challenge church doctrine and set the scene for bitter struggles. Even the Communist Party was loath to carry out reforms that might split the electorate by alienating the devoutly catholic sectors, and that fear was fueled further by the example of Chile and the murder of Allende in 1973.

Italy had the additional problem that from its south, especially from Sicily, emanated an economy based on violence, and a violence that was ritualised and mystified as a measure of masculinity (*omertà*). The Mafia has a long history: it originally evolved in 19th century Sicily as a parallel system of power exerted locally against the authority of the Bourbons and, later, against the Piedmontese governments, and developed as an aberration of rural capitalism. Its leaders were typically wealthy men of the rural middle class, capitalist farmers and contractors (Hobsbawm, 1974: 37). It is one organisation that benefited from US occupation by its establishing a link to the USA and encouraging international routes of black-marketeering and drug-trafficking. The Mafia has not been stamped out to this day despite some postwar measures against it, and while it may have started out as a movement of 'primitive rebels' (Hobsbawm, 1974) against foreign rulers, its system of *omertà* and *onore* is cowardly: in essence, it permits the denunciation only of the weak and the defeated (Hobsbawm, 1974: 32). Women are certainly in the latter category. Machismo values are not just held by the *mafioso* but have spread and been maintained by large sections of southern Italy. Machismo values are tolerant of rape and the kidnapping of a girl as long as the 'suitor' then marries her. It condones male violence against women when the latter have in any way offended or impaired the male code of honour (Moss, 1988: 77). Much of that honour is invested in men's proprietary role over women which required women, amongst other things, to remain pure and entirely unblemished. A survey conducted at the height of the women's movement in the mid-1970s revealed that 39 percent of all men interviewed in the north of Italy wanted a virgin for a wife and in the south a staggering 72 percent of men insisted on the virginity of the bride as a prerequisite of marriageability (Glaab, 1980: 70). The belief in the desirability of virginity was coupled with a paranoid system of supervision of young girls and women, and seemingly justified a myriad of mechanisms for women's oppression. Bielli noted that in the south, wives were more readily seen as a slaves than as companions (1976: 106). Neither the church nor male heads of families were likely to give up vested interests with ease. Nor would one expect fast and voluntary changes amongst men who had so thoroughly incorporated the machismo of the honour system in the south. How alive the issues of machismo still are is exemplified, among other things, by a most unusual feminist organisation. A 1982 organisation, formed by Mafia widows, made it its explicit goal to fight against the culture of male violence and female submissiveness (Morgan, 1984: 370).

When the new wave began, the stage was thus set for violent clashes and confrontations against a misogyny that was deeply entrenched in Italian thinking. The fourth phase of Italian feminism expanded to a true mass movement, which exploded in 1970 and died down around 1978. Its strength was an index of the strength of the opposition to women's liberation or just to women's rights. Indeed, the opposition had been formidable. But women were well 'armed' to meet the challenge both in terms of their political skills and organisational abilities and in terms of the knowledge of their own oppression and their tradition of fighting against it. But unlike movements in other countries, its concern was not to participate in the political agenda but, 'to determine the content' of this agenda (Beckwith, 1985: 20).

It was in 1970 that the Women's Liberation Movement (Movimento di liberazione della donna—Mld) was officially founded in Rome, but there were groups which preceded the foundation of this organisation. The very first political group which demanded a separate analysis of women's position in society emerged out of the worker's movement as early as 1967, calling itself DEMAU for *demistificazione autoritaria* (demystification of authority). Another group, formed during the student uprising of 1969, was called the Cerchio spezzato (Broken Circle). This group used as the basis for their analysis a quote from Marx: 'The necessity to do without the illusions concerning one's own condition is the necessity to do without conditions that need illusions', setting the scene for an agenda of a radical transformation of society (Wunderle, 1977: 61, 70; see also Spagnoletti, 1971). Perhaps not surprisingly, the first new-wave feminist group in Italy was founded in Turin (Collettivo delle Compagne), formed by women who had also been members of a new-left organisation called Communicazioni Rivoluzionarie. These political groups had sprung up in Turin, Rome and Milan and their ideology had been informed not just by the northern triangle worker tradition but also by radical groups of the US, such as the Young Lords or the Black Panthers with whom they corresponded (Hellman, 1987: 119). New types of feminist collectives (*alternativa femminista*) developed in the early 1970s and from then on other groups developed very quickly throughout Italy, many of them as consciousness-raising groups (*autocoscienza*), but many beginning to be active in unions and within the political party structure.

Broadly speaking, it has been possible to identify four different strands of the movement which evolved in the early 1970s (Pisciotta, 1986: 27). One was the autonomous branch, forming the backbone of the extra-parliamentary opposition, a second one developed out of the new left, a third grouping was led and organised by the Udi and a fourth was the Mld. Another group founded in 1970, Rivolta Femminile, eventually developed into the famous collective Lotta Femminile (Feminist Struggle). Mld and the Colletivo Femminista Romana, later called Pompeo Magno, belonged to the autonomous strand. The Mld and the Udi initially had very strong ties with political parties. The Mld was part of the left Socialist Party and the Udi was still the same mass organisation for women that the Pci had formed in the immediate postwar years. In 1975, a split in the Mld led to the founding of Movimento di Liberazione della Donna Autonomo (Mlda) which maintained a strong association with workers.

One of the earliest and still most significant documents of the movement (Bassnet, 1986: 108) was the manifesto *Sputiamo su Hegel* (we spit on Hegel) by Rivolta Femminile, and another was a pamphlet by the Mld on the issue of abortion. A number of large-scale events took place at this time, among them a 'smile strike' by Naples cashiers, who refused to be nice to customers until work conditions and salaries were improved (Morgan, 1984: 369). The movement continued to produce a myriad of groups, all with their own agenda and political programme (see Birnbaum, 1986: 91 for listing of most groups). The year 1976 marked a caesura in Italian life in as much as it brought to a close the 'period of widespread mobilisation that had been inaugurated by the students' revolt' (Ergas, 1982: 272).

The first large-scale mobilisation of women occurred on International Women's Day in 1974 in Mestre near Venice. It was undoubtedly the abortion issue that helped to create cohesion between feminist groups and brought out a wide net of women supporters for the new wave. In 1972 alone, the pope had spoken on six separate occasions in favour of maintaining the anti-abortion law and he adamantly supported the severe punishment that the fascist law meted out to offenders. Despite papal opposition to many proposed changes, civil divorce became possible in 1974, the issue having been settled in parliament more or less by men without much input from feminists. The abortion issue carried with it a far larger lobby of disapproval, however, and anti-abortion speeches by representatives of the Vatican were frequent. It was a fight in which women were very much on their own.

In 1973 a socialist parliamentarian first presented a very meek abortion law reform proposal. His submission unleashed an outcry from the church and its ecolites. In the first instance, this lobby was powerful enough to prevent the bill from being discussed within parliament. When women learned of the demise of the bill proposal, they went on hunger strikes and demonstrations, but achieved absolutely nothing. On the contrary, following these demonstrations, there was a court case made against a member of Lotta Femminista for having aborted. In 1974 in Trient, 263 women were charged with the crime of abortion and in January 1975 the illicit abortion clinic in Florence was raided and closed down by police. Leading doctors and 40 patients, some of them still under anaesthetic, were charged and arrested. We need to remember that abortion carried very severe and long prison terms at the time. The outrage of women around the country was so overwhelming that the movement at once grew substantially and became noticeably more demonstrative and radical in its protest. Self-accusatorial, 'I have aborted' campaigns' followed in the wake of the first provocations. A 1974 survey in *Panorama* showed that the mood of the public had swung strongly in favour of the removal of the fascist anti-abortion law (Pisciotta, 1986: 35). In 1975 feminists in Rome set up a committee for abortion and contraceptives (Comitato Romano aborto contracettivo). In 1975 another abortion bill was drafted but this time it managed to get to the House for discussion, mainly because public pressure had increased. It stated that decisions on abortion were to be in the hands of a medical commission. When women learned of this they were provoked by the prospect of a decision about their own bodies and their own lives being handed over to a committee of medical men. Large demonstrations were the result, and on 6 December 1975 women gathered in their tens of thousands in Rome. Out of this demonstration grew the Collective of 6 December which made it its business to deal exclusively with the abortion issue (Wunderle, 1977: 21–5).

The problem with the abortion issue was that even progressive parties were loath to take it on board for fear of alienating the catholic masses. In the abortion debates of 1976 there were mass demonstrations in favour of abolishing the law and replacing it by a humane new law. At the same time a secret ballot inside parliament revealed that a very small majority of politicians (about 290 votes) still wished to see abortion as a crime. The issue was powerful enough in 1976 to topple the Moro government. The new feminist tactic then changed to the party room, with the Udi beginning to exert pressure on the Pci. The Udi forced the Pci to change the abortion bill to a 'right to choose' bill, and Udi members did so by lobbying for more women candidates. The tactic succeeded well enough at the time because the feminist lobby in the Pci managed to increase the number of women deputies from 21 (1972) to 45. Yet the abortion bill was still not on its way to success. First it was blocked in parliament and then, in 1977, the conservatives launched a right-to-life movement (Movimento per la Vita), well organised and with its campaigns richly endowed by the catholic church.

It took yet another year before a new modified bill managed to be passed in parliament. It was extremely restrictive and nowhere near fulfilled the demands feminists had made. It specified that the minimum age for an abortion was 18 years of age, and the maximum period within which an abortion could be carried out was 90 days and then only under very specific conditions. It specified furthermore that 'conscientious objection' was a legitimate claim by a doctor to refuse to carry out an abortion, a proviso which predictably would make it almost impossible for a woman in the more traditional south to obtain one. Yet despite these severe restrictions, during the first year after the law had been passed over 187 000 abortions were registered and three years later more than a quarter of a million abortions had been performed legally. This was not the end of the abortion issue, however. The bill was challenged twice in the coming years and mass rallies continued to be needed to safeguard the little that had been achieved. In each of the challenges, the feminist lobby won (Pisciotta, 1986: 40–3). Pisciotta rightly points out that even in this restrictive form, the abortion bill was a major success of the movement. Indeed, it represented a cultural revolution in which the population won against the most powerful of Italian institutions, the church.

Throughout the 1970s, the publicity about feminist issues increased dramatically, due to women's own initiative. Publishing houses were founded, such as Edizione delle Donna, I libretti verdi and La Tartaruga, publishing some of the material from the immense proliferation of women's writing in this period. The first regular feminist publication, apart from *Noi Donne*, still published by the Udi, was the monthly magazine *Effe*, which was founded in 1973 and produced its first volume in 1974. Three years later its circulation was 27 000, thereafter 50 000 and, for a long time, it was the largest feminist magazine in western Europe. It had a wide appeal and was purchasable at any newsstand. In 1978 this was followed by *Quotidiano Donna*, and then by several other newspapers, magazines and journals, such as *Differenze*, *Rosa*, *Sottosopra*, *Donnawomanfemme*, and *Memoria*. Wunderle claims that, unlike West German feminist publishing, the Italian movement produced fewer pamphlets and small publications but instead had several magazines, journals and newspapers with very large circulations (Wunderle, 1977: 43). This, however, is debatable. I counted at least 30 journals and magazines, amongst them small publications, which had attracted attention as feminist publications. The Italian feminists also managed to secure their own television and radio programmes. The programme 'Si dice donna' (Thus says the woman), for instance, had eight million viewers. The radio programme 'noi, voi, loro, donna' (we, you, they, woman) was also very popular (Colombo, 1981: 466). Radio stations and newspapers generally took on board debates of feminist issues, indicating the great importance attributed to the movement in Italy. From 1973 on there was also a multitude of cultural associations and activities, such as feminist art and fine art exhibitions, feminist bookshops (such as La Maddalena in Rome) and theatre collectives.

In conjunction with these developments, the Pci experienced a spectacular revival in the years 1973 to 1976, attracting an enormously large membership (Pinto, 1981: 14–17). In 1976 the Pci had a membership of 1.8 million people and gained 34.4 percent of the votes in the parliamentary elections (Barkan, 1980: 49, 62). The importance of the Pci during the 1970s cannot be exaggerated and it is not without significance that these coincided with the peak years of the feminist movement. Nor can one ignore the conclusions that the Pci drew from contemporary events. While historically it had guided and supervised much of its own women's organisation (Udi) and activities, the party now agreed that social movements needed to remain largely separate and independent of the party if they were to follow their own momentum and agenda successfully. Unlike most other communist parties in western Europe, the Italian Pci was adaptable and willing to gear its programmes to local political realities. As a result of the Hungarian Uprising in 1956 and Soviet intervention in Czecho-slovakia in 1968, the party had weakened ties with the USSR, and after the invasion of Afghanistan it eventually broke them. As a party, it had made attempts to offer a political programme that was relevant to larger segments of Italian society rather than just its working class. Of crucial relevance also to the women's movement was the party's willingness to support a 'third way' (*terza via*) towards social transformation in Italy (Beckwith, 1985: 27). Conversely, the feminist movement did its share in promoting the left ahead of the conservative Christian Democrats, who saw their membership steadily eroded throughout the 1970s, reaching an all time low of 33 percent in 1983, the year when the first socialist prime minister in Italian history was sworn in. Enrico Berlinguer, the Pci party secretary, acknowledged that women have caused the downfall of 'one government after another'. In agreement with Berlinguer, feminists claimed credit for the decline of the Christian Democrats (Birnbaum, 1986: 95).

## Violence and gender warfare

The 1970s polarised Italian society, making change in any direction a difficult feat. At the same time as progressive forces made very radical and novel plans for a thorough reassessment of values and norms, another force threatened to destroy or undermine all advances made. The Movimento Sociale Italiano, a new neo-fascist force, attracted increasing voter interest and, in the 1972 elections, managed to gain 8.7 percent of the vote. This ultra-right group specialised in terrorist activities. In its bombing of a Milanese bank in 1972 it wanted to provoke a 'strategy of tension'. Soon after, subversive left-wing terrorism followed suit. Terrorism in Italy, as in Spain and West Germany, was like the outbreak of a belated and virulent disease inherited from the nightmare of fascism.

Hence, the Italy of the 1970s had to contend not only with massive unrest and with the uprising of various movements and their legitimate claims, but also with the worst terrorism experienced in any western European country. These forces led the anti-democratic backlash. As in West Germany, terrorist activities continued throughout the 1970s and spilled into the 1980s, causing the loss of many lives. The 1978 kidnapping and murder of Aldo Moro, the president of the Christian Democratic Party, was just one example (Galleni, 1978: 82 ff). Another was a fascist bomb attack on the railway station at Bologna in 1980, which created a bloodbath, a literal massacre of innocent people, and this tragedy stirred millions to participate in mass demonstrations. Official estimates claim that, in the 1970s, the terrorism of the new fascists and the left added up to about 14 000 acts of violence, the deaths of 409 persons and injuries to a further 1366. Italian history shows many examples of political violence but the 1970s saw an unusual concentration and increase in acts of violence which members of the Red Brigade terrorist group defined as a move from a '*creeping* civil war' to a '*full-scale* civil war' (Bertini, 1978: 63).

Birnbaum maintains that, unlike the experience in West Germany, Italian governments did not panic. Their calm and firm response to these terrorist crises has been widely admired in Italy as showing, above all, the tenacity of the country's commitment to democracy (1986: 219). This view, however, is not held by many observers who do not recognise the government's response as 'calm and firm'. Other writers see the long hesitation in responding to the terrorist crisis with its international (Arab and Armenian) elements, as the result of 'endemically unstable governments which are dependent upon heterogeneous and faction-ridden multiparty coalitions' (Pisano, 1986: 196). Once the government adopted anti-terrorist measures in 1979 they came under fire from the left for having breached important democratic principles. A person suspected of terrorist activities could be held without trial for up to two years; rigid wire-tapping laws were relaxed; house searches were permitted on the mere suspicion of a terrorist hide-out in the general area; and provisional apprehension of those suspected of links with terrorism was allowed (Pisano, 1986: 197).

Here too, as in West Germany, the tension between government and feminists grew as a consequence of terrorist activities and led to arrests and reprisals. In 1979, for instance, the well-known feminist theorist MariaRosa Dalla Costa, who had expounded the idea of wages for housework, was arrested and charged for writing subversive material (Morgan, 1984: 370). Left-wing activists have claimed (with a good deal of justification) that state repression of terrorism in Italy had a very negative influence on left-wing politics as a whole. Braidotti points out that the state reprisals against terrorism altered the strategies of women's protest and shifted the ground of activities from the street to the written word (1986: 129).

Terrorism, directed against the state but strategically carried out against people, was underscored by a different kind of violence which had similar origins in Italian tradition. This was the violence against recalcitrant women who were determined to break the spell of machismo and the value hierarchies expounded in official attitudes of the church and the state. The 1970s can only be described as an extraordinary spectacle of open gender-warfare. To my knowledge, Italy is the only country in which the new wave was accompanied by so much violence. In 1971 at the first conference of the Mld, men turned up in large numbers and disrupted the meeting by hurling verbal abuse and obscenities at the women. The second meeting, which took place a little later at the University of Rome, brought male political groups to the scene. They threw condoms filled with water through windows, again shouting abuse throughout the meeting. At the end, when women filed out of the room, they were met with physical violence. In the same year a member of the group Rivolta Femminile was banned from teaching because she had discussed the group's manifesto with her students. In 1972, a peaceful sit-in of 60 women and their children in an open market place was met and watched by helmeted policemen in full armour, 'carrying shields and heavy truncheons'. Women then sang a song: 'Although we are women, we have no fear', which so totally unnerved the police that they launched a full attack. Many women and children were injured (Colombo, 1981: 462). In 1975, men stormed a peaceful march by women in Rome (Barkan, 1984: 133). In 1977, rallies of students in Rome and Padua led to violence by men against their party political female colleagues so that men had to be excluded from assemblies. Also in 1977, local authorities prohibited a particular demonstration but feminists decided to go ahead and found themselves blocked by no less than 1000 police and civil police. Fights broke out and a 19-year-old woman was killed: the death of Giorgiana Masi, as a result of police brutality, 'demonstrated dramatically that the *piazza* was no longer a place for meeting and discussion but had become the scene of violent conflict with no room for mediation' (Zancan, 1988: 57). In 1978, Catanian women in Sicily were beaten, stoned and arrested by male bystanders and the police alike when they staged a pro-abortion march. One year later neo-fascist gunmen broke into the recording studios of Radio Donna in Rome, shooting and seriously wounding several women (Bassnet, 1986: 97).

Violence against and the contempt for women found its clearest public expression in the number of rapes that were recorded. The number of reported rapes in Italy was incomparably higher than in other nations of similar size. In the early 1970s, the beginning of the new women's movement, there were 16 000 reported rapes per annum, compared with 7000 in West Germany (Glaab, 1980: 118). One may wonder whether these astronomical figures reflect a higher incidence of rape or a lower threshold of tolerance for it on the part of Italian women. The incidence of vengeful rapes as a response against feminists might have increased during this period, but this is not clear. It was certainly in the interest of feminists to make their outrage known by having the details of certain cases as publicly stated as possible. And in many instances, these cases afforded a good deal of political mileage and offered opportunities for staging mass rallies. Conversely, the persistence of blatantly sexist and victimising attitudes of the courts and the police in the face of public outcry against rape rightly incensed women, and the murders of raped women shocked the whole nation.

The legal profession had been closed to women until 1963. As late as 1982 only 66 women, or 2.7 percent of female candidates (as against 3.1 percent of male candidates), passed the state examination in law. Altogether, 35 percent of law graduates in 1980 were women (Lovenduski, 1986: 227–8). While this was a vast improvement over the figures in the 1960s and early 1970s, the number of women who had taken up law *and* turned feminist was absolutely minute. Legislators like Maria Eletta Martini and Nilde Jotti, who were at the forefront of the family law reform of 1975, were still a rarity. Hence there were as yet no organisations comparable with Choisir in France and there were no feminist lawyers like Halimi who could and would take on the fight with the law on its own territory. Women had no choice but to take to the streets and use every means of public protest in order to influence opinion against the practices of the legal establishment and the law enforcing agencies.

One publicly debated case was that of a 16-year-old girl who had accepted a lift from her ex-boyfriend and another boy who later raped her. When she tried to report this to the police, the police refused to take the protocol. This occurred in Pomigliano d'Arco (east of Naples), where the specific southern value system reigns. In all likelihood the police rejected the idea of making the rape public in order to protect the girl's family (that is, its male members) from shame and loss of honour. It became an important case in so far as it highlighted the problems between the north and the south (*mezzogiorno*), and showed up the contradiction between the assumptions of modern democracy and ingrained social custom. Apparently the girl was subsequently rejected by her family and village, and pack-raped in revenge. The 1982 criminal code amendment that made rape a punishable crime has its origin in the extensive lobbying by feminists which resulted from this case. Then there was Rosaria Lopez, who was raped and murdered near Rome in 1976, a famous case, which was seen as an example of 'punishment' for a woman who had dared to abandon her traditional role (Glaab, 1980: 119). There was also the case of Claudia Caputi in Rome in 1977. Claudia Caputi was pack-raped by eighteen youths and she later identified and testified against seven of them. The court discredited her as a prostitute and freed the men, four of whom sought her out and subsequently raped her again. This time Claudia Caputi was found injured and unconscious in the gutter, but once again the law moved on the side of these men. This case evoked extreme anger amongst feminists who gathered in Rome and in other cities in their thousands, and the court attitude even stimulated women in the conservative south to stage sit-ins in front of court houses (Chotjewitz-Häfner, 1977: 4–9).

The problem was that Italian law had no provisions at all to protect women against sexual violence (Beckwith, 1987: 162). In the past, social custom had taken care of that lack of protection by requiring a girl or a woman to be accompanied at all times (*accompagnamento*), especially at night. Up to the new feminist wave it was indeed considered unthinkable for a woman to be about at night on her own. But in modern city life, this was often a difficult rule to follow. What if a woman worked late shift in a factory, or attended lectures till after dusk, or wanted to go to the theatre or attend a meeting at night? These experiences were in constant conflict with a tradition that first arose in rural environments. In the rural lifestyle many of the modern urban problems were unlikely to occur and the tradition might have appeared more sensible and even somewhat less restrictive. Many women, no doubt, had little choice but to break this cumbersome social rule of *accompagnamento*. The problem was rather that the alternatives could be dangerous. If a woman were to venture out alone, she could risk rape or at least being accosted and sexually harassed. At the least, most women would experience anxiety.

The interrelationship between a woman's right to move about on her own and her right in a democratic law-governed society to be safe from sexual abuse was more than evident to feminists. Hence, at the peak of the movement and at the time of the much publicised rape cases, women in Italy, as in France and England, held protest actions to reclaim the night for themselves. The '*Riprendiamoci la Notte*' action in 1976 involved about 100 000 women in Rome alone and many more thousands in other cities. In Rome up to 20 000 women marched arm in arm each and every night, shouting slogans such as '*La notte ci piace, vogliam uscir in pace*' (we like the night, we want to go out in peace) to make the point that they were no longer going to tolerate victimisation. They insisted that they had a right to be safe, a right to determine their own movements (Chotjewitz-Häfner, 1977: 11). In the same year, feminists in Rome founded the Centre against Violence and two years later, the Mld and *Effe* organised an International Convention on Violence in order to devise direct strategies and proposals for the reduction and elimination of violence against women (Beckwith, 1987: 163). Italian feminists were well aware of the opposition and obviously willing and courageous enough to face that opposition very squarely in an array of militant and well-executed acts of protest. Indeed, the new Italian feminist wave was the most violence-prone movement in western Europe. Its famous slogan became almost emblematic of Italian feminism (Bassnet, 1986: 94–5), and even if it had an element of irony in it, was understood by men very much as a declaration of war: *'tremate, tremate, le streghe sono tornate'* (tremble, tremble, the witches are back).

'Feminism is no pacifism' exclaimed the new movement, and its tackling of the incipient hatred of women turned into violent confrontations on more than one occasion. Women themselves, even if only in relatively small groups, turned to violence as a means of self-defence. Female terrorist squads (commando groups) were trained and maintained. They perceived their struggle as revolution and sought to set up new power structures within their organisations in order to change women from passive, alienated creatures who were mere commodities in a male world into active participants in history. They used shotguns and revolvers but, unlike male terrorist activists at the same time, they aimed not at killing but at maiming key figures of the male establishment, usually shooting the 'enemies' in the knee.

Bassnet suggested that, in a sense, Italian feminism had always been militant and violent. Resistance in Italy had in fact always meant active military participation, whether during the time of the *risorgimento*, when we find Garibaldi's wife Anita as a participant in the Redshirt campaigns, or the violent labour conflicts of the early 20th century, or the resistance to fascism (Bassnet, 1986: 97–105). Depending on political orientation, some people referred to this period as civil war and others as revolution. Whatever its ideological underpinning might have been, it certainly was violent and women were caught in the middle of these events, sometimes as victims, but mostly as conscious political actors.

## The status of Italian women

Despite the violence, the bitterness and the seemingly endless struggle over a decade, it is generally agreed that the new-wave Italian feminist movement was extremely influential in Italian life and politics in several ways. The movement was strong enough to topple governments, taken seriously enough to be regularly reported on in the mainstream daily press, and persistent enough to effect change. The magnitude of that change and the ideological packaging of some of that change when it finally did occur may have left many radical Italian feminists disillusioned and disappointed, but whatever change took place was mostly attributable to the efforts of the movement itself.

These successes ranged from a number of significant and gender-specific changes in Italian law to new services and new feminist networks. The laws relating to the family and to reproduction were certainly key changes that affected not only women's general freedom of movement and of decision making but their general well being and physical health. The family law reform bills of 1975, with their clear statement on women's equality in marriage, finally did away with the last shadow of fascist influence. A 1977 law for the equality of treatment (*legge di parità*) eradicated a number of anomalies and discriminatory policies concerning pensions and family allowances, and it made much more explicit the unacceptability of discrimination on the basis of sex in relation to jobs and promotion. Women had fought for and had succeeded in getting the *consultori pubblici* set up in 1975. These were publicly funded health centres which enabled women to gain access to free medical examinations, with provision for birth control counselling.

The abortion law of 1978, despite its limitations, was a major victory against the institution of the church and against the right-to-life lobbyists, amongst them neo-fascist and other ultra right-wing groups. Since abortion has been legalised, the death rate of women due to abortion has declined sharply. The 1984 central statistics revealed that almost a quarter of a million abortions are performed each year, most of them (73.4 percent) on married women. The official figure for sexual violence against women is noticeably lower than the estimates given in the 1970s. In 1980, the movement was able to register a further victory for the new-wave movement when feminists marched for a bill on violence against women. It was an important display of solidarity. Feminism in Italy was as diverse and fractured as in other countries but on important issues they had now learned to act as one: the 30 000 women marching in Rome represented the Mld, the Roman feminists and the Udi. Colombo rightly claims that because of this unity this march represented a 'great achievement for the women's movement' (1981: 461). Since 1982, rape has been punishable by three to eight years imprisonment, with stiffer sentences applying for pack-rape and additional debilitating damage. Unfortunately, we shall never know whether the number has really dropped or whether there was then and is now an unrevealed percentage of violence. One tremendous disappointment for feminists concerned the violence bill of 1984. The bill excludes husbands and lovers as perpetrators and thus, despite years of remonstrances, implicitly continues to give licence to domestic violence. In 1984, a Commission for Equal Opportunities was set up by the government as a consultative body for the prime minister.

There are noticeable changes in the marital status of women and these appear to have become a trend in the 1980s. Between the 1970s and the 1980s the number of marriages per year has declined by 28 percent, even though the rate of separation and divorce has remained amongst the lowest in western Europe. In 1984, for instance, only 1 percent of women was either divorced or separated while the percentage of the married category had fallen to 48.8 percent. It is clear that this trend is related to women's attitudes and greater degree of independence. In the late 1980s, over 40 percent of women were financially independent, although often at very low incomes. The majority of those living as 'singles', as single parents or widowed, were women.

Italian feminists, as feminists elsewhere, were the movers for identifying needs and appropriate services for women. In addition, the activities of the new wave have cast a net of supportive and woman-identified social spaces. As a result, the Italy of the 1980s and 1990s has refuges and health centres, legal abortions and contraceptives, rape crisis centres, feminist advice and healing centres, centres against violence, self-help groups, feminist radio stations and a myriad of cultural and political feminist groups. In September 1986, a meeting was called in Siena in order to achieve a national forum and feminist umbrella structure to coordinate regional achievements and regional groups. There are now well over 100 feminist research and documentation centres sprinkled throughout Italy. Feminist bookshops exist in every larger town or city. Women's centres lead an independent existence. Apart from *Quotidiano* and *Effe*, all other major feminist journals of the heyday of the new wave have survived and enjoy a large readership. Other magazines and daily newspapers, such as *Il Manifesto*, carry regular sections on feminism (Braidotti, 1986). As in other western European, and indeed western industrialised countries, there are feminist courses offered at most universities in Italy. In 1987, the first Italian Feminist Studies Conference was held in Modena, attracting over 400 delegates (Cicioni, 1987: 132).

Italian feminists have cut across taboos and managed to open debates on the body and on sexuality. They discovered and openly defended women's right to an autonomous sexuality, and this broke the church-imposed nexus between sex and motherhood (Caldwell, 1981: 59). Indeed, one of the last movement events, in 1977, was a national feminist conference on sexuality and the body, held in Paestum (Zancan, 1988: 57). Interestingly, the issue of lesbianism remained rather mute. There had been a gay movement of Fiori in the 1970s and several meetings of lesbians had taken place but, ironically, the lesbians in the movement began to thrive only once the mainstream new-wave movement subsided. The first lesbian anthology of poetry was published in 1976 and that of 'coming out' stories in 1979. The first congress of lesbian feminists took place in 1981 and the first national conference in 1983 in Bologna. These conferences have continued into the present but, despite the increasing visibility and public debate, the unease of feminists on the issue seems to have persisted (Fiocchetto, 1987; Borghi et al., 1988: 60–5).

In terms of paid work, women have regained most of the ground lost since the late 19th century (38.4 percent in 1881 and 35.2 percent in 1988; see Moss, 1988: 71), but very little has changed in terms of the segregation of the labour market and the unsavoury practice of home-based labour. The earning capacity of women has slowly crept up over the years but not nearly far enough to warrant great enthusiasm. In 1978, women's incomes on average were 74.1 percent of male earnings (Barkan, 1984: 10), and this was so despite the fact that the Italian parliament had accepted salary equality between the sexes as early as 1956. Feminists spent a great deal of time in the attempt to improve women's position in factories. None of these efforts appeared have to been very successful. If, in their own opinion, feminists had failed to democratise the political and the union structure, they had at least succeeded in setting up strong women's networks within both. They fought for and managed to implement, in 1973, a special educational deal for women workers in the metal workers' union with the new and creative idea of the '150-hour' programme, which allowed women to learn and attend classes during working hours (Caldwell, 1983: 74).

The controversial and outright exploitative form of home-based labour has not been extinguished and far too little is still known about it. In the beginning of the 1970s more than 1.5 million adult women worked in home-based labour. Piecework at home carries no pension entitlements, paid holidays or any other benefits, such as insurance and sickness benefits. It is also poorly paid and usually does not exceed half of the officially set minimum income. Another unofficial and statistically not measurable figure concerns women's work in other households. A survey of 1974 revealed that the average Italian woman works twelve hours per day and up to sixteen hours when she has a paid job. Farmhands and farm workers are even worse off at times than the city-dwelling woman engaged in home-based labour; for instance, in the 1980s Sicilian women earned about the equivalent of US$2–5 for a night's work, harvesting yasmin from 1:00 a.m. to 10:00 a.m., standing in the fields all night with their feet in the water, and of course suffering great health risks. In addition, housework, especially in the south, has often remained a difficult chore in the absence of amenities, let alone modern appliances. In Sicily, 68 percent of households were without a bath and many had no kitchen, forcing women to cook outside on woodburners (Glaab, 1980: 79–83). The problems of the *mezzogiorno* and the *battaglia meridionale* (battle for the south) are far from over. It is also telling that a far larger proportion of women than men have suffered the fate of unemployment. In 1980, to take a typical year, female unemployment rates were 13.1 percent as compared to 4.8 percent for men. It is interesting to note that in Italy, the debate on whether housework should be paid or not has raged hard and long (since 1972) and, in 1986, it led to the formation of a new housewives' association. A survey in the same year in Italy's TV guide, the best selling weekly magazine *Sorrisi e Canzoni* (Smiles and Songs), showed that 65 percent of women interviewed were keen to get some part-time work outside the home. Eighty-five percent said that they deserved social security benefits and half of those interviewed agreed that they should receive some form of salary for all the work they do.

For those women who do work in gainful employment outside the home the maternity law of 1971 was a substantial improvement on their previous position. It secures their jobs for one year after the birth of a child. For the first five months of maternity leave women are paid 80 percent of their last wage and this is funded by health insurance and the employer. A further half year can be taken off but only on 30 percent of the last pay, funded entirely by the health fund. Men too have the right to some paternal leave but this right is counteracted by the fact that it does not protect men from losing their jobs on their return to work. In reality then, very few men make use of that right.

A marked change has occurred in the professional gender profile. Women have now begun to enter professions in greater numbers than ever before and certain educational paths have opened up for them again (such as law and university teaching). In comparison with western European averages, however, the number has remained low (see table 6.7).

Women's role in politics has not appreciably improved over the postwar years. If anything, present participation rates of women merely suggest that the losses from the immediate postwar years have just been recouped and it remains to be seen whether the momentary impact of the women's movement will have

Table 6.7 Comparative data on the occupational status of Italian women and men, 1984

|  | % women | % men |
|---|---|---|
| **In gainful employment** | 32.4 | 67.6 |
| of these in industry | 24.6 | 75.4 |
| in public service | 62.6 | 37.4 |
| self employed | 13.7 | 86.3 |
| in agriculture | 12.8 | 87.2 |
| **Occupations** | | |
| primary school teachers | 88.1 | 11.9 |
| nurses | 67.1 | 32.9 |
| employees | 41.2 | 58.8 |
| pharmacists | 41.0 | 59.0 |
| business owners | 38.9 | 61.1 |
| university staff | 34.9 | 65.1 |
| sales staff | 31.6 | 68.4 |
| factory workers | 23.1 | 76.9 |
| surgeons | 15.8 | 84.2 |
| dentists | 8.7 | 91.3 |
| solicitors | 8.4 | 91.6 |
| entrepreneurs | 8.4 | 91.6 |
| medical doctors (GP) | 7.3 | 92.7 |
| barristers | 3.4 | 96.6 |
| judges and senior law | 2.9 | 97.1 |
| **Education** | | |
| primary schooling incomplete | 23.8 | 18.4 |
| completed tertiary ed. | 2.1 | 3.6 |

*Source*: adapted from Fiocchetto, 1988: 31, based on ISTAT, Central Institute for Statistics in Italy of 1984

a lasting effect. The only increase so far to be recorded is solely in the category of senators. Overall, however, the participation rate of women in Italian politics in the 1980s fell below the western European average (see table 6.8).

The presence of Italian women in the European parliament is also dismally small. In 1988, only eight women out of an Italian contingent of 89 were voted in as delegates. The reason for this poor representation was its method of selection from a pool in which only a few women are found, such as a limited number of constituencies, economic interest groups and large newspaper editorial staff. The cynicism Maurizio Cotta expressed in his article of 1979, 'Classe politice e Parlamento in Italia', was borne out in subsequent years. He argued that even the most progressive parties will accept women to represent the party only in extreme cases: namely, when it serves to improve the party's image at a time when there is very strong electoral competition, especially from moderate parties with a high level of female support, or when the electorate exerts considerable pressure to have more women standing for election (Zincone, 1988: 166–8). Italy perhaps offers the clearest example of gender bias in formal politics in western Europe. Throughout this chapter, it has been argued and shown that Italian women are politically highly literate. The movement has shown that women use that literacy in active forms. Hence, under no circumstances can their absence in power politics be explained away by claiming that this absence shows a lack of interest in politics or a lack of political skills.

In the 1980s, the movement subsided and began to disappear from public view, after having been an 'obligatory point of reference for parties and political forces' for years (Pasquinelli, 1984: 131). It is interesting that two very strong branches of the movement, the Mld and the Udi, had initially very strong ties with political parties—the Mld with the left Socialist Party and the Udi with the Pci. Once they decided to sever their ties with the parties in the early 1980s both groups perished in the process. The Udi had been a strong women's organisation for four decades, but did not survive its transition from a party-connected organisation to a feminist anti-hierarchical organisation. Italian feminism, as feminist movements elsewhere in western Europe, began to live in calmer waters and had to learn to live with less than perfect results in their endeavour to change social reality. Like other western European countries, Italy was affected by ecological and pacifist movements, which slowly spread during the mid-1980s. In the peace groups in particular, women have a strong presence. But as elsewhere, the emphasis of the 1980s in general has been on policy implementation and on structurally consolidating past interests of the movement.

The power of the church has not been broken but it has been undermined. In 1984 the Concordat with the papacy was reconfirmed with the amendment that religious instruction in schools was to be based on voluntary student participation. Indeed, between the encroaching secularisation and the general popu-

**Table 6.8   Percentage of Italian women in politics, 1948–1988**

| Legislature | | | | | | | | |
|---|---|---|---|---|---|---|---|---|
| I | II | III | IV | V | VI | VII | VIII | IX |
| 1948–53 | 1953–58 | 1958–63 | 1963–68 | 1968–72 | 1972–76 | 1976–79 | 1979–83 | 1983–88 |
| MPs       7.8 | 5.7 | 4.1 | 4.6 | 2.8 | 4.1 | 8.5 | 8.2 | 7.9 |
| Senators 0.9 | 0.4 | 0.8 | 1.9 | 3.4 | 1.8 | 3.4 | 3.4 | 4.9 |

*Source*: Zincone, 1988: 161–2

lation's deep-seated religiosity, also present amongst feminists, a new compromise was struck. Religion in Italy has gradually shifted from signifying catholicism to being an expression of personal conscience as 'believers' (*credente*). In any case, the Concordat now means much less than it once did, because the introduction of civil divorce, of contraceptives and abortion rights cut deeply into catholic dogma and effectively overruled, or sidestepped, canon law.

Despite a number of important events in the 1980s it is noteworthy that the new feeling of Italian feminists is often characterised by *disagio* (discomfort) and *scacco* (defeat), as a 1983 document entitled *Più donne che uomini* (More women than men) so aptly identified. The unease has not left Italian feminists, either in terms of the achievements of the movement or in terms of their own lives and social relationships. One manner of overcoming either feeling, some recent feminist arguments suggest, is to create something beyond the network practices of the past, creating a new *affidamento* (dependence) amongst women. This *affidamento*, unfortunately, has implied a rejection, or is at least an undermining of, the egalitarian ideology of the movement. *Affidamento* propagates the idea that women should learn to value and depend on other women with more highly developed skills and greater knowledge (Cicioni 1987: 136). Whether the recognition of difference and an implied acceptance of some form of hierarchy will ultimately help to strengthen women's networks and women's political agenda remains to be seen. The shifts raise the question of whether Italian women and women in other western European countries are on the way to a new conservatism or, through a newly found ability to accommodate pluralism within their own ranks, are headed to a much needed new level of solidarity. Here Hannah Arendt was right in suggesting that the idea of sisterhood and solidarity are fundamentally different in consequence. Sisterhood, or fraternity, is a psychological substitute for the loss of the common world and therefore politically irrelevant. Solidarity, she believes, is the stronger concept of the two for it is a political concept which 'makes political demands and preserves reference to the world' (Arendt, 1968: 25).

In summary, the feminist movement in Italy of the 1970s was extremely strong by any empirical or ideological measure. The movement mobilised high numbers of women for specific demonstrations and actions. On certain issues the numbers ran into the tens and even hundreds of thousands. When the movement wanted signatures for referenda, it managed to collect half a million within three months. In the case of abortion law reform demonstrations, the number of signatories was 900 000 in 1975 alone (Chotjewitz-Häfner, 1977: 22). Moreover, despite the diversity of groups they were extremely efficient in communicating with one another, not just within one town or city but right across Italy. National rallies never counted fewer than 50 000 women and usually more (Colombo, 1981: 465). A splendid sense of coordination and purpose made it possible for demonstrations to occur simultaneously throughout Italy. The new-wave movement was indeed a national movement. From Sicily to Frinli, from Potenza to Milan, there were feminist groups in the smallest towns, feminist collectives in schools, feminist councils and feminist collectives in every suburb and every city quarter. In a town the size of Florence, there were twenty such major collectives (Chotjewitz-Häfner, 1977: 12). This ability to mobilise well and quickly and rouse large numbers of women into action nationally was a feat unmatched by any other western European movement.

Part of the reason, one suspects, why the Italian movement acquired such enormous energies and momentum, was the constant overt hostility displayed against the movement, and this reminder of a 'common enemy' served to bring women more closely together. Women managed to tackle and question, head on, the two chief institutions of Italian life: the family and the catholic church, and, in addition, question its two ideological blocs: the catholic and the Marxist. More positive and interesting in terms of our discussion on the legitimacy of protest is the Italian constitution's stating that, as long as a minimum of 500 000 signatories (who must be registered voters) can be found for a bill within a three-month period, the Italian government will be obliged to discuss that bill in both houses. In other words, the Italian constitution has inbuilt a clause which not only permits the general population a voice but actually invites mobilisation of dissenters. The fact that the constitution incorporates the principle of participatory democracy not just via referenda but via the channel of legislature is a recognition that dissent is a part, and an important part, of democracy. The women's movement learned to use this legitimate channel extremely effectively. Moreover, the movement argued that its concerns were not just those of a small minority group but of a very large number in the electorate. There was no need for women to collect as many as 900 000 signatures, as occurred on the issue of abortion, but they did so to indicate that there was substantial community support for the bills they proposed. A third reason for the movement's power and impetus is a consequence of Italian social history. As we identified, Italian women had been organised in women's organisations for most of this century, and many of them in dissenting political groups. Indeed, Italy is the 'only country in Europe where a strong mass organisation of women has existed since the end of the war' (Colombo, 1981: 467). The political astuteness and brilliance of Italian women's organisations today, after all, were based on long and bitter experience. There is an Italian tradition which argues that there can be no true democracy without the existence and vocalisation of political conflict. If this is so then the Italian feminist new wave has certainly contributed substantially to the democratisation of Italy. Eugenio Manca said in a published article in 1982: 'Everyone knows that if all of Italian society today feels more free, mature, and civil, this is owed to the results that women have produced' (cit. in Birnbaum, 1986: 214).

*THE MODEL EXAMINED*

The southern European countries—Portugal, Spain, Italy and Greece—have often been described as the 'new Mediterranean democracies' (Pridham, 1984). Indeed, all four countries had suffered major failures and setbacks in sustaining stable democratic politics in the past. All four had authoritarian interludes or long-standing dictatorial rule and they either have emerged from these very recently or, as with Italy, in the post–World War II period. When the dictators had gone, one of the first steps towards change was always to ensure that human rights and democratic procedures were firmly enshrined in written constitutions, which were often drafted and sealed within months. Not all western nations have written constitutions (e.g. New Zealand, Israel, or the UK), but in most western European countries such a measure was seen as absolutely essential, either as a blueprint for national identity or as a consequence of the experience of fascism. There is every reason to believe that these new 'Mediterranean' constitutions are evidence of a fear of a resurgence of dictatorship held by those who spearheaded the new democracies. While the content of the southern European constitutions is extremely progressive, the fear is identifiable by the rigidity and patrimonialism of the democratic system they devised: all four countries, not unlike West Germany, have written constitutions which are very difficult to change and are subject to a judicial review (Lijphart et al., 1988: 15). Patrimonial systems are characterised by elaborate networks of patron–client relations and involve a 'top-down' rule. They stress permanence and immutability and will limit and channel social mobilisation (Wiarda, 1982: 26–7). Within such a framework, the very idea of social democracy is at odds with the patrimonial system, for the former implies a willingness for change. It seems to follow that social movements should have very little chance of success. How can they affect change from below, from grassroots level, if power is so clearly structured from above?

For a movement like the feminist new wave, there were additional stumbling blocks in the southern European countries which, in the form they took, rarely if ever occurred elsewhere in Europe. Feminism entered the political arena against a stronger bulwark of misogyny than elsewhere in Europe. Until the eve of the fall of the dictatorships, laws claimed that women were immutably, innately and fundamentally inferior to men and therefore in need of control and supervision by men. They harnassed women's activities by making domestic labour a duty by law. They stated the right of physical chastisement, of sexual assault and rape as part of the marriage contract against which women had absolutely no right of appeal. Of course, many of these measures and laws had also existed in most other countries, but they had slowly been eroded in the wake of new bourgeois values and the new demands of industrialisation. And of course, the new constitutions eradicated the worst excesses of this misogyny at once. Yet often this legal and formal change was coeval with the feminist movement but not with changes in attitudes of the population at large.

One of the reasons for this powerful opposition can be found in the changes that did not happen in southern Europe as they had already happened in other parts of Europe. The speed of the transformation from dictatorship to democracy and from agricultural economies to urban industrialisation meant that none of the former centres of power had been dismantled or substantially weakened. This is particularly true of Greece, Spain, and Portugal. But even Italy, with a much longer period of democracy and industrialisation than any of the other three countries, had retained power blocs which were hostile to arguments on equality. Here, the church had directly re-entered power politics in 1929. In Portugal, Spain and Greece, it was the military that had held sway. These power structures were intact right up to the end of Salazar's (and Caeto's) rule in Portugal and the advent of the Carnation Revolution in 1974, to the fall of the colonels in Greece in 1975, and the death of Franco in 1975 in Spain. In other words, although there was some evidence that the alliances between military, church, governments and aristocracy were crumbling, the political power centres had not shifted before the social protest movements began. The redistribution of power in the new democratic governments occurred more or less simultaneously with the protest movements.

By contrast, in most other western European nations the role of the military, of the church, and even of the ruling classes had lost sway over governments well before the protest movements evolved. The process of a steady erosion of vested class or church interests and secularisation of governments had been completed either in the 19th or in the early part of the 20th century. Democratic governments had effectively relegated the military to civil control. The power of the church and the old ruling classes had been diffused or minimised because maturing democracies increasingly strove to represent the entire country rather than specific-interest groups. In southern European states, however, these processes had been arrested and, with the help of powerful dictatorships, frozen in time. Thus, in southern Europe, a number of very substantial developments, which had often occurred over long periods of time elsewhere, came together suddenly and intersected at that moment when protest movements erupted.

Except for Italy, which underwent a period of very rapid economic growth in the postwar decades, industrialisation arrived late in the southern European countries. This in itself does not support the assumption that rapid economic development and parliamentary democracy intrinsically belong together. Tipton and Aldrich rightly argue that for the southern development this easy equation, often made, is proven wrong, for here the transition came 'in the teeth of crisis' (1987: 257). In everyday life this crisis was partly expressed by the extremely drastic measures which a significant proportion of the population had to make in order to eke out a living, namely by having to conscript themselves as guest labourers to other countries. Families were separated for long periods of time, sometimes years and, on an individual basis, often paid an inordinately high price for personal survival. In the period of 1962 to 1964 over 40 percent of West Germany's recruitment requirements for qualified labour were met by Greece, Portugal, Spain and chiefly by Italy (Kindleberger, 1967: 190). Women had to fend for their households, farms, children, parents and parents-in-law by themselves. All these were experiences of independent management, running counter to the idea of minority and female submissiveness to the male head of the household.

Given these apparent restrictions, one may well ask why the women's movement in Italy became so powerful and why the Spanish movement was a good deal stronger than were the Portuguese and Greek feminist waves. These questions await further research, but it would not appear far-fetched to hypothesise at least on two grounds. One of them concerns the economic and demographic distribution of the population. Social change in rural areas tends to take much longer than in urban areas. In Portugal and Greece, two countries with the weakest movements, the rural population is significantly larger than in Spain or Italy. In 1988, the Portuguese rural and semi-rural population still accounted for 69 percent of the total population and in Greece for 42 percent, as against Italy's 33 and Spain's 23 percent (*Fischer Weltalmanach '90*, 1989).

Second, the Mediterranean democracies are not so similar as has often been suggested. As Lijphart argued, one should not expect them to be so (Lijphart et al., 1988). Their histories had similarities, but were also very different, as we showed in this chapter. In Italy, the potential rigidity of the patrimonial system has been broken in at least two ways. On one hand, the political management has never been quite stabilised due to in-faction fighting, intense competition between parties and the sheer lack of clear majority rule, which has forced almost all Italian governments into coalition arrangements. On the other hand, Italy enjoys, as perhaps no other country in western Europe, a sub-system of power, a grassroots-based unionism and labour movement that has claimed and retained a surprising degree of autonomy. Many of the women's groups have their tradition and origin in worker, union, or labour movement-based activity of the industrial northern Italian triangle. From the vantage point of semi-autonomy, and equipped with the strategies of political action, against which the state had proven fairly powerless before, the new feminist wave of Italy had a greater chance of generally destabilising the patrimonialist state than, say, the one in Greece ever had. In Greece the unions have been kept weak and divided by state intervention and favouritism, and similar developments took place in Portugal.

The case for Spain is not so easily made. Lidia Falcón, one of the doyennes of Spanish feminism, called the post-Franco feminist movement 'the most aggressive, explosive, and brilliant feminist movement in all of Europe' (Falcón, 1984: 628). How it could have been so in Spain and not in Portugal or Greece invites consideration. It is true that the Spanish outburst was brief. In 1980 the Feminist Coordinatorship in Barcelona and the Feminist Platform in Madrid simply disappeared. But for five years the (urban) movement was extremely powerful, angry and vocal. In Spain, the transition from dictatorship to democracy was almost smooth but it was a democracy that was guided by monarchy and to an extent had to be underwritten by the military. King Don Carlos specifically sought out the generals to be assured of their good will. There can be no doubt that the Spanish democracy is indeed rigid and patrimonial but, and herein lies one of its major differences, Spain was never a unitary country like modern Greece or Portugal. Its various regions, even characterised by different languages, had always maintained some sub-system of independent local government, irrespective of whether that had always been legitimate or not. Over the last two decades, the Catalans (Barcelona and environs) have demanded more exposure to their language, more cultural recognition and more self-determination. The Basques, vocally led by local and 'nationalistic' terrorist groups, have even demanded full autonomy and independence. Historically, particularism has been very pronounced and has remained so to this day, so that writers on Spain have rightly suggested that the present Spanish model of democracy approaches federalism. The notion of federalism, however, is not a symbol of a unitary, strongly centralised state which will be able to rule 'top-down' in unimpeded ways, despite attempts to make it so. Power is diffused through the second, regional layer. There are loopholes and spaces created regionally which resists the patrimonism of the central government. Basque struggles for independence are the extreme case for 'winning space' but Catalonia is not far removed. I am suggesting here that the simple model of a hierarchy of power is not entirely applicable to Spain. The 'top-down' rule is intercepted at various levels, and by default it may also allow discrepant groups like feminists to rally against the state as if the demands were based on a regional claim. Clearly, the regional protests were aimed at achieving autonomy and were an expression of resistance—two claims that *mutatis mutandis* were translatable to the broader socio-political aims of women's movements and other protests. Moreover, the legacy of the Spanish Civil War of the 1930s and the feminist struggle within it was never forgotten. As in Italy, there was a clandestine continuity of dissent, which even the Franco regime never managed to wipe out.

The feminist protest movements of southern Europe reveal more overtly and more unambiguously than any other new-wave movement in the western world that the fight for equality and liberation was a fight against a specific code of ethics. We have touched upon this by describing some of the facets of the honour system. We know that amongst the sanctions against non-conformism are psychological regulators such as *shame* and *guilt*. The enormous energy *and* courage of feminists to break the nexus between external authority (prevailing code of ethics) and the attempt to legitimate their own 'devious' behaviour is astounding. What feminists in southern European countries have done is, in Sartre's terms, no less than the radicalisation of evil. The judgement of the community is accepted but turned around. What was seen as a deviation from the norm is now the norm. The table is turned on others. In other words, it is not I who should be ashamed but you, for the imposition of rules and values which are cruel to me and self-serving for you. It is a way of reciprocating shame and guilt and of putting the onus of responsibility on the makers of the code of ethics. Turning the table is a radically necessary exercise for change and also one that alienates and infuriates those on whom the table is turned and who feel that they too are mere abiders of the rules and caught in their own web. We may possibly consider that the extreme violence that the feminist movements in the south of Europe provoked was a response to the 'turning of the table'.

For women to have become active participants in history was a formidable achievement. It carried its own rewards, to be sure. For the attempt of breaking with prevailing ideals, when achieved, gave women a sense of liberation from imposed ideals and contributed to a feeling of empowerment (Fisher, 1984: 193). Or, as Marcuse has argued, the liberatory impulse of the social process lay in the dynamics of negativity; that is, in the negation of existing norms. The rules of the game had to be refused, the absent made present, because 'the greater part of the truth is in that which is absent' (see Cornell and Thurschwell, 1987). The act of rebellion was nevertheless a deeply courageous one. It is profound because it required a major conceptual revolution. Astonishingly, the most oppressive laws *and* practices vanished from southern European law books and custom almost overnight and one may count this as a revolutionary transformation of their respective societies.

Of course, the rebellion and the radical rethinking of predominant social norms did not happen in a vacuum but in concert with the political parties on the left. That link was vital and came to mean something special in southern European countries, especially since the political left in all four southern European countries existed solely as resistance groups for long stretches of time. The implications were twofold. The tactics of groups forced underground vary markedly from political groups and parties which are part of the mainstream. All political parties on the left, be these anarcho-syndicalist, socialist or communist, had to learn to survive extreme oppression and persecution. They also had to learn to find allies and thus were open to inviting people into their ranks, who, in mainstream politics, would barely have gained entry. It is significant that all resistance groups throughout Europe and especially in southern Europe counted substantial numbers of women amongst their active members. Indeed, most resistance movements in western Europe consisted of between 40 to 80 percent of women, at a guess. The underground movements gave women an equal place amongst their male comrades and, in addition, part of the ideological package of the left said that women should neither be discriminated against nor singled out for specific tasks commensurate with traditional role concepts of 'womanhood'. Women thus often accomplished dangerous and very important missions and became a vital part in all resistance groups. In the upsurge of the postwar movements of the 1970s, these underground experiences became important skills. Italy is perhaps the best example of how a working-class movement and a resistance movement can culminate in a highly sophisticated, politically astute and well-organised political force in peacetime. Since the end of the war Italy has also had the only mass movement of women found anywhere in Europe, and one that was well equipped to address issues of oppression.

We have seen that in Portugal and Spain, and to a lesser extent also in Greece, the power of the dictatorship and repression of any different party or any other political views eventually led to the effective disenfranchisement and political ignorance of an entire generation. The groups with any memory or knowledge of political activity had become dismally small. The majority of the population had never gone to the polls, had never expressed a political opinion and had never been engaged in political activity of any kind. Nearly all the essential political knowledge, so vital for the functioning of democracy, had been wiped out. In Portugal and Spain, the political ignorance was underscored by sparse educational facilities and opportunities so that illiteracy, especially for women, remained extremely high. It is not surprising that, after the fall of the dictatorships in all four countries, political leadership was derived from those very groups which, at their peril, had continued to engage in political activity. Only those groups had the political literacy necessary to accept the challenge of government and make a clear break with the past.

Political literacy can be gained in a variety of ways independently of the formal channels of political parties. In Greece, the population had never been so thoroughly depoliticised by dictatorship as it had been in Spain and Portugal. First, no Greek dictatorship had lasted as long as in either of the other southern European countries. Second, there was little in the Greek mentality that compared with the Portuguese *patiência* or the Spanish *pasitamo*. On the contrary, Greeks were angry, impatient and ready for a thorough reevaluation of culture and nation. Third, Greeks had never been depoliticised, 'thanks' to the slipshod despotic style of their bureaucracy. The bureaucracy, as most Greeks would have agreed, was useless and irrational but also extremely powerful and fickle. It could decide what was being built where, and who was granted what and when, without ever feeling compelled to explain its actions. In order to deal with this bureaucracy, as everyone would have had to at one time or another, it was extremely important for all Greeks to be politically well informed (Choisi, 1988: 71–3). Finally, there were a number of Greek values which had not died but actually been strengthened in the various phases of iron rule, war and dictatorships, such as the virtue of *leventis*—magnanimity and bravery—and *pallikar*—fighting for an ideal such as liberty and social justice—(Kourvetaris and Dobratz, 1987: 5). These values, including the Greek anti-authoritarianism, had a great deal to do with Turkish occupation and oppression and were easily adapted to an imposed internal dictatorship. Indeed, it was more than evident in the post-1974 period that within Greece a revolutionary spirit and an eagerness for change, even for drastic social transformation, had survived and quickly surfaced despite US interference, which very nearly broke the backbone of Greek society. In Italy, the very core of the resistance movement was called into the political arena immediately after the war. The church tried to condemn communists by excommunicating them but the Pci and Psi survived the period of cold war and, as we saw, rose in status and importance particularly in the 1970s and 1980s.

Common to all these parties was a belief in participatory and rank-and-file democracy amongst the new urban proletariat and skilled working class. Anarchosyndicalism has left a deep mark, especially on Spain and Italy: the Spanish Confederacion National del Trebajo (National Workers' Federation), which was founded in 1910 and worked closely with the Federacion Anarquista Iberica, provided instruction and training for workers' self-management and collectivisation, and developed and maintained decentralisation and initiative at anarchist workers' collectives. Wage equalisation (the elimination of huge profit margins for a few) increased the money held in the hands of the collective to buy new equipment and create better conditions. The Peasant Federation of Levant included no less than 900 and in Aragon there were over 500 such collectives. Their immediate aims were the achievement of a higher standard of living, but the underlying ideals were concerned with economic equality, individual freedom and self-expression and collective cooperation. Such ideals and aims, which were widely advertised in books and pamphlets and followed up by concrete training and educational classes, ultimately had to be in stark contrast to the realities of women's position in their respective societies. Equality and freedom were decidedly not meant to be theirs in the world at large, but in these collectives they practised those rights.

The interrelationship between the women, feminist movements and the parties on the left in southern European countries is thus a very special one, and it is not easy to tease out the influence of one on the other or vice versa. It appears fairly clear, however, that in Portugal and Greece many of the legal and social changes in favour of women were instigated by the newly appointed leftist governments, that is, from above. Deutsch's claim that change is forged from above and cascades downwards to mass level has concrete empirical evidence here. The achievements of both the Portuguese constitution and of the PASOK governments in Greece can only be described as extraordinary. The introduction of the abortion law in Greece, Greece being one of the few western European countries which now allows abortion on demand, was an astounding feat in the presence of a very unliberated army and amidst a set of social values steeped in religion. The Portuguese constitution in one stroke of the pen removed from the law books all medieval oppression of women and became one of the very few countries in the world that recognised women as equal in all aspects of life (law, marriage, family, and work). It is a masterpiece of modern democratic thought that, remarkably, was forged within a year after the fall of a protracted and sinister dictatorship.

Yet one wonders how meaningfully one may use the terms of 'above' and 'below' when one wishes to describe the reforms that have taken place. By the mid-1980s all four countries had elected socialist governments. After all, the governments that did emerge after the end of their respective dictatorships were governments whose beliefs and practices had sprung from the very centre of grassroots resistance movements. This is true of the coalition governments of Italy in the 1970s and of the PASOK government in Greece in the 1980s, whose mandate it was to initiate the very reforms that the broader public had demanded, women and feminists included. In Italy, the circumstances of women's liberation were in several respects very different from other southern European countries. To Italian feminists of the 1970s it had become eminently clear that the framework of the parties of the left was too narrow to accommodate gender demands within the universalist classist appeal and arguments. As they had to take their fight further than any framework provided, women often steered on the course of confrontation rather than collaboration with the left. Many of the changes made in Italy were thus effected by the constant pressure that feminist political activity exerted and, if one wishes to speak of a transformation from below, it is surely the Italian example one has to quote. Spanish feminists too lay claim to having substantially influenced legislation. Hence Falcón writes of the feminist activism: 'It had taken two years of struggle to eliminate the adultery law which sent only women to prison; three years to legalise contraception; and six years to obtain a divorce law with equality of spouses regarding child custody, family rights, and responsibilities' (1984: 629). Thus, while the grassroots activities were hard work, they gave results, showing a 'bubbling up' of dissenting views from the established norms.

This argument aside, the freedoms women were granted in all four countries were in *practice* nowhere near comparable to, say, those of the Scandinavian women, despite advanced legislation that was often akin to Scandinavian laws. In some ways, Italy does not fit this model any more, certainly not Italy's industrial north. Nevertheless, the difference between the Scandinavian countries and southern European countries is not so much one of ideology or difference in perception of democracy, but rather one of wealth. The north and the south, more so than the west and the centre of Europe, believe in social democracy. Northern Europe, however, is also a good deal wealthier than the south. We have said that social engineering takes money. One needs to add here something rather basic and so obvious that it is rarely mentioned. There are liberties that are dependent on money, or rather on consumer items such as appliances, on the availability of health care and social services, on general services, including such basis things as energy supply, water supply, transport, and on more sophisticated institutions such as schools and universities. The shortage of all these things, per capita, and especially in rural and semi-rural environments, means that in everyday life the workload of those women is not likely to change very much or very quickly. What has changed very dramatically is the way in which women's role is assessed and the way in which the law formally protects women from the worst ghosts of institutionalised misogyny that still haunt the pillars of the establishment.

*NOTES*

1 By 1988, however, the government had turned to the right to centre, and once again approached the issue of a constitutional amendment. On 1 June it succeeded in eliminating from the 1976 constitution all Marxist passages which, among other things, had assured the inevocability of the nationalisation of key industries and of the agrarian reform programme. This change was certainly not in the spirit of the constitution but, predictably, this recent change has been welcomed by the western European business community.

2 At the end of 1989, the Committee on the Status of Women published an extensive bibliography of studies, articles, laws and testimony on the status of women in Portugal between 1974 and 1988. Unfortunately, the publication was too late to be incorporated in this book. It is called *A Mulher em Textos e contextos—un recenseamento bibliográfico* (Cadernos Conciçao Feminina, no. 26), Presidencia da Conselho de Ministros, available from the Commissao da Condiçao Feminina, Ave. da Republica, 32/1, 1093 Lisboa Codex, Portgual.

3 The annual number of Spanish emigrants in the 1960s was rather low in comparison with other countries, particularly when one considers that many of the other countries have much smaller populations than Spain (40 mill.): Italy: 853 300; Turkey: 686 000; Yugoslavia: 606 000; Portugal: 472 900; Spain: 390 000; Ireland: 232 000; and Greece: 177 800 (Tipton and Aldrich, 1987: 171).

4 In 1985 there were about 600 women's organisations in Spain of which just over 100 were overtly feminist (Duran & Gallego, 1986: 204–5)

5 There are some discrepancies here in dates and background information in a number

of secondary sources. In Morgan, 1984: 271, for instance, this foundation is recorded as having taken place in 1879, and the first women's journal, called *Ladies' Daily*, was apparently launched in 1888. According to other sources (as indicated) there were a number of feminist/women's journals preceding the *Daily*.

6   The percentage of those who believed that total domestic role-sharing was the best role division within the home was as follows: Greece 51 percent; Denmark 46 percent; Italy 41 percent; France 40 percent; Netherlands 38 percent; United Kingdom 37 percent; Belgium 31 percent; Ireland 30 percent; and West Germany 26 percent (*European Women and Men in 1983*: 30).

# PART III

Outlook

# 7    Into the 1990s

In recent debates it has become fashionable to talk about 'post-feminism', as if a post-mortem were required for something that had irretrievably disappeared or gone terribly wrong. To argue thus is not entirely unjustified. Amongst feminists and post-feminists there is a sense of disillusionment and of disaffection with a movement that rode high on anger and the idealism of an enlightenment tradition, and promised the coming of a new age. The new age was to be much like that which radical thinkers of the French Revolution promised, a world of equality and fraternity, enriched now by the new *fellow*ship of women in the ranks of the enlightened. The utopian visions of a fundamental transformation of society have not turned into images within grasp, the dream of a just society has not yet come true, and the movements have dispersed before their work was completed. One may ask whether one could seriously have hoped for such radical change in a mere two decades. History tells us that even the most profound upheavals in human history have a substantial gestation period. A valid criticism made by contemporary feminist theorists is, however, that the hope for the realisation of equality and fraternity (amongst women too) is in fact not just two decades, but two centuries old. It is therefore timely to question that faith itself (Young, 1986: 382).

Indeed, feminism seems historically condemned to suffer a 'permanent state of incompletion' (Riot-Sarcey & Varikas, 1986: 443). Radical feminists of the 1970s sought no collaboration with the state. If anything, by steering a course of conflict and confrontation, they ensured that the myth of democratic stability and alleged concensus politics was false. These radical 'schools' (communist, anarchist, utopian, socialist, communitarian), it is true, have had few inheritors, not so much in their ideas as in practice. Bourgeois, liberal feminist reform movements, on the other hand, have faired better in the sense that from the outset their methods and goals were more manageable within existing structures. They were also less threatening and demanding (Benhabib, 1987: 367 ff). Whatever the movements were, they are gone, and the fear is that too little is left to sustain the machinery that started turning in women's favour.

Yet everywhere in western Europe there are unmistakable signs that societies have changed, formally and informally. As Hoskyns concedes, countries with existing legislation, such as Britain, have been forced to make amendments. Countries with inadequate legislation have introduced new legislation, such as West Germany, France and Italy. Others, which had no provisions at all, such as Portugal, Spain and Greece, have all adopted profound changes to their legislation since the mid-1970s (Hoskyns, 1985: 85–6). In Scandinavian countries the change has been slow but steady over most of the 20th century, while in most other western European countries the jolt came swiftly and massively. That change, it seems to me, may well be read as the beginning of a process of transformation.

I fail to see grounds for pessimism, both in terms of a change of women's role and in terms of the continuity of knowledge of feminism. This time round in human history, the parameters have been set differently, the questions have been greater and the political and legal processes accompanying the changes and development of feminist ideas have been more consistent and widespread, and they have become more entrenched overall than at any previous time. Rossana Rossanda, the eminent Italian writer, said recently that feminists had a formidable task. They 'faced exactly the problems which Georg Lukács had raised and developed in his book *History and Class-Consciousness* (1923): how can a class which is neither perceived nor thought of perceive itself and the world, and how must that class think in order to change the world?' (Rossanda, 1988: 162, trans GK). Western European feminism has done precisely that. It has asked the same questions and started to 'perceive itself', not as a class in the socio-economic sense of the old working class, but as loose, horizontal, democratic associations with a strong collective identity (Cohen, 1985: 667). It has done splendidly in carving out a niche for women in new and challenging ways. A 'niche' here refers to having created a space that, at least for a decade, was not swallowed up by mainstream culture or relegated to marginality. Moreover, the second-wave women were fully cognisant of the fact that 'one exists only to the extent as one is thought of by others' (Lukács, cit. in Rossanda, 1988: 162). The strategies they employed in the second wave went far beyond the reformist goals of the first feminist wave. And even if the goals of the more radical strands of western European feminism have not been met, they have been *raised*.

Conceptual frontiers have been explored and the intellectual frameworks in which this has happened have been expanded. Intellectual history has been questioned and the levels of analysis have led to profoundly different interpretations of the world. Indeed, it would be hard to deny that no less than the entire intellectual tradition of philosophy, of political theory and practice, and of sociology has come under fire. Whatever was thought to be universal, gender-neutral, valid in the profoundest and universalist way has been exposed as mere constructs of a particular male bias. At only a few times in recorded history has the sum total of human thought been so thoroughly challenged and interrogated. There is no turning back from this intellectual uncertainty. It is equally impossible to pretend that there is no bias once it has been shown to exist. In all the feminist work so far accomplished, be this in the most abstract or grassroots work, one of the motivating forces was to exorcise the ghost of oppression from humanity. No one can doubt that important groundwork for the future has been laid so that women may never become invisible victims and silent majorities again. Expressed in more formal terms: 'The new social movements began where existing large-scale formal organisations leave off; to expand, redefine, and democratise social spaces in which collective identities, new meanings, new solidarities and forms of democratic association can emerge' (Arato & Cohen, 1984: 269).

The concept of collective identity (Pizzorno, 1978, 1983) implies a commitment to collective action as well as some notion of the possible effects of that action for the purpose of effecting change. It stands to reason that the question on 'how must that class think in order to change the world' is tied up with the formation of such an identity and has preoccupied the new social movements throughout western Europe. In the process of developing such a collective identity as part of an orientation towards group member needs, women have resorted to new forms of action which have continued to safeguard and promote a collective identity, as in self-management of services, of alternative business ventures, and new solidarity groups and structures (Diani & Melucci, 1988: 338).

Whether one ought to fear an increasing erosion of the movements' three most valued ideological achievements: collective identity, feminist consciousness and solidarity (Cohen, 1985: 685), and therefore expect a re-emerging marginalisation of women's issues, is a different matter. In some respects, feminist ideas have merged into mainstream culture. But instead of arguing that the integration into mainstream culture is a loss to the movements, it may be much more appropriate to demonstrate that those beliefs represent the first infiltration into the mainstream and will possibly alter the system eventually.

Feminism in the western Europe of today is alive and well but it is wearing a different garb. If there is a fundamental difference between now and the 1970s, it is the feminists' role vis-à-vis the state. As movements of radical opposition, feminism has vanished from the scene to make room for extensive networks of structured groups, of representatives at all levels in culture, education, government, and legislature. Feminists run feminist shops, bookshops, film crews, publishing houses and theatres. They are serving on committees and on boards. They are involved in the slow grinding machine of institutional amendments and public opinion education. To be sure, where they have ventured into institutions or private enterprise they are often fighting in isolation, and they are exposed and vulnerable because in their particular work/life environment the concrete support for their views may be small. But women are in positions in which they have not been before and thus may wield influence or even power. Furthermore, there are countless examples of women having gained substantial political experience and political confidence throughout the decade of the 1970s, as demonstrated in the world conference of the UN Decade for Women in Copenhagen in 1980 (Barry, 1981: 41–3). Feminist ability to conduct meetings, assert themselves on the political floor and make binding resolutions has improved markedly. We now see very polished political performances by women, which would have been relatively atypical twenty years ago. Offe makes the point that such non-institutional politics was able to play to the full its claim that 'the means of action can be recognized as legitimate and the ends of action can become binding for the wider community' (1985: 827). In the political reality, however, 'movements are incapable of negotiating because they do not have anything to offer in return for any concessions made to their demands' (Offe, 1985: 830). In the present climate, negotiation is the one venue open in the absence of an active movement. It is therefore perhaps regrettable that the life cycles of the movements have come to an end. But it is not regrettable that in their stead, women have found a way into the maze of formal structures from which negotiations are at least possible and seen as necessary.

Having said this, there is of course room for criticism. Post-mortems usually reveal weaknesses much more readily than strengths. I shall proceed to name a few of these weaknesses, as I have perceived them, even if this seems to contradict my basic optimism about the future of feminism.

At the risk of psychologising complex socio-political events, I do want to bring up at least two interrelated psycho-historical blind spots in the movements. There is a generational question here which I have rarely seen addressed in contemporary debates. This issue was openly discussed in the first-wave feminism in Europe, when sharp differences and communication problems with the next generation of young women, who were supposed to inherit the fruits of all the work, were discussed at length. By contrast, it is my impression that the younger generation of western European women is not so much disaffected with the feminists of the former movements as disinterested and bored. Boredom chiefly stems from two sources. Young women today are the recipients of the changes for which the preceding generation fought. For the young women of the 1990s stories of oppression, as told by their mothers (the feminists of the 1970s) and grandmothers, sound like stories from a different age, no longer relevant. Many of the irksome restrictions have fallen away, and the road has been paved for a freer life. Freedom is like fresh air and easily taken for granted. At this point it appears as if there are no particular feminist issues on which the generation born in the late 1960s or early 1970s feels it has to mobilise. Rather, current popular concerns have shifted to peace and environmental issues, which a small minority of young women actively support. Apart from some exceptions, as for instance in Greece, political meetings have become less widespread and feminist consciousness-raising activities have generally dropped off. 'Women's groups', which were once the hub of movements, have declined in numbers and often are no longer even specifically feminist. They have moved into the periphery of the contemporary feminist scene (Carden, 1978: 181). In their stead, education, including feminist education, and a feminist culture have emerged as the two constant sources of information and dissipation of ideas. The present trend has not happened in a vacuum, of course, but is part and parcel of a general swing to the political right all across western Europe. Since the mid-1970s even strong social democratic parties, such as those in Austria, Denmark, UK, Norway, Sweden, the Netherlands and West Germany, have had to accept electoral defeat, and so have social democratic parties in Greece and Portugal.

Furthermore, I have seen few if any attempts by the 'old guard' of feminists to woo the young generation before it quietly disappeared into a 'Barbie Doll's golden cage' of mindless consumerism (Marcone, 1987: 123). On the contrary— it was barely noticed in the 1980s that for young women the feminist 'message' of the 1970s, or rather the way in which it was delivered was anything but attractive. Since the beginning of the days of the second wave, women have heard from other women that they are exploited and oppressed. The constant reinforcement of these bleak tidings worked at the height of the movements because it helped to keep up the level of anger and create cohesion and a sense of purpose. It also worked as long as consciousness-raising groups, fun and positive cultural events gave a healthy counterweight to the stories of gloom. At the same time as women were being told how they were downtrodden, they were also being told that they could change that state of affairs and their own perception of themselves. They learned to take action, to take pride in their position, capacities, and combined power. With the disappearance of the strong action-oriented energies of the movement the sole remaining story of oppression looms large and ominously for the successors. For feminist thinking to remain relevant, constant reappraisals will be necessary.

As to who the movements were meant for and who they actually addressed, opinions differ. We have discovered an age bias here, and in earlier chapters we also pointed out that in some places and countries there was a distinct class bias. To these we have to add an ethnic bias as well. The new movements were said to be heterogeneous in character. To an extent that is true. They tried to appeal to women of all social strata, occupational and income groups. On specific-issue campaigns, such as abortion, the strategy worked well. But apart from those one-off events of mobilisation for specific reasons, the supposed heterogeneity never quite worked at local level. The ideal of an all inclusive global solidarity of women has found its best expression in international gatherings. In European movements the problem of racial and ethnic pluralism was generally of minor concern, although it surfaces here and there either via socialist feminism or by trickling through from across the English Channel. Some European feminists may have hoped for a new kind of global sisterhood, but in too many western European countries the issue of class and ethnic difference was neglected and lost in the fragmentation of movements. Ironically, the very idea, let alone practice, of building a pluralist movement inclusive of women of many different cultural, ethnic and class identities, is surfacing more strongly after the event. I agree with Nancy Fraser that this kind of solidarity amongst women today exists at best in a 'prefigurative form' (1986: 429).

From the middle of the 1970s the political dimensions of western European feminist movements were steadily being overshadowed by a new form of introspective activity. Frigga Haug, at a European feminist gathering, said that 'feminism has attacked all levels of bourgeois culture. It has exposed the male bias of their language, dethroned their high culture and ridiculed their science. But it has got bogged down in its own critique, absorbed by its own preoccupations' (Haug, 1986: 6). I agree with her argument entirely. 'Getting bogged down in its own critique' is a luxury no movement or set of ideas intent on changing the world can permit itself. It is indeed apolitical, for it leads away from the public and the political arena. Introspectivity of organisations, groups, and activities results in missing cues for actions. Any self-imposed ghettoisation, culturally and intellectually, is ultimately sentencing those ideas to death or to a loss of the vital audience. The 'vital' audience consists of policy makers, politicians, and women and men at every level of activity.

In a sense, however, this self-imposed ghettoisation was built into the movements from their very onset because the movements spoke to women alone and mobilised women only. This created a lopsided revolution in which only half of the members of society was addressed. Put bluntly, in a revolution there are basically only three things one can do with those individuals or groups who are identified as the oppressors: kill them, force them to leave, or force them to undergo ideological re-education. In all cases, power and control has to be taken away from them or the revolution has failed. As said before, women could not eradicate or overpower half of humanity. Familial, physical, and sexual ties made this unthinkable and somewhat impractical, although in Monique Wittig's *Les Guérillères* the utopian vision builds precisely on those revolutionary practices. In reality, women were not in the position to wrest the power and control from the institutions, or individuals. Nevertheless, some more thought could have been given to the ideological re-education of men (as the weakest but nevertheless real option in revolutionary practice). Of course, there have always been very good reasons for excluding men from feminist meetings, from discussion groups, and especially from consciousness-raising gatherings. Apart from demonstrations and policy submissions, however, when and where can men hear feminist views and arguments consistently debated? There have been such attempts, but in western Europe they have remained rather isolated and therefore largely inconsequential.

Interestingly, a 1968 report to the United Nations on the position of women in Sweden spelled out very clearly that men had to be re-educated to learn to become parenting fathers, learn domestic role-sharing and shared family responsibilities, if women were to be relieved of carrying the totality of that burden and even of a dual workload. In a minor way, a male liberation move-ment has developed in the USA. Herb Goldberg's book *The Hazards of Being Male: Surviving the Myth of Masculine Privilege* (1976), argued that men languished away in the prison of their 'masculine role'. Admittedly, this did not bring many tears to feminists' eyes. But there has been some grassroots work amongst men that has shown a good deal of promise, such as MOVE (Men Overcoming Violence), an organisation counselling battering men, and appar-ently, fighting for gender justice (Lichterman, 1989: 187). Except for a few 'masculinist' publications coeval with the onset of the second wave, such as a book by the Austrian writer Karl Bednarik *The Male in Crisis* (1970), and the Swedish government-supported programmes for men (since 1985), there is, overall, little activity on that front in western Europe.

When the second-wave movements erupted, one of the first questions femi-nists asked was how women could be liberated from their present yoke and become people (citizens) with a sense of autonomy, self-determination, and freedom. Unequivocally, the answer was and still is that women need an in-dependent income in order to make independent decisions. If women were to remain at home to raise children, then there was an argument for receiving some sort of remuneration for that work. In West Germany (Bock, 1984), Italy (Costa, 1972), and England (Cowan, 1985), the debates on housework raged long and hard. But the options and the ways of translating these ideas into practice continuously ran into difficulties. The other, much more feasible option, espe-cially at times of full employment in the early 1970s, was to propose and defend women's right to seek work, and careers, outside the home, and to gain equal access to education and training towards those ends. In the late 1980s some of the criticism that should be levied against the very forces that prevent women from pursuing careers, ironically and unfairly, have been charged against feminism. In this period of 'post-feminism', the resentment is turned against feminism for having forced women into a horrible double yoke of household and paid work.

These ideas were not necessarily wrong or over-dramatised, but too many other things needed to change in conjunction with these ideas in order to achieve the goal of getting women into positions of financial independence. Feminists throughout Europe have lobbied strenuously for adequate services that would especially help mothers to seek a field of activity outside the home. As it was shown in earlier chapters, very few of the other necessary changes in fact occurred or kept pace with rising demands for these services as the number of women in the workforce increased. Throughout western Europe there are only very few countries now in which child-care facilities are at anywhere near adequate levels (e.g. Sweden and Denmark). In only a few countries has a workable parental leave been introduced, which men can claim without penalty or fear of losing their jobs. In most countries, it falls entirely to the woman to take time off from work when a child is ill. In other words, the infrastructure necessary to follow the feminist blueprint for a woman's liberation is either barely established or non-existent.

Unfortunately, largely as a consequence of the lopsidedness of the feminist movements, little of the feminist teaching has trickled into everyday life and into the domestic sphere. We said that even in countries with the most advanced gender policies domestic role-sharing is practised by a small minority. In only few cases, usually involving the younger generation of men, has the burden of child care become a shared responsibility of both parents. In most cases, the major workload for household and child rearing has remained a woman's lot.

Thus, a lack of infrastructure in society at large is mirrored by a lack of support systems within the nuclear family itself. And of course, for married working women in particular, there is an additional psychological burden of *sole responsibility* which is rarely put in perspective. We need to remember that over the last 100 years or so the European family has undergone a profound change in its familial structures, as has the family in new world countries. Probably the most important loss to the modern nuclear family has been a loss of support structures (of aunts, uncles, grandparents etc.). A European woman of the 20th century looking after a child is arguably in a worse position than she might have been in the 19th century. Her job might not have been easier a century ago, the housework was likely to have been more time consuming and backbreaking, but the psychological strains might have been fewer for the sheer knowledge of shared responsibilities. In addition, present-day career paths for women have produced inordinate psychological pressures, and, despite enormous efforts, women are not making inroads into upper status and upper-income brackets at a rate one might have hoped for twenty years ago. None of this augurs well for women's happiness or freedom. Stress management courses are not accidentally dominated by them.

In summary, then, there may be a hotchpotch of reasons why the feminist recipe of women and work has not necessarily produced the desired results. We are here counting the 'victims' of the new philosophy rather than the success stories. Nobody has taken account of whether there are more losers or winners within this new constellation. I suspect that there may be more winners but the numbers of women who were negatively affected cannot be ignored. No doubt, there has been a sense of disillusionment with feminist thinking amongst the latter. For many of them, the liberation that had been hoped for has either not happened or has become a limp horse that tired riders try to move along. Much of the discomfort and unease in fact is expressed by working women. Sylvia Hewlett's book, *A Lesser Life,* illustrates the frustrations and the bleak humdrum of the lives of women who have chosen to combine motherhood and work (Rosenfelt & Stacey, 1987: 79). Some of the key words of the second wave, such as autonomy, self-determination and economic independence, ring faintly in the ears of women who have taken on the double burden of work and motherhood. Some women have inevitably ended up in a vicious circle strictly defined by the double life and regulated hour by hour. The glory of autonomy, for many, has turned into a nightmare of obligations from which there is no reprieve. Apart from the very few women on above-average incomes, for most there is little compensation via economic rewards. The feminist message may have sugar-coated the pill for a while but the bitter core is now revealed. Without the re-education of men to act as co-houseworkers and co-parents, or provide the constant support of another adult, the strains become immense. The difficulties that working women with children experience today, sadly come at a crossroad that might see the feminist options slide away. Women have taken the punt and taken on careers and full-time jobs. In many cases, of course, this did not happen because feminists told them to do so, but because they needed an income. Unfortunately, fundamental changes in attitudes and role model education might not come for years. Meanwhile too many women have grown tired of their 'freedom' and have been worn out by its specific idiosyncracies.

Remarkably, the problems that are being raised now are almost identical to the problems and complaints raised in the 1920s. Women then argued that feminism had betrayed them and had guided them into the worst enslavement they had ever experienced. These arguments, throughout western Europe, but strongly developed in the Weimar Republic of Germany, led directly into a pronounced anti-feminism and into a celebration of feminine virtues and of family life (Kaplan & Adams, 1990). This new pro-family ideology made it relatively easy for rising fascist governments to gradually remove women from the workplace.

It seems that the disillusionment and disappointments of some women have created a spiritual void and a need to find something to believe in, about themselves, and about their futures. It is at such vulnerable psycho-historical moments that we see the rise of ideologies which revert to concepts and beliefs that have been tried before and have failed. Some women have come to the conclusion that they have virtues and strengths precisely because they are biologically and 'intrinsically' different from men. This 'special value perspective' as we discussed in Part I, argues that women possess specific feminine virtues (nurturing, mothering, etc.) for which little recognition is given. Indeed, there is a good deal of work women do and there are a good many qualities women have that are not being rewarded because these skills happen to fall outside the paid labour force. I fail to see why such valid observations need to be underpinned with highly questionable biological arguments. What this argument overlooks, of course, is that the 'feminine virtues' are *social* virtues, long nurtured and fostered in socialisation processes, and praised and rewarded as manifest behaviours.

The feminist movements of the new wave clearly have not convinced everyone that biology, in the wider social reality, must not matter. Nor have they always spelt out clearly where the demarcation lines are between biology and the social world. Ironically, the new-wave movements have developed and strengthened women's identity *as women*. The movements arose for gender-specific reasons, ones that were tied to women's biology: the fight for abortion was the most biologically based revolt by women and, in Europe, this single issue also attracted the largest number of supporters amongst feminists and women outside the movement. But within the movement and its ideological framework, women's biological and socially conditioned 'womanhood' fell largely into oblivion in the general scramble for equality and emancipation. This is a rather gross generalisation because analyses were made, books were written and debates were held on these issues too. It would be hard to find a topic that the second wave has not raised. This is not the point. Rather, the energies more often than not moved into the political realm of citizenship, concerns for social parity (anti-discrimination) and equal opportunity in education and job markets. There is nothing wrong with this strategy, and at the time it was highly necessary. Yet all these emphases deny, and often radically so, the concept of 'difference'. They may concede a socially constructed inferiority (the deficiency model), but only to outline strategies on how to overcome difference (i.e. deficiency).

Conceptually, however, it is difficult for many to see that women can overcome being women in a strict theoretical sense, as Monique Wittig has argued. While various movements were not proposing that womanhood should be overcome, many suggested implicitly or explicitly that biology ultimately must not matter. And of course it does, at least in so far at it has mattered socially, culturally and politically to this date, and it will continue to matter in a purely reproductive sense. The post-feminist dilemma came to the surface in most western European countries at the latest by the mid-1980s and was taken up as a concern by a socialist feminist gathering. Haug wrote of it: ' ... the earlier emphasis on the disadvantage of women and how to overcome it has been replaced by a tendency of feminists looking for hidden strengths, to stress the virtues of femininity, the value of housework and the importance of family culture. The strength of the women's movement is in danger of becoming the strength of right wing politics' (Haug, 1986: 6). Haug is right in calling this development a 'danger' because the present politics of the Christian Democrats in Germany for instance, as we described in chapter 4, is firmly steered on a strong pro-motherhood course. Hoskyns sees a 'disturbing convergence' between some new feminist arguments appealing to the 'special value perspective' (that is, the special *biological* value of women) and statements by the Kohl government in Germany, which idealise the special qualities of women and attribute 'the lack of "warmth" in German society' to the fact that too many women work (Hoskyns, 1985: 86). Leaving aside the obvious sexism of Kohl's remark (as if men were unable to provide 'warmth'!) Germany has one of the lowest rates of work participation by women in western Europe. All over western Europe 'motherliness' and 'womanhood', often understood in the most traditional ways, have been rediscovered and praised (Beck-Gernsheim, 1984) in fiction and non-fiction alike. Throughout the 1980s, books on breastfeeding, on pregnancy and on motherhood regularly made it to bestseller status across western Europe.

The shift from seeing women as political subjects to the subjectivity of women, that is, from asking 'what we want' to 'who we are' has led some dangerously close to essentialist views of femininity, attributing much of the 'eternal feminine' once again to biology, and to 'intrinsic' differences. Bowlby pointed out some years ago that such attitudes, espoused to some extent also by French writers such as Irigaray, came close to the concept of *negritude* of the 1930s and 1940s in which the subject was exalted 'into closer association with the primitive nature, with the fertility of the land, with the pantheistic religion of the cosmos and with childhood' (Bowlby, 1983: 54).

With some minor exceptions, the last decade has seen a substantial shift to the political right in western Europe, as well as in other western industrialised countries. It would be superficial and not quite appropriate to attribute any present-day disillusionment with feminism entirely to feminist political errors. The swing towards greater conservatism and new right-wing values, however, has not been without repercussions within feminist circles themselves. Feminists have also looked for 'true values' and, sadly, have come up with nothing newer than ideas of 'natural' predetermination of the sexes, and the discovery of a 'new femininity' and 'new masculinity' (see Guillaumin's critique, 1985: 67 ff).

I fail to understand how these values and beliefs keep resurfacing when it must be well understood that they have always led to the exclusion of women from the public realm. The praise of women's 'feminine virtues', if one needs to recall this here, has usually been employed as a lever to rationalise why women are unable to take an active part in politics and to justify women's relegation to the private domain. From ancient times onwards, political life 'has been conceptualized in opposition to the mundane world of necessity, the body, the sexual passions and birth' (Pateman, 1988: 115; see also Elshtain, 1981). Authorities of the stature of Rousseau or Hegel expressed cognisance of women's ability for love and nurturing, but both authors derived from this insight the conclusion that women had to be excluded from the public realm of citizenship *because* they are caretakers 'of affectivity, desire, and the body'. Those three elements, according to enlightenment ideas and modern ethics, have to be excluded if moral reason, with its key ideal of impartiality, can be achieved.

Young argues that the 'will to unity expressed by this ideal of impartial and universal reason generates an oppressive opposition between reason and desire or affectivity' (Young, 1986: 382, 387–9). As diametrically opposed to enlightenment ideas and to modern liberal ethics as fascism appears, it is nevertheless indebted to this particularly sexist tradition of thought. We do not need to repeat the ideological packaging of motherhood in fascist regimes here other than to say that the celebration of motherhood, femininity and womanhood was the only compensation for very unequivocal rules barring women from the realms of the public.

It has taken women to this latter part of the 20th century to create for themselves a public voice in a public sphere. It is my firm belief that any model which suggests a retreat from that public sphere must indeed be regarded as a 'danger'. Such an atrophy would slowly erode any form of control by women over their own affairs. My own responses are obviously political in this regard rather than theoretical, but to date I have not been persuaded that the 'special value perspective' can be argued without having overwhelmingly negative consequences in politico-historical terms. To date, I have also found it difficult to believe that such traits as caring and nurturing should be vested in only half of humanity, and that they could not be developed, allowed to surface and supported in men. In other words, women have the choice of opting out of the niche that philosophy, political theory, and even the most disparate political ideologies and practices have created for them over centuries, and refusing to remain or be caretakers of 'affectivity, desire and the body'. If, on the other hand, feminist theorists decide that there is merit in retaining that role then, as indeed quite a number of feminists have argued, political theory has to be challenged. And more than that: they must draw the conclusion that emancipatory ethics and politics cannot work with modern traditions of moral and political life. They must reject the enlightenment ideals because they are in essence sexist (Okin, 1978). They have to break the nexus of enlightenment ideals even if, on the surface, the very basis of the new feminist movements appears to be a realisation of the potential of those ideals.

Debates on 'difference' and 'equality' too often have remained in the lower echelons of political belief. A 1983 conference in Turin on women and employment produced papers, including one by Piva and Ingrao, directly confronting the issue. They rightly saw that the arguments on gender 'difference' and gender 'equality' had split political activists and theorists into two camps. Those who advocated 'difference' made no attempt to transform the workplace or to negotiate; those who adhered to the notion of 'equality' entered bargaining initiatives, both within the trade union movements and the parties of the left. They proposed that a synthesis was timely: 'equality' brought women into the workforce and 'difference' will transform the workplace once women are installed (Piva & Ingrao, 1984). Such a synthesis would of course require the defenders of equality to accept that 'difference' exists in more fundamental than merely socialised ways. The position in western world feminist thinking is probably at a theoretical impasse and we may expect a good deal more work in future that addresses the issue of 'equality' and 'difference'. Politically, the former has remained to the forefront and has been the guiding light for legislative reform. The latter, however, as uncomfortable as the term is, harbours not just a very conservative and revisionist element but also a very radical one: only if we can accept social and cultural 'difference'—without using this exploitatively— will we put into place a more just world. In other words, if we opt for pluralism and heterogeneity in a context of equality of treatment and access in general, the argument of biology, historically purposely overrated, can fall away. This does not mean that the reproductive difference is ignored. It is not defensible that a whole gammut of punitive and restrictive measures is derived from this clearly definable state. What follows after the biological event, for which two people are of course responsible, is in the realm of social accountability of man and woman. In my opinion, there is not a single good reason why the burden of *that* responsibility should be shifted to one party only.


## THE COMING EUROPE

The Europe of the 1990s, of the new century and millennium, is likely to be a very different political entity from the Europe it has been up to now. For the third time this century it stands at a significant historical threshold. This time not to make war, but to move towards unification. The first step is imminent— 1992—and further steps are likely to follow. Some degree of success for the unification of western European countries seems assured, along with the pro- gressive integration of other European countries. The Common Market has been tried and tested, and it has worked for some time. Discussions on the possibilities of unification of Europe have been seriously pondered since the end of World War II and a good many measures have since been taken in moving towards this goal. For some decades, the idea of a unified Europe has increasingly claimed support from very disparate groups. Historically, the position of the Vatican on unification has always been the same. The Vatican has championed the idea of a unified Europe as if it were a 'substitute' for the Holy Roman Empire. Also, the Vatican has strong ideological objections to socialism. It has always supported the christian democratic parties. By the 1960s even the European left, in many ways the very antithesis to the catholic church, succumbed to the idea of unification. Italian communists then argued that a unified Europe was to be welcomed because multinationals can only be fought with multinational powers, and these powers 'can be efficacious only if they have a democratic basis by means of elections by universal suffrage to the European Parliament' (cit. in Kaldor, 1979: 191). In France the idea of joining was rationalised by the left with the rather chauvinistic argument that they would help liberate the domi- nation of capital, democratise its institutions and support the workers' claims.

There is nothing rash about the new proposals. European countries have been at peace with each other long enough to allow these processes to mature and to take effect structurally, legally, and in the dynamics of interaction. But this is only one side of the coin. In the year 1990, the process of unification has taken on a different meaning. What was ideologically considered as Europe is now just 'western' Europe. 'Eastern' Europe (including, geographically central Europe) is now coming into sharp relief.

The year 1989 to 1990 changed things dramatically, taking even close political observers by surprise. Trevor-Roper put it well:

> The year 1989–1990 has been one of the most dramatic in remembered history: a general revolution in Europe, unparalleled in time of peace, at least since 'the year of revolutions', 1848. Indeed, it has many similarities with that year: the crumbling of an imposed international order; the rediscovery, by the nations of Eastern Europe, of their national identity, their long-suppressed individualism, their continuous history. (1990: 8)

These events call into question the wisdom of the Yalta and Potsdam agreements, and topple the artificial constructs of a divided Europe. The firm ideological and economic divisions between western and eastern Europe have been blurred and are in some cases in the process of disappearing. There is a shift westward, to democratic and free-enterprise strategies, in many of the eastern bloc countries. These countries, among them Poland, Czechoslovakia, and Hungary, are now making moves to rejoin Europe.

High on the list of the extraordinary events of 1989 to 1990 was the collapse of the German Democratic Republic, once the stronghold and steadfast outpost of Stalinist Russia, and the sudden, almost quiet, reunification of Germany which occurred, de facto, on 1 July 1990, when the East German currency was withdrawn and, *de jure*, accomplished by the end of 1990. Leaving the enormous internal problems of this process aside, the reunification is likely to have the effect of accelerating the process of (western) European unification in an effort to prevent old historical questions of the balance of power and of European hegemony from surfacing again. The Romanian Revolution has vanquished the dictatorship of Ceaucescu and forcefully installed an interim democratic government. Lithuania has tried to take a stand for independence. There is Yugoslavia in turmoil. In Slovenia and Croatia, the newly elected leaders have 'called for a pluralist system, a market economy, and a greater degree of independence for their republic' (Scammel, 1990: 37). In Poland, as Michnik claims, 'communism is dead' (1990: 7). He calls it a miracle that 'the Poles including both the Communists and the opposition—[have] come to an understanding with one another. This miracle—something that seemed to me utterly impossible—actually occurred in my country. The prisoners and their guards sat down at a table and began to negotiate. The result is that communism has ceased to exist in Poland.' (Michnik, 1990: 7).

There is the possibility for a 'new' central Europe, one that is geographically central, but politically moving westwards. Czechoslovakia, Hungary and Austria might see themselves fulfilling new roles, and the 'tragedy of central Europe' (Kundera, 1984) might be over. Austria has taken steps to join the European Community, not a small feat in view of the fact that Austria was given its independence in 1945 on the undertaking that it was to be neutral forever and never to enter into a military pact with Germany (Bodi, 1989). In Hungary, the restoration of freedom is coupled with strategies to join western-style markets (Trevor-Roper, 1990: 8). In the present joint Viennese–Budapest preparation for the 1995 Expo, the Mayor of Vienna significantly referred to the preparatory efforts as a central European one, adding: 'Should we, at some later date, succeed in changing the Vienna–Budapest axis into a triangle that also includes Prague, then we could demonstrate to the world how strongly the European heart can beat' (cit. in Bodi, 1991).

At this time of massive transition the question 'What is Europe? Where is Europe?', as Seton-Watson asked in 1985, will have to be asked anew. Eastern bloc countries are economically in crisis and need to think of more workable economic strategies in future, and western Europe cannot hope to survive international market pressures unless it pulls and stays together. In other words, economic considerations are probably the strongest motivators in the present restructuring of Europe. All other issues have to follow in their wake and be somehow accommodated. Such economic pragmatism has guided much of western European development and thinking in the post–World War II decades, and issues of regional and national interest might have to continue to take a back seat in this new European theatre. Yet there are many unanswered questions and uncertainties.

What has all this to do with women, and how will women fare in the new Europe? I have been asked these questions with great regularity. In the context of German reunification it has been said how wonderful it would be if the best of socialism and capitalism would come together in a new kind of synthesis and help women in their struggle for equality. I would regard such hopes as naive pipe dreams. There are clearly risks during the process of liberalisation for eastern bloc countries of which their astute inhabitants are well aware. Michnik argues that with the threat of communist governments disappearing, there surfaces other threats, possibly opening a Pandora's box of evils, so to speak, which, if some of them were to gain the upper hand, would certainly not aid women's cause: 'The greatest threat to democracy today is no longer communism, either as a political movement or as an ideology. The threat grows instead from a combination of chauvinism, xenophobia, populism, and authoritarianism' (Michnik, 1990: 7). He asks himself whether chauvinism would ever again gain the upper hand:

> Whether the victors will be those in Berlin and Dresden who screamed *Polen raus*, or wrote those words on walls, in November and December of last year; those in Bulgaria who deny Muslims the right to their own names; those in Transylvania who deny Hungarians the right to their own schools; those in Poland who promote anti-Semitism and a country without Jews. These people could be victorious. They have their chance because we do not know what will flow into the great vacuum left behind by the death of communism (1990: 7)

Michnik has a point, namely that liberation from any coercive political force also 'liberates' qualities that had been successfully oppressed before. Male chauvinism, to some extent, also belongs in the catalogue of attitudes and values which eastern bloc countries have fairly successfully suppressed. The problem is that ideas that have not developed from grassroots level and have had no time to mature amongst the general populace have also had little chance to be adopted with conviction by that populace. The only lesson that people learn in dictatorships is to sidestep rules by devious means where possible, to develop an Orwellian double-think, and to keep quiet but not to reason.

Jirina Siklová, a long-time Czechoslovakian dissident, is particularly concerned about the future of women in her country. There is fear that welfare programmes which protected women and children will be dismantled, and a number of women's rights will disappear. There exist already signs that women see staying at home as 'new and progressive'. Rosen argues that such fears are not unwarranted. There is 'a call for Christian renewal, for traditional values, and for support for the "traditional family"', which 'finds a receptive audience among both sexes'. Rosen continues:

> Propaganda which seeks to send women home is pervasive. From the church, the media, and pro-life groups comes the familiar chant that women's participation in the labor force and absence from the home is responsible for the high divorce rate, juvenile delinquency, alcoholism—even men's high rate of heart attacks in Hungary. As unemployment rises, according to Siklová, economists plan to retire women and the elderly to ease the economic plight of working-age men. The calculation is simple: dismantling the crèches and bringing women home with their children is cheaper than keeping women in the labor force and paying their childcare. (1990: 11)

In the new Europe, a good deal of thinking will need to take place. The situation now is precarious, and it remains to be seen which models for change are going to be adopted: the Spanish model of peaceful negotiation between *ancien régime* and democratic forces, the German and French model of expiation ('denazification'), involving revenge and punishment, or the resurrection of dictatorships in a new garb (Michnik, 1990: 7). One may hope that economic and pragmatic considerations may win the day, so that in several eastern bloc countries at least an approximation of the Spanish model may become a reality.

Despite the obvious complexities of the present situation, in terms of women's status the fusion of east and west would not involve much adaptation for women on either side of the iron curtain. In some respects, eastern bloc countries and western European countries have come almost to the same point of gender parity, as is particularly obvious in the field of education. Somewhat ironically, for all the assumptions about democracy, self-expression and individual liberty, women in western European countries have just begun to catch up to women's educational status and labour force participation rates in eastern European countries. In socialist countries, no post–World War II protest movements took place but the communist governments instigated change from above at a very rapid rate, outstripping gender inequalities of the west as early as the 1960s. The gap was beginning to close in the 1980s:

Table 7.1  **Percentage of women in higher education in western and eastern European countries, 1950–1976**

| Country | 1950 | 1960 | 1970 | 1976 |
|---|---|---|---|---|
| Austria | 21 | 23 | 29 | 39 |
| Belgium | 15 | 26 | 29 | 40 |
| Bulgaria | 33 | 40 | 51 | 58 |
| CSSR | 20 | 34 | 38 | 41 |
| Denmark | 24 | 33 | 37 | 47 |
| Finland | 37 | 46 | 48 | 50 |
| France | 34 | 40 | 45 | 50 |
| Germany, East | 19 | 25 | 36 | 48 |
| Germany, West | 20 | 23 | 27 | 39 |
| Hungary | 24 | 29 | 43 | 50 |
| Norway | 16 | 21 | 30 | 43 |
| Poland | 35 | 35 | 47 | 55 |
| Romania | 33 | 34 | 43 | 44 |
| Spain | 14 | 23 | 27 | 38 |
| Sweden | 23 | 33 | 37 | 41 |
| UK | 36 | 34 | 33 | 36 |
| USSR | 53 | 43 | 49 | 51 |
| Yugoslavia | 33 | 29 | 39 | 40 |
| (USA | 32 | 37 | 41 | 47) |

*Source*: Wolchik, 1981: 449

The social provisions for old age, the widely distributed social services for children and women in eastern bloc countries, have often been the envy of feminists in the west, who have had to fight for every single creche, only to see the principles of access eroded again when governments claimed a shortage of funds. There is no doubt that in the range of services that affect women and child care, and also in the diversity of trades and professions, women in many eastern bloc countries are used to a better treatment and better provisions than in the west. This is not to say that they necessarily perceive their own treatment as better. So hated was the communist regime that anything initiated by them might be viewed with suspicion. If becoming a housewife features as a 'progressive' step, there is really little chance that socialist ideas will continue to play a dominant role. On the other hand, every former eastern bloc country now has its own feminist groups, combining well-seasoned dissenters and intellectuals, and new recruits for the women's cause. This is suggesting that, despite the supposed liberation of women in formerly communist countries, there has been a long stowed up residue of resentment born from political paralysis under state socialism.

In the past, social questions, including women's liberation, have always disappeared from the political agenda when major political events seemed to demand a nation's complete attention. The European Community, however, already has a good number of structures and laws in place to enforce women's more equitable position in society. The present changes could see a caesura, but hopefully not a backlash. Deutsch's cascade model, which we have referred to throughout this book, is relevant in a new way. There may be no feminist movements in the near future but the work that the protest movements have begun as an extra-parliamentary opposition have merged into mainstream politics, if often only in the narrowest sense. Will the new European power elites feel that they have to continue to honour the rules they have made, and will they want to promote a gender policy in line with their own avowed principles? We have not mentioned the working classes. The welfare state, as Michjael Shalev quite rightly argued, is a class issue. Its principal proponents and defenders are movements of the working class. The only serious left-wing contenders for government power have been those that align themselves with the middle classes and propose very limited reformist programmes (Shalev, 1983: 319). European economic pragmatism, however, is committed to no such goals other than management of its economic resources. The larger the federal structure, the less likely it is, so the US example shows, that social rules are unified. Indeed, it is in those structures that the greatest variation occurs, because in order to create unity in one of the many elements of social and political life, it is easier to achieve a pay off by allowing autonomy in areas that are seen as being of lesser importance. On the other hand, the likely future of the social structure of western European democratic welfare states, as Offe speculates, will see an increase rather than a decrease of the new middle class and the 'peripheral' and 'decommodified' segments of the population (Offe, 1985: 836)—the very groups which according to him, formed the basis of the new social movements in western Europe, including the feminist movements. It will be a major task of women's organisations and international groups to ensure that feminist thinking, which involves all humanity, is not cast aside in the grand sweep of historical events.

# Appendix
# Feminist research addresses

FFBIZ, Danckelmannstr. 15 and 17, 1000 Berlin 19
Feministisches Archiv und Dokumentationszentrum, Arndtstr, 18, 6000 Ff/M.
Bibliothèque Marguerite Durand, 21, Place du Panthéon, F-75005 Paris
Fawcett Library, City of London Polytechnic, Old Castle St, London E-1
Feminist Library and Information Centre (WRRC) Hungerford House, Victoria Embankment, London, WC2N 6PA
ISIS International, Via Santa Maria del' Anima, 30, I-00186  Rome
Internationaal Archief voor de Vrouwenbeweging, Keizergracht 10, NL-1015 CN Amsterdam
Isis Women's International Cross-Cultural Exchange (WICCE) C.P.24 71, CH-1211 Genf 2
The Swedish Institute, Hamngatan 27, P.O. Box 7434, S-103 91 Stockholm, Sweden
Council for Equality between Men and Women, Ministry of Social Affairs and Health, Tasa-Arvovaltuutetun Toimisto, PL Box 267, 00171 Helsinki, Finland
Multinational Women's Liberation Group, Mavromichalis 69, Athens, Greece
Women's Information Service, Directorate-General Information, Communication, Culture, Commission of the European Communities, Rue de la Loi, 200, B-1049 Brussels
Centre for Research on European Women (CREW), 38 Rue Stevin, 1040 Brussels, Belgium (coordinates the European Network of Women (ENOW)
British section of ENOW (UK), 53/54 Featherstone St, London EC1

# References

## Alphabetical

Abel, Christopher and Torrents, Nissa (eds) (1984) *Spain: Conditional Democracy*, London: Croom Helm, New York: St Martin's Press

Abelshauser, Werner (1983) *Wirtschaftsgeschichte der Bundesrepublik Deutschland 1945–1980*, Frankfurt/M.: Edition Suhrkamp

Ackelsberg, Martha A. (1985) '"Separate and Equal"? Mujeres Libres and Anarchist Strategy for Women's Emancipation' *Feminist Studies*, vol. 11, no. 1, spring, 63–84

Adams, Carolyn T. and Winston, Katherine T. (1980) *Mothers at Work: Public Policies in the United States, Sweden and China*, New York and London: Longman

Adorno, Theodor W. (1963) *Eingriffe*, Frankfurt/M.: Edition Suhrkamp 10

*Aktuell. Das Lexikon der Gegenwart* (1984), Dortmund: Chronik Verlag

Alba, Víctor (1978) *Transition in Spain. From Franco to Democracy*, trans. by B. Lotito, New Brunswick, New Jersey: Transaction Books

Albistur, Maïté and Armogathe, Daniel (1977) *Histoire du féminisme français du moyen-âge à nos jours*, Paris: Des Femmes

Alcobendas, Tirado, Pilar, María (1982) *Women's Employment in Spain*, Report for and published by the Commission of the European Communities, File V/2163/82-EN, Directorate General for Employment, Social Affairs and Education, Brussels

Alemann, Claudia V., Jallamion, Dominique, Schäfer, Bettina (1981) *Das nächste Jahrhundert wird uns gehören. Frauen und Utopie 1830 bis 1840*, Frankfurt/M.: Fischer Taschenbuchverlag

Alexiou, K. (1981) 'The Greek women's movement', *Tribune*, 4 March, 12–13

Altbach, Edith (1984) 'The New German Women's Movement' in *German Feminism: Readings in Politics and Literature*, ed. by E. Altbach et al., Albany: State University of New York Press, 3–26

Altbach, Edith, Clause, J., Schultz, D. and Stephan, N. (eds) (1984) *German Feminism: Readings in Politics and Literature*, Albany: State University of New York Press

Ambjørnsen, Ingvar and Hæfs, Gabriele (eds) (1988) *Norwegen. Ein politisches Reisebuch*, Hamburg: VSA-Verlag

Amos, Valerie and Parmar, Pratibha (1984) 'Challenging Imperial Feminism' *Feminist Review*, 17, autumn, 3–19

Andersen, Otto (1977) *The Population of Denmark*, Copenhagen: Cicred

Anderson, Perry (1974) *Lineages of the Absolutist State*, London: N.L.B. Humanities Press

Andreucci, Franco (1981) '"Subversiveness" and Anti-Fascism in Italy' in *People's History and Socialist Theory*, ed. by R. Samuel, London, Boston, Henley: Routledge & Kegan Paul, 199–204

Anthony, Katherine (1915) *Feminism in Germany and Scandinavia*, New York: Henry Holt

Arato, Andrew and Cohen, Jean (1984) 'Social Movements, Civil Society, and the Problem of Sovereignty' *Praxis International*, vol. 4/3, Oct.

Arato, Andrew and Cohen, Jean (1988) 'Civil Society and Social Theory' *Thesis Eleven*, no. 21, 40–64

Arendt, Hannah (1951) *The Origins of Totalitarianism*, New York: Harcourt Brace Jovanovich
——(1968) 'On Humanity in Dark Times: Thoughts about Lessing' in *Men in Dark Times*, New York: Harcourt Brace Jovanovich, 3–31
——(1973) 'Thoughts on Politics and Revolution. A Commentary' in *Crises of the Republic*, Harmondsworth: Penguin
——(1973a) *On Revolution*, 2nd ed., Harmondsworth: Penguin
Argue, Robert, Emanuel, Barbara and Graham, Stephen (1978) *The Sun Builders: A People's Guide to Solar, Wind and Wood Energy in Canada*, Toronto: Renewable Energy in Canada
Ås, Berit (1984) 'More power to women!' in *Sisterhood is Global*, ed. by R. Morgan, New York: Anchor Press/Doubleday, 509–514
Astin, Helen S., Parelman, A. and Fischer, A. (1975) *Sex Roles: A Research Bibliography*, Center for Human Services, National Institute of Mental Health, Washington D.C.
Ayres, Russel W. (1975) 'Policing Plutonium: The Civil Liberties Fallout' *Harvard Civil Rights-Civil Liberties Law Review*, 10, 374–443
Badham, Richard (1984) 'The Sociology of Industrial and Post-Industrial Societies' *Current Sociology*, 32 (1), 1–94
Balbo, Laura (1988) 'Women's studies in Italy: a hypothesis' in *Altro Polo. Studies of Contemporary Italy*, ed. by I. Grosart and S. Trambaiolo, Frederick May Foundation for Italian Studies, University of Sydney, Australia, 61–67
Baldock, Cora V. and Cass, Bettina (eds) (1983) *Women, Social Welfare and the State in Australia*, Sydney: Allen & Unwin
Barbosa, Madelena (1981) 'Women in Portugal' in Bradshaw, ed., special issue of *Women's Studies International Quarterly*, vol. 4, no. 4, 477–480
Barkan, Joanne (1980) 'Italian Communism at the Crossroads' in *The Politics of Eurocommunism. Socialism in Transition*, ed. by C. Boggs and D. Plotke, Montreal: Black Rose Books, 49–76
——(1984) *Visions of Emancipation: The Italian Workers' Movement Since 1945*, New York: Praeger
Barnes, Barry and Edge, David (eds) (1982) *Science in Context. Readings in the Sociology of Science*, Milton Keynes: Open University Press
Barnes, Samuel H. (1977) *Representation in Italy. Institutionalized Tradition and Electoral Choice*, Chicago and London: The University of Chicago Press
Barnes, Samuel H. and Kaase, Max (1979) *Political Action: Mass Participation in Five Western Democracies*, Beverly Hills and London: Sage Publications
Barreno, Maria I., Horta, Maria T., Velho da Costa, Maria (1975) *New Portuguese Letters* (original: *Novas Cartas Portuguesas*, 1973, Lisbon: Estudios Cor), trans. by H. R. Lane and F. Gillespie, London: Victor Gollancz, Ltd. (proof copy)
Barry, Kathleen (1981) 'International Feminism: Sexual Politics and the World Conference of Women in Copenhagen' *Feminist Issues*, summer, 37–49
Barry, Ursula and Jackson, Pauline (1988) 'Women on the Edge of Time: Part-time Work in Ireland, North and South', ch. 5 in *Women, Equality and Europe*, ed. by M. Buckley and M. Anderson, London: Macmillan Press, 78–94
Bartuch, Ewald, Böhm, Christian and Gross, Inge (1984) *Die wirtschaftliche Rolle der Frau in Österreich*, Bundesministerium für Soziale Verwaltung, Vienna
Barwick, Linda (1984) 'Patterns of Powerlessness: Women in Italian Popular Song' *Social Alternatives*, vol. 4, no. 3, 35–39
Bashevkin, Sylvia (ed.) (1985) *Women and Politics in Western Europe*, London: Frank Cass
Bassnett, Susan (1986) *Feminist Experiences. The Women's Movement in Four Cultures*, London: Allen & Unwin
Batiot, Anne (1986) 'Radical democracy and feminist discourse: the case of France', in *The New Women's Movement. Feminism and Political Power in Europe and the USA*, ed. by D. Dahlerup, London, Beverly Hills & Newbury Park, New Delhi: Sage Publications, 85–102

Baumann, Bommi (1977) *How it all Began. The Personal Account of a West German Urban Guerilla*, with statements by Heinrich Böll and Daniel Cohn-Bendit, trans. by H. Ellenbogen and W. Parker, Vancouver: Pulp Press

Beauvoir, Simone de (1949) *Le Deuxième Sexe*, Paris: Gallimard

——(1952) *The Second Sex*, New York: Bantham

——(1982) *A Very Easy Death*, trans. by P. O'Brian, Harmondsworth: Penguin (original *Une Mort Très Douce*, 1964, Paris: Gallimard)

——(1984) 'France: Feminism–Alive, Well and in Constant Danger' in *Sisterhood is Global*, ed. by R. Morgan, New York: Anchor Press, 229–235

Becalli, Bianca (1984) 'From Equality to Difference: Women and Trade Unions in Italy' part of 'Trade Unions and the Radicalizing of Socialist Feminism' by C. Cockburn et al., *Feminist Review*, no. 16, summer, 43–73

——(1984) 'Working Class Militancy, Feminism and Trade Union Politics' *Radical America*, vol. 18, no. 5, Sept.–Oct., 39–51

Beck-Gernsheim, Elisabeth (1984) *Vom Geburtenrückgang zur neuen Mütterlichkeit?*, Frankfurt/M.: Fischer Verlag

Beckwith, Karen (1980) 'Women and Parliamentary Politics in Italy, 1946–1979' in H. R. Penniman (ed.) *Italy at the Polls 1979*, Washington and London: American Enterprise Institute

——(1985) 'Feminism and Leftist Politics in Italy: The Case of UDI-PCI Relations' in S. Bashevkin (ed.) *Women and Politics in Western Europe*, London: Frank Cass, 19–37

Bednarik, Karl (1970) *The Male in Crisis*, New York: Knopf

Benard, Cheryl and Schlaffer, Edit (1984) 'Benevolent Despotism Versus the Contemporary Feminist Movement' in R. Morgan (ed.) *Sisterhood is Global*, Garden City, New York: Anchor Press/Doubleday, 72–76

Benhabib, Seyla and Cornell, Drucilla (1987) *Feminism as Critique. Essays on the Politics of Gender in Late-Capitalist Societies*, Cambridge: Polity Press (previously as special issue, vol. 5, no. 4, Jan. 1986 of *Praxis International*)

Benn, Melissa (1987) 'In and Against the European Left: Socialist Feminists Get Organized' *Feminist Review*, no. 26, summer, 83–92

Benz, Wolfgang (1983) 'Neutrale Staaten' in *Fischer Weltgeschichte. Das Zwanzigste Jahrhundert II. Europa nach dem Zweiten Weltkrieg*, Frankfurt/M.: Fischer Taschenbuch Verlag, 206–224

——(ed.) (1984) *Rechtsextremismus in der Bundesrepublik*, Frankfurt/M.: Fischer

Benz, Wolfgang and Graml, Hermann (1983) 'Abschied vom alten Europa' in *Fischer Weltgeschichte, Europa nach dem Zweiten Weltkrieg*, Frankfurt/M.: Fischer Taschenbuch Verlag, 13–22

Berger, Hartwig, Heßler, Manfred, Kavemann, Barbara (1978) '*Brot für heute, Hunger für morgen'. Landarbeiter in Südspanien. Ein Sozialbericht*, Frankfurt/M.: Suhrkamp Verlag

Berger, Renate, Kolb, Ingrid and Janssen-Jurreit, Marielouise (1984) 'Fragmented Selves. A collage' in *Sisterhood is Global*, ed. by R. Morgan, New York: Anchor Press/Doubleday, 248–254

Bergman, Solveig and Vehkakoski, Vellamo (1988) 'Eine Ehe zwischen "Staatsfeminismus" und Politik der Unterschiede' in *Frauenbewegungen in der Welt*, vol. 1: *Westeuropa*, ed. by the collective Autonome Frauenredaktion Argument, Berlin: Argument, 77–94

Bernecker, Walther L. (1984) *Spaniens Geschichte seit dem Bürgerkrieg*, Munich: Beck Verlag

Bertini, Bruno (1978) 'Italy: a guide to the armed party' in *Terrorism today in Italy and Western Europe*, ed. by B.di Biase Sydney: Circolo 'G. D. Vittorio', 62–65

Beyer, Johanna, Lamott, Franziska, and Meyer, Birgit (eds) (1983) *Frauenhandlexikon. Stichworte zur Selbstbestimmung*, Munich: C. H. Beck

Bielli, Carla (1976) 'Some Aspects of the Condition of Women in Italy' in *Women in the World. A Comparative Study*, ed. by L. B. Iglitzin and R. Ross, trans. by B. Springer, Santa Barbara, Oxford: Clio Books, 105–114

Birnbaum, Lucia Chiavola (1986) *Liberazione della donna. feminism in Italy*, Middletown, Connecticut: Wesleyan University Press

Bobbio, Norberto (1987) *The Future of Democracy. A Defence of the Rules of the Game*, trans. by R. Griffin, ed. by R. Bellamy, Minneapolis: University of Minnesota Press

Bock, Gisela (1984) 'Wages for Housework as a Perspective of the Women's Movement' in *German Feminism*, ed. by E. Altbach et al., Albany: State University of New York Press, 246–250

——(1984a) 'Racism and Sexism in National Socialist Germany: Motherhood, Compulsory Sterilization, and the State' in Bridenthal, R. et al. *When Biology Became Destiny. Women in Weimar and Nazi Germany*, New York: Monthly Review Press, 271–296

——(1986) *Zwangssterilisation im Nationalsozialismus*, Opladen

Bodi, Leslie (1991) 'Europe, Central Europe and the Austrian Identity' in *The Idea of Europe. Problems of National and Transnational Identity*, 2 vols., ed. by B. Nelson, London: Berg Publishers (in press)

Borchers, Elisabeth and Müller-Schwefe, H.-U. (1984) *Im Jahrhundert der Frau*, Frankfurt/M.: Suhrkamp Verlag

Borghi, Liana, Corsi, G., Perini, A.de, Spinelli, S. (1988) 'Zeichen und Spuren: Lesben in Italien' in *Italien der Frauen*, ed. by M. Savier and R. Fiocchetto, Munich: Frauenoffensive, 52–65

Bottomley, Gill (1984) 'Women on the move: migration and feminism.', ch. 6 in *Ethnicity, Class and Gender in Australia*, ed. by G. Bottomley and M. de Lepervanche, Sydney, London: Allen & Unwin

——(1986) 'A world divided: studies of gender relations in modern Greece' *Mankind*, vol. 16, no. 3, 181–189

Bowlby, Rachel (1983) 'The Feminine Female' *Social Text*, no. 7, spring/summer, 54–68

Bradshaw, Jan (ed.) (1981) 'Special Issue: The Women's Liberation Movement—Europe and North America' *Women's Studies International Quarterly*, vol. 4, no. 4

Braidotti, Rosi (1986) 'The Italian Women's Movement in the 1980s', *Australian Feminist Studies*, no. 3, summer, 129–135

Branca, Patricia (1978) *Women in Europe since 1750*, London: Croom Helm

Brand, Karl-Werner (ed.) (1985) *Neue Soziale Bewegungen in Westeuropa und den USA. Ein internationaler Vergleich*, Frankfurt/M., New York: Campus

Brand, K. W., Büsser, D. and Rucht, D. (1984) *Aufbruch in eine andere Gesellschaft. Neue soziale Bewegungen in der Bundesrepublik*, Frankfurt/M.: Campus Verlag

Brantenberg, Gerd (1985) *The Daughters of Egalia*, trans. from Norwegian by L. Mackay, London and West Nyack, NY: Journeyman Press, (1st ed. Oslo, *Egalias døtre*, 1977)

——(1986) *What Comes Naturally*, trans. by author, London: Women's Press, (1st ed. Oslo: Gyldendals Forlag, as *Opp Jordens Homofile*, 1973)

Breed Platform Vrouwen voor Economische Zelfstandigeid (1984) *Van vrouwen en de dingen die aan haar voorbijgaan*, Den Hague

Bridenthal, Renate and Koonz, Claudia (eds) (1977) *Becoming Visible: Women in European History*, Boston: Houghton Mifflin Comp

Bridenthal, Renate, Grossmann, Atina and Kaplan, Marion (eds) (1984) *When Biology Became Destiny. Women in Weimar and Nazi Germany*, New York: Monthly Review Press

Briët, Martien, Klandermans, Bert and Kroon, Frederike (1987) 'How Women Become Involved in the Women's Movement of the Netherlands', ch. 2 in *The Women's Movements of the United States and Western Europe*, ed. by M. F. Katzenstein and C. M. Mueller, Philadelphia: Temple University Press

Brooks, J. E. (1983) 'Left-wing mobilisation and socio-economic equality' *Comparative Political Studies*, 16 (3), 393–416

Brown, Connie (1976) 'Book Reviews' (*The New Portuguese Letters*), *Womanspeak*, vol. 2, no. 2, 6–7

Brox-Brochot, Delphine (1984) 'Manifesto of the "Green" Women' in *German Feminism. Readings in Politics and Literature*, ed. by E. Altbach et al., Albany: State University Press, 315–317

Brugmans, I. J. (1961) *Paardenkracht en Mensenmacht*, Den Haag: Nÿhoff

Buckley, Mary and Anderson, Malcolm (eds) (1988) *Women, Equality and Europe*, London: Macmillan

Bundesministerium des Inneren (1982) *Sicherheit in der Demokratie. Die Gefährdung des Rechtsstaats durch Extremismus*, Bonn

Burke, Carolyn (1978) 'Report from Paris: Women's Writing and the Women's Movement' *Signs*, vol. 3, no. 4: 843–855

Butragueño, María de Los Angeles J. (1982) 'Protective legislation and equal opportunity and treatment for women in Spain' *International Labour Review*, vol. 121, no. 2, Mar.–Apr., 185–198

Buttafuoco, Annarita (1980) 'Italy: The Feminist Challenge', ch. 7 in *The Politics of Eurocommunism*, ed. by C. Boggs and D. Plotke, Montreal: Black Rose Books, 197–217

Caldwell, Lesley (1981) 'Abortion in Italy' *Feminist Review*, vol. 27, spring, 49–64

——(1983) 'Courses for Women: The Example of the 150 hours in Italy' *Feminist Review*, vol. 14, summer, 71–83

Calhoun, Craig ((1989) 'Introduction: Social Issues in the Study of Culture' *Comparative Social Research*, vol. 11, 1–29

Cantarow, Ellen (1976) 'Abortion and Feminism in Italy: Women against Church and State' *Radical America*, vol. 10, no. 6, Nov.–Dec., 8–27

Carden, Maren Lockwood (1978) 'The Proliferation of a Social Movement: Ideology and Individual Incentives in the Contemporary Feminist Movement' *Research in Social Movements, Conflicts and Change*, vol. 1, 179–196

Carr, Raymond (1977) *The Spanish Tragedy. The Civil War in Perspective*, London: Weidenfeld and Nicolson

——(1980) *Modern Spain 1875–1980*, Oxford, New York, Toronto, Melbourne: Oxford University Press

——(1982) *Spain 1808–1975*, (2nd ed.) Oxford: Clarendon Press

Carsten, F. L. (1972) *Revolution in Central Europe 1918–1919*, Berkeley and Los Angeles: University of California Press

Castles, Stephen (1984) *Here for good. Western Europe's New Ethnic Minorities*, together with Heather Booth and Tina Wallace, London, Sydney: Pluto Press

Cavounidis, J. (1983) 'Capitalist Development and Women's Work in Greece' *Journal of Modern Greek Studies*, vol. 1, no. 2, Oct., 321–338

Cerny, Karl H. (ed.) (1977) *Scandinavia at the Polls. Recent political trends in Denmark, Norway, and Sweden*, Washington, D.C.: American Enterprise Institute for Public Policy Research

Chafetz, Janet Salzman and Dworkin, Anthony Gary (1986) *Female Revolt. Women's Movements in World and Historical Perspective*, Totowa, N.J.: Rowman & Allanheld

Childs, David and Johnson, Jeffrey (1981) *West Germany. Politics and Society*, London: Croom Helm

Choisi, Jeanette, (ed.) (1988) *Griechenland. Ein politisches Reisebuch*, Hamburg: VSA

Choisir Association (1975) *Abortion: The Bobigny Affair. A Law on Trial*, with an introd. by S. de Beauvoir, Sydney: Wild & Woolley

Chotjewitz-Häfner, Renate (1977) *Feminismus ist kein Pazifismus. Dokumente aus der italienischen Frauenbewegung*, Frankfurt/M.: Freie Gesellschaft

Christian, Barbara (1985) 'No More Buried Lives: The Theme of Lesbianism in Lorde, Naylor, Shange, Walker' *Feminist Issues*, vol. 5, no. 1, spring, 3–20

Cicioni, Mirna (1987) 'Women Subjects and Women's Projects: The First Italian Feminist Studies Conference', *Australian Feminist Studies*, no. 4, autumn, 133–137

——(1989) 'Love and Respect, Together': The Theory and Practice of *Affidamento* in Italian Feminism', *Australian Feminist Studies*, no. 10., summer, 71–83

Cixous, Hélène (1985) *Angst*, trans. from French by J. Levy, (1st French ed. 1977), London: John Calder, New York: Riverrun Press

Cockburn, Cynthia (1985) 'Caught in the wheels: the high cost of being a female cog in the male machinery of engineering', in *The Social Shaping of Technology*, ed. by D. MacKenzie and J. Wajcman, Milton Keynes, Philadelphia: Open University Press

——(1985) 'The material of male power', ch. 11 in *The Social Shaping of Technology*, ed. by D. MacKenzie and J. Wajcman, Milton Keynes, Philadelphia: Open University Press

Cohen, Jean L. (1985) 'Strategy or Identity: New Theoretical Paradigms and Contemporary Social Movements' *Social Research*, vol. 52, no. 4, winter, 663–716

——(1982) 'Between Crisis Management and Social Movements: The Place of Institutional Reform' *Telos*, no. 52, summer, 21–40

——(1983) 'Rethinking Social Movements.' *Berkeley Journal of Sociology*, vol. 28, 97–113

Cohen, Yolande (1983) 'Student Protest in the Welfare State: France and West Germany in the 1960s' *Comparative Social Research*, vol. 6, 299–312

Colombo, Daniela (1981) 'The Italian Feminist Movement' *Women's Studies International Quarterly*, vol. 4, no. 4, 461–469

Conley, Verena Andermatt (1984) *Hélène Cixous: Writing the Feminine*, Lincoln and London: University of Nebraska Press

Cook, Alice, Lorwin, Val and Daniels, Arlene Kaplan (1984) *Women and Trade Unions in Eleven Industrialized Countries*, Philadelphia: Temple University Press

Coquillat, Michelle (1988) 'The Achievements of the French Ministry of Women's Rights: 1981–1986', ch. 11 in *Women, Equality and Europe*, ed. by M. Buckley and M. Anderson, London: Macmillan Press, 177–184

Cornelisen, Ann (1976) *Women of the Shadows*, An Atlantic Monthly Press Book, Boston, Toronto: Little, Brown and Company

Cornell, Drucilla and Thurschwell, Adam (1987) 'Feminism, Negativity, Intersubjectivity' in *Feminism as Critique*, ed. by S. Benhabib and D. Cornell, Cambridge: Polity Press

Costain, Anne N. (1982) 'Representing Women: The Transition from Social Movement to Interest Group' in *Women, Power and Policy*, ed. by E. Bonaparth, New York: Pergamon Press, 19–37

Coyle, Angela (1985) 'Going Private: The Implications of Privatization for Women's Work' *Feminist Review*, vol. 21, 5–23

Cowan, Ruth Schwartz (1985) 'Gender and technological change', ch. 3 in *The Social Shaping of Technology. How the refrigerator got its hum*, ed. by D. MacKenzie and J. Wajcman, Milton Keyes, Philadelphia: Open University Press

——(1985a) 'The industrial revolution in the home', ch. 14 in *The Social Shaping of Technology*, ed. by D. MacKenzie and J. Wajcman

Christensen, Jens (1983) *Rural Denmark 1750–1980*, Copenhagen: Central Cooperative Committee of Denmark

Dahlerup, Drude (ed.) (1986) *The New Women's Movement. Feminism and Political Power in Europe and the USA*, London, Beverly Hills & Newbury Park, New Delhi: Sage Publications

Dahrendorf, Ralf (1972) *Gesellschaft und Demokratie in Deutschland*, 1st ed. 1968, Munich: Deutscher Taschenbuchverlag

Dalla Costa, Mariarosa (1972) *Potere femminile e sovversione sociale*, Padua

Dalla Costa, Mariarosa and James, Selma (1975) *The Power of Women and the Subversion of the Community*, Bristol, England: Falling Wall Press

Dawidowicz, Lucy S. (1986) *The War Against the Jews 1933–1945*, New York, London: Seth Press and Free Press, Division of Macmillan

Delphy, Christine (1981) 'Women's Liberation in France: The Tenth Year' *Feminist Issues*, vol. 1, no. 2, winter, 103–112

Demmer, H., Kuepper, B. and Kutzner, E. (1983) 'Frauenarbeitsschutz: Gesundheitsschutz oder Ideologie?' *Beiträge zur feministischen Theorie und Praxis*, 9/10, 24–31

De Vries, Petra (1981) 'Feminism in the Netherlands' *Women's Studies International Quarterly*, vol. 4, no. 4, 389–407

Deutsch, K.-W. (1968) *The Analysis of International Relations*, Englewood Cliff, NJ: Prentice Hall

Diamandouros, P. Nikiforos (1984) 'Transition to, and Consolidation of, Democratic Politics in Greece, 1974–1983: A Tentative Assessment.' in *The New Mediterranean Democracies: Regime Transition in Spain, Greece and Portugal*, ed. by G. Pridham, London: Frank Cass

Diani, Mario and Melucci, Alberto (1988) 'Searching for autonomy: the sociology of social movements in Italy' *Social Science Information*, 27, 3, 333–353

Dittrich, Kathinka (1980) 'Wohin stürmst Du, Eva? Beispiellos: Frauenverlage und Zeitschriften in Holland' *Börsenblatt für den deutschen Buchhandel*, vol. 24, March 1980, 655–658

Doering, Dörte (1981) 'Frauen und Parteipolitik' in *Wohin geht die Frauenbewegung*, ed. by G. Gassen, Frankfurt/M.: Fischer Taschenbuchverlag, 45–53

Dominelli, Lena and Jonsdottir, Gudrun (1988) 'Feminist Political Organization in Iceland: Some Reflections on the Experience of Kwenna Frambothid' *Feminist Review*, no. 30, autumn, 36–60

Doormann, Lottemi (ed.) (1979) 'Die neue Frauenbewegung in der Bundesrepublik' in (idem): *Keiner schiebt uns weg. Zwischenbilanz der Frauenbewegung in der Bundesrepublik.*, Weinheim and Basel: Beltz, 16–70

——(1983) 'Die neue Frauenbewegung: Zur Entwicklung seit 1968.' in *Geschichte der deutschen Frauenbewegung*, ed. by F. Hervé, Cologne: Pahl-Rugenstein, 237–272

Dritsas, M. (1981) 'Changes in the character of the Greek Parliament.' *The Greek Review of Social Research*, Jan.–April, 2–5

D'Souza, Dinesh (1986) 'The New Feminist Revolt; This Time It's Against Feminism' *Policy Review*, 35, winter, 46–52

Duchen, Claire (1986) *Feminism in France. From May '68 to Mitterand*, London, Boston and Henley: Routledge & Kegan Paul

Duran and Gallego (1986) Spain

Eaubonne, Françoise d' (1977) *Feminismus oder Tod* ('Le Féminisme ou la mort') trans. G. Giert, Munich: Verlag Frauenoffensive

——(1978) *Feminismus und 'Terror'* (Contre-Violence ou la résistance à l'Etat), trans. R. Weiss, Munich: Trikont

Eder, Klaus (1985) 'The "New Social Movements": Moral Crusades, Political Pressure Groups, or Social Movements?' *Social Research*, vol. 52, no. 4, winter, 869–900

Eder, Richard (1974) 'Portuguese Revolt: Smiles Arguments and Meetings' *New York Times*, May 14

Ehrlich, Paul R. (1968) *The Population Bomb*, London: Ballantine/Friends of the Earth Books

Einarsdóttir, Else M. (1976) 'Women of Iceland... a great "day-off"', *International Women's News*, vol. 71, no. 2, 18

Elshtain, Jean (1981) *Public Man, Private Woman: Women in Social and Political Thought*, Princeton: Princeton University Press

*Emancipation in the Netherlands* (1980) World Conference of the United Nations Decade for Women: Equality, Development and Peace, Copenhagen: Ministry of Cultural Affairs, Recreation and Social Welfare

Emancipatieraad (1984) *Sociale Zekerheid en Emancipatie*, Emancipatieraad, The Hague

Encel, Sol, MacKenzie, Norman and Tebutt, Margaret (1974) *Women and Society. An Australian Study*, London: Cheshire

Epstein, Cynthia Fuchs and Coser, Rose Laub, (eds) (1981) *Access to Power: Cross National Studies of Women and Elites*, London: George Allen & Unwin

Eskola, Irja and Haavio-Mannila, Elina (1975) 'The careers of professional women and men in Finland' *Acta Sociologica*, vol. 18, no. 5, 2–3, 174–201

*Equal Rights and Opportunities for Women in the Netherlands* (1986), Ministry of Social Affairs and Employment, Public Relations Division, The Hague

Ergas, Yasmine (1982) '1968–79—Feminism and the Italian Party System: Women's Politics in a Decade of Turmoil' *Comparative Politics*, vol. 14, no. 3, April, 253–280

——(1988) 'Zwischen Sexualität und Geschlecht' in *Frauenbewegungen in der Welt*, vol. 1: *Westeuropa*, trans. by E. Helfenstein and E. Opromolla, ed. by Autonome Frauenredaktion, Hamburg: Argument, 148–155, (first appeared under title 'Tra sesso e genere' in *memoria. rivista di storia delle donne*, 19–20, 1987)

European Trade Union Institute (1983) *Information 6. Women's Representation in Trade Unions*

Evans, Richard J. (1976) *The feminist movement in Germany 1894–1933*, London and Beverley Hills: Sage Publications

Evans, Sara (1979) *Personal Politics: The Roots of Women's Liberation in the Civil Rights Movement and the New Left*, New York: Vintage

Falcón, Lidia (1984) 'Women are the conscience of our country' in *Sisterhood is Global*, ed. by R. Morgan, Garden City, New York: Anchor Press/Doubleday, 626–631

Fallaci, Oriana (1987) *Brief an ein nie geborenes Kind* (original: *Lettere a un bambino mai nato*, 1975, Milan: Rizzoli), trans. by H. Riedt, Frankfurt /M.: Fischer Taschenbuch

Feigl, Susanne (1985) *Frauen in Österreich 1975–1985*, Vienna: Staatssekretariat für allgemeine Frauenfragen im Bundeskanzleramt

Felski, Rita (1986) 'German Feminist Aesthetics' review essay in *Australian Feminist Studies*, summer, 143–151

Ferree, Myra Marx (1987) 'Equality and Autonomy: Feminist Politics in the United States and West Germany' in *The Women's Movements of the United States and Western Europe*, ed. by M. F. Katzenstein & C. Mc Mueller, Philadelphia: Temple University Press, 172–195

Ferreira, Hugo Gil and Marshall, Michael W. (1986) *Portugal's Revolution: ten years on*, Cambridge, London, New York, Sydney: Cambridge University Press

Fetscher, Iring (1978) *Terrorismus und Reaktion*, Frankfurt/M.: Europäische Verlagsanstalt

Figgis, J. N. (1960) *Studies in Political Thought from Gerson to Grotius 1414–1625*, Cambridge, New York: Harper & Row

Fiocchetto, Rosanna (1987) *L'amante celeste—La distruzione scientifica della lesbica*, Florence: Estro

——(1988) 'Die Geschichte der italienischen Frauenbewegung' in *Italien der Frauen*, ed. by M. Savier and R. Fiocchetto, Munich: Frauenoffensive

Fischer, Erica (1988) 'Frauenbewegung in Österreich' in *Frauenbewegungen in der Welt*, vol. 1: *Westeuropa*, ed. by Autonome Frauenredaktion, Hamburg: Argument, 184–188

*Fischer Weltalmanach*, '81, 1980; '90, 1989, Frankfurt/M.: Fischer Taschenbuchverlag

Fisher, Berenice (1984) 'Guilt and Shame in the Women's Movement: The Radical Ideal of Action and Its Meaning for Feminist Intellectuals', *Feminist Studies*, vol. 10, no. 2 summer, 185–212

Fishman, Robert M. (1982) 'The Labor Movement in Spain: From Authoritarianism to Democracy' *Comparative Politics*, vol. 14, no. 3, April, 281–306

Fitzmaurice, John (1981) *Politics in Denmark*, London: Hurst

Flanz, G. H. (1983) *Comparative Women's Rights and Political Participation in Europe*, New York: Transnational

Folguera, Pilar (1983) 'Research on women in Spain' in *The Changing Role of Women in Society. A Documentation of Current Research. Research Projects in Progress 1981–1983*, ed. by W. Richter et al. (1985) for the European Cooperation in Social Science Information and Documentation (ECSSID) Programme coordinated by the European Coordination Centre for Research and Documentation in Social Sciences, Berlin: Akademie Verlag, 779–781

Fontana, Joseph and Nadal, Jordi (1976) 'Spain 1914–1970' in *The Fontana Economic History of Europe*, vol. 6, Glasgow: Collins/Fontana Books, 460–529

Forester, Tom (ed.) (1980) *Microelectronics Revolution: The Complete Guide to the New Technology and its Impact on Society*, Oxford: Blackswell

Forsås-Scott, Helena (1980) 'A Woman of her time — and of ours' *Swedish Books, An Independent Quarterly*, vol. 1/4, special issues: Writing by Women, 11–15

Fox-Lockert, Lucía (1979) *Women novelists in Spain and Spanish America*, Metuchen, N.J. and London: Scarecrow Press

Foweraker, Joe (1989) *Making Democracy in Spain. Grassroots struggle in the South 1955–1975*, Cambridge: Cambridge University Press

Frabotta, B. (ed.) (1976) *La politica del femminismo*, Rome

Francome, Colin (1984) *Abortion Freedom. A Worldwide Movement*, London, Boston, Sydney: George Allen & Unwin

Frank, Miriam (1978) 'Feminist Publications in West Germany Today' *New German Critique*, 13, winter, 181–194

Fraser, Nancy (1986) 'Toward a Discourse Ethic of Solidarity' *Praxis International*, vol. 5, 4 Jan., 425–429

Fraser, Ronald (1981) 'The Spanish Civil War' in *People's History and Socialist Theory*, ed. by R. Samuel, London, Boston, Henley: Routledge & Kegan Paul, 196–199

Friedan, Betty (1985) 'How to Get the Women's Movement Moving Again' *New York Times Magazine*, 3 Nov., 26 ff

Friedl, E. (1976) 'The position of women: appearance and reality' *Anthropological Quarterly*, 40, no. 3, 97–108

Froggett, Lynn (1981) 'Feminism and the Italian Trade Unions: *L'Acqua in Gabbia*: A Summary and Discussion' *Feminist Review*, vol. 40, summer, 35–42

Froncillo, Rosetta (1983) *Confusa Desio. Eine Reise in Abschweifungen*, trans. by P. Biermann, München: Frauenoffensive

Gadourek, I. (1982) *Social Change as Redefinition of Roles. A study of structural and causal relationships in the Netherlands of the 'seventies'*, Assen/Netherlands: Van Gorcum

Galleni Mauro (1978) 'Four months of terrorism in Italy' in *Terrorism today in Italy and Western Europe*, ed. by B.di Biase, Sydney: Circolo 'G. D. Vittorio', 82–84

Gamble, Andrew and Walton, Paul (1976) *Capitalism in Crisis*, London and Basingstoke: Macmillan

Gamson, William A. (1975) *The Strategy of Social Protest*, Homewood, Ill: Dorsey Press

Gassen, Gisela (ed.) (1981) *Wohin geht die Frauenbewegung? 22 Protokolle*, Frankfurt/M.: Fischer Verlag

——(1981) 'Frauen in den Medien-Frauenarbeitsgruppe des Senders Freies Berlin (SFB)' in idem: *Wohin geht die Frauenbewegung*, ed. by G. Gassen Frankfurt/M.: Fischer Verlag, 216–225

Gelfand, Elissa D. and Hules, Virginia Thorndike (1985) *French Feminist Criticism: Women, Language and Literature*, An Annotated Bibliography, New York, London: Garland Publishing

Gerhard, Ute (1982) 'A Hidden and Complex Heritage: Reflections on the History of Germany's Women's Movements' *Women's Studies International Forum*, 5, no. 6, 561–567

Gerlach, Lattier, and Hine, Virginia (1970) *People, Power, Change: Movements of Social Transformation*, Indianapolis, Ind.: Bobbs-Merrill

Gerlach-Nielsen, Merete (1980) *New Trends in the Danish Women's Movement, 1970–1978*, Roskilde: Emmeline Press

Gersão, Teolinda (1987) *Das Schweigen* (original: *O Silencio*, Lissabon: *Edições O Jornal*, 1981), trans by K. von Schweder-Schreiner, Munich: Frauenbuchverlag

Ginsberg, M. (1953) *The Idea of Progress: A Revaluation*, London: Methuen

Giray, A. de (1980) 'Les femmes et la politique en Grece', in idem. *Femmes et Politiques autour de la Méditerrannée*, Paris: L'Harmattan

Giroud, Françoise (1974) *I give you my word*, trans. by R. Seaver, Boston: Houghton Mifflin Co. (1st ed. 1972, original: *Si je mens. Conversations avec Claude Glayman*, Paris: Société-Express-Union and Éditions Stock)

Glaab, Liana (1980) *Die unbekannte Italienerin. Aufbruch in die Emanzipation. Ein Situationsbericht*, Freiburg/Br., Basel, Wien: Herder Verlag

González, Anabel (1979) *El Feminismo en España, hoy*, Madrid: ZERO

Gordon, L. (1977) *Woman's Body, Woman's Right. A Social History of Birth Control in America*, Harmondsworth: Penguin

Gough, I. (1979) *The Political Economy of the Welfare State*, London: Macmillan

Gould, Julius and Kolb, William L. (eds) (1964) *A Dictionary of the Social Sciences*, London: Tavistock Publications

Green, Kenneth, Coombs, Rod and Holroyd, Keith (1982) *The Effects of Microelectronic Technologies on Employment Prospects: A Case Study of Tameside*, Aldershot: Gower

Greenwood, Karen and King, Lucy (1981) 'Contraception and Abortion' in *Women in Society*, ed. by the Cambridge Women's Study Group, London: Virago

Grosart, Ian and Trambaiolo, Silvio (eds) (1988) *Altro Polo. Studies of Contemporary Italy*, Frederick May Foundation for Italian Studies, University of Sydney, Australia

Grossmann, Atina (1983) '"Satisfaction is Domestic Happiness": Mass Working Class Sex Reform Organizations in the Weimar Republic' in *Towards the Holocaust. The*

*Economic and Social Collapse of the Weimar Republic*, ed. by Michael N. Dobkowski and Isidor Wallimann, London: Greenwood Press, 265–293

Gubbels, Robert (1976) 'The Female Labor Force in Western Europe', in *Women in the World: A Comparative Study*, ed. by L. B. Iglitzin and R. Ross, Santa Barbara, Oxford: Clio Books, 149–162

Guillaumin, Colette (1985) 'The Masculine: Denotations/Connotations' *Feminist Issues*, vol. 5, no. 1, spring, 65–74

Gunn, J. (1980) 'Greece-women organise for change', *Tribune*, 5 Nov., 6

Gustafsson, Göran (1987) 'Religious change in the five Scandinavian countries, 1930–1980' *Comparative Social Research*, vol. 10, 145–181

Haavio-Mannila, Elina (1968) *Suomalainen nainen ja mies* (The Finnish Man and the Finnish Woman), Porvoo

——(1975) 'Women in the Economic, Political and Cultural Elites in Finland' in *Access to Power: Cross. National Studies of Women and Elites*, ed. by C. F. Epstein and R. L. Coser, London: George Allen & Unwin, 53–75

——(1979) 'How Women Become Political Actors: Female Candidates in Finnish Elections' *Scandinavian Political Studies*, vol. 2, new series, no. 4

——et al. (eds) (1983) *Det Uferdige Demokratiet*, Oslo: Nordisk Ministerråd, trans. (1985) *Unfinished Democracy. Women in Nordic Politics*, Oxford: Pergamon

——Haavio-Mannila, Elina and Husu, Liisa (1985) 'Research on Women in Finland' in *The Changing Role of Women in Society. A Documentation of Current Research. Research Projects in Progress 1981–1983*, ed. by W. Richter et al. (1985) for the European Cooperation in Social Science Information and Documentation (ECSSID) Programme coordinated by the European Coordination Centre for Research and Documentation in Social Sciences, Berlin: Akademie Verlag, 755–758

Habermas, Jürgen (ed.) (1980) *Stichworte zur 'Geistigen Situation der Zeit'* vol. 1: *Nation und Republik*, vol. 2: *Politik und Kultur*, Frankfurt/M.: Edition Suhrkamp

Hakim, C. (1979) 'Occupational Segregation: A Comparative Study of the Degree and Pattern of Differentiation between Men's and Women's Work in Britain, the US and other Countries' *Research Paper no. 9*, Dept. of Employment, London

Halimi, Gisèle (1977) *The right to choose*, trans. by R. Morgan, Brisbane: University of Queensland Press (1st ed. Paris: Bernard Grasset as *La Cause des Femmes*, 1973)

Hanmer, Jalna (1981) 'Violence and the Social Control of Women' *Feminist Issues*, vol. 1, no. 2, winter, 29–46

Hansen, Preben, Rying, Bent, Borre, Thorkild (eds) (1985) *Women in Denmark in the 1980s*, Copenhagen: Royal Danish Ministry of Foreign Affairs

Hanson, Katherine (ed.) (1984) *An Everyday Story. Norwegian Women's Fiction*, Washington, Seattle: The Seal Press

Harrington, Michael (1986) *The Other America. Poverty in the United States*, Harmondsworth: Penguin (1st ed. Macmillan, 1962)

Harsgor, Michael (1976) *Portugal in Revolution*, The Washington Papers, The Centre for Strategic and International Studies, Beverly Hills, London: Sage Publications

Haslund, Ebba (1987) *Nothing Happened*, trans by B.Wilson (first appeared in 1948 in Norway under the title *Det hendte ingenting*) Seattle, WA: Seal Press

Hastings, E. H. and Hastings, P. K. (1980) *Index to International Public Opinion 1978–1979*, Westport: Greenwood Press

Haug, Frigga (1986) 'Women and Politics' *European Forum of Socialist-Feminists*, no. 1, Feb., 4–6, 29

——(1987) *Female Sexualisation*, London: Verso Press

——(1988) 'Lehren aus den Frauenbewegungen in Westeuropa' in *Frauenbewegungen in der Welt*, vol. 1: *Westeuropa*, ed. by the collective Autonome Frauenredaktion Argument, Berlin: Argument, 6–13

Haukaa, Runa (1988) 'Norwegen: Nostalgie und neue Herausforderung' in *Frauenbewegungen in der Welt*, vol.1: *Westeuropa*, ed. by the collective Autonome Frauenredaktion Argument, Berlin: Argument, 170–183

Heidenheimer, Arnold J., Heclo, Hugh and Adams, Carolyn Teich (1983) *Compa-*

*rative Public Policy. The Politics of Social Choice in Europe and America*, London: Macmillan

Heller, Agnes (1978) *Renaissance Man*, trans. from Hungarian by R. E. Allen, London, Henley and Boston: Routledge & Kegan Paul

——(1980) 'Die Eigenart der Geschichtsphilosophie aus der Sicht der Wissenssoziologie' trans. from English by Gisela T. Kaplan, *Kölner Zeitschrift für Soziologie und Sozialpsychologie*, special issue, no. 22, 140–152

——(1988) 'On Formal Democracy' in *Civil Society and the State*, ed. by John Keane, London and New York: Verso, 129–145

Hellman, Judith Adler (1987) *Journeys Among Women. Feminism in five Italian cities*, Cambridge, Oxford: Polity Press in association with Basil Blackwell

Henry, Ruth (1978) *Jeanne und die anderen. Stationen einer französischen Emanzipation*, Freiburg, Breisgau: Herder Verlag

Herman, Sondra R. (1972) 'The liberated women of Sweden' *Massachusetts Review*, vol. 13, winter–spring, 45–64

Hernes, Helga Maria (1985) 'Women's Research in Norway' in *The Changing Role of Women in Society. A Documentation of Current Research. Research Projects in Progress 1981–1983*, ed. by W. Richter et al. (1985) for the European Cooperation in Social Science Information and Documentation (ECSSID) Programme coordinated by the European Coordination Centre for Research and Documentation in Social Sciences, Berlin: Akademie Verlag, 773–77

Hervé, Florence (ed.) (1983) *Geschichte der deutschen Frauenbewegung*, Köln: Pahl-Rugenstein Verlag

Herzfeld, M. (1982) *Ours once more: folklore, ideology and the making of modern Greece*, Austin: University of Texas Press

Hewitt, C. (1977) 'The Effect of Political Democracy and Social Democracy on Equality in Industrial Societies: A Cross-National Comparison' *American Sociological Review*, vol. 42, 450–464

Hine, D. (1977) 'Social Democracy in Italy' in *Social Democratic Parties in Western Europe*, ed. by W. E. Paterson, and A. H. Thomas, London: Croom Helm

Hinn, Vilma (1988) 'Helvetiens Töchter. 20 Jahre Frauenbewegung in der Schweiz' in *Frauenbewegungen in der Welt*, vol. 1: *Westeuropa*, Berlin: Argument, 204–209

Hobsbawm, E. J. (1974) *Primitive Rebels. Studies in Archaic Forms of Social Movements in the 19th and 20th Centuries*, Manchester: Manchester University Press

Högbacka, Riitta (1987) 'Summary of an International Literature Review' in *Sexual Harassment*, Series E: Abstracts 2, Equality Reports, Ministry of Social Affairs and Health, Finland, Helsinki: Valtion Painatuskeskus, 1–8

Högbacka, Riitta, Kandolin, Irja, Haavio-Mannila, Elina et al. (1987) 'Sexual Harassment in the Workplace: Results of a survey of Finns' in *Sexual Harassment*, Series E: Abstracts 2, Equality Reports, Ministry of Social Affairs and Health, Finland, Helsinki: Valtion Painatuskeskus, 9–64 (incl. detailed bibliography)

Hogeweg-de Haart, H. P. (1978) 'The History of the Women's Movement in the Netherlands' *The Netherlands Journal of Sociology/ Sociologia Neerlandica*, 14, 1, July, 19–40

Höhn, C. and Otto, J. (1985) 'Bericht über die demographische Lage in der Bundesrepublik Deutschland und über die Weltbevölkerungstrends' *Zeitschrift für Bevölkerungswissenschaft*, 11, 4, 445–518

Hoskyns, Catherine (1985) 'Women's Equality and the European Community—A Feminist Perspective' *Feminist Review*, no. 20, 71–88

Howard, Judith Jeffrey (1980) 'Patriot Mothers in the Post Risorgimento' in *Women, War, and Revolution*, ed. by C. R. Berkin and C. M. Lovett, New York

Hunt, Richard N. (1964) *German Social Democracy 1918–1933*, New Haven

Huizinga, J. (1968) *Dutch Civilisation in the Seventeenth Century and other Essays*, London: F. Ungar Publishing Co.

Hvidtfeldt, Kirsten, Jørgensen, Kirsten, Nielsen, Ruth (eds) (1982) 'Strategies for integrating women into the labour market', *European Women's Studies in Social Sciences*, no. 1, Copenhagen, 1–350

Iglitzin, Lynn B. and Ross, Ruth (eds) (1976) *Women in the World*. Santa Barbara, Cal., and Oxford, England: Clio Books

Iglitzin, Lynn B. and Ross, Ruth (eds) (1986) *Women in the World. 1975–1985, The Women's Decade*, 2nd rev. ed., Santa Barbara, Cal., and Oxford, England: Clio Books

Inglehart, Margaret L. (1981) 'Political Interest in West European Women: An Historical and Empirical Comparative Analysis' *Comparative Political Studies*, vol. 14, no. 3, 299–326

Institut Für Marxistische Studien Und Forschungen (IMSF), (1978) 'Wirtschaftskrise und Frauenemanzipation in der BRD', Informationsbericht Nr. 31, Fulda: Fuldaer Verlag

Jacobs, Denise and Mazzone, Rean (1978) *Donna in Sicilia*, Palma, Palermo and S. Paulo, Brasil: NEF, Ilapalma

Jacobs, Monica (1978) 'Civil Rights and Women's Rights in the Federal Republic of Germany Today', *New German Critique*, no. 13, winter, 165–174

Jaeggi, Urs (1973) *Kapital und Arbeit in der Bundesrepublik*, originally *Macht und Herrschaft in der BRD* (1969), Frankfurt/M.: Fischer Taschenbuch Verlag

Jallinoja, Riitta (1986) 'Independence or integration: the women's movement and political parties in Finland' in *The New Women's Movement. Feminism and Political Power in Europe and the USA*, ed. by D. Dahlerup, London, Beverly Hills & Newbury Park, New Delhi: Sage Publications, 158–178

Janke, Peter (1980) *Spanish Separatism: E.T.A.'s threat to Basque democracy*, London: The Institute for the Study of Conflict

Janssen-Jurreit, Marielouise (1985) S*exismus. Über die Abtreibung der Frauenfrage*, Frankfurt/M.: Fischer Verlag

Jardine, Alice (1979) 'Interview with Simone de Beauvoir', *Signs*, vol. 5, no. 2, winter, 224–236

Jeffries, Sheila (1983) 'Sex Reform and Anti-feminism in the 1920s' in *The Sexual Dynamics of History*, ed. by the London Feminist History Group, London: Pluto, 177–202

Joeken, Susan P. (1987) *Women in the World Economy. An Instraw Study*, United Nations International Research and Training Institute for the Advancement of Women, New York, Oxford: Oxford University Press

Johansen, Margaret (1983) 'The Office Party' in *An Everyday Story. Norwegian Women's Fiction*, Washington, Seattle: The Seal Press

Jong, de Uulkje (1982) 'The Improvement of the Position of Girls in Education in a Feminist Perspective', Association Paper, International Sociological Association, Canada Public

Jouve, Nicole Ward (1981) *Shades of Grey*, London: Virago (1st ed. Paris: Editions des femmes, as *Le Spectre du Gris*, 1977)

Jowkar, Forouz (1986) 'Honour and Shame: A feminist view from within', *Feminist Issues*, vol. 6, no. 1, 45–65

Juillard, Joelle Rutherford (1976) 'Women in France' in *Women in the World. A Comparative Study*, ed. by L. B. Iglitzin and R. Ross, Santa Barbara, Oxford: Clio Books, 115–128

Jungwirth, Nikolaus and Kromschröder, Gerhard (1978) *Die Pubertät der Republik*, Reinbek

Jutikkala, Eino and Pirinen, (1984) *A brief history of Finland*, Espoo: Weilin and Göös

Juusola-Halonen, Elina (1981) 'The Women's Liberation Movement in Finland' in Bradshaw (ed.), special issue of *Women's Studies International Quarterly*, vol. 4, no. 4, 453–460

Kaldor, Mary (1979) *The Disintegrating West*, Harmondsworth: Penguin

Kandolin, Irja and Uusitalo, Hannu (1980) *Scandinavian Men and Women: A Welfare Comparison*, Research Group for Comparative Sociology, University of Helsinki, Research Reports, no. 28, Helsinki

Kaplan, Gisela and Adams, Carole E. (1988) 'Das Frauenideal national-sozialistischer Frauen vor 1933: Wider Weimarer Feminismus und männlich definierte Sexualität', trans. by G. Kaplan, in *'The Attractions of Fascism.' Traditionen und Traditionssuche des Deutschen Faschismus*, ed. by G. Hartung, special issue of *Wissenschaftliche Beiträge* 1988/55 (F 83) Halle, Saale, GDR, 3–25

Kaplan, Gisela and Kessler, Clive (eds) (1989) *Hannah Arendt: Thinking, Judging, Freedom*, London, Boston, Wellington, Sydney: Allen & Unwin

Kaplan, Gisela (1989) 'Hannah Arendt: the life of a Jewish woman' in *Hannah Arendt. Thinking, Judging, Freedom*, ed. by idem and C. Kessler, London, Boston, Wellington, Sydney: Allen & Unwin, 71–89

Kaplan, Gisela and Adams, Carole E. (1990) 'Early Women Supporters of National Socialism in *The Attractions of Fascism*, ed. by J. Milfull, Oxford, Hamburg, New York: Berg Publishers, 186–203

Kaplan, Gisela and Rogers, Lesley (1990) 'Scientific constructions, cultural productions: scientific narratives of sexual attraction' ch. 12 in *Feminine, Masculine and Representation*, ed. by T. Threadgold and A. Cranny-Francis, London, Boston, Wellington, Sydney: Allen & Unwin, 211–230

Kaplan, Gisela and Rogers, Lesley (1990a) 'The Definition of Male and Female: Biological Determinism and the Sanctions of Normality', ch. 7 in *Feminist Knowledge, Critique and Construct*, ed. by S. Gunew, London: Routledge: 205–228

Kaplan, Temma (1977) 'Women and Spanish Anarchism' in *Becoming Visible: Women in European History*, ed. by R. Bridenthal and C. Koonz, Boston: Houghton Mifflin Comp

Kaplanski, Louise K. (1984) 'German Feminism and the Peace Movement' *Potomac Review*, 1984–85, vol. 26–27, 33–50

Katzenstein, Mary Fainsod and Mueller, Carol McClurg (eds) (1987) *The Women's Movements of the United States and Western Europe. Consciousness, Political Opportunity, and Public Policy*, Philadelphia: Temple University Press

Kavemann, Barbara (1978) 'Das Leben der Frauen im Dorf', ch. 5 in «*Brot für heute, Hunger für morgen*». *Landarbeiter in Südspanien. Ein Sozialbericht*, by H. Berger, M. Heßler and B. Kavemann, Frankfurt/M.: Suhrkamp

Keane, John (ed.) (1988) *Civil Society and the State. New European Perspectives*, London, New York: Verso

Kertzer, David I. (1982) 'The Liberation of Evelina Zaghi: The Life of an Italian Communist' *Signs. Journal of Women in Culture and Society*, vol. 8, no. 1, autumn, 45–67

Ketting, Evert and Praag, Philip van (1986) 'The marginal relevance of legislation relating to induced abortion' *The New Politics of Abortion*, ed. by J. Lovenduski and J. Outshoorn, London, Beverly Hills and Newbury Park, New Delhi: Sage Publications, 154–169

Kindleberger, Charles P. (1967) *Europe's Postwar Growth*, Cambridge, Mass.: Harvard University Press

Kjønstad, Asbjørn (1987) *Norwegian Social Law*, Oslo: Norwegian University Press, distributed by Oxford University Press

Klein, Kurt (1980) 'Frauenkarrieren im gesamtberuflichen Zusammenhang in Österreich' in I. Lamel (ed.) *Managementkarrieren im gesellschaftlichen Umbruch*, Vienna

Kleinert, Ulfrid (ed.) (1981) *Gewaltfrei widerstehen. Brokdorf-Protokolle gegen Schlagstöcke und Steine*, Reinbek/Hamburg: Rororo

Kohler, Beate (1982) *Political Forces in Spain, Greece and Portugal*, trans. by F. Carter and G. Hole, London: Butterworth Scientific

Kolinsky, Martin and Paterson, William E. (1976) *Social and Political Movements in Western Europe*, London: Croom Helm

Koonz, Claudia (1986) 'Some Political Implications of Separatism: German Women between Democracy and Nazism, 1928–1934' in *Women in Culture and Politics. A Century of Change*, ed. by J. Friedlander et al., Bloomington: Indiana University Press, 269–285

——(1987) *Mothers in the Fatherland. Women, the Family, and Politics*, London: Jonathan Cape

Korpi, Walter (1978) *The Working Class in Welfare Capitalism: Work, Unions and Politics in Sweden*, London: Routledge & Kegan Paul

Kostash, M. (1982) 'Women in Greece: democracy at home?' *Broadside*, 4, 2 Nov., 8–9

Kourvetaris, Yorgos A. and Dobratz, Betty A. (1987) *A Profile of Modern Greece in Search of Identity*, Oxford: Clarendon Press

Krichmar, Albert (1977) *The Women's Movement in the Seventies: An International English-Language Bibliography*, Metuchen, N. J. & London: The Scarecrow Press

Kundera, Milan (1984) 'The Tragedy of Central Europe' *The New York Review of Books*, April 26, 33–39

*Kvinnor och Män i Norden. Fakta on jämställndheten*, (1988), Nordic Council of Ministers, Nord 1988: 58, Stockholm

*La Libération de la femme* (1975), Paris, Barcelona: Robert Laffont-Grammont

Lamel, Ingrid (ed.) (1980) *Managementkarrieren im gesellschaftlichen Umbruch*, Vienna

Lange, Peter (1979) 'Crisis and Consent' *West European Politics*, II–3

——(1979) 'Change and Compromise: Dilemmas of Italian Communism in the 1970s' *West European Politics*, II–3

Lange, Peter and Tarrow, Sidney (eds) (1980) *Italy in Transition. Conflict and Consensus*, London: Frank Cass

Lappe, Lothar (1981) *Die Arbeitssituation erwerbstätiger Frauen*, Frankfurt/M: Campus Verlag

Laqueur, Walter (1970) *Europa aus der Asche. Geschichte seit 1945*, Munich, Zurich, Vienna; English ed. *Europe since Hitler. The rebirth of Europe* (1982) Harmondsworth: Penguin

——(1985) *Was ist los mit den Deutschen?* Frankfurt/M., Berlin: Ullstein Verlag; simultaneous with English ed. *Germany today*, London: Weidenfeld and Nicolson

Latey, Maurice (1972) *Tyranny. A Study in the Abuse of Power*, Harmondsworth: Penguin

Leackok, Eleanor and Safa, Helen I. (eds) (1986) *Women's Work. Development and the Division of Labor by Gender*, Massachusetts: Bergin and Garvey Publishers

Leduc, Violette (1973) *In the Prison of Her Skin*, trans. by D. Coltman, St Albans: Panther Books, (1st ed. Paris: Librairie Gallimard, as *L'Asphyxie*, 1946)

Léger, Danièle (1982) *Le feminisme en France*, Paris: Éditions Sycomore, excerpts also in *Frauenbewegungen in der Welt*, vol. 1, trans. by B. Jansen, Hamburg: Autonome Frauenredaktion, 95–104

Lesselier, Claudie (1987) 'Social Categorizations and Construction of a Lesbian Subject', trans. by M. J. Lakeland, *Feminist Issues*, vol. 7, no. 1, spring, 89–93

Letessier, Dorothée (1985) *Eine kurze Reise. Aufzeichungen einer Frau*, trans. by Ch. Mäder-Viragh, Frankfurt/M.: Fischer Taschenbuch, (1st ed. Paris: Édition du Seuil, as *Le voyage à Paimpol*, 1980)

Lever, Alison (1988) Capital, Gender and Skill: Women Homeworkers in Rural Spain' *Feminist Review*, no. 30, autumn, 3–23

Levin, Tobe (1986) 'Introducing Elfriede Jelinek: Double Agent of Feminist Aesthetics' *Women's Studies International Forum*, vol. 9, no. 4, 435–442

*Libreria delle donne di Milano. Wie weibliche Freiheit entsteht. Eine neue politische Praxis* (1989) (original: *Non credere di avere dei diritti*, 1987, Turin: Rosenberg and Sellier Editori), trans. by T. Sattler, foreword by C. Bernardoni, Berlin: Orlando Frauenverlag

Lichterman, Paul (1989) 'Making A Politics of Masculinity' *Comparative Social Research*, vol. 11, 185–208

Lijphart, Arend (1984) *Democracies*, New Haven: Yale University Press

——, Bruneau, Thomas C., Diamandouros P. Nikiforos and Gunther, Richard (1988) 'A Mediterranean Model of Democracy? The Southern European Democracies in Comparative Perspective' *West European Politics*, vol. 11, no. 1, Jan., 7–25

Liljeström, Rita (1984) 'Similarity, Singularity, and Sisterhood' in *Sisterhood is Global*, ed. by R. Morgan, Garden City, New York: Anchor Press/Doubleday, 661–666

Lindemann, Albert S. (1983) *A History of European Socialism*, New Haven and London: Yale University Press

Lloyd, Genevieve (1984) *The Man of Reason*, Minneapolis: University of Minnesota Press

Logan, John R. (1977) 'Affluence, class structure, and working-class consciousness in modern Spain' *American Journal of Sociology*, vol. 83, no. 2, Sept., 386–402

——(1983) 'Social Welfare, Equality, and the Labour Movement in Denmark and Sweden' *Comparative Social Research*, vol. 6, 243–277

Lomax, Bill (1983) 'Ideology and Illusion in the Portuguese Revolution: The Role of the Left' in *In Search of Modern Portugal. The Revolution & its Consequences*, ed. by L. S. Graham and D. L. Wheeler, Madison, Wisconsin: The University of Wisconsin Press, 105–133

Lovenduski, Joni (1986) *Women and European Politics. Contemporary Feminism and Public Policy*, Brighton, Sussex: Harvester Press, Wheatsheaf Books

Lovenduski, Joni and Outshoorn, Joyce (eds) (1986) *The New Politics of Abortion*, London, Beverly Hills and Newbury Park, New Delhi: Sage Publications

Lucas, J. R. (1976) *Democracy and Participation*, Harmondsworth: Penguin

Lynch, Lesley (1984) 'Bureaucratic Feminisms: Bossism and Beige Suits' *Refractory Girl*, May, 38–44

Macciocchi, Maria Antonietta (1979) 'Female Sexuality in Fascist Ideology' *Feminist Review*, vol. 1, 68–69

——(1979a) *Les Femmes et Leurs Maitres*, Paris

MacKenzie, Donald and Wajcman, Judy (eds) (1985) *The Social Shaping of Technology. How the refrigerator got its hum*, Milton Keynes, Philadelphia: Open University Press

Maddox, Graham (1974) 'Democratic theory and the face to face society', *Politics*, IX (1) May, 56–62

——(1986) 'Contours of a Democratic Polity', *Politics*, XXI (2) Nov., 1–11

Mäkelä, Matti (1987) 'The Great Move in Finnish Literature in the 1960s and 1970s' *Books from Finland*, vol. 1, 36–38

Mannheim, Karl (1969) *Ideologie und Utopie*, 5th ed., Frankfurt/M.: Suhrkamp

Mandel, Ernest (1969) *Die deutsche Wirtschaftskrise. Lehren der Rezession 1966/67*, Frankfurt/M.: Europäische Verlagsanstalt

Mandel, R. (1983) 'Sacrifice at the Bridge of Arta: Sex Roles and the Manipulation of Power' *Journal of Modern Greek Studies*, vol. 1, no.1, May, 173–184

Maraini, Dacia (1984) *Women at War* (original: *Donna in Guerra*, 1975, Rome: Einaudi) trans. by M. Benetti and E. Spottiswood, London: Lighthouse Books

——(1987) *Letters to Marina* (original: *Lettere a Marina*, 1981), trans. by D. Kitto and E. Spottiswood, London: Camden Press

——(1985) *Zug nach Helsinki* (original: *It treno per Helsinki*, 1984, Rome: Einaudi), trans. by G. Jäger and P. Biermann, Berlin: Rotbuch Verlag (an English edition forecast as *Train to Helsinki*)

Marcone, Maria (1987) *A Woman and Her Family*, London: The Women's Press, (original: *Analisi in Famiglia* (1977) Milan: G. Feltrinelli Editore)

Marks, Elaine (1978) 'Women and Literature in France' *Signs*, vol. 3, no. 4, 832–842

Marks, Elaine and Courtivron, Isabelle de (eds) (1981) *New French Feminisms: An Anthology*, New York: Schocken Books

Markus, Maria (1985) 'Formation and Restructuration of Civil Society: Is there a General Meaning in the Polish Paradigm?' *International Review of Sociology*, series II, vol. XXI no. 1–3, April–August–Dec., 5–24

——(1986) 'The Antinomies of civil society and the feminist movement' Paper delivered at the conference on New Perspectives on Democracy and Civil Society, London, ms of author, University of New South Wales

——(1986) 'Women, Success, and Civil Society: Submission to, or Subversion of, the Achievement Principle', *Praxis International*, 5, iv

——(1989) 'The 'Anti-Feminism' of Hannah Arendt' in *Hannah Arendt: Thinking, Judging, Freedom*, ed. by G. Kaplan and C. S. Kessler, Sydney, Boston, Wellington, London: Allen & Unwin

Mathiasson, C. J., (ed.) (1974) *Many Sisters: Women in Cross-Cultural Perspectives*, New York: Free Press

Mathieu, Nicole-Claude (1980) 'Masculinity/Femininity' *Feminist Issues*, vol. 1, no. 1, (the English language edition of *Questions Feministes*), 51–69

Mayer, Margit (1978) 'The German October of 1977' *New German Critique*, no. 13, winter, 155–164

McNeil, William H. (1978) *The Metamorphosis of Greece since World War II*, Chicago, London: The University of Chicago Press

Means, Ingunn Norderval (1972) 'Political recruitment of Women in Norway' *Western Political Quarterly*, vol. 25, Sept., 491–521

Meissner, Michael (1980) *Massenmedien und Journalismus in den Niederlanden und in Dänemark. Mit einer Darstellung zur Journalistenausbildung*, Frankfurt/M.: Rita G. Fischer Publishing House

Melucci, Alberto (1988) 'Social Movements and the Democratization of Everyday Life' in *Civil Society and the State*, ed. by J. Keane, London and New York: Verso, 245–260

Menschik, Jutta (1977) *Gleichberechtigung oder Emanzipation. Die Frau im Erwerbsleben der Bundesrepublik*, Frankfurt/M.: Fischer Taschenbuchverlag

Merkl, Peter H. (1976) 'The Politics of Sex: West Germany' in *Women in the World. A Comparative Study*, ed. by L. B. Iglitzin and R. Ross, Santa Barbara and Oxford: Clio Books

Meulenbelt, Anja (1980) *Feminismus und Sozialismus*, trans. by J. van Soer and T. Huber-Hönck, Hamburg: Konkret Literatur Verlag, (1st ed. Amsterdam: Uitgeverij en boekhandel Van Gennep, 1975)

——(1982) *Feminismus. Aufsätze zur Frauenbefreiung*, trans. from Dutch by B. Dominick and S. Lange, Munich: Frauenoffensive, (1st. ed. Amsterdam: 1982)

——(1985) *Weiter als die Wut*, Aufsätze, trans. by B. Dominick and S. Lange, Munich: Frauenoffensive (1st ed. Amsterdam: Feministische Uitgeverij, 1983)

——(1986) *Ich wollte nur dein Bestes*, trans. by S. Lange, Reinbek: Rowohlt Verlag, (1st ed. Amsterdam: Uitgeverij Van Gennep, as *Een kleine moeite*, 1985)

——, Outshoorn, Joyce, Sevenhuijsen, Selma and de Vries, Petra (1984) *A Creative Tension. Explorations in Socialist Feminism*, trans. by D. Couling, London and Sydney: Pluto Press (1st ed. Amsterdam: Feministische Uitgeverij Sara, from anthologies *Socialisties-Feministiese Teksten*, 1980–1983)

Michel, Andrée (1971) 'Interaction and Goal Attainment in Parisian Working Wives Families' in *Family issues of employed women in Europe and America*, ed. by A. Michel, Leiden: E. J. Brill, 43–65

Michnik, Adam (1990) 'The Two Faces of Europe' *The New York Review of Books*, vol. 37, no. 12, July 19, 7

Millet, Kate (1971) *Sexual Politics*, London: Hart-Davis

Ministry of Social Affairs and Health, Finland (1988)

Mitchell, Juliet and Oakley, Ann (eds) (1976) *The Rights and Wrongs of Women*, Harmondsworth: Penguin

Mitterauer, Michael and Sieder, Reinhard (1983) *The European Family. Patriarchy to Partnership. From the Middle Ages to the Present*, Oxford: Basil Blackwell

Mohr, J. (1978) *Abortion in America*, New York: Oxford University Press

Moi, Toril (ed.) (1987) *French Feminist Thought. A Reader*, Oxford, New York: Basil Blackwell

Morgan, R. (ed.) (1984) *Sisterhood is Global*, New York: Anchor Press

Molvaer, Janitha et al. (eds) (1984) *Foreign Women in Greece*, Athens: Eleftheros

Mørch, Dea Trier (1986) *Winter's Child*, trans. by J. Tate, London: Serpent's Tale, (1st ed. Copenhagen: Gyldendal, as *Vinterbørn*, 1976)

——(1988) *Evening Star*, trans. by J. Tate, London: Serpent's Tale, (1st ed. Copenhagen: Vindrose, as *Aftenstjernen*, 1982)

Moreau-Bisseret, Noëll (1986) 'A Scientific Warranty for Sexual Politics: Demographic Discourse on "Reproduction" (France 1945–1985)' in *Feminist Issues*, vol. 6, no. 1, spring, 67–86

Morrison, Rodney J. (1981) *Portugal: Revolutionary Change in an Open Economy*, Boston, Mass.: Auburn House Publishing Co.

Moss, David (1988) 'Notes on honour, sexuality and the state' in *Altro Polo: Studies of*

*Contemporary Italy*, ed. by I. Grosart and S. Trambaiolo, Frederick May Foundation for Italian Studies, University of Sydney, Australia, 69–79

Mossuz-Lavau, J. and Sineau, M. (1984) *The Situation of Women in the Political Process in Europe*, Council of Europe, Strasbourg

Mossuz-Lavau, Janine (1986) 'Abortion policy in France under governments of the Right and Left (1973–1984)' trans. by J. Forbes, in *The New Politics of Abortion*, ed. by J. Lovenduski and J. Outshoorn, London, Beverly Hills and Newbury Park, New Delhi: Sage Publications

Mouffe, Chantal (1988) 'The civic lesson' *New Statesman and Society*, 7 Oct., 28–31

Mouzelis, N. M. (1978) *Modern Greece. Facets of Underdevelopment*, London: Macmillan

Mozzoni, Anna Maria (1975) *La liberazione della donna*, ed. by F. P. Bortolotti, Milan

Mullaney, Marie Marmo (1983) *Revolutionary Women: Gender and the Socialist Revolutionary Role*, New York

Mumford, Lewis (1964) 'Authoritarian and Democratic Technics' *Technology and Culture*, 5, 1–8

Nagle, John David (1970) *The National Democratic Party. Right Radicalism in the Federal Republic of Germany*, Berkeley, Los Angeles and London: University of California Press

*Naisten asema* (1984) Tilastokeskus (Central Statistical Office of Finland), Helsinki

Nash, Mary (1979) *Mujeres Libres 1936–1978*, trans. from Spanish by T. Kleinspehn, German ed., Berlin: Karin Kramer Verlag

Nienhaus, Ursula (1981) 'Frauenforschungs-, Bildungs- und Informationszentrum (FFBIZ)' in *Wohin geht die Frauenbewegung*, ed. by G. Gassen, Frankfurt/M.: Fischer Taschenbuch Verlag, 25–35

Norderval, Ingunn (1985) 'Party and Legislative Participation among Scandinavian Women' *West European Politics*, vol. 8, no. 4, 71–89

——(1986) 'Elusive Equality: The Limits of Public Policy' in *Women in the World 1975–1985*, 2nd rev. ed., Santa Barbara, Cal., Oxford, England: Clio, 53–81

Norris, Pippa (1985) 'Women's Legislative Participation in Western Europe' *West European Politics*, vol. 8 no. 4, 90–101 also reprinted in *Women and Politics in Western Europe*, ed. by S. Bashevkin, London: Frank Cass

——(1987) *Politics and Sexual Equality. The Comparative Position of Women in Western Democracies*, Brighton/Sussex: Wheatsheaf Books and Boulder, Colorado: Rienner Publishers

——(1988) 'The Impact of Parties on Economic Equality' in *Women, Equality and Europe*, ed. by M. Buckley and M. Anderson, Basingstoke, Hampshire and London: Macmillan Press, 142–159

Nowotny, Helga (1981) 'Women in Public Life in Austria' in *Access to Power: Cross National Studies of Women and Elites*, ed. by C. F. Epstein and R. L. Coser, London: George Allen & Unwin, 147–156

Oakley, Ann (1983) 'Women and Health Policy' in *Women's Welfare: Women's Rights*, ed. by J. Lewis, London and Canberra: Croom Helm

Oberschall, Anthony (1973) *Social Conflict and Social Movements*, Englewood Cliffs, N.J.: Prentice-Hall

Offe, Claus (1985) 'New Social Movements: Challenging the Boundaries of Institutional Politics' *Social Research*, vol. 52, no. 4, winter, 817–868

ÖH-Frauenreferat (1989) *Frauen an österreichischen Universitäten*, Vienna: Edition ÖH, ÖH-Wirtschaftsbetriebe GmbH

Okin, Susan (1978) *Women in Western Political Thought*, Princeton: Princeton University Press

Olsen, Tillie (1979) *Silences*, New York: Dell-Delta

Olson, Mancur (1977) *The Logic of Collective Action: Public Goods and the Theory of Groups*, Cambridge, Mass.: Harvard University Press

Ostriker, Alicia (1983) *Writing Like a Woman*, Ann Arbor: The University of Michigan Press

Ottolenghi, Claudia (1981) *Women in Spain*, suppl. no. 8 to *Women of Europe*, Commission of the European Communities, Brussels

Oudijk, Corrine (1984) 'In the Unions, the Parties, the Streets, and the Bedrooms' in *Sisterhood is Global*, ed. by R. Morgan, Garden City, New York: Anchor Press/ Doubleday, 469–475

Outshoorn, Joyce (1986) 'The feminist movement and abortion policy in the Netherlands' ch. 3 in *The New Women's Movement. Feminism and Political Power in Europe and the USA*, ed. by D. Dahlerup, London, Beverly Hills & Newbury Park, New Delhi: Sage Publications

——(1986a) 'The rules of the game: abortion politics in the Netherlands' ch. 2 in *The New Politics of Abortion*, ed. by J. Lovenduski and J. Outshoorn, London, Beverley Hills and Newbury Park, New Delhi: SAGE Publications

——(1988) 'Abortion Law Reform: A Woman's Right to Choose? in *Women, Equality and Europe*, ed. by M. Buckley and M. Anderson, London: Macmillan, 204–220

Papandreou, Margaret (1984) 'A village sisterhood' in *Sisterhood is Global*, ed. by R. Morgan, Garden City, New York: Anchor Press/Doubleday, 272–277

Pasquinelli, Carla (1984) 'Beyond the Longest Revolution: The Impact of the Italian Women's Movement on Cultural and Social Change' *Praxis International*, vol. 4, no. 2, July, 131–136

París, Juan N. García-Nieto (1979) 'The current evolution of trade unionism in Spain' *Labour and Society*, vol. 4, no. 1, Jan., 26–48

Parson, Talcott (1970) 'Equality and Inequality in Modern Society' *Social Inquiry*, vol. 40, spring, 13–72

Pateman, Carole (1988) 'The Fraternal Social Contract' in *Civil Society and the State: New European Perspectives*, ed. by J. Keane, London, New York: Verso, 101–127

Paukert, Liba (1982) 'Personal Preference, Social Change or Economic Necessity? Why Women Work', *Labour and Society*, vol. 7, no. 4, 311–331

Pauli, Ruth (1986) *Emanzipation in Österreich. Der lange Marsch in die Sackgasse*, Wien, Köln, Graz: Hermann Böhlaus Nachf

Petchesky, Rosalind Pollock (1981) 'Antiabortion, Antifeminism and the Rise of the New Right' *Feminist Studies*, vol. 7, no. 2, summer, 206–246

Petersen, Herbert (1981) *Schweden, Bewährte Demokratie und neue Zeit*, Köln: Verlag Wissenschaft und Politik

Peterson, Abby (1985) 'The New Women's Movement—Where Have All The Women Gone? Women And The Peace Movement In Sweden' *Women's Studies International Forum*, vol. 8, no. 6, 631–638

Petzold, Ruth (1980) 'Die Situation der Frauen in der österreichischen Landwirtschaft' *Der Förderungsdienst*, 6, 161

Pietilä, Hilkka (1984) 'The right to be oneself' in *Sisterhood is Global*, ed. by R. Morgan, Garden City, New York: Anchor Press/Doubleday, 218–224

Pinson, Koppel S. (1966) *Modern Germany. Its History and Civilization*, 2nd. ed. New York: Macmillan

Pintasilgo, Maria de Lourdes (1984) 'Daring to be different' in *Sisterhood is Global*, ed. by R. Morgan, Garden City, New York: Anchor Press/Doubleday, 571–575

Pinto, Diana, (ed.) (1981) *Contemporary Italian Sociology. A Reader*, trans. and with an introd. by D. Pinto, London, Cambridge: Cambridge University Press and Paris: Editions de la Maison des sciences de l'homme

Pisan, Annie de and Tristan, Anne (1977) *Histoires du MLF*, preface by S. de Beauvoir, Paris: Calmann-Lévy

Pisano, Vittorfranco S. (1986) 'The Red Brigades: A Challenge to Italian Democracy' in *The New Terrorism*, ed. by W. Gutteridge, London: Mansell Publishing Ltd, 167–198

Pisciotta, Eleonore Eckmann (1986) 'The strength and the powerlessness of the new Italian women's movement: the case of abortion', ch. 1 in *The New Women's Movement. Feminism and Political Power in Europe and the USA*, ed. by D. Dahlerup, London, Beverly Hills & Newbury Park, New Delhi: Sage Publications, 26–47

Pitch, Tamar (1979) 'Notes from within the Italian Women's Movement: How We Talk of Marxism and Feminism', *Contemporary Crises*, vol. 3, no. 2, Jan., 1–16

Piva, Paola and Ingrao, Chiara (1984) 'Women's Subjectivity, Union Power and the Problem of Work' part of C. Cockburn et al. 'Trade Unions and the Radicalizing of Socialist Feminism' *Feminist Review*, no. 16, summer, 43–73

Piven, Frances Fox and Cloward, Richard (1979) *Poor People's Movements*, New York: Vintage

Pizzorno, A. (1978) 'Political Exchange and Collective Identity in Industrial Conflict' in *The Resurgence of Class Conflict in Western Europe since 1968*, ed. by C. Crouch and A. Pizzorno, London: Macmillan

——(1983) 'Identità ed interesse' in *Identità*, ed. by L. Sciolla, Turin: Rosenberg and Sellier

Plamenatz, John (1958) 'Electoral Studies and Democratic Theory', *Political Studies*, 6, 1–9

Pletscher, Marianne (1977) *Weggehen ist nicht so einfach. Gewalt gegen Frauen in der Schweiz. Gespräche und Informationen*, Zurich: Limmal Verlagsgenossenschaft

Plogstedt, Sibylle (1984) 'Has Violence Arrived in the Women's Movement?' in *German Feminism*, ed. by E. H. Altbach et al., Albany: State University of New York Press, 336–341

Pollard, Sidney (1981) *Peaceful Conquest. The Industrialization of Europe 1760–1970*, Oxford: Oxford University Press

Pollmann, Dorlies (1976) 'Der Kongreß der arbeitenden Frauen Portugals' in *Deutsche Volkszeitung*, Düsseldorf, 14 Oct. 1976

——(1979) 'Wider die weibliche Untugend Geduld. Portugals Frauen entwickeln Phantasie im Kampf um ihre Rechte' in *Deutsche Volkszeitung*, Düsseldorf, 18 Jan. 1979

Population Crisis Committee (1988) 'Country Rankings of the Status of Women: Poor, Powerless and Pregnant' *Population Briefing Paper*, no. 20, June, 1120 19th Street, N.W., Washington, D.C., 20036

Postan, M. M. (1967) *An Economic History of Western Europe 1945–1964*, London: Methuen & Co

Poulantzas, Nicos (1976) *The Crisis of the Dictatorships*, London: Atlantic Highlands, N.J.: NLB Humanities Press

Pridham, Geoffrey (ed.) (1984) *The New Mediterranean Democracies: Regime Transition in Spain, Greece and Portugal*, London: Frank Cass

Prokopp, Ulrike (1978) 'Production and the Context of Women's Daily Life' *New German Critique*, no. 13 winter, 13–33

Pross, Helge (1972) *Kapitalismus und Demokratie. Studien über westdeutsche Sozialstrukturen*, Frankfurt/M.: Athenäum Fischer Taschenbuch Verlag

——(1973) *Gleichberechtigung im Beruf*, Frankfurt/M.: Suhrkamp

Prou, Suzanne (1984) *Die Schöne*, trans. by L. Birk, Hamburg: Hoffmann und Campe, (1st ed. Paris: Calmann-Lévy, as *Le pré aux narcisses*, 1983)

Psacharopoulos, G. (1983) 'Sex Discrimination in the Greek Labour Market' *Journal of Modern Greek Studies*, vol. 1, no. 2, Oct., 339–372

Radusch, Hilde 'Lesben-Gruppe L (Lesbos) 74' in *Wohin geht die Frauenbewegung? 22 Protokolle*, ed. by G. Gassen, Frankfurt/M.: Fischer Taschenbuchverlag

Rague-Arias, Maria-Jose (1981) 'Spain: Feminism In Our Time.' *Women's Studies International Quarterly*, vol. 4, no. 4, 471–476

Randall, Vicky (1982) *Women and Politics*, London and Basingstoke: Macmillan

Rang, Brita (1988) 'Guck doch einfach auch mal, was sich bei den Platelandfrauen tut' in *Frauenbewegungen in der Welt*, vol. 1: *Westeuropa*, Berlin: Argument, 164–169

Räsänen, Leila (1984) 'Katsaus tasa-arvolain säädännön Kelutyseen vuosina 1970–1982' (A survey of the development of laws of equality 1970–1982) In *Mies-nainen- in minen. Opet usministeriö*. Helsinki, 147–168

Raulff, Heiner (1983) 'Frankreich' in *Fischer Weltgeschichte, Europa nach dem Zweiten Weltkrieg*, Frankfurt /M.: Fischer Taschenbuch Verlag, 312–320

——(1983) 'Die Militärdiktatur in Griechenland' in *Fischer Weltgeschichte, Europa nach dem Zweiten Weltkrieg*, Frankfurt /M.: Fischer Taschenbuch Verlag, 344–346

Ravaioli, Carla (1977) *Frauenbefreiung und Arbeiterbewegung* (original: 'La questione femminile'), Hamburg/Berlin: USA

Ravera, Camilla (1978) *Breve storia del movimento femminile in Italia*, Rome

Reader, Keith A. (1987) *Intellectuals and the Left in France since 1968*, Basingstoke: Macmillan

Rehn, Gösta and Petersen, K. Helvig (1980) *Education and Youth Employment in Sweden and Denmark*, Berkeley, Cal.: Carnegie Council on Policy Studies in Higher Education

Resnick, Margery (1984) *Women Writers in Translation. An annotated bibliography, 1945–1982*, Garland reference library of the humanities, vol. 228

Rich, Adrienne (1977) *On Lies, Secrets and Silence: Selected Prose 1966–1978*, London: Virago

Richter, Werner, Hogeweg-de Haart, Huberta and Kiuzadjan, Liparit (1985) *The Changing Role of Women in Society. A Documentation of Current Research. Research Projects in Progress 1981–1983*, for the European Cooperation in Social Science Information and Documentation (ECSSID) Programme coordinated by the European Coordination Centre for Research and Documentation in Social Sciences, Berlin: Akademie Verlag

Riegelhaupt, Joyce Firstenberg (1983) 'Introduction' to *In Search of Modern Portugal: The Revolution & its Consequences*, ed. by L. S. Graham and D. L. Wheeler, Madison, Wisconsin: The University of Wisconsin Press, 3–13

Riemer, Eleanor S. & Fout, John C. (eds) (1983) *European Women. A Documentary History 1789–1945*, Brighton/Sussex: The Harvester Press

Rights of Women Europe (1983) *Women's Rights and the EEC*, London: Rights of Women Europe

Riot-Sarcey, Michèle and Varikas, Eleni (1986) 'Feminist Consciousness in the Nineteenth Century: A Pariah Consciousness? *Praxis International* (special issue, entitled *Feminism as Critique*, ed. by S. Benhabib and D. Cornell), vol. 5, Jan., 443–465

Rochefort, Christiane (1986) *Die Welt ist wie zwei Pferde*, trans. by E. Helmlé, Frankfurt/M.: Suhrkamp (1st ed. Paris Editions Grasset & Fasquelle, as *Le monde est comme deux chevaux*, 1984)

Rogerat, Chantal (1988) 'Frauenbewegung und Frauenforschung in Frankreich' trans. by C. Ottomeyer-Hervieu and B. Jansen, in *Frauenbewegungen in der Welt*, vol. 1, ed. by Autonome Frauenredaktion, Hamburg: Argument, 108–111

Roïdis, E. (1896) *The Greek Literary Women*, Athens

Rose, Hilary (1984) 'The New International and Gender Division of Employment and Welfare. Weltweite Feminisierung der Lohnarbeit' *Das Argument*, no. 26, vol. 144, March–April, 185–198

Rosen, Ruth (1990) 'Male Democracies, Female Dissidents' *Tikkun*, vol. 5, no. 5, 11–16, 100–101

Rosenfelt, Deborah and Stacey, Judith (1987) 'Review Essay: Second Thoughts on the Second Wave' *Feminist Review*, no. 27, Sept., 77–95

Rossanda, Rossana (1988) 'Die Emanzipierte, die keine Buße tun will.' trans. from Italian by E. Helfenstein, P. Jehle and E. Opromolla, in *Frauenbewegungen in der Welt*, vol. 1: *Westeuropa*, ed. by Autonome Frauenredaktion, Hamburg: Argument, 156–163, (first appeared under the title 'L'impenitente emancipata' in *memoria, rivista di storia delle donne*, 19–20, 1987)

Roth, Roland (1985) 'Neue soziale Bewegungen in der politischen Kultur der Bundesrepublik- eine vorläufige Skizze' in *Neue soziale Bewegungen in Westeuropa und den USA*, ed. by K.-W. Brand, Frankfurt/M., New York: Campus, 20–82

Rowley, Hazel and Reismann, Renate (1981) 'Interview with Simone de Beauvoir', *Hecate*, vol. VII, no. 2, 90–96

Russell, Bertrand (1945) *A History of Western Philosophy*, New York

Russell, Diana E. H. and Van de Ven, Nicole (eds) (1984) *Crimes Against Women: Proceedings of the International Tribunal*

Ruth (1984) 'Waiting for a miracle' excerpt trans. in *German Feminism*, ed. by E. H. Altbach, Albany: State University of New York Press, 170–176; origin. in *Guten Morgen, du Schöne. Frauen in der DDR*, ed. by M. Wander, 1978, Darmstadt and Neuwied: Luchterhand Verlag, 78–87

Sá e Melo, Maria Teresa (1988) 'Frauenorganisationen in Portugal 1988' in *Frauenbewegungen in der Welt*, (Women's Movements in the World), vol. 1: *Westeuropa*, Hamburg: Argument, 189–194

Safa, Helen I. (1986) 'Runaway Shops and Female Employment: The Search for Cheap Labour' ch. 4 in *Women's Work*, ed. by E. Leacock and H. I. Safa, Massachusetts: Bergin & Garvey Publishers, Inc.

Sandel, Cora (1968) *Krane's Café: An Interior with Figures*, trans. from the Norwegian by E. Rokkan, London: The Women's Press (1st ed. *Kranes Konditori*, 1946)

Saraceno, Chiara (1984) 'Shifts in Public and Private Boundaries: Women as Mothers and Service Workers in Italian Daycare' *Feminist Studies*, vol. 10, no. 1, spring, 7–29

Sarraute, Nathalie (1977) *Fools say*, trans. by M. Jolas, London: John Calder, (1st ed. Paris: Éditions Gallimard, as *Disent les imbéciles*, 1976)

——(1983) *The Use of Speech*, trans. by B. Wright, London: John Calder, (1st ed. Paris: Éditions Gallimard, as *L'usage de la parole*, 1980)

Sartori, Giovanni (1987) *The Theory of Democracy Revisited*, part I: The Contemporary Debate, Chatham, New Jersey: Chatham House Publishers Inc.

Sauter-Bailliet, Theresia (1981) 'The Feminist Movement in France, *Women's Studies International Quarterly*, vol. 4, no. 4, 409–420

Savier, Monika and Fiocchetto, Rosanna (eds) (1988) *Italien der Frauen*, Munich: Frauenoffensive

Scammel, Michael (1990) 'The New Yugoslavia' *The New York Review of Books*, vol. 37, no. 12, July 19, 37–42

Schatzberg, Karin (ed.) (1986) *Frauenarchive und Frauenbibliotheken: Entstehungsgeschichte-Organisation-inhaltliche Schwerpunkte*, Aachen: Rader Wissenschaftliche Publikationen

Schelsky, H. (1965) *Auf der Suche nach Wirklichkeit*, Köln and Düsseldorf: Eugen Diederichs

Schenk, Herrad (1980) *Die feministische Herausforderung: 150 Jahre Frauenbewegung in Deutschland*, München: C.H. Beck

Schlaeger, Hilke (1978) 'The West German Women's Movement' *New German Critique*, 13, Winter, 60–68

Schmidt-Harzbach, Ingrid (1981) 'Frauengesprächskreise an Berliner Volkshochschulen' in *Wohin geht die Frauenbewegung?* ed. by G. Gassen, Frankfurt/M.: Fischer Taschenbuchverlag, 226–247

Schor, Naomi (1981) 'Female Paranoia: The Case for Psychoanalytic Feminist Criticism' *Yale French Studies*, no. 62, 204–219

Schultz, Dora (1984) 'The German Women's Movement in 1982' in *German Feminism: Readings in Politics and Literature*, ed. by E. Altbach, J. Clause et al., Albany: State University of New York Press, 368–377

Schümann, Beate and Müller, Anton-Peter (1986) *Portugal. Ein politisches Reisebuch*, Hamburg: VSA Verlag

Schuster, V. (1982) 'Serie Nachkrieg IV: Freiheit, Gleichheit, und unsere verfluchte Lust, glücklich zu sein' *Courage*, 7, Sept., 39–47

Schwarzer, Alice (1977) *Der 'kleine Unterschied' und seine großen Folgen*, Frankfurt/M.: Fischer Taschenbuchverlag

Schwarzer, Alice (1981) *10 Jahre Frauenbefreiung. So fing es an!*, Köln: Emma Frauenverlag

——(1983) *Simone de Beauvoir*, Reinbeck/Hamburg: Rowohlt

——(1985) *Lohn: Liebe*, Frankfurt/M.: Suhrkamp Verlag (previously known and published under the title: *Frauenarbeit, Frauenbefreiung*, 1973)

Scott, Hilda (1982) *Sweden's Right to be Human*, New York: M.E. Sharpe

Scroppo, E. (1979) *Donna, privato e politico*, Milan: Mazzotta

Seager, Joni and Olson, Ann (1986) *Women in the World*, London and Sydney: Pan Books

Sellers, Susan (1986) 'Writing Women: Hélène Cixous' Political "Sexts"', *Women's Studies International Forum*, vol. 9, no. 4, 443–447

Semyovonov, M. (1980) 'The Social Context of Women's Labor Force Participation: A Comparative Analysis' *American Journal of Sociology*, vol. 86, no. 3, 534–549

Seton-Watson, Hugh (1985) 'What is Europe? Where is Europe? From Mystique to Politique' *Encounter*, 2, 65, July-Aug., 9–17

Shalev, Michael (1983) 'The Social Democratic Model and Beyond: Two "Generations" Comparative Research on the Welfare State' *Comparative Social Research*, vol. 6, 315–351

Shapin, Steven (1982) 'History of Science and its Sociological Reconstruction' *History of Science*, 20, 157–211

Shields, Graham J. (compiler) (1985) *Spain*, (vol. 60 in the *World Bibliographical Series*), Oxford, Engl., Santa Barbara, Cal., Denver, Col.: CLIO Press

Showalter, Elaine (1978) *A Literature of Their Own*, London: Virago

SINUS (1981) *5 Millionen Deutsche: "Wir sollten wieder einen Führer haben."* SINUS-Studie über rechtsextremistische Einstellung bei den Deutschen

Sjerps, Ina (1988) 'Indirect Discrimination in Social Security in the Netherlands: Demands of the Dutch Women's Movement', ch. 6 in *Women, Equality and Europe*, ed. by M. Buckley and M. Anderson, London: Macmillan Press, 95–106

Skard, Torild (1981) 'Progress for Women. Increased Female Representation in Political Elites in Norway', in *Access to Power*, ed. by C. F. Epstein and R. L. Coser, Sydney, London: Allen & Unwin, 76–89

Slaughter, Jane and Kern, Robert (eds) (1981) *European Women on the Left: Socialism, feminism and the problems faced by political women, 1880 to the present*, London: Greenwood Press

Slupik,V. (1982) 'Gefährlicher Schutz' *Emma*, May, 27–30

Smyth, Ailbhe (1983) 'Contemporary French Feminism. An Annotated Shortlist of Recent Works' *Hecate*, vol. 9, 203–236

Snow, David, Louis A. Zurcher, and Ekland-Olson, Sheldon (1980) 'Social Networks and Social Movements: A Microstructural Approach to Differential Recruitment' *American Sociological Review*, 45, 787–801

Sombart, W. (1967) *The Quintessence of Capitalism*, New York: H. Fertig

Søndergaard, Dorte M. (1988) 'Die Frauenbewegung in Dänemark' in *Frauenbewegungen in der Welt*, vol. 1, Berlin: Argument, 53–66

Spagnoletti, R. (ed.) (1971) *I Movimenti femministi in Italia*, Rome

Spanidou, Irini (1987) *God's Snake*, London: Secker & Warburg

Spanish Women's Abortion Support Group (1988) 'Spanish Women and the Alton Bill' *Feminist Review: Abortion, The International Agenda*, no. 29, spring, 72–74

Spivak, Gayarti Chakravorty (1981) 'French Feminism in an International Frame', *Yale French Studies*, no. 62, 154–184

Spotts, Frederic and Wieser, Theodore (1986) *Italy: A Difficult Democracy. A survey of Italian politics*, Cambridge: Cambridge University Press

Stäbler, Eva (1986) 'Guaranteed Minimum Income. A Critique' *European Forum of Socialist-Feminists*, no. 1, Feb., 14–15

Stamiris, Eleni (1988) 'Die Frauenbewegung in Griechenland' in *Frauenbewegungen in der Welt*, vol. 1, Westeuropa, Hamburg: Argument, 113–130

Stanton, Theodore (ed.) (1884) *The Woman Question in Europe. A series of original essays*, New York, London, Paris: G.P. Putnam's Sons

Stefan, Venera (1979) *Shedding* (original: *Häutungen*, Munich: Verlag Frauenoffensive), trans. by J. Moore and B. Weckmüller, London: The Women's Press

Stephenson, Jill (1983) 'National Socialism and Women before 1933' in *Die Nazi Machtergreifung*, ed. by Peter D. Stachura, London: Allen & Unwin, 49–67

Stetson, Dorothy Mc Bride (1987) *Women's Rights in France*, New York, Westport/Conn., London: Greenwood Press

Stocker de Sousa, Maria M. and Dominguez, Maria C. P. (n.d.*) *Women in Portugal*, suppl. no. 11 to *Women of Europe*, Commission of the European Communities, Brussels, *(possibly 1986, according to content), 59

Stolk, Bram van and Wouters, Cas (1987) *Frauen im Zwiespalt. Beziehungsprobleme im*

*Wohlfahrtsstaat,* forward by N. Elias, trans. by M. Schröter, Frankfurt/M.: Suhrkamp, (1st Dutch ed. Deventer: Van Loghum Slaterus, as *Vrouwen in tweestrijd. Tussen thuis en tehuis- Relatieproblemen in de verzorgingsstaat, opgetekend in een crisiscentrum,* 1983)

Stone, Oliver M. (1972) 'The rebirth of the Women's Movement' *Contemporary Review,* vol. 221, Aug., 74–81

Streijffert, Helena (1974) 'The Women's Movement. A theoretical discussion' *Acta Sociologica,* vol. 17, no. 4, 344–366

Styrkársdóttir, Audur (1986) 'From social movement to political party: the new women's movement in Iceland' in *The New Women's Movement. Feminism and Political Power in Europe and the USA,* ed. by D. Dahlerup, London, Beverly Hills & Newbury Park, New Delhi: Sage Publications, 140–157

Suleiman, Susan R. (1986) '(Re)Writing The Body: The Politics and Poetics Of Female Eroticism' in *The Female Body in Western Culture, comparative perspectives,* ed. by idem., London and Cambridge, Mass: Harvard University Press, 7–29

Sullerot, Evelyne (1971) *Women, Society and Change,* trans. from the French by M. Scotford Archer, London: Weidenfels and Nicolson

Summers, Anne (1986) 'Femocrats: Mandarins and Missionaries' in *Australian Women: New Feminist Perspectives,* ed. by N. Grieve and A. Burns, Melbourne, London: Oxford University Press

Swedish Institute (1968) 'Report to the United Nations, 1968: The Status of Women in Sweden', repr. in parts in *Voices of the New Feminism,* (1970), ed. by M. L. Thompson, Boston: Beacon Press

Szymanski, Al (1976) 'The Socialisation of Women's Oppression: A Marxist Theory of the Changing Position of Women in Advanced Capitalist Society' *Insurgent Sociologist,* 6, 31–58

Tarrow, Sidney (1980) 'Italy: Crisis, Crises or Transition?' in *Italy in Transition: Conflict and Consensus,* ed. by P. Lange and S. Tarrow, Totowa, N.J.: Frank Cass, 166–187

Tatalovich, R. and Daynes, B. W. (1981) *The Politics of Abortion: A Study of Community Conflict in Public Policy,* New York: Praeger

Taylor, A. J. P. (1970) *The Habsburg Monarchy,* Harmondsworth: Penguin

Theweleit, Klaus (1987) *Male fantasies,* trans. by S. Conway with E. Carter and C. Turner, Minneapolis: University of Minnesota Press

Thönnesson, Werner (1973) *The Emancipation of Women: The Rise and Decline of the Women's Movement in German Social Democracy, 1863–1933,* trans. by J. de Bres, London: Pluto Press

Threlfall, Monica (1985) 'The Women's Movement in Spain' *New Left Review,* no. 151, 44–75

Threlfall, Monica (1988) 'Die Frauenbewegung in Spanien' in *Frauenbewegungen in der Welt,* vol. 1: *Westeuropa* ed. by the collective Autonome Frauenredaktion Argument, Berlin: Argument

Tikkanen, Märta (1988) *Wie vergewaltige ich einen Mann?,* trans. by V. Reichel, Reinbeck: Rowohlt Taschenbuchverlag (1st ed. Stockholm: Bokförlaget Trevi, as *Män kan inte våldtas,* 1975)

——(1987) *Ein Traum von Männern, nein, von Wölfen,* trans. by V. Reichel, Reinbeck: Rowohlt Taschenbuchverlag, (1st ed. Stockholm: Bokförlaget Trevi, as *Rödluvan,* 1986)

Tilly, Louise A., and Scott, Joan W. (1978) *Women, Work and Family,* New York: Holt, Rinehart & Winston

Tipton, Frank B. and Aldrich, Robert (1987) *An Economic and Social History of Europe. From 1939 to the present,* Basingstoke, Hampshire and London: Macmillan Education Ltd.

Tisdall, Cardine (1982) 'Chronology of Events in Italy 1960–1982' Published by the Arts Council of Great Britain on the occasion of the exhibition 'Arte Italiana 1960–1982' at the Hayward Gallery, London

Tomasson, Richard F. (1980) *Iceland. The First New Society,* University of Minnesota Press: Minneapolis

Torchi, Antonia (1981) 'Feminist Responses to the Book' (ref. to *L'Acqua in Gabbia*), *Feminist Review*, vol. 40, summer, 43–48

Törnudd, K. (1986) *Finland and the International Norms of Human Rights*, Dordrecht, Boston, Lancaster: Martinus Nijhoff Publishers

Touraine, Alain (1971) *The May Movement. Revolt and Reform*, New York: Random House

——(1977) *The Self-Production of Society*, trans. by D. Coltman, Chicago and London: The University of Chicago Press

——(1981) *The voice and the eye. An analysis of social movements*, foreword by R. Sennett, trans. by A. Duff, Cambridge, London, New York, New Rochelle, Melbourne, Sydney: Cambridge University Press

——(1988) *Return of the Actor. Social Theory in Postindustrial Society*, foreward by S. Aronowitz, trans. by M. Godzich, Minneapolis: University of Minnesota Press

Trevor-Roper, H. R. (1990) 'Reunion in Budapest' *The New York Review of Books*, vol. 37, no. 12, July 19, 8–11

Tröger, Annemarie (1978) 'Summer Universities for Women: The Beginning of Women's Studies in Germany?' *New German Critique*, 13, winter, 175–180

Turner, Ralph H. (1983) 'Figure and Ground in the Analysis of Social Movements' *Symbolic Interaction*, 6, 175–181

Tusquets, Esther (1985) *Love is a solitary game* (original: *Elamores un juego solitalo*, 1979, Barcelona: Editorial Lumen) trans. by B. Penman, London: John Calder, New York: Riverrun Press

Tuttle, Lisa (1987) *Encyclopedia of Feminism*, London: Arrow Books

Vammen, Tinne (1984) 'Letter from a troubled Copenhagen Redstocking' in *Sisterhood is Global*, ed. by R. Morgan, Garden City, New York: Anchor Press/Doubleday, 181–186

Van der Wee, Herman (1987) *Prosperity and Upheaval. The World Economy 1945–1980*, Harmondsworth: Penguin

Vedder-Schults, Nancy (1978) 'Introduction' to 'The West German Women's Movement' by Hilke Schlaeger, *New German Critique*, no. 13, winter, 59–60

Verba, Sydney, Nie, Norma H., Jae-on, Kim (1978) *Participation and Political Equality. A Seven-Nation Comparison*, London, New York, New Rochelle, Melbourne, Sydney, Cambridge: Cambridge University Press

Vicens-Vives, J. (1969) *An Economic History of Spain*, Princeton, N.J.: Princeton University Press

VSSTÖ (1988) 'Jede 50. Professor der Uni ist eine Frau: Frauen and den Unis' brochure published by the Association of Socialist Students (VSSTÖ), Vienna: REMAprint

Walsh, Vivian (1980) 'Contraception. The Growth of a Technology' ch. 9 in *Alice through the microscope. The Power of Science over Women's Lives*, by The Brighton Women and Science Group, ed. by L. Birke, W. Faulkner, S. Best, D. Janson-Smith and K. Overfield, London: Virago

Walzer, Michael (1983) *Spheres of Justice. A Defence of Pluralism and Equality*, Oxford: Basil Blackwell

Wassmo, Herbjørg (1987) *The House with the Blind Glass Windows*, trans. by R. Lloyd and A. Simpson, Seattle, Washington: The Seal Press (1st ed. Oslo: Gyldendal Norsk Forlag, as *Huset med den blinde glassveranda*, 1981)

Weiland, Daniela (1983) *Geschichte der Frauenemanzipation in Deutschland und Österreich*, Hermes Handlexikon, Düsseldorf: Econ Taschenbuchverlag

Weinzierl, Erika (1975) *Emanzipation? Österreichische Frauen im 20. Jahrhundert*, Vienna and Munich: Verlag Jugend und Volk

Welsch, Erwin K. (1974) *Feminism in Denmark, 1850–1875*, PhD, Indiana University, 336

Whitford, Frank (1984) *Bauhaus*, Thames and Hudson: London

Wiarda, Howard J. (1982) 'From Corporatism to Neo-Syndicalism: The state, organized labor, and the changing industrial relations system of Southern Europe' *Comparative Social Research*, vol. 5, 3–57

Winner, Langdon (1985) 'Do artifacts have politics?' ch. 1 in *The Social Shaping of*

*Technology. How the refrigerator got its hum*, ed. by D. MacKenzie and J. Wajcman, Milton Keynes, Philadelphia: Open University Press

Wistrand, Birgitta (1981) *Swedish Women On The Move*, ed. and trans. by J. Rosen, Stockholm: The Swedish Institute

Wittig, Monique, Wittig, Gille, Rothenburg, Marcia, and Stephenson, Margaret (1970) 'Combat pour la libération de la femme' in *L'Idiot International*, no. 6, 13–16

——(1972) *The Guérillères*, trans. by D. Le Vay, London: Picador, Pan Books, (1st ed. Paris: Les Éditions de Minuit as *Les Guérillères*, 1969)

——(1980) 'The Straight Mind' *Feminist Issues*, vol. 1, no. 1, (the English language edition of *Questions Feministes*), 103–111

——(1981) 'One is Not Born A Woman' *Feminist Issues*, vol. 1, no. 2, winter, 47–54

——(1987) *Across the Acheron*, trans. by D. le Vay and M. Crosland, London: Peter Owen (1st ed. Paris: Les Éditions de Minuit, as *Virgile, Non*, 1985)

Wohmann, Gabriele (1976) *Ausflug mit der Mutter*, Darmstadt and Neuwied: Luchterhand

Wolchik, A. (1981) 'The Status of Women' *Comparative Political Studies*, vol. 13, no. 4, Jan.

Woller, Hans (1983) 'Die Benelux Staaten' in *Das Zwanzigste Jahrhundert*, vol. II: *Europa nach dem Zweiten Weltkrieg*, (= Fischer Weltgeschichte), Frankfurt/M.: Fischer Taschenbuchverlag, 158–164

*Womanspeak* (1982) 'French Women's Right to Know' 'Roundabout' *Womanspeak*, vol. 7, no. 2, Aug.–Sept., 14

*Women and Men of Europe 1983*, (1983) Commission of European Communities, Brussels

*Women in Agriculture* ( 1988), supplement no. 29 to *Women of Europe*, text drafted by the Secretariat of the Copa Women's Committee, Women's Information Service, Commission of the European Communities, Brussels

*Women in Statistics* (1984), supplement no. 14 to *Women of Europe*, Directorate-General, Information for Women's Organisations and Press, prep. by M. J. Gonzalez, Commission of the European Communities, Brussels

*Women of Europe*, no. 46, 1986; no. 50, 1987; no. 54, 1988; no. 56, 1988; no. 60, 1989; no. 63, 1990, Commission of European Communities, Brussels

Woodtli, Susanna (1975) *Gleichberechtigung. Der Kampf um die politischen Rechte der Frau in der Schweiz*, Frauenfeld: Huber & Co

*Working papers in women's law* (1983) no. 1, Oslo: University of Oslo, Dept. of Women's Law

Wunderle, Michaela (ed.) (1977) *Politik der Subjektivität. Texte der italienischen Frauenbewegung*, Frankfurt/M.: Suhrkamp Verlag

Wyss, Laure (1985) 'Epilogue' to *Eine kurze Reise. Aufzeichungen einer Frau*, by D. Letessier, trans. by Ch. Mäder-Viragh, Frankfurt/M.: Fischer Taschenbuch

Xiradiki, K. (1898) *Kalliopi Papalexopoulou (1809–1898)*, Athens

Yans-McLaughlin, Virginia (1977) 'Italian Women and Work' in *Class, Sex and the Woman Worker*, ed. by M. Cantor and B. Laurie, Westport/Conn.: Greenwood Press

Young, Iris Marion (1986) 'Impartiality and the Civic Public: Some Implications of Feminist Critiques of Moral and Political Theory' *Praxis International* (special issue, entitled *Feminism as Critique*, ed. by S. Benhabib and D. Cornell), vol. 5, Jan., 381–401

Young-Bruehl, Elisabeth (1982) *Hannah Arendt. For Love of the World*, New Haven and London: Yale University Press

Zaccaria, Paola (1984) 'Italy: A Mortified Thirst for Living' in *Sisterhood is Global: The International Women's Movement Anthology*, ed. by R. Morgan, Garden City, New York: Anchor Press/Doubleday, 370–375

Zald, Mayer, and McCarthy, John D. (1979) *The Dynamics of Social Movements: Resource Mobilization, Social Control and Tactics*, Cambridge, Mass.:Winthrop

Zancan, Marina (1988) 'Some reflections on women's initiatives in Italy after the feminist movement' in *Altro Polo. Studies of Contemporary Italy*, ed. by I. Grosart and S. Trambaiolo, Frederick May Foundation for Italian Studies, University of Sydney, Australia, 55–59

Zeit im Bild (ed.) (1978) *100 years of August Bebel's 'Women and Socialism'. Women in the GDR* Dresden: Zeit im Bild

Zincone, Giovanna (1983) *Decision-Making Arenas Affecting Women at Work in Four European Countries*, final report to Directorate-General Employment, Social Affairs and Education of the Commission of the European Community

Zincone, Giovanna (1988) 'Women in Decision Making Arenas: Italy' in W*omen, Equality and Europe*, ed. by M. Buckley and M. Anderson, London: MacMillan, 160–176

Zöllner, Erich (1974) *Geschichte Österreichs. Von den Anfängen bis zur Gegenwart*, Vienna: Verlag für Geschichte und Politik

Zuccotti, Susan (1987) *The Italians and the Holocaust. Persecution, Rescue and Survival*, London: Peter Halban

# Cross reference by country

Europe (general)
Individual countries/geopolitical regions
Benelux countries: Belgium, Netherlands, Luxembourg
France
Germanic countries: Austria, Switzerland, West Germany
Greece
The Iberian Peninsula: Portugal, Spain
Italy
Scandinavian countries: Denmark, Iceland, Finland, Sweden, Norway
Social movements

## EUROPE (GENERAL)

*Aktuell. Das Lexikon der Gegenwart* (1984), Dortmund: Chronik Verlag
Alemann, Claudia V., Jallamion, Dominique, Schäfer, Bettina (1981) *Das nächste Jahrhundert wird uns gehören. Frauen und Utopie 1830 bis 1840*, Frankfurt/M.: Fischer Taschenbuchverlag
Anderson, Perry (1974) *Lineages of the Absolutist State*, London: NLB Humanities Press
Arendt, Hannah (1951) *The Origins of Totalitarianism*, New York: Harcourt Brace Jovanovich
——(1968) 'On Humanity in Dark Times: Thoughts about Lessing.' in *Men in Dark Times*, New York: Harcourt Brace Jovanovich, 3–31
——(1973) 'Thoughts on Politics and Revolution. A Commentary' in *Crises of the Republic*, Harmondsworth: Penguin
Barnes, Samuel H. and Kaase, Max (1979) *Political Action: Mass Participation in Five Western Democracies*, Beverly Hills and London: Sage Publications
Barry, Ursula and Jackson, Pauline (1988) 'Women on the Edge of Time: Part-time Work in Ireland, North and South', ch. 5 in *Women, Equality and Europe*, ed. by M. Buckley and M. Anderson, London: Macmillan Press, 78–94
Bashevkin, Sylvia (ed.) (1985) *Women and Politics in Western Europe*, London: Frank Cass
Benn, Melissa (1987) 'In and Against the European Left: Socialist Feminists Get Organized' *Feminist Review*, no. 26, summer, 83–92
Benz, Wolfgang (1983) 'Neutrale Staaten' in *Fischer Weltgeschichte. Das Zwanzigste Jahrhundert II. Europa nach dem Zweiten Weltkrieg*, Frankfurt/M.: Fischer Taschenbuch Verlag, 206–224
Benz, Wolfgang and Graml, Hermann (1983) 'Abschied vom alten Europa' in *Fischer Weltgeschichte, Europa nach dem Zweiten Weltkrieg*, Frankfurt/M.: Fischer Taschenbuch Verlag, 13–22
Bodi, Leslie (1989) 'Europe, Central Europe and the Austrian Identity' *The Idea of Europe: Problems of National and Transnational Identity*, 2 vols., ed. by B. Nelson, London: Berg Publishers (in press)
Borchers, Elisabeth and Müller-Schwefe, H.-U. (1984) *Im Jahrhundert der Frau*, Frankfurt/M.: Suhrkamp Verlag
Bradshaw, Jan, (ed.) (1981) 'Special Issue: The Women's Liberation Movement—Europe and North America' *Women's Studies International Quarterly*, vol. 4, no. 4
Branca, Patricia (1978) *Women in Europe since 1750*, London: Croom Helm
Bridenthal, Renate and Koonz, Claudia (eds) (1977) *Becoming Visible: Women in European History*, Boston: Houghton Mifflin Company
Buckley, Mary and Anderson, Malcolm (eds) (1988) *Women, Equality and Europe*, London: Macmillan
Carsten, F. L. (1972) *Revolution in Central Europe 1918–1919*, Berkeley and Los Angeles: University of California Press

Castles, Stephen (1984) *Here for good. Western Europe's New Ethnic Minorities*, together with Heather Booth and Tina Wallace, London, Sydney: Pluto Press

Cohen, Yolande (1983) 'Student Protest in the Welfare State: France and West Germany in the 1960s' *Comparative Social Research*, vol. 6, 299–312

Cook, Alice, Lorwin,Val and Daniels, Arlene Kaplan (1984) *Women and Trade Unions in Eleven Industrialized Countries*, Philadelphia: Temple University Press

Dahlerup, Drude (ed.) (1986) *The New Women's Movement. Feminism and Political Power in Europe and the USA*, London, Beverly Hills & Newbury Park, New Delhi: Sage Publications

Dawidowicz, Lucy S. (1986) *The War Against the Jews 1933–1945,* New York, London: Seth Press and Free Press, Division of Macmillan

Epstein, Cynthia Fuchs and Coser, Rose Laub, (eds) (1981) *Access to Power: Cross National Studies of Women and Elites*, London: George Allen & Unwin

European Trade Union Institute (1983) *Information 6. Women's Representation in Trade Unions*

*Der Fischer Weltalmanach*, Frankfurt/M. (annual publ.): Fischer Taschenbuchverlag

Flanz, G. H. (1983) *Comparative Women's Rights and Political Participation in Europe*, New York: Transnational

Gamble, Andrew and Walton, Paul (1976) *Capitalism in Crisis*, London and Basingstoke: Macmillan

Gough, I. (1979) *The Political Economy of the Welfare State*, London: Macmillan

Gubbels, Robert (1976) 'The Female Labor Force in Western Europe', *Women in the World: A Comparative Study*, ed. by L. B. Iglitzin and R. Ross, Santa Barbara, Oxford: Clio Books, 149–162

Haavio-Mannila, Elina et al. (eds) (1983) *Det Uferdige Demokratiet*, Oslo: Nordisk Minister-råd, trans. 1985: *Unfinished Democracy. Women in Nordic Politics,* Oxford: Pergamon

Hakim, C. (1979) 'Occupational Segregation: A Comparative Study of the Degree and Pattern of Differentiation between Men's and Women's Work in Britain, the US and other Countries' *Research Paper No. 9*, Dept. of Employment, London

Hastings, E. H. and Hastings, P. K. (1980) *Index to International Public Opinion 1978–1979*, Westport: Greenwood Press

Haug, Frigga (1986) 'Women and Politics' *European Forum of Socialist-Feminists*, no. 1, Feb., 4–6, 29

——(1988) 'Lehren aus den Frauenbewegungen in Westeuropa' *Frauenbewegungen in der Welt,* vol. 1: *Westeuropa*, ed. by the collective Autonome Frauenredaktion Argument, Berlin: Argument, 6–13

Heidenheimer, Arnold J., Heclo, Hugo and Adams, Carolyn Teich (1983) *Comparative Public Policy. The Politics of Social Choice in Europe and America*, London: Macmillan.

Heller, Agnes (1978) *Renaissance Man*, trans. from Hungarian by R. E. Allen, London, Henley and Boston: Routledge & Kegan Paul

Hewitt, C. (1977) 'The Effect of Political Democracy and Social Democracy on Equality in Industrial Societies: A Cross-National Comparison' *American Sociological Review*, vol. 42, 450–464

Hobsbawm, E. J. (1974) *Primitive Rebels. Studies in Archaic Forms of Social Movement in the 19th and 20th Centuries*, Manchester: Manchester University Press

Hoskyns, Catherine (1985) 'Women's Equality and the European Community—A Feminist Perspective' *Feminist Review*, no. 20, 71–88

Iglitzin, Lynn B. and Ross, Ruth (eds) (1986) *Women in the World, 1975–1985, The Women's Decade*, 2nd rev. ed., Santa Barbara, Cal., and Oxford, England: CLIO

Inglehart, Margaret L. (1981) 'Political Interest in West European Women: An Historical and Empirical Comparative Analysis' *Comparative Political Studies*, vol. 14, no. 3, 299–326

Kaldor, Mary (1979) *The Disintegrating West*, Harmondsworth: Penguin

Katzenstein, Mary Fainsod and Mueller, Carol McClurg (eds) (1987) *The Women's*

*Movements of the United States and Western Europe. Consciousness, Political Opportunity, and Public Policy,* Philadelphia: Temple University Press

Keane, John (ed.) (1988) *Civil Society and the State. New European Perspectives,* London, New York: Verso.

Kindleberger, Charles P. (1967) *Europe's Postwar Growth,* Cambridge, Mass.: Harvard University Press

Kohler, Beate (1982) *Political Forces in Spain, Greece and Portugal,* trans. by F. Carter and G. Hole, London: Butterworth Scientific

Kolinsky, Martin and Paterson, William E. (1976) *Social and Political Movements in Western Europe,* London: Croom Helm

Krichmar, Albert (1977) *The Women's Movement in the Seventies: An International English-Language Bibliography,* Metuchen, N.J. & London: The Scarecrow Press

Kundera, Milan (1984) 'The Tragedy of Central Europe' *The New York Review of Books,* April 26, 33–39

*Kvinnor och Män i Norden. Fakta on jämställndheten* (1988) Nordic Council of Ministeres, Nord 1988, Stockholm, 58

Laqueur, Walter (1970) *Europa aus der Asche. Geschichte seit 1945,* Munich, Zurich, Vienna; English ed. *Europe since Hitler. The rebirth of Europe* (1982) Harmondsworth: Penguin

Lindemann, Albert S. (1983) *A History of European Socialism,* New Haven and London: Yale University Press

Lovenduski, Joni (1986) *Women and European Politics: Contemporary Feminism and Public Policy,* Brighton, Sussex: Harvester Press, Wheatsheaf Books

Mathiasson, C. J. (ed.) (1974) *Many Sisters: Women in Cross-Cultural Perspectives,* New York: Free Press

Michnik, Adam (1990) 'The Two Faces of Europe' *The New York Review of Books,* vol. 37, no. 12, July 19, 7

Mitterauer, Michael and Sieder, Reinhard (1983) *The European Family. Patriarchy to Partnership. From the Middle Ages to the Present,* Oxford: Basil Blackwell

Morgan, R. (ed.) (1984) *Sisterhood is Global,* New York: Anchor Press

Mossuz-Lavau, J. and Sineau, M. (1984) *The Situation of Women in the Political Process in Europe,* Council of Europe, Strasbourg

Mullaney, Marie Marmo (1983) *Revolutionary Women: Gender and the Socialist Revolutionary Role,* New York

Norderval, Ingunn (1985) 'Party and Legislative Participation among Scandinavian Women' *West European Politics,* vol. 8, no. 4, 71–89

Norris, Pippa (1985) 'Women's Legislative Participation in Western Europe' *West European Politics,* vol. 8. no. 4, 90–101 in *Women and Politics in Western Europe,* ed. by S. Bashevkin, London: Frank Cass

——(1987) *Politics and Sexual Equality. The Comparative Position of Women in Western Democracies,* Brighton/Sussex: Wheatsheaf Books and Boulder, Colorado: Rienner Publishers

Pickles, Dorothy (1971) *Democracy,* London: Methuen & Co.

Population Crisis Committee (1988) 'Country Rankings of the Status of Women: Poor, Powerless and Pregnant' *Population Briefing Paper,* no. 20, June, 1120 19th Street, N.W., Washington, D.C.-20036

Postan, M. M. (1967) *An Economic History of Western Europe 1945–1964,* London: Methuen & Co

Pollard, Sidney (1981) *Peaceful Conquest. The Industrialization of Europe 1760–1970,* Oxford: Oxford University Press

Pridham, Geoffrey (ed.) (1984) *The New Mediterranean Democracies: Regime Transition in Spain, Greece and Portugal,* London: Frank Cass

Richter, Werner, Hogeweg-de Haart, Huberta and Kiuzadjan, Liparit (1985) *The Changing Role of Women in Society. A Documentation of Current Research. Research Projects in Progress 1981–1983,* for the European Cooperation in Social Science Information and Documentation (ECSSID) Programme coordinated by the European

Coordination Centre for Research and Documentation in Social Sciences, Berlin: Akademie Verlag

Riemer, Eleanor S. and Fout, John C. (eds) (1983) *European Women. A Documentary History 1789–1945*, Brighton/Sussex: The Harvester Press

Rights of Women Europe (1983) *Women's Rights and the EEC*, London: Rights of Women Europe

Rosen, Ruth (1990) 'Male Democracies, Female Dissidents' *Tikkun*, vol. 5, no. 5, 11–16, 100–101

Russell, Diana E. H. and Van de Ven, Nicole (eds) (1984) *Crimes Against Women: Proceedings of the International Tribunal*

Scammel, Michael (1990) 'The New Yugoslavia' *The New York Review of Books*, vol. 37, no. 12, July 19, 37–42

Seton-Watson, Hugh (1985) 'What is Europe? Where is Europe? From Mystique to Politique' *Encounter*, 2, 65, July–Aug., 9–17

Slaughter, Jane and Kern, Robert (eds) (1981) *European Women on the Left: Socialism, Feminism and the problems faced by political women, 1880 to the present*, London: Greenwood Press

Stäbler, Eva (1986) 'Guaranteed Minimum Income. A Critique' *European Forum of Socialist-Feminists*, no.1, Feb., 14–15

Stanton, Theodore (ed.) (1884) *The Woman Question in Europe. A series of original essays*, New York, London, Paris: G.P. Putnam's Sons

Tipton, Frank B. and Aldrich, Robert (1987) *An Economic and Social History of Europe. From 1939 to the present*, Basingstoke, Hampshire and London: Macmillan Education Ltd.

Trevor-Roper, H. R. (1990) 'Reunion in Budapest' *The New York Review of Books*, vol. 37, no. 12, July 19, pp. 8–11

Van der Wee, Herman (1987) *Prosperity and Upheaval. The World Economy 1945–1980*, Harmondsworth: Penguin

Verba, Sydney, Nie, Norma H., Jae-on, Kim (1976) *Participation and Political Equality. A Seven-Nation Comparison*, London, New York, New Rochelle, Melbourne, Sydney, Cambridge: Cambridge University Press

Wiarda, Howard J. (1982) 'From Corporatism to Neo-Syndicalism: The state, organized labor, and the changing industrial relations system of Southern Europe' *Comparative Social Research*, vol. 5, 3–57

Wolchik, A. (1981) 'The Status of Women' *Comparative Political Studies*, vol. 13, no. 4 (Jan.)

*Women in Agriculture* ( 1988), supplement no. 29 to *Women of Europe*, text drafted by the Secretariat of the Copa Women's Committee, Women's Information Service, Commission of the European Communities, Brussels

*Women in Statistics* (1984), supplement no. 14 to *Women of Europe,* Directorate-General, Information for Women's Organisations and Press, prep. by M. J. Gonzalez, Commission of the European Communities, Brussels

*Women of Europe*, no. 46, 15 May/15 July 1986; no. 50, 15 March/15 July 1987, no. 54, April/May 1988, no. 56, September/October 1988, Commission of European Communities, Brussels

Zincone, Giovanna (1983) *Decision-Making Arenas Affecting Women at Work in Four European Countries*, final report to Directorate-General Employment, Social Affairs and Education of the Commission of the European Community

*INDIVIDUAL COUNTRIES/GEOGRAPHIC REGIONS*

## Benelux countries: Belgium, Netherlands, Luxembourg

Breed Platform Vrouwen voor Economische Zelfstandigeid (1984) *Van vrouwen en de dingen die aan haar voorbijgaan*, Den Hague

Briët, Martien, Klandermans, Bert and Kroon, Frederike (1987) 'How Women Become Involved in the Women's Movement of the Netherlands', ch. 2 in *The Women's Movements of the United States and Western Europe*, ed. by M. F. Katzenstein and C. M. Mueller, Philadelphia: Temple University Press

Brugmans, I. J. (1961) *Paardenkracht en Mensenmacht*, Den Haag: Nÿhoff

De Vries, Petra (1981) 'Feminism in the Netherlands' *Women's Studies International Quarterly*, vol. 4, no. 4, 389–407

Dittrich, Kathinka (1980) 'Wohin stürmst Du, Eva? Beispiellos: Frauenverlage und-Zeitschriften in Holland' *Börsenblatt für den deutschen Buchhandel*, vol. 24, March 1980, 655–658

Emancipatieraad (1984) *Sociale Zekerheid en Emancipatie*, Emancipatieraad, The Hague

*Emancipation in the Netherlands* (1980) World Conference of the United Nations Decade for Women: Equality, Development and Peace, Copenhagen: Ministry of Cultural Affairs, Recreation and Social Welfare

*Equal Rights and Opportunities for Women in the Netherlands* (1986) Ministry of Social Affairs and Employment, Public Relations Division, The Hague

Gadourek, I. (1982) *Social Change as Redefinition of Roles. A study of structural and causal relationships in the Netherlands of the 'seventies'*, Assen/Netherlands: Van Gorcum

Hogeweg-de Haart, H. P. (1978) 'The History of the Women's Movement in the Netherlands' *The Netherlands Journal of Sociology/ Sociologia Neerlandica*, 14, 1, July, 19–40

Huizinga, J. (1968) *Dutch Civilisation in the Seventeenth Century and other Essays*, London: F. Ungar Publishing Co.

Jong, de Uulkje (1982) 'The Improvement of the Position of Girls in Education in a Feminist Perspective', Association Paper, International Sociological Association, Canada Public

Meissner, Michael (1980) *Massenmedien und Journalismus in den Niederlanden und in Dänemark. Mit einer Darstellung zur Journalistenausbildung*, Frankfurt/M.: Rita G. Fischer Publishing House

Meulenbelt, Anja (1980) *Feminismus und Sozialismus*, trans. by J. van Soer and T. Huber-Hönck, Hamburg: Konkret Literatur Verlag, (1st ed. Amsterdam: Uitgeverij en boekhandel Van Gennep, 1975)

——(1982) *Feminismus. Aufsätze zur Frauenbefreiung*, trans. from Dutch by B. Dominick and S. Lange, Munich: Frauenoffensive, (1st ed. Amsterdam:1982)

——(1985) *Weiter als die Wut*, Aufsätze, trans. by B. Dominick and S. Lange, Munich: Frauenoffensive (1st ed. Amsterdam: Feministische Uitgeverij, 1983)

——(1986) *Ich wollte nur dein Bestes*, trans. by S. Lange, Reinbek: Rowohlt Verlag, (1st ed. Amsterdam: Uitgeverij Van Gennep, as *Een kleine moeite*, 1985)

Meulenbelt, Anja, Outshoorn, Joyce, Sevenhuijsen, Selma and de Vries, Petra (1984) *A Creative Tension. Explorations in Socialist Feminism*, trans. by D. Couling, London and Sydney: Pluto Press (1st ed. Amsterdam: Feministische Uitgeverij Sara, from anthologies *Socialisties-Feministiese Teksten*, 1980–1983)

Oudijk, Corrine (1984) 'In the Unions, the Parties, the Streets, and the Bedrooms.' in *Sisterhood is Global*, ed. by R. Morgan, Garden City, New York: Anchor Press/ Doubleday, 469–475

Outshoorn, Joyce (1986) 'The feminist movement and abortion policy in the Netherlands' ch. 3 in *The New Women's Movement. Feminism and Political Power in Europe and the USA*, ed. by D. Dahlerup, London, Beverly Hills & Newbury Park, New Delhi: Sage Publications

Outshoorn, Joyce (1986) 'The rules of the game: abortion politics in the Netherlands' ch. 2 in *The New Politics of Abortion*, ed. by J. Lovenduski and J. Outshoorn, London, Beverley Hills and Newbury Park, New Delhi: SAGE Publications

Rang, Brita (1988) 'Guck doch einfach auch mal, was sich bei den Platelandfrauen tut' in *Frauenbewegungen in der Welt*, vol. 1: *Westeuropa*, Berlin: Argument, 164–169

Sjerps, Ina (1988) 'Indirect Discrimination in Social Security in the Netherlands:

Demands of the Dutch Women's Movement', in *Women, Equality and Europe*, ed. by M. Buckley and M. Anderson, London: Macmillan Press, 95–106

Stolk, Bram van and Wouters, Cas (1987) *Frauen im Zwiespalt. Beziehungsprobleme im Wohlfahrtsstaat*, forward by N. Elias, trans. by M. Schröter, Frankfurt/M.: Suhrkamp, (1st Dutch ed. Deventer: Van Loghum Slaterus, as *Vrouwen in tweestrijd. Tussen thuis en tehuis- RElatieproblemen in de verzorgingsstaat, opgetekend in een crisiscentrum*, 1983)

Woller, Hans (1983) 'Die Benelux Staaten' in *Das Zwanzigste Jahrhundert*, vol. II: *Europa nach dem Zweiten Weltkrieg*, (= Fischer Weltgeschichte), Frankfurt/M.: Fischer Taschenbuchverlag, 158–164

## France

Albistur, Maïté and Armogathe, Daniel (1977) *Histoire du féminisme français du moyen-âge à nos jours*, Paris: Des Femmes

Batiot, Anne (1986) 'Radical democracy and feminist discourse: the case of France', in *The New Women's Movement. Feminism and Political Power in Europe and the USA*, ed. by D. Dahlerup, London, Beverly Hills & Newbury Park, New Delhi: Sage Publications, 85–102

Beauvoir, Simone de (1949) *Le Deuxième Sexe*, Paris: Gallimard

——(1952) *The Second Sex*, New York: Bantham

——(1982) *A Very Easy Death*, trans. by P. O'Brian, Harmondsworth: Penguin (original *Une Mort Très Douce*, 1964, Paris: Gallimard)

——(1984) 'France: Feminism—Alive, Well and in Constant Danger' in *Sisterhood is Global*, ed. by R. Morgan, New York: Anchor Press, 229–235

Burke, Carolyn (1978) 'Report from Paris: Women's Writing and the Women's Movement' *Signs*, vol. 3, no. 4, 843–855

Choisir Association (1975) *Abortion: The Bobigny Affairs. A Law on Trial*, with an introd. by S. de Beauvoir, Sydney: Wild & Woolley

Cixous, Hélène (1985) *Angst*, trans by J. Levy, (1st French ed. 1977), London: John Calder, New York: Riverrun Press

Conley, Verena Andermatt (1984) *Hélène Cixous: Writing the Feminine*, Lincoln and London: University of Nebraska Press

Coquillat, Michelle (1988) 'The Achievements of the French Ministry of Women's Rights: 1981–1986', ch. 11 in *Women, Equality and Europe*, ed. by M. Buckley and M. Anderson, London: Macmillan Press, 177–184

Delphy, Christine (1981) 'Women's Liberation in France: The Tenth Year' *Feminist Issues*, vol. 1, no. 2, winter, 103–112

Duchen, Claire (1986) *Feminism in France. From May '68 to Mitterand*, London, Boston and Henley: Routledge & Kegan Paul

Eaubonne, Françoise d' (1977) *Feminismus oder Tod* ('Le Féminisme ou la mort') trans. G. Giert, Munich: Verlag Frauenoffensive

——(1978) *Feminismus und 'Terror'* (Contre-Violence ou la résistance à l'Etat), trans. R. Weiss, Munich: Trikont

Gelfand, Elissa D. and Hules, Virginia Thorndike (1985) *French Feminist Criticism: Women, Language, and Literature*, An Annotated Bibliography, New York, London: Garland Publishing

Giroud, Françoise (1974) *I give you my word*, trans. by R. Seaver, Boston: Houghton Mifflin Co. (1st ed. 1972, original: *Si je mens. Conversations avec Claude Glayman*, Paris: Société-Express-Union and Éditions Stock)

Guillaumin, Colette (1985) 'The Masculine: Denotations/Connotations' *Feminist Issues*, vol. 5, no. 1, spring, 65–74

Halimi, Gisèle (1977) *The right to choose*, trans. by R. Morgan, Brisbane: University of Queensland Press (1st ed. Paris: Bernard Grasset as *La Cause des Femmes*, 1973)

Henry, Ruth (1978) *Jeanne und die anderen. Stationen einer französischen Emanzipation*, Freiburg, Breisgau: Herder Verlag

Jardine, Alice (1979) 'Interview with Simone de Beauvoir', *Signs*, vol. 5, no. 2, winter, 224–236

Jouve, Nicole Ward (1981) *Shades of Grey*, London: Virago (1st ed. Paris: Editions des femmes, as *Le Spectre du Gris*, 1977)

Juillard, Joelle Rutherford (1976) 'Women in France' in *Women in the World. A Comparative Study*, ed. by L. B. Iglitzin and R. Ross, Santa Barbara, Oxford: Clio Books, 115–128

*La Libération de la femme* (1975) Paris, Barcelona: Robert Laffont-Grammont

Leduc, Violette (1973) *In the Prison of Her Skin*, trans. by D. Coltman, St. Albans: Panther Books, (1st ed. Paris: Librairie Gallimard, as *L'Asphyxie*, 1946)

Léger, Danièle (1982) *Le feminisme en France*, Paris: Éditions Sycomore, excerpts also in *Frauenbewegungen in der Welt*, vol. 1, Hamburg: Autonome Frauenredaktion, trans. by B. Jansen, 95–104

Lesselier, Claudie (1987) 'Social Categorizations and Construction of a Lesbian Subject', trans. by M. J. Lakeland, *Feminist Issues*, vol. 7, no. 1, spring, 89–94

Letessier, Dorothée (1985) *Eine kurze Reise. Aufzeichnungen einer Frau*, trans. by C. Mäder-Viragh, Frankfurt/M.: Fischer Taschenbuch, (1st ed. Paris: Édition du Seuil, as *Le voyage à Paimpol*, 1980)

Marks, Elaine (1978) 'Women and Literature in France' *Signs*, vol. 3, no. 4, 832–842

Marks, Elaine and Courtivron, Isabelle de (eds) (1981) *New French Feminisms. An Anthology*, New York: Schocken Books

Mathieu, Nicole-Claude (1980) 'Masculinity/Femininity' *Feminist Issues*, vol. 1, no. 1, (the English language edition of *Questions Feministes*), 51–69

Michel, Andrée (1971) 'Interaction and Goal Attainment in Parisian Working Wives Families' in *Family issues of employed women in Europe and America*, ed. by A. Michel, Leiden: E. J. Brill, 43–65

Moi, Toril (ed.) (1987) *French Feminist Thought. A Reader*, Oxford, New York: Basil Blackwell

Moreau-Bisseret, Noëll (1986) 'A Scientific Warranty for Sexual Politics: Demographic Discourse on "Reproduction" (France 1945–1985)' in *Feminist Issues*, vol. 6, no. 1, spring, 67–86

Mossuz-Lavau, Janine (1986) 'Abortion policy in France under governments of the Right and Left (1973–1984)' trans. by J. Forbes, in *The New Politics of Abortion*, ed. by J. Lovenduski and J. Outshoorn, London, Beverly Hills and Newbury Park, New Delhi: Sage Publications

Pisan, Annie de and Tristan, Anne (1977) *Histoires du MLF*, preface by S. de Beauvoir, Paris: Calmann-Lévy

Prou, Suzanne (1984) *Die Schöne*, trans. by L. Birk, Hamburg: Hoffmann und Campe, (1st ed. Paris: Calmann-Lévy, as *Le pré aux narcisses*, 1983)

Raulff, Heiner (1983) 'Frankreich' in *Fischer Weltgeschichte, Europa nach dem Zweiten Weltkrieg*, Frankfurt/M.: Fischer Taschenbuch Verlag, 312–320

Reader, Keith A. (1987) *Intellectuals and the Left in France since 1968*, Basingstoke: Macmillan

Rochefort, Christiane (1986) *Die Welt ist wie zwei Pferde*, trans. by E. Helmlé, Frankfurt/M.: Suhrkamp (1st ed. Paris Editions Grasset & Fasquelle, as *Le monde est comme deux chevaux*, 1984)

Rogerat, Chantal (1988) 'Frauenbewegung und Frauenforschung in Frankreich' trans. by C. Ottomeyer-Hervieu and B. Jansen, in *Frauenbewegungen in der Welt*, vol. 1, ed. by Autonome Frauenredaktion, Hamburg: Argument, 108–111

Rowley, Hazel and Reismann, Renate (1981) 'Interview with Simone de Beauvoir', *Hecate*, vol. VII, no. 2, 90–96

Sarraute, Nathalie (1977) *Fools say*, trans. by M. Jolas, London: John Calder, (1st ed. Paris: Éditions Gallimard, as *Disent les imbéciles*, 1976)

——(1983) *The Use of Speech*, trans. by B. Wright, London: John Calder, (1st ed. Paris: Éditions Gallimard, as *L'usage de la parole*, 1980)

Sauter-Bailliet, Theresia (1981) 'The Feminist Movement in France', *Women's Studies International Quarterly*, vol. 4, no. 4, 409–420

Schor, Naomi (1981) 'Female Paranoia: The Case for Psychoanalytic Feminist Criticism', *Yale French Studies*, no. 62, 204–219

Schwarzer, Alice (1983) *Simone de Beauvoir*, Reinbeck/Hamburg: Rowohlt

Sellers, Susan (1986) 'Writing Women: Hélène Cixous' Political "Sexts"', *Women's Studies International Forum*, vol. 9, no. 4, 443–447

Smyth, Ailbhe (1983) 'Contemporary French Feminism. An Annotated Shortlist of Recent Works' *Hecate*, vol. 9, 203–236

Stetson, Dorothy Mc Bride (1987) *Women's Rights in France*, New York, Westport/Conn., London: Greenwood Press

Spivak, Gayarti Chakravorty (1981) 'French Feminism in an International Frame' *Yale French Studies*, no. 62, 154–184

Suleiman, Susan R. (1986) '(Re)Writing The Body: The Politics And Poetics Of Female Eroticism' in *The Female Body in Western Culture, comparative perspectives*, ed. by idem., London and Cambridge, Mass: Harvard University Press, 7–29

Sullerot, Evelyne (1971) *Women, Society and Change*, trans. from the French by M. Scotford Archer, London: Weidenfels and Nicolson

Touraine, Alain (1971) *The May Movement. Revolt and Reform*, New York: Random House

Wittig, Monique, Wittig, Gille, Rothenburg, Marcia, and Stephenson, Margaret (1970) 'Combat pour la libération de la femme' in *L'Idiot International*, no. 6, 13–16

——(1972) *The Guérillères*, trans. by D. Le Vay, London: Picador, Pan Books, (1st ed. Paris: Les Éditions de Minuit as *Les Guérillères*, 1969)

——(1980) 'The Straight Mind' *Feminist Issues,* vol. 1, no. 1, (the English language edition of *Questions Feministes*), 103–111

——(1981) 'One is Not Born A Woman' *Feminist Issues*, vol. 1, no. 2, winter, 47–54

——(1987) *Across the Acheron*, trans. by D. le Vay and M. Crosland, London: Peter Owen (1st ed. Paris: Les Éditions de Minuit, as *Virgile, Non*, 1985)

*Womanspeak* (1982) 'French Women's Right to Know' 'Roundabout' *Womanspeak*, vol. 7, no. 2, Aug.–Sept., 14

Wyss, Laure (1985) 'Epilogue' to *Eine kurze Reise. Aufzeichungen einer Frau*, by D. Letessier, trans. by Ch.Mäder-Viragh, Frankfurt/M.: Fischer Taschenbuch

## Germanic countries:   Austria, Switzerland, Germany

Abelshauser, Werner (1983) *Wirtschaftsgeschichte der Bundesrepublik Deutschland 1945–1980*, Frankfurt/M.: edition Suhrkamp

Altbach, Edith (1984) 'The New German Women's Movement' in *German Feminism: Readings in Politics and Literature*, ed. by E. Altbach et al., Albany: State University of New York Press, 3–26

Altbach, Edith, Clause, J., Schultz, D. and Stephan, N. (eds) (1984) *German Feminism: Readings in Politics and Literature*, Albany: State University of New York Press

Anthony, Katherine (1915) *Feminism in Germany and Scandinavia*, New York: Henry Holt and Co.

Bartuch, Ewald, Böhm, Christian and Gross, Inge (1984) *Die wirtschaftliche Rolle der Frau in Österreich*, Bundesministerium für Soziale Verwaltung, Vienna

Baumann, Bommi (1977) *How it all Began. The Personal Account of a West German Urban Guerilla*, with statements by Heinrich Böll and Daniel Cohn-Bendit, trans. by H. Ellenbogen and W. Parker, Vancouver: Pulp Press

Beck-Gernsheim, Elisabeth (1984) *Vom Geburtenrückgang zur neuen Mütterlichkeit*, Frankfurt/M.: Fischer Verlag

Bednarik, Karl (1970) *The Male in Crisis*, New York: Knopf

Benard, Cheryl and Schlaffer, Edit (1984) 'Benevolent Despotism Versus the Contemporary Feminist Movement' in *Sisterhood is Global*, ed. by R. Morgan, Garden City, New York: Anchor Press/Doubleday, 72–76

Benz, Wolfgang (ed.) (1984) *Rechtsextremismus in der Bundesrepublik*, Frankfurt/M.: Fischer Verlag

Berger, Renate, Kolb, Ingrid and Janssen-Jurreit, Marielouise (1984) 'Fragmented Selves. A collage' in *Sisterhood is Global*, ed. by R. Morgan, New York: Anchor Press/ Doubleday, 248–254

Bock, Gisela (1984) 'Wages for Housework as a Perspective of the Women's Movement' in *German Feminism*, ed. by E. Altbach et al. Albany: State University of New York Press, 246–250

——(1984a) 'Racism and Sexism in National Socialist Germany: Motherhood, Compulsory Sterilization, and the State' in Bridenthal, R. et al. *When Biology Became Destiny. Women in Weimar and Nazi Germany*, New York: Monthly Review Press, 271–296

——(1986) *Zwangssterilisation im Nationalsozialismus*, Opladen

Bodi, Leslie (1989) 'Europe, Central Europe and the Austrian Identity' in *The Idea of Europe. Problems of National and Transnational Identity*, 2 vols., ed. by B. Nelson, London: Berg Publishers (in press)

Brand, K. W., Büsser, D. and Rucht, D. (1984) *Aufbruch in eine andere Gesellschaft. Neue soziale Bewegungen in der Bundesrepublik*, Frankfurt/M.: Campus Verlag

Bridenthal, Renate; Grossmann, Atina and Kaplan, Marion (eds) (1984) *When Biology Became Destiny. Women in Weimar and Nazi Germany*, New York: Monthly Review Press

Brox-Brochot, Delphine (1984) 'Manifesto of the "Green" Women' in *German Feminism. Readings in Politics and Literature*, ed. by E. Altbach et al., Albany: State University Press, 315–317

Bundesministerium des Inneren (1982) *Sicherheit in der Demokratie. Die Gefährdung des Rechtsstaats durch Extremismus*, Bonn

Childs, David and Johnson, Jeffrey (1981) West Germany. *Politics and Society*, London: Croom Helm

Dahrendorf, Ralf (1972) *Gesellschaft und Demokratie in Deutschland*, 1st ed. 1968, Munich: Deutscher Taschenbuchverlag

Demmer, H., Kuepper, B. and Kutzner, E. (1983) 'Frauenarbeitsschutz: Gesundheitsschutz oder Ideologie?' *Beiträge zur feministischen Theorie und Praxis*, 9/10, 24–31

Doering, Dörte (1981) 'Frauen und Parteipolitik' in *Wohin geht die Frauenbewegung*, ed. by G. Gassen, Frankfurt/M.: Fischer Taschenbuchverlag, 45–53

Doormann, Lottemi (ed.) (1979) 'Die neue Frauenbewegung in der Bundesrepublik' in (idem):*Keiner schiebt uns weg. Zwischenbilanz der Frauenbewegung in der Bundesrepublik.*, Weinheim and Basel: Beltz, 16–70

Doormann, Lottemi (1983) 'Die neue Frauenbewegung: Zur Entwicklung seit 1968' in *Geschichte der deutschen Frauenbewegung*, ed. by F. Hervé, Cologne: Pahl-Rugenstein, 237–272

Evans, Richard J. (1976) *The feminist movement in Germany 1894–1933*, London and Beverley Hills: Sage Publications

Feigl, Susanne (1985) *Frauen in Österreich 1975–1985*, Vienna: Staatssekretariat für allgemeine Frauenfragen im Bundeskanzleramt

Felski, Rita (1986) 'German Feminist Aesthetics' Review Essay in *Australian Feminist Studies*, summer, 143–151

Ferree, Myra Marx (1987) 'Equality and Autonomy: Feminist Politics in the United States and West Germany' in *The Women's Movements of the United States and Western Europe*, ed. by M. F. Katzenstein & C. Mc. Mueller, Philadelphia: Temple University Press, 172–195

Fetscher, Iring (1978) *Terrorismus und Reaktion*, Frankfurt/M.: Europäische Verlagsanstalt

Fischer, Erica (1988) 'Frauenbewegung in Österreich' in *Frauenbewegungen in der Welt*, vol. 1: *Westeuropa*, ed. by Autonome Frauenredaktion, Hamburg: Argument, 184–188

Frank, Miriam (1978) 'Feminist Publications in West Germany Today' *New German Critique*, 13, winter, 181–194

Gassen, Gisela (ed.) (1981) *Wohin geht die Frauenbewegung? 22 Protokolle*, Frankfurt/ M.: Fischer Verlag

——(1981) 'Frauen in den Medien-Frauenarbeitsgruppen des Senders Freies Berlin (SFB)' in *idem: Wohin geht die Frauenbewegung*, ed. by G. Gassen Frankfurt/M.: Fischer Verlag, 216–225

Gerhard, Ute (1982) 'A Hidden and Complex Heritage: Reflections on the History of Germany's Women's Movements' *Women's Studies International Forum*, 5, no. 6, 561–567

Grossmann, Atina (1983) '"Satisfaction is Domestic Happiness": Mass Working Class Sex Reform Organizations in the Weimar Republic,' in *Towards the Holocaust. The Economic and Social Collapse of the Weimar Republic*, ed. by Michael N. Dobkowski and Isidor Wallimann, London: Greenwood Press, 265–293

Habermas, Jürgen (ed.) (1980) *Stichworte zur 'Geistigen Situation der Zeit'* vol. 1: *Nation und Republik*, vol. 2: *Politik und Kultur*, Frankfurt/M.: edition suhrkamp

Haug, Frigga (1987) *Female Sexualisation*, London: Verso Press

Hervé, Florence (ed.) (1983) *Geschichte der deutschen Frauenbewegung*, Köln: Pahl-Rugenstein Verlag

Hinn, Vilma (1988) 'Helvetiens Töchter. 20 Jahre Frauenbewegung in der Schweiz' in *Frauenbewegungen in der Welt*, vol. 1: *Westeuropa*, Berlin: Argument: 204–209

Höhn, C. and Otto, J. (1985) 'Bericht über die demographische Lage in der Bundesrepublik Deutschland und über die Weltbevölkerungstrends' *Zeitschrift für Bevölkerungswissenschaft*, 11, 4, 445–518

Hunt, Richard N. (1964) *German Social Democracy 1918–1933*, New Haven

Institut Für Marxistische Studien Und Forschungen (IMSF), (1978) 'Wirtschaftskrise und Frauenemanzipation in der BRD', Informationsbericht Nr. 31, Fulda: Fuldaer Verlagsanstalt.

Jacobs, Monica (1978) 'Civil Rights and Women's Rights in the Federal Republic of Germany Today', *New German Critique*, no. 13, winter, 165–174

Jaeggi, Urs (1973) *Kapital und Arbeit in der Bundesrepublik*, originally *Macht und Herrschaft in der BRD* (1969), Frankfurt/M.: Fischer Taschenbuch Verlag

Janssen-Jurreit, Marielouise (1985) *Sexismus. Über die Abtreibung der Frauenfrage*, Frankfurt/M.: Fischer Verlag

Jeffries, Sheila (1983) 'Sex Reform and Anti-feminism in the 1920s' in *The Sexual Dynamics of History*, ed. by the London Feminist History Group, London: Pluto, 177–202

Jungwirth, Nikolaus and Kromschröder, Gerhard (1978) *Die Pubertät der Republik*, Reinbek

Kaplan, Gisela and Adams, Carole E. (1988) 'Das Frauenideal nationalsozialistischer Frauen vor 1933: Wider Weimarer Feminismus und männlich definierte Sexualität', trans. by G. Kaplan, in *"The Attractions of Fascism" Traditionen und Traditionssuche des Deutschen Faschismus*, ed. by G. Hartung, special issue of *Wissenschaftliche Beiträge* 1988/55 (F 83) Halle, Saale, GDR, 3–25

Kaplan, Gisela and Adams, Carole E. (1990) 'Early Women Supporters of National Socialism' in *The Attractions of Fascism*, ed. by J. Milfull, Oxford, Hamburg, New York: Berg Publishers, 186–203

Kaplanski, Louise K. (1984) 'German Feminism and the Peace Movement' *Potomac Review*, 1984–85, vol. 26–27, 33–50

Klein, Kurt (1980) 'Frauenkarrieren im gesamtberuflichen Zusammenhang in Österreich' in I. Lamel ed. *Managementkarrieren im gesellschaftlichen Umbruch*, Vienna

Kleinert, Ulfrid (ed.) (1981) *Gewaltfrei widerstehen. Brokdorf-Protokolle gegen Schlagstöcke und Steine*, Reinbek/Hamburg: Rororo

Koonz, Claudia (1986) 'Some Political Implications of Separatism: German Women between Democracy and Nazism, 1928–1934' in *Women in Culture and Politics. A Century of Change*, ed. by Judith Friedlander et al., Bloomington: Indiana University Press, 269–285

Koonz, Claudia (1987) *Mothers in the Fatherland. Women, the Family, and Politics*, London: Jonathan Cape

Lamel, Ingrid (ed.) (1980) *Managementkarrieren im gesellschaftlichen Umbruch*, Vienna

Lappe, Lothar (1981) *Die Arbeitssituation erwerbsttätiger Frauen*, Frankfurt/M: Campus Verlag

Laqueur, Walter (1985) *Was ist los mit den Deutschen?* Frankfurt/M., Berlin: Ullstein Verlag; simultaneous with English ed. *Germany today*, London: Weidenfeld and Nicolson

Levin, Tobe (1986) 'Introducing Elfriede Jelinek: Double Agent of Feminist Aesthetics' *Women's Studies International Forum*, vol. 9, no. 4: 435–442

Mandel, Ernest (1969) *Die deutsche Wirtschaftskrise. Lehren der Rezession 1966/67*, Frankfurt/M.: Europäische Verlagsanstalt

Mayer, Margit (1978) 'The German October of 1977' *New German Critique*, no. 13, winter, 155–164

Menschik, Jutta (1977) *Gleichberechtigung oder Emanzipation. Die Frau im Erwerbsleben der Bundesrepublik*, Frankfurt/M.:Fischer Taschenbuchverlag

Merkl, Peter H. (1976) 'The Politics of Sex: West Germany' in *Women in the World. A Comparative Study*, ed. by L. B. Iglitzin and R. Ross, Santa Barbara and Oxford: Clio Books

Nagle, John David (1970) *The National Democratic Party. Right Radicalism in the Federal Republic of Germany*, Berkeley, Los Angeles, and London: University of California Press

Nienhaus, Ursula (1981) 'Frauenforschungs-, Bildungs- und Informationszentrum (FFBIZ)' in *Wohin geht die Frauenbewegung*, ed. by G. Gassen, Frankfurt/M.: Fischer Taschenbuch Verlag, 25–35

Nowotny, Helga (1981) 'Women in Public Life in Austria' in *Access to Power: Cross. National Studies of Women and Elites*, ed. by C. F. Epstein and R. L. Coser, London: George Allen & Unwin, 147–156

ÖH-Frauenreferat (1989) *Frauen an österreichischen Universitäten*, Vienna: Edition ÖH, ÖH-Wirtschaftsbetriebe GmbH

Pauli, Ruth (1986) *Emanzipation in Österreich. Der lange Marsch in die Sackgasse*, Wien, Köln, Graz: Hermann Böhlaus Nachf.

Petzold, Ruth (1980) 'Die Situation der Frauen in der österreichischen Landwirtschaft' *Der Förderungsdienst*, 6, 161

Pinson, Koppel S. (1966) *Modern Germany. Its History and Civilization*, 2nd. ed. New York: Macmillan

Pletscher, Marianne (1977) *Weggehen ist nicht so einfach. Gewalt gegen Frauen in der Schweiz. Gespräche und Informationen*, Zurich: Limmal Verlagsgenossenschaft

Plogstedt, Sibylle (1984) 'Has Violence Arrived in the Women's Movement?' in *German Feminism*, ed. by E. H. Altbach et al., Albany: State University of New York Press, 336–341

Prokopp, Ulrike (1978) 'Production and the Context of Women's Daily Life.' *New German Critique*, no. 13 winter, 13–33

Pross, Helge (1972) *Kapitalismus und Demokratie. Studien über westdeutsche Sozialstrukturen*, Frankfurt/M.: Athenäum Fischer Taschenbuch Verlag

Pross, Helge (1973) *Gleichberechtigung im Beruf*, Frankfurt/M.: Suhrkamp

Radusch, Hilde 'Lesben-Gruppe L (Lesbos) 74' in *Wohin geht die Frauenbewegung? 22 Protokolle*, ed. by G. Gassen, Frankfurt/M.: Fischer Taschenbuchverlag

Roth, Roland (1985) 'Neue soziale Bewegungen in der politischen Kultur der Bundesrepublik-eine vorläufige Skizze' in *Neue soziale Bewegungen in Westeuropa und den USA*, ed. by K.-W. Brand, Frankfurt/M., New York: Campus, 20–82

Ruth (1984) 'Waiting for a miracle' excerpt trans. in *German Feminism*, ed. by E. H. Altbach, Albany: State University of New York Press: 170–176; origin. in *Guten Morgen, du Schöne. Frauen in der DDR*, ed. by M. Wander, 1978, Darmstadt and Neuwied: Luchterhand Verlag, 78–87

Schatzberg, Karin (ed.) (1986) *Frauenarchive und Frauenbibliotheken: Entstehungsgeschichte-Organisation-inhaltliche Schwerpunkte*, Aachen: Rader Wissenschaftliche Publikationen

Schelsky, Helmut (1965) *Auf der Suche nach Wirklichkeit*, Köln and Düsseldorf: Eugen Diederichs

Schenk, Herrad (1980) *Die feministische Herausforderung: 150 Jahre Frauenbewegung in Deutschland*, München: C. H. Beck

Schlaeger, Hilke (1978) 'The West German Women's Movement' *New German Critique*, 13, winter, 60–68

Schmidt-Harzbach, Ingrid (1981) 'Frauengesprächskreise an Berliner Volkshochschulen' in *Wohin geht die Frauenbewegung?*, ed. by G. Gassen, Frankfurt/M.: Fischer Taschenbuchverlag, 226–247

Schultz, Dora (1984) 'The German Women's Movement in 1982' in *German Feminism: Readings in Politics and Literature*, ed. by E. Altbach, J. Clause et al., Albany: State University of New York Press, 368–377

Schuster, V. (1982) 'Serie Nachkrieg IV: Freiheit, Gleichheit, und unsere verfluchte Lust, glücklich zu sein.' *Courage*, 7, Sept., 39–47

Schwarzer, Alice (1977) *Der 'kleine Unterschied' und seine großen Folgen*, Frankfurt/M.: Fischer Taschenbuchverlag

——(1981) *10 Jahre Frauenbefreiung. So fing es an!*, Köln: Emma Frauenverlag

——(1985) *Lohn: Liebe*, Frankfurt/M.: Suhrkamp Verlag (previously known and published under the title: *Frauenarbeit, Frauenbefreiung*, 1973)

SINUS (1981) *5 Millionen Deutsche:'Wir sollten wieder einen Führer haben'* SINUS-Studie über rechtsextremistische Einstellung bei den Deutschen

Slupik,V. (1982) 'Gefährlicher Schutz.' *Emma*, May, 27–30

Stefan, Venera (1979) *Shedding* (original: *Häutungen*, Munich: Verlag Frauenoffensive), trans. by J. Moore and B. Weckmüller, London: The Women's Press

Stephenson, Jill (1983) 'National Socialism and Women before 1933' in *Die Nazi Machtergreifung*, ed. by Peter D. Stachura, London: Allen & Unwin, 49–67

Taylor, A. J. P. (1970) *The Habsburg Monarchy*, Harmondsworth: Penguin

Thönnesson, Werner (1973) *The Emancipation of Women: The Rise and Decline of the Women's Movement in German Social Democracy, 1863–1933*, trans. by J. de Bres, London: Pluto Press

Tröger, Annemarie (1978) 'Summer Universities for Women: The Beginning of Women's Studies in Germany?' *New German Critique*, 13, winter, 175–180

Vedder-Schults, Nancy (1978) 'Introduction' to "The West German Women's Movement" by Hilke Schlaeger, *New German Critique*, no. 13, winter, 59–60

VSSTÖ (1988) 'Jede 50. Professor der Uni ist eine Frau: Frauen and den Unis', brochure published by the Association of Socialist Students (VSSTÖ), Vienna: REMAprint

Weiland, Daniela (1983) *Geschichte der Frauenemanzipation in Deutschland und Österreich*, Hermes Handlexikon, Düsseldorf: Econ Taschenbuchverlag

Weinzierl, Erika (1975) *Emanzipation? Österreichische Frauen im 20. Jahrhundert*, Vienna:

Whitford, Frank (1984) *Bauhaus*, Thames & Hudson: London

Wohmann, Gabriele (1976) *Ausflug mit der Mutter*, Darmstadt and Neuwied: Luchterhand

Woodtli, Susanna (1975) *Gleichberechtigung. Der Kampf um die politischen Rechte der Frau in der Schweiz*, Frauenfeld: Huber & Co

Zöllner, Erich (1974) *Geschichte Österreichs. Von den Anfängen bis zur Gegenwart*, Vienna: Verlag für Geschichte und Politik

## Greece

Alexiou, K. (1981) 'The Greek women's movement', *Tribune*, 4 March, 12–13

Bottomley, Gill (1984) 'Women on the move: migration and feminism', ch. 6 in *Ethnicity, Class and Gender in Australia*, ed. by G. Bottomley, M. de Lepervanche, Sydney, London: George Allen & Unwin

——(1986) 'A world divided: studies of gender relations in modern Greece' *Mankind*, vol. 16, no. 3, 181–189

Cavounidis, J. (1983) 'Capitalist Development and Women's Work in Greece' *Journal of Modern Greek Studies*, vol. 1, no. 2, Oct., 321–338

Choisi, Jeanette, (ed.) (1988) *Griechenland. Ein politisches Reisebuch*, Hamburg: VSA

Diamandouros, P. Nikiforos (1984) 'Transition to, and Consolidation of, Democratic Politics in Greece, 1974–1983: A Tentative Assessment' in *The New Mediterranean Democracies: Regime Transition in Spain, Greece and Portugal*, ed. by G. Pridham, London: Frank Cass

Dritsas, M. (1981) 'Changes in the character of the Greek Parliament' *The Greek Review of Social Research*, Jan.–April, 2–5

Friedl, E. (1976) 'The position of women: appearance and reality' *Anthropological Quarterly*, 40, no. 3, 97–108

Giray, A. de (1980) 'Les femmes et la politique en Grece', in idem. *Femmes et Politiques autour de la Méditerrannée*, Paris: L'Harmattan

Gunn, J. (1980) 'Greece—women organise for change', *Tribune*, 5 Nov., 6

Herzfeld, M. (1982) *Ours once more: folklore, ideology and the making of modern Greece*, Austin: University of Texas Press

Kostash, M. (1982) 'Women in Greece: democracy at home?' *Broadside*, 4, 2, Nov., 8–9

Kourvetaris, Yorgos A. and Dobratz, Betty A. (1987) *A Profile of Modern Greece in Search of Identity*, Oxford: Clarendon Press

Mandel, R. (1983) 'Sacrifice at the Bridge of Arta: Sex Roles and the Manipulation of Power' *Journal of Modern Greek Studies*, vol. 1, no. 1, May, 173–184

McNeil, William H. (1978) *The Metamorphosis of Greece since World War II*, Chicago, London: The University of Chicago Press

Molvaer, Janitha et al. (eds) (1984) *Foreign Women in Greece*, Athens: Eleftheros

Mouzelis, N. M. (1978) *Modern Greece. Facets of Underdevelopment*, London: Macmillan

Papandreou, Margaret (1984) 'A village sisterhood' in *Sisterhood is Global*, ed. by R. Morgan, Garden City, New York: Anchor Press/Doubleday, 272–277

Psacharopoulos, G. (1983) 'Sex Discrimination in the Greek Labour Market' *Journal of Modern Greek Studies*, vol. 1, no. 2, Oct., 339–372

Raulff, Heiner (1983) 'Die Militärdiktatur in Griechenland' in *Fischer Weltgeschichte, Europa nach dem Zweiten Weltkrieg*, Frankfurt/M.: Fischer Taschenbuch Verlag, 344–346

Riot-Sarcey, Michèle and Varikas, Eleni (1986) 'Feminist Consciousness in the Nineteenth Century: A Pariah Consciousness?' *Praxis International* (special issue, entitled *Feminism as Critique*, ed. by S. Benhabib and D. Cornell), vol. 5, Jan., 443–465

Roïdis, E. (1896) *The Greek Literary Women*, Athens

Spanidou, Irini (1987) *God's Snake*, London: Secker & Warburg

Stamiris, Eleni (1988) 'Die Frauenbewegung in Griechenland' in *Frauenbewegungen in der Welt*, vol. 1: Westeuropa, Hamburg: Argument, 113–130

Xiradiki, K. (1898) *Kalliopi Papalexopoulou (1809–1898)*, Athens

## The Iberian Peninsula: Portugal, Spain

Abel, Christopher and Torrents, Nissa (eds) (1984) *Spain: Conditional Democracy*, London: Croom Helm, New York: St Martin's Press

Ackelsberg, Martha A. (1985) '"Separate and Equal"? Mujeres Libres and Anarchist Strategy for Women's Emancipation' *Feminist Studies*, vol. 11, no. 1, spring, 63–84

Alba, Víctor (1978) *Transition in Spain. From Franco to Democracy*, trans. by B. Lotito, New Brunswick, New Jersey: Transaction Books

Alcobendas Tirado, María Pilar (1982) *Women's Employment in Spain*, Report for and published by the Commission of the European Communities, File V/2163/82-EN, Directorate General for Employment, Social Affairs and Education, Brussels

Barbosa, Madelena (1981) 'Women in Portugal' in Bradshaw, ed., special issue of *Women's Studies International Quarterly*, vol. 4, no. 4, 477–480

Barreno, Maria I., Horta, Maria T., Velho da Costa, Maria (1975) *New Portuguese Letters* (original: *Novas Cartas Portuguesas*, 1973, Lisbon: Estudios Cor), trans. by H. R. Lane and F. Gillespie, London: Victor Gollancz, Ltd. (proof copy)

Berger, Hartwig, Heßler, Manfred, Kavemann, Barbara (1978) '*Brot für heute, Hunger für morgen'. Landarbeiter in Südspanien. Ein Sozialbericht*, Frankfurt/M.: Suhrkamp Verlag

Bernecker, Walther L. (1984) *Spaniens Geschichte seit dem Bürgerkrieg*, Munich: Beck Verlag

Brown, Connie (1976?) 'Book Reviews' (*The New Portuguese Letters*), *Womanspeak*, vol. 2, no. 2, 6–7

Butragueño, María de Los Angeles J. (1982) 'Protective legislation and equal opportunity and treatment for women in Spain' *International Labour Review*, vol. 121, no. 2, Mar.–Apr., 185–198

Carr, Raymond (1977) *The Spanish Tragedy. The Civil War in Perspective*, London: Weidenfeld and Nicolson

——(1980) *Modern Spain 1875–1980*, Oxford, New York, Toronto, Melbourne: Oxford University Press

——(1982) *Spain 1808–1975*, 2nd ed., Oxford: Clarendon Press

Eder, Richard (1974) 'Portuguese Revolt: Smiles Arguments and Meetings' *New York Times*, May 14

Falcón, Lidia (1984) 'Women are the conscience of our country' in *Sisterhood is Global*, ed. by R. Morgan, Garden City, New York: Anchor Press/Doubleday, 626–631

Ferreira, Hugo Gil and Marshall, Michael W. (1986) *Portugal's Revolution: ten years on*, Cambridge, London, New York, Sydney: Cambridge University Press

Fishman, Robert M. (1982) 'The Labor Movement in Spain: From Authoritarianism to Democracy' *Comparative Politics*, vol. 14, no. 3, April, 281–306

Folguera, Pilar (1983) 'Research on women in Spain' in *The Changing Role of Women in Society. A Documentation of Current Research. Research Projects in Progress 1981–1983*, ed. by W. Richter et al. (1985) for the European Cooperation in Social Science Information and Documentation (ECSSID) Programme coordinated by the European Coordination Centre for Research and Documentation in Social Sciences, Berlin: Akademie Verlag, 779–781

Fontana, Joseph and Nadal, Jordi (1976) 'Spain 1914–1970' in *The Fontana Economic History of Europe*, vol. 6, Glasgow: Collins/Fontana Books, 460–529

Foweraker, Joe (1989) *Making Democracy in Spain. Grassroots struggle in the South 1955–1975*, Cambridge: Cambridge University Press

Fox-Lockert, Lucía (1979) *Women novelists in Spain and Spanish America*, Metuchen, N. J. and London: Scarecrow Press

Fraser, Ronald (1981) 'The Spanish Civil War' in *People's History and Socialist Theory*, ed. by R. Samuel, London, Boston, Henley: Routledge & Kegan Paul, 196–199

Gersão, Teolinda (1987) *Das Schweigen* (original: *O Silencio*, Lissabon: Edições O Jornal, 1981), trans. by K. von Schweder Schreiner, Munich: Frauenbuch-verlag

González, Anabel (1979) *El Feminismo en España, hoy*, Madrid: ZERO

Harsgor, Michael (1976) *Portugal in Revolution*, The Washington Papers, The Centre for Strategic and International Studies, Beverly Hills, London: Sage Publications

Janke, Peter (1980) *Spanish Separatism: E.T.A.'s threat to Basque democracy*, London: The Institute for the Study of Conflict

Kaplan, Temma (1977) 'Women and Spanish Anarchism' in Bridenthal and Koonz eds, *Becoming Visible: Women in European History*, Boston: Houghton Mifflin Comp.

Kavemann, Barbara (1978) 'Das Leben der Frauen im Dorf', ch. 5 in «*Brot für heute, Hunger für morgen». Landarbeiter in Südspanien. Ein Sozialbericht*, by H. Berger, M. Heßler and B. Kavemann, Frankfurt/M.: Suhrkamp

Lever, Alison (1988) 'Capital, Gender and Skill: Women Homeworkers in Rural Spain' *Feminist Review*, no. 30, autumn, 3–23

Logan, John R. (1977) 'Affluence, class structure, and working-class consciousness in modern Spain' *American Journal of Sociology*, vol. 83, no. 2, Sept., 386–402

Lomax, Bill (1983) 'Ideology and Illusion in the Portuguese Revolution: The Role of the Left' in *In Search of Modern Portugal. The Revolution & its Consequences*, ed. by L. S. Graham and D. L. Wheeler, Madison, Wisconsin: The University of Wisconsin Press, 105–133

Morrison, Rodney J. (1981) *Portugal: Revolutionary Change in an Open Economy*, Boston, Mass.: Auburn House Publishing Co.

Nash, Mary (1979) *Mujeres Libres 1936–1978*, sel. and trans. from Spanish by T. Kleinspehn, German ed., Berlin: Karin Kramer Verlag

Ottolenghi, Claudia (1981) *Women in Spain*, suppl. no. 8 to *Women of Europe*, Commission of the European Communities, Brussels

París, Juan N. García-Nieto (1979) 'The current evolution of trade unionism in Spain.' *Labour and Society*, vol. 4, no. 1, Jan., 26–48

Pintasilgo, Maria de Lourdes (1984) 'Daring to be different' in *Sisterhood is Global*, ed. by R. Morgan, Garden City, New York, Anchor Press/Doubleday, 571–575

Pollmann, Dorlies (1976) 'Der Kongreß der arbeitenden Frauen Portugals' in *Deutsche Volkszeitung*, Düsseldorf, 14 Oct. 1976

Pollmann, Dorlies (1979) 'Wider die weibliche Untugend Geduld. Portugals Frauen entwicklen Phantasie im Kampf um ihre Rechte' in *Deutsche Volkszeitung*, Düsseldorf, 18 Jan. 1979

Poulantzas, Nicos (1976) *The Crisis of the Dictatorships*, London: Atlantic Highlands, N. J.: NLB Humanities Press

Rague-Arias, Maria-Jose (1981) 'Spain: Feminism In Our Time' *Women's Studies International Quarterly*, vol. 4, no. 4, 471–476

Riegelhaupt, Joyce Firstenberg (1983) 'Introduction' to *In Search of Modern Portugal. The Revolution & its Consequences*, ed. by L. S. Graham and D. L. Wheeler, Madison, Wisconsin: The University of Wisconsin Press, 3–13

Sá e Melo, Maria Teresa (1988) 'Frauenorganisationen in Portugal 1988' in *Frauenbewegungen in der Welt*, vol. 1: *Westeuropa*, Hamburg: Argument, 189–194

Schümann, Beate and Müller, Anton-Peter (1986) *Portugal. Ein politisches Reisebuch*, Hamburg: VSA Verlag

Shields, Graham J. (compiler) (1985) *Spain*, (vol. 60 in the *World Bibliographical Series*), Oxford, Engl., Santa Barbara, Cal., Denver, Col.: CLIO Press

Spanish Women's Abortion Support Group (1988) 'Spanish Women and the Alton Bill' *Feminist Review: Abortion, The International Agenda*, no. 29, spring: 72–74

Stocker de Sousa, Maria M. and Dominguez, Maria C. P. (n.d.*) *Women in Portugal*, suppl. no.11 to *Women of Europe*, Commission of the European Communities, Brussels *(possibly 1986, according to content), 59

Threlfall, Monica (1985) 'The Women's Movement in Spain' *New Left Review*, no. 151, 44–75

Threlfall, Monica (1988) 'Die Frauenbewegung in Spanien' in *Frauenbewegungen in der Welt* vol. 1 *Westeuropa* ed. by the collective Autonome Frauenredaktion Argument, Berlin: Argument

Tusquets, Esther (1985) *Love is a solitary game* (original: *Elamores un juego solitalo*, 1979, Barcelona: Editorial Lumen) trans. by B. Penman, London: John Calder, New York: Riverrun Press

Vicens-Vives, J. (1969) *An Economic History of Spain*, Princeton, N.J.: Princeton University Press

## Italy

Andreucci, Franco (1981) "'Subversiveness' and 'Anti-Fascism in Italy' in *People's History and Socialist Theory*, ed. by R. Samuel, London, Boston, Henley: Routledge & Kegan Paul, 199–204

Balbo, Laura (1988) 'Women's studies in Italy: a hypothesis' in *Altro Polo, Studies of Contemporary Italy*, ed. by I. Grosart and S. Trambaiolo, Frederick May Foundation for Italian Studies, University of Sydney, Australia, 61–67

Barkan, Joanne (1980) 'Italian Communism at the Crossroads' in *The Politics of Eurocommunism, Socialism in Transition*, ed. by C. Boggs and D. Plotke, Montreal: Black Rose Books, 49–76

——(1984) *Visions of Emancipation: The Italian Workers' Movement Since 1945*, New York

Barnes, Samuel H. (1977) *Representation in Italy. Institutionalized Tradition and Electoral Choice*, Chicago and London: The University of Chicago Press

Barwick, Linda (1984) 'Patterns of Powerlessness: Women in Italian Popular Song' *Social Alternatives*, vol. 4, no. 3, 35–39

Bassnett, Susan (1986) *Feminist Experiences. The Women's Movement in Four Cultures*, (ch. 3: 'Italy'), London: Allen & Unwin

Becalli, Bianca (1984) 'From Equality to Difference: Women and Trade Unions in Italy' part of 'Trade Unions and the Radicalizing of Socialist Feminism' by C. Cockburn et al., *Feminist Review*, no. 16, summer, 43–73

——(1984) 'Working Class Militancy, Feminism and Trade Union Politics' *Radical America*, vol. 18, no. 5, Sept.–Oct., 39–51

Beckwith, Karen (1980) 'Women and Parliamentary Politics in Italy, 1946–1979' in H. R. Penniman (ed.), *Italy at the Polls 1979*, Washington and London: American Enterprise Institute

——(1985) 'Feminism and Leftist Politics in Italy: The Case of UDI-PCI Relations' in S. Bashevkin (ed.), *Women and Politics in Western Europe*, London: Frank Cass, 19–37

Bertini Bruno (1978) 'Italy: a guide to the armed party' in *Terrorism today in Italy and Western Europe*, ed. by B. di Biase, Sydney: Circolo 'G. D. Vittorio', 62–65

Bielli, Carla (1976) 'Some Aspects of the Condition of Women in Italy' in *Women in the World: A Comparative Study*, ed. by L. B. Iglitzin and R. Ross, trans. by B. Springer, Santa Barbara, Oxford: Clio Books, 105–114

Birnbaum, Lucia Chiavola (1986) *Liberazione della donna. feminism in Italy*, Middletown, Connecticut: Wesleyan University Press

Borghi, Liana, Corsi, G., Perini, A. de, Spinelli, S. (1988) 'Zeichen und Spuren: Lesben in Italien' in *Italien der Frauen*, ed. by M. Savier and R. Fiocchetto, Munich: Frauenoffensive, 52–65

Braidotti, Rosi (1986) 'The Italian Women's Movement in the 1980s', *Australian Feminist Studies*, no. 3, summer, 129–135

Buttafuoco, Annarita (1980) 'Italy: The Feminist Challenge', ch. 7 in *The Politics of Eurocommunism*, ed. by C. Boggs and D. Plotke, Montreal: Black Rose Books, 197–217

Caldwell, Lesley (1981) 'Abortion in Italy' *Feminist Review*, vol. 27, spring, 49–64

——(1983) 'Courses for Women: The Example of the 150 hours in Italy' *Feminist Review*, vol. 14, summer, 71–83

Cantarow, Ellen (1976) 'Abortion and Feminism in Italy: Women against Church and State' *Radical America*, vol. 10, no. 6, Nov.–Dec., 8–27

Chotjewitz-Häfner, Renate (1977) *Feminismus ist kein Pazifismus. Dokumente aus der italienischen Frauenbewegung*, Frankfurt/M.: Freie Gesellschaft

Cicioni, Mirna (1987) 'Women Subjects and Women's Projects: the first Italian Feminist Studies Conference, *Australian Feminist Studies*, no. 4, autumn, 133–137

——(1989) '"Love and Respect, Together": The Theory and Practice of *Affidamento* in Italian Feminism', *Australian Feminist Studies*, no. 10, summer, 71–83

Colombo, Daniela (1981) 'The Italian Feminist Movement' *Women's Studies International Quarterly*, vol. 4, no. 4, 461–469

Cornelisen, Ann (1976) *Women of the Shadows*, An Atlantic Monthly Press Book, Boston, Toronto: Little, Brown and Company

Dalla Costa, Mariarosa (1972) *Potere femminile e sovversione sociale*, Padua

Dalla Costa, Mariarosa and James, Selma (1975) *The Power of Women and the Subversion of the Community*, Bristol, England: Falling Wall Press

Diani, Mario and Melucci, Alberto (1988) 'Searching for autonomy: the sociology of social movements in Italy' *Social Science Information*, 27, 3, 333–353

Ergas, Yasmine (1982) '1968–79—Feminism and the Italian Party System: Women's Politics in a Decade of Turmoil' *Comparative Politics*, vol. 14, no. 3, April, 253–280

——(1988) 'Zwischen Sexualität und Geschlecht.' in *Frauenbewegungen in der Welt*, vol. 1: *Westeuropa*, trans. by E. Helfenstein and E. Opromolla, ed. by Autonome Frauenredaktion, Hamburg: Argument, 148–155, (first appeared under title 'Tra sesso e genere' in *memoria, rivista di storia delle donne*, 19–20, 1987)

Fallaci, Oriana (1987) *Brief an ein nie geborenes Kind* (original: *Lettere a un bambino mai nato*, 1975, Milan: Rizzoli), trans. by H. Riedt, Frankfurt /M.: Fischer Taschenbuch

Fiocchetto, Rosanna (1987) *L'amante celeste—La distruzione scientifica della lesbica*, Florence: Estro

——(1988) 'Die Geschichte der italienischen Frauenbewegung' in *Italien der Frauen*, ed. by M. Savier and R. Fiocchetto, Munich: Frauenoffensive

Frabotta, B. (ed.) (1976) *La politica del femminismo*, Rome

Froggett, Lynn (1981) 'Feminism and the Italian Trade Unions: *L'Acqua in Gabbia:* A Summary and Discussion' *Feminist Review*, vol. 40, summer, 35–42

Froncillo, Rosetta (1983) *Confusa Desio. Eine Reise in Abschweifungen*, trans. by P. Biermann, München: Frauenoffensive

Galleni, Mauro (1978) 'Four months of terrorism in Italy' in *Terrorism today in Italy and Western Europe*, ed. by B. di Biase and E. Hobsbawm, Sydney: Circolo 'G. D. Vittorio', 82–84

Glaab, Liana (1980) *Die unbekannte Italienerin. Aufbruch in die Emanzipation. Ein Situationsbericht*, Freiburg/Br., Basel, Wien: Herder Verlag

Grosart, Ian and Trambaiolo, Silvio (eds) (1988) *Altro Polo. Studies of Contemporary Italy*, Frederick May Foundation for Italian Studies, University of Sydney, Australia

Hellman, Judith Adler (1987) *Journeys Among Women. Feminism in five Italian cities*, Cambridge, Oxford: Polity Press in association with Basil Blackwell

Hine, D. (1977) 'Social Democracy in Italy' in *Social Democratic Parties in Western Europe*, ed. by W. E. Paterson, and A. H. Thomas, London: Croom Helm

Hobsbawm, E. J. (1974) 'Mafia.' ch. 3 in *Primitive Rebels. Studies in Archaic Forms of Social Movement in the 19th and 20th Centuries*, Manchester: Manchester University Press, 30–56

Howard, Judith Jeffrey (1980) 'Patriot Mothers in the Post Risorgimento' in *Women, War, and Revolution*, ed. by C. R. Berkin and C. M. Lovett, New York

Jacobs, Denise and Mazzone, Rean (1978) *Donna in Sicilia*, Palma, Palermo and S. Paulo, Brasil: NEF, Ilapalma

Kertzer, David I. (1982) 'The Liberation of Evelina Zaghi: The Life of an Italian Communist' *Signs: Journal of Women in Culture and Society*, vol. 8, no. 1, autumn, 45–67

Lange, Peter (1979) 'Change and Compromise: Dilemmas of Italian Communism in the 1970s' *West European Politics*, II–3

Lange, Peter and Tarrow, Sidney, (eds) (1980) *Italy in Transition. Conflict and Consensus,* London: Frank Cass

*Libreria delle donne di Milano. Wie weibliche Freiheit entsteht. Eine neue politische Praxis* (1989) (original: *Non credere di avere dei diritti*, 1987, Turin: Rosenberg and Sellier Editori), trans. by T. Sattler, foreword by C. Bernardoni, Berlin: Orlando Frauenverlag

Macciocchi, Maria Antonietta (1979) 'Female Sexuality in Fascist Ideology' *Feminist Review*, vol. 1, 68–69

Macciocchi, Maria Antonietta (1979a) *Les Femmes et Leurs Maitres*, Paris

Maraini, Dacia (1984) *Women at War* (original: *Donna in Guerra*, 1975, Rome: Einaudi) trans. by M. Benetti and E. Spottiswood, London: Lighthouse Books

——(1987) *Letters to Marina* (original: *Lettere a Marina*, 1981), trans. by D. Kitto and E. Spottiswood, London: Camden Press

——(1985) *Zug nach Helsinki* (original: *Il treno per Helsinki*, 1984, Rome: Einaudi), trans. by G. Jäger and P. Biermann, Berlin: Rotbuch Verlag (an English edition forecast as *Train to Helsinki*)

——(1987) *A Woman and Her Family*, London: The Women's Press, (original: *Analisi in Famiglia* (1977) Milan: G. Feltrinelli Editore)

Moss, David (1988) 'Notes on honour, sexuality and the state' in *Altro Polo: Studies of Contemporary Italy*, ed. by I. Grosart and S. Trambaiolo, Frederick May Foundation for Italian Studies, University of Sydney, Australia, 69–79

Mozzoni, Anna Maria (1975) *La liberazione della donna*, ed. by F. P. Bortolotti, Milan

Pasquinelli, Carla (1984) 'Beyond the Longest Revolution: The Impact of the Italian Women's Movement on Cultural and Social Change' *Praxis International*, vol. 4, no. 2, July, 131–136

Pinto, Diana, (ed) (1981) *Contemporary Italian Sociology: A Reader*, trans. and with an introd. by D. Pinto, London, Cambridge: Cambridge University Press and Paris: Editions de la Maison des sciences de l'homme

Pisano, Vittorfranco S. (1986) 'The Red Brigades: A Challenge to Italian Democracy' in *The New Terrorism*, ed. by W. Gutteridge, London: Mansell Publishing Ltd, 167–198

Pisciotta, Eleonore Eckmann (1986) 'The strength and the powerlessness of the new Italian women's movement: the case of abortion', ch. 1 in *The New Women's Movement: Feminism and Political Power in Europe and the USA*, ed. by D. Dahlerup, London, Beverly Hills & Newbury Park, New Delhi: Sage Publications, 26–47

Pitch, Tamar (1979) 'Notes from within the Italian Women's Movement: How We Talk of Marxism and Feminism', *Contemporary Crises*, vol. 3, no. 2, January, 1–16

Piva, Paola and Ingrao, Chiara (1984) 'Women's Subjectivity, Union Power and the Problem of Work' part of C. Cockburn et al. 'Trade Unions and the Radicalizing of Socialist Feminism,' *Feminist Review*, no. 16, summer, 43–73

Pizzorno, A. (1978) 'Political Exchange and Collective Identity in Industrial Conflict' in *The Resurgence of Class Conflict in Western Europe since 1968*, ed. by C. Crouch and A. Pizzorno, London: Macmillan

——(1983) 'Identità ed interesse' in *Identità*, ed. by L. Sciolla, Turin: Rosenberg and Sellier

Ravaioli, Carla (1977) *Frauenbefreiung und Arbeiterbewegung* (original: 'La questione femminile'), Hamburg/Berlin: USA

Ravera, Camilla (1978) *Breve storia del movimento femminile in Italia*, Rome

Rossanda, Rossana (1988) 'Die Emanzipierte, die keine Buße tun will' trans. from Italian by E. Helfenstein, P. Jehle and E. Opromolla, in *Frauenbewegungen in der Welt*, vol. 1: *Westeuropa*, ed. by Autonome Frauenredaktion, Hamburg: Argument, 156–163, (first appeared under the title 'L'impenitente emancipata' in *memoria, rivista di storia delle donne*, 19–20, 1987.)

Saraceno, Chiara (1984) 'Shifts in Public and Private Boundaries: Women as Mothers and Service Workers in Italian Daycare' *Feminist Studies*, vol. 10, no. 1, spring, 7–29

Savier, Monika and Fiocchetto, Rosanna, (eds) (1988) *Italien der Frauen*, Munich: Frauenoffensive

Scroppo, E. (1979) *Donna, privato e politico*, Milan: Mazzotta

Spagnoletti, R. (ed.) (1971) *I Movimenti femministi in Italia*, Rome:

Spotts, Frederic and Wieser Theodore (1986) *Italy: A Difficult Democracy. A survey of Italian politics*, Cambridge: Cambridge University Press

Tarrow, Sidney (1980) 'Italy: Crisis, Crises or Transition?' in *Italy in Transition: Conflict and Consensus*, ed. by P. Lange and S. Tarrow, Totowa, N.J.: Frank Cass

Tisdall, Cardine (1982) 'Chronology of Events in Italy 1960–1982' Published by the Arts Council of Great Britain on the occasion of the exhibition 'Arte Italiana 1960–1982' at the Hayward Gallery, London

Torchi, Antonia (1981) 'Feminist Responses to the Book' (ref. to *L'Acqua in Gabbia*), *Feminist Review*, vol. 40, summer, 43–48

Wunderle, Michaela (ed.) (1977) *Politik der Subjektivität. Texte der italienischen Frauenbewegung*, Frankfurt/M.: Suhrkamp Verlag

Yans-McLaughlin, Virginia (1977) 'Italian Women and Work' in *Class, Sex and the Woman Worker*, ed. by M. Cantor and B. Laurie, Westport/Conn.: Greenwood Press

Zaccaria, Paola (1984) 'Italy: A Mortified Thirst for Living' in *Sisterhood is Global: The International Women's Movement Anthology*, ed. by R. Morgan, Garden City, New York: Anchor Press/Doubleday: 370–375

Zancan, Marina (1988) 'Some reflections on women's initiatives in Italy after the feminist movement' in *Altro Polo. Studies of Contemporary Italy*, ed. by I. Grosart and S. Trambaiolo, Frederick May Foundation for Italian Studies, University of Sydney, Australia, 55–59

Zincone, Giovanna (1988) 'Women in Decision Making Arenas: Italy' in *Women, Equality and Europe*, ed. by M. Buckley and M. Anderson, London: Macmillan, 160–176

Zuccotti, Susan (1987) *The Italians and the Holocaust. Persecution, Rescue and Survival*, London: Peter Halban

## Scandinavian Countries: Denmark, Iceland, Finland, Sweden, Norway

Adams, Carolyn T. and Winston, Katherine T. (1980) *Mothers at Work: Public Policies in the United States, Sweden and China*, New York and London: Longman
Ambjørnsen, Ingvar and Haefs, Gabriele (eds) (1988) *Norwegen. Ein politisches Reisebuch*, Hamburg: VSA-Verlag
Andersen, Otto (1977) *The Population of Denmark*, Copenhagen: Cicred
Ås, Berit (1984) 'More power to women!' in *Sisterhood is Global*, ed. by R. Morgan, New York: Anchor Press/Doubleday, 509–514
Bergman, Solveig and Vehkakoski, Vellamo (1988) 'Eine Ehe zwischen 'Staatsfeminismus und Politik der Unterschiede' in *Frauenbewegungen in der Welt*, vol. 1: *Westeuropa*, ed. by the collective Autonome Frauenredaktion Argument, Berlin: Argument, 77–94
Brantenberg, Gerd (1985) *The Daughters of Egalia*, trans. from Norwegian by L. Mackay, London and West Nyack, NY: Journeyman Press, (1st ed. Oslo, as *Egalias døtre*, 1977)
——(1986) *What Comes Naturally*, trans. by author, London: Women's Press, (1st ed. Oslo: Gyldendals Forlag, as *Opp Jordens Homofile*, 1973)
Cerny, Karl H. (ed.) (1977) *Scandinavia at the Polls. Recent political trends in Denmark, Norway, and Sweden*, American Enterprise Institute for Public Policy Research, Washington, D.C.
Christensen, Jens (1983) *Rural Denmark 1750–1980*, Copenhagen: Central Cooperative Committee of Denmark
Dominelli, Lena and Jonsdottir, Gudrun (1988) 'Feminist Political Organization in Iceland: Some Reflections on the Experience of Kwenna Frambothid' *Feminist Review*, no. 30, autumn, 36–60
Einarsdóttir, Else M. (1976) 'Women of Iceland…a great "day-off"', *International Women's News*, vol. 71, no. 2, 18
Eskola, Irja and Haavio-Mannila, Elina (1975) 'The careers of professional women and men in Finland' *Acta Sociologica*, vol. 18, no. 2–3, 174–201
Fitzmaurice, John (1981) *Politics in Denmark*, London: Hurst
Forsås-Scott, Helena (1980) 'A woman of her time—and of ours.' *Swedish Books, An Independent Quarterly*, vol. 1/4, special issues: Writing by Women, 11–15
Gerlach-Nielsen, Merete (1980) *New Trends in the Danish Women's Movement, 1970–1978*, Roskilde: Emmeline Press
Gustafsson, Göran (1987) 'Religious change in the five Scandinavian countries, 1930–1980' *Comparative Social Research*, vol. 10, 145–181
Haavio-Mannila, Elina (1968) *Suomalainen nainen ja mies* (The Finnish Man and the Finnish Woman), Porvoo
Haavio-Mannila, Elina (1975) 'Women in the Economic, Political and Cultural Elites in Finland' in *Access to Power: Cross. National Studies of Women and Elites*, ed. by C. F. Epstein and R. L. Coser, London: George Allen & Unwin, 53–75
——(1979) 'How Women Become Political Actors: Female Candidates in Finnish Elections' *Scandinavian Political Studies*, vol. 2, new series, no. 4
Haavio-Mannila, Elina et al (eds) (1983) *Det Uferdige Demokratiet*, Oslo: Nordisk Ministerråd, trans. (1985) *Unfinished Democracy. Women in Nordic Politics*, Oxford: Pergamon
Haavio-Mannila, Elina and Husu, Liisa (1985) 'Research on Women in Finland' in *The Changing Role of Women in Society. A Documentation of Current Research. Research Projects in Progress 1981–1983*, ed. by W. Richter et al. (1985) for the European Cooperation in Social Science Information and Documentation (ECSSID) Programme coordinated by the European Coordination Centre for Research and Documentation in Social Sciences, Berlin: Akademie Verlag, 755–758
Hansen, Preben, Rying, Bent, Borre, Thorkild (eds) (1985) *Women in Denmark in the 1980s*, Copenhagen: Royal Danish Ministry of Foreign Affairs

Hanson, Katherine (ed.) (1984) *An Everyday Story. Norwegian Women's Fiction*, Washington, Seattle: The Seal Press

Haslund, Ebba (1987) *Nothing Happened*, trans. by B. Wilson (first appeared in 1948 in Norway under the title *Det hendte ingenting*) Seattle, WA: Seal Press

Haukaa, Runa (1988) 'Norwegen: Nostalgie und neue Herausforderung' in *Frauenbewegungen in der Welt*, vol. 1: *Westeuropa*, ed. by the collective 'Autonome Frauenredaktion Argument', Berlin: Argument, 170–183

Herman, Sondra R. (1972) 'The liberated women of Sweden' *Massachusetts Review*, vol. 13, winter–spring, 45–64

Hernes, Helga Maria (1985) 'Women's Research in Norway' in *The Changing Role of Women in Society. A Documentation of Current Research. Research Projects in Progress 1981–1983*, ed. by W. Richter et al. (1985) for the European Cooperation in Social Science Information and Documentation (ECSSID) Programme coordinated by the European Coordination Centre for Research and Documentation in Social Sciences, Berlin: Akademie Verlag: 773–777

Högbacka, Riitta (1987) 'Summary of an International Literature Review' in *Sexual Harassment*, Series E: Abstracts 2, Equality Reports, Ministry of Social Affairs and Health, Finland, Helsinki: Valtion Painatuskeskus, 1–8

Högbacka, Riitta, Kandolin, Irja, Haavio-Mannila, Elina et al. (1987) 'Sexual Harassment in the Workplace: Results of a survey of Finns' in *Sexual Harassment*, Series E: Abstracts 2, Equality Reports, Ministry of Social Affairs and Health, Finland, Helsinki: Valtion Painatuskeskus, 9–64 (incl. detailed bibliography)

Hvidtfeldt, Kirsten, Jørgensen, Kirsten, Nielsen, Ruth (eds) (1982) 'Strategies for integrating women into the labour market', *European Women's Studies in Social Sciences*, no. 1, Copenhagen, 1–350

Jallinoja, Riitta (1986) 'Independence or integration: the women's movement and political parties in Finland' in *The New Women's Movement. Feminism and Political Power in Europe and the USA*, ed. by D. Dahlerup, London, Beverly Hills & Newbury Park, New Delhi: Sage Publications, 158–178

Johansen, Margaret (1983) 'The Office Party' in *An Everyday Story: Norwegian Women's Fiction*, Washington, Seattle: The Seal Press

Jutikkala, Eino and Pirinen, (1984) *A brief history of Finland*, Espoo: Weilin and Göös

Juusola-Halonen, Elina (1981) 'The Women's Liberation Movement in Finland' in Bradshaw (ed.), special issue of *Women's Studies International Quarterly*, vol. 4, no. 4, 453–460

Kandolin, Irja and Uusitalo, Hannu (1980) *Scandinavian Men and Women: A Welfare Comparison*, Research Group for Comparative Sociology, University of Helsinki, Research Reports, no. 28, Helsinki

Kjønstad, Asbjørn (1987) *Norwegian Social Law*, Oslo: Norwegian University Press, distributed by Oxford University Press

Korpi, Walter (1978) *The Working Class in Welfare Capitalism: Work, Unions and Politics in Sweden*, London: Routledge & Kegan Paul

*Kvinnor och Män i Norden. Fakta on jämställndheten*, (1988), Nordic Council of Ministers, Nord 1988: 58, Stockholm

Liljeström, Rita (1984) 'Similarity, Singularity, and Sisterhood' in *Sisterhood is Global*, ed. by R. Morgan, Garden City, New York: Anchor Press/Doubleday, 661–666

Logue, John (1983) 'Social Welfare, Equality, and the Labour Movement in Denmark and Sweden' *Comparative Social Research*, vol. 6, 243–277

Mäkelä, Matti (1987) 'The Great Move in Finnish Literature in the 1960s and 1970s' *Books from Finland*, vol. 1, 36–38

Means, Ingunn Norderval (1972) 'Political recruitment of Women in Norway' *Western Political Quarterly*, vol. 25, Sept., 491–521

Meissner, Michael (1980) *Massenmedien und Journalismus in den Niederlanden und in Dänemark. Mit einer Darstellung zur Journalistenausbildung*, Frankfurt/M.: Rita G. Fischer Publishing House.

Mørch, Dea Trier (1986) *Winter's Child*, trans. by J. Tate, London: Serpent's Tale, (1st ed. Copenhagen: Gyldendal, as *Vinterbørn*, 1976)
——(1988) *Evening Star*, trans. by J. Tate, London: Serpent's Tale, (1st ed. Copenhagen: Vindrose, as *Aftenstjernen*, 1982)
*Naisten asema* (1984) Tilastokeskus (Central Statistical Office of Finland), Helsinki
Norderval, Ingunn (1985) 'Party and Legislative Participation among Scandinavian Women' *West European Politics*, vol. 8, no. 4, 71–89
——(1986) 'Elusive Equality: The Limits of Public Policy' in *Women in the World 1975–1985*, 2nd. rev. ed., Santa Barbara, Cal., Oxford, England: Clio, 53–81
Petersen, Herbert (1981) *Schweden, Bewährte Demokratie und neue Zeit*, Köln: Verlag Wissenschaft und Politik
Peterson, Abby (1985) 'The New Women's Movement—Where Have All The Women Gone? Women And The Peace Movement In Sweden, *Women's Studies International Forum*, vol. 8, no. 6, 631–638
Pietilä, Hilkka (1984) 'The right to be oneself' in *Sisterhood is Global*, ed. by R. Morgan, Garden City, New York: Anchor Press/Doubleday, 218–224
Räsänen, Leila (1984) 'Katsaus tasa-arvolain säädännön Kelutyseen vuosina 1970–1982' (A survey of the development of laws of equality 1970–1982) In *Mies—nainen—in minen*. Opet usministeriö. Helsinki, 147–168
Rehn, Gösta and Petersen, K. Helvig (1980) *Education and Youth Employment in Sweden and Denmark*, Berkeley, Cal.: Carnegie Council on Policy Studies in Higher Education
Sandel, Cora (1968) *Krane's Café. An Interior with Figures*, trans. from the Norwegian by E. Rokkan, London: The Women's Press (1st ed. *Kranes Konditori*, 1946)
Scott, Hilda (1982) *Sweden's Right to be Human*, New York: M. E. Sharpe
Skard, Torild (1981) 'Progress for Women. Increased Female Representation in Political Elites in Norway', in *Access to Power*, ed. by C. F. Epstein and R. L. Coser, Sydney, London: Allen & Unwin
Søndergaard, Dorte M. (1988) 'Die Frauenbewegung in Dänemark' in *Frauenbewegungen in der Welt*, vol. 1, Berlin: Argument, 53–66
Styrkársdóttir, Audur (1986) 'From social movement to political party: the new women's movement in Iceland' in *The New Women's Movement. Feminism and Political Power in Europe and the USA*, ed. by D. Dahlerup, London, Beverly Hills & Newbury Park, New Delhi: Sage Publications, 140–157
Swedish Institute (1968) 'Report to the United Nations, 1968: The Status of Women in Sweden', repr. in parts in *Voices of the New Feminism*, (1970), ed. by M. L. Thompson, Boston: Beacon Press
Tikkanen, Märta (1988) *Wie vergewaltige ich einen Mann?*, trans. by V. Reichel, Reinbeck: Rowohlt Taschenbuchverlag (1st ed. Stockholm: Bokförlaget Trevi, as *Män kan inte våldtas*, 1975)
——(1987) *Ein Traum von Männern, nein, von Wölfen*, trans. by V. Reichel, Reinbeck: Rowohlt Taschenbuchverlag, (1st ed. Stockholm: Bokförlaget Trevi, as *Rödluvan*, 1986)
Tomasson, Richard F. (1980) *Iceland The First New Society*, University of Minnesota Press: Minneapolis
Törnudd, K. (1986) *Finland and the International Norms of Human Rights*, Dordrecht, Boston, Lancaster: Martinus Nijhoff Publishers
Vammen, Tinne (1984) 'Letter from a troubled Copenhagen Redstocking' in *Sisterhood is Global*, ed. by R. Morgan, Garden City, New York: Anchor Press/Doubleday: 181–186
Wassmo, Herbjørg (1987) *The House with the Blind Glass Windows*, trans. by R. Lloyd and A. Simpson, Seattle, Washington: The Seal Press (1st ed. Oslo: Gyldendal Norsk Forlag, as *Huset med den blinde glassveranda*, 1981)
Welsch, Erwin K. (1974) *Feminism in Denmark, 1850–1875*, PhD, Indiana University, 336
Wistrand, Birgitta (1981) *Swedish Women On The Move*, ed. and trans. by J. Rosen, Stockholm: The Swedish Institute

*Working papers in women's law* (1983) no. 1, Oslo: University of Oslo, Dept. of Women's Law

## SOCIAL MOVEMENTS

Brand, Karl-Werner (ed.) (1985) *Neue Soziale Bewegungen in Westeuropa und den USA. Ein internationaler Vergleich*, Frankfurt/M., New York: Campus

Brand, K. W., Büsser, D. and Rucht, D. (1984) *Aufbruch in eine andere Gesellschaft. Neue soziale Bewegungen in der Bundesrepublik*, Frankfurt/M.: Campus Verlag

Carden, Maren Lockwood (1978) 'The Proliferation of a Social Movement: Ideology and Individual Incentives in the Contemporary Feminist Movement.' *Research in Social Movements, Conflicts and Change*, vol. 1, 179–196

Chafetz, Janet Salzman and Dworkin, Anthony Gary (1986) *Female Revolt. Women's Movements in World and Historical Perspective*, Totowa, N.J.: Rowman & Allanheld

Cohen, Jean L. (1985) 'Strategy or Identity: New Theoretical Paradigms and Contemporary Social Movements' *Social Research*, vol. 52, no. 4, winter, 663–716

——(1982) 'Between Crisis Mangement and Social Movements: The Place of Institutional Reform' *Telos*, no. 52, summer, 21–40

——(1983) 'Rethinking Social Movements' *Berkeley Journal of Sociology*, vol. 28, 97–113

Costain, Anne N. (1982) 'Representing Women: The Transition from Social Movement to Interest Group' in *Women, Power and Policy*, ed. by E. Bonaparth, New York: Pergamon Press, 19–37

Eder, Klaus (1985) 'The "New Social Movements": Moral Crusades, Political Pressure Groups, or Social Movements?' *Social Research*, vol. 52, no. 4, winter, 869–900

Evans, Sara (1979) *Personal Politics: The Roots of Women's Liberation in the Civil Rights Movement and the New Left*, New York: Vintage

Gerlach, Lattier, and Hine, Virginia (1970) *People, Power, Change: Movements of Social Transformation*, Indianapolis, Ind.: Bobbs-Merrill

Oberschall, Anthony (1973) *Social Conflict and Social Movements*, Englewood Cliffs, N.J.: Prentice-Hall

Offe, Claus (1985) 'New Social Movements: Challenging the Boundaries of Institutional Politics' *Social Research*, vol. 52, no. 4, winter, 817–868

Olson, Mancur (1977) *The Logic of Collective Action: Public Goods and the Theory of Groups*, Cambridge, Mass.: Harvard University Press

Piven, Frances Fox and Cloward, Richard (1979) *Poor People's Movements*, New York: Vintage

Snow, David, Zurcher, Louis A. and Ekland-Olson, Sheldon (1980) 'Social Networks and Social Movements: A Microstructural Approach to Differential Recruitment' *American Sociological Review*, 45, 787–801

Turner, Ralph H. (1983) 'Figure and Ground in the Analysis of Social Movements' *Symbolic Interaction*, 6, 175–181

Zald, Mayer, and McCarthy, John D. (1979) *The Dynamics of Social Movements: Resource Mobilization, Social Control and Tactics*, Cambridge, Mass.: Winthrop

# Index

Names of the countless feminist organisations mentioned in the book are not listed separately here. Instead, a guide is provided in the subject index under 'women's organisations' by countries. The same principle governs the listing of political organisations/parties: see subject index under 'political organisations/parties' ordered by country.

(Number in italics refers to tables, in bold means topic is subject of a sub-chapter.)